50 Best Jobs™ for Your Personality

Part of JIST's Best Jobs™ series

Michael Farr and Laurence Shatkin, Ph.D.

Foreword by Kristine Dobson, Director, Career Information Delivery System, Utah Career Resource Network

Also in JIST's Best Jobs Series

◎ *Best Jobs for the 21st Century*

◎ *300 Best Jobs Without a Four-Year Degree*

◎ *200 Best Jobs for College Graduates*

◎ *250 Best Jobs Through Apprenticeships*

JIST Works
America's Career Publisher

50 Best Jobs for Your Personality

© 2005 by JIST Publishing

Published by JIST Works, an imprint of JIST Publishing, Inc.
8902 Otis Avenue
Indianapolis, IN 46216-1033

Phone: 1-800-648-JIST   Fax: 1-800-JIST-FAX   E-mail: info@jist.com   Web site: www.jist.com

Some Other Books by the Authors

Michael Farr

The Quick Resume & Cover Letter Book
Getting the Job You Really Want
The Very Quick Job Search

Laurence Shatkin

Quick Guide to College Majors and Careers
Quick Guide to Career Training in Two Years
or Less

Quantity discounts are available for JIST products. Have future editions of JIST books automatically delivered to you on publication through our convenient standing order program. Please call 1-800-648-JIST or visit www.jist.com for a free catalog and more information.

Visit www.jist.com for information on JIST, free job search information, book excerpts, and ordering information on our many products.

Acquisitions Editor: Susan Pines
Development Editor: Stephanie Koutek
Cover and Interior Designer: Aleata Howard
Printed in the United States of America

Interior Layout: Carolyn J. Newland
Proofreader: Jeanne Clark
Indexer: Kelly D. Henthorne

10 09 08 07   9 8 7 6 5

Library of Congress Cataloging-in-Publication Data

Farr, J. Michael.
    50 best jobs for your personality / Michael Farr and Laurence Shatkin.
        p. cm. -- (JIST's best jobs series)
    Includes index.
    ISBN 1-59357-177-1 (alk. paper)
    1. Vocational guidance--Psychological aspects. 2. Career
development--Psychological aspects. 3. Personality and occupation. 4.
Vocational interests. 5. Occupations--Psychological aspects. I. Title:
Fifty best jobs for your personality. II. Shatkin, Laurence. III. Title. IV.
Series.
    HF5381.15.F3618 2005
    331.702--dc22
                              2005005153

ISBN 978-1-59357-177-1

This Is a Big Book, But It Is Very Easy to Use

Psychologists have long understood a principle that many of us consider just common sense: that people have an aspect called *personality* that makes them feel more comfortable in some situations than in others. People who have a certain personality feel more capable of doing certain things and dealing with certain problems; they also feel more accepted when they are among people with personalities similar to their own. This is especially true for one place where people spend a major portion of their time: at work. People want to feel they fit in with the people and with the activities where they work.

If personality is the key to this feeling of fitting in, then you need to consider this question: *What kind of personality do you have?* Maybe you can come up with a few ways to describe yourself, such as "sunny," "energetic," "conscientious," "loyal," "outgoing," "funny," or "competitive." But what do those terms suggest for the kind of work you might enjoy and do well? What terms might be *more* useful?

This book can help you think about your personality in terms that have proven relevance to the world of work. You'll learn about the personality types that many psychologists and guidance practitioners use to describe people and jobs. You'll take a quick assessment to help you clarify your dominant personality type. Then you'll dig into a gold mine of facts about the jobs that are the best fit for your personality type—and that are the best for other reasons, such as their wages and job openings. The lists of "best jobs" will help you zero in on promising careers, and the descriptive profiles of the jobs will open your eyes to career choices that previously you may not have known much about.

We all want to fit in somewhere. And there are probably several different careers where each of us could fit in. But why not do it in a *really good job?* That's what this book can help you choose.

(continued)

(continued)

Credits and Acknowledgments: While the authors created this book, it is based on the work of many others. The occupational information is based on data obtained from the U.S. Department of Labor and the U.S. Census Bureau. These sources provide the most authoritative occupational information available. The job titles and their related descriptions are from the O*NET database, which was developed by researchers and developers under the direction of the U.S. Department of Labor. They, in turn, were assisted by thousands of employers who provided details on the nature of work in the many thousands of job samplings used in the database's development. We used the most recent version of the O*NET database, release 7. We appreciate and thank the staff of the U.S. Department of Labor for their efforts and expertise in providing such a rich source of data.

Table of Contents

Summary of Major Sections

Introduction. A short overview to help you better understand and use the book. *Starts on page 1.*

Part I: Overview of Personality and Career. Part I is an overview of personality and of personality types. This section also explores the relationship between personality and career. *Starts on page 11.*

Part II: What's Your Personality Type? Take an Assessment. This part helps you discover your personality type with a short, easy-to-complete assessment. *Starts on page 17.*

Part III: The Best Jobs Lists: Jobs for Each of the Six Personality Types. The 140 lists in Part III show you the best jobs in terms of high salaries, fast growth, and plentiful job openings for each of the six personality types. You can also see which jobs are best when these factors are combined. Further lists classify the jobs according to education and training required and several other features, such as jobs with the highest percentage of women and of men and jobs with high rates of self-employment and part-time workers. Although there are a lot of lists, they are easy to understand because they have clear titles and are organized into groupings of related lists. *Starts on page 27.*

Part IV: Descriptions of the 50 Best Jobs for Each Personality. This part provides a brief but information-packed description of the 50 jobs from each personality type that met our criteria for high pay, fast growth, or many openings. Each description contains information on earnings, projected growth, education and training required, job duties, skills, related job titles, related knowledge and courses, and many other details. The descriptions are presented in alphabetical order within each personality type. This structure makes it easy to look up a job that you've identified in a list from Part III and that you want to learn more about. *Starts on page 119.*

Part V: Appendixes. Appendix A contains a list of occupations in this book and their two-letter Personality codes. Appendix B explains the various skills listed in the job descriptions in Part IV. Appendix C lists the GOE interest fields and work groups, and Appendix D defines the related knowledges and courses listed in the job descriptions in Part IV. *Starts on page 427.*

Detailed Table of Contents

Part IV: Descriptions of the 50 Best Jobs for Each Personality 119

Descriptions for all the jobs in this book are included in this part in alphabetical order. The titles are presented below, along with the page numbers where each description begins. We suggest that you use Part III to identify job titles that interest you and then locate their descriptions in Part IV.

Foreword

Whether you're a counselor or a career explorer, this book is a must-have resource!

For more than 20 years, I have used assessment tools based on career guidance researcher John Holland's work when assisting students and adults. I have found that helping individuals identify their personality types according to six primary codes, also called the Holland codes, is a valuable first step that establishes the counselor as an ally in the career exploration process yet empowers individuals to move forward on their own with new information about themselves.

If you are making decisions about your career, this book will not only guide you in identifying your personality type; it will also help you to take that important next step. That is, you will discover some key occupations that are likely to fit your individual personality type, and—at the same time—you will learn about the education, outlook, and salary for occupations of interest. This book is uniquely organized to encourage you to consider a range of information as you explore potential occupations.

The O*NET (Occupational Information Network, a database of career information created by the U.S. Department of Labor) structure, from which the job descriptions in this book were derived, and the in-depth descriptions of occupations that have grown out of it, are of huge significance. The O*NET has provided career professionals and others with more easily understood information about the world of work. It was thrilling to see Holland's six personality types reflected in the O*NET occupational descriptions, as this validated the prominence of the Holland codes in career counseling.

This book takes advantage of the vast amount of information in the O*NET database and organizes it in a number of ways to advance the career exploration process. Though the focus is on personality type, other important occupational information is presented in a clear and user-friendly manner.

As a career counseling professional, I have experienced firsthand the gratification that comes with helping individuals understand how their personal characteristics relate to occupational choice. I have witnessed the effects, both in terms of job satisfaction and of productivity, when there is a good match between an individual's personality and an environment that supports his/her personality traits. It's an exciting process, one that will be furthered through the use of this book.

Kristine Dobson
Director
Career Information Delivery System
Utah Career Resource Network

Introduction

Before we get started finding the best jobs for your personality type, here are a few things to know about the information in this book and how it is organized.

Where the Information Came From

The information we used in creating this book came mostly from databases created by the U.S. Department of Labor and the U.S. Census Bureau:

- We started with the jobs included in the Department of Labor's O*NET (Occupational Information Network) database, which is now the primary source of detailed information on occupations. The Labor Department updates the O*NET on a regular basis, and we used the most recent one available—O*NET release 7.

- Because we wanted to include earnings, growth, number of openings, and other data not in the O*NET, we cross-referenced information on earnings developed by the U.S. Bureau of Labor Statistics (BLS) and the U.S. Census Bureau. This information on earnings is the most reliable data we could obtain. For data on earnings, projected growth, and number of openings, the BLS uses a slightly different set of job titles than the O*NET uses. Data about part-time workers, age of workers, and the male-female breakdown of workers was derived from the Census Bureau, which also uses a slightly different set of job titles. By linking the BLS and Census data to the O*NET job titles in this book, we tied information about growth, earnings, and characteristics of workers to all the job titles in this book.

Of course, information in a database format can be boring and even confusing, so we did many things to help make the data useful and present it to you in a form that is easy to understand.

How the Jobs in This Book Were Selected

Here is the procedure we followed to select the 300 jobs (50 for each personality type) we included in this book:

1. We began by creating our own database from the O*NET, the Census Bureau, and other sources to include the information that we wanted. This database covered about 1,000 job titles, 900 of which were rated in terms of the six RIASEC personality types. ("RIASEC" stands for "Realistic," "Investigative," "Artistic," "Social," "Enterprising," and "Conventional"—the six personality types developed by the researcher John Holland. For more information about the RIASEC personality types, see "The RIASEC Personality Types" in Part I.)

2. From these 900 occupations, we were able to create comprehensive lists of occupations that primarily fit into one of the six personality types. The six lists ranged in size from 51 jobs for the Artistic type to 455 for the Realistic type.

3. Next, for each of the six comprehensive lists, we created three sub-lists that ranked the jobs by annual earnings, projected growth, and number of job openings projected per year. Each of these sub-lists was then sorted from highest to lowest, and the jobs were assigned a number score. For example, the highest-paying job on the list of 455 Realistic jobs received an earnings score of 455, and the lowest-paying Realistic job received an earnings score of 1.

4. We then added the number scores from all three sub-lists—the earnings score, the growth score, and the job-openings score—for each job and created a new list that presented all the jobs for that personality type in order from highest to lowest *total* score for all three measures.

5. To emphasize jobs that tend to pay more, are likely to grow more rapidly, and have more job openings, we selected the 50 job titles with the highest total scores from each of the six final lists. These 300 jobs are the focus of this book.

For example, Accountants is the Conventional job with the highest combined score for earnings, growth, and number of job openings, so Accountants is listed first in our "50 Best Conventional Jobs" list even though it is not the best-paying Conventional job (which is Air Traffic Controllers), the fastest-growing Conventional job (which is Medical Records and Health Information Technicians), or the Conventional job with the most openings (which is Cashiers).

Understand the Limits of the Data in This Book

In this book we use the most reliable and up-to-date information available on earnings, projected growth, number of openings, and other topics. The data came from the U.S. Department of Labor source known as Occupation and Employment Statistics. As you look at the data, keep in mind that the figures are estimates. They give you a general idea about the number of workers employed, annual earnings, rate of job growth, and annual job openings.

Understand that a problem with such data is that it describes an average. Just as there is no precisely average person, there is no such thing as a statistically average example of a particular job. We say this because data, while helpful, can also be misleading.

Take, for example, the yearly earnings information in this book. This is highly reliable data obtained from a very large U.S. working population sample by the Bureau of Labor Statistics. It tells us the average annual pay received as of May 2003 by people in various job titles (actually, it is the median annual pay, which means that half earned more and half less).

This sounds great, except that half of all people in that occupation earned less than that amount. For example, people who are new to the occupation or with only a few years of work experience often earn much less than the average amount. People who live in rural areas or who work for smaller employers typically earn less than those who do similar work in cities (where the cost of living is higher) or for bigger employers. People in certain areas of the country earn less than those in others. Other factors also influence how much you are likely to earn in a given job in your area. For example, Lawn Service Managers (an Enterprising job) have median earnings of $33,770, but those in cold climate areas would work only part of the year.

Also keep in mind that the figures for job growth and number of openings are projections by labor economists—their best guesses about what we can expect between now and 2012. They are not guarantees. A major economic downturn, war, or technological breakthrough could change the actual outcome.

Finally, because different government agencies classify jobs in slightly different ways, sometimes we had to treat two jobs as if they were identical in terms of earnings, growth, openings, or some other topic. For example, in this book we treat Accountants and Auditors as two different jobs because the O*NET database provides separate descriptions for them. However, information about their earnings is available only for the *combined* occupation called "Accountants and Auditors." As a result, when you look at the list called "The 20 Best-Paying Conventional Jobs," you will find them listed side by side with the exact same earnings.

So, in reviewing the information in this book, please understand the limitations of data. You need to use common sense in career decision making as in most other things in life. We hope that, using that approach, you find the information helpful and interesting.

How This Book Is Organized

The information in this book moves from the general to the highly specific. It starts by explaining how personality relates to career choice and presents a widely used model for making that connection. An assessment helps you focus on your dominant personality type (or types), and then you can consult a wealth of lists that itemize the best jobs for your personality type. These lists let you look at the jobs from several different perspectives—for example, which pay the best, which employ the most young people, and which require an associate's degree for entry. Finally, you can get highly detailed information about any of these career choices in the fact-packed job descriptions that make up the last part of the book.

Part I: Overview of Personality and Career

Part I is an overview of how personality relates to careers—the basic theory, plus the six personality types that were originally described by John Holland and have since become the basis of many guidance resources. This section may clear up some misunderstandings you have about what personality means in the context of career choice, and it will help you understand a useful way of looking at yourself and the world of work.

Part II: What's Your Personality Type? Take an Assessment

You probably are not reading this book simply to educate yourself about career development theory. Rather, the odds are that you have a more practical goal: making a career choice. To help you, we've included a paper-and-pencil assessment that can help you clarify your dominant personality type or types. The Personality Type Inventory usually takes about 20 to 30 minutes to complete, but there is no time limit, nor are there any right or wrong answers.

After taking the Personality Type Inventory, you can use what you've learned about your personality type to identify a job that suits you well. This book makes that task easy because all of the information about jobs is grouped by the dominant personality type of the jobs. That means you don't have to waste time exploring jobs that are unlikely to be a good match for your personality. Also, because this book focuses on the 50 most rewarding jobs for each personality type, you don't have to complicate your search by considering jobs with low earnings or highly limited odds of being employed.

Part III: The Best Jobs Lists: Jobs for Each of the Six Personality Types

For many people, the 141 lists in Part III are the most interesting section of the book. Here you can see which jobs for each personality type are best in terms of high salaries, fast growth, and plentiful job openings and best when these three factors are combined. Other lists break out the best of each type according to the level of education or training required and several other features of the jobs and the people who hold them. Look in the Table of Contents for a complete list of lists. Although there are a lot of lists, they are not difficult to understand because they have clear titles and are organized into groupings of related lists.

People who prefer to think about careers in terms of economic rewards will want to browse the lists that show the best jobs in terms of earnings, growth, and openings. On the other hand, some people think first in terms of opportunities for young people or representation of women, and these people will find other useful lists that reflect these interests.

We suggest that you use the lists that make the most sense for you. Following are the names of each group of lists along with short comments on each group. You will find additional information in a brief introduction provided at the beginning of each group of lists in Part III.

Best Jobs Overall for Each Personality Type: Jobs with the Highest Pay, Fastest Growth, and Most Openings

This group has four sets of six lists, and they are the ones that most people want to see first. The first set of lists presents, for each personality type, all 50 jobs that are included in this book in order of their total scores for earnings, growth, and number of job openings. These jobs are used in the more specialized lists that follow and in the descriptions in Part IV. Three more sets of lists in this group present, for each personality type, specialized lists of jobs extracted from the best 50 overall: the 20 best-paying, the 20 fastest-growing, and the 20 with the most openings.

Best Jobs for Each Personality Type Sorted by Education or Training Required

When considering a career choice, many people put a lot of emphasis on how long it takes to prepare for the job and what kind of preparation is appropriate—education, training, or work experience. Just as it's important to choose a job that suits your personality, it can be helpful to choose a learning style that suits your preferences and abilities. Your financial circumstances also may shape your plans for career preparation because higher education can be expensive (even with financial aid) and the years you spend in college will postpone the years in which you will earn a salary. This set of lists sorts the jobs linked to each personality type into groups according to what preparation method is the fastest route to career entry. Within each group, the jobs are sorted by their overall ranking for earnings, growth, and openings.

Best Jobs for Each Personality Type with a High Percentage of Women and Men

This group includes 24 lists in all: For each personality type, you can see the jobs that have the highest percentage of workers who are women and men. That would make up 12 lists, but each of these lists is also re-sorted to show these predominantly male or predominantly female jobs ordered by their overall ranking for earnings, growth, and openings.

Best Jobs for Each Personality Type with a High Percentage of Workers Age 16–24

This section provides lists of the jobs for each personality type that have the highest percentage of workers age 16–24. Like the lists in the previous section, each list is then re-sorted to present these youthful jobs in order of their total combined scores for earnings, growth, and number of openings. Thus there is a total of 12 lists in this section.

Best Jobs for Each Personality Type with a High Percentage of Workers Age 65 and Over

The 12 lists in this section were assembled in the same manner as the lists in the previous section, except that these jobs have a high percentage of workers age 65 and over.

Best Jobs for Each Personality Type with a High Percentage of Part-Time Workers

There are 12 lists in this group, and they extract the jobs from our 50 best jobs that have a high percentage of part-time workers. Again, they are ordered first in terms of percentage of part-time workers, so you can easily find the jobs with the most opportunities for part-timers, and then they are re-sorted in order of their total combined score for earnings, growth, and number of openings.

Best Jobs for Each Personality Type with a High Percentage of Self-Employed Workers

The 12 lists in this section show you the jobs that have the highest percentage of self-employed workers. Once again, the lists for the six personality types are re-sorted in order of their total combined score for earnings, growth, and number of openings.

Part IV: Descriptions of the 50 Best Jobs for Each Personality

This part of the book provides a brief but information-packed description of each of the 300 best jobs that met our criteria for this book. The descriptions are divided into six groups, one for each personality type, and are presented in alphabetical order within each group. This structure makes it easy to look up a job that you've identified in a list from Part III and that you want to learn more about.

We used the most current information from a variety of government sources to create the descriptions. Although we've tried to make the descriptions easy to understand, the sample job description that follows—and the explanation of each of its parts—may help you better understand and use the descriptions.

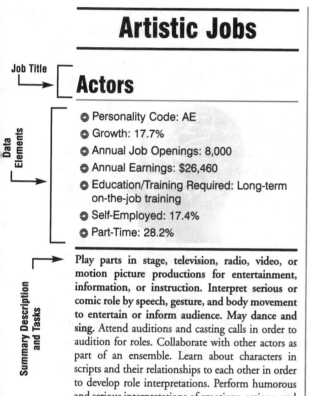

Artistic Jobs

Job Title

Actors

Data Elements

- Personality Code: AE
- Growth: 17.7%
- Annual Job Openings: 8,000
- Annual Earnings: $26,460
- Education/Training Required: Long-term on-the-job training
- Self-Employed: 17.4%
- Part-Time: 28.2%

Summary Description and Tasks

Play parts in stage, television, radio, video, or motion picture productions for entertainment, information, or instruction. Interpret serious or comic role by speech, gesture, and body movement to entertain or inform audience. May dance and sing. Attend auditions and casting calls in order to audition for roles. Collaborate with other actors as part of an ensemble. Learn about characters in scripts and their relationships to each other in order to develop role interpretations. Perform humorous and serious interpretations of emotions, actions, and situations, using body movements, facial expressions, and gestures. Portray and interpret roles, using speech, gestures, and body movements in order to entertain, inform, or instruct radio, film, television, or live audiences. Sing and/or dance during dramatic or comedic performances. Study and rehearse roles from scripts in order to interpret, learn, and memorize lines, stunts, and cues as directed. Work closely with directors, other actors, and playwrights to find the interpretation most suited to the role. Manipulate strings, wires, rods, or fingers to animate puppets or dummies in synchronization with talking, singing, or recorded programs. Perform original and stock tricks of illusion to entertain and mystify audiences, occasionally including audi-

ence members as participants. Promote productions using means such as interviews about plays or movies. Read from scripts or books to narrate action or to inform or entertain audiences, utilizing few or no stage props. Tell jokes; perform comic dances, songs and skits; impersonate mannerisms and voices of others; contort face; and use other devices to amuse audiences. Work with other crewmembers responsible for lighting, costumes, makeup, and props. Write original or adapted material for dramas, comedies, puppet shows, narration, or other performances. Construct puppets and ventriloquist dummies and sew accessory clothing, using hand tools and machines. Dress in comical clown costumes and makeup and perform comedy routines to entertain audiences. Introduce performances and performers in order to stimulate excitement and coordinate smooth transition of acts during events. Prepare and perform action stunts for motion picture, television, or stage productions. **SKILLS**— Speaking; Monitoring; Social Perceptiveness; Repairing; Coordination; Active Learning; Reading Comprehension; Equipment Maintenance.

Skills

GOE—Interest Area: 01. Arts, Entertainment, and Media. **Work Group:** 01.05. Performing Arts. **Other Jobs in This Work Group:** Choreographers; Composers; Dancers; Directors—Stage, Motion Pictures, Television, and Radio; Entertainers and Performers, Sports and Related Workers, All Other; Music Arrangers and Orchestrators; Music Directors; Music Directors and Composers; Musicians and Singers; Musicians, Instrumental; Public Address System and Other Announcers; Radio and Television Announcers; Singers; Talent Directors.

GOE

EDUCATION/TRAINING PROGRAM(S)— Acting; Directing and Theatrical Production; Drama and Dramatics/Theatre Arts, General; Dramatic/Theatre Arts and Stagecraft, Other. **RELATED KNOWLEDGE/COURSES**—Fine Arts; Communications and Media; English Language.

Related Knowledge/Courses

Here are some details on each of the major parts of the job descriptions you will find in Part IV:

- **Job Title**—This is the job title for the job as defined by the U.S. Department of Labor and used in its O*NET database.

- **Data Elements**—This information comes from various U.S. Department of Labor and Census databases for this occupation, as explained elsewhere in this introduction.

- **Summary Description and Tasks**—The bold sentences provide a summary description of the occupation. This is followed by a listing of tasks that are generally performed by people who work in this job. We followed the listing of tasks in the O*NET database, except that where necessary we edited the tasks to keep them from exceeding 2200 characters.

- **Skills**—The government provides data on many skills; we decided to list only those that were most important for each job rather than list pages of unhelpful details. For each job, we identified any skill with a rating that was higher than the average rating for that skill for all jobs. If there were more than eight, we included only those eight with the highest ratings, and we present them from highest to lowest score (that is, in terms of by how much its score exceeds the average score). We include up to 10 skills if scores were tied for eighth place. You can find definitions of the skills in Appendix B.

- **GOE**—This information cross-references the *Guide for Occupational Information* (or the *GOE*), a system that organizes jobs based on interests and is used in a variety of career information systems. We use the third edition of the *Guide for Occupational Information,* as published by JIST. The description includes the major Interest Area the job fits into, its more specific Work Group, and a list of related job titles that are in this same GOE Work Group. This will help you identify other jobs that relate to similar interests or require similar skills. You can find more information on the *GOE* Interest Areas in Appendix C.

- **Education/Training Program(s)**—This part gives the names of one or more programs for preparing for the job. The titles are based on the U.S. Department of Education *Classification of Instructional Programs.* A particular college major or training program may not have the identical title—for example, there probably is no college that offers a major called "Political Science and Government, General," but you are likely to find a major called "Political Science" or "Government." In a few cases we edited the list of programs to keep it from exceeding 2000 characters.

- **Related Knowledge/Courses**—This entry can help you understand the most important knowledge areas that are required for a job and the types of subjects you will likely study in the training or curriculum that prepares you for the job. We used information in the O*NET database for this entry. We went through a process similar to the one we used for skills (earlier in this list) to determine which entries were most important for each job. In this case, however, we listed at least two knowledge areas for each job, even if the ratings for those knowledge areas were lower than the average for all jobs. You can find definitions of related knowledge/courses in Appendix D.

How to Use This Book

This is a book that you can dive right into:

◉ **If you don't know much about what personality types are,** you'll want to read Part I, which is an overview of the theory behind using personality types as a way of making career choices. You'll also see definitions of the six personality types that are used in this book.

◉ **If you want to understand your own personality type,** you'll want to do the assessment in Part II. It takes only 20 to 30 minutes to complete and can guide you to jobs that suit you.

◉ **If you like lists and want an easy way to compare jobs,** you should turn to Part III. Here you can browse lists showing the 50 jobs for each personality type with the best pay, the fastest growth, and the most job openings. You can see these "best jobs" broken down in various ways, such as by amount of education or training required.

◉ **For detailed information about jobs,** turn to Part IV and read the profiles of the jobs. We include 300 jobs and itemize their major tasks, their top skills, their educational or training programs, and other facts you won't learn from the lists in Part III.

On the other hand, **if you like to do things in a methodical way,** you may want to read the sections in order:

◉ Part I will give you useful background on how personality type can be a guide in choosing a career.

◉ The assessment in Part II will help you identify your dominant personality type.

◉ With a clearer understanding of your personality type, you can browse the appropriate lists of "best jobs" in Part III and take notes on the jobs that have the greatest appeal for you.

◉ Then you can look up the descriptions of these jobs in Part IV and narrow down your list. Ask yourself, Do the work tasks interest me? Does the required education or training discourage me?

PART I

Overview of Personality and Career

Why Use Personality to Choose a Career?

M any psychological theorists and practicing career counselors believe that you will be most satisfied and productive in a career if it suits your personality. There are two main aspects of a job that determine whether it is a good fit:

- ◉ The nature of the work tasks and the skills and knowledge you use on the job must be a good match for the things you like to do and the subjects that interest you. For example, if you like to help other people and promote learning and personal development and if you like communication more than working with things or ideas, then a career in social work might be one that you would enjoy and do well in.

- ◉ The people you work with must share your personality traits so that you feel comfortable and can accomplish good work in their company. For an example of the opposite, think of how a person who enjoys following set procedures and working with data and detail might feel if forced to work with a group of conceptual artists who constantly seek self-expression and the inspiration for unconventional new artistic ideas.

Personality theorists believe that people with similar personality types naturally tend to associate with one another in the workplace (among other places). As they do so, they create a working environment that is hospitable to their personality type. For example, a workplace with a lot of Artistic types tends to reward creative thinking and behavior. Therefore, your personality type not only predicts how well your skills will match the demands of the work tasks in a particular job; it also predicts how well you will fit in with the culture of the work site as shaped by the people who will surround you and interact with you. Your personality type thus affects your satisfaction with the job, your productivity in it, and the likelihood that you will persist in this type of work.

One of the advantages of using personality as a key to career choice is that it is *economical*— it provides a tidy summary of many aspects of people and of careers. Consider how knotty a career decision could get if you were to break down the components of the work environment into highly specific aspects and reflect on how well you fit them. For example, you could focus on the skills required and your ability to meet them. Next you could analyze the kinds of knowledge that are used on the job and decide how much you enjoy working with those topics. Then you could consider a broad array of satisfactions, such as variety, creativity, and independence; for each one, you would evaluate its importance to you and then determine the potential of various career options to satisfy this need. You can see that, when looked at under a microscope like this, career choice gets extremely complex.

But the personality-based approach allows you to view the career alternatives from 40,000 feet. When you compare yourself or a job to certain basic personality types, you encounter much less complexity. With fewer ideas and facts to sort through and consider, the task of deciding becomes much easier.

Describing Personality Types

You probably have heard many labels that describe people's personalities: "He's a perfectionist." "She's a control freak." "He's a go-getter." "She's very self-confident." "He's pushy." "She's wishy-washy." "He has a short fuse." "She's a drama queen." The list could go on and on.

These everyday terms for personality types have some bearing on work, but they are not very useful for several reasons: They don't differentiate well between jobs (for example, self-confidence is useful in just about every job); some of them are too specific (for example, "control freak" focuses on one small aspect of how a person functions at work); and worst of all, most of them are too negative for people to want to apply to themselves.

Now that it's clear what kinds of personality labels we *don't* want to use, let's consider what would characterize a useful set of personality types:

- They should differentiate well between kinds of work.
- They should differentiate well between people.
- They should be broad enough that a small number of these categories can cover the whole universe of jobs and people.
- They should have neutral connotations, neither negative nor positive.

The RIASEC Personality Types

During the 1950s, the career guidance researcher John Holland was trying to find a meaningful new way to arrange the output of an interest inventory and relate it to occupations. He devised a set of six personality types that would meet the criteria listed in the previous section, and he called them Realistic, Investigative, Artistic, Social, Enterprising, and Conventional. (The acronym *RIASEC* is a convenient way to remember them.)

The following table shows how these labels apply to both people and work:

Personality Type	How It Applies to People	How It Applies to Work
Realistic	Realistic personalities like work activities that include practical, hands-on problems and solutions. They enjoy dealing with plants, animals, and real-world materials like wood, tools, and machinery. They enjoy outside work. Often they do not like occupations that mainly involve doing paperwork or working closely with others.	Realistic occupations frequently involve work activities that include practical, hands-on problems and solutions. They often deal with plants, animals, and real-world materials like wood, tools, and machinery. Many of the occupations require working outside and do not involve a lot of paperwork or working closely with others.
Investigative	Investigative personalities like work activities that have to do with ideas and thinking more than with physical activity. They like to search for facts and figure out problems mentally rather than to persuade or lead people.	Investigative occupations frequently involve working with ideas and require an extensive amount of thinking. These occupations can involve searching for facts and figuring out problems mentally.
Artistic	Artistic personalities like work activities that deal with the artistic side of things, such as forms, designs, and patterns. They like self-expression in their work. They prefer settings where work can be done without following a clear set of rules.	Artistic occupations frequently involve working with forms, designs, and patterns. They often require self-expression and the work can be done without following a clear set of rules.
Social	Social personalities like work activities that assist others and promote learning and personal development. They prefer to communicate more than to work with objects, machines, or data. They like to teach, to give advice, to help, or otherwise to be of service to people.	Social occupations frequently involve working with, communicating with, and teaching people. These occupations often involve helping or providing service to others.
Enterprising	Enterprising personalities like work activities having to do with starting up and carrying out projects, especially business ventures. They like persuading and leading people and making decisions. They like taking risks for profit. These personalities prefer action rather than thought.	Enterprising occupations frequently involve starting up and carrying out projects. These occupations can involve leading people and making many decisions. They sometimes require risk taking and often deal with business.
Conventional	Conventional personalities like work activities that follow set procedures and routines. They prefer working with data and details rather than with ideas. They prefer work in which there are precise standards rather than work in which you have to judge things by yourself. These personalities like working where the lines of authority are clear.	Conventional occupations frequently involve following set procedures and routines. These occupations can include working with data and details more than with ideas. Usually there is a clear line of authority to follow.

Holland went further by arranging these six personality types on a hexagon:

Figure 1: Holland's hexagon of personality types.

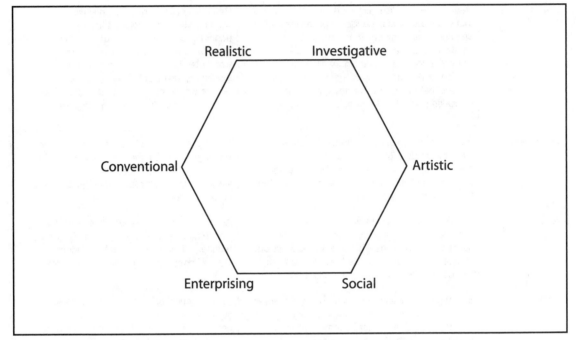

(After Holland, *A Theory of Vocational Choice*, 1959.)

He used this diagram to explain that people tend to resemble one type primarily but they may also have aspects of one or more adjacent types. Each personality type tends to have little in common with the types on the opposite side of the hexagon. Therefore, for example, a person might be primarily Realistic, with an additional but smaller resemblance to the Conventional type. Such a person would be described by the two-letter code RC and might be well suited to work as a Radiologic Technician or a Rough Carpenter (both coded RC). This person would have little in common with a Social personality type and likely would not be very happy or productive as a Special Education Teacher (coded SA). But this person could get along well with both Realistic and Conventional personalities and, to a lesser extent, with Investigative personalities.

Although Holland originally applied this model to academic advising, he soon extended it to the larger question of career choice, and since then hundreds of researchers and practitioners have investigated the RIASEC framework and have applied it to real-life decisions and situations. Researchers have even found it useful for predicting who will have the most traffic accidents or what kinds of drug abuse people are likely to engage in. More relevant to the theme of this book, however, is the fact that a number of career decision-making assessments have been developed to help people determine what personality type best describes them (and perhaps an additional adjacent type or types that are also important). You can find one such assessment in Part II of this book.

Although the RIASEC scheme does a good job of covering the whole world of work, the symmetrical hexagon shape used to illustrate it may be a little misleading because when you count the different jobs in our economy and the number of people working in those jobs, you'll find that some sectors of the hexagon are much more heavily populated than others. Here is a breakdown of the 900 RIASEC-coded occupations in the Department of Labor's O*NET database:

Personality Type	Number of Occupations	Number of Workers 2002
Realistic	455	79,183,000
Investigative	99	5,654,000
Artistic	51	8,218,000
Social	93	40,311,000
Enterprising	111	33,680,000
Conventional	91	36,336,000

As the United States shifts from a manufacturing economy to an information economy, employment in the Realistic sector is declining and employment in the Investigative sector is growing, but a large imbalance is likely to continue for the foreseeable future.

The six sectors are asymmetrical in other ways, too. As you'll see when you look at the lists in Part III, Social jobs employ a lot more women than Realistic jobs. Enterprising jobs employ a lot more men than Conventional jobs. Likewise, there are differences when you consider where large numbers of young people and older people work.

The differences get really significant when you look at the amounts of education or training required by jobs linked to the various personality types. For example, for Realistic and Conventional jobs the most common entry route is on-the-job training, whereas for Investigative jobs a college degree is usually needed. John Holland and other researchers have explained that these differences reflect the different levels of cognitive complexity to be found in the jobs. Realistic jobs deal mainly with manipulating things physically—moving them, cleaning them, repairing them, and so forth. Conventional jobs deal mainly with data at the level of organizing it according to pre-determined patterns—filing it, keying it in, and so forth. Investigative jobs, on the other hand, deal mainly with ideas and solving problems mentally, so the level of cognitive complexity is high and a college education becomes a necessity.

You should not be troubled by this lack of symmetry in the RIASEC model (even if you are an Artistic type). It does not indicate a weakness in the theory. But it does create some problems for a book like this. Although we have attempted to give equal coverage to each of the six personality types, you will notice that some of the sets of lists in Part III are not of equal size. Also, since there are only 51 O*NET occupations coded as Artistic, the "Best 50 Artistic Jobs" actually include *all* the Artistic jobs except one, which means that when you scan that list you may want to concentrate on the higher-ranked choices. On the other hand, the list of the "Best 50 Realistic Jobs" truly represents the upper crust of that large group of 455 jobs. These differences simply reflect the nature of the United States workforce.

No theory can perfectly describe the infinite variety of personalities to be found in our culture and the messy distribution of jobs that a free economy produces. You should note that the RIASEC scheme for describing personality types is not the only one that is used in career decision-making. However, it is the most popular and most thoroughly researched one, so it is the best one to use in this book.

Other Assessments with RIASEC Output

Apart from the assessment in Part II of this book, you may want to use any of these free assessments to explore your personality type in RIASEC terms:

- The O*NET Computerized Interest Profiler (for Windows), which you can download at www.onetcenter.org/CIP.html (the assessment in Part II is based on it)
- The University of Missouri's Career Center Career Interests Game at career.missouri.edu/modules.php?name=News&file=article&sid=146
- The Work Interest Quiz at www.myfuture.com/toolbox/workinterest.html
- The Keirsey Temperament Sorter at www.advisorteam.com/default.html (registration required)

You also have a number of options if you are willing to pay a fee. For example, you can access John Holland's own Self-Directed Search at www.self-directed-search.com/.

Keep in mind that although all of these assessments produce outputs with RIASEC codes and some of them also link these codes to occupations, they will not necessarily produce the exact same output. Assessment of personality is not as exact a science as, say, chemistry. Neither is the task of linking personalities to occupations.

You should not regard the output of *any* personality assessment as the final word on what career will suit you best. Use a variety of approaches to decide what kind of person you are and narrow down the kinds of work you enjoy. Actual work experience is probably the best way to test a tentative choice.

PART II

What's Your Personality Type? Take an Assessment

In this section, you can take a Personality Type Inventory that will help you determine your primary RIASEC personality type and perhaps one or two secondary RIASEC personality types. It asks if you like or dislike various activities and then lets you score your responses. You can use your scores in the following sections of the book to identify specific highly rewarding jobs to explore.

It's easy to use the Personality Type Inventory—just turn the page and follow the directions beginning with Step 1. This is not a test, so there are no right or wrong answers. There is also no time limit for completing this inventory.

If someone else will be using this book, you should photocopy the inventory pages and mark your responses on the photocopy.

Note: This inventory is based on the O*NET Interest Profiler, Version 3.0, developed by the U.S. Department of Labor (DOL). The DOL's edition consists of several components, including the Interest Profiler Instrument, Interest Profiler Score Report, and Interest Profiler O*NET Occupations Master List. The DOL provides a separate Interest Profiler User's Guide with information on the Profiler's development and validity as well as tips for professionals using it in career counseling. Additional information on these items is available at www.onetcenter.org, which is maintained by the DOL. This Personality Type Inventory is a version of the DOL's O*NET Interest Profiler that uses its work activity items and scoring system but has shorter directions, format changes, and additional content.

Restrictions for use: This and any other form of the O*NET Interest Profiler should be used for career exploration, career planning, and vocational counseling purposes only, and no other use has been authorized or is valid. Results should not be used for employment or hiring decisions or for applicant screening for jobs or training programs. Please see the DOL's separate "O*NET User's Agreement" at www.onetcenter.org/agree/tools for additional details on restrictions and use. The word "O*NET" is a trademark of the U.S. Department of Labor, Employment and Training Administration.

JIST Publishing offers a color foldout version of this assessment. It is called the *O*NET Career Interests Inventory* and is sold in packages of 25.

Step 1: Respond to the Statements

Carefully read each work activity (items 1 through 180). For each item, fill in just one of the three circles as follows:

If you think you would LIKE the activity, fill in the circle containing the L, like this:

If you think you would DISLIKE the activity, fill in the circle containing the D, like this:

If you are UNSURE whether you would like the activity, fill in the circle with the ?, like this:

$$\text{(L)} \qquad \text{(?)} \qquad \text{(D)}$$

As you respond to each activity, don't consider whether you have the education or training needed for it or how much money you might earn if it were part of your job. Simply fill in the circle based on whether you would like, would dislike, or aren't sure about the activity.

After you respond to all 180 activities, you'll score your responses in Step 2.

Would you LIKE the activity or DISLIKE the activity, or are you UNSURE?

		L	?	D
1.	Build kitchen cabinets	L	**?**	D
2.	Guard money in an armored car	**L**	?	D
3.	Operate a dairy farm	L	?	**D**
4.	Lay brick or tile	**L**	?	D
5.	Monitor a machine on an assembly line	L	?	**D**
6.	Repair household appliances	L	?	**D**
7.	Drive a taxicab	L	?	**D**
8.	Install flooring in houses	L	**?**	D
9.	Raise fish in a fish hatchery	L	**?**	D
10.	Build a brick walkway	**L**	?	D
11.	Assemble electronic parts	**L**	?	D
12.	Drive a truck to deliver packages to offices and homes	L	?	**D**
13.	Paint houses	L	**?**	D
14.	Enforce fish and game laws	L	**?**	D
15.	Operate a grinding machine in a factory	L	?	**D**
16.	Work on an offshore oil-drilling rig	L	?	**D**
17.	Perform lawn care services	**L**	?	D
18.	Assemble products in a factory	L	?	**D**
19.	Catch fish as a member of a fishing crew	L	?	**D**
20.	Refinish furniture	**L**	?	D
21.	Fix a broken faucet	**L**	?	D
22.	Do cleaning or maintenance work	L	?	**D**
23.	Maintain the grounds of a park	**L**	?	D
24.	Operate a machine on a production line	L	?	**D**
25.	Spray trees to prevent the spread of harmful insects	L	**?**	D
26.	Test the quality of parts before shipment	L	?	**D**
27.	Operate a motorboat to carry passengers	L	?	**D**
28.	Repair and install locks	L	**?**	D
29.	Set up and operate machines to make products	L	**?**	D
30.	Put out forest fires	L	?	**D**

9
Page Score for **R**

Would you LIKE the activity or DISLIKE the activity, or are you UNSURE?

31. Study space travel	L	?	D
32. Make a map of the bottom of an ocean	L	?	D
33. Study the history of past civilizations	L	?	D
34. Study animal behavior	L	?	D
35. Develop a new medicine	L	?	D
36. Plan a research study	L	?	D
37. Study ways to reduce water pollution	L	?	D
38. Develop a new medical treatment or procedure	L	?	D
39. Determine the infection rate of a new disease	L	?	D
40. Study rocks and minerals	L	?	D
41. Diagnose and treat sick animals	L	?	D
42. Study the personalities of world leaders	L	?	D
43. Conduct chemical experiments	L	?	D
44. Conduct biological research	L	?	D
45. Study the population growth of a city	L	?	D
46. Study whales and other types of marine life	L	?	D
47. Investigate crimes	L	?	D
48. Study the movement of planets	L	?	D
49. Examine blood samples using a microscope	L	?	D
50. Investigate the cause of a fire	L	?	D
51. Study the structure of the human body	L	?	D
52. Develop psychological profiles of criminals	L	?	D
53. Develop a new way to better predict the weather	L	?	D
54. Work in a biology lab	L	?	D
55. Invent a replacement for sugar	L	?	D
56. Study genetics	L	?	D
57. Study the governments of different countries	L	?	D
58. Do research on plants or animals	L	?	D
59. Do laboratory tests to identify diseases	L	?	D
60. Study weather conditions	L	?	D

_____ Page Score for I

Would you LIKE the activity or DISLIKE the activity, or are you UNSURE?

61. Conduct a symphony orchestra   Ⓛ   ⓵   **Ⓓ**
62. Write stories or articles for magazines   **Ⓛ**   ⓵   Ⓓ
63. Direct a play   **Ⓛ**   ⓵   Ⓓ
64. Create dance routines for a show   Ⓛ   **⓵**   Ⓓ
65. Write books or plays   **Ⓛ**   ⓵   Ⓓ
66. Play a musical instrument   Ⓛ   **⓵**   Ⓓ
67. Perform comedy routines in front of an audience   Ⓛ   ⓵   **Ⓓ**
68. Perform as an extra in movies, plays, or television shows   **Ⓛ**   ⓵   Ⓓ
69. Write reviews of books or plays   **Ⓛ**   ⓵   Ⓓ
70. Compose or arrange music   Ⓛ   ⓵   **Ⓓ**
71. Act in a movie   **Ⓛ**   ⓵   Ⓓ
72. Dance in a Broadway show   Ⓛ   ⓵   **Ⓓ**
73. Draw pictures   **Ⓛ**   ⓵   Ⓓ
74. Sing professionally   Ⓛ   ⓵   **Ⓓ**
75. Perform stunts for a movie or television show   Ⓛ   ⓵   **Ⓓ**
76. Create special effects for movies   Ⓛ   ⓵   **Ⓓ**
77. Conduct a musical choir   Ⓛ   ⓵   **Ⓓ**
78. Act in a play   **Ⓛ**   ⓵   Ⓓ
79. Paint sets for plays   Ⓛ   **⓵**   Ⓓ
80. Audition singers and musicians for a musical show   **Ⓛ**   ⓵   Ⓓ
81. Design sets for plays   Ⓛ   **⓵**   Ⓓ
82. Announce a radio show   Ⓛ   ⓵   **Ⓓ**
83. Write scripts for movies or television shows   **Ⓛ**   ⓵   Ⓓ
84. Write a song   Ⓛ   ⓵   **Ⓓ**
85. Perform jazz or tap dance   Ⓛ   ⓵   **Ⓓ**
86. Direct a movie   Ⓛ   **⓵**   Ⓓ
87. Sing in a band   Ⓛ   **⓵**   Ⓓ
88. Design artwork for magazines   **Ⓛ**   ⓵   Ⓓ
89. Edit movies   **Ⓛ**   ⓵   Ⓓ
90. Pose for a photographer   Ⓛ   ⓵   **Ⓓ**

Page Score for A

Would you LIKE the activity or DISLIKE the activity, or are you UNSURE?

91. Teach an individual an exercise routine — L (?) D
92. Perform nursing duties in a hospital — L ? D
93. Give CPR to someone who has stopped breathing — L ? D
94. Help people with personal or emotional problems — L ? D
95. Teach children how to read — L (?) D
96. Work with mentally disabled children — L (?) D
97. Teach an elementary school class — L (?) D
98. Give career guidance to people — L ? D
99. Supervise the activities of children at a camp — L (?) D
100. Help people with family-related problems — L ? D
101. Perform rehabilitation therapy — L ? D
102. Do volunteer work at a nonprofit organization — L ? D
103. Help elderly people with their daily activities — L (?) D
104. Teach children how to play sports — L (?) D
105. Help disabled people improve their daily living skills — L ? D
106. Teach sign language to people with hearing disabilities — L ? D
107. Help people who have problems with drugs or alcohol — L ? D
108. Help conduct a group therapy session — L ? D
109. Help families care for ill relatives — L (?) D
110. Provide massage therapy to people — L ? D
111. Plan exercises for disabled students — L ? D
112. Counsel people who have a life-threatening illness — L ? D
113. Teach disabled people work and living skills — L ? D
114. Organize activities at a recreational facility — L (?) D
115. Take care of children at a day-care center — L ? D
116. Organize field trips for disabled people — L ? D
117. Assist doctors in treating patients — L ? D
118. Work with juveniles on probation — L ? D
119. Provide physical therapy to people recovering from an injury — L ? D
120. Teach a high school class — L ? D

_14_ **Page Score for S**

Would you LIKE the activity or DISLIKE the activity, or are you UNSURE?

121. Buy and sell stocks and bonds — L — ? — D
122. Manage a retail store — L — ? — D
123. Sell telephone and other communication equipment — L — ? — D
124. Operate a beauty salon or barbershop — L — ? — D
125. Sell merchandise over the telephone — L — ? — D
126. Run a stand that sells newspapers and magazines — L — ? — D
127. Give a presentation about a product you are selling — L — ? — D
128. Buy and sell land — L — ? — D
129. Sell compact discs at a music store — L — ? — D
130. Run a toy store — L — ? — D
131. Manage the operations of a hotel — L — ? — D
132. Sell houses — L — ? — D
133. Sell candy and popcorn at sports events — L — ? — D
134. Manage a supermarket — L — ? — D
135. Manage a department within a large company — L — ? — D
136. Sell a soft drink product line to stores and restaurants — L — ? — D
137. Sell refreshments at a movie theater — L — ? — D
138. Sell hair-care products to stores and salons — L — ? — D
139. Start your own business — L — ? — D
140. Negotiate business contracts — L — ? — D
141. Represent a client in a lawsuit — L — ? — D
142. Negotiate contracts for professional athletes — L — ? — D
143. Be responsible for the operation of a company — L — ? — D
144. Market a new line of clothing — L — ? — D
145. Sell newspaper advertisements — L — ? — D
146. Sell merchandise at a department store — L — ? — D
147. Sell automobiles — L — ? — D
148. Manage a clothing store — L — ? — D
149. Sell restaurant franchises to individuals — L — ? — D
150. Sell computer equipment in a store — L — ? — D

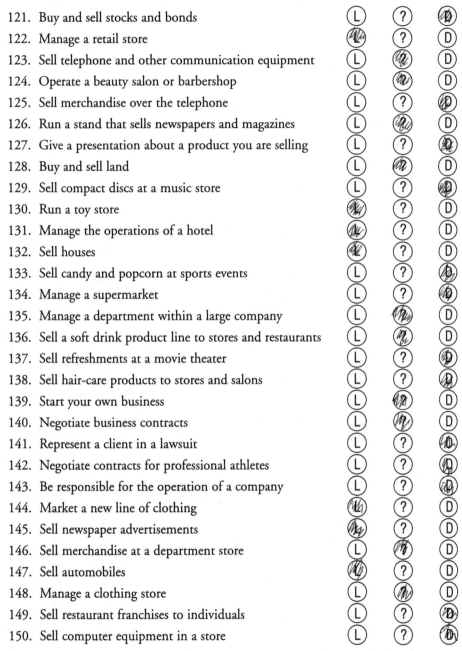

Page Score for E

Would you LIKE the activity or DISLIKE the activity, or are you UNSURE?

		L	?	D
151.	Develop a spreadsheet using computer software	L	?	D
152.	Proofread records or forms	L	?	D
153.	Use a computer program to generate customer bills	L	?	D
154.	Schedule conferences for an organization	L	?	D
155.	Keep accounts payable/receivable for an office	L	?	D
156.	Load computer software into a large computer network	L	?	D
157.	Transfer funds between banks using a computer	L	?	D
158.	Organize and schedule office meetings	L	?	D
159.	Use a word processor to edit and format documents	L	?	D
160.	Operate a calculator	L	?	D
161.	Direct or transfer phone calls for a large organization	L	?	D
162.	Perform office filing tasks	L	?	D
163.	Compute and record statistical and other numerical data	L	?	D
164.	Generate the monthly payroll checks for an office	L	?	D
165.	Take notes during a meeting	L	?	D
166.	Keep shipping and receiving records	L	?	D
167.	Calculate the wages of employees	L	?	D
168.	Assist senior-level accountants in performing bookkeeping tasks	L	?	D
169.	Type labels for envelopes and packages	L	?	D
170.	Inventory supplies using a hand-held computer	L	?	D
171.	Develop an office filing system	L	?	D
172.	Keep records of financial transactions for an organization	L	?	D
173.	Record information from customers applying for charge accounts	L	?	D
174.	Photocopy letters and reports	L	?	D
175.	Record rent payments	L	?	D
176.	Enter information into a database	L	?	D
177.	Keep inventory records	L	?	D
178.	Maintain employee records	L	?	D
179.	Stamp, sort, and distribute mail for an organization	L	?	D
180.	Handle customers' bank transactions	L	?	D

Page Score for C

Step 2: Score Your Responses

Do the following to score your responses:

1. **Score the responses on each page.** On each page of responses, go from top to bottom and add the number of "L"s you filled in. Then write that number in the "Page Score" box at the bottom of the page. Go on to the next page and do the same there.

2. **Determine your primary interest area.** Which Page Score has your highest score: **R, I, A, S, E,** or **C**? Enter the letter for that personality type on the following line.

My Primary Personality Type: SA

You will use your Primary Personality Type *first* to explore careers. (If two Page Scores are tied for the highest scores or are within 5 points of each other, use both of them for your Primary Personality Type. You are equally divided between two types.)

- ◉ R = Realistic
- ◉ I = Investigative
- ◉ A = Artistic
- ◉ S = Social
- ◉ E = Enterprising
- ◉ C = Conventional

3. **Determine your secondary interest areas.** Which Page Score has your next highest score? Which has your third highest score? Enter the letters for those areas on the following lines.

My Secondary Personality Types: R I

(If you do not find many occupations that you like using your Primary Personality Type, you can use your Secondary Personality Types to look at more career options.)

Step 3: Find Jobs That Suit Your Personality Type

Start with your Primary Personality Type. Turn to Part III and look at the Best Jobs lists for your type. Find lists that suit your particular priorities and see what job titles appear there. Don't rule out a job just because the title is not familiar to you.

When you find job titles that interest you or that you want to learn more about, turn to Part IV. The job descriptions there are grouped by Primary Personality Types and are listed alphabetically within each type. Of course, you can also look at jobs that are linked to one of your Secondary Personality Types.

If you want to find jobs that *combine* your Primary Personality Type and a Secondary Personality Type, turn to Appendix A. All 300 jobs in this book are listed there by their one- or two-letter personality codes. For example, if your Primary Personality Type is Social and your Secondary Personality Type is Enterprising, you would look in Appendix A for the letter S and then for jobs coded SE, such as Personal Financial Advisors and Training and Development Specialists.

You may discover that you can't find an appealing job in your Primary Personality Type that *also* is coded for one of your Secondary Personality Types. That is not necessarily a problem. John Holland himself has remarked, "You cannot expect a single job to satisfy all aspects of your personality." This is why we have hobbies. Use recreational time for activities related to your Secondary Personality Types. Volunteer work can be another outlet for these interests and abilities.

PART III

The Best Jobs Lists: Jobs for Each of the Six Personality Types

This part contains a lot of interesting lists, and it's a good place for you to start using the book. Here are some suggestions for using the lists to explore career options:

- The Table of Contents at the beginning of this book presents a complete listing of the list titles in this section. You can browse the lists or use the Table of Contents to find those that interest you most.

- We gave the lists clear titles, so most require little explanation. We provide comments for each group of lists.

- As you review the lists, one or more of the jobs may appeal to you enough that you want to seek additional information. As this happens, mark that job (or, if someone else will be using this book, write it on a separate sheet of paper) so that you can look up the description of the job in Part IV.

- Keep in mind that all jobs in these lists meet our basic criteria for being included in this book. All lists, therefore, are organized by personality type and emphasize occupations with high pay, high growth, or large numbers of openings. These measures are easily quantified and are often presented in lists of best jobs in the newspapers and other media. While earnings, growth, and openings are important, there are other factors to consider in your career planning. For example, location, having an opportunity to serve others, and enjoying your work are a few of many factors that may define the ideal job for you. These measures are difficult or impossible to quantify and thus are not used in this book, so you will need to consider the importance of these issues yourself.

- All data used to create these lists comes from the U.S. Department of Labor. The earnings figures are based on the average annual pay received by full-time workers. Because the earnings represent the national averages, actual pay rates can vary greatly by location, amount of previous work experience, and other factors.

Best Jobs Overall for Each Personality Type: Jobs with the Highest Pay, Fastest Growth, and Most Openings

The four sets of lists that follow are the most important lists in this book. The first set of lists presents, for each personality type, the jobs with the highest combined scores for pay, growth, and number of openings. These are very appealing lists because they represent jobs with the very highest quantifiable measures from our labor market. The 300 jobs in these six lists are the ones that are described in detail in Part IV.

The three additional sets of lists present, for each personality type, jobs with the highest scores in each of three measures: annual earnings, projected percentage growth, and largest number of openings.

The 50 Best Jobs for Each Personality Type

These are the lists that most people want to see first. For each personality type, you can see the jobs that have the highest overall combined ratings for earnings, projected growth, and number of openings. (The section in the Introduction on "How the Jobs in This Book Were Selected" explains in detail how we rated jobs to assemble this list.)

Although each list covers one personality type, you'll notice a wide variety of jobs on the list. For example, among the top 10 Investigative jobs are some in the fields of high technology, higher education, and medicine. Among the top 10 Conventional jobs are some in the financial, legal, law enforcement, and manufacturing industries. We included each job's personality code, which indicates its Primary and Secondary (if any) Personality Types.

A look at one list will clarify how we ordered the jobs—take the Realistic list as an example. Highway Patrol Pilots was the occupation with the best total score, and it is on the top of the list. The other occupations follow in descending order based on their total scores. Many jobs had tied scores and were simply listed one after another, so there are often only very small or even no differences between the scores of jobs that are near each other on the list. All other jobs lists in this book use these jobs as their source list. You can find descriptions for each of these jobs in Part IV, beginning on page 119.

The 50 Best Realistic Jobs

Job	Personality Code	Annual Earnings	Percent Growth	Annual Openings
1. Highway Patrol Pilots	RE	$44,020	24.7%	67,000
2. Electricians	RI	$41,680	23.4%	65,000
3. Pipe Fitters	R	$40,950	18.7%	56,000
4. Pipelaying Fitters	R	$40,950	18.7%	56,000
5. Plumbers	R	$40,950	18.7%	56,000
6. Heating and Air Conditioning Mechanics	RC	$35,160	31.8%	35,000
7. Refrigeration Mechanics	RC	$35,160	31.8%	35,000
8. Tractor-Trailer Truck Drivers	RC	$33,310	19.0%	299,000
9. Truck Drivers, Heavy	R	$33,310	19.0%	299,000
10. Radiologic Technicians	RC	$40,620	22.9%	21,000
11. Radiologic Technologists	RI	$40,620	22.9%	21,000
12. Refractory Materials Repairers, Except Brickmasons	R	$36,910	16.3%	155,000
13. Correctional Officers and Jailers	RS	$33,160	24.2%	49,000
14. Forest Fire Fighters	RS	$37,060	20.7%	29,000
15. Municipal Fire Fighters	RS	$37,060	20.7%	29,000
16. Sheet Metal Workers	R	$35,000	19.8%	30,000
17. Forest Fire Fighting and Prevention Supervisors	RE	$57,000	18.7%	8,000
18. Municipal Fire Fighting and Prevention Supervisors	RE	$57,000	18.7%	8,000
19. Technical Directors/Managers	RA	$48,200	18.3%	10,000
20. Airline Pilots, Copilots, and Flight Engineers	RE	$125,030	18.5%	6,000
21. Brickmasons and Blockmasons	R	$41,550	14.2%	21,000
22. Telecommunications Line Installers and Repairers	R	$39,540	18.8%	13,000
23. Boat Builders and Shipwrights	RC	$34,250	10.1%	193,000
24. Brattice Builders	R	$34,250	10.1%	193,000
25. Carpenter Assemblers and Repairers	RC	$34,250	10.1%	193,000
26. Construction Carpenters	R	$34,250	10.1%	193,000
27. Rough Carpenters	RC	$34,250	10.1%	193,000
28. Ship Carpenters and Joiners	R	$34,250	10.1%	193,000
29. First-Line Supervisors and Manager/ Supervisors—Landscaping Workers	RE	$33,770	21.6%	18,000
30. Calibration and Instrumentation Technicians	RC	$43,650	10.0%	24,000
31. Electrical Engineering Technicians	RI	$43,650	10.0%	24,000

(continued)

(continued)

The 50 Best Realistic Jobs

Job	Personality Code	Annual Earnings	Percent Growth	Annual Openings
32. Electronics Engineering Technicians	RI	$43,650	10.0%	24,000
33. Ceiling Tile Installers	R	$33,670	21.4%	17,000
34. Drywall Installers	R	$33,670	21.4%	17,000
35. Cement Masons and Concrete Finishers	R	$30,780	26.1%	24,000
36. Maintenance and Repair Workers, General	RC	$29,800	16.3%	155,000
37. Pressure Vessel Inspectors	RC	$46,780	9.8%	20,000
38. Bus and Truck Mechanics and Diesel Engine Specialists	RC	$34,970	14.2%	28,000
39. Brazers	RC	$29,640	17.0%	71,000
40. Solderers	RC	$29,640	17.0%	71,000
41. Welder-Fitters	RI	$29,640	17.0%	71,000
42. Welders and Cutters	RC	$29,640	17.0%	71,000
43. Welders, Production	R	$29,640	17.0%	71,000
44. Roofers	R	$30,020	18.6%	38,000
45. Grader, Bulldozer, and Scraper Operators	RC	$35,030	10.4%	45,000
46. Operating Engineers	RI	$35,030	10.4%	45,000
47. Civil Engineers	RI	$61,850	8.0%	17,000
48. Surgical Technologists	RS	$32,130	27.9%	13,000
49. Automotive Master Mechanics	RC	$31,130	12.4%	100,000
50. Automotive Specialty Technicians	RC	$31,130	12.4%	100,000

The 50 Best Investigative Jobs

Job	Personality Code	Annual Earnings	Percent Growth	Annual Openings
1. Engineering Teachers, Postsecondary	IR	$69,700	38.1%	216,000
2. Computer Software Engineers, Systems Software	IR	$76,240	45.5%	39,000
3. Computer Software Engineers, Applications	IR	$72,530	45.5%	55,000
4. Agricultural Sciences Teachers, Postsecondary	IS	$65,470	38.1%	216,000
5. Forestry and Conservation Science Teachers, Postsecondary	IS	$64,500	38.1%	216,000
6. Physics Teachers, Postsecondary	IS	$62,880	38.1%	216,000

The 50 Best Investigative Jobs

Job	Personality Code	Annual Earnings	Percent Growth	Annual Openings
7. Health Specialties Teachers, Postsecondary	IS	$61,790	38.1%	216,000
8. Anesthesiologists	IR	over $145,000	19.5%	38,000
9. Internists, General	I	over $145,000	19.5%	38,000
10. Obstetricians and Gynecologists	I	over $145,000	19.5%	38,000
11. Surgeons	IR	over $145,000	19.5%	38,000
12. Pediatricians, General	I	$134,170	19.5%	38,000
13. Computer Systems Analysts	IC	$64,160	39.4%	68,000
14. Psychiatrists	IA	$133,970	19.5%	38,000
15. Family and General Practitioners	I	$133,340	19.5%	38,000
16. Pharmacists	IC	$80,530	30.1%	23,000
17. Biological Science Teachers, Postsecondary	IS	$55,840	38.1%	216,000
18. Chemistry Teachers, Postsecondary	IS	$55,420	38.1%	216,000
19. Physician Assistants	IS	$65,670	48.9%	7,000
20. Network Systems and Data Communications Analysts	IR	$59,120	57.0%	29,000
21. Computer Science Teachers, Postsecondary	IC	$51,030	38.1%	216,000
22. Mathematical Science Teachers, Postsecondary	IS	$50,910	38.1%	216,000
23. Database Administrators	IC	$58,200	44.2%	16,000
24. Computer Security Specialists	IR	$56,050	37.4%	35,000
25. Computer Programmers	IR	$61,340	14.6%	45,000
26. Veterinarians	IR	$64,750	25.1%	4,000
27. Financial Analysts	IC	$60,050	18.7%	22,000
28. Market Research Analysts	IE	$54,670	23.4%	18,000
29. Medical Scientists, Except Epidemiologists	IR	$59,210	26.9%	6,000
30. Chiropractors	IR	$65,990	23.3%	3,000
31. Clinical Psychologists	IA	$52,220	24.4%	17,000
32. Educational Psychologists	IS	$52,220	24.4%	17,000
33. Electronics Engineers, Except Computer	IR	$71,370	9.4%	11,000
34. Natural Sciences Managers	IE	$85,860	11.3%	5,000
35. Optometrists	IR	$85,430	17.1%	2,000
36. Computer Support Specialists	IC	$39,440	30.3%	71,000
37. Dentists, General	IR	$120,330	4.1%	7,000
38. Oral and Maxillofacial Surgeons	IR	$120,330	4.1%	7,000
39. Orthodontists	IR	$120,330	4.1%	7,000
40. Prosthodontists	IR	$120,330	4.1%	7,000

(continued)

(continued)

The 50 Best Investigative Jobs

Job	Personality Code	Annual Earnings	Percent Growth	Annual Openings
41. Biochemists	IR	$62,300	22.9%	2,000
42. Biophysicists	IR	$62,300	22.9%	2,000
43. Compensation, Benefits, and Job Analysis Specialists	IC	$46,860	28.0%	15,000
44. Economists	IE	$70,250	13.4%	2,000
45. Respiratory Therapists	IR	$41,150	34.8%	10,000
46. Computer Hardware Engineers	IR	$75,980	6.1%	6,000
47. Geologists	IR	$68,460	11.5%	2,000
48. Environmental Scientists and Specialists, Including Health	IR	$48,790	23.7%	6,000
49. Electrical Engineers	IR	$69,640	2.5%	11,000
50. Medical and Clinical Laboratory Technologists	IR	$43,640	19.3%	21,000

The 50 Best Artistic Jobs

Job	Personality Code	Annual Earnings	Percent Growth	Annual Openings
1. Art, Drama, and Music Teachers, Postsecondary	AS	$47,980	38.1%	216,000
2. English Language and Literature Teachers, Postsecondary	AS	$47,120	38.1%	216,000
3. Foreign Language and Literature Teachers, Postsecondary	AS	$46,780	38.1%	216,000
4. Advertising and Promotions Managers	AE	$60,350	25.0%	13,000
5. Graphic Designers	AE	$36,630	21.9%	29,000
6. Directors—Stage, Motion Pictures, Television, and Radio	AE	$48,200	18.3%	10,000
7. Producers	AE	$48,200	18.3%	10,000
8. Talent Directors	AE	$48,200	18.3%	10,000
9. Technical Writers	AI	$51,590	27.1%	6,000
10. Architects, Except Landscape and Naval	AR	$57,950	17.3%	8,000
11. Musicians, Instrumental	A	$37,380	17.1%	25,000
12. Singers	AE	$37,380	17.1%	25,000
13. Caption Writers	AS	$42,330	16.1%	23,000
14. Copy Writers	AE	$42,330	16.1%	23,000
15. Costume Attendants	AR	$25,410	27.8%	66,000

The 50 Best Artistic Jobs

Job	Personality Code	Annual Earnings	Percent Growth	Annual Openings
16. Creative Writers	A	$42,330	16.1%	23,000
17. Poets and Lyricists	AI	$42,330	16.1%	23,000
18. Interior Designers	AE	$40,120	21.7%	8,000
19. Landscape Architects	AR	$50,480	22.2%	2,000
20. Art Directors	AE	$62,260	11.4%	8,000
21. Film and Video Editors	A	$40,600	26.4%	3,000
22. Commercial and Industrial Designers	AR	$52,320	14.7%	7,000
23. Librarians	AC	$44,140	10.1%	15,000
24. Editors	AS	$41,460	11.8%	14,000
25. Interpreters and Translators	AS	$33,490	22.1%	4,000
26. Actors	AE	$26,460	17.7%	8,000
27. Cartoonists	AE	$35,420	16.5%	4,000
28. Painters and Illustrators	AR	$35,420	16.5%	4,000
29. Sculptors	AR	$35,420	16.5%	4,000
30. Sketch Artists	AR	$35,420	16.5%	4,000
31. Exhibit Designers	AR	$35,150	20.9%	2,000
32. Set Designers	AR	$35,150	20.9%	2,000
33. Curators	AI	$35,660	17.0%	2,000
34. Museum Technicians and Conservators	AR	$35,660	17.0%	2,000
35. Photographers, Scientific	AR	$25,050	13.6%	18,000
36. Professional Photographers	AR	$25,050	13.6%	18,000
37. Composers	A	$32,530	13.5%	8,000
38. Fashion Designers	AE	$52,860	10.6%	2,000
39. Music Arrangers and Orchestrators	A	$32,530	13.5%	8,000
40. Music Directors	AS	$32,530	13.5%	8,000
41. Camera Operators, Television, Video, and Motion Picture	AR	$34,330	13.4%	4,000
42. Floral Designers	AR	$19,660	12.4%	13,000
43. Makeup Artists, Theatrical and Performance	AR	$29,320	18.2%	fewer than 500
44. Merchandise Displayers and Window Trimmers	AR	$22,030	11.3%	10,000
45. Choreographers	AS	$31,030	15.8%	3,000
46. Broadcast News Analysts	AS	$31,240	6.2%	6,000
47. Reporters and Correspondents	AI	$31,240	6.2%	6,000
48. Radio and Television Announcers	AS	$20,940	–10.1%	8,000
49. Models	AE	$24,270	14.5%	1,000
50. Photographic Retouchers and Restorers	AR	$20,370	5.4%	4,000

The 50 Best Social Jobs

Job	Personality Code	Annual Earnings	Percent Growth	Annual Openings
1. Economics Teachers, Postsecondary	SI	$64,950	38.1%	216,000
2. Anthropology and Archeology Teachers, Postsecondary	SI	$59,710	38.1%	216,000
3. Political Science Teachers, Postsecondary	SI	$57,340	38.1%	216,000
4. Area, Ethnic, and Cultural Studies Teachers, Postsecondary	SI	$55,060	38.1%	216,000
5. Psychology Teachers, Postsecondary	SI	$54,170	38.1%	216,000
6. Sociology Teachers, Postsecondary	SI	$52,770	38.1%	216,000
7. History Teachers, Postsecondary	SI	$52,180	38.1%	216,000
8. Nursing Instructors and Teachers, Postsecondary	SI	$50,920	38.1%	216,000
9. Vocational Education Teachers, Postsecondary	SR	$39,740	38.1%	216,000
10. Registered Nurses	SI	$49,550	27.3%	215,000
11. Personal Financial Advisors	SE	$58,700	34.6%	18,000
12. Graduate Teaching Assistants	SI	$24,570	38.1%	216,000
13. Dental Hygienists	SC	$56,360	43.1%	9,000
14. Physical Therapists	SR	$57,710	35.3%	16,000
15. Special Education Teachers, Secondary School	SA	$44,240	30.0%	59,000
16. Medical Assistants	SC	$24,170	58.9%	78,000
17. Special Education Teachers, Preschool, Kindergarten, and Elementary School	SA	$42,920	30.0%	59,000
18. Social and Human Service Assistants	SC	$23,860	48.7%	63,000
19. Special Education Teachers, Middle School	SA	$42,010	30.0%	59,000
20. Occupational Therapists	SR	$52,550	35.2%	10,000
21. Education Administrators, Elementary and Secondary School	SE	$73,490	20.7%	31,000
22. Self-Enrichment Education Teachers	SA	$29,820	40.1%	39,000
23. Police Patrol Officers	SR	$44,020	24.7%	67,000
24. Sheriffs and Deputy Sheriffs	SE	$44,020	24.7%	67,000
25. Training and Development Specialists	SE	$44,160	27.9%	35,000
26. Dental Assistants	SR	$27,700	42.5%	35,000
27. Fitness Trainers and Aerobics Instructors	SR	$24,510	44.5%	38,000
28. Home Health Aides	SR	$18,240	48.1%	141,000
29. Secondary School Teachers, Except Special and Vocational Education	SA	$44,580	18.2%	118,000
30. Social and Community Service Managers	SE	$45,450	27.7%	19,000
31. Security Guards	SE	$19,660	31.9%	228,000

The 50 Best Social Jobs

Job	Personality Code	Annual Earnings	Percent Growth	Annual Openings
32. Personal and Home Care Aides	SR	$16,450	40.5%	154,000
33. Physical Therapist Assistants	SR	$36,610	44.6%	10,000
34. Counseling Psychologists	SI	$52,220	24.4%	17,000
35. Instructional Coordinators	SI	$47,470	25.4%	18,000
36. Kindergarten Teachers, Except Special Education	SA	$40,160	27.2%	34,000
37. Preschool Teachers, Except Special Education	SA	$19,820	36.2%	88,000
38. Elementary School Teachers, Except Special Education	SA	$42,160	15.2%	183,000
39. Employment Interviewers, Private or Public Employment Service	SE	$40,770	27.3%	29,000
40. Speech-Language Pathologists	SI	$50,050	27.2%	10,000
41. Nursing Aides, Orderlies, and Attendants	SR	$20,490	24.9%	302,000
42. Radiation Therapists	SR	$54,190	31.6%	1,000
43. Medical and Public Health Social Workers	SI	$38,430	28.6%	18,000
44. Mental Health and Substance Abuse Social Workers	SI	$33,020	34.5%	17,000
45. Emergency Medical Technicians and Paramedics	SR	$24,440	33.1%	32,000
46. Licensed Practical and Licensed Vocational Nurses	SR	$32,390	20.2%	105,000
47. Occupational Therapist Assistants	SR	$37,400	39.2%	3,000
48. Child, Family, and School Social Workers	S	$33,810	23.2%	45,000
49. Educational, Vocational, and School Counselors	SA	$44,640	15.0%	32,000
50. Teacher Assistants	SC	$19,000	23.0%	259,000

The 50 Best Enterprising Jobs

Job	Personality Code	Annual Earnings	Percent Growth	Annual Openings
1. Sales Managers	EC	$80,470	30.5%	54,000
2. Management Analysts	EC	$62,580	30.4%	78,000

(continued)

(continued)

The 50 Best Enterprising Jobs

Job	Personality Code	Annual Earnings	Percent Growth	Annual Openings
3. Computer and Information Systems Managers	EC	$89,740	36.1%	39,000
4. Financial Managers, Branch or Department	EC	$77,300	18.3%	71,000
5. Treasurers, Controllers, and Chief Financial Officers	EC	$77,300	18.3%	71,000
6. Government Service Executives	EC	$134,740	16.7%	63,000
7. Medical and Health Services Managers	ES	$64,550	29.3%	33,000
8. Private Sector Executives	EC	$134,740	16.7%	63,000
9. Marketing Managers	EC	$83,210	21.3%	30,000
10. Lawyers	EC	$91,490	17.0%	53,000
11. Sales Representatives, Agricultural	ER	$57,120	19.3%	44,000
12. Sales Representatives, Chemical and Pharmaceutical	ES	$57,120	19.3%	44,000
13. Sales Representatives, Electrical/Electronic	ER	$57,120	19.3%	44,000
14. Sales Representatives, Instruments	ER	$57,120	19.3%	44,000
15. Sales Representatives, Mechanical Equipment and Supplies	ER	$57,120	19.3%	44,000
16. Sales Representatives, Medical	ES	$57,120	19.3%	44,000
17. Administrative Services Managers	EC	$56,940	19.8%	40,000
18. Education Administrators, Postsecondary	ES	$66,640	25.9%	19,000
19. Sales Representatives, Wholesale and Manufacturing, Except Technical and Scientific Products	ES	$43,860	19.1%	160,000
20. Compensation and Benefits Managers	ES	$68,800	19.4%	21,000
21. Human Resources Managers	ES	$68,800	19.4%	21,000
22. Training and Development Managers	ES	$68,800	19.4%	21,000
23. Construction Managers	ER	$66,470	12.0%	47,000
24. Public Relations Specialists	EA	$42,590	32.9%	28,000
25. Storage and Distribution Managers	EC	$63,590	19.7%	13,000
26. Transportation Managers	EC	$63,590	19.7%	13,000
27. Personnel Recruiters	ES	$40,770	27.3%	29,000
28. Sales Engineers	ER	$67,790	19.9%	7,000
29. First-Line Supervisors and Manager/Supervisors—Construction Trades Workers	ER	$48,730	14.1%	67,000
30. First-Line Supervisors and Manager/Supervisors—Extractive Workers	ER	$48,730	14.1%	67,000

The 50 Best Enterprising Jobs

Job	Personality Code	Annual Earnings	Percent Growth	Annual Openings
31. Sales Agents, Financial Services	EC	$60,530	13.0%	39,000
32. Sales Agents, Securities and Commodities	EC	$60,530	13.0%	39,000
33. Paralegals and Legal Assistants	EC	$37,930	28.7%	29,000
34. Child Support, Missing Persons, and Unemployment Insurance Fraud Investigators	ES	$52,390	22.4%	11,000
35. Criminal Investigators and Special Agents	EI	$52,390	22.4%	11,000
36. Police Detectives	ES	$52,390	22.4%	11,000
37. First-Line Supervisors/Managers of Mechanics, Installers, and Repairers	ER	$48,620	15.4%	42,000
38. Loan Officers	ES	$46,640	18.8%	30,000
39. First-Line Supervisors/Managers of Non-Retail Sales Workers	EC	$55,690	6.8%	72,000
40. Agents and Business Managers of Artists, Performers, and Athletes	ES	$54,640	27.8%	2,000
41. First-Line Supervisors/Managers of Food Preparation and Serving Workers	ER	$24,700	15.5%	154,000
42. Engineering Managers	ER	$94,470	9.2%	16,000
43. First-Line Supervisors/Managers of Police and Detectives	ES	$62,350	15.3%	14,000
44. First-Line Supervisors/Managers of Production and Operating Workers	ER	$43,720	9.5%	66,000
45. Insurance Adjusters, Examiners, and Investigators	EI	$44,040	14.2%	31,000
46. Hosts and Hostesses, Restaurant, Lounge, and Coffee Shop	ES	$15,380	16.4%	95,000
47. Lawn Service Managers	ER	$33,770	21.6%	18,000
48. Program Directors	EA	$48,200	18.3%	10,000
49. Retail Salespersons	ES	$18,090	14.6%	1,014,000
50. First-Line Supervisors, Administrative Support	EC	$39,490	6.6%	140,000

The 50 Best Conventional Jobs

Job	Personality Code	Annual Earnings	Percent Growth	Annual Openings
1. Accountants	CE	$49,060	19.5%	119,000
2. Auditors	CE	$49,060	19.5%	119,000
3. Adjustment Clerks	CE	$26,500	24.3%	419,000
4. Customer Service Representatives, Utilities	CE	$26,500	24.3%	419,000
5. Cost Estimators	CE	$48,290	18.6%	25,000
6. Legal Secretaries	CE	$35,660	18.8%	39,000
7. Immigration and Customs Inspectors	CE	$52,390	22.4%	11,000
8. Police Identification and Records Officers	CR	$52,390	22.4%	11,000
9. Bill and Account Collectors	CE	$27,000	24.5%	76,000
10. Production, Planning, and Expediting Clerks	CE	$34,820	14.1%	51,000
11. Claims Examiners, Property and Casualty Insurance	CE	$44,040	14.2%	31,000
12. Human Resources Assistants, Except Payroll and Timekeeping	CE	$31,060	19.3%	36,000
13. Executive Secretaries and Administrative Assistants	CE	$34,080	8.7%	210,000
14. Receptionists and Information Clerks	CE	$21,320	29.5%	296,000
15. Assessors	CE	$43,610	17.6%	11,000
16. Credit Analysts	CE	$45,020	18.7%	9,000
17. Dispatchers, Except Police, Fire, and Ambulance	CR	$30,390	14.4%	28,000
18. Counter and Rental Clerks	CE	$17,640	26.3%	144,000
19. Interviewers, Except Eligibility and Loan	CS	$22,590	28.0%	46,000
20. Budget Analysts	CE	$54,520	14.0%	8,000
21. Licensing Examiners and Inspectors	CE	$46,780	9.8%	20,000
22. Pharmacy Technicians	CR	$22,760	28.8%	39,000
23. Medical Secretaries	CE	$26,000	17.2%	50,000
24. Actuaries	CI	$72,520	14.9%	2,000
25. Medical Records and Health Information Technicians	C	$24,520	46.8%	24,000
26. Audio and Video Equipment Technicians	CS	$30,810	26.7%	5,000
27. Mapping Technicians	CR	$29,520	23.1%	10,000
28. Bookkeeping, Accounting, and Auditing Clerks	CE	$27,760	3.0%	274,000
29. Insurance Underwriters	CE	$47,330	10.0%	12,000
30. Construction and Building Inspectors	CR	$42,650	13.8%	10,000
31. Air Traffic Controllers	CR	$96,260	12.6%	2,000
32. Hotel, Motel, and Resort Desk Clerks	CE	$17,450	23.9%	46,000

The 50 Best Conventional Jobs

Job	Personality Code	Annual Earnings	Percent Growth	Annual Openings
33. Office Clerks, General	C	$22,450	10.4%	550,000
34. Cashiers	CE	$15,760	13.2%	1,221,000
35. Billing, Cost, and Rate Clerks	CE	$26,290	7.9%	78,000
36. Billing, Posting, and Calculating Machine Operators	CR	$26,290	7.9%	78,000
37. Statement Clerks	CE	$26,290	7.9%	78,000
38. Tax Preparers	CE	$26,530	23.2%	11,000
39. Cargo and Freight Agents	CR	$31,990	15.5%	8,000
40. Insurance Claims Clerks	CE	$28,520	3.6%	41,000
41. Insurance Policy Processing Clerks	CE	$28,520	3.6%	41,000
42. Cartographers and Photogrammetrists	CR	$44,170	15.1%	1,000
43. Postal Service Mail Carriers	CR	$39,620	–0.5%	20,000
44. Freight Inspectors	CR	$49,590	7.7%	5,000
45. Marine Cargo Inspectors	CR	$49,590	7.7%	5,000
46. Reservation and Transportation Ticket Agents	CE	$26,220	12.2%	35,000
47. Travel Clerks	CS	$26,220	12.2%	35,000
48. Library Assistants, Clerical	CR	$19,930	21.5%	27,000
49. Audio-Visual Collections Specialists	CS	$32,590	16.3%	2,000
50. Court Clerks	CE	$27,450	12.3%	14,000

The 20 Best-Paying Jobs for Each Personality Type

In the following six lists you'll find the 20 best-paying jobs for each personality type that met our criteria for this book. These are popular lists, for obvious reasons.

If you compare these six lists, you may notice that some personality types have better income possibilities than others. For example, the best-paying Investigative and Enterprising jobs command much higher incomes than the best-paying Artistic and Conventional jobs. Keep in mind that these figures are only averages; there are a few artists (for example, think of movie stars) who are earning more than obstetricians. Also remember what we said earlier about how earnings can vary by region of the country and amount of experience and because of many other factors.

The 20 Best-Paying Realistic Jobs

Job	Annual Earnings
1. Airline Pilots, Copilots, and Flight Engineers	$125,030
2. Civil Engineers	$61,850
3. Forest Fire Fighting and Prevention Supervisors	$57,000
4. Municipal Fire Fighting and Prevention Supervisors	$57,000
5. Technical Directors/Managers	$48,200
6. Pressure Vessel Inspectors	$46,780
7. Highway Patrol Pilots	$44,020
8. Calibration and Instrumentation Technicians	$43,650
9. Electrical Engineering Technicians	$43,650
10. Electronics Engineering Technicians	$43,650
11. Electricians	$41,680
12. Brickmasons and Blockmasons	$41,550
13. Pipe Fitters	$40,950
14. Pipelaying Fitters	$40,950
15. Plumbers	$40,950
16. Radiologic Technicians	$40,620
17. Radiologic Technologists	$40,620
18. Telecommunications Line Installers and Repairers	$39,540
19. Forest Fire Fighters	$37,060
20. Municipal Fire Fighters	$37,060

The 20 Best-Paying Investigative Jobs

Job	Annual Earnings
1. Anesthesiologists	over $145,000
2. Internists, General	over $145,000
3. Obstetricians and Gynecologists	over $145,000
4. Surgeons	over $145,000
5. Pediatricians, General	$134,170
6. Psychiatrists	$133,970
7. Family and General Practitioners	$133,340
8. Dentists, General	$120,330
9. Oral and Maxillofacial Surgeons	$120,330
10. Orthodontists	$120,330
11. Prosthodontists	$120,330
12. Natural Sciences Managers	$85,860

The 20 Best-Paying Investigative Jobs

Job	Annual Earnings
13. Optometrists	$85,430
14. Pharmacists	$80,530
15. Computer Software Engineers, Systems Software	$76,240
16. Computer Hardware Engineers	$75,980
17. Computer Software Engineers, Applications	$72,530
18. Electronics Engineers, Except Computer	$71,370
19. Economists	$70,250
20. Engineering Teachers, Postsecondary	$69,700

The 20 Best-Paying Artistic Jobs

Job	Annual Earnings
1. Art Directors	$62,260
2. Advertising and Promotions Managers	$60,350
3. Architects, Except Landscape and Naval	$57,950
4. Fashion Designers	$52,860
5. Commercial and Industrial Designers	$52,320
6. Technical Writers	$51,590
7. Landscape Architects	$50,480
8. Directors—Stage, Motion Pictures, Television, and Radio	$48,200
9. Producers	$48,200
10. Talent Directors	$48,200
11. Art, Drama, and Music Teachers, Postsecondary	$47,980
12. English Language and Literature Teachers, Postsecondary	$47,120
13. Foreign Language and Literature Teachers, Postsecondary	$46,780
14. Librarians	$44,140
15. Caption Writers	$42,330
16. Copy Writers	$42,330
17. Creative Writers	$42,330
18. Poets and Lyricists	$42,330
19. Editors	$41,460
20. Film and Video Editors	$40,600

The 20 Best-Paying Social Jobs

Job	Annual Earnings
1. Education Administrators, Elementary and Secondary School	$73,490
2. Economics Teachers, Postsecondary	$64,950
3. Anthropology and Archeology Teachers, Postsecondary	$59,710
4. Personal Financial Advisors	$58,700
5. Physical Therapists	$57,710
6. Political Science Teachers, Postsecondary	$57,340
7. Dental Hygienists	$56,360
8. Area, Ethnic, and Cultural Studies Teachers, Postsecondary	$55,060
9. Radiation Therapists	$54,190
10. Psychology Teachers, Postsecondary	$54,170
11. Sociology Teachers, Postsecondary	$52,770
12. Occupational Therapists	$52,550
13. Counseling Psychologists	$52,220
14. History Teachers, Postsecondary	$52,180
15. Nursing Instructors and Teachers, Postsecondary	$50,920
16. Speech-Language Pathologists	$50,050
17. Registered Nurses	$49,550
18. Instructional Coordinators	$47,470
19. Social and Community Service Managers	$45,450
20. Educational, Vocational, and School Counselors	$44,640

The 20 Best-Paying Enterprising Jobs

Job	Annual Earnings
1. Government Service Executives	$134,740
2. Private Sector Executives	$134,740
3. Engineering Managers	$94,470
4. Lawyers	$91,490
5. Computer and Information Systems Managers	$89,740
6. Marketing Managers	$83,210
7. Sales Managers	$80,470
8. Financial Managers, Branch or Department	$77,300
9. Treasurers, Controllers, and Chief Financial Officers	$77,300
10. Compensation and Benefits Managers	$68,800
11. Human Resources Managers	$68,800
12. Training and Development Managers	$68,800

The 20 Best-Paying Enterprising Jobs

Job	Annual Earnings
13. Sales Engineers	$67,790
14. Education Administrators, Postsecondary	$66,640
15. Construction Managers	$66,470
16. Medical and Health Services Managers	$64,550
17. Storage and Distribution Managers	$63,590
18. Transportation Managers	$63,590
19. Management Analysts	$62,580
20. First-Line Supervisors/Managers of Police and Detectives	$62,350

The 20 Best-Paying Conventional Jobs

Job	Annual Earnings
1. Air Traffic Controllers	$96,260
2. Actuaries	$72,520
3. Budget Analysts	$54,520
4. Immigration and Customs Inspectors	$52,390
5. Police Identification and Records Officers	$52,390
6. Freight Inspectors	$49,590
7. Marine Cargo Inspectors	$49,590
8. Accountants	$49,060
9. Auditors	$49,060
10. Cost Estimators	$48,290
11. Insurance Underwriters	$47,330
12. Licensing Examiners and Inspectors	$46,780
13. Credit Analysts	$45,020
14. Cartographers and Photogrammetrists	$44,170
15. Claims Examiners, Property and Casualty Insurance	$44,040
16. Assessors	$43,610
17. Construction and Building Inspectors	$42,650
18. Postal Service Mail Carriers	$39,620
19. Legal Secretaries	$35,660
20. Production, Planning, and Expediting Clerks	$34,820

The 20 Fastest-Growing Jobs for Each Personality Type

From the six lists of 50 jobs that met our criteria for this book, these six lists show the 20 for each personality type that are projected to have the highest percentage increase in the numbers of people employed through 2012.

You will notice that just as income opportunities vary among the lists of the best-paying jobs, job opportunities vary among the personality types. The top Investigative and Social jobs have better opportunities (an average of about 40 percent growth) than do the top jobs in the other groups (an average of about 24 percent growth). This is partly because the kind of work done by Investigative and Social workers typically cannot be done by computers or by overseas workers. An aging population with greater need for medical and personal care also will demand more Investigative and Social workers.

The 20 Fastest-Growing Realistic Jobs

Job	Percent Growth
1. Heating and Air Conditioning Mechanics	31.8%
2. Refrigeration Mechanics	31.8%
3. Surgical Technologists	27.9%
4. Cement Masons and Concrete Finishers	26.1%
5. Highway Patrol Pilots	24.7%
6. Correctional Officers and Jailers	24.2%
7. Electricians	23.4%
8. Radiologic Technicians	22.9%
9. Radiologic Technologists	22.9%
10. First-Line Supervisors and Manager/Supervisors—Landscaping Workers	21.6%
11. Ceiling Tile Installers	21.4%
12. Drywall Installers	21.4%
13. Forest Fire Fighters	20.7%
14. Municipal Fire Fighters	20.7%
15. Sheet Metal Workers	19.8%
16. Tractor-Trailer Truck Drivers	19.0%
17. Truck Drivers, Heavy	19.0%
18. Telecommunications Line Installers and Repairers	18.8%
19. Forest Fire Fighting and Prevention Supervisors	18.7%
20. Municipal Fire Fighting and Prevention Supervisors	18.7%

The 20 Fastest-Growing Investigative Jobs

Job	Percent Growth
1. Network Systems and Data Communications Analysts	57.0%
2. Physician Assistants	48.9%
3. Computer Software Engineers, Applications	45.5%
4. Computer Software Engineers, Systems Software	45.5%
5. Database Administrators	44.2%
6. Computer Systems Analysts	39.4%
7. Agricultural Sciences Teachers, Postsecondary	38.1%
8. Biological Science Teachers, Postsecondary	38.1%
9. Chemistry Teachers, Postsecondary	38.1%
10. Computer Science Teachers, Postsecondary	38.1%
11. Engineering Teachers, Postsecondary	38.1%
12. Forestry and Conservation Science Teachers, Postsecondary	38.1%
13. Health Specialties Teachers, Postsecondary	38.1%
14. Mathematical Science Teachers, Postsecondary	38.1%
15. Physics Teachers, Postsecondary	38.1%
16. Computer Security Specialists	37.4%
17. Respiratory Therapists	34.8%
18. Computer Support Specialists	30.3%
19. Pharmacists	30.1%
20. Compensation, Benefits, and Job Analysis Specialists	28.0%

The 20 Fastest-Growing Artistic Jobs

Job	Percent Growth
1. Art, Drama, and Music Teachers, Postsecondary	38.1%
2. English Language and Literature Teachers, Postsecondary	38.1%
3. Foreign Language and Literature Teachers, Postsecondary	38.1%
4. Costume Attendants	27.8%
5. Technical Writers	27.1%
6. Film and Video Editors	26.4%
7. Advertising and Promotions Managers	25.0%
8. Landscape Architects	22.2%
9. Interpreters and Translators	22.1%
10. Graphic Designers	21.9%
11. Interior Designers	21.7%
12. Exhibit Designers	20.9%

(continued)

(continued)

The 20 Fastest-Growing Artistic Jobs

Job	Percent Growth
13. Set Designers	20.9%
14. Directors—Stage, Motion Pictures, Television, and Radio	18.3%
15. Producers	18.3%
16. Talent Directors	18.3%
17. Makeup Artists, Theatrical and Performance	18.2%
18. Actors	17.7%
19. Architects, Except Landscape and Naval	17.3%
20. Musicians, Instrumental	17.1%

The 20 Fastest-Growing Social Jobs

Job	Percent Growth
1. Medical Assistants	58.9%
2. Social and Human Service Assistants	48.7%
3. Home Health Aides	48.1%
4. Physical Therapist Assistants	44.6%
5. Fitness Trainers and Aerobics Instructors	44.5%
6. Dental Hygienists	43.1%
7. Dental Assistants	42.5%
8. Personal and Home Care Aides	40.5%
9. Self-Enrichment Education Teachers	40.1%
10. Occupational Therapist Assistants	39.2%
11. Anthropology and Archeology Teachers, Postsecondary	38.1%
12. Area, Ethnic, and Cultural Studies Teachers, Postsecondary	38.1%
13. Economics Teachers, Postsecondary	38.1%
14. Graduate Teaching Assistants	38.1%
15. History Teachers, Postsecondary	38.1%
16. Nursing Instructors and Teachers, Postsecondary	38.1%
17. Political Science Teachers, Postsecondary	38.1%
18. Psychology Teachers, Postsecondary	38.1%
19. Sociology Teachers, Postsecondary	38.1%
20. Vocational Education Teachers, Postsecondary	38.1%

The 20 Fastest-Growing Enterprising Jobs

Job	Percent Growth
1. Computer and Information Systems Managers	36.1%
2. Public Relations Specialists	32.9%
3. Sales Managers	30.5%
4. Management Analysts	30.4%
5. Medical and Health Services Managers	29.3%
6. Paralegals and Legal Assistants	28.7%
7. Agents and Business Managers of Artists, Performers, and Athletes	27.8%
8. Personnel Recruiters	27.3%
9. Education Administrators, Postsecondary	25.9%
10. Child Support, Missing Persons, and Unemployment Insurance Fraud Investigators	22.4%
11. Criminal Investigators and Special Agents	22.4%
12. Police Detectives	22.4%
13. Lawn Service Managers	21.6%
14. Marketing Managers	21.3%
15. Sales Engineers	19.9%
16. Administrative Services Managers	19.8%
17. Storage and Distribution Managers	19.7%
18. Transportation Managers	19.7%
19. Compensation and Benefits Managers	19.4%
20. Human Resources Managers	19.4%

The 20 Fastest-Growing Conventional Jobs

Job	Percent Growth
1. Medical Records and Health Information Technicians	46.8%
2. Receptionists and Information Clerks	29.5%
3. Pharmacy Technicians	28.8%
4. Interviewers, Except Eligibility and Loan	28.0%
5. Audio and Video Equipment Technicians	26.7%
6. Counter and Rental Clerks	26.3%
7. Bill and Account Collectors	24.5%
8. Adjustment Clerks	24.3%
9. Customer Service Representatives, Utilities	24.3%
10. Hotel, Motel, and Resort Desk Clerks	23.9%
11. Tax Preparers	23.2%
12. Mapping Technicians	23.1%

(continued)

(continued)

The 20 Fastest-Growing Conventional Jobs

Job	Percent Growth
13. Immigration and Customs Inspectors	22.4%
14. Police Identification and Records Officers	22.4%
15. Library Assistants, Clerical	21.5%
16. Accountants	19.5%
17. Auditors	19.5%
18. Human Resources Assistants, Except Payroll and Timekeeping	19.3%
19. Legal Secretaries	18.8%
20. Credit Analysts	18.7%

The 20 Jobs with the Most Openings for Each Personality Type

From the six lists of 50 jobs that met our criteria for this book, this list shows the 20 jobs for each personality type that are projected to have the largest number of job openings per year through 2012.

Jobs with many openings present several advantages that may be attractive to you. Because there are many openings, these jobs can be easier to obtain, particularly for those just entering the job market. These jobs may also offer more opportunities to move from one employer to another with relative ease. Though some of these jobs have average or below-average pay, some also pay quite well and can provide good long-term career opportunities or the ability to move up to more responsible roles.

It is interesting but not surprising that job openings are dramatically more scarce in the Artistic list than in the other five lists; this is a category where keen competition for non-teaching jobs is the rule. If sales jobs were set aside, comparatively few openings also would be found among the Enterprising jobs; this also tends to be a competitive arena. The two personality types with outstanding figures for job openings are Conventional and Social.

On all the lists, the jobs that are expected to have the greatest number of openings tend to be those that require hands-on or in-person work—for example, truck drivers, teachers, salespeople, or cashiers. These workers are less likely to be replaced by technology or by overseas workers.

The 20 Realistic Jobs with the Most Openings

Job	Annual Openings
1. Tractor-Trailer Truck Drivers	299,000
2. Truck Drivers, Heavy	299,000
3. Boat Builders and Shipwrights	193,000
4. Brattice Builders	193,000
5. Carpenter Assemblers and Repairers	193,000
6. Construction Carpenters	193,000
7. Rough Carpenters	193,000
8. Ship Carpenters and Joiners	193,000
9. Maintenance and Repair Workers, General	155,000
10. Refractory Materials Repairers, Except Brickmasons	155,000
11. Automotive Master Mechanics	100,000
12. Automotive Specialty Technicians	100,000
13. Brazers	71,000
14. Solderers	71,000
15. Welder-Fitters	71,000
16. Welders and Cutters	71,000
17. Welders, Production	71,000
18. Highway Patrol Pilots	67,000
19. Electricians	65,000
20. Pipe Fitters	56,000

The 20 Investigative Jobs with the Most Openings

Job	Annual Openings
1. Agricultural Sciences Teachers, Postsecondary	216,000
2. Biological Science Teachers, Postsecondary	216,000
3. Chemistry Teachers, Postsecondary	216,000
4. Computer Science Teachers, Postsecondary	216,000
5. Engineering Teachers, Postsecondary	216,000
6. Forestry and Conservation Science Teachers, Postsecondary	216,000
7. Health Specialties Teachers, Postsecondary	216,000
8. Mathematical Science Teachers, Postsecondary	216,000
9. Physics Teachers, Postsecondary	216,000
10. Computer Support Specialists	71,000
11. Computer Systems Analysts	68,000
12. Computer Software Engineers, Applications	55,000

(continued)

(continued)

The 20 Investigative Jobs with the Most Openings

Job	Annual Openings
13. Computer Programmers	45,000
14. Computer Software Engineers, Systems Software	39,000
15. Anesthesiologists	38,000
16. Family and General Practitioners	38,000
17. Internists, General	38,000
18. Obstetricians and Gynecologists	38,000
19. Pediatricians, General	38,000
20. Psychiatrists	38,000

The 20 Artistic Jobs with the Most Openings

Job	Annual Openings
1. Art, Drama, and Music Teachers, Postsecondary	216,000
2. English Language and Literature Teachers, Postsecondary	216,000
3. Foreign Language and Literature Teachers, Postsecondary	216,000
4. Costume Attendants	66,000
5. Graphic Designers	29,000
6. Musicians, Instrumental	25,000
7. Singers	25,000
8. Caption Writers	23,000
9. Copy Writers	23,000
10. Creative Writers	23,000
11. Poets and Lyricists	23,000
12. Photographers, Scientific	18,000
13. Professional Photographers	18,000
14. Librarians	15,000
15. Editors	14,000
16. Advertising and Promotions Managers	13,000
17. Floral Designers	13,000
18. Directors—Stage, Motion Pictures, Television, and Radio	10,000
19. Merchandise Displayers and Window Trimmers	10,000
20. Producers	10,000

The 20 Social Jobs with the Most Openings

Job	Annual Openings
1. Nursing Aides, Orderlies, and Attendants	302,000
2. Teacher Assistants	259,000
3. Security Guards	228,000
4. Anthropology and Archeology Teachers, Postsecondary	216,000
5. Area, Ethnic, and Cultural Studies Teachers, Postsecondary	216,000
6. Economics Teachers, Postsecondary	216,000
7. Graduate Teaching Assistants	216,000
8. History Teachers, Postsecondary	216,000
9. Nursing Instructors and Teachers, Postsecondary	216,000
10. Political Science Teachers, Postsecondary	216,000
11. Psychology Teachers, Postsecondary	216,000
12. Sociology Teachers, Postsecondary	216,000
13. Vocational Education Teachers, Postsecondary	216,000
14. Registered Nurses	215,000
15. Elementary School Teachers, Except Special Education	183,000
16. Personal and Home Care Aides	154,000
17. Home Health Aides	141,000
18. Secondary School Teachers, Except Special and Vocational Education	118,000
19. Licensed Practical and Licensed Vocational Nurses	105,000
20. Preschool Teachers, Except Special Education	88,000

The 20 Enterprising Jobs with the Most Openings

Job	Annual Openings
1. Retail Salespersons	1,014,000
2. Sales Representatives, Wholesale and Manufacturing, Except Technical and Scientific Products	160,000
3. First-Line Supervisors/Managers of Food Preparation and Serving Workers	154,000
4. First-Line Supervisors, Administrative Support	140,000
5. Hosts and Hostesses, Restaurant, Lounge, and Coffee Shop	95,000
6. Management Analysts	78,000
7. First-Line Supervisors/Managers of Non-Retail Sales Workers	72,000
8. Financial Managers, Branch or Department	71,000
9. Treasurers, Controllers, and Chief Financial Officers	71,000
10. First-Line Supervisors and Manager/Supervisors—Construction Trades Workers	67,000
11. First-Line Supervisors and Manager/Supervisors—Extractive Workers	67,000

(continued)

(continued)

The 20 Enterprising Jobs with the Most Openings

Job	Annual Openings
12. First-Line Supervisors/Managers of Production and Operating Workers	66,000
13. Government Service Executives	63,000
14. Private Sector Executives	63,000
15. Sales Managers	54,000
16. Lawyers	53,000
17. Construction Managers	47,000
18. Sales Representatives, Agricultural	44,000
19. Sales Representatives, Chemical and Pharmaceutical	44,000
20. Sales Representatives, Electrical/Electronic	44,000

The 20 Conventional Jobs with the Most Openings

Job	Annual Openings
1. Cashiers	1,221,000
2. Office Clerks, General	550,000
3. Adjustment Clerks	419,000
4. Customer Service Representatives, Utilities	419,000
5. Receptionists and Information Clerks	296,000
6. Bookkeeping, Accounting, and Auditing Clerks	274,000
7. Executive Secretaries and Administrative Assistants	210,000
8. Counter and Rental Clerks	144,000
9. Accountants	119,000
10. Auditors	119,000
11. Billing, Cost, and Rate Clerks	78,000
12. Billing, Posting, and Calculating Machine Operators	78,000
13. Statement Clerks	78,000
14. Bill and Account Collectors	76,000
15. Production, Planning, and Expediting Clerks	51,000
16. Medical Secretaries	50,000
17. Hotel, Motel, and Resort Desk Clerks	46,000
18. Interviewers, Except Eligibility and Loan	46,000
19. Insurance Claims Clerks	41,000
20. Insurance Policy Processing Clerks	41,000

The Best Jobs for Each Personality Type Sorted by Education or Training Required

The lists that follow cover each personality type and separate the top 50 jobs that met the criteria for this book into lists based on the education or training typically required for entry. Next to each job title you'll find the job's annual earnings, percent growth, and annual job openings, and these measures are used to order the jobs within each grouping. Thus you can easily find the best overall jobs for a given level of education or training within a given personality type.

You can use these lists in a variety of ways. For example, they can help you identify a job that has higher potential than a job you now hold that requires a similar level of education.

You can also use these lists to figure out additional job possibilities that would open up if you were to get additional training, education, or work experience. For example, maybe you are a high school graduate working in a job associated with the Social personality type. There are many jobs in this field at all levels of education, but especially at higher levels. You can identify the job you're interested in and the related training you need (you'll find more details in Part IV) so you can move ahead in the Social personality type.

The lists of jobs by education should also help you when you're planning your education. For example, you might be thinking about a job within the Realistic personality type, but you aren't sure what kind of work you want to do. The lists show that a job as a Pipelaying Fitter requires moderate-term on-the-job training and pays $40,950, while various welding jobs require long-term on-the-job training but pay an average of $29,640. If you want higher earnings without lengthy training, this information might make a difference in your choice.

If you compare the different personality types, you'll note something that was discussed in the Introduction: some personality types (especially Investigative) offer most of their opportunities to people who are willing to get college degrees, whereas for other types (especially Realistic and Conventional) the most common entry route is on-the-job training.

The Education Levels

⊚ *Short-term on-the-job training.* It is possible to work in these occupations and achieve an average level of performance within a few days or weeks through on-the-job training.

⊚ *Moderate-term on-the-job training.* Occupations that require this type of training can be performed adequately after a 1- to 12-month period of combined on-the-job and informal training. Typically, untrained workers observe experienced workers performing tasks and are gradually moved into progressively more difficult assignments.

- *Long-term on-the-job training.* This training requires more than 12 months of on-the-job training or combined work experience and formal classroom instruction. This includes occupations that use formal apprenticeships for training workers that may take up to four years. It also includes intensive occupation-specific, employer-sponsored training such as police academies. Furthermore, it includes occupations that require natural talent that must be developed over many years.
- *Work experience in a related occupation.* This type of job requires experience in a related occupation. For example, Forest Fire Fighting and Prevention Supervisors are selected based on their experience as Forest Fire Fighters.
- *Postsecondary vocational training.* This requirement involves an amount of training that can vary from a few months to about one year. In a few instances, there may be as many as four years of training.
- *Associate's degree.* This degree usually requires two years of full-time academic work beyond high school.
- *Bachelor's degree.* This degree requires approximately four to five years of full-time academic work beyond high school.
- *Work experience plus degree.* Jobs in this category are often management-related and require some experience in a related nonmanagerial position.
- *Master's degree.* Completion of a master's degree usually requires one to two years of full-time study beyond the bachelor's degree.
- *Doctoral degree.* This degree normally requires two or more years of full-time academic work beyond the bachelor's degree.
- *First professional degree.* This type of degree normally requires a minimum of two years of education beyond the bachelor's degree and frequently requires three years.

Another Warning About the Data

We warned you in the Introduction to use caution in interpreting the data we use, and we want to do it again here. The occupational data we use is the most accurate available anywhere, but it has its limitations. For example, the education or training requirements for entry into a job are those typically required as a minimum—but some people working in those jobs may have considerably more or different credentials. For example, most Registered Nurses now have a four-year bachelor's degree, although the two-year associate's degree is the minimum level of training the job requires.

In a similar way, people with jobs that require long-term on-the-job training typically earn more than people with jobs that require short-term on-the-job training. However, some people with short-term on-the-job training do earn more than the average for the highest-paying occupations listed in this book. On the other hand, some people with long-term on-the-job training earn much less than the average shown in this book—this is particularly true early in a person's career.

So as you browse the lists that follow, please use them as a way to be encouraged rather than discouraged. Education and training are very important for success in the labor market of the future, but so are ability, drive, initiative, and, yes, luck.

Having said this, we encourage you to get as much education and training as you can. It used to be that you got your schooling and never went back, but this is not a good attitude to have now. You will probably need to continue learning new things throughout your working life. You can do so by going to school, and this is a good thing for many people to do. But there are also many other ways to learn, such as workshops, certification programs, employer training, professional conferences, Internet training, reading related books and magazines, and many others. Upgrading your computer and other technical skills is particularly important in our rapidly changing workplace, and you avoid doing so at your peril.

An old saying goes, "The harder you work, the luckier you get." It is just as true now as it ever was.

Best Realistic Jobs Requiring Short-Term On-the-Job Training

Job	Annual Earnings	Percent Growth	Annual Openings
1. Truck Drivers, Heavy	$33,310	19.0%	299,000
2. Refractory Materials Repairers, Except Brickmasons	$36,910	16.3%	155,000
3. Brazers	$29,640	17.0%	71,000
4. Solderers	$29,640	17.0%	71,000
5. Welders, Production	$29,640	17.0%	71,000

Best Realistic Jobs Requiring Moderate-Term On-the-Job Training

Job	Annual Earnings	Percent Growth	Annual Openings
1. Pipelaying Fitters	$40,950	18.7%	56,000
2. Tractor-Trailer Truck Drivers	$33,310	19.0%	299,000
3. Correctional Officers and Jailers	$33,160	24.2%	49,000
4. Sheet Metal Workers	$35,000	19.8%	30,000
5. Brattice Builders	$34,250	10.1%	193,000
6. Carpenter Assemblers and Repairers	$34,250	10.1%	193,000
7. Rough Carpenters	$34,250	10.1%	193,000
8. Ship Carpenters and Joiners	$34,250	10.1%	193,000
9. Ceiling Tile Installers	$33,670	21.4%	17,000
10. Drywall Installers	$33,670	21.4%	17,000
11. Roofers	$30,020	18.6%	38,000
12. Grader, Bulldozer, and Scraper Operators	$35,030	10.4%	45,000
13. Operating Engineers	$35,030	10.4%	45,000

Best Realistic Jobs Requiring Long-Term On-the-Job Training

Job	Annual Earnings	Percent Growth	Annual Openings
1. Highway Patrol Pilots	$44,020	24.7%	67,000
2. Electricians	$41,680	23.4%	65,000
3. Pipe Fitters	$40,950	18.7%	56,000
4. Plumbers	$40,950	18.7%	56,000
5. Heating and Air Conditioning Mechanics	$35,160	31.8%	35,000
6. Refrigeration Mechanics	$35,160	31.8%	35,000
7. Forest Fire Fighters	$37,060	20.7%	29,000
8. Municipal Fire Fighters	$37,060	20.7%	29,000
9. Technical Directors/Managers	$48,200	18.3%	10,000
10. Brickmasons and Blockmasons	$41,550	14.2%	21,000
11. Telecommunications Line Installers and Repairers	$39,540	18.8%	13,000
12. Boat Builders and Shipwrights	$34,250	10.1%	193,000
13. Construction Carpenters	$34,250	10.1%	193,000
14. Cement Masons and Concrete Finishers	$30,780	26.1%	24,000
15. Maintenance and Repair Workers, General	$29,800	16.3%	155,000
16. Pressure Vessel Inspectors	$46,780	9.8%	20,000
17. Welder-Fitters	$29,640	17.0%	71,000
18. Welders and Cutters	$29,640	17.0%	71,000

Best Realistic Jobs Requiring Work Experience in a Related Occupation

Job	Annual Earnings	Percent Growth	Annual Openings
1. Forest Fire Fighting and Prevention Supervisors	$57,000	18.7%	8,000
2. Municipal Fire Fighting and Prevention Supervisors	$57,000	18.7%	8,000
3. First-Line Supervisors and Manager/Supervisors—Landscaping Workers	$33,770	21.6%	18,000

Best Realistic Jobs Requiring Postsecondary Vocational Training

Job	Annual Earnings	Percent Growth	Annual Openings
1. Bus and Truck Mechanics and Diesel Engine Specialists	$34,970	14.2%	28,000
2. Surgical Technologists	$32,130	27.9%	13,000
3. Automotive Master Mechanics	$31,130	12.4%	100,000
4. Automotive Specialty Technicians	$31,130	12.4%	100,000

Best Realistic Jobs Requiring an Associate's Degree

Job	Annual Earnings	Percent Growth	Annual Openings
1. Radiologic Technicians	$40,620	22.9%	21,000
2. Radiologic Technologists	$40,620	22.9%	21,000
3. Calibration and Instrumentation Technicians	$43,650	10.0%	24,000
4. Electrical Engineering Technicians	$43,650	10.0%	24,000
5. Electronics Engineering Technicians	$43,650	10.0%	24,000

Best Realistic Jobs Requiring a Bachelor's Degree

Job	Annual Earnings	Percent Growth	Annual Openings
1. Airline Pilots, Copilots, and Flight Engineers	$125,030	18.5%	6,000
2. Civil Engineers	$61,850	8.0%	17,000

Best Investigative Jobs Requiring an Associate's Degree

Job	Annual Earnings	Percent Growth	Annual Openings
1. Computer Support Specialists	$39,440	30.3%	71,000
2. Respiratory Therapists	$41,150	34.8%	10,000

Best Investigative Jobs Requiring a Bachelor's Degree

Job	Annual Earnings	Percent Growth	Annual Openings
1. Computer Software Engineers, Systems Software	$76,240	45.5%	39,000
2. Computer Software Engineers, Applications	$72,530	45.5%	55,000
3. Computer Systems Analysts	$64,160	39.4%	68,000
4. Physician Assistants	$65,670	48.9%	7,000
5. Network Systems and Data Communications Analysts	$59,120	57.0%	29,000
6. Database Administrators	$58,200	44.2%	16,000
7. Computer Security Specialists	$56,050	37.4%	35,000
8. Computer Programmers	$61,340	14.6%	45,000
9. Financial Analysts	$60,050	18.7%	22,000

(continued)

(continued)

Best Investigative Jobs Requiring a Bachelor's Degree

Job	Annual Earnings	Percent Growth	Annual Openings
10. Market Research Analysts	$54,670	23.4%	18,000
11. Electronics Engineers, Except Computer	$71,370	9.4%	11,000
12. Compensation, Benefits, and Job Analysis Specialists	$46,860	28.0%	15,000
13. Economists	$70,250	13.4%	2,000
14. Computer Hardware Engineers	$75,980	6.1%	6,000
15. Geologists	$68,460	11.5%	2,000
16. Environmental Scientists and Specialists, Including Health	$48,790	23.7%	6,000
17. Electrical Engineers	$69,640	2.5%	11,000
18. Medical and Clinical Laboratory Technologists	$43,640	19.3%	21,000

Best Investigative Jobs Requiring Work Experience Plus Degree

Job	Annual Earnings	Percent Growth	Annual Openings
1. Natural Sciences Managers	$85,860	11.3%	5,000

Best Investigative Jobs Requiring a Master's Degree

Job	Annual Earnings	Percent Growth	Annual Openings
1. Engineering Teachers, Postsecondary	$69,700	38.1%	216,000
2. Agricultural Sciences Teachers, Postsecondary	$65,470	38.1%	216,000
3. Forestry and Conservation Science Teachers, Postsecondary	$64,500	38.1%	216,000
4. Physics Teachers, Postsecondary	$62,880	38.1%	216,000
5. Health Specialties Teachers, Postsecondary	$61,790	38.1%	216,000
6. Biological Science Teachers, Postsecondary	$55,840	38.1%	216,000
7. Chemistry Teachers, Postsecondary	$55,420	38.1%	216,000
8. Computer Science Teachers, Postsecondary	$51,030	38.1%	216,000
9. Mathematical Science Teachers, Postsecondary	$50,910	38.1%	216,000
10. Clinical Psychologists	$52,220	24.4%	17,000
11. Educational Psychologists	$52,220	24.4%	17,000

Best Investigative Jobs Requiring a Doctoral Degree

Job	Annual Earnings	Percent Growth	Annual Openings
1. Medical Scientists, Except Epidemiologists	$59,210	26.9%	6,000
2. Biochemists	$62,300	22.9%	2,000
3. Biophysicists	$62,300	22.9%	2,000

Best Investigative Jobs Requiring a First Professional Degree

Job	Annual Earnings	Percent Growth	Annual Openings
1. Anesthesiologists	over $145,000	19.5%	38,000
2. Internists, General	over $145,000	19.5%	38,000
3. Obstetricians and Gynecologists	over $145,000	19.5%	38,000
4. Surgeons	over $145,000	19.5%	38,000
5. Pediatricians, General	$134,170	19.5%	38,000
6. Psychiatrists	$133,970	19.5%	38,000
7. Family and General Practitioners	$133,340	19.5%	38,000
8. Pharmacists	$80,530	30.1%	23,000
9. Veterinarians	$64,750	25.1%	4,000
10. Chiropractors	$65,990	23.3%	3,000
11. Optometrists	$85,430	17.1%	2,000
12. Dentists, General	$120,330	4.1%	7,000
13. Oral and Maxillofacial Surgeons	$120,330	4.1%	7,000
14. Orthodontists	$120,330	4.1%	7,000
15. Prosthodontists	$120,330	4.1%	7,000

Best Artistic Jobs Requiring Moderate-Term On-the-Job Training

Job	Annual Earnings	Percent Growth	Annual Openings
1. Caption Writers	$42,330	16.1%	23,000
2. Costume Attendants	$25,410	27.8%	66,000
3. Camera Operators, Television, Video, and Motion Picture	$34,330	13.4%	4,000
4. Floral Designers	$19,660	12.4%	13,000
5. Merchandise Displayers and Window Trimmers	$22,030	11.3%	10,000
6. Radio and Television Announcers	$20,940	–10.1%	8,000
7. Models	$24,270	14.5%	1,000
8. Photographic Retouchers and Restorers	$20,370	5.4%	4,000

Best Artistic Jobs Requiring Long-Term On-the-Job Training

Job	Annual Earnings	Percent Growth	Annual Openings
1. Talent Directors	$48,200	18.3%	10,000
2. Musicians, Instrumental	$37,380	17.1%	25,000
3. Singers	$37,380	17.1%	25,000
4. Interpreters and Translators	$33,490	22.1%	4,000
5. Actors	$26,460	17.7%	8,000
6. Cartoonists	$35,420	16.5%	4,000
7. Painters and Illustrators	$35,420	16.5%	4,000
8. Sculptors	$35,420	16.5%	4,000
9. Sketch Artists	$35,420	16.5%	4,000
10. Photographers, Scientific	$25,050	13.6%	18,000
11. Professional Photographers	$25,050	13.6%	18,000

Best Artistic Jobs Requiring Work Experience in a Related Occupation

Job	Annual Earnings	Percent Growth	Annual Openings
1. Choreographers	$31,030	15.8%	3,000

Best Artistic Jobs Requiring Postsecondary Vocational Training

Job	Annual Earnings	Percent Growth	Annual Openings
1. Makeup Artists, Theatrical and Performance	$29,320	18.2%	fewer than 500

Best Artistic Jobs Requiring a Bachelor's Degree

Job	Annual Earnings	Percent Growth	Annual Openings
1. Graphic Designers	$36,630	21.9%	29,000
2. Technical Writers	$51,590	27.1%	6,000
3. Architects, Except Landscape and Naval	$57,950	17.3%	8,000
4. Copy Writers	$42,330	16.1%	23,000
5. Creative Writers	$42,330	16.1%	23,000
6. Poets and Lyricists	$42,330	16.1%	23,000

Best Artistic Jobs Requiring a Bachelor's Degree

Job	Annual Earnings	Percent Growth	Annual Openings
7. Interior Designers	$40,120	21.7%	8,000
8. Landscape Architects	$50,480	22.2%	2,000
9. Film and Video Editors	$40,600	26.4%	3,000
10. Commercial and Industrial Designers	$52,320	14.7%	7,000
11. Editors	$41,460	11.8%	14,000
12. Exhibit Designers	$35,150	20.9%	2,000
13. Set Designers	$35,150	20.9%	2,000
14. Fashion Designers	$52,860	10.6%	2,000
15. Music Arrangers and Orchestrators	$32,530	13.5%	8,000
16. Broadcast News Analysts	$31,240	6.2%	6,000
17. Reporters and Correspondents	$31,240	6.2%	6,000

Best Artistic Jobs Requiring Work Experience Plus Degree

Job	Annual Earnings	Percent Growth	Annual Openings
1. Advertising and Promotions Managers	$60,350	25.0%	13,000
2. Directors—Stage, Motion Pictures, Television, and Radio	$48,200	18.3%	10,000
3. Producers	$48,200	18.3%	10,000
4. Art Directors	$62,260	11.4%	8,000

Best Artistic Jobs Requiring a Master's Degree

Job	Annual Earnings	Percent Growth	Annual Openings
1. Art, Drama, and Music Teachers, Postsecondary	$47,980	38.1%	216,000
2. English Language and Literature Teachers, Postsecondary	$47,120	38.1%	216,000
3. Foreign Language and Literature Teachers, Postsecondary	$46,780	38.1%	216,000
4. Librarians	$44,140	10.1%	15,000
5. Curators	$35,660	17.0%	2,000
6. Museum Technicians and Conservators	$35,660	17.0%	2,000
7. Composers	$32,530	13.5%	8,000
8. Music Directors	$32,530	13.5%	8,000

Best Social Jobs Requiring Short-Term On-the-Job Training

Job	Annual Earnings	Percent Growth	Annual Openings
1. Home Health Aides	$18,240	48.1%	141,000
2. Security Guards	$19,660	31.9%	228,000
3. Personal and Home Care Aides	$16,450	40.5%	154,000
4. Nursing Aides, Orderlies, and Attendants	$20,490	24.9%	302,000
5. Teacher Assistants	$19,000	23.0%	259,000

Best Social Jobs Requiring Moderate-Term On-the-Job Training

Job	Annual Earnings	Percent Growth	Annual Openings
1. Medical Assistants	$24,170	58.9%	78,000
2. Social and Human Service Assistants	$23,860	48.7%	63,000
3. Dental Assistants	$27,700	42.5%	35,000

Best Social Jobs Requiring Long-Term On-the-Job Training

Job	Annual Earnings	Percent Growth	Annual Openings
1. Police Patrol Officers	$44,020	24.7%	67,000
2. Sheriffs and Deputy Sheriffs	$44,020	24.7%	67,000

Best Social Jobs Requiring Work Experience in a Related Occupation

Job	Annual Earnings	Percent Growth	Annual Openings
1. Vocational Education Teachers, Postsecondary	$39,740	38.1%	216,000
2. Self-Enrichment Education Teachers	$29,820	40.1%	39,000

Best Social Jobs Requiring Postsecondary Vocational Training

Job	Annual Earnings	Percent Growth	Annual Openings
1. Fitness Trainers and Aerobics Instructors	$24,510	44.5%	38,000
2. Emergency Medical Technicians and Paramedics	$24,440	33.1%	32,000
3. Licensed Practical and Licensed Vocational Nurses	$32,390	20.2%	105,000

Best Social Jobs Requiring an Associate's Degree

Job	Annual Earnings	Percent Growth	Annual Openings
1. Registered Nurses	$49,550	27.3%	215,000
2. Dental Hygienists	$56,360	43.1%	9,000
3. Physical Therapist Assistants	$36,610	44.6%	10,000
4. Radiation Therapists	$54,190	31.6%	1,000
5. Occupational Therapist Assistants	$37,400	39.2%	3,000

Best Social Jobs Requiring a Bachelor's Degree

Job	Annual Earnings	Percent Growth	Annual Openings
1. Personal Financial Advisors	$58,700	34.6%	18,000
2. Special Education Teachers, Secondary School	$44,240	30.0%	59,000
3. Special Education Teachers, Preschool, Kindergarten, and Elementary School	$42,920	30.0%	59,000
4. Special Education Teachers, Middle School	$42,010	30.0%	59,000
5. Occupational Therapists	$52,550	35.2%	10,000
6. Training and Development Specialists	$44,160	27.9%	35,000
7. Secondary School Teachers, Except Special and Vocational Education	$44,580	18.2%	118,000
8. Social and Community Service Managers	$45,450	27.7%	19,000
9. Kindergarten Teachers, Except Special Education	$40,160	27.2%	34,000
10. Preschool Teachers, Except Special Education	$19,820	36.2%	88,000
11. Elementary School Teachers, Except Special Education	$42,160	15.2%	183,000
12. Employment Interviewers, Private or Public Employment Service	$40,770	27.3%	29,000
13. Medical and Public Health Social Workers	$38,430	28.6%	18,000
14. Child, Family, and School Social Workers	$33,810	23.2%	45,000

Best Social Jobs Requiring Work Experience Plus Degree

Job	Annual Earnings	Percent Growth	Annual Openings
1. Education Administrators, Elementary and Secondary School	$73,490	20.7%	31,000

Best Social Jobs Requiring a Master's Degree

Job	Annual Earnings	Percent Growth	Annual Openings
1. Economics Teachers, Postsecondary	$64,950	38.1%	216,000
2. Anthropology and Archeology Teachers, Postsecondary	$59,710	38.1%	216,000
3. Political Science Teachers, Postsecondary	$57,340	38.1%	216,000
4. Area, Ethnic, and Cultural Studies Teachers, Postsecondary	$55,060	38.1%	216,000
5. Psychology Teachers, Postsecondary	$54,170	38.1%	216,000
6. Sociology Teachers, Postsecondary	$52,770	38.1%	216,000
7. History Teachers, Postsecondary	$52,180	38.1%	216,000
8. Nursing Instructors and Teachers, Postsecondary	$50,920	38.1%	216,000
9. Graduate Teaching Assistants	$24,570	38.1%	216,000
10. Physical Therapists	$57,710	35.3%	16,000
11. Counseling Psychologists	$52,220	24.4%	17,000
12. Instructional Coordinators	$47,470	25.4%	18,000
13. Speech-Language Pathologists	$50,050	27.2%	10,000
14. Mental Health and Substance Abuse Social Workers	$33,020	34.5%	17,000
15. Educational, Vocational, and School Counselors	$44,640	15.0%	32,000

Best Enterprising Jobs Requiring Short-Term On-the-Job Training

Job	Annual Earnings	Percent Growth	Annual Openings
1. Hosts and Hostesses, Restaurant, Lounge, and Coffee Shop	$15,380	16.4%	95,000
2. Retail Salespersons	$18,090	14.6%	1,014,000

Best Enterprising Jobs Requiring Moderate-Term On-the-Job Training

Job	Annual Earnings	Percent Growth	Annual Openings
1. Sales Representatives, Agricultural	$57,120	19.3%	44,000
2. Sales Representatives, Chemical and Pharmaceutical	$57,120	19.3%	44,000
3. Sales Representatives, Electrical/Electronic	$57,120	19.3%	44,000
4. Sales Representatives, Instruments	$57,120	19.3%	44,000
5. Sales Representatives, Mechanical Equipment and Supplies	$57,120	19.3%	44,000
6. Sales Representatives, Medical	$57,120	19.3%	44,000
7. Sales Representatives, Wholesale and Manufacturing, Except Technical and Scientific Products	$43,860	19.1%	160,000

Best Enterprising Jobs Requiring Long-Term On-the-Job Training

Job	Annual Earnings	Percent Growth	Annual Openings
1. Insurance Adjusters, Examiners, and Investigators	$44,040	14.2%	31,000

Best Enterprising Jobs Requiring Work Experience in a Related Occupation

Job	Annual Earnings	Percent Growth	Annual Openings
1. Storage and Distribution Managers	$63,590	19.7%	13,000
2. Transportation Managers	$63,590	19.7%	13,000
3. First-Line Supervisors and Manager/Supervisors—Construction Trades Workers	$48,730	14.1%	67,000
4. First-Line Supervisors and Manager/Supervisors—Extractive Workers	$48,730	14.1%	67,000
5. Child Support, Missing Persons, and Unemployment Insurance Fraud Investigators	$52,390	22.4%	11,000
6. Criminal Investigators and Special Agents	$52,390	22.4%	11,000
7. Police Detectives	$52,390	22.4%	11,000
8. First-Line Supervisors/Managers of Mechanics, Installers, and Repairers	$48,620	15.4%	42,000
9. First-Line Supervisors/Managers of Non-Retail Sales Workers	$55,690	6.8%	72,000

(continued)

(continued)

Best Enterprising Jobs Requiring Work Experience in a Related Occupation

Job	Annual Earnings	Percent Growth	Annual Openings
10. First-Line Supervisors/Managers of Food Preparation and Serving Workers	$24,700	15.5%	154,000
11. First-Line Supervisors/Managers of Police and Detectives	$62,350	15.3%	14,000
12. First-Line Supervisors/Managers of Production and Operating Workers	$43,720	9.5%	66,000
13. Lawn Service Managers	$33,770	21.6%	18,000
14. First-Line Supervisors, Administrative Support	$39,490	6.6%	140,000

Best Enterprising Jobs Requiring an Associate's Degree

Job	Annual Earnings	Percent Growth	Annual Openings
1. Paralegals and Legal Assistants	$37,930	28.7%	29,000

Best Enterprising Jobs Requiring a Bachelor's Degree

Job	Annual Earnings	Percent Growth	Annual Openings
1. Construction Managers	$66,470	12.0%	47,000
2. Public Relations Specialists	$42,590	32.9%	28,000
3. Personnel Recruiters	$40,770	27.3%	29,000
4. Sales Engineers	$67,790	19.9%	7,000
5. Sales Agents, Financial Services	$60,530	13.0%	39,000
6. Sales Agents, Securities and Commodities	$60,530	13.0%	39,000
7. Loan Officers	$46,640	18.8%	30,000

Best Enterprising Jobs Requiring Work Experience Plus Degree

Job	Annual Earnings	Percent Growth	Annual Openings
1. Sales Managers	$80,470	30.5%	54,000
2. Management Analysts	$62,580	30.4%	78,000
3. Computer and Information Systems Managers	$89,740	36.1%	39,000
4. Financial Managers, Branch or Department	$77,300	18.3%	71,000
5. Treasurers, Controllers, and Chief Financial Officers	$77,300	18.3%	71,000
6. Government Service Executives	$134,740	16.7%	63,000
7. Medical and Health Services Managers	$64,550	29.3%	33,000
8. Private Sector Executives	$134,740	16.7%	63,000
9. Marketing Managers	$83,210	21.3%	30,000
10. Administrative Services Managers	$56,940	19.8%	40,000
11. Education Administrators, Postsecondary	$66,640	25.9%	19,000
12. Compensation and Benefits Managers	$68,800	19.4%	21,000
13. Human Resources Managers	$68,800	19.4%	21,000
14. Training and Development Managers	$68,800	19.4%	21,000
15. Agents and Business Managers of Artists, Performers, and Athletes	$54,640	27.8%	2,000
16. Engineering Managers	$94,470	9.2%	16,000
17. Program Directors	$48,200	18.3%	10,000

Best Enterprising Jobs Requiring a First Professional Degree

Job	Annual Earnings	Percent Growth	Annual Openings
1. Lawyers	$91,490	17.0%	53,000

Best Conventional Jobs Requiring Short-Term On-the-Job Training

Job	Annual Earnings	Percent Growth	Annual Openings
1. Bill and Account Collectors	$27,000	24.5%	76,000
2. Production, Planning, and Expediting Clerks	$34,820	14.1%	51,000
3. Human Resources Assistants, Except Payroll and Timekeeping	$31,060	19.3%	36,000
4. Receptionists and Information Clerks	$21,320	29.5%	296,000
5. Counter and Rental Clerks	$17,640	26.3%	144,000

(continued)

(continued)

Best Conventional Jobs Requiring Short-Term On-the-Job Training

Job	Annual Earnings	Percent Growth	Annual Openings
6. Interviewers, Except Eligibility and Loan	$22,590	28.0%	46,000
7. Hotel, Motel, and Resort Desk Clerks	$17,450	23.9%	46,000
8. Office Clerks, General	$22,450	10.4%	550,000
9. Cashiers	$15,760	13.2%	1,221,000
10. Billing, Cost, and Rate Clerks	$26,290	7.9%	78,000
11. Billing, Posting, and Calculating Machine Operators	$26,290	7.9%	78,000
12. Statement Clerks	$26,290	7.9%	78,000
13. Postal Service Mail Carriers	$39,620	–0.5%	20,000
14. Reservation and Transportation Ticket Agents	$26,220	12.2%	35,000
15. Travel Clerks	$26,220	12.2%	35,000
16. Library Assistants, Clerical	$19,930	21.5%	27,000
17. Court Clerks	$27,450	12.3%	14,000

Best Conventional Jobs Requiring Moderate-Term On-the-Job Training

Job	Annual Earnings	Percent Growth	Annual Openings
1. Adjustment Clerks	$26,500	24.3%	419,000
2. Customer Service Representatives, Utilities	$26,500	24.3%	419,000
3. Executive Secretaries and Administrative Assistants	$34,080	8.7%	210,000
4. Dispatchers, Except Police, Fire, and Ambulance	$30,390	14.4%	28,000
5. Pharmacy Technicians	$22,760	28.8%	39,000
6. Mapping Technicians	$29,520	23.1%	10,000
7. Bookkeeping, Accounting, and Auditing Clerks	$27,760	3.0%	274,000
8. Tax Preparers	$26,530	23.2%	11,000
9. Cargo and Freight Agents	$31,990	15.5%	8,000
10. Insurance Claims Clerks	$28,520	3.6%	41,000
11. Insurance Policy Processing Clerks	$28,520	3.6%	41,000
12. Audio-Visual Collections Specialists	$32,590	16.3%	2,000

Best Conventional Jobs Requiring Long-Term On-the-Job Training

Job	Annual Earnings	Percent Growth	Annual Openings
1. Claims Examiners, Property and Casualty Insurance	$44,040	14.2%	31,000
2. Licensing Examiners and Inspectors	$46,780	9.8%	20,000
3. Audio and Video Equipment Technicians	$30,810	26.7%	5,000
4. Air Traffic Controllers	$96,260	12.6%	2,000

Best Conventional Jobs Requiring Work Experience in a Related Occupation

Job	Annual Earnings	Percent Growth	Annual Openingss
1. Immigration and Customs Inspectors	$52,390	22.4%	11,000
2. Police Identification and Records Officers	$52,390	22.4%	11,000
3. Construction and Building Inspectors	$42,650	13.8%	10,000
4. Freight Inspectors	$49,590	7.7%	5,000
5. Marine Cargo Inspectors	$49,590	7.7%	5,000

Best Conventional Jobs Requiring Postsecondary Vocational Training

Job	Annual Earnings	Percent Growth	Annual Openings
1. Legal Secretaries	$35,660	18.8%	39,000
2. Assessors	$43,610	17.6%	11,000
3. Medical Secretaries	$26,000	17.2%	50,000

Best Conventional Jobs Requiring an Associate's Degree

Job	Annual Earnings	Percent Growth	Annual Openings
1. Medical Records and Health Information Technicians	$24,520	46.8%	24,000

Best Conventional Jobs Requiring a Bachelor's Degree

Job	Annual Earnings	Percent Growth	Annual Openings
1. Accountants	$49,060	19.5%	119,000
2. Auditors	$49,060	19.5%	119,000
3. Cost Estimators	$48,290	18.6%	25,000
4. Credit Analysts	$45,020	18.7%	9,000
5. Budget Analysts	$54,520	14.0%	8,000
6. Insurance Underwriters	$47,330	10.0%	12,000
7. Cartographers and Photogrammetrists	$44,170	15.1%	1,000

Best Conventional Jobs Requiring Work Experience Plus Degree

Job	Annual Earnings	Percent Growth	Annual Openings
1. Actuaries	$72,520	14.9%	2,000

Best Jobs for Each Personality Type with a High Percentage of Women and Men

We knew we would create some controversy when we first included the best jobs lists with high percentages of men and women. But these lists are not meant to restrict women or men from considering job options—one reason for including these lists is exactly the opposite. We hope the lists will help people see possibilities that they might not otherwise have considered. For example, we suggest that women browse the lists of jobs that employ high percentages of men. Many of these occupations pay quite well, and women who want to do them and are willing to undertake the education or training should consider them.

To create the lists, we sorted the jobs of each personality type that met the criteria for this book and included only those employing 70 percent or more of women or men. For the Realistic, Investigative, and Enterprising personality types, the list of predominantly male jobs is much longer than the list of predominantly female jobs. For the Social and Conventional personality types, we found the opposite to be true. For the Artistic personality type, the lists were roughly equal.

We also produced "best overall" lists in which these predominantly male jobs and predominantly female jobs are sorted by their combined ranking in terms of annual earnings, percent growth, and annual job openings. In these lists, we list these facts for each job so you can compare their potential rewards.

In the following lists, if you compare the occupations employing a high percentage of women with those employing a high percentage of men, you may notice some distinct differences beyond the obvious. For example, you may notice that the jobs with a high percentage of women are growing somewhat faster than those with a high percentage of men. We've done the math and discovered that the different is an average growth rate of 24 percent for the jobs that employ mostly women versus an average rate of 18 percent for the jobs that employ mostly men. The number of annual job openings shows a similar pattern. Occupations with a high percentage of men average 49,719 openings per year, while more than double that number of openings, 102,808, are projected on average for occupations with a high percentage of women.

This discrepancy reflects the trend that men have had more problems than women in adapting to an economy dominated by service and information-based jobs. Many women may simply be better prepared for these jobs, possessing more appropriate skills for the jobs that are now growing rapidly and have more job openings.

On the other hand, you may notice that on average the jobs with a high percentage of men have higher wages (an average of $51,075) than do the jobs with a high percentage of women ($32,088). This indicates that women interested in improving their earnings may want to consider jobs traditionally dominated by men. Remember that a time-honored gender imbalance is not always a barrier to women. Some employers are seeking female recruits to counterbalance a traditional male dominance.

Realistic Jobs with the Highest Percentage of Women

Job	Percent Women
1. Surgical Technologists	80.7%
2. Radiologic Technicians	71.7%
3. Radiologic Technologists	71.7%

Best Realistic Jobs Overall Employing 70 Percent or More Women

Job	Percent Women	Annual Earnings	Percent Growth	Annual Openings
1. Radiologic Technicians	71.7%	$40,620	22.9%	21,000
2. Radiologic Technologists	71.7%	$40,620	22.9%	21,000
3. Surgical Technologists	80.7%	$32,130	27.9%	13,000

Realistic Jobs with the Highest Percentage of Men

Job	Percent Men
1. Brickmasons and Blockmasons	98.9%
2. Bus and Truck Mechanics and Diesel Engine Specialists	98.8%
3. Cement Masons and Concrete Finishers	98.6%
4. Roofers	98.4%
5. Pipe Fitters	98.3%
6. Pipelaying Fitters	98.3%
7. Plumbers	98.3%
8. Heating and Air Conditioning Mechanics	98.2%
9. Refrigeration Mechanics	98.2%
10. Boat Builders and Shipwrights	98.1%
11. Brattice Builders	98.1%
12. Carpenter Assemblers and Repairers	98.1%
13. Construction Carpenters	98.1%
14. Rough Carpenters	98.1%
15. Ship Carpenters and Joiners	98.1%
16. Automotive Master Mechanics	98.1%
17. Automotive Specialty Technicians	98.1%
18. Grader, Bulldozer, and Scraper Operators	97.8%
19. Operating Engineers	97.8%
20. Electricians	97.4%
21. Ceiling Tile Installers	97.3%
22. Drywall Installers	97.3%
23. Forest Fire Fighting and Prevention Supervisors	97.1%
24. Municipal Fire Fighting and Prevention Supervisors	97.1%
25. Forest Fire Fighters	96.4%
26. Municipal Fire Fighters	96.4%
27. Refractory Materials Repairers, Except Brickmasons	96.2%
28. Airline Pilots, Copilots, and Flight Engineers	96.0%
29. Sheet Metal Workers	95.9%
30. Maintenance and Repair Workers, General	95.9%
31. Tractor-Trailer Truck Drivers	94.1%
32. Truck Drivers, Heavy	94.1%
33. Telecommunications Line Installers and Repairers	93.5%
34. First-Line Supervisors and Manager/Supervisors—Landscaping Workers	93.3%
35. Brazers	92.6%
36. Solderers	92.6%

Realistic Jobs with the Highest Percentage of Men

Job	Percent Men
37. Welder-Fitters	92.6%
38. Welders and Cutters	92.6%
39. Welders, Production	92.6%
40. Civil Engineers	89.9%
41. Highway Patrol Pilots	86.9%
42. Calibration and Instrumentation Technicians	80.9%
43. Electrical Engineering Technicians	80.9%
44. Electronics Engineering Technicians	80.9%
45. Correctional Officers and Jailers	74.0%

Best Realistic Jobs Overall Employing 70 Percent or More Men

Job	Percent Men	Annual Earnings	Percent Growth	Annual Openings
1. Highway Patrol Pilots	86.9%	$44,020	24.7%	67,000
2. Electricians	97.4%	$41,680	23.4%	65,000
3. Pipe Fitters	98.3%	$40,950	18.7%	56,000
4. Pipelaying Fitters	98.3%	$40,950	18.7%	56,000
5. Plumbers	98.3%	$40,950	18.7%	56,000
6. Heating and Air Conditioning Mechanics	98.2%	$35,160	31.8%	35,000
7. Refrigeration Mechanics	98.2%	$35,160	31.8%	35,000
8. Tractor-Trailer Truck Drivers	94.1%	$33,310	19.0%	299,000
9. Truck Drivers, Heavy	94.1%	$33,310	19.0%	299,000
10. Refractory Materials Repairers, Except Brickmasons	96.2%	$36,910	16.3%	155,000
11. Correctional Officers and Jailers	74.0%	$33,160	24.2%	49,000
12. Forest Fire Fighters	96.4%	$37,060	20.7%	29,000
13. Municipal Fire Fighters	96.4%	$37,060	20.7%	29,000
14. Sheet Metal Workers	95.9%	$35,000	19.8%	30,000
15. Forest Fire Fighting and Prevention Supervisors	97.1%	$57,000	18.7%	8,000
16. Municipal Fire Fighting and Prevention Supervisors	97.1%	$57,000	18.7%	8,000
17. Airline Pilots, Copilots, and Flight Engineers	96.0%	$125,030	18.5%	6,000
18. Brickmasons and Blockmasons	98.9%	$41,550	14.2%	21,000

(continued)

Best Realistic Jobs Overall Employing 70 Percent or More Men

Job	Percent Men	Annual Earnings	Percent Growth	Annual Openings
19. Telecommunications Line Installers and Repairers	93.5%	$39,540	18.8%	13,000
20. Boat Builders and Shipwrights	98.1%	$34,250	10.1%	193,000
21. Brattice Builders	98.1%	$34,250	10.1%	193,000
22. Carpenter Assemblers and Repairers	98.1%	$34,250	10.1%	193,000
23. Construction Carpenters	98.1%	$34,250	10.1%	193,000
24. Rough Carpenters	98.1%	$34,250	10.1%	193,000
25. Ship Carpenters and Joiners	98.1%	$34,250	10.1%	193,000
26. First-Line Supervisors and Manager/Supervisors—Landscaping Workers	93.3%	$33,770	21.6%	18,000
27. Calibration and Instrumentation Technicians	80.9%	$43,650	10.0%	24,000
28. Electrical Engineering Technicians	80.9%	$43,650	10.0%	24,000
29. Electronics Engineering Technicians	80.9%	$43,650	10.0%	24,000
30. Ceiling Tile Installers	97.3%	$33,670	21.4%	17,000
31. Drywall Installers	97.3%	$33,670	21.4%	17,000
32. Cement Masons and Concrete Finishers	98.6%	$30,780	26.1%	24,000
33. Maintenance and Repair Workers, General	95.9%	$29,800	16.3%	155,000
34. Bus and Truck Mechanics and Diesel Engine Specialists	98.8%	$34,970	14.2%	28,000
35. Brazers	92.6%	$29,640	17.0%	71,000
36. Solderers	92.6%	$29,640	17.0%	71,000
37. Welder-Fitters	92.6%	$29,640	17.0%	71,000
38. Welders and Cutters	92.6%	$29,640	17.0%	71,000
39. Welders, Production	92.6%	$29,640	17.0%	71,000
40. Roofers	98.4%	$30,020	18.6%	38,000
41. Grader, Bulldozer, and Scraper Operators	97.8%	$35,030	10.4%	45,000
42. Operating Engineers	97.8%	$35,030	10.4%	45,000
43. Civil Engineers	89.9%	$61,850	8.0%	17,000
44. Automotive Master Mechanics	98.1%	$31,130	12.4%	100,000
45. Automotive Specialty Technicians	98.1%	$31,130	12.4%	100,000

Investigative Jobs with the Highest Percentage of Women

Job	Percent Women
1. Medical and Clinical Laboratory Technologists	73.9%

Best Investigative Jobs Overall Employing 70 Percent or More Women

Job	Percent Women	Annual Earnings	Percent Growth	Annual Openings
1. Medical and Clinical Laboratory Technologists	73.9%	$43,640	19.3%	21,000

Investigative Jobs with the Highest Percentage of Men

Job	Percent Men
1. Electronics Engineers, Except Computer	91.3%
2. Electrical Engineers	91.3%
3. Computer Hardware Engineers	83.7%
4. Dentists, General	82.1%
5. Oral and Maxillofacial Surgeons	82.1%
6. Orthodontists	82.1%
7. Prosthodontists	82.1%
8. Chiropractors	77.8%
9. Computer Security Specialists	76.7%
10. Environmental Scientists and Specialists, Including Health	75.9%
11. Geologists	75.9%
12. Computer Software Engineers, Systems Software	75.3%
13. Computer Software Engineers, Applications	75.3%
14. Network Systems and Data Communications Analysts	73.5%
15. Anesthesiologists	73.2%
16. Internists, General	73.2%
17. Family and General Practitioners	73.2%
18. Obstetricians and Gynecologists	73.2%
19. Pediatricians, General	73.2%
20. Psychiatrists	73.2%
21. Surgeons	73.2%
22. Computer Programmers	72.5%
23. Optometrists	72.4%

Best Investigative Jobs Overall Employing 70 Percent or More Men

Job	Percent Men	Annual Earnings	Percent Growth	Annual Openings
1. Computer Software Engineers, Systems Software	75.3%	$76,240	45.5%	39,000
2. Computer Software Engineers, Applications	75.3%	$72,530	45.5%	55,000
3. Anesthesiologists	73.2%	over $145,000	19.5%	38,000
4. Internists, General	73.2%	over $145,000	19.5%	38,000
5. Obstetricians and Gynecologists	73.2%	over $145,000	19.5%	38,000
6. Surgeons	73.2%	over $145,000	19.5%	38,000
7. Pediatricians, General	73.2%	$134,170	19.5%	38,000
8. Psychiatrists	73.2%	$133,970	19.5%	38,000
9. Family and General Practitioners	73.2%	$133,340	19.5%	38,000
10. Network Systems and Data Communications Analysts	73.5%	$59,120	57.0%	29,000
11. Computer Security Specialists	76.7%	$56,050	37.4%	35,000
12. Computer Programmers	72.5%	$61,340	14.6%	45,000
13. Chiropractors	77.8%	$65,990	23.3%	3,000
14. Electronics Engineers, Except Computer	91.3%	$71,370	9.4%	11,000
15. Optometrists	72.4%	$85,430	17.1%	2,000
16. Dentists, General	82.1%	$120,330	4.1%	7,000
17. Oral and Maxillofacial Surgeons	82.1%	$120,330	4.1%	7,000
18. Orthodontists	82.1%	$120,330	4.1%	7,000
19. Prosthodontists	82.1%	$120,330	4.1%	7,000
20. Computer Hardware Engineers	83.7%	$75,980	6.1%	6,000
21. Geologists	75.9%	$68,460	11.5%	2,000
22. Environmental Scientists and Specialists, Including Health	75.9%	$48,790	23.7%	6,000
23. Electrical Engineers	91.3%	$69,640	2.5%	11,000

Artistic Jobs with the Highest Percentage of Women

Job	Percent Women
1. Makeup Artists, Theatrical and Performance	88.8%
2. Choreographers	84.2%
3. Librarians	82.6%
4. Models	77.4%

Best Artistic Jobs Overall Employing 70 Percent or More Women

Job	Percent Women	Annual Earnings	Percent Growth	Annual Openings
1. Librarians	82.6%	$44,140	10.1%	15,000
2. Makeup Artists, Theatrical and Performance	88.8%	$29,320	18.2%	fewer than 500
3. Choreographers	84.2%	$31,030	15.8%	3,000
4. Models	77.4%	$24,270	14.5%	1,000

Artistic Jobs with the Highest Percentage of Men

Job	Percent Men
1. Film and Video Editors	81.1%
2. Camera Operators, Television, Video, and Motion Picture	81.1%
3. Architects, Except Landscape and Naval	79.7%
4. Landscape Architects	79.7%
5. Radio and Television Announcers	78.1%

Best Artistic Jobs Overall Employing 70 Percent or More Men

Job	Percent Men	Annual Earnings	Percent Growth	Annual Openings
1. Architects, Except Landscape and Naval	79.7%	$57,950	17.3%	8,000
2. Landscape Architects	79.7%	$50,480	22.2%	2,000
3. Film and Video Editors	81.1%	$40,600	26.4%	3,000
4. Camera Operators, Television, Video, and Motion Picture	81.1%	$34,330	13.4%	4,000
5. Radio and Television Announcers	78.1%	$20,940	–10.1%	8,000

Social Jobs with the Highest Percentage of Women

Job	Percent Women
1. Kindergarten Teachers, Except Special Education	97.8%
2. Preschool Teachers, Except Special Education	97.8%
3. Dental Hygienists	97.7%
4. Dental Assistants	97.1%
5. Speech-Language Pathologists	95.1%

(continued)

(continued)

Social Jobs with the Highest Percentage of Women

Job	Percent Women
6. Licensed Practical and Licensed Vocational Nurses	93.0%
7. Registered Nurses	92.4%
8. Teacher Assistants	91.6%
9. Occupational Therapists	90.0%
10. Medical Assistants	88.0%
11. Home Health Aides	87.8%
12. Nursing Aides, Orderlies, and Attendants	87.8%
13. Personal and Home Care Aides	87.3%
14. Occupational Therapist Assistants	87.2%
15. Special Education Teachers, Secondary School	86.6%
16. Special Education Teachers, Preschool, Kindergarten, and Elementary School	86.6%
17. Special Education Teachers, Middle School	86.6%
18. Elementary School Teachers, Except Special Education	79.0%
19. Medical and Public Health Social Workers	78.5%
20. Mental Health and Substance Abuse Social Workers	78.5%
21. Child, Family, and School Social Workers	78.5%
22. Physical Therapist Assistants	76.0%
23. Physical Therapists	70.4%

Best Social Jobs Overall Employing 70 Percent or More Women

Job	Percent Women	Annual Earnings	Percent Growth	Annual Openings
1. Registered Nurses	92.4%	$49,550	27.3%	215,000
2. Dental Hygienists	97.7%	$56,360	43.1%	9,000
3. Physical Therapists	70.4%	$57,710	35.3%	16,000
4. Special Education Teachers, Secondary School	86.6%	$44,240	30.0%	59,000
5. Medical Assistants	88.0%	$24,170	58.9%	78,000
6. Special Education Teachers, Preschool, Kindergarten, and Elementary School	86.6%	$42,920	30.0%	59,000
7. Special Education Teachers, Middle School	86.6%	$42,010	30.0%	59,000
8. Occupational Therapists	90.0%	$52,550	35.2%	10,000
9. Dental Assistants	97.1%	$27,700	42.5%	35,000
10. Home Health Aides	87.8%	$18,240	48.1%	141,000
11. Personal and Home Care Aides	87.3%	$16,450	40.5%	154,000
12. Physical Therapist Assistants	76.0%	$36,610	44.6%	10,000

Best Social Jobs Overall Employing 70 Percent or More Women

Job	Percent Women	Annual Earnings	Percent Growth	Annual Openings
13. Kindergarten Teachers, Except Special Education	97.8%	$40,160	27.2%	34,000
14. Preschool Teachers, Except Special Education	97.8%	$19,820	36.2%	88,000
15. Elementary School Teachers, Except Special Education	79.0%	$42,160	15.2%	183,000
16. Speech-Language Pathologists	95.1%	$50,050	27.2%	10,000
17. Nursing Aides, Orderlies, and Attendants	87.8%	$20,490	24.9%	302,000
18. Medical and Public Health Social Workers	78.5%	$38,430	28.6%	18,000
19. Mental Health and Substance Abuse Social Workers	78.5%	$33,020	34.5%	17,000
20. Licensed Practical and Licensed Vocational Nurses	93.0%	$32,390	20.2%	105,000
21. Occupational Therapist Assistants	87.2%	$37,400	39.2%	3,000
22. Child, Family, and School Social Workers	78.5%	$33,810	23.2%	45,000
23. Teacher Assistants	91.6%	$19,000	23.0%	259,000

Social Jobs with the Highest Percentage of Men

Job	Percent Men
1. Police Patrol Officers	86.9%
2. Sheriffs and Deputy Sheriffs	86.9%
3. Security Guards	79.0%

Best Social Jobs Overall Employing 70 Percent or More Men

Job	Percent Men	Annual Earnings	Percent Growth	Annual Openings
1. Police Patrol Officers	86.9%	$44,020	24.7%	67,000
2. Sheriffs and Deputy Sheriffs	86.9%	$44,020	24.7%	67,000
3. Security Guards	79.0%	$19,660	31.9%	228,000

Enterprising Jobs with the Highest Percentage of Women

Job	Percent Women
1. Hosts and Hostesses, Restaurant, Lounge, and Coffee Shop	87.3%
2. Paralegals and Legal Assistants	86.1%

Best Enterprising Jobs Overall Employing 70 Percent or More Women

Job	Percent Women	Annual Earnings	Percent Growth	Annual Openings
1. Paralegals and Legal Assistants	86.1%	$37,930	28.7%	29,000
2. Hosts and Hostesses, Restaurant, Lounge, and Coffee Shop	87.3%	$15,380	16.4%	95,000

Enterprising Jobs with the Highest Percentage of Men

Job	Percent Men
1. First-Line Supervisors and Manager/Supervisors—Construction Trades Workers	97.2%
2. First-Line Supervisors and Manager/Supervisors—Extractive Workers	97.2%
3. Sales Engineers	94.0%
4. Engineering Managers	93.4%
5. Lawn Service Managers	93.3%
6. Construction Managers	93.2%
7. First-Line Supervisors/Managers of Mechanics, Installers, and Repairers	91.8%
8. First-Line Supervisors/Managers of Police and Detectives	87.2%
9. Storage and Distribution Managers	82.9%
10. Transportation Managers	82.9%
11. Government Service Executives	81.2%
12. Private Sector Executives	81.2%
13. First-Line Supervisors/Managers of Production and Operating Workers	79.1%
14. Child Support, Missing Persons, and Unemployment Insurance Fraud Investigators	79.0%
15. Criminal Investigators and Special Agents	79.0%
16. Police Detectives	79.0%
17. Sales Representatives, Agricultural	73.9%
18. Sales Representatives, Chemical and Pharmaceutical	73.9%
19. Sales Representatives, Electrical/Electronic	73.9%
20. Sales Representatives, Instruments	73.9%
21. Sales Representatives, Mechanical Equipment and Supplies	73.9%
22. Sales Representatives, Medical	73.9%

Enterprising Jobs with the Highest Percentage of Men

Job	Percent Men
23. Sales Representatives, Wholesale and Manufacturing, Except Technical and Scientific Products	73.9%
24. Lawyers	71.3%
25. Computer and Information Systems Managers	70.3%

Best Enterprising Jobs Overall Employing 70 Percent or More Men

Job	Percent Men	Annual Earnings	Percent Growth	Annual Openings
1. Computer and Information Systems Managers	70.3%	$89,740	36.1%	39,000
2. Government Service Executives	81.2%	$134,740	16.7%	63,000
3. Private Sector Executives	81.2%	$134,740	16.7%	63,000
4. Lawyers	71.3%	$91,490	17.0%	53,000
5. Sales Representatives, Agricultural	73.9%	$57,120	19.3%	44,000
6. Sales Representatives, Chemical and Pharmaceutical	73.9%	$57,120	19.3%	44,000
7. Sales Representatives, Electrical/Electronic	73.9%	$57,120	19.3%	44,000
8. Sales Representatives, Instruments	73.9%	$57,120	19.3%	44,000
9. Sales Representatives, Mechanical Equipment and Supplies	73.9%	$57,120	19.3%	44,000
10. Sales Representatives, Medical	73.9%	$57,120	19.3%	44,000
11. Sales Representatives, Wholesale and Manufacturing, Except Technical and Scientific Products	73.9%	$43,860	19.1%	160,000
12. Construction Managers	93.2%	$66,470	12.0%	47,000
13. Storage and Distribution Managers	82.9%	$63,590	19.7%	13,000
14. Transportation Managers	82.9%	$63,590	19.7%	13,000
15. Sales Engineers	94.0%	$67,790	19.9%	7,000
16. First-Line Supervisors and Manager/Supervisors—Construction Trades Workers	97.2%	$48,730	14.1%	67,000
17. First-Line Supervisors and Manager/Supervisors—Extractive Workers	97.2%	$48,730	14.1%	67,000
18. Child Support, Missing Persons, and Unemployment Insurance Fraud Investigators	79.0%	$52,390	22.4%	11,000
19. Criminal Investigators and Special Agents	79.0%	$52,390	22.4%	11,000
20. Police Detectives	79.0%	$52,390	22.4%	11,000

(continued)

(continued)

Best Enterprising Jobs Overall Employing 70 Percent or More Men

Job	Percent Men	Annual Earnings	Percent Growth	Annual Openings
21. First-Line Supervisors/Managers of Mechanics, Installers, and Repairers	91.8%	$48,620	15.4%	42,000
22. Engineering Managers	93.4%	$94,470	9.2%	16,000
23. First-Line Supervisors/Managers of Police and Detectives	87.2%	$62,350	15.3%	14,000
24. First-Line Supervisors/Managers of Production and Operating Workers	79.1%	$43,720	9.5%	66,000
25. Lawn Service Managers	93.3%	$33,770	21.6%	18,000

Conventional Jobs with the Highest Percentage of Women

Job	Percent Women
1. Legal Secretaries	96.5%
2. Executive Secretaries and Administrative Assistants	96.5%
3. Medical Secretaries	96.5%
4. Receptionists and Information Clerks	92.7%
5. Medical Records and Health Information Technicians	91.0%
6. Bookkeeping, Accounting, and Auditing Clerks	89.4%
7. Billing, Cost, and Rate Clerks	88.5%
8. Billing, Posting, and Calculating Machine Operators	88.5%
9. Statement Clerks	88.5%
10. Insurance Claims Clerks	85.9%
11. Insurance Policy Processing Clerks	85.9%
12. Office Clerks, General	83.9%
13. Library Assistants, Clerical	81.9%
14. Human Resources Assistants, Except Payroll and Timekeeping	81.1%
15. Pharmacy Technicians	80.7%
16. Court Clerks	78.2%
17. Cashiers	76.0%
18. Interviewers, Except Eligibility and Loan	71.4%
19. Bill and Account Collectors	71.0%

50 Best Jobs for Your Personality © JIST Works

Best Conventional Jobs Overall Employing 70 Percent or More Women

Job	Percent Women	Annual Earnings	Percent Growth	Annual Openings
1. Legal Secretaries	96.5%	$35,660	18.8%	39,000
2. Bill and Account Collectors	71.0%	$27,000	24.5%	76,000
3. Human Resources Assistants, Except Payroll and Timekeeping	81.1%	$31,060	19.3%	36,000
4. Executive Secretaries and Administrative Assistants	96.5%	$34,080	8.7%	210,000
5. Receptionists and Information Clerks	92.7%	$21,320	29.5%	296,000
6. Interviewers, Except Eligibility and Loan	71.4%	$22,590	28.0%	46,000
7. Pharmacy Technicians	80.7%	$22,760	28.8%	39,000
8. Medical Secretaries	96.5%	$26,000	17.2%	50,000
9. Medical Records and Health Information Technicians	91.0%	$24,520	46.8%	24,000
10. Bookkeeping, Accounting, and Auditing Clerks	89.4%	$27,760	3.0%	274,000
11. Office Clerks, General	83.9%	$22,450	10.4%	550,000
12. Cashiers	76.0%	$15,760	13.2%	1,221,000
13. Billing, Cost, and Rate Clerks	88.5%	$26,290	7.9%	78,000
14. Billing, Posting, and Calculating Machine Operators	88.5%	$26,290	7.9%	78,000
15. Statement Clerks	88.5%	$26,290	7.9%	78,000
16. Insurance Claims Clerks	85.9%	$28,520	3.6%	41,000
17. Insurance Policy Processing Clerks	85.9%	$28,520	3.6%	41,000
18. Library Assistants, Clerical	81.9%	$19,930	21.5%	27,000
19. Court Clerks	78.2%	$27,450	12.3%	14,000

Conventional Jobs with the Highest Percentage of Men

Job	Percent Men
1. Mapping Technicians	91.1%
2. Construction and Building Inspectors	90.2%
3. Cost Estimators	88.0%
4. Audio and Video Equipment Technicians	85.8%
5. Freight Inspectors	83.8%
6. Marine Cargo Inspectors	83.8%
7. Cartographers and Photogrammetrists	82.0%
8. Air Traffic Controllers	81.6%
9. Immigration and Customs Inspectors	79.0%
10. Police Identification and Records Officers	79.0%
11. Cargo and Freight Agents	73.1%

Best Conventional Jobs Overall Employing 70 Percent or More Men

Job	Percent Men	Annual Earnings	Percent Growth	Annual Openings
1. Cost Estimators	88.0%	$48,290	18.6%	25,000
2. Immigration and Customs Inspectors	79.0%	$52,390	22.4%	11,000
3. Police Identification and Records Officers	79.0%	$52,390	22.4%	11,000
4. Audio and Video Equipment Technicians	85.8%	$30,810	26.7%	5,000
5. Mapping Technicians	91.1%	$29,520	23.1%	10,000
6. Construction and Building Inspectors	90.2%	$42,650	13.8%	10,000
7. Air Traffic Controllers	81.6%	$96,260	12.6%	2,000
8. Cargo and Freight Agents	73.1%	$31,990	15.5%	8,000
9. Cartographers and Photogrammetrists	82.0%	$44,170	15.1%	1,000
10. Freight Inspectors	83.8%	$49,590	7.7%	5,000
11. Marine Cargo Inspectors	83.8%	$49,590	7.7%	5,000

The Best Jobs for Each Personality Type with a High Percentage of Workers Age 16–24

In the following lists, we sorted the best 50 jobs for each personality type and included only those that employ the highest percentage of workers age 16–24. Workers in this age bracket make up 14.1 percent of the workforce, and jobs in the lists that follow include at least 10 percent of these workers.

Though young workers are employed in virtually all major occupations, and therefore in settings associated with all six personality types, you may notice that the jobs for the Realistic, Conventional, and Artistic personality types are considerably "younger" than those for the Investigative and Enterprising personality types. This largely reflects the fact that careers in the Investigative and Enterprising categories often require a lot of prior education or time spent rising through the ranks to a supervisory role, whereas on-the-job training requiring less commitment of time may be sufficient preparation for many jobs for the other personality types. In the Artistic category, for some of the jobs—such as Actors, Models, and Singers—youth may actually be an advantage, although it is also possible to have a lifelong career in these occupations.

Keep in mind that the young people who hold the jobs listed in this section may not stay in those jobs, or even in jobs related to the same personality type, for a whole career. Some people are "late bloomers" who do not recognize at an early age what their personality type is and how to find a job appropriate to that type. Others may take a job related to an inappropriate personality type because it offers the opportunity to enter the labor market, earn some money, gain basic job skills, and acquire the experience necessary for moving up to a job that is a better fit.

Realistic Jobs with the Highest Percentage of Workers Age 16–24

Job	Percent Workers Age 16–24
1. Surgical Technologists	24.7%
2. Roofers	22.7%
3. Drywall Installers	19.5%
4. Ceiling Tile Installers	19.5%
5. Automotive Specialty Technicians	18.6%
6. Automotive Master Mechanics	18.6%
7. Brattice Builders	15.7%
8. Ship Carpenters and Joiners	15.7%
9. Boat Builders and Shipwrights	15.7%
10. Carpenter Assemblers and Repairers	15.7%
11. Construction Carpenters	15.7%
12. Rough Carpenters	15.7%
13. Plumbers	13.9%
14. Pipe Fitters	13.9%
15. Pipelaying Fitters	13.9%
16. Refrigeration Mechanics	13.4%
17. Heating and Air Conditioning Mechanics	13.4%
18. Brickmasons and Blockmasons	12.4%
19. Cement Masons and Concrete Finishers	11.7%
20. Sheet Metal Workers	11.6%
21. Electricians	10.9%
22. Operating Engineers	10.1%
23. Grader, Bulldozer, and Scraper Operators	10.1%

Best Realistic Jobs Overall Employing 10 Percent or More Workers Age 16–24

Job	Percent Workers Age 16–24	Annual Earnings	Percent Growth	Annual Openings
1. Electricians	10.9%	$41,680	23.4%	65,000
2. Pipe Fitters	13.9%	$40,950	18.7%	56,000
3. Pipelaying Fitters	13.9%	$40,950	18.7%	56,000
4. Plumbers	13.9%	$40,950	18.7%	56,000
5. Heating and Air Conditioning Mechanics	13.4%	$35,160	31.8%	35,000
6. Refrigeration Mechanics	13.4%	$35,160	31.8%	35,000

(continued)

(continued)

Best Realistic Jobs Overall Employing 10 Percent or More Workers Age 16–24

Job	Percent Workers Age 16–24	Annual Earnings	Percent Growth	Annual Openings
7. Sheet Metal Workers	11.6%	$35,000	19.8%	30,000
8. Brickmasons and Blockmasons	12.4%	$41,550	14.2%	21,000
9. Boat Builders and Shipwrights	15.7%	$34,250	10.1%	193,000
10. Brattice Builders	15.7%	$34,250	10.1%	193,000
11. Carpenter Assemblers and Repairers	15.7%	$34,250	10.1%	193,000
12. Construction Carpenters	15.7%	$34,250	10.1%	193,000
13. Rough Carpenters	15.7%	$34,250	10.1%	193,000
14. Ship Carpenters and Joiners	15.7%	$34,250	10.1%	193,000
15. Ceiling Tile Installers	19.5%	$33,670	21.4%	17,000
16. Drywall Installers	19.5%	$33,670	21.4%	17,000
17. Cement Masons and Concrete Finishers	11.7%	$30,780	26.1%	24,000
18. Roofers	22.7%	$30,020	18.6%	38,000
19. Operating Engineers	10.1%	$35,030	10.4%	45,000
20. Grader, Bulldozer, and Scraper Operators	10.1%	$35,030	10.4%	45,000
21. Surgical Technologists	24.7%	$32,130	27.9%	13,000
22. Automotive Master Mechanics	18.6%	$31,130	12.4%	100,000
23. Automotive Specialty Technicians	18.6%	$31,130	12.4%	100,000

Investigative Jobs with the Highest Percentage of Workers Age 16–24

Job	Percent Workers Age 16–24
1. Computer Support Specialists	11.8%
2. Network Systems and Data Communications Analysts	11.7%
3. Market Research Analysts	11.3%
4. Financial Analysts	10.4%
5. Natural Sciences Managers	10.0%

Best Investigative Jobs Overall Employing 10 Percent or More Workers Age 16–24

Job	Percent Workers Age 16–24	Annual Earnings	Percent Growth	Annual Openings
1. Network Systems and Data Communications Analysts	11.7%	$59,120	57.0%	29,000
2. Financial Analysts	10.4%	$60,050	18.7%	22,000
3. Market Research Analysts	11.3%	$54,670	23.4%	18,000
4. Natural Sciences Managers	10.0%	$85,860	11.3%	5,000
5. Computer Support Specialists	11.8%	$39,440	30.3%	71,000

Artistic Jobs with the Highest Percentage of Workers Age 16–24

Job	Percent Workers Age 16–24
1. Costume Attendants	52.4%
2. Photographic Retouchers and Restorers	48.7%
3. Choreographers	46.9%
4. Radio and Television Announcers	23.0%
5. Actors	20.0%
6. Camera Operators, Television, Video, and Motion Picture	17.9%
7. Film and Video Editors	17.9%
8. Professional Photographers	17.8%
9. Photographers, Scientific	17.8%
10. Models	15.1%
11. Music Arrangers and Orchestrators	14.5%
12. Composers	14.5%
13. Singers	14.5%
14. Music Directors	14.5%
15. Musicians, Instrumental	14.5%
16. Makeup Artists, Theatrical and Performance	13.8%
17. Editors	10.4%
18. Advertising and Promotions Managers	10.1%
19. Broadcast News Analysts	10.0%
20. Reporters and Correspondents	10.0%

Best Artistic Jobs Overall Employing 10 Percent or More Workers Age 16–24

Job	Percent Workers Age 16–24	Annual Earnings	Percent Growth	Annual Openings
1. Advertising and Promotions Managers	10.1%	$60,350	25.0%	13,000
2. Musicians, Instrumental	14.5%	$37,380	17.1%	25,000
3. Singers	14.5%	$37,380	17.1%	25,000
4. Costume Attendants	52.4%	$25,410	27.8%	66,000
5. Film and Video Editors	17.9%	$40,600	26.4%	3,000
6. Editors	10.4%	$41,460	11.8%	14,000
7. Actors	20.0%	$26,460	17.7%	8,000
8. Photographers, Scientific	17.8%	$25,050	13.6%	18,000
9. Professional Photographers	17.8%	$25,050	13.6%	18,000
10. Composers	14.5%	$32,530	13.5%	8,000
11. Music Arrangers and Orchestrators	14.5%	$32,530	13.5%	8,000
12. Music Directors	14.5%	$32,530	13.5%	8,000
13. Camera Operators, Television, Video, and Motion Picture	17.9%	$34,330	13.4%	4,000
14. Makeup Artists, Theatrical and Performance	13.8%	$29,320	18.2%	fewer than 1,000
15. Choreographers	46.9%	$31,030	15.8%	3,000
16. Broadcast News Analysts	10.0%	$31,240	6.2%	6,000
17. Reporters and Correspondents	10.0%	$31,240	6.2%	6,000
18. Radio and Television Announcers	23.0%	$20,940	–10.1%	8,000
19. Models	15.1%	$24,270	14.5%	1,000
20. Photographic Retouchers and Restorers	48.7%	$20,370	5.4%	4,000

Social Jobs with the Highest Percentage of Workers Age 16–24

Job	Percent Workers Age 16–24
1. Fitness Trainers and Aerobics Instructors	29.1%
2. Medical Assistants	21.5%
3. Security Guards	20.6%
4. Emergency Medical Technicians and Paramedics	19.0%
5. Self-Enrichment Education Teachers	18.4%
6. Dental Assistants	17.9%
7. Home Health Aides	16.6%
8. Nursing Aides, Orderlies, and Attendants	16.6%

Social Jobs with the Highest Percentage of Workers Age 16–24

Job	Percent Workers Age 16–24
9. Physical Therapist Assistants	15.5%
10. Occupational Therapist Assistants	14.3%
11. Teacher Assistants	14.1%
12. Kindergarten Teachers, Except Special Education	13.4%
13. Preschool Teachers, Except Special Education	13.4%
14. Personal and Home Care Aides	12.7%
15. Educational, Vocational, and School Counselors	11.1%

Best Social Jobs Overall Employing 10 Percent or More Workers Age 16–24

Job	Percent Workers Age 16–24	Annual Earnings	Percent Growth	Annual Openings
1. Medical Assistants	21.5%	$24,170	58.9%	78,000
2. Self-Enrichment Education Teachers	18.4%	$29,820	40.1%	39,000
3. Dental Assistants	17.9%	$27,700	42.5%	35,000
4. Fitness Trainers and Aerobics Instructors	29.1%	$24,510	44.5%	38,000
5. Home Health Aides	16.6%	$18,240	48.1%	141,000
6. Security Guards	20.6%	$19,660	31.9%	228,000
7. Personal and Home Care Aides	12.7%	$16,450	40.5%	154,000
8. Physical Therapist Assistants	15.5%	$36,610	44.6%	10,000
9. Kindergarten Teachers, Except Special	13.4%	$40,160	27.2%	34,000
10. Preschool Teachers, Except Special Education	13.4%	$19,820	36.2%	88,000
11. Nursing Aides, Orderlies, and Attendants	16.6%	$20,490	24.9%	302,000
12. Emergency Medical Technicians and Paramedics	19.0%	$24,440	33.1%	32,000
13. Occupational Therapist Assistants	14.3%	$37,400	39.2%	3,000
14. Educational, Vocational, and School Counselors	11.1%	$44,640	15.0%	32,000
15. Teacher Assistants	14.1%	$19,000	23.0%	259,000

Enterprising Jobs with the Highest Percentage of Workers Age 16–24

Job	Percent Workers Age 16–24
1. Hosts and Hostesses, Restaurant, Lounge, and Coffee Shop	77.8%
2. Retail Salespersons	30.5%
3. First-Line Supervisors/Managers of Food Preparation and Serving Workers	24.3%
4. Agents and Business Managers of Artists, Performers, and Athletes	17.5%
5. Public Relations Specialists	10.9%

Best Enterprising Jobs Overall Employing 10 Percent or More Workers Age 16–24

Job	Percent Workers Age 16–24	Annual Earnings	Percent Growth	Annual Openings
1. Public Relations Specialists	10.9%	$42,590	32.9%	28,000
2. Agents and Business Managers of Artists, Performers, and Athletes	17.5%	$54,640	27.8%	2,000
3. First-Line Supervisors/Managers of Food Preparation and Serving Workers	24.3%	$24,700	15.5%	154,000
4. Hosts and Hostesses, Restaurant, Lounge, and Coffee Shop	77.8%	$15,380	16.4%	95,000
5. Retail Salespersons	30.5%	$18,090	14.6%	1,014,000

Conventional Jobs with the Highest Percentage of Workers Age 16–24

Job	Percent Workers Age 16–24
1. Cashiers	49.1%
2. Hotel, Motel, and Resort Desk Clerks	46.0%
3. Counter and Rental Clerks	42.2%
4. Receptionists and Information Clerks	27.6%
5. Library Assistants, Clerical	26.7%
6. Pharmacy Technicians	24.7%
7. Office Clerks, General	23.3%
8. Interviewers, Except Eligibility and Loan	20.6%
9. Medical Records and Health Information Technicians	20.6%
10. Adjustment Clerks	20.5%
11. Customer Service Representatives, Utilities	20.5%

Conventional Jobs with the Highest Percentage of Workers Age 16–24

Job	Percent Workers Age 16–24
12. Credit Analysts	20.0%
13. Bill and Account Collectors	19.6%
14. Mapping Technicians	16.0%
15. Reservation and Transportation Ticket Agents	14.0%
16. Travel Clerks	14.0%
17. Cost Estimators	12.0%
18. Human Resources Assistants, Except Payroll and Timekeeping	11.3%
19. Dispatchers, Except Police, Fire, and Ambulance	11.2%
20. Audio and Video Equipment Technicians	10.6%
21. Insurance Claims Clerks	10.6%
22. Insurance Policy Processing Clerks	10.6%

Best Conventional Jobs Overall Employing 10 Percent or More Workers Age 16–24

Job	Percent Workers Age 16–24	Annual Earnings	Percent Growth	Annual Openings
1. Adjustment Clerks	20.5%	$26,500	24.3%	419,000
2. Customer Service Representatives, Utilities	20.5%	$26,500	24.3%	419,000
3. Cost Estimators	12.0%	$48,290	18.6%	25,000
4. Bill and Account Collectors	19.6%	$27,000	24.5%	76,000
5. Human Resources Assistants, Except Payroll and Timekeeping	11.3%	$31,060	19.3%	36,000
6. Receptionists and Information Clerks	27.6%	$21,320	29.5%	296,000
7. Credit Analysts	20.0%	$45,020	18.7%	9,000
8. Dispatchers, Except Police, Fire, and Ambulance	11.2%	$30,390	14.4%	28,000
9. Counter and Rental Clerks	42.2%	$17,640	26.3%	144,000
10. Interviewers, Except Eligibility and Loan	20.6%	$22,590	28.0%	46,000
11. Pharmacy Technicians	24.7%	$22,760	28.8%	39,000
12. Medical Records and Health Information Technicians	20.6%	$24,520	46.8%	24,000
13. Audio and Video Equipment Technicians	10.6%	$30,810	26.7%	5,000
14. Mapping Technicians	16.0%	$29,520	23.1%	10,000
15. Hotel, Motel, and Resort Desk Clerks	46.0%	$17,450	23.9%	46,000
16. Office Clerks, General	23.3%	$22,450	10.4%	550,000

(continued)

(continued)

Best Conventional Jobs Overall Employing 10 Percent or More Workers Age 16–24

Job	Percent Workers Age 16–24	Annual Earnings	Percent Growth	Annual Openings
17. Cashiers	49.1%	$15,760	13.2%	1,221,000
18. Insurance Claims Clerks	10.6%	$28,520	3.6%	41,000
19. Insurance Policy Processing Clerks	10.6%	$28,520	3.6%	41,000
20. Reservation and Transportation Ticket Agents	14.0%	$26,220	12.2%	35,000
21. Travel Clerks	14.0%	$26,220	12.2%	35,000
22. Library Assistants, Clerical	26.7%	$19,930	21.5%	27,000

The Best Jobs for Each Personality Type with a High Percentage of Workers Age 65 and Over

In the following lists, we sorted the best 50 jobs for each personality type and included only those that employ the highest percentage of workers age 65 and over. Workers in this age bracket make up about 3.3 percent of the labor market. We included occupations in the lists if the percentage of workers 65 and over was 4 percent or higher.

One use for these lists is to help you identify jobs that might be interesting to you as you decide to change careers or approach retirement. Some jobs are on the lists because they are attractive to older workers wanting part-time work to supplement their retirement income—for example, Tax Preparers. Other occupations on the lists, such as several jobs in music (Artistic), medicine and science (Investigative), psychology (Social), and college teaching (several personality types), take many years of training and experience. People who are established in such careers often have many incentives to continue working at ages when workers in other fields are ready to retire. These jobs also may not be as physically demanding as some other jobs, especially compared to those linked to the Realistic personality type, and therefore may be easier for older workers to perform.

You may be surprised to find Models topping the list of Artistic jobs with the most workers age 65 and older, but you should know that the employment information about workers in this job applies to the somewhat broader category of "Models, Demonstrators, and Product Promoters"; many of these workers never strut down a runway. Likewise, the information about Singers is based on the larger category of "Musicians, Singers, and Related Workers."

Realistic Jobs with the Highest Percentage of Workers Age 65 and Over

Job	Percent Workers Age 65 and Over
1. Maintenance and Repair Workers, General	5.5%
2. Civil Engineers	4.3%
3. Brickmasons and Blockmasons	4.1%

Best Realistic Jobs Overall Employing 4 Percent or More Workers Age 65 and Over

Job	Percent Workers Age 65 and Over	Annual Earnings	Percent Growth	Annual Openings
1. Brickmasons and Blockmasons	4.1%	$41,550	14.2%	21,000
2. Maintenance and Repair Workers, General	5.5%	$29,800	16.3%	155,000
3. Civil Engineers	4.3%	$61,850	8.0%	17,000

Investigative Jobs with the Highest Percentage of Workers Age 65 and Over

Job	Percent Workers Age 65 and Over
1. Optometrists	8.1%
2. Clinical Psychologists	7.6%
3. Educational Psychologists	7.6%
4. Veterinarians	6.8%
5. Pharmacists	6.5%
6. Dentists, General	6.4%
7. Oral and Maxillofacial Surgeons	6.4%
8. Orthodontists	6.4%
9. Prosthodontists	6.4%
10. Agricultural Sciences Teachers, Postsecondary	5.5%
11. Biological Science Teachers, Postsecondary	5.5%
12. Chemistry Teachers, Postsecondary	5.5%
13. Computer Science Teachers, Postsecondary	5.5%
14. Engineering Teachers, Postsecondary	5.5%
15. Forestry and Conservation Science Teachers, Postsecondary	5.5%
16. Health Specialties Teachers, Postsecondary	5.5%

(continued)

(continued)

Investigative Jobs with the Highest Percentage of Workers Age 65 and Over

Job	Percent Workers Age 65 and Over
17. Mathematical Science Teachers, Postsecondary	5.5%
18. Physics Teachers, Postsecondary	5.5%
19. Anesthesiologists	5.4%
20. Family and General Practitioners	5.4%
21. Internists, General	5.4%
22. Obstetricians and Gynecologists	5.4%
23. Pediatricians, General	5.4%
24. Psychiatrists	5.4%
25. Surgeons	5.4%
26. Financial Analysts	4.2%

Best Investigative Jobs Overall Employing 4 Percent or More Workers Age 65 and Over

Job	Percent Workers Age 65 and Over	Annual Earnings	Percent Growth	Annual Openings
1. Engineering Teachers, Postsecondary	5.5%	$69,700	38.1%	216,000
2. Agricultural Sciences Teachers, Postsecondary	5.5%	$65,470	38.1%	216,000
3. Forestry and Conservation Science Teachers, Postsecondary	5.5%	$64,500	38.1%	216,000
4. Physics Teachers, Postsecondary	5.5%	$62,880	38.1%	216,000
5. Health Specialties Teachers, Postsecondary	5.5%	$61,790	38.1%	216,000
6. Anesthesiologists	5.4%	over $145,000	19.5%	38,000
7. Internists, General	5.4%	over $145,000	19.5%	38,000
8. Obstetricians and Gynecologists	5.4%	over $145,000	19.5%	38,000
9. Surgeons	5.4%	over $145,000	19.5%	38,000
10. Pediatricians, General	5.4%	$134,170	19.5%	38,000
11. Psychiatrists	5.4%	$133,970	19.5%	38,000
12. Family and General Practitioners	5.4%	$133,340	19.5%	38,000
13. Pharmacists	6.5%	$80,530	30.1%	23,000
14. Biological Science Teachers, Postsecondary	5.5%	$55,840	38.1%	216,000
15. Chemistry Teachers, Postsecondary	5.5%	$55,420	38.1%	216,000
16. Computer Science Teachers, Postsecondary	5.5%	$51,030	38.1%	216,000
17. Mathematical Science Teachers, Postsecondary	5.5%	$50,910	38.1%	216,000
18. Veterinarians	6.8%	$64,750	25.1%	4,000

Best Investigative Jobs Overall Employing 4 Percent or More Workers Age 65 and Over

Job	Percent Workers Age 65 and Over	Annual Earnings	Percent Growth	Annual Openings
19. Financial Analysts	4.2%	$60,050	18.7%	22,000
20. Clinical Psychologists	7.6%	$52,220	24.4%	17,000
21. Educational Psychologists	7.6%	$52,220	24.4%	17,000
22. Optometrists	8.1%	$85,430	17.1%	2,000
23. Dentists, General	6.4%	$120,330	4.1%	7,000
24. Oral and Maxillofacial Surgeons	6.4%	$120,330	4.1%	7,000
25. Orthodontists	6.4%	$120,330	4.1%	7,000
26. Prosthodontists	6.4%	$120,330	4.1%	7,000

Artistic Jobs with the Highest Percentage of Workers Age 65 and Over

Job	Percent Workers Age 65 and Over
1. Models	20.5%
2. Composers	10.6%
3. Music Arrangers and Orchestrators	10.6%
4. Music Directors	10.6%
5. Musicians, Instrumental	10.6%
6. Singers	10.6%
7. Caption Writers	7.4%
8. Copy Writers	7.4%
9. Creative Writers	7.4%
10. Poets and Lyricists	7.4%
11. Costume Attendants	7.1%
12. Art Directors	5.7%
13. Cartoonists	5.7%
14. Painters and Illustrators	5.7%
15. Sketch Artists	5.7%
16. Sculptors	5.7%
17. Art, Drama, and Music Teachers, Postsecondary	5.5%
18. English Language and Literature Teachers, Postsecondary	5.5%
19. Foreign Language and Literature Teachers, Postsecondary	5.5%

Best Artistic Jobs Overall Employing 4 Percent or More Workers Age 65 and Over

Job	Percent Workers Age 65 and Over	Annual Earnings	Percent Growth	Annual Openings
1. Art, Drama, and Music Teachers, Postsecondary	5.5%	$47,980	38.1%	216,000
2. English Language and Literature Teachers, Postsecondary	5.5%	$47,120	38.1%	216,000
3. Foreign Language and Literature Teachers, Postsecondary	5.5%	$46,780	38.1%	216,000
4. Musicians, Instrumental	10.6%	$37,380	17.1%	25,000
5. Singers	10.6%	$37,380	17.1%	25,000
6. Caption Writers	7.4%	$42,330	16.1%	23,000
7. Copy Writers	7.4%	$42,330	16.1%	23,000
8. Costume Attendants	7.1%	$25,410	27.8%	66,000
9. Creative Writers	7.4%	$42,330	16.1%	23,000
10. Poets and Lyricists	7.4%	$42,330	16.1%	23,000
11. Art Directors	5.7%	$62,260	11.4%	8,000
12. Cartoonists	5.7%	$35,420	16.5%	4,000
13. Painters and Illustrators	5.7%	$35,420	16.5%	4,000
14. Sculptors	5.7%	$35,420	16.5%	4,000
15. Sketch Artists	5.7%	$35,420	16.5%	4,000
16. Composers	10.6%	$32,530	13.5%	8,000
17. Music Arrangers and Orchestrators	10.6%	$32,530	13.5%	8,000
18. Music Directors	10.6%	$32,530	13.5%	8,000
19. Models	20.5%	$24,270	14.5%	1,000

Social Jobs with the Highest Percentage of Workers Age 65 and Over

Job	Percent Workers Age 65 and Over
1. Security Guards	8.5%
2. Personal and Home Care Aides	8.4%
3. Counseling Psychologists	7.6%
4. Anthropology and Archeology Teachers, Postsecondary	5.5%
5. Area, Ethnic, and Cultural Studies Teachers, Postsecondary	5.5%
6. Economics Teachers, Postsecondary	5.5%

Social Jobs with the Highest Percentage of Workers Age 65 and Over

Job	Percent Workers Age 65 and Over
7. Graduate Teaching Assistants	5.5%
8. History Teachers, Postsecondary	5.5%
9. Nursing Instructors and Teachers, Postsecondary	5.5%
10. Political Science Teachers, Postsecondary	5.5%
11. Psychology Teachers, Postsecondary	5.5%
12. Sociology Teachers, Postsecondary	5.5%
13. Vocational Education Teachers, Postsecondary	5.5%
14. Self-Enrichment Education Teachers	5.1%

Best Social Jobs Overall Employing 4 Percent or More Workers Age 65 and Over

Job	Percent Workers Age 65 and Over	Annual Earnings	Percent Growth	Annual Openings
1. Economics Teachers, Postsecondary	5.5%	$64,950	38.1%	216,000
2. Anthropology and Archeology Teachers, Postsecondary	5.5%	$59,710	38.1%	216,000
3. Political Science Teachers, Postsecondary	5.5%	$57,340	38.1%	216,000
4. Area, Ethnic, and Cultural Studies Teachers, Postsecondary	5.5%	$55,060	38.1%	216,000
5. Psychology Teachers, Postsecondary	5.5%	$54,170	38.1%	216,000
6. Sociology Teachers, Postsecondary	5.5%	$52,770	38.1%	216,000
7. History Teachers, Postsecondary	5.5%	$52,180	38.1%	216,000
8. Nursing Instructors and Teachers, Postsecondary	5.5%	$50,920	38.1%	216,000
9. Vocational Education Teachers Postsecondary	5.5%	$39,740	38.1%	216,000
10. Graduate Teaching Assistants	5.5%	$24,570	38.1%	216,000
11. Self-Enrichment Education Teachers	5.1%	$29,820	40.1%	39,000
12. Security Guards	8.5%	$19,660	31.9%	228,000
13. Personal and Home Care Aides	8.4%	$16,450	40.5%	154,000
14. Counseling Psychologists	7.6%	$52,220	24.4%	17,000

Enterprising Jobs with the Highest Percentage of Workers Age 65 and Over

Job	Percent Workers Age 65 and Over
1. Management Analysts	6.8%
2. Retail Salespersons	5.5%
3. Government Service Executives	5.3%
4. Private Sector Executives	5.3%
5. Lawyers	5.0%
6. Agents and Business Managers of Artists, Performers, and Athletes	5.0%
7. Administrative Services Managers	4.9%
8. Sales Agents, Financial Services	4.1%
9. Sales Agents, Securities and Commodities	4.1%

Best Enterprising Jobs Overall Employing 4 Percent or More Workers Age 65 and Over

Job	Percent Workers Age 65 and Over	Annual Earnings	Percent Growth	Annual Openings
1. Management Analysts	6.8%	$62,580	30.4%	78,000
2. Government Service Executives	5.3%	$134,740	16.7%	63,000
3. Private Sector Executives	5.3%	$134,740	16.7%	63,000
4. Lawyers	5.0%	$91,490	17.0%	53,000
5. Administrative Services Managers	4.9%	$56,940	19.8%	40,000
6. Sales Agents, Financial Services	4.1%	$60,530	13.0%	39,000
7. Sales Agents, Securities and Commodities	4.1%	$60,530	13.0%	39,000
8. Agents and Business Managers of Artists, Performers, and Athletes	5.0%	$54,640	27.8%	2,000
9. Retail Salespersons	5.5%	$18,090	14.6%	1,014,000

Conventional Jobs with the Highest Percentage of Workers Age 65 and Over

Job	Percent Workers Age 65 and Over
1. Tax Preparers	13.2%
2. Assessors	9.2%
3. Cost Estimators	7.0%
4. Bookkeeping, Accounting, and Auditing Clerks	6.6%
5. Construction and Building Inspectors	6.3%
6. Receptionists and Information Clerks	5.6%
7. Air Traffic Controllers	5.3%
8. Library Assistants, Clerical	5.2%
9. Interviewers, Except Eligibility and Loan	5.0%
10. Cartographers and Photogrammetrists	4.9%
11. Counter and Rental Clerks	4.4%

Best Conventional Jobs Overall Employing 4 Percent or More Workers Age 65 and Over

Job	Percent Workers Age 65 and Over	Annual Earnings	Percent Growth	Annual Openings
1. Cost Estimators	7.0%	$48,290	18.6%	25,000
2. Receptionists and Information Clerks	5.6%	$21,320	29.5%	296,000
3. Assessors	9.2%	$43,610	17.6%	11,000
4. Counter and Rental Clerks	4.4%	$17,640	26.3%	144,000
5. Interviewers, Except Eligibility and Loan	5.0%	$22,590	28.0%	46,000
6. Bookkeeping, Accounting, and Auditing Clerks	6.6%	$27,760	3.0%	274,000
7. Construction and Building Inspectors	6.3%	$42,650	13.8%	10,000
8. Air Traffic Controllers	5.3%	$96,260	12.6%	2,000
9. Tax Preparers	13.2%	$26,530	23.2%	11,000
10. Cartographers and Photogrammetrists	4.9%	$44,170	15.1%	1,000
11. Library Assistants, Clerical	5.2%	$19,930	21.5%	27,000

The Best Jobs for Each Personality Type with a High Percentage of Part-Time Workers

Starting with the 50 jobs that met our criteria for each personality type in this book, we created lists that include those jobs with 15 percent or more part-time workers.

If you want to work part time, these lists will be helpful in identifying where most others are finding opportunities for this kind of work in the personality type most compatible with you. Many people prefer to work less than full time. For example, people who are attending school or who have young children may prefer the flexibility of part-time work. People also work part time for money-related reasons, such as supplementing income from a full-time job or working two or more part-time jobs because one desirable full-time job is not available.

If you are the Enterprising type of personality, you will note that few occupations suited to you have a lot of part-timers. Keep in mind that even in occupations where few people work part-time it may be possible for you to carve out a position for yourself that does not require a 40-hour work week.

Many of these jobs can be learned quickly, offer flexible work schedules, are easy to obtain, and offer other desirable advantages. Although many people think of part-time jobs as requiring few skills and providing low pay, this is not always the case. Some of these jobs pay quite well, require substantial training or experience, or are growing rapidly.

Realistic Jobs with the Highest Percentage of Part-Time Workers

Job	Percent Part-Time Workers
1. Surgical Technologists	23.0%
2. Radiologic Technicians	17.5%
3. Radiologic Technologists	17.5%

Best Realistic Jobs Overall Employing 15 Percent or More Part-Time Workers

Job	Percent Part-Time Workers	Annual Earnings	Percent Growth	Annual Openings
1. Radiologic Technicians	17.5%	$40,620	22.9%	21,000
2. Radiologic Technologists	17.5%	$40,620	22.9%	21,000
3. Surgical Technologists	23.0%	$32,130	27.9%	13,000

Investigative Jobs with the Highest Percentage of Part-Time Workers

Job	Percent Part-Time Workers
1. Agricultural Sciences Teachers, Postsecondary	27.7%
2. Biological Science Teachers, Postsecondary	27.7%
3. Chemistry Teachers, Postsecondary	27.7%
4. Computer Science Teachers, Postsecondary	27.7%
5. Engineering Teachers, Postsecondary	27.7%
6. Forestry and Conservation Science Teachers, Postsecondary	27.7%
7. Health Specialties Teachers, Postsecondary	27.7%
8. Mathematical Science Teachers, Postsecondary	27.7%
9. Physics Teachers, Postsecondary	27.7%
10. Clinical Psychologists	27.2%
11. Educational Psychologists	27.2%
12. Optometrists	25.1%
13. Dentists, General	22.3%
14. Oral and Maxillofacial Surgeons	22.3%
15. Orthodontists	22.3%
16. Prosthodontists	22.3%
17. Chiropractors	22.2%
18. Pharmacists	17.3%
19. Physician Assistants	16.3%
20. Medical and Clinical Laboratory Technologists	16.0%
21. Respiratory Therapists	15.5%

Best Investigative Jobs Overall Employing 15 Percent or More Part-Time Workers

Job	Percent Part-Time Workers	Annual Earnings	Percent Growth	Annual Openings
1. Engineering Teachers, Postsecondary	27.7%	$69,700	38.1%	216,000
2. Agricultural Sciences Teachers, Postsecondary	27.7%	$65,470	38.1%	216,000
3. Forestry and Conservation Science Teachers, Postsecondary	27.7%	$64,500	38.1%	216,000
4. Physics Teachers, Postsecondary	27.7%	$62,880	38.1%	216,000
5. Health Specialties Teachers, Postsecondary	27.7%	$61,790	38.1%	216,000

(continued)

(continued)

Best Investigative Jobs Overall Employing 15 Percent or More Part-Time Workers

Job	Percent Part-Time Workers	Annual Earnings	Percent Growth	Annual Openings
6. Pharmacists	17.3%	$80,530	30.1%	23,000
7. Biological Science Teachers, Postsecondary	27.7%	$55,840	38.1%	216,000
8. Chemistry Teachers, Postsecondary	27.7%	$55,420	38.1%	216,000
9. Physician Assistants	16.3%	$65,670	48.9%	7,000
10. Computer Science Teachers, Postsecondary	27.7%	$51,030	38.1%	216,000
11. Mathematical Science Teachers, Postsecondary	27.7%	$50,910	38.1%	216,000
12. Chiropractors	22.2%	$65,990	23.3%	3,000
13. Clinical Psychologists	27.2%	$52,220	24.4%	17,000
14. Educational Psychologists	27.2%	$52,220	24.4%	17,000
15. Optometrists	25.1%	$85,430	17.1%	2,000
16. Dentists, General	22.3%	$120,330	4.1%	7,000
17. Oral and Maxillofacial Surgeons	22.3%	$120,330	4.1%	7,000
18. Orthodontists	22.3%	$120,330	4.1%	7,000
19. Prosthodontists	22.3%	$120,330	4.1%	7,000
20. Respiratory Therapists	15.5%	$41,150	34.8%	10,000
21. Medical and Clinical Laboratory Technologists	16.0%	$43,640	19.3%	21,000

Artistic Jobs with the Highest Percentage of Part-Time Workers

Job	Percent Part-Time Workers
1. Models	52.5%
2. Costume Attendants	51.9%
3. Composers	39.5%
4. Music Arrangers and Orchestrators	39.5%
5. Music Directors	39.5%
6. Musicians, Instrumental	39.5%
7. Singers	39.5%
8. Radio and Television Announcers	34.2%
9. Choreographers	33.8%
10. Makeup Artists, Theatrical and Performance	29.5%

Artistic Jobs with the Highest Percentage of Part-Time Workers

Job	Percent Part-Time Workers
11. Actors	28.2%
12. Art, Drama, and Music Teachers, Postsecondary	27.7%
13. English Language and Literature Teachers, Postsecondary	27.7%
14. Foreign Language and Literature Teachers, Postsecondary	27.7%
15. Interpreters and Translators	26.3%
16. Photographic Retouchers and Restorers	24.3%
17. Caption Writers	24.2%
18. Copy Writers	24.2%
19. Creative Writers	24.2%
20. Poets and Lyricists	24.2%
21. Photographers, Scientific	24.0%
22. Professional Photographers	24.0%
23. Art Directors	23.1%
24. Cartoonists	23.1%
25. Painters and Illustrators	23.1%
26. Sculptors	23.1%
27. Sketch Artists	23.1%
28. Librarians	23.1%
29. Camera Operators, Television, Video, and Motion Picture	20.4%
30. Film and Video Editors	20.4%
31. Commercial and Industrial Designers	16.5%
32. Exhibit Designers	16.5%
33. Fashion Designers	16.5%
34. Floral Designers	16.5%
35. Graphic Designers	16.5%
36. Interior Designers	16.5%
37. Merchandise Displayers and Window Trimmers	16.5%
38. Set Designers	16.5%

Best Artistic Jobs Overall Employing 15 Percent or More Part-Time Workers

Job	Percent Part-Time Workers	Annual Earnings	Percent Growth	Annual Openings
1. Art, Drama, and Music Teachers, Postsecondary	27.7%	$47,980	38.1%	216,000
2. English Language and Literature Teachers, Postsecondary	27.7%	$47,120	38.1%	216,000
3. Foreign Language and Literature Teachers, Postsecondary	27.7%	$46,780	38.1%	216,000
4. Graphic Designers	16.5%	$36,630	21.9%	29,000
5. Musicians, Instrumental	39.5%	$37,380	17.1%	25,000
6. Singers	39.5%	$37,380	17.1%	25,000
7. Caption Writers	24.2%	$42,330	16.1%	23,000
8. Copy Writers	24.2%	$42,330	16.1%	23,000
9. Costume Attendants	51.9%	$25,410	27.8%	66,000
10. Creative Writers	24.2%	$42,330	16.1%	23,000
11. Poets and Lyricists	24.2%	$42,330	16.1%	23,000
12. Interior Designers	16.5%	$40,120	21.7%	8,000
13. Art Directors	23.1%	$62,260	11.4%	8,000
14. Film and Video Editors	20.4%	$40,600	26.4%	3,000
15. Commercial and Industrial Designers	16.5%	$52,320	14.7%	7,000
16. Librarians	23.1%	$44,140	10.1%	15,000
17. Interpreters and Translators	26.3%	$33,490	22.1%	4,000
18. Actors	28.2%	$26,460	17.7%	8,000
19. Cartoonists	23.1%	$35,420	16.5%	4,000
20. Painters and Illustrators	23.1%	$35,420	16.5%	4,000
21. Sculptors	23.1%	$35,420	16.5%	4,000
22. Sketch Artists	23.1%	$35,420	16.5%	4,000
23. Exhibit Designers	16.5%	$35,150	20.9%	2,000
24. Set Designers	16.5%	$35,150	20.9%	2,000
25. Photographers, Scientific	24.0%	$25,050	13.6%	18,000
26. Professional Photographers	24.0%	$25,050	13.6%	18,000
27. Composers	39.5%	$32,530	13.5%	8,000
28. Fashion Designers	16.5%	$52,860	10.6%	2,000
29. Music Arrangers and Orchestrators	39.5%	$32,530	13.5%	8,000
30. Music Directors	39.5%	$32,530	13.5%	8,000
31. Camera Operators, Television, Video, and Motion Picture	20.4%	$34,330	13.4%	4,000
32. Floral Designers	16.5%	$19,660	12.4%	13,000

Best Artistic Jobs Overall Employing 15 Percent or More Part-Time Workers

Job	Percent Part-Time Workers	Annual Earnings	Percent Growth	Annual Openings
33. Makeup Artists, Theatrical and Performance	29.5%	$29,320	18.2%	fewer than 500
34. Merchandise Displayers and Window Trimmers	16.5%	$22,030	11.3%	10,000
35. Choreographers	33.8%	$31,030	15.8%	3,000
36. Radio and Television Announcers	34.2%	$20,940	−10.1%	8,000
37. Models	52.5%	$24,270	14.5%	1,000
38. Photographic Retouchers and Restorers	24.3%	$20,370	5.4%	4,000

Social Jobs with the Highest Percentage of Part-Time Workers

Job	Percent Part-Time Workers
1. Dental Hygienists	57.8%
2. Teacher Assistants	41.1%
3. Self-Enrichment Education Teachers	41.0%
4. Fitness Trainers and Aerobics Instructors	35.6%
5. Dental Assistants	35.6%
6. Personal and Home Care Aides	34.0%
7. Occupational Therapists	31.1%
8. Speech-Language Pathologists	28.1%
9. Anthropology and Archeology Teachers, Postsecondary	27.7%
10. Area, Ethnic, and Cultural Studies Teachers, Postsecondary	27.7%
11. Economics Teachers, Postsecondary	27.7%
12. Graduate Teaching Assistants	27.7%
13. History Teachers, Postsecondary	27.7%
14. Nursing Instructors and Teachers, Postsecondary	27.7%
15. Political Science Teachers, Postsecondary	27.7%
16. Psychology Teachers, Postsecondary	27.7%
17. Sociology Teachers, Postsecondary	27.7%
18. Vocational Education Teachers, Postsecondary	27.7%
19. Counseling Psychologists	27.2%
20. Occupational Therapist Assistants	25.5%
21. Medical Assistants	25.3%

(continued)

(continued)

Social Jobs with the Highest Percentage of Part-Time Workers

Job	Percent Part-Time Workers
22. Kindergarten Teachers, Except Special Education	24.9%
23. Preschool Teachers, Except Special Education	24.9%
24. Physical Therapists	23.8%
25. Physical Therapist Assistants	22.8%
26. Registered Nurses	22.0%
27. Nursing Aides, Orderlies, and Attendants	21.9%
28. Home Health Aides	21.9%
29. Licensed Practical and Licensed Vocational Nurses	19.1%
30. Instructional Coordinators	16.5%
31. Security Guards	15.1%

Best Social Jobs Overall Employing 15 Percent or More Part-Time Workers

Job	Percent Part-Time Workers	Annual Earnings	Percent Growth	Annual Openings
1. Economics Teachers, Postsecondary	27.7%	$64,950	38.1%	216,000
2. Anthropology and Archeology Teachers, Postsecondary	27.7%	$59,710	38.1%	216,000
3. Political Science Teachers, Postsecondary	27.7%	$57,340	38.1%	216,000
4. Area, Ethnic, and Cultural Studies Teachers, Postsecondary	27.7%	$55,060	38.1%	216,000
5. Psychology Teachers, Postsecondary	27.7%	$54,170	38.1%	216,000
6. Sociology Teachers, Postsecondary	27.7%	$52,770	38.1%	216,000
7. History Teachers, Postsecondary	27.7%	$52,180	38.1%	216,000
8. Nursing Instructors and Teachers, Postsecondary	27.7%	$50,920	38.1%	216,000
9. Vocational Education Teachers, Postsecondary	27.7%	$39,740	38.1%	216,000
10. Registered Nurses	22.0%	$49,550	27.3%	215,000
11. Graduate Teaching Assistants	27.7%	$24,570	38.1%	216,000
12. Dental Hygienists	57.8%	$56,360	43.1%	9,000
13. Physical Therapists	23.8%	$57,710	35.3%	16,000
14. Medical Assistants	25.3%	$24,170	58.9%	78,000
15. Occupational Therapists	31.1%	$52,550	35.2%	10,000
16. Self-Enrichment Education Teachers	41.0%	$29,820	40.1%	39,000

Best Social Jobs Overall Employing 15 Percent or More Part-Time Workers

Job	Percent Part-Time Workers	Annual Earnings	Percent Growth	Annual Openings
17. Dental Assistants	35.6%	$27,700	42.5%	35,000
18. Fitness Trainers and Aerobics Instructors	35.6%	$24,510	44.5%	38,000
19. Home Health Aides	21.9%	$18,240	48.1%	141,000
20. Security Guards	15.1%	$19,660	31.9%	228,000
21. Personal and Home Care Aides	34.0%	$16,450	40.5%	154,000
22. Physical Therapist Assistants	22.8%	$36,610	44.6%	10,000
23. Counseling Psychologists	27.2%	$52,220	24.4%	17,000
24. Instructional Coordinators	16.5%	$47,470	25.4%	18,000
25. Kindergarten Teachers, Except Special Education	24.9%	$40,160	27.2%	34,000
26. Preschool Teachers, Except Special Education	24.9%	$19,820	36.2%	88,000
27. Speech-Language Pathologists	28.1%	$50,050	27.2%	10,000
28. Nursing Aides, Orderlies, and Attendants	21.9%	$20,490	24.9%	302,000
29. Licensed Practical and Licensed Vocational Nurses	19.1%	$32,390	20.2%	105,000
30. Occupational Therapist Assistants	25.5%	$37,400	39.2%	3,000
31. Teacher Assistants	41.1%	$19,000	23.0%	259,000

Enterprising Jobs with the Highest Percentage of Part-Time Workers

Job	Percent Part-Time Workers
1. Hosts and Hostesses, Restaurant, Lounge, and Coffee Shop	66.9%
2. Retail Salespersons	32.6%
3. Agents and Business Managers of Artists, Performers, and Athletes	15.2%

Best Enterprising Jobs Overall Employing 15 Percent or More Part-Time Workers

Job	Percent Part-Time Workers	Annual Earnings	Percent Growth	Annual Openings
1. Agents and Business Managers of Artists, Performers, and Athletes	15.2%	$54,640	27.8%	2,000
2. Hosts and Hostesses, Restaurant, Lounge, and Coffee Shop	66.9%	$15,380	16.4%	95,000
3. Retail Salespersons	32.6%	$18,090	14.6%	1,014,000

Conventional Jobs with the Highest Percentage of Part-Time Workers

Job	Percent Part-Time Workers
1. Library Assistants, Clerical	50.4%
2. Cashiers	44.8%
3. Counter and Rental Clerks	35.9%
4. Receptionists and Information Clerks	31.5%
5. Interviewers, Except Eligibility and Loan	30.4%
6. Hotel, Motel, and Resort Desk Clerks	27.2%
7. Office Clerks, General	25.7%
8. Bookkeeping, Accounting, and Auditing Clerks	25.0%
9. Pharmacy Technicians	23.0%
10. Tax Preparers	20.3%
11. Medical Records and Health Information Technicians	17.6%
12. Executive Secretaries and Administrative Assistants	17.5%
13. Legal Secretaries	17.5%
14. Medical Secretaries	17.5%
15. Audio-Visual Collections Specialists	16.5%
16. Billing, Cost, and Rate Clerks	16.1%
17. Billing, Posting, and Calculating Machine Operators	16.1%
18. Statement Clerks	16.1%
19. Reservation and Transportation Ticket Agents	15.7%
20. Travel Clerks	15.7%
21. Human Resources Assistants, Except Payroll and Timekeeping	15.1%

Best Conventional Jobs Overall Employing 15 Percent or More Part-Time Workers

Job	Percent Part-Time Workers	Annual Earnings	Percent Growth	Annual Openings
1. Legal Secretaries	17.5%	$35,660	18.8%	39,000
2. Human Resources Assistants, Except Payroll and Timekeeping	15.1%	$31,060	19.3%	36,000
3. Executive Secretaries and Administrative Assistants	17.5%	$34,080	8.7%	210,000
4. Receptionists and Information Clerks	31.5%	$21,320	29.5%	296,000
5. Counter and Rental Clerks	35.9%	$17,640	26.3%	144,000
6. Interviewers, Except Eligibility and Loan	30.4%	$22,590	28.0%	46,000
7. Pharmacy Technicians	23.0%	$22,760	28.8%	39,000
8. Medical Secretaries	17.5%	$26,000	17.2%	50,000
9. Medical Records and Health Information Technicians	17.6%	$24,520	46.8%	24,000
10. Bookkeeping, Accounting, and Auditing Clerks	25.0%	$27,760	3.0%	274,000
11. Hotel, Motel, and Resort Desk Clerks	27.2%	$17,450	23.9%	46,000
12. Office Clerks, General	25.7%	$22,450	10.4%	550,000
13. Cashiers	44.8%	$15,760	13.2%	1,221,000
14. Billing, Cost, and Rate Clerks	16.1%	$26,290	7.9%	78,000
15. Billing, Posting, and Calculating Machine Operators	16.1%	$26,290	7.9%	78,000
16. Statement Clerks	16.1%	$26,290	7.9%	78,000
17. Tax Preparers	20.3%	$26,530	23.2%	11,000
18. Reservation and Transportation Ticket Agents	15.7%	$26,220	12.2%	35,000
19. Travel Clerks	15.7%	$26,220	12.2%	35,000
20. Library Assistants, Clerical	50.4%	$19,930	21.5%	27,000
21. Audio-Visual Collections Specialists	16.5%	$32,590	16.3%	2,000

The Best Jobs for Each Personality Type with a High Percentage of Self-Employed Workers

About 8 percent of all working people are self-employed or own their own business. This substantial part of our workforce gets little mention in most career books.

The jobs in the lists in this section are selected from the 50 best jobs for each personality type, and all have 15 percent or more self-employed workers. Many jobs in these lists, such as the various types of artists, are held by people who operate one- or two-person businesses and who may also do this work part time. Those in other occupations, such as Rough Carpenters, often work on a per-job basis under the supervision of others.

As you will see from these lists, self-employed people hold a wide range of jobs at all levels of pay and skill. Many are in the arts (Artistic), construction (Realistic), or health (Investigative) professions, but many other fields are also represented. Also, while the lists do not include data on age and gender, older workers and women make up a rapidly growing part of the self-employed population. For example, some highly experienced older workers set up consulting and other small businesses following a layoff or as an alternative to full retirement. Large numbers of women are forming small businesses or creating self-employment opportunities as an alternative to traditional employment.

Realistic Jobs with the Highest Percentage of Self-Employed Workers

Job	Percent Self-Employed Workers
1. First-Line Supervisors and Manager/Supervisors—Landscaping Workers	34.7%
2. Technical Directors/Managers	32.8%
3. Roofers	31.9%
4. Boat Builders and Shipwrights	29.7%
5. Brattice Builders	29.7%
6. Carpenter Assemblers and Repairers	29.7%
7. Construction Carpenters	29.7%
8. Rough Carpenters	29.7%
9. Ship Carpenters and Joiners	29.7%
10. Brickmasons and Blockmasons	27.9%
11. Ceiling Tile Installers	18.4%
12. Drywall Installers	18.4%
13. Automotive Master Mechanics	15.5%
14. Automotive Specialty Technicians	15.5%
15. Heating and Air Conditioning Mechanics	15.4%
16. Refrigeration Mechanics	15.4%

Best Realistic Jobs Overall with 15 Percent or More Self-Employed Workers

Job	Percent Self-Employed Workers	Annual Earnings	Percent Growth	Annual Openings
1. Heating and Air Conditioning Mechanics	15.4%	$35,160	31.8%	35,000
2. Refrigeration Mechanics	15.4%	$35,160	31.8%	35,000
3. Technical Directors/Managers	32.8%	$48,200	18.3%	10,000
4. Brickmasons and Blockmasons	27.9%	$41,550	14.2%	21,000
5. Boat Builders and Shipwrights	29.7%	$34,250	10.1%	193,000
6. Brattice Builders	29.7%	$34,250	10.1%	193,000
7. Carpenter Assemblers and Repairers	29.7%	$34,250	10.1%	193,000
8. Construction Carpenters	29.7%	$34,250	10.1%	193,000
9. Rough Carpenters	29.7%	$34,250	10.1%	193,000
10. Ship Carpenters and Joiners	29.7%	$34,250	10.1%	193,000
11. First-Line Supervisors and Manager/Supervisors—Landscaping Workers	34.7%	$33,770	21.6%	18,000
12. Ceiling Tile Installers	18.4%	$33,670	21.4%	17,000
13. Drywall Installers	18.4%	$33,670	21.4%	17,000
14. Roofers	31.9%	$30,020	18.6%	38,000
15. Automotive Master Mechanics	15.5%	$31,130	12.4%	100,000
16. Automotive Specialty Technicians	15.5%	$31,130	12.4%	100,000

Investigative Jobs with the Highest Percentage of Self-Employed Workers

Job	Percent Self-Employed Workers
1. Chiropractors	58.5%
2. Dentists, General	39.9%
3. Oral and Maxillofacial Surgeons	39.9%
4. Orthodontists	39.9%
5. Prosthodontists	39.9%
6. Optometrists	29.2%
7. Veterinarians	27.7%
8. Clinical Psychologists	25.4%
9. Educational Psychologists	25.4%
10. Network Systems and Data Communications Analysts	23.6%

(continued)

(continued)

Investigative Jobs with the Highest Percentage of Self-Employed Workers

Job	Percent Self-Employed Workers
11. Anesthesiologists	16.9%
12. Family and General Practitioners	16.9%
13. Internists, General	16.9%
14. Obstetricians and Gynecologists	16.9%
15. Pediatricians, General	16.9%
16. Psychiatrists	16.9%
17. Surgeons	16.9%

Best Investigative Jobs Overall with 15 Percent or More Self-Employed Workers

Job	Percent Self-Employed Workers	Annual Earnings	Percent Growth	Annual Openings
1. Anesthesiologists	16.9%	over $145,000	19.5%	38,000
2. Internists, General	16.9%	over $145,000	19.5%	38,000
3. Obstetricians and Gynecologists	16.9%	over $145,000	19.5%	38,000
4. Surgeons	16.9%	over $145,000	19.5%	38,000
5. Pediatricians, General	16.9%	$134,170	19.5%	38,000
6. Psychiatrists	16.9%	$133,970	19.5%	38,000
7. Family and General Practitioners	16.9%	$133,340	19.5%	38,000
8. Network Systems and Data Communications Analysts	23.6%	$59,120	57.0%	29,000
9. Veterinarians	27.7%	$64,750	25.1%	4,000
10. Chiropractors	58.5%	$65,990	23.3%	3,000
11. Clinical Psychologists	25.4%	$52,220	24.4%	17,000
12. Educational Psychologists	25.4%	$52,220	24.4%	17,000
13. Optometrists	29.2%	$85,430	17.1%	2,000
14. Dentists, General	39.9%	$120,330	4.1%	7,000
15. Oral and Maxillofacial Surgeons	39.9%	$120,330	4.1%	7,000
16. Orthodontists	39.9%	$120,330	4.1%	7,000
17. Prosthodontists	39.9%	$120,330	4.1%	7,000

Artistic Jobs with the Highest Percentage of Self-Employed Workers

Job	Percent Self-Employed Workers
1. Caption Writers	67.9%
2. Copy Writers	67.9%
3. Creative Writers	67.9%
4. Poets and Lyricists	67.9%
5. Cartoonists	55.5%
6. Painters and Illustrators	55.5%
7. Sculptors	55.5%
8. Sketch Artists	55.5%
9. Art Directors	53.6%
10. Photographers, Scientific	52.5%
11. Professional Photographers	52.5%
12. Makeup Artists, Theatrical and Performance	50.6%
13. Models	49.1%
14. Composers	39.3%
15. Music Arrangers and Orchestrators	39.3%
16. Music Directors	39.3%
17. Musicians, Instrumental	38.3%
18. Singers	38.3%
19. Radio and Television Announcers	34.4%
20. Directors—Stage, Motion Pictures, Television, and Radio	32.8%
21. Producers	32.8%
22. Talent Directors	32.8%
23. Floral Designers	32.5%
24. Exhibit Designers	32.2%
25. Interior Designers	32.2%
26. Set Designers	32.2%
27. Graphic Designers	31.8%
28. Commercial and Industrial Designers	31.0%
29. Merchandise Displayers and Window Trimmers	30.9%
30. Fashion Designers	29.3%
31. Camera Operators, Television, Video, and Motion Picture	23.8%
32. Landscape Architects	23.4%
33. Film and Video Editors	21.9%
34. Architects, Except Landscape and Naval	21.4%
35. Interpreters and Translators	19.6%
36. Actors	17.4%
37. Choreographers	16.7%

Best Artistic Jobs Overall with 15 Percent or More Self-Employed Workers

Job	Percent Self-Employed Workers	Annual Earnings	Percent Growth	Annual Openings
1. Graphic Designers	31.8%	$36,630	21.9%	29,000
2. Directors—Stage, Motion Pictures, Television, and Radio	32.8%	$48,200	18.3%	10,000
3. Producers	32.8%	$48,200	18.3%	10,000
4. Talent Directors	32.8%	$48,200	18.3%	10,000
5. Architects, Except Landscape and Naval	21.4%	$57,950	17.3%	8,000
6. Musicians, Instrumental	38.3%	$37,380	17.1%	25,000
7. Singers	38.3%	$37,380	17.1%	25,000
8. Caption Writers	67.9%	$42,330	16.1%	23,000
9. Copy Writers	67.9%	$42,330	16.1%	23,000
10. Creative Writers	67.9%	$42,330	16.1%	23,000
11. Poets and Lyricists	67.9%	$42,330	16.1%	23,000
12. Interior Designers	32.2%	$40,120	21.7%	8,000
13. Landscape Architects	23.4%	$50,480	22.2%	2,000
14. Art Directors	53.6%	$62,260	11.4%	8,000
15. Film and Video Editors	21.9%	$40,600	26.4%	3,000
16. Commercial and Industrial Designers	31.0%	$52,320	14.7%	7,000
17. Interpreters and Translators	19.6%	$33,490	22.1%	4,000
18. Actors	17.4%	$26,460	17.7%	8,000
19. Cartoonists	55.5%	$35,420	16.5%	4,000
20. Painters and Illustrators	55.5%	$35,420	16.5%	4,000
21. Sculptors	55.5%	$35,420	16.5%	4,000
22. Sketch Artists	55.5%	$35,420	16.5%	4,000
23. Exhibit Designers	32.2%	$35,150	20.9%	2,000
24. Set Designers	32.2%	$35,150	20.9%	2,000
25. Photographers, Scientific	52.5%	$25,050	13.6%	18,000
26. Professional Photographers	52.5%	$25,050	13.6%	18,000
27. Composers	39.3%	$32,530	13.5%	8,000
28. Fashion Designers	29.3%	$52,860	10.6%	2,000
29. Music Arrangers and Orchestrators	39.3%	$32,530	13.5%	8,000
30. Music Directors	39.3%	$32,530	13.5%	8,000
31. Camera Operators, Television, Video, and Motion Picture	23.8%	$34,330	13.4%	4,000
32. Floral Designers	32.5%	$19,660	12.4%	13,000

Best Artistic Jobs Overall with 15 Percent or More Self-Employed Workers

Job	Percent Self-Employed Workers	Annual Earnings	Percent Growth	Annual Openings
33. Makeup Artists, Theatrical and Performance	50.6%	$29,320	18.2%	fewer than 500
34. Merchandise Displayers and Window Trimmers	30.9%	$22,030	11.3%	10,000
35. Choreographers	16.7%	$31,030	15.8%	3,000
36. Radio and Television Announcers	34.4%	$20,940	–10.1%	8,000
37. Models	49.1%	$24,270	14.5%	1,000

Social Jobs with the Highest Percentage of Self-Employed Workers

Job	Percent Self-Employed Workers
1. Personal Financial Advisors	37.7%
2. Counseling Psychologists	25.4%
3. Self-Enrichment Education Teachers	19.9%

Best Social Jobs Overall with 15 Percent or More Self-Employed Workers

Job	Percent Self-Employed Workers	Annual Earnings	Percent Growth	Annual Openings
1. Personal Financial Advisors	37.7%	$58,700	34.6%	18,000
2. Self-Enrichment Education Teachers	19.9%	$29,820	40.1%	39,000
3. Counseling Psychologists	25.4%	$52,220	24.4%	17,000

Enterprising Jobs with the Highest Percentage of Self-Employed Workers

Job	Percent Self-Employed Workers
1. Construction Managers	46.9%
2. First-Line Supervisors/Managers of Non-Retail Sales Workers	44.7%
3. Lawn Service Managers	34.7%
4. Program Directors	32.8%
5. Management Analysts	29.8%
6. Agents and Business Managers of Artists, Performers, and Athletes	27.0%
7. Lawyers	26.8%
8. First-Line Supervisors and Manager/Supervisors—Construction Trades Workers	20.1%
9. First-Line Supervisors and Manager/Supervisors—Extractive Workers	20.1%

Best Enterprising Jobs Overall with 15 Percent or More Self-Employed Workers

Job	Percent Self-Employed Workers	Annual Earnings	Percent Growth	Annual Openings
1. Management Analysts	29.8%	$62,580	30.4%	78,000
2. Lawyers	26.8%	$91,490	17.0%	53,000
3. Construction Managers	46.9%	$66,470	12.0%	47,000
4. First-Line Supervisors and Manager/Supervisors—Construction Trades Workers	20.1%	$48,730	14.1%	67,000
5. First-Line Supervisors and Manager/Supervisors—Extractive Workers	20.1%	$48,730	14.1%	67,000
6. First-Line Supervisors/Managers of Non-Retail Sales Workers	44.7%	$55,690	6.8%	72,000
7. Agents and Business Managers of Artists, Performers, and Athletes	27.0%	$54,640	27.8%	2,000
8. Lawn Service Managers	34.7%	$33,770	21.6%	18,000
9. Program Directors	32.8%	$48,200	18.3%	10,000

Conventional Jobs with the Highest Percentage of Self-Employed Workers

Job	Percent Self-Employed Workers
1. Assessors	34.8%
2. Tax Preparers	26.2%

Best Conventional Jobs Overall with 15 Percent or More Self-Employed Workers

Job	Percent Self-Employed Workers	Annual Earnings	Percent Growth	Annual Openings
1. Assessors	34.8%	$43,610	17.6%	11,000
2. Tax Preparers	26.2%	$26,530	23.2%	11,000

PART IV

Descriptions of the 50 Best Jobs for Each Personality

This part provides descriptions for all the jobs included in one or more of the lists in Part III. The book's introduction gives more details on how to use and interpret the job descriptions, but here are the highlights, along with some additional information.

◎ The job descriptions that follow met our criteria for inclusion in this book, as we describe in the Introduction. The jobs in this book scored among the 50 highest in each personality type for earnings, projected growth, and number of job openings. Many good jobs do not meet one or more of these criteria, but we think the jobs that do are the best ones to consider in your career planning.

◎ The job descriptions are arranged by personality type and in alphabetical order by job title within each personality type. This approach allows you to find a description quickly if you know its title from one of the lists in Part III. If you have not browsed the lists in Part III, consider spending some time there. The lists are interesting and will help you identify job titles that you can look up in the descriptions that follow.

◎ Refer to the Introduction, beginning on page 1, for details on interpreting the job descriptions' content.

◎ The GOE job description section includes a subsection titled Other Jobs in This Work Group to help you identify similar jobs. Not all of the jobs listed here are among the top 50 for each personality type.

◎ When reviewing the descriptions, keep in mind that the jobs meet our criteria for being among the top 50 jobs for each personality type based on their total scores for earnings, growth, and number of openings—but one or more of these measures may not be among the highest. For example, an occupation that has high pay may be included, even though growth rate and number of job openings are below average.

"Well," you might ask, "doesn't this mean that at least some 'bad' jobs are described in this part?" Our answer is yes and no. Some jobs with high scores for all measures, such as Sales Managers—the Enterprising job with the highest total for pay, growth, and number of openings—would be a very bad job for people who dislike or are not good at that sort of work. On the other hand, many people love working as Lawn Service Managers even though that job has lower earnings, a lower projected growth rate, and fewer openings. Descriptions for both jobs are included in this book.

Possibly somewhere a former sales manager works as a lawn service manager and loves it. This person may even have figured out how to make more money (say, by specializing in golf courses), have a more flexible schedule, have more fun, or have other advantages not available to a sales manager.

The point is that each job is right for somebody, perhaps at a certain time in their lives. We are all likely to change careers and jobs several times, and it's not always money that motivates us. So browse the job descriptions that follow and know that somewhere there is a good place for you. We hope you find it.

Realistic Jobs

Airline Pilots, Copilots, and Flight Engineers

- Personality Code: RE
- Growth: 18.5%
- Annual Job Openings: 6,000
- Annual Earnings: $125,030
- Education/Training Required: Bachelor's degree
- Self-Employed: 0%
- Part-Time: 12.9%

Pilot and navigate the flight of multi-engine aircraft in regularly scheduled service for the transport of passengers and cargo. Requires Federal Air Transport rating and certification in specific aircraft type used. File instrument flight plans with air traffic control to ensure that flights are coordinated with other air traffic. Inspect aircraft for defects and malfunctions according to pre-flight checklists. Make announcements regarding flights, using public address systems. Monitor engine operation, fuel consumption, and functioning of aircraft systems during flights. Monitor gauges, warning devices, and control panels to verify aircraft performance and to regulate engine speed. Order changes in fuel supplies, loads, routes, or schedules to ensure safety of flights. Plan and formulate flight activities and test schedules and prepare flight evaluation reports. Respond to and report in-flight emergencies and malfunctions. Start engines, operate controls, and pilot airplanes to transport passengers, mail, or freight while adhering to flight plans, regulations, and procedures. Steer aircraft along planned routes with the assistance of autopilot and flight management computers. Work as part of a flight team with other crew members, especially during takeoffs and landings. Brief crews about flight details such as destinations, duties, and responsibilities. Check passenger and cargo distributions and fuel amounts to ensure that weight and balance specifications are met. Choose routes, altitudes, and speeds that will provide the fastest, safest, and smoothest flights. Confer with flight dispatchers and weather forecasters to keep abreast of flight conditions. Contact control towers for takeoff clearances, arrival instructions, and other information, using radio equipment. Coordinate flight activities with ground crews and air-traffic control and inform crew members of flight and test procedures. Direct activities of aircraft crews during flights. Conduct in-flight tests and evaluations at specified altitudes and in all types of weather in order to determine the receptivity and other characteristics of equipment and systems. Evaluate other pilots or pilot-license applicants for proficiency. Instruct other pilots and student pilots in aircraft operations and the principles of flight. Load smaller aircraft, handling passenger luggage and supervising refueling. **SKILLS**—Operation and Control; Operation Monitoring; Instructing; Science; Coordination; Systems Evaluation; Judgment and Decision Making; Systems Analysis.

GOE—Interest Area: 07. Transportation. **Work Group:** 07.03. Air Vehicle Operation. **Other Jobs in This Work Group:** Commercial Pilots.

EDUCATION/TRAINING PROGRAM(S)—Airline/Commercial/Professional Pilot and Flight Crew; Flight Instructor. **RELATED KNOWLEDGE/COURSES—**Transportation; Geography; Public Safety and Security; Education and Training; Mechanical Devices; Physics.

Automotive Master Mechanics

- Personality Code: RC
- Growth: 12.4%
- Annual Job Openings: 100,000
- Annual Earnings: $31,130
- Education/Training Required: Postsecondary vocational training
- Self-Employed: 15.5%
- Part-Time: 4.3%

Repair automobiles, trucks, buses, and other vehicles. Master mechanics repair virtually any part on the vehicle or specialize in the transmission system. Examine vehicles to determine extent of damage or malfunctions. Test drive vehicles and test components and systems, using equipment such as infrared engine analyzers, compression gauges, and computerized diagnostic devices. Repair, reline, replace, and adjust brakes. Review work orders and discuss work with supervisors. Follow checklists to ensure all important parts are examined, including belts, hoses, steering systems, spark plugs, brake and fuel systems, wheel bearings, and other potentially troublesome areas. Plan work procedures, using charts, technical manuals, and experience. Test and adjust repaired systems to meet manufacturers' performance specifications. Confer with customers to obtain descriptions of vehicle problems and to discuss work to be performed and future repair requirements. Perform routine and scheduled maintenance services such as oil changes, lubrications, and tune-ups. Disassemble units and inspect parts for wear, using micrometers, calipers, and gauges. Overhaul or replace carburetors, blowers, generators, distributors, starters, and pumps. Repair and service air conditioning, heating, engine-cooling, and electrical systems. Repair or replace parts such as pistons, rods, gears, valves, and bearings. Tear down, repair, and rebuild faulty assemblies such as power systems, steering systems, and linkages. Rewire ignition systems, lights, and instrument panels. Repair radiator leaks. Install and repair accessories such as radios, heaters, mirrors, and windshield wipers. Repair manual and automatic transmissions. Repair or replace shock absorbers. Align vehicles' front ends. Rebuild parts such as crankshafts and cylinder blocks. **SKILLS**—Troubleshooting; Repairing; Installation; Equipment Maintenance; Active Learning; Complex Problem Solving; Instructing; Equipment Selection.

GOE—Interest Area: 05. Mechanics, Installers, and Repairers. **Work Group:** 05.03. Mechanical Work. **Other Jobs in This Work Group:** Aircraft Body and Bonded Structure Repairers; Aircraft Engine Specialists; Aircraft Mechanics and Service Technicians; Airframe-and-Power-Plant Mechanics; Automotive Body and Related Repairers; Automotive Glass Installers and Repairers; Automotive Service Technicians and Mechanics; Automotive Specialty Technicians; Bicycle Repairers; Bridge and Lock Tenders; Bus and Truck Mechanics and Diesel Engine Specialists; Camera and Photographic Equipment Repairers; Coin, Vending, and Amusement Machine Servicers and Repairers; Control and Valve Installers and Repairers, Except Mechanical Door; Farm Equipment Mechanics; Gas Appliance Repairers; Hand and Portable Power Tool Repairers; Heating and Air Conditioning Mechanics; Heating, Air Conditioning, and Refrigeration Mechanics and Installers; Helpers—Electricians; Helpers—Installation, Maintenance, and Repair Workers; Industrial Machinery Mechanics; Installation, Maintenance, and Repair Workers, All Other; Keyboard Instrument Repairers and Tuners; Locksmiths and Safe Repairers; Maintenance and Repair Workers, General; Maintenance Workers, Machinery; Mechanical Door Repairers; Medical Appliance Technicians; Medical Equipment Repairers; Meter Mechanics; Millwrights; Mobile Heavy Equipment Mechanics, Except Engines; Motorboat Mechanics; Motorcycle Mechanics; Musical Instrument Repairers and Tuners; Ophthalmic Laboratory Technicians; Optical Instrument Assemblers; Outdoor Power Equipment and Other Small Engine Mechanics; Painters, Transportation Equipment; Percussion Instrument

Repairers and Tuners; Precision Instrument and Equipment Repairers, All Other; Rail Car Repairers; Railroad Inspectors; Recreational Vehicle Service Technicians; Reed or Wind Instrument Repairers and Tuners; Refrigeration Mechanics; Stringed Instrument Repairers and Tuners; Tire Repairers and Changers; Valve and Regulator Repairers; Watch Repairers.

EDUCATION/TRAINING PROGRAM(S)— Alternative Fuel Vehicle Technology/Technician; Automobile/Automotive Mechanics Technology/ Technician; Automotive Engineering Technology/Technician; Medium/Heavy Vehicle and Truck Technology/Technician; Vehicle Emissions Inspection and Maintenance Technology/Technician. **RELATED KNOWLEDGE/COURSES—**Mechanical Devices; Computers and Electronics; Physics; Engineering and Technology; Education and Training; Customer and Personal Service.

Automotive Specialty Technicians

- Personality Code: RC
- Growth: 12.4%
- Annual Job Openings: 100,000
- Annual Earnings: $31,130
- Education/Training Required: Postsecondary vocational training
- Self-Employed: 15.5%
- Part-Time: 4.3%

Repair only one system or component on a vehicle, such as brakes, suspension, or radiator. Align and repair wheels, axles, frames, torsion bars, and steering mechanisms of automobiles, using special alignment equipment and wheel-balancing machines. Examine vehicles, compile estimates of repair costs, and secure customers' approval to perform repairs. Install and repair air conditioners and service components such as compressors, condensers, and controls. Rebuild, repair, and test automotive fuel injection units. Remove and replace defective mufflers and tailpipes. Repair and rebuild clutch systems. Repair and replace automobile leaf springs. Repair and replace defective ball joint suspensions, brake shoes, and wheel bearings. Repair, overhaul, and adjust automobile brake systems. Repair, replace, and adjust defective carburetor parts and gasoline filters. Test electronic computer components in automobiles to ensure that they are working properly. Tune automobile engines to ensure proper and efficient functioning. Use electronic test equipment to locate and correct malfunctions in fuel, ignition, and emissions control systems. Convert vehicle fuel systems from gasoline to butane gas operations and repair and service operating butane fuel units. Inspect and test new vehicles for damage; then record findings so that necessary repairs can be made. Repair, install, and adjust hydraulic and electromagnetic automatic lift mechanisms used to raise and lower automobile windows, seats, and tops. **SKILLS—**Installation; Repairing; Troubleshooting; Equipment Maintenance; Quality Control Analysis; Technology Design; Operation Monitoring; Management of Material Resources.

GOE—Interest Area: 05. Mechanics, Installers, and Repairers. **Work Group:** 05.03. Mechanical Work. **Other Jobs in This Work Group:** Aircraft Body and Bonded Structure Repairers; Aircraft Engine Specialists; Aircraft Mechanics and Service Technicians; Airframe-and-Power-Plant Mechanics; Automotive Body and Related Repairers; Automotive Glass Installers and Repairers; Automotive Master Mechanics; Automotive Service Technicians and Mechanics; Bicycle Repairers; Bridge and Lock Tenders; Bus and Truck Mechanics and Diesel Engine Specialists; Camera and Photographic Equipment Repairers; Coin, Vending, and Amusement Machine Servicers and Repairers; Control and Valve Installers and Repairers, Except Mechanical Door; Farm Equipment Mechanics; Gas Appliance Repairers; Hand and Portable Power Tool Repairers; Heating and Air Conditioning Mechanics; Heating,

Air Conditioning, and Refrigeration Mechanics and Installers; Helpers—Electricians; Helpers—Installation, Maintenance, and Repair Workers; Industrial Machinery Mechanics; Installation, Maintenance, and Repair Workers, All Other; Keyboard Instrument Repairers and Tuners; Locksmiths and Safe Repairers; Maintenance and Repair Workers, General; Maintenance Workers, Machinery; Mechanical Door Repairers; Medical Appliance Technicians; Medical Equipment Repairers; Meter Mechanics; Millwrights; Mobile Heavy Equipment Mechanics, Except Engines; Motorboat Mechanics; Motorcycle Mechanics; Musical Instrument Repairers and Tuners; Ophthalmic Laboratory Technicians; Optical Instrument Assemblers; Outdoor Power Equipment and Other Small Engine Mechanics; Painters, Transportation Equipment; Percussion Instrument Repairers and Tuners; Precision Instrument and Equipment Repairers, All Other; Rail Car Repairers; Railroad Inspectors; Recreational Vehicle Service Technicians; Reed or Wind Instrument Repairers and Tuners; Refrigeration Mechanics; Stringed Instrument Repairers and Tuners; Tire Repairers and Changers; Valve and Regulator Repairers; Watch Repairers.

EDUCATION/TRAINING PROGRAM(S)— Alternative Fuel Vehicle Technology/Technician; Automobile/Automotive Mechanics Technology/ Technician; Automotive Engineering Technology/Technician; Medium/Heavy Vehicle and Truck Technology/Technician; Vehicle Emissions Inspection and Maintenance Technology/Technician. **RELATED KNOWLEDGE/COURSES—**Mechanical Devices; Computers and Electronics; Design; Physics; Engineering and Technology; Chemistry.

Boat Builders and Shipwrights

- Personality Code: RC
- Growth: 10.1%
- Annual Job Openings: 193,000
- Annual Earnings: $34,250
- Education/Training Required: Long-term on-the-job training
- Self-Employed: 29.7%
- Part-Time: 5.3%

Construct and repair ships or boats according to blueprints. Cuts and forms parts, such as keel, ribs, sidings, and support structures and blocks, using woodworking hand tools and power tools. Constructs and shapes wooden frames, structures, and other parts according to blueprint specifications, using hand tools, power tools, and measuring instruments. Attaches metal parts such as fittings, plates, and bulkheads to ship, using brace and bits, augers, and wrenches. Establishes dimensional reference points on layout and hull to make template of parts and locate machinery and equipment. Smoothes and finishes ship surfaces, using power sander, broadax, adz, and paint, and waxes and buffs surface to specified finish. Cuts out defect, using power tools and hand tools, and fits and secures replacement part, using caulking gun, adhesive, or hand tools. Assembles and installs hull timbers and other structures in ship, using adhesive, measuring instruments, and hand tools or power tools. Measures and marks dimensional lines on lumber, following template and using scriber. Consults with customer or supervisor and reads blueprint to determine necessary repairs. Attaches hoist to sections of hull and directs hoist operator to align parts over blocks according to layout of boat. Marks outline of boat on building dock, shipway, or mold loft according to blueprint specifications, using measuring instruments and crayon. Inspects boat to determine location and extent of defect. Positions and secures support structures on construction area. **SKILLS**—Installation; Repairing; Operations Analysis; Technology Design; Equipment Selection; Equipment Maintenance; Mathematics; Quality Control Analysis.

GOE—Interest Area: 06. Construction, Mining, and Drilling. **Work Group:** 06.02. Construction. **Other Jobs in This Work Group:** Boilermakers; Brattice Builders; Brickmasons and Blockmasons; Carpenters; Carpet Installers; Ceiling Tile Installers; Cement Masons and Concrete Finishers; Commercial Divers; Construction and Related Workers, All Other; Construction Carpenters; Drywall and Ceiling Tile Installers; Drywall Installers; Electricians; Explosives Workers, Ordnance Handling Experts, and Blasters; Fence Erectors; Floor Layers, Except Carpet, Wood, and Hard Tiles; Floor Sanders and Finishers; Glaziers; Grader, Bulldozer, and Scraper Operators; Hazardous Materials Removal Workers; Insulation Workers, Floor, Ceiling, and Wall; Insulation Workers, Mechanical; Manufactured Building and Mobile Home Installers; Operating Engineers; Operating Engineers and Other Construction Equipment Operators; Painters, Construction and Maintenance; Paperhangers; Paving, Surfacing, and Tamping Equipment Operators; Pile-Driver Operators; Pipe Fitters; Pipelayers; Pipelaying Fitters; Plasterers and Stucco Masons; Plumbers; Plumbers, Pipefitters, and Steamfitters; Rail-Track Laying and Maintenance Equipment Operators; Refractory Materials Repairers, Except Brickmasons; Reinforcing Iron and Rebar Workers; Riggers; Roofers; Rough Carpenters; Security and Fire Alarm Systems Installers; Segmental Pavers; Sheet Metal Workers; Ship Carpenters and Joiners; Stone Cutters and Carvers; Stonemasons; Structural Iron and Steel Workers; Tapers; Terrazzo Workers and Finishers; Tile and Marble Setters.

EDUCATION/TRAINING PROGRAM(S)—Carpentry/Carpenter. **RELATED KNOWLEDGE/COURSES**—Building and Construction; Design; Mechanical Devices; Engineering and Technology; Production and Processing; Physics.

Brattice Builders

- Personality Code: R
- Growth: 10.1%
- Annual Job Openings: 193,000
- Annual Earnings: $34,250
- Education/Training Required: Moderate-term on-the-job training
- Self-Employed: 29.7%
- Part-Time: 5.3%

Build doors or brattices (ventilation walls or partitions) in underground passageways to control the proper circulation of air through the passageways and to the working places. Installs rigid and flexible air ducts to transport air to work areas. Drills and blasts obstructing boulders to reopen ventilation shafts. Erects partitions to support roof in areas unsuited to timbering or bolting. **SKILLS**—Installation; Technology Design; Operations Analysis; Equipment Selection; Quality Control Analysis.

GOE—Interest Area: 06. Construction, Mining, and Drilling. **Work Group:** 06.02. Construction. **Other Jobs in This Work Group:** Boat Builders and Shipwrights; Boilermakers; Brickmasons and Blockmasons; Carpenters; Carpet Installers; Ceiling Tile Installers; Cement Masons and Concrete Finishers; Commercial Divers; Construction and Related Workers, All Other; Construction Carpenters; Drywall and Ceiling Tile Installers; Drywall Installers; Electricians; Explosives Workers, Ordnance Handling Experts, and Blasters; Fence Erectors; Floor Layers, Except Carpet, Wood, and Hard Tiles; Floor Sanders and Finishers; Glaziers; Grader, Bulldozer, and Scraper Operators; Hazardous Materials Removal Workers; Insulation Workers, Floor, Ceiling, and Wall; Insulation Workers, Mechanical; Manufactured Building and Mobile Home Installers; Operating Engineers; Operating Engineers and Other Construction Equipment Operators; Painters, Construction and Maintenance; Paperhangers; Paving, Surfacing, and Tamping Equipment Operators; Pile-Driver Operators; Pipe

Fitters; Pipelayers; Pipelaying Fitters; Plasterers and Stucco Masons; Plumbers; Plumbers, Pipefitters, and Steamfitters; Rail-Track Laying and Maintenance Equipment Operators; Refractory Materials Repairers, Except Brickmasons; Reinforcing Iron and Rebar Workers; Riggers; Roofers; Rough Carpenters; Security and Fire Alarm Systems Installers; Segmental Pavers; Sheet Metal Workers; Ship Carpenters and Joiners; Stone Cutters and Carvers; Stonemasons; Structural Iron and Steel Workers; Tapers; Terrazzo Workers and Finishers; Tile and Marble Setters.

EDUCATION/TRAINING PROGRAM(S)— Carpentry/Carpenter. **RELATED KNOWLEDGE/ COURSES**—Building and Construction; Physics; Engineering and Technology; Mechanical Devices.

Brazers

- Personality Code: RC
- Growth: 17.0%
- Annual Job Openings: 71,000
- Annual Earnings: $29,640
- Education/Training Required: Short-term on-the-job training
- Self-Employed: 5.6%
- Part-Time: 2.1%

Braze together components to assemble fabricated metal parts, using torch or welding machine and flux. Connects hoses from torch to regulator valves and cylinders of oxygen and specified fuel gas, acetylene or natural. Turns valves to start flow of gases, lights flame, and adjusts valves to obtain desired color and size of flame. Brushes flux onto joint of workpiece or dips braze rod into flux to prevent oxidation of metal. Aligns and secures workpieces in fixtures, jigs, or vise, using rule, square, or template. Melts and separates brazed joints to remove and straighten damaged or misaligned components, using hand torch or furnace. Selects torch tip, flux,

and brazing alloy from data charts or work order. Adjusts electric current and timing cycle of resistance welding machine to heat metal to bonding temperature. Guides torch and rod along joint of workpieces to heat to brazing temperature, melt braze alloy, and bond workpieces together. Cuts carbon electrodes to specified size and shape, using cut-off saw. Removes workpiece from fixture, using tongs, and cools workpiece, using air or water. Cleans joints of workpieces, using wire brush or by dipping them into cleaning solution. Examines seam and rebrazes defective joints or broken parts. **SKILLS**—Operation and Control; Operation Monitoring; Installation; Equipment Selection; Science; Quality Control Analysis.

GOE—Interest Area: 08. Industrial Production. **Work Group:** 08.03. Production Work. **Other Jobs in This Work Group:** Assemblers and Fabricators, All Other; Bakers, Manufacturing; Bindery Machine Operators and Tenders; Cementing and Gluing Machine Operators and Tenders; Chemical Equipment Controllers and Operators; Chemical Equipment Operators and Tenders; Chemical Equipment Tenders; Cleaning, Washing, and Metal Pickling Equipment Operators and Tenders; Coating, Painting, and Spraying Machine Operators and Tenders; Coil Winders, Tapers, and Finishers; Combination Machine Tool Operators and Tenders, Metal and Plastic; Computer-Controlled Machine Tool Operators, Metal and Plastic; Cooling and Freezing Equipment Operators and Tenders; Crushing, Grinding, and Polishing Machine Setters, Operators, and Tenders; Cutters and Trimmers, Hand; Cutting and Slicing Machine Operators and Tenders; Cutting and Slicing Machine Setters, Operators, and Tenders; Design Printing Machine Setters and Set-Up Operators; Electrolytic Plating and Coating Machine Operators and Tenders, Metal and Plastic; Electrolytic Plating and Coating Machine Setters and Set-Up Operators, Metal and Plastic; Electrotypers and Stereotypers; Embossing Machine Set-Up Operators; Engraver Set-Up Operators; Extruding and Forming Machine Operators and Tenders, Synthetic or Glass Fibers; Extruding and Forming Machine Setters, Operators, and Tenders, Synthetic and Glass Fibers; Extruding, Forming, Pressing, and Compacting Machine Operators and Tenders; Fabric and Apparel Patternmakers; Fiber Product Cutting Machine Setters and Set-Up Operators; Fiberglass Laminators and Fabricators; Film Laboratory Technicians; Fitters, Structural Metal—Precision; Food and Tobacco Roasting, Baking, and Drying Machine Operators and Tenders; Food Batchmakers; Food Cooking Machine Operators and Tenders; Furnace, Kiln, Oven, Drier, and Kettle Operators and Tenders; Glass Cutting Machine Setters and Set-Up Operators; Graders and Sorters, Agricultural Products; Grinding and Polishing Workers, Hand; Hand Compositors and Typesetters; Heaters, Metal and Plastic; Helpers—Production Workers; Job Printers; Letterpress Setters and Set-Up Operators; Marking and Identification Printing Machine Setters and Set-Up Operators; Meat, Poultry, and Fish Cutters and Trimmers; Metal Fabricators, Structural Metal Products; Metal-Refining Furnace Operators and Tenders; Mixing and Blending Machine Setters, Operators, and Tenders; Mold Makers, Hand; Molding and Casting Workers; Nonelectrolytic Plating and Coating Machine Operators and Tenders, Metal and Plastic; Nonelectrolytic Plating and Coating Machine Setters and Set-Up Operators, Metal and Plastic; Numerical Control Machine Tool Operators and Tenders, Metal and Plastic; Offset Lithographic Press Setters and Set-Up Operators; Packaging and Filling Machine Operators and Tenders; Painting, Coating, and Decorating Workers; Photoengraving and Lithographing Machine Operators and Tenders; Photographic Hand Developers; Photographic Process Workers; Photographic Processing Machine Operators; Photographic Reproduction Technicians; Photographic Retouchers and Restorers; Plate Finishers; Platemakers; Plating and Coating Machine Setters, Operators, and Tenders, Metal and Plastic; Pourers and Casters, Metal; Precision Printing Workers; Prepress Technicians and Workers; Pressing Machine Operators and Tenders—Textile, Garment, and Related Materials; Printing Machine Operators; Printing Press Machine Operators and Tenders; Production

Helpers; Production Laborers; Production Workers, All Other; Sawing Machine Operators and Tenders; Sawing Machine Setters and Set-Up Operators; Sawing Machine Setters, Operators, and Tenders, Wood; Scanner Operators; Semiconductor Processors; Separating, Filtering, Clarifying, Precipitating, and Still Machine Setters, Operators, and Tenders; Sewers, Hand; Sewing Machine Operators; Sewing Machine Operators, Garment; Sewing Machine Operators, Non-Garment; Shoe Machine Operators and Tenders; Slaughterers and Meat Packers; Solderers; Soldering and Brazing Machine Operators and Tenders; Stone Sawyers; Strippers; Structural Metal Fabricators and Fitters; Team Assemblers; Textile Bleaching and Dyeing Machine Operators and Tenders; Tire Builders; Welder-Fitters; Welders and Cutters; Welders, Cutters, Solderers, and Brazers; Welders, Production; Welding Machine Operators and Tenders; Woodworking Machine Operators and Tenders, Except Sawing.

EDUCATION/TRAINING PROGRAM(S)—Welding Technology/Welder. **RELATED KNOWLEDGE/COURSES**—Engineering and Technology; Building and Construction; Mechanical Devices; Chemistry.

Brickmasons and Blockmasons

- Personality Code: R
- Growth: 14.2%
- Annual Job Openings: 21,000
- Annual Earnings: $41,550
- Education/Training Required: Long-term on-the-job training
- Self-Employed: 27.9%
- Part-Time: 5.3%

Lay and bind building materials, such as brick, structural tile, concrete block, cinder block, glass block, and terra-cotta block, with mortar and other substances to construct or repair walls, partitions, arches, sewers, and other structures. Construct corners by fastening in plumb position a corner pole or building a corner pyramid of bricks and then filling in between the corners, using a line from corner to corner to guide each course, or layer, of brick. Measure distance from reference points and mark guidelines to lay out work, using plumb bobs and levels. Calculate angles and courses and determine vertical and horizontal alignment of courses. Fasten or fuse brick or other building material to structure with wire clamps, anchor holes, torch, or cement. Break or cut bricks, tiles, or blocks to size, using trowel edge, hammer, or power saw. Remove excess mortar with trowels and hand tools and finish mortar joints with jointing tools for a sealed, uniform appearance. Interpret blueprints and drawings to determine specifications and to calculate the materials required. Apply and smooth mortar or other mixture over work surface. Mix specified amounts of sand, clay, dirt, or mortar powder with water to form refractory mixtures. Examine brickwork or structure to determine need for repair. Clean working surface to remove scale, dust, soot, or chips of brick and mortar, using broom, wire brush, or scraper. Lay and align bricks, blocks, or tiles to build or repair structures or high temperature equipment, such as cupola, kilns, ovens, or furnaces. Remove burned or damaged brick or mortar, using sledgehammer, crowbar, chipping gun, or chisel. **SKILLS**—Equipment Maintenance; Mathematics; Instructing; Installation; Coordination; Social Perceptiveness; Management of Financial Resources; Technology Design.

GOE—Interest Area: 06. Construction, Mining, and Drilling. **Work Group:** 06.02. Construction. **Other Jobs in This Work Group:** Boat Builders and Shipwrights; Boilermakers; Brattice Builders; Carpenters; Carpet Installers; Ceiling Tile Installers; Cement Masons and Concrete Finishers; Commercial Divers; Construction and Related Workers, All Other; Construction Carpenters; Drywall and Ceiling Tile Installers; Drywall Installers; Electricians; Explosives Workers, Ordnance Handling Experts, and Blasters; Fence Erectors; Floor Layers, Except Carpet, Wood, and Hard Tiles; Floor Sanders and Finishers; Glaziers; Grader, Bulldozer, and Scraper Operators; Hazardous Materials Removal Workers; Insulation Workers, Floor, Ceiling, and Wall; Insulation Workers, Mechanical; Manufactured Building and Mobile Home Installers; Operating Engineers; Operating Engineers and Other Construction Equipment Operators; Painters, Construction and Maintenance; Paperhangers; Paving, Surfacing, and Tamping Equipment Operators; Pile-Driver Operators; Pipe Fitters; Pipelayers; Pipelaying Fitters; Plasterers and Stucco Masons; Plumbers; Plumbers, Pipefitters, and Steamfitters; Rail-Track Laying and Maintenance Equipment Operators; Refractory Materials Repairers, Except Brickmasons; Reinforcing Iron and Rebar Workers; Riggers; Roofers; Rough Carpenters; Security and Fire Alarm Systems Installers; Segmental Pavers; Sheet Metal Workers; Ship Carpenters and Joiners; Stone Cutters and Carvers; Stonemasons; Structural Iron and Steel Workers; Tapers; Terrazzo Workers and Finishers; Tile and Marble Setters.

EDUCATION/TRAINING PROGRAM(S)—Mason/Masonry. **RELATED KNOWLEDGE/COURSES**—Building and Construction; Design; Public Safety and Security; Mathematics; Production and Processing; Mechanical Devices.

Bus and Truck Mechanics and Diesel Engine Specialists

- Personality Code: RC
- Growth: 14.2%
- Annual Job Openings: 28,000
- Annual Earnings: $34,970
- Education/Training Required: Postsecondary vocational training
- Self-Employed: 3.9%
- Part-Time: 2.5%

Diagnose, adjust, repair, or overhaul trucks, buses, and all types of diesel engines. Includes mechanics working primarily with automobile diesel engines. Use handtools such as screwdrivers, pliers, wrenches, pressure gauges, and precision instruments, as well as power tools such as pneumatic wrenches, lathes, welding equipment, and jacks and hoists. Inspect brake systems, steering mechanisms, wheel bearings, and other important parts to ensure that they are in proper operating condition. Perform routine maintenance such as changing oil, checking batteries, and lubricating equipment and machinery. Adjust and reline brakes, align wheels, tighten bolts and screws, and reassemble equipment. Raise trucks, buses, and heavy parts or equipment, using hydraulic jacks or hoists. Test-drive trucks and buses to diagnose malfunctions or to ensure that they are working properly. Inspect, test, and listen to defective equipment to diagnose malfunctions, using test instruments such as handheld computers, motor analyzers, chassis charts, and pressure gauges. Examine and adjust protective guards, loose bolts, and specified safety devices. Inspect and verify dimensions and clearances of parts to ensure conformance to factory specifications. Specialize in repairing and maintaining parts of the engine, such as fuel injection systems. Attach test instruments to equipment and read dials and gauges in order to diagnose mal-

functions. Rewire ignition systems, lights, and instrument panels. Recondition and replace parts, pistons, bearings, gears, and valves. Repair and adjust seats, doors, and windows and install and repair accessories. Inspect, repair, and maintain automotive and mechanical equipment and machinery such as pumps and compressors. Disassemble and overhaul internal combustion engines, pumps, generators, transmissions, clutches, and differential units. Rebuild gas and/or diesel engines. Align front ends and suspension systems. **SKILLS**—Equipment Maintenance; Repairing; Troubleshooting; Installation; Learning Strategies; Coordination; Instructing; Technology Design.

GOE—Interest Area: 05. Mechanics, Installers, and Repairers. **Work Group:** 05.03. Mechanical Work. **Other Jobs in This Work Group:** Aircraft Body and Bonded Structure Repairers; Aircraft Engine Specialists; Aircraft Mechanics and Service Technicians; Airframe-and-Power-Plant Mechanics; Automotive Body and Related Repairers; Automotive Glass Installers and Repairers; Automotive Master Mechanics; Automotive Service Technicians and Mechanics; Automotive Specialty Technicians; Bicycle Repairers; Bridge and Lock Tenders; Camera and Photographic Equipment Repairers; Coin, Vending, and Amusement Machine Servicers and Repairers; Control and Valve Installers and Repairers, Except Mechanical Door; Farm Equipment Mechanics; Gas Appliance Repairers; Hand and Portable Power Tool Repairers; Heating and Air Conditioning Mechanics; Heating, Air Conditioning, and Refrigeration Mechanics and Installers; Helpers—Electricians; Helpers—Installation, Maintenance, and Repair Workers; Industrial Machinery Mechanics; Installation, Maintenance, and Repair Workers, All Other; Keyboard Instrument Repairers and Tuners; Locksmiths and Safe Repairers; Maintenance and Repair Workers, General; Maintenance Workers, Machinery; Mechanical Door Repairers; Medical Appliance Technicians; Medical Equipment Repairers; Meter Mechanics; Millwrights; Mobile Heavy Equipment Mechanics, Except Engines; Motorboat Mechanics; Motorcycle Mechanics; Musical Instru-

Realistic-B

ment Repairers and Tuners; Ophthalmic Laboratory Technicians; Optical Instrument Assemblers; Outdoor Power Equipment and Other Small Engine Mechanics; Painters, Transportation Equipment; Percussion Instrument Repairers and Tuners; Precision Instrument and Equipment Repairers, All Other; Rail Car Repairers; Railroad Inspectors; Recreational Vehicle Service Technicians; Reed or Wind Instrument Repairers and Tuners; Refrigeration Mechanics; Stringed Instrument Repairers and Tuners; Tire Repairers and Changers; Valve and Regulator Repairers; Watch Repairers.

EDUCATION/TRAINING PROGRAM(S)— Diesel Mechanics Technology/Technician; Medium/Heavy Vehicle and Truck Technology/ Technician. RELATED KNOWLEDGE/COURSES—Mechanical Devices; Transportation; Public Safety and Security; Engineering and Technology; Law and Government; Physics; Chemistry.

Calibration and Instrumentation Technicians

- Personality Code: RC
- Growth: 10.0%
- Annual Job Openings: 24,000
- Annual Earnings: $43,650
- Education/Training Required: Associate's degree
- Self-Employed: 0.4%
- Part-Time: 5.0%

Develop, test, calibrate, operate, and repair electrical, mechanical, electromechanical, electrohydraulic, or electronic measuring and recording instruments, apparatus, and equipment. Plans sequence of testing and calibration program for instruments and equipment according to blue-prints, schematics, technical manuals, and other specifications. Performs preventative and corrective maintenance of test apparatus and peripheral equipment. Confers with engineers, supervisor, and other technical workers to assist with equipment installation, maintenance, and repair techniques. Analyzes and converts test data, using mathematical formulas, and reports results and proposed modifications. Sets up test equipment and conducts tests on performance and reliability of mechanical, structural, or electromechanical equipment. Selects sensing, telemetering, and recording instrumentation and circuitry. Disassembles and reassembles instruments and equipment, using hand tools, and inspects instruments and equipment for defects. Sketches plans for developing jigs, fixtures, instruments, and related nonstandard apparatus. Modifies performance and operation of component parts and circuitry to specifications, using test equipment and precision instruments. SKILLS—Technology Design; Equipment Maintenance; Quality Control Analysis; Science; Equipment Selection; Troubleshooting; Installation; Operations Analysis.

GOE—Interest Area: 02. Science, Math, and Engineering. Work Group: 02.08. Engineering Technology. Other Jobs in This Work Group: Aerospace Engineering and Operations Technicians; Architectural and Civil Drafters; Architectural Drafters; Cartographers and Photogrammetrists; Civil Drafters; Civil Engineering Technicians; Construction and Building Inspectors; Drafters, All Other; Electrical and Electronic Engineering Technicians; Electrical and Electronics Drafters; Electrical Drafters; Electrical Engineering Technicians; Electro-Mechanical Technicians; Electronic Drafters; Electronics Engineering Technicians; Engineering Technicians, Except Drafters, All Other; Environmental Engineering Technicians; Industrial Engineering Technicians; Mapping Technicians; Mechanical Drafters; Mechanical Engineering Technicians; Numerical Tool and Process Control Programmers; Pressure Vessel Inspectors; Surveying and Mapping Technicians; Surveying Technicians; Surveyors.

EDUCATION/TRAINING PROGRAM(S)—Computer Engineering Technology/Technician; Computer Technology/Computer Systems Technology; Electrical and Electronic Engineering Technologies/Technicians, Other; Electrical, Electronic and Communications Engineering Technology/Technician; Telecommunications Technology/Technician. **RELATED KNOWLEDGE/COURSES**—Design; Mathematics; Computers and Electronics; Engineering and Technology; Mechanical Devices; Physics.

Carpenter Assemblers and Repairers

- Personality Code: RC
- Growth: 10.1%
- Annual Job Openings: 193,000
- Annual Earnings: $34,250
- Education/Training Required: Moderate-term on-the-job training
- Self-Employed: 29.7%
- Part-Time: 5.3%

Perform a variety of tasks requiring a limited knowledge of carpentry, such as applying siding and weatherboard to building exteriors or assembling and erecting prefabricated buildings. Measures and marks location of studs, leaders, and receptacle openings, using tape measure, template, and marker. Cuts sidings and moldings, sections of weatherboard, openings in sheetrock, and lumber, using hand tools and power tools. Lays out and aligns materials on worktable or in assembly jig according to specified instructions. Removes surface defects, using knife, scraper, wet sponge, electric iron, and sanding tools. Trims overlapping edges of wood or weatherboard, using portable router or power saw and hand tools. Installs prefabricated windows and doors; insulation; wall, ceiling, and floor panels; or siding, using adhesives, hoists, hand tools, and power tools. Aligns and fastens materials together, using hand tools and power tools, to form building or bracing. Repairs or replaces defective locks, hinges, cranks, and pieces of wood, using glue, hand tools, and power tools. Applies stain, paint, or crayons to defects and filter to touch up the repaired area. Directs crane operator in positioning floor, wall, ceiling, and roof panel on house foundation. Moves panel or roof section to other work stations or to storage or shipping area, using electric hoist. Studies blueprints, specification sheets, and drawings to determine style and type of window or wall panel required. Fills cracks, seams, depressions, and nail holes with filler. Examines wood surfaces for defects, such as nicks, cracks, or blisters. Measures cut materials to determine conformance to specifications, using tape measure. Realigns windows and screens to fit casements and oils moving parts. **SKILLS**—Repairing; Installation; Management of Material Resources; Equipment Maintenance; Operation and Control.

GOE—Interest Area: 06. Construction, Mining, and Drilling. **Work Group:** 06.04. Hands-on Work in Construction, Extraction, and Maintenance. **Other Jobs in This Work Group:** Construction Laborers; Extraction Workers, All Other; Grips and Set-Up Workers, Motion Picture Sets, Studios, and Stages; Helpers, Construction Trades, All Other; Helpers—Brickmasons, Blockmasons, Stonemasons, and Tile and Marble Setters; Helpers—Carpenters; Helpers—Extraction Workers; Helpers—Painters, Paperhangers, Plasterers, and Stucco Masons; Helpers—Pipelayers, Plumbers, Pipefitters, and Steamfitters; Helpers—Roofers; Highway Maintenance Workers; Septic Tank Servicers and Sewer Pipe Cleaners.

EDUCATION/TRAINING PROGRAM(S)—Carpentry/Carpenter. **RELATED KNOWLEDGE/COURSES**—Building and Construction; Design; Engineering and Technology.

Realistic—C

Ceiling Tile Installers

- Personality Code: R
- Growth: 21.4%
- Annual Job Openings: 17,000
- Annual Earnings: $33,670
- Education/Training Required: Moderate-term on-the-job training
- Self-Employed: 18.4%
- Part-Time: 5.9%

Apply or mount acoustical tiles or blocks, strips, or sheets of shock-absorbing materials to ceilings and walls of buildings to reduce or reflect sound. Materials may be of decorative quality. Includes lathers who fasten wooden, metal, or rockboard lath to walls, ceilings, or partitions of buildings to provide support base for plaster, fire-proofing, or acoustical material. Applies cement to back of tile and presses tile into place, aligning with layout marks and joints of previously laid tile. Applies acoustical tiles or shock-absorbing materials to ceilings and walls of buildings to reduce or reflect sound and to decorate rooms. Washes concrete surfaces with washing soda and zinc sulfate solution before mounting tile to increase adhesive qualities of surfaces. Inspects furrings, mechanical mountings, and masonry surface for plumbness and level, using spirit or water level. Hangs dry lines (stretched string) to wall molding to guide positioning of main runners. Nails or screws molding to wall to support and seals joint between ceiling tile and wall. Scribes and cuts edges of tile to fit wall where wall molding is not specified. Nails channels or wood furring strips to surfaces to provide mounting for tile. Measures and marks surface to lay out work according to blueprints and drawings. Cuts tiles for fixture and borders, using keyhole saw, and inserts tiles into supporting framework. **SKILLS**—None met the criteria.

GOE—Interest Area: 06. Construction, Mining, and Drilling. **Work Group:** 06.02. Construction. **Other Jobs in This Work Group:** Boat Builders and Shipwrights; Boilermakers; Brattice Builders; Brickmasons and Blockmasons; Carpenters; Carpet Installers; Cement Masons and Concrete Finishers; Commercial Divers; Construction and Related Workers, All Other; Construction Carpenters; Drywall and Ceiling Tile Installers; Drywall Installers; Electricians; Explosives Workers, Ordnance Handling Experts, and Blasters; Fence Erectors; Floor Layers, Except Carpet, Wood, and Hard Tiles; Floor Sanders and Finishers; Glaziers; Grader, Bulldozer, and Scraper Operators; Hazardous Materials Removal Workers; Insulation Workers, Floor, Ceiling, and Wall; Insulation Workers, Mechanical; Manufactured Building and Mobile Home Installers; Operating Engineers; Operating Engineers and Other Construction Equipment Operators; Painters, Construction and Maintenance; Paperhangers; Paving, Surfacing, and Tamping Equipment Operators; Pile-Driver Operators; Pipe Fitters; Pipelayers; Pipelaying Fitters; Plasterers and Stucco Masons; Plumbers; Plumbers, Pipefitters, and Steamfitters; Rail-Track Laying and Maintenance Equipment Operators; Refractory Materials Repairers, Except Brickmasons; Reinforcing Iron and Rebar Workers; Riggers; Roofers; Rough Carpenters; Security and Fire Alarm Systems Installers; Segmental Pavers; Sheet Metal Workers; Ship Carpenters and Joiners; Stone Cutters and Carvers; Stonemasons; Structural Iron and Steel Workers; Tapers; Terrazzo Workers and Finishers; Tile and Marble Setters.

EDUCATION/TRAINING PROGRAM(S)— Drywall Installation/Drywaller. **RELATED KNOWLEDGE/COURSES—**Building and Construction; Design; Mathematics; Physics.

Cement Masons and Concrete Finishers

◉ Personality Code: R

◉ Growth: 26.1%

◉ Annual Job Openings: 24,000

◉ Annual Earnings: $30,780

◉ Education/Training Required: Long-term on-the-job training

◉ Self-Employed: 5.2%

◉ Part-Time: 5.0%

Smooth and finish surfaces of poured concrete, such as floors, walks, sidewalks, roads, or curbs, using a variety of hand and power tools. Align forms for sidewalks, curbs, or gutters; patch voids; use saws to cut expansion joints. Wet surface to prepare for bonding, fill holes and cracks with grout or slurry, and smooth, using trowel. Build wooden molds and clamp molds around area to be repaired, using hand tools. Cut out damaged areas, drill holes for reinforcing rods, and position reinforcing rods to repair concrete, using power saw and drill. Direct the casting of the concrete and supervise laborers who use shovels or special tools to spread it. Install anchor bolts, steel plates, door sills, and other fixtures in freshly poured concrete and/or pattern or stamp the surface to provide a decorative finish. Polish surface, using polishing or surfacing machine. Produce rough concrete surface, using broom. Push roller over surface to embed chips in surface. Signal truck driver to position truck to facilitate pouring concrete and move chute to direct concrete on forms. Sprinkle colored marble or stone chips, powdered steel, or coloring powder over surface to produce prescribed finish. Cut metal division strips and press them into terrazzo base so that top edges form desired design or pattern. Fabricate concrete beams, columns, and panels. Operate power vibrator to compact concrete. Spread roofing paper on surface of foundation and spread concrete onto roofing paper with trowel to form terrazzo base. Apply hard-ening and sealing compounds to cure surface of concrete and waterproof or restore surface. Apply muriatic acid to clean surface and rinse with water. Check the forms that hold the concrete to see that they are properly constructed. Chip, scrape, and grind high spots, ridges, and rough projections to finish concrete, using pneumatic chisels, power grinders, or hand tools. Clean chipped area, using wire brush, and feel and observe surface to determine if it is rough or uneven. Mix cement, sand, and water to produce concrete, grout, or slurry, using hoe, trowel, tamper, scraper, or concrete-mixing machine. Mold expansion joints and edges, using edging tools, jointers, and straightedge. Monitor how the wind, heat, or cold affects the curing of the concrete throughout the entire process. Set and align the forms that hold concrete to the desired pitch and depth. **SKILLS**—Technology Design; Repairing; Operations Analysis; Installation; Science.

GOE—Interest Area: 06. Construction, Mining, and Drilling. **Work Group:** 06.02. Construction. **Other Jobs in This Work Group:** Boat Builders and Shipwrights; Boilermakers; Brattice Builders; Brickmasons and Blockmasons; Carpenters; Carpet Installers; Ceiling Tile Installers; Commercial Divers; Construction and Related Workers, All Other; Construction Carpenters; Drywall and Ceiling Tile Installers; Drywall Installers; Electricians; Explosives Workers, Ordnance Handling Experts, and Blasters; Fence Erectors; Floor Layers, Except Carpet, Wood, and Hard Tiles; Floor Sanders and Finishers; Glaziers; Grader, Bulldozer, and Scraper Operators; Hazardous Materials Removal Workers; Insulation Workers, Floor, Ceiling, and Wall; Insulation Workers, Mechanical; Manufactured Building and Mobile Home Installers; Operating Engineers; Operating Engineers and Other Construction Equipment Operators; Painters, Construction and Maintenance; Paperhangers; Paving, Surfacing, and Tamping Equipment Operators; Pile-Driver Operators; Pipe Fitters; Pipelayers; Pipelaying Fitters; Plasterers and Stucco Masons; Plumbers; Plumbers, Pipefitters, and Steamfitters;

Realistic—C

Rail-Track Laying and Maintenance Equipment Operators; Refractory Materials Repairers, Except Brickmasons; Reinforcing Iron and Rebar Workers; Riggers; Roofers; Rough Carpenters; Security and Fire Alarm Systems Installers; Segmental Pavers; Sheet Metal Workers; Ship Carpenters and Joiners; Stone Cutters and Carvers; Stonemasons; Structural Iron and Steel Workers; Tapers; Terrazzo Workers and Finishers; Tile and Marble Setters.

EDUCATION/TRAINING PROGRAM(S)— Concrete Finishing/Concrete Finisher. **RELATED KNOWLEDGE/COURSES**—Building and Construction; Engineering and Technology; Fine Arts; Design; Geography.

Civil Engineers

- Personality Code: RI
- Growth: 8.0%
- Annual Job Openings: 17,000
- Annual Earnings: $61,850
- Education/Training Required: Bachelor's degree
- Self-Employed: 6.7%
- Part-Time: 3.3%

Perform engineering duties in planning, designing, and overseeing construction and maintenance of building structures, and facilities, such as roads, railroads, airports, bridges, harbors, channels, dams, irrigation projects, pipelines, power plants, water and sewage systems, and waste disposal units. Includes architectural, structural, traffic, ocean, and geo-technical engineers. Analyze survey reports, maps, drawings, blueprints, aerial photography, and other topographical or geologic data to plan projects. Plan and design transportation or hydraulic systems and structures, following construction and government standards and using design software and drawing tools. Compute load and grade requirements, water flow rates, and mate-

rial stress factors to determine design specifications. Inspect project sites to monitor progress and ensure conformance to design specifications and safety or sanitation standards. Direct construction, operations, and maintenance activities at project site. Direct or participate in surveying to lay out installations and establish reference points, grades, and elevations to guide construction. Estimate quantities and cost of materials, equipment, or labor to determine project feasibility. Prepare or present public reports, such as bid proposals, deeds, environmental impact statements, and property and right-of-way descriptions. Test soils and materials to determine the adequacy and strength of foundations, concrete, asphalt, or steel. Provide technical advice regarding design, construction, or program modifications and structural repairs to industrial and managerial personnel. **SKILLS**—Coordination; Science; Persuasion; Negotiation; Mathematics; Instructing; Operations Analysis; Monitoring; Service Orientation; Technology Design.

GOE—Interest Area: 02. Science, Math, and Engineering. **Work Group:** 02.07. Engineering. **Other Jobs in This Work Group:** Aerospace Engineers; Agricultural Engineers; Architects, Except Landscape and Naval; Biomedical Engineers; Chemical Engineers; Computer Hardware Engineers; Computer Software Engineers, Applications; Computer Software Engineers, Systems Software; Electrical Engineers; Electronics Engineers, Except Computer; Engineers, All Other; Environmental Engineers; Fire-Prevention and Protection Engineers; Health and Safety Engineers, Except Mining Safety Engineers and Inspectors; Industrial Engineers; Industrial Safety and Health Engineers; Landscape Architects; Marine Architects; Marine Engineers; Marine Engineers and Naval Architects; Materials Engineers; Mechanical Engineers; Mining and Geological Engineers, Including Mining Safety Engineers; Nuclear Engineers; Petroleum Engineers; Product Safety Engineers; Sales Engineers.

EDUCATION/TRAINING PROGRAM(S)— Civil Engineering, General; Civil Engineering, Other; Transportation and Highway Engineering;

Water Resources Engineering. **RELATED KNOWLEDGE/COURSES**—Engineering and Technology; Design; Building and Construction; Mathematics; Customer and Personal Service; Transportation; Physics.

Construction Carpenters

- Personality Code: R
- Growth: 10.1%
- Annual Job Openings: 193,000
- Annual Earnings: $34,250
- Education/Training Required: Long-term on-the-job training
- Self-Employed: 29.7%
- Part-Time: 5.3%

Construct, erect, install, and repair structures and fixtures of wood, plywood, and wallboard, using carpenter's hand tools and power tools. Measure and mark cutting lines on materials, using ruler, pencil, chalk, and marking gauge. Follow established safety rules and regulations and maintain a safe and clean environment. Verify trueness of structure, using plumb bob and level. Shape or cut materials to specified measurements, using hand tools, machines, or power saw. Study specifications in blueprints, sketches, or building plans to prepare project layout and determine dimensions and materials required. Assemble and fasten materials to make framework or props, using hand tools and wood screws, nails, dowel pins, or glue. Build or repair cabinets, doors, frameworks, floors, and other wooden fixtures used in buildings, using woodworking machines, carpenter's hand tools, and power tools. Erect scaffolding and ladders for assembling structures above ground level. Remove damaged or defective parts or sections of structures and repair or replace, using hand tools. Install structures and fixtures, such as windows, frames, floorings, and trim, or hardware, using carpenter's hand and power tools. Select and order lumber and other required materials. Maintain records, document actions, and present written progress reports. Finish surfaces of woodwork or wallboard in houses and buildings, using paint, hand tools, and paneling. Prepare cost estimates for clients or employers. Arrange for subcontractors to deal with special areas such as heating and electrical wiring work. **SKILLS**—Management of Personnel Resources; Management of Financial Resources; Management of Material Resources; Equipment Maintenance; Repairing; Quality Control Analysis; Service Orientation; Speaking; Time Management.

GOE—Interest Area: 06. Construction, Mining, and Drilling. **Work Group:** 06.02. Construction. **Other Jobs in This Work Group:** Boat Builders and Shipwrights; Boilermakers; Brattice Builders; Brickmasons and Blockmasons; Carpenters; Carpet Installers; Ceiling Tile Installers; Cement Masons and Concrete Finishers; Commercial Divers; Construction and Related Workers, All Other; Drywall and Ceiling Tile Installers; Drywall Installers; Electricians; Explosives Workers, Ordnance Handling Experts, and Blasters; Fence Erectors; Floor Layers, Except Carpet, Wood, and Hard Tiles; Floor Sanders and Finishers; Glaziers; Grader, Bulldozer, and Scraper Operators; Hazardous Materials Removal Workers; Insulation Workers, Floor, Ceiling, and Wall; Insulation Workers, Mechanical; Manufactured Building and Mobile Home Installers; Operating Engineers; Operating Engineers and Other Construction Equipment Operators; Painters, Construction and Maintenance; Paperhangers; Paving, Surfacing, and Tamping Equipment Operators; Pile-Driver Operators; Pipe Fitters; Pipelayers; Pipelaying Fitters; Plasterers and Stucco Masons; Plumbers; Plumbers, Pipefitters, and Steamfitters; Rail-Track Laying and Maintenance Equipment Operators; Refractory Materials Repairers, Except Brickmasons; Reinforcing Iron and Rebar Workers; Riggers; Roofers; Rough Carpenters; Security and Fire Alarm Systems Installers;

Segmental Pavers; Sheet Metal Workers; Ship Carpenters and Joiners; Stone Cutters and Carvers; Stonemasons; Structural Iron and Steel Workers; Tapers; Terrazzo Workers and Finishers; Tile and Marble Setters.

EDUCATION/TRAINING PROGRAM(S)— Carpentry/Carpenter. **RELATED KNOWLEDGE/COURSES—**Building and Construction; Production and Processing; Engineering and Technology; Design; Public Safety and Security; Mechanical Devices.

Correctional Officers and Jailers

- Personality Code: RS
- Growth: 24.2%
- Annual Job Openings: 49,000
- Annual Earnings: $33,160
- Education/Training Required: Moderate-term on-the-job training
- Self-Employed: 0%
- Part-Time: 1.3%

Guard inmates in penal or rehabilitative institution in accordance with established regulations and procedures. May guard prisoners in transit between jail, courtroom, prison, or other point. Includes deputy sheriffs and police who spend the majority of their time guarding prisoners in correctional institutions. Monitor conduct of prisoners, according to established policies, regulations, and procedures, in order to prevent escape or violence. Inspect conditions of locks, window bars, grills, doors, and gates at correctional facilities in order to ensure that they will prevent escapes. Search prisoners, cells, and vehicles for weapons, valuables, or drugs. Guard facility entrances in order to screen visitors. Search for and recapture escapees. Inspect mail for the presence of contraband. Take prisoners into custody and escort to locations within and outside of facility, such as visiting room, courtroom, or airport. Record information such as prisoner identification, charges, and incidences of inmate disturbance. Use weapons, handcuffs, and physical force to maintain discipline and order among prisoners. Conduct fire, safety, and sanitation inspections. Provide to supervisors oral and written reports of the quality and quantity of work performed by inmates, inmate disturbances and rule violations, and unusual occurrences. Settle disputes between inmates. Drive passenger vehicles and trucks used to transport inmates to other institutions, courtrooms, hospitals, and work sites. Arrange daily schedules for prisoners, including library visits, work assignments, family visits, and counseling appointments. Assign duties to inmates, providing instructions as needed. Issue clothing, tools, and other authorized items to inmates. Serve meals and distribute commissary items to prisoners. Investigate crimes that have occurred within an institution or assist police in their investigations of crimes and inmates. Maintain records of prisoners' identification and charges. Supervise and coordinate work of other correctional service officers. Sponsor inmate recreational activities such as newspapers and self-help groups. **SKILLS—**Social Perceptiveness; Persuasion; Negotiation; Instructing; Monitoring; Speaking; Writing; Critical Thinking; Coordination.

GOE—Interest Area: 04. Law, Law Enforcement, and Public Safety. **Work Group:** 04.03. Law Enforcement. **Other Jobs in This Work Group:** Animal Control Workers; Bailiffs; Child Support, Missing Persons, and Unemployment Insurance Fraud Investigators; Criminal Investigators and Special Agents; Crossing Guards; Detectives and Criminal Investigators; Fire Investigators; Fish and Game Wardens; Forensic Science Technicians; Gaming Surveillance Officers and Gaming Investigators; Highway Patrol Pilots; Immigration and Customs Inspectors; Lifeguards, Ski Patrol, and Other Recreational Protective Service Workers; Parking Enforcement Workers; Police and Sheriff's Patrol Officers; Police Detectives; Police Identification and Records Officers; Police Patrol Officers; Private Detectives and Investigators; Protective Service Workers, All Other; Security Guards; Sheriffs and Deputy Sheriffs; Transit and Railroad Police.

EDUCATION/TRAINING PROGRAM(S)— Corrections; Corrections and Criminal Justice, Other; Juvenile Corrections. **RELATED KNOWLEDGE/COURSES**—Psychology; Public Safety and Security; Law and Government; Philosophy and Theology; Sociology and Anthropology; Transportation; Education and Training.

Drywall Installers

- ◉ Personality Code: R
- ◉ Growth: 21.4%
- ◉ Annual Job Openings: 17,000
- ◉ Annual Earnings: $33,670
- ◉ Education/Training Required: Moderate-term on-the-job training
- ◉ Self-Employed: 18.4%
- ◉ Part-Time: 5.9%

Apply plasterboard or other wallboard to ceilings and interior walls of buildings. Trims rough edges from wallboard to maintain even joints, using knife. Fits and fastens wallboard or sheetrock into specified position, using hand tools, portable power tools, or adhesive. Measures and marks cutting lines on framing, drywall, and trim, using tape measure, straightedge or square, and marking devices. Installs blanket insulation between studs and tacks plastic moisture barrier over insulation. Removes plaster, drywall, or paneling, using crowbar and hammer. Assembles and installs metal framing and decorative trim for windows, doorways, and bents. Reads blueprints and other specifications to determine method of installation, work procedures, and material and tool requirements. Lays out reference lines and points, computes position of framing and furring channels, and marks position, using chalkline. Suspends angle iron grid and channel iron from ceiling, using wire. Installs horizontal and vertical metal or wooden studs for attachment of wallboard on interior walls, using hand tools. Cuts metal or wood framing, angle and channel iron, and trim to size, using cutting tools. Cuts openings into board for electrical outlets, windows, vents, or fixtures, using keyhole saw or other cutting tools. **SKILLS**—Installation; Equipment Selection.

GOE—Interest Area: 06. Construction, Mining, and Drilling. **Work Group:** 06.02. Construction. **Other Jobs in This Work Group:** Boat Builders and Shipwrights; Boilermakers; Brattice Builders; Brickmasons and Blockmasons; Carpenters; Carpet Installers; Ceiling Tile Installers; Cement Masons and Concrete Finishers; Commercial Divers; Construction and Related Workers, All Other; Construction Carpenters; Drywall and Ceiling Tile Installers; Electricians; Explosives Workers, Ordnance Handling Experts, and Blasters; Fence Erectors; Floor Layers, Except Carpet, Wood, and Hard Tiles; Floor Sanders and Finishers; Glaziers; Grader, Bulldozer, and Scraper Operators; Hazardous Materials Removal Workers; Insulation Workers, Floor, Ceiling, and Wall; Insulation Workers, Mechanical; Manufactured Building and Mobile Home Installers; Operating Engineers; Operating Engineers and Other Construction Equipment Operators; Painters, Construction and Maintenance; Paperhangers; Paving, Surfacing, and Tamping Equipment Operators; Pile-Driver Operators; Pipe Fitters; Pipelayers; Pipelaying Fitters; Plasterers and Stucco Masons; Plumbers; Plumbers, Pipefitters, and Steamfitters; Rail-Track Laying and Maintenance Equipment Operators; Refractory Materials Repairers, Except Brickmasons; Reinforcing Iron and Rebar Workers; Riggers; Roofers; Rough Carpenters; Security and Fire Alarm Systems Installers; Segmental Pavers; Sheet Metal Workers; Ship Carpenters and Joiners; Stone Cutters and Carvers; Stonemasons; Structural Iron and Steel Workers; Tapers; Terrazzo Workers and Finishers; Tile and Marble Setters.

EDUCATION/TRAINING PROGRAM(S)— Drywall Installation/Drywaller. **RELATED**

Realistic—D

KNOWLEDGE/COURSES—Building and Construction; Design; Engineering and Technology; Mechanical Devices.

Electrical Engineering Technicians

◎ Personality Code: RI

◎ Growth: 10.0%

◎ Annual Job Openings: 24,000

◎ Annual Earnings: $43,650

◎ Education/Training Required: Associate's degree

◎ Self-Employed: 0.4%

◎ Part-Time: 5.0%

Apply electrical theory and related knowledge to test and modify developmental or operational electrical machinery and electrical control equipment and circuitry in industrial or commercial plants and laboratories. Usually work under direction of engineering staff. Provide technical assistance and resolution when electrical or engineering problems are encountered before, during, and after construction. Assemble electrical and electronic systems and prototypes according to engineering data and knowledge of electrical principles, using hand tools and measuring instruments. Install and maintain electrical control systems and solid state equipment. Modify electrical prototypes, parts, assemblies, and systems to correct functional deviations. Set up and operate test equipment to evaluate performance of developmental parts, assemblies, or systems under simulated operating conditions and record results. Collaborate with electrical engineers and other personnel to identify, define, and solve developmental problems. Build, calibrate, maintain, troubleshoot, and repair electrical instruments or testing equipment. Analyze and interpret test information to resolve design-related problems. Write commission-

ing procedures for electrical installations. Prepare project cost and work-time estimates. Evaluate engineering proposals, shop drawings, and design comments for sound electrical engineering practice and conformance with established safety and design criteria and recommend approval or disapproval. Draw or modify diagrams and write engineering specifications to clarify design details and functional criteria of experimental electronics units. Conduct inspections for quality control and assurance programs, reporting findings and recommendations. Prepare contracts and initiate, review, and coordinate modifications to contract specifications and plans throughout the construction process. Plan, schedule, and monitor work of support personnel to assist supervisor. Review existing electrical engineering criteria to identify necessary revisions, deletions, or amendments to outdated material. Perform supervisory duties such as recommending work assignments, approving leaves, and completing performance evaluations. Plan method and sequence of operations for developing and testing experimental electronic and electrical equipment. SKILLS—Troubleshooting; Repairing; Installation; Technology Design; Operations Analysis; Equipment Maintenance; Mathematics; Science.

GOE—Interest Area: 02. Science, Math, and Engineering. Work Group: 02.08. Engineering Technology. Other Jobs in This Work Group: Aerospace Engineering and Operations Technicians; Architectural and Civil Drafters; Architectural Drafters; Calibration and Instrumentation Technicians; Cartographers and Photogrammetrists; Civil Drafters; Civil Engineering Technicians; Construction and Building Inspectors; Drafters, All Other; Electrical and Electronic Engineering Technicians; Electrical and Electronics Drafters; Electrical Drafters; Electro-Mechanical Technicians; Electronic Drafters; Electronics Engineering Technicians; Engineering Technicians, Except Drafters, All Other; Environmental Engineering Technicians; Industrial Engineering Technicians; Mapping Technicians; Mechanical Drafters; Mechanical Engineering Technicians; Numerical Tool and Process

Control Programmers; Pressure Vessel Inspectors; Surveying and Mapping Technicians; Surveying Technicians; Surveyors.

EDUCATION/TRAINING PROGRAM(S)— Computer Engineering Technology/Technician; Computer Technology/Computer Systems Technology; Electrical and Electronic Engineering Technologies/Technicians, Other; Electrical, Electronic and Communications Engineering Technology/Technician; Telecommunications Technology/Technician. **RELATED KNOWLEDGE/COURSES—** Engineering and Technology; Design; Computers and Electronics; Physics; Mechanical Devices; Telecommunications.

Electricians

- Personality Code: RI
- Growth: 23.4%
- Annual Job Openings: 65,000
- Annual Earnings: $41,680
- Education/Training Required: Long-term on-the-job training
- Self-Employed: 9.1%
- Part-Time: 2.2%

Install, maintain, and repair electrical wiring, equipment, and fixtures. Ensure that work is in accordance with relevant codes. May install or service street lights, intercom systems, or electrical control systems. Assemble, install, test, and maintain electrical or electronic wiring, equipment, appliances, apparatus, and fixtures, using hand tools and power tools. Diagnose malfunctioning systems, apparatus, and components, using test equipment and hand tools, to locate the cause of a breakdown and correct the problem. Connect wires to circuit breakers, transformers, or other components. Inspect electrical systems, equipment, and components to identify hazards, defects, and the need for adjustment or repair and to ensure compliance with codes. Advise management on whether continued operation of equipment could be hazardous. Test electrical systems and continuity of circuits in electrical wiring, equipment, and fixtures, using testing devices such as ohmmeters, voltmeters, and oscilloscopes, to ensure compatibility and safety of system. Maintain current electrician's license or identification card to meet governmental regulations. Plan layout and installation of electrical wiring, equipment, and fixtures based on job specifications and local codes. Direct and train workers to install, maintain, or repair electrical wiring, equipment, and fixtures. Prepare sketches or follow blueprints to determine the location of wiring and equipment and to ensure conformance to building and safety codes. Use a variety of tools and equipment, such as power construction equipment; measuring devices; power tools; and testing equipment, including oscilloscopes, ammeters, and test lamps. Install ground leads and connect power cables to equipment such as motors. Perform business management duties such as maintaining records and files, preparing reports, and ordering supplies and equipment. Repair or replace wiring, equipment, and fixtures, using hand tools and power tools. Work from ladders, scaffolds, and roofs to install, maintain, or repair electrical wiring, equipment, and fixtures. Place conduit (pipes or tubing) inside designated partitions, walls, or other concealed areas and pull insulated wires or cables through the conduit to complete circuits between boxes. Construct and fabricate parts, using hand tools and specifications. **SKILLS—**Installation; Troubleshooting; Repairing; Equipment Maintenance; Technology Design; Management of Financial Resources; Equipment Selection; Operations Analysis.

GOE—Interest Area: 06. Construction, Mining, and Drilling. **Work Group:** 06.02. Construction. **Other Jobs in This Work Group:** Boat Builders and Shipwrights; Boilermakers; Brattice Builders; Brickmasons and Blockmasons; Carpenters; Carpet Installers; Ceiling Tile Installers; Cement Masons and Concrete Finishers; Commercial Divers; Construction and Related Workers, All Other; Construction Carpenters; Drywall and Ceiling Tile Installers; Drywall Installers; Explosives Workers, Ordnance Handling Experts, and Blasters; Fence Erectors; Floor Layers, Except Carpet, Wood, and Hard Tiles; Floor Sanders and Finishers; Glaziers; Grader, Bulldozer, and Scraper Operators; Hazardous Materials Removal Workers; Insulation Workers, Floor, Ceiling, and Wall; Insulation Workers, Mechanical; Manufactured Building and Mobile Home Installers; Operating Engineers; Operating Engineers and Other Construction Equipment Operators; Painters, Construction and Maintenance; Paperhangers; Paving, Surfacing, and Tamping Equipment Operators; Pile-Driver Operators; Pipe Fitters; Pipelayers; Pipelaying Fitters; Plasterers and Stucco Masons; Plumbers; Plumbers, Pipefitters, and Steamfitters; Rail-Track Laying and Maintenance Equipment Operators; Refractory Materials Repairers, Except Brickmasons; Reinforcing Iron and Rebar Workers; Riggers; Roofers; Rough Carpenters; Security and Fire Alarm Systems Installers; Segmental Pavers; Sheet Metal Workers; Ship Carpenters and Joiners; Stone Cutters and Carvers; Stonemasons; Structural Iron and Steel Workers; Tapers; Terrazzo Workers and Finishers; Tile and Marble Setters.

EDUCATION/TRAINING PROGRAM(S)— Electrician. **RELATED KNOWLEDGE/ COURSES**—Building and Construction; Mechanical Devices; Design; Production and Processing; Customer and Personal Service; Physics.

Electronics Engineering Technicians

- Personality Code: RI
- Growth: 10.0%
- Annual Job Openings: 24,000
- Annual Earnings: $43,650
- Education/Training Required: Associate's degree
- Self-Employed: 0.4%
- Part-Time: 5.0%

Lay out, build, test, troubleshoot, repair, and modify developmental and production electronic components, parts, equipment, and systems, such as computer equipment, missile control instrumentation, electron tubes, test equipment, and machine tool numerical controls, applying principles and theories of electronics, electrical circuitry, engineering mathematics, electronic and electrical testing, and physics. Usually work under direction of engineering staff. Test electronics units, using standard test equipment, and analyze results to evaluate performance and determine need for adjustment. Perform preventative maintenance and calibration of equipment and systems. Read blueprints, wiring diagrams, schematic drawings, and engineering instructions for assembling electronics units, applying knowledge of electronic theory and components. Identify and resolve equipment malfunctions, working with manufacturers and field representatives as necessary to procure replacement parts. Maintain system logs and manuals to document testing and operation of equipment. Assemble, test, and maintain circuitry or electronic components according to engineering instructions, technical manuals, and knowledge of electronics, using hand and power tools. Adjust and replace defective or improperly functioning circuitry and electronics components, using hand tools and soldering iron. Procure parts and maintain inventory and related documentation. Maintain working knowledge of state-of-the-art tools, software, etc., through reading and/or attending conferences, workshops, or other training. Provide user applications and engineering support and recommendations for new and existing equipment with regard to installation, upgrades, and enhancement. Write reports and record data on testing techniques, laboratory equipment, and specifications to assist engineers. Provide customer support and education, working with users to identify needs, determine sources of problems, and provide information on product use. Design basic circuitry and draft sketches for clarification of details and design documentation under engineers' direction, using drafting instruments and computer-aided design equipment. Build prototypes from rough sketches or plans. Develop and upgrade preventative maintenance procedures for components, equipment, parts, and systems. Fabricate parts, such as coils, terminal boards, and chassis, using bench lathes, drills, or other machine tools. Research equipment and component needs, sources, competitive prices, delivery times, and ongoing operational costs. **SKILLS**—Repairing; Troubleshooting; Equipment Maintenance; Installation; Technology Design; Operation Monitoring; Service Orientation; Systems Evaluation.

GOE—Interest Area: 02. Science, Math, and Engineering. **Work Group:** 02.08. Engineering Technology. **Other Jobs in This Work Group:** Aerospace Engineering and Operations Technicians; Architectural and Civil Drafters; Architectural Drafters; Calibration and Instrumentation Technicians; Cartographers and Photogrammetrists; Civil Drafters; Civil Engineering Technicians; Construction and Building Inspectors; Drafters, All Other; Electrical and Electronic Engineering Technicians; Electrical and Electronics Drafters; Electrical Drafters; Electrical Engineering Technicians; Electro-Mechanical Technicians; Electronic Drafters; Engineering Technicians, Except Drafters, All Other; Environmental Engineering Technicians; Industrial Engineering Technicians; Mapping Technicians; Mechanical Drafters; Mechanical Engineering Technicians; Numerical Tool and Process Control Programmers; Pressure Vessel Inspectors; Surveying and Mapping Technicians; Surveying Technicians; Surveyors.

EDUCATION/TRAINING PROGRAM(S)—Computer Engineering Technology/Technician; Computer Technology/Computer Systems Technology; Electrical and Electronic Engineering Technologies/Technicians, Other; Electrical, Electronic and Communications Engineering Technology/Technician; Telecommunications Technology/Technician. **RELATED KNOWLEDGE/COURSES**—Engineering and Technology; Computers and Electronics; Mechanical Devices; Mathematics; Design; Telecommunications.

First-Line Supervisors and Manager/Supervisors—Landscaping Workers

- Personality Code: RE
- Growth: 21.6%
- Annual Job Openings: 18,000
- Annual Earnings: $33,770
- Education/Training Required: Work experience in a related occupation
- Self-Employed: 34.7%
- Part-Time: 5.9%

Directly supervise and coordinate activities of landscaping workers. Manager/Supervisors are generally found in smaller establishments, where they perform both supervisory and management functions, such as accounting, marketing, and personnel work, and may also engage in the same landscaping work as the workers they supervise. Directs workers in maintenance and repair of driveways, walkways, benches, graves, and mausoleums.

Observes ongoing work to ascertain if work is being performed according to instructions and will be completed on time. Determines work priority and crew and equipment requirements and assigns workers tasks such as planting, fertilizing, irrigating, and mowing. Directs and assists workers engaged in maintenance and repair of equipment such as power mower and backhoe, using hand tools and power tools. Confers with manager to develop plans and schedules for maintenance and improvement of grounds. Keeps employee time records and records daily work performed. Interviews, hires, and discharges workers. Assists workers in performing work when completion is critical. Tours grounds, such as park, botanical garden, cemetery, or golf course, to inspect conditions. Trains workers in tasks such as transplanting and pruning trees and shrubs, finishing cement, using equipment, and caring for turf. Mixes and prepares spray and dust solutions and directs application of fertilizer, insecticide, and fungicide. **SKILLS**—Management of Personnel Resources; Coordination; Management of Material Resources; Instructing; Systems Evaluation; Time Management; Systems Analysis; Speaking.

GOE—Interest Area: 03. Plants and Animals. **Work Group:** 03.01. Managerial Work in Plants and Animals. **Other Jobs in This Work Group:** Agricultural Crop Farm Managers; Farm Labor Contractors; Farmers and Ranchers; First-Line Supervisors and Manager/Supervisors—Agricultural Crop Workers; First-Line Supervisors and Manager/Supervisors—Animal Care Workers, Except Livestock; First-Line Supervisors and Manager/Supervisors—Animal Husbandry Workers; First-Line Supervisors and Manager/Supervisors—Fishery Workers; First-Line Supervisors and Manager/Supervisors—Horticultural Workers; First-Line Supervisors and Manager/Supervisors—Logging Workers; First-Line Supervisors/Managers of Farming, Fishing, and Forestry Workers; First-Line Supervisors/Managers of Landscaping, Lawn Service, and Groundskeeping Workers; Fish Hatchery Managers; Lawn Service Managers; Nursery and Greenhouse Managers.

EDUCATION/TRAINING PROGRAM(S)—Landscaping and Groundskeeping; Ornamental Horticulture; Turf and Turfgrass Management. **RELATED KNOWLEDGE/COURSES**—Personnel and Human Resources; Administration and Management; Chemistry; Mechanical Devices; Biology; Building and Construction.

Forest Fire Fighters

- Personality Code: RS
- Growth: 20.7%
- Annual Job Openings: 29,000
- Annual Earnings: $37,060
- Education/Training Required: Long-term on-the-job training
- Self-Employed: 0%
- Part-Time: 1.1%

Control and suppress fires in forests or vacant public land. Maintain contact with fire dispatchers at all times in order to notify them of the need for additional firefighters and supplies or to detail any difficulties encountered. Rescue fire victims and administer emergency medical aid. Collaborate with other firefighters as a member of a firefighting crew. Patrol burned areas after fires to locate and eliminate hot spots that may restart fires. Extinguish flames and embers to suppress fires, using shovels or engine- or hand-driven water or chemical pumps. Fell trees, cut and clear brush, and dig trenches in order to create firelines, using axes, chainsaws, or shovels. Maintain knowledge of current firefighting practices by participating in drills and by attending seminars, conventions, and conferences. Operate pumps connected to high-pressure hoses. Participate in physical training in order to maintain high levels of physical fitness. Establish water supplies, connect hoses, and direct water onto fires. Maintain fire equipment and firehouse living quarters. Inform and educate the public about fire prevention. Take action to contain any hazardous chemicals that could catch fire, leak, or spill. Organize fire caches, positioning equipment for the most effective response. Transport personnel and cargo to and from fire areas. Participate in fire prevention and inspection programs. Perform forest maintenance and improvement tasks such as cutting brush, planting trees, building trails, and marking timber. Test and maintain tools, equipment, jump gear, and parachutes in order to ensure readiness for fire suppression activities. Observe forest areas from fire lookout towers in order to spot potential problems. Orient self in relation to fire, using compass and map, and collect supplies and equipment dropped by parachute. Serve as fully trained lead helicopter crewmember and as helispot manager. Drop weighted paper streamers from aircraft to determine the speed and direction of the wind at fire sites. SKILLS—Management of Personnel Resources; Service Orientation; Equipment Maintenance; Coordination; Repairing; Instructing; Equipment Selection; Operation Monitoring.

GOE—Interest Area: 04. Law, Law Enforcement, and Public Safety. Work Group: 04.04. Public Safety. Other Jobs in This Work Group: Agricultural Inspectors; Aviation Inspectors; Compliance Officers, Except Agriculture, Construction, Health and Safety, and Transportation; Emergency Medical Technicians and Paramedics; Environmental Compliance Inspectors; Equal Opportunity Representatives and Officers; Financial Examiners; Fire Fighters; Fire Inspectors; Fire Inspectors and Investigators; Forest Fire Inspectors and Prevention Specialists; Government Property Inspectors and Investigators; Licensing Examiners and Inspectors; Marine Cargo Inspectors; Municipal Fire Fighters; Nuclear Monitoring Technicians; Occupational Health and Safety Specialists; Occupational Health and Safety Technicians; Protective Service Workers, All Other; Public Transportation Inspectors.

EDUCATION/TRAINING PROGRAM(S)— Fire Protection, Other; Fire Science/Firefighting. RELATED KNOWLEDGE/COURSES—Customer and Personal Service; Geography; Education

and Training; Public Safety and Security; Mechanical Devices; Personnel and Human Resources.

Forest Fire Fighting and Prevention Supervisors

- Personality Code: RE
- Growth: 18.7%
- Annual Job Openings: 8,000
- Annual Earnings: $57,000
- Education/Training Required: Work experience in a related occupation
- Self-Employed: 0%
- Part-Time: 0.1%

Supervise firefighters who control and suppress fires in forests or vacant public land. Inspect all stations, uniforms, equipment, and recreation areas in order to ensure compliance with safety standards, taking corrective action as necessary. Monitor fire suppression expenditures in order to ensure that they are necessary and reasonable. Parachute to major fire locations in order to direct fire containment and suppression activities. Recommend equipment modifications or new equipment purchases. Regulate open burning by issuing burning permits, inspecting problem sites, issuing citations for violations of laws and ordinances, and educating the public in proper burning practices. Lead work crews in the maintenance of structures and access roads in forest areas. Investigate special fire issues such as railroad fire problems, right-of-way burning, and slash disposal problems. Communicate fire details to superiors, subordinates, and interagency dispatch centers, using two-way radios. Direct investigations of suspected arsons in wildfires, working closely with other investigating agencies. Direct the loading of fire suppression equipment into aircraft and the parachuting of equipment to crews on the ground. Evaluate size, location, and condition of

Realistic—F

forest fires in order to request and dispatch crews and position equipment so fires can be contained safely and effectively. Identify staff training and development needs in order to ensure that appropriate training can be arranged. Maintain fire suppression equipment in good condition, checking equipment periodically in order to ensure that it is ready for use. Maintain knowledge of forest fire laws and fire prevention techniques and tactics. Monitor prescribed burns to ensure that they are conducted safely and effectively. Observe fires and crews from air to determine fire-fighting force requirements and to note changing conditions that will affect fire-fighting efforts. Operate wildland fire engines and hoselays. Perform administrative duties such as compiling and maintaining records, completing forms, preparing reports, and composing correspondence. Recruit and hire forest fire–fighting personnel. Review and evaluate employee performance. **SKILLS**—Management of Personnel Resources; Management of Material Resources; Service Orientation; Systems Evaluation; Coordination; Systems Analysis; Instructing; Judgment and Decision Making; Time Management.

GOE—Interest Area: 04. Law, Law Enforcement, and Public Safety. **Work Group:** 04.01. Managerial Work in Law, Law Enforcement, and Public Safety. **Other Jobs in This Work Group:** Emergency Management Specialists; First-Line Supervisors/ Managers of Correctional Officers; First-Line Supervisors/Managers of Fire Fighting and Prevention Workers; First-Line Supervisors/Managers of Police and Detectives; First-Line Supervisors/ Managers, Protective Service Workers, All Other; Municipal Fire Fighting and Prevention Supervisors.

EDUCATION/TRAINING PROGRAM(S)— Fire Protection and Safety Technology/Technician; Fire Services Administration. **RELATED KNOWLEDGE/COURSES**—Public Safety and Security; Transportation; Education and Training; Geography; Administration and Management; Chemistry.

Grader, Bulldozer, and Scraper Operators

- Personality Code: RC
- Growth: 10.4%
- Annual Job Openings: 45,000
- Annual Earnings: $35,030
- Education/Training Required: Moderate-term on-the-job training
- Self-Employed: 3.7%
- Part-Time: 2.6%

Operate machines or vehicles equipped with blades to remove, distribute, level, or grade earth. Starts engine; moves throttle, switches, and levers; and depresses pedals to operate machines, equipment, and attachments. Drives equipment in successive passes over working area to achieve specified result, such as grade terrain or remove, dump, or spread earth and rock. Aligns machine, cutterhead, or depth gauge marker with reference stakes and guidelines on ground or positions equipment, following hand signals of assistant. Fastens bulldozer blade or other attachment to tractor, using hitches. Greases, oils, and performs minor repairs on tractor, using grease gun, oilcans, and hand tools. Signals operator to guide movement of tractor-drawn machine. Connects hydraulic hoses, belts, mechanical linkage, or power takeoff shaft to tractor. **SKILLS**—Operation and Control; Repairing; Operation Monitoring; Equipment Maintenance; Equipment Selection.

GOE—Interest Area: 06. Construction, Mining, and Drilling. **Work Group:** 06.02. Construction. **Other Jobs in This Work Group:** Boat Builders and Shipwrights; Boilermakers; Brattice Builders; Brickmasons and Blockmasons; Carpenters; Carpet Installers; Ceiling Tile Installers; Cement Masons and Concrete Finishers; Commercial Divers; Construction and Related Workers, All Other; Construction Carpenters; Drywall and Ceiling Tile Installers; Drywall Installers; Electricians; Explosives

Workers, Ordnance Handling Experts, and Blasters; Fence Erectors; Floor Layers, Except Carpet, Wood, and Hard Tiles; Floor Sanders and Finishers; Glaziers; Hazardous Materials Removal Workers; Insulation Workers, Floor, Ceiling, and Wall; Insulation Workers, Mechanical; Manufactured Building and Mobile Home Installers; Operating Engineers; Operating Engineers and Other Construction Equipment Operators; Painters, Construction and Maintenance; Paperhangers; Paving, Surfacing, and Tamping Equipment Operators; Pile-Driver Operators; Pipe Fitters; Pipelayers; Pipelaying Fitters; Plasterers and Stucco Masons; Plumbers; Plumbers, Pipefitters, and Steamfitters; Rail-Track Laying and Maintenance Equipment Operators; Refractory Materials Repairers, Except Brickmasons; Reinforcing Iron and Rebar Workers; Riggers; Roofers; Rough Carpenters; Security and Fire Alarm Systems Installers; Segmental Pavers; Sheet Metal Workers; Ship Carpenters and Joiners; Stone Cutters and Carvers; Stonemasons; Structural Iron and Steel Workers; Tapers; Terrazzo Workers and Finishers; Tile and Marble Setters.

EDUCATION/TRAINING PROGRAM(S)—Construction/Heavy Equipment/Earthmoving Equipment Operation; Mobil Crane Operation/Operator. **RELATED KNOWLEDGE/COURSES**—Mechanical Devices; Transportation; Physics.

Heating and Air Conditioning Mechanics

- Personality Code: RC
- Growth: 31.8%
- Annual Job Openings: 35,000
- Annual Earnings: $35,160
- Education/Training Required: Long-term on-the-job training
- Self-Employed: 15.4%
- Part-Time: 3.1%

Install, service, and repair heating and air conditioning systems in residences and commercial establishments. Obtain and maintain required certification(s). Comply with all applicable standards, policies, and procedures, including safety procedures and the maintenance of a clean work area. Repair or replace defective equipment, components, or wiring. Test electrical circuits and components for continuity, using electrical test equipment. Reassemble and test equipment following repairs. Inspect and test system to verify system compliance with plans and specifications and to detect and locate malfunctions. Discuss heating-cooling system malfunctions with users to isolate problems or to verify that malfunctions have been corrected. Record and report all faults, deficiencies, and other unusual occurrences, as well as the time and materials expended on work orders. Test pipe or tubing joints and connections for leaks, using pressure gauge or soap-and-water solution. Adjust system controls to setting recommended by manufacturer to balance system, using hand tools. Recommend, develop, and perform preventive and general maintenance procedures such as cleaning, power-washing, and vacuuming equipment; oiling parts; and changing filters. Lay out and connect electrical wiring between controls and equipment according to wiring diagram, using electrician's hand tools. Install auxiliary components to heating-cooling equipment, such as expansion and discharge valves, air ducts, pipes, blowers, dampers, flues, and stokers, following blueprints. Assist with other work in coordination with repair and maintenance teams. Install, connect, and adjust thermostats, humidistats, and timers, using hand tools. Generate work orders that address deficiencies in need of correction. Join pipes or tubing to equipment and to fuel, water, or refrigerant source to form complete circuit. Assemble, position, and mount heating or cooling equipment, following blueprints. Study blueprints, design specifications, and manufacturers' recommendations to ascertain the configuration of heating or cooling equipment components and to ensure the proper installation of components. Cut and drill holes in floors, walls, and roof to install equipment, using power saws and drills. **SKILLS**—Installation; Repairing; Equipment Maintenance; Troubleshooting; Coordination; Systems Evaluation; Negotiation; Persuasion.

GOE—Interest Area: 05. Mechanics, Installers, and Repairers. **Work Group:** 05.03. Mechanical Work. **Other Jobs in This Work Group:** Aircraft Body and Bonded Structure Repairers; Aircraft Engine Specialists; Aircraft Mechanics and Service Technicians; Airframe-and-Power-Plant Mechanics; Automotive Body and Related Repairers; Automotive Glass Installers and Repairers; Automotive Master Mechanics; Automotive Service Technicians and Mechanics; Automotive Specialty Technicians; Bicycle Repairers; Bridge and Lock Tenders; Bus and Truck Mechanics and Diesel Engine Specialists; Camera and Photographic Equipment Repairers; Coin, Vending, and Amusement Machine Servicers and Repairers; Control and Valve Installers and Repairers, Except Mechanical Door; Farm Equipment Mechanics; Gas Appliance Repairers; Hand and Portable Power Tool Repairers; Heating, Air Conditioning, and Refrigeration Mechanics and Installers; Helpers—Electricians; Helpers—Installation, Maintenance, and Repair Workers; Industrial Machinery Mechanics; Installation, Maintenance, and Repair Workers, All Other; Keyboard Instrument Repairers and Tuners; Locksmiths and Safe Repairers; Maintenance and Repair Workers, General; Maintenance Workers, Machinery; Mechanical Door Repairers; Medical Appliance Technicians; Medical Equipment Repairers; Meter Mechanics; Millwrights; Mobile Heavy Equipment Mechanics, Except Engines; Motorboat Mechanics; Motorcycle Mechanics; Musical Instrument Repairers and Tuners; Ophthalmic Laboratory Technicians; Optical Instrument Assemblers; Outdoor Power Equipment and Other Small Engine Mechanics; Painters, Transportation Equipment; Percussion Instrument Repairers and Tuners; Precision Instrument and Equipment Repairers, All Other; Rail Car Repairers; Railroad Inspectors; Recreational Vehicle Service Technicians; Reed or Wind Instrument Repairers and Tuners; Refrigeration Mechanics; Stringed

Instrument Repairers and Tuners; Tire Repairers and Changers; Valve and Regulator Repairers; Watch Repairers.

EDUCATION/TRAINING PROGRAM(S)—Heating, Air Conditioning and Refrigeration Technology/Technician (ACH/ACR/ACHR/HRAC/HVAC/AC Technology); Heating, Air Conditioning, Ventilation, and Refrigeration Maintenance Technology/Technician (HAC, HACR, HVAC, HVACR); Solar Energy Technology/Technician. **RELATED KNOWLEDGE/COURSES**—Mechanical Devices; Building and Construction; Design; Customer and Personal Service; Engineering and Technology; Physics.

Highway Patrol Pilots

- Personality Code: RE
- Growth: 24.7%
- Annual Job Openings: 67,000
- Annual Earnings: $44,020
- Education/Training Required: Long-term on-the-job training
- Self-Employed: 0%
- Part-Time: 1.4%

Pilot aircraft to patrol highway and enforce traffic laws. Pilots airplane to maintain order, respond to emergencies, enforce traffic and criminal laws, and apprehend criminals. Investigates traffic accidents and other accidents to determine causes and to determine if crimes were committed. Arrests perpetrator of criminal act or submits citation or warning to violator of motor vehicle ordinance. Informs ground personnel where to re-route traffic in case of emergencies. Informs ground personnel of traffic congestion or unsafe driving conditions to ensure traffic flow and reduce incidence of accidents. Reviews facts to determine if criminal act or statute violation are involved. Expedites processing of prisoners, prepares and maintains records of prisoner bookings, and maintains record of prisoner status during booking and pre-trial process. Prepares reports to document activities. Relays complaint and emergency request information to appropriate agency dispatcher. Evaluates complaint and emergency request information to determine response requirements. Renders aid to accident victims and other persons requiring first aid for physical injuries. Testifies in court to present evidence or act as witness in traffic and criminal cases. Records facts, photographs and diagrams crime or accident scene, and interviews witnesses to gather information for possible use in legal action or safety programs. **SKILLS**— Operation and Control; Social Perceptiveness; Service Orientation; Operation Monitoring; Judgment and Decision Making; Active Listening; Critical Thinking; Reading Comprehension.

GOE—**Interest Area:** 04. Law, Law Enforcement, and Public Safety. **Work Group:** 04.03. Law Enforcement. **Other Jobs in This Work Group:** Animal Control Workers; Bailiffs; Child Support, Missing Persons, and Unemployment Insurance Fraud Investigators; Correctional Officers and Jailers; Criminal Investigators and Special Agents; Crossing Guards; Detectives and Criminal Investigators; Fire Investigators; Fish and Game Wardens; Forensic Science Technicians; Gaming Surveillance Officers and Gaming Investigators; Immigration and Customs Inspectors; Lifeguards, Ski Patrol, and Other Recreational Protective Service Workers; Parking Enforcement Workers; Police and Sheriff's Patrol Officers; Police Detectives; Police Identification and Records Officers; Police Patrol Officers; Private Detectives and Investigators; Protective Service Workers, All Other; Security Guards; Sheriffs and Deputy Sheriffs; Transit and Railroad Police.

EDUCATION/TRAINING PROGRAM(S)— Criminal Justice/Police Science; Criminalistics and Criminal Science. **RELATED KNOWLEDGE/ COURSES**—Public Safety and Security; Transportation; Law and Government; Customer and Personal Service; Medicine and Dentistry; Psychology; Geography.

Maintenance and Repair Workers, General

- ◎ Personality Code: RC
- ◎ Growth: 16.3%
- ◎ Annual Job Openings: 155,000
- ◎ Annual Earnings: $29,800
- ◎ Education/Training Required: Long-term on-the-job training
- ◎ Self-Employed: 0.9%
- ◎ Part-Time: 4.5%

Perform work involving the skills of two or more maintenance or craft occupations to keep machines, mechanical equipment, or the structure of an establishment in repair. Duties may involve pipe fitting; boiler making; insulating; welding; machining; carpentry; repairing electrical or mechanical equipment; installing, aligning, and balancing new equipment; and repairing buildings, floors, or stairs. Repair or replace defective equipment parts, using hand tools and power tools, and reassemble equipment. Perform routine preventive maintenance to ensure that machines continue to run smoothly, building systems operate efficiently, and the physical condition of buildings does not deteriorate. Inspect drives, motors, and belts; check fluid levels; replace filters; and perform other maintenance actions, following checklists. Use tools ranging from common hand and power tools, such as hammers, hoists, saws, drills, and wrenches, to precision measuring instruments and electrical and electronic testing devices. Assemble, install, and/or repair wiring, electrical and electronic components, pipe systems and plumbing, machinery, and equipment. Diagnose mechanical problems and determine how to correct them, checking blueprints, repair manuals, and parts catalogs as necessary. Inspect, operate, and test machinery and equipment in order to diagnose machine malfunctions. Record maintenance and repair work performed and the costs of the work. Clean and lubricate shafts, bearings, gears, and other parts of machinery. Dismantle devices to gain access to and remove defective parts, using hoists, cranes, hand tools, and power tools. Plan and lay out repair work, using diagrams, drawings, blueprints, maintenance manuals, and schematic diagrams. Order parts, supplies, and equipment from catalogs and suppliers or obtain them from storerooms. Adjust functional parts of devices and control instruments, using hand tools, levels, plumb bobs, and straightedges. Paint and repair roofs, windows, doors, floors, woodwork, plaster, drywall, and other parts of building structures. Operate cutting torches or welding equipment to cut or join metal parts. Align and balance new equipment after installation. Inspect used parts to determine changes in dimensional requirements, using rules, calipers, micrometers, and other measuring instruments. Set up and operate machine tools to repair or fabricate machine parts, jigs and fixtures, and tools. Maintain and repair specialized equipment and machinery found in cafeterias, laundries, hospitals, stores, offices, and factories. **SKILLS**—Equipment Maintenance; Installation; Repairing; Troubleshooting; Operation Monitoring; Equipment Selection; Operation and Control; Critical Thinking.

GOE—Interest Area: 05. Mechanics, Installers, and Repairers. **Work Group:** 05.03. Mechanical Work. **Other Jobs in This Work Group:** Aircraft Body and Bonded Structure Repairers; Aircraft Engine Specialists; Aircraft Mechanics and Service Technicians; Airframe-and-Power-Plant Mechanics; Automotive Body and Related Repairers; Automotive Glass Installers and Repairers; Automotive Master Mechanics; Automotive Service Technicians and Mechanics; Automotive Specialty Technicians; Bicycle Repairers; Bridge and Lock Tenders; Bus and Truck Mechanics and Diesel Engine Specialists; Camera and Photographic Equipment Repairers; Coin, Vending, and Amusement Machine Servicers and Repairers; Control and Valve Installers and Repairers, Except Mechanical Door; Farm Equipment Mechanics; Gas Appliance Repairers; Hand and Portable Power Tool Repairers; Heating and Air Conditioning Mechanics; Heating, Air Conditioning, and Refrigeration Mechanics and Installers; Helpers—Electricians; Helpers—Installation, Maintenance, and Repair Workers; Industrial Machinery Mechanics; Installation, Maintenance, and Repair Workers, All Other; Keyboard Instrument Repairers and Tuners; Locksmiths and Safe Repairers; Maintenance Workers, Machinery; Mechanical Door Repairers; Medical Appliance Technicians; Medical Equipment Repairers; Meter Mechanics; Millwrights; Mobile Heavy Equipment Mechanics, Except Engines; Motorboat Mechanics; Motorcycle Mechanics; Musical Instrument Repairers and Tuners; Ophthalmic Laboratory Technicians; Optical Instrument Assemblers; Outdoor Power Equipment and Other Small Engine Mechanics; Painters, Transportation Equipment; Percussion Instrument Repairers and Tuners; Precision Instrument and Equipment Repairers, All Other; Rail Car Repairers; Railroad Inspectors; Recreational Vehicle Service Technicians; Reed or Wind Instrument Repairers and Tuners; Refrigeration Mechanics; Stringed Instrument Repairers and Tuners; Tire Repairers and Changers; Valve and Regulator Repairers; Watch Repairers.

EDUCATION/TRAINING PROGRAM(S)—Building/Construction Site Management/Manager. **RELATED KNOWLEDGE/COURSES**—Mechanical Devices; Building and Construction; Design; Public Safety and Security; Engineering and Technology; Physics.

Municipal Fire Fighters

- ◎ Personality Code: RS
- ◎ Growth: 20.7%
- ◎ Annual Job Openings: 29,000
- ◎ Annual Earnings: $37,060
- ◎ Education/Training Required: Long-term on-the-job training
- ◎ Self-Employed: 0%
- ◎ Part-Time: 1.1%

Control and extinguish municipal fires, protect life and property, and conduct rescue efforts. Administer first aid and cardiopulmonary resuscitation to injured persons. Rescue victims from burning buildings and accident sites. Search burning buildings to locate fire victims. Drive and operate firefighting vehicles and equipment. Dress with equipment such as fire-resistant clothing and breathing apparatus. Move toward the source of a fire, using knowledge of types of fires, construction design, building materials, and physical layout of properties. Position and climb ladders in order to gain access to upper levels of buildings or to rescue individuals from burning structures. Take action to contain hazardous chemicals that might catch fire, leak, or spill. Assess fires and situations and report conditions to superiors in order to receive instructions, using two-way radios. Respond to fire alarms and other calls for assistance, such as automobile and industrial accidents. Operate pumps connected to high-pressure hoses. Select and attach hose nozzles, depending on fire type, and direct streams of water or chemicals onto fires. Create openings in buildings for ventilation or entrance, using axes, chisels, crowbars, electric saws, or core cutters. Inspect fire sites after flames have been extinguished in order to ensure that there is no further danger. Lay hose lines and connect them to water supplies. Protect property from water and smoke, using waterproof salvage covers, smoke ejectors, and deodorants. Participate in physical training activities in order to maintain a high level of physical fitness. Salvage property by removing broken glass, pumping out water, and ventilating buildings to remove smoke. Participate in fire drills and demonstrations of firefighting techniques. Clean and maintain fire stations and firefighting equipment and apparatus. Collaborate with police to respond to accidents, disasters, and arson investigation calls. Establish firelines to prevent unauthorized persons from entering areas near fires. Inform and educate the public on fire prevention. Inspect buildings for fire hazards and compliance with fire prevention ordinances, testing and checking smoke alarms, and fire suppression equipment as necessary. **SKILLS**—Service Orientation; Equipment Maintenance; Social Perceptiveness; Equipment Selection; Coordination; Learning Strategies; Critical Thinking; Complex Problem Solving; Operation Monitoring.

GOE—Interest Area: 04. Law, Law Enforcement, and Public Safety. **Work Group:** 04.04. Public Safety. **Other Jobs in This Work Group:** Agricultural Inspectors; Aviation Inspectors; Compliance Officers, Except Agriculture, Construction, Health and Safety, and Transportation; Emergency Medical Technicians and Paramedics; Environmental Compliance Inspectors; Equal Opportunity Representatives and Officers; Financial Examiners; Fire Fighters; Fire Inspectors; Fire Inspectors and Investigators; Forest Fire Fighters; Forest Fire Inspectors and Prevention Specialists; Government Property Inspectors and Investigators; Licensing Examiners and Inspectors; Marine Cargo Inspectors; Nuclear Monitoring Technicians; Occupational Health and Safety Specialists; Occupational Health and Safety Technicians; Protective Service Workers, All Other; Public Transportation Inspectors.

EDUCATION/TRAINING PROGRAM(S)— Fire Protection, Other; Fire Science/Firefighting. **RELATED KNOWLEDGE/COURSES—**Customer and Personal Service; Medicine and Dentistry; Physics; Public Safety and Security; Psychology; Building and Construction.

Realistic—M

Municipal Fire Fighting and Prevention Supervisors

- Personality Code: RE
- Growth: 18.7%
- Annual Job Openings: 8,000
- Annual Earnings: $57,000
- Education/Training Required: Work experience in a related occupation
- Self-Employed: 0%
- Part-Time: 0.1%

Supervise firefighters who control and extinguish municipal fires, protect life and property, and conduct rescue efforts. Assign firefighters to jobs at strategic locations in order to facilitate rescue of persons and maximize application of extinguishing agents. Provide emergency medical services as required and perform light to heavy rescue functions at emergencies. Assess nature and extent of fire, condition of building, danger to adjacent buildings, and water supply status in order to determine crew or company requirements. Instruct and drill fire department personnel in assigned duties, including firefighting, medical care, hazardous materials response, fire prevention, and related subjects. Evaluate the performance of assigned firefighting personnel. Direct the training of firefighters, assigning of instructors to training classes, and providing of supervisors with reports on training progress and status. Prepare activity reports listing fire call locations, actions taken, fire types and probable causes, damage estimates, and situation dispositions. Maintain required maps and records. Attend in-service training classes to remain current in knowledge of codes, laws, ordinances, and regulations. Evaluate fire station procedures in order to ensure efficiency and enforcement of departmental regulations. Direct firefighters in station maintenance duties and participate in these duties. Compile and maintain equipment and personnel records, including accident reports. Direct investigation of cases of suspected arson, hazards, and false alarms and submit reports outlining findings. Recommend personnel actions related to disciplinary procedures, performance, leaves of absence, and grievances. Supervise and participate in the inspection of properties in order to ensure that they are in compliance with applicable fire codes, ordinances, laws, regulations, and standards. Write and submit proposals for repair, modification, or replacement of firefighting equipment. Coordinate the distribution of fire prevention promotional materials. Identify corrective actions needed to bring properties into compliance with applicable fire codes and ordinances and conduct follow-up inspections to see if corrective actions have been taken. **SKILLS**—Service Orientation; Management of Personnel Resources; Equipment Maintenance; Coordination; Instructing; Judgment and Decision Making; Management of Material Resources; Social Perceptiveness.

GOE—Interest Area: 04. Law, Law Enforcement, and Public Safety. **Work Group:** 04.01. Managerial Work in Law, Law Enforcement, and Public Safety. **Other Jobs in This Work Group:** Emergency Management Specialists; First-Line Supervisors/Managers of Correctional Officers; First-Line Supervisors/Managers of Fire Fighting and Prevention Workers; First-Line Supervisors/Managers of Police and Detectives; First-Line Supervisors/Managers, Protective Service Workers, All Other; Forest Fire Fighting and Prevention Supervisors.

EDUCATION/TRAINING PROGRAM(S)—Fire Protection and Safety Technology/Technician; Fire Services Administration. **RELATED KNOWLEDGE/COURSES**—Public Safety and Security; Customer and Personal Service; Education and Training; Building and Construction; Medicine and Dentistry; Psychology.

Operating Engineers

- Personality Code: RI
- Growth: 10.4%
- Annual Job Openings: 45,000
- Annual Earnings: $35,030
- Education/Training Required: Moderate-term on-the-job training
- Self-Employed: 3.7%
- Part-Time: 2.6%

Operate several types of power construction equipment, such as compressors, pumps, hoists, derricks, cranes, shovels, tractors, scrapers, or motor graders, to excavate, move and grade earth, erect structures, or pour concrete or other hard-surface pavement. May repair and maintain equipment in addition to other duties. Adjusts handwheels and depresses pedals to drive machines and control attachments, such as blades, buckets, scrapers, and swing booms. Turns valves to control air and water output of compressors and pumps. Repairs and maintains equipment. **SKILLS**—Repairing; Operation and Control; Equipment Maintenance; Operation Monitoring; Troubleshooting.

GOE—Interest Area: 06. Construction, Mining, and Drilling. **Work Group:** 06.02. Construction. **Other Jobs in This Work Group:** Boat Builders and Shipwrights; Boilermakers; Brattice Builders; Brickmasons and Blockmasons; Carpenters; Carpet Installers; Ceiling Tile Installers; Cement Masons and Concrete Finishers; Commercial Divers; Construction and Related Workers, All Other; Construction Carpenters; Drywall and Ceiling Tile Installers; Drywall Installers; Electricians; Explosives Workers, Ordnance Handling Experts, and Blasters; Fence Erectors; Floor Layers, Except Carpet, Wood, and Hard Tiles; Floor Sanders and Finishers; Glaziers; Grader, Bulldozer, and Scraper Operators; Hazardous Materials Removal Workers; Insulation Workers, Floor, Ceiling, and Wall; Insulation Workers, Mechanical; Manufactured Building and Mobile Home Installers; Operating Engineers and Other Construction Equipment Operators; Painters, Construction and Maintenance; Paperhangers; Paving, Surfacing, and Tamping Equipment Operators; Pile-Driver Operators; Pipe Fitters; Pipelayers; Pipelaying Fitters; Plasterers and Stucco Masons; Plumbers; Plumbers, Pipefitters, and Steamfitters; Rail-Track Laying and Maintenance Equipment Operators; Refractory Materials Repairers, Except Brickmasons; Reinforcing Iron and Rebar Workers; Riggers; Roofers; Rough Carpenters; Security and Fire Alarm Systems Installers; Segmental Pavers; Sheet Metal Workers; Ship Carpenters and Joiners; Stone Cutters and Carvers; Stonemasons; Structural Iron and Steel Workers; Tapers; Terrazzo Workers and Finishers; Tile and Marble Setters.

EDUCATION/TRAINING PROGRAM(S)—Construction/Heavy Equipment/Earthmoving Equipment Operation; Mobil Crane Operation/Operator. **RELATED KNOWLEDGE/COURSES**—Mechanical Devices; Building and Construction; Sales and Marketing; Physics; Engineering and Technology; Public Safety and Security.

Pipe Fitters

- Personality Code: R
- Growth: 18.7%
- Annual Job Openings: 56,000
- Annual Earnings: $40,950
- Education/Training Required: Long-term on-the-job training
- Self-Employed: 10.3%
- Part-Time: 3.4%

Lay out, assemble, install, and maintain pipe systems, pipe supports, and related hydraulic and pneumatic equipment for steam, hot water, heating, cooling, lubricating, sprinkling, and industrial production and processing systems. Cut, thread, and hammer pipe to specifications, using tools such as saws, cutting torches, and pipe threaders and benders. Assemble and secure pipes, tubes, fittings, and related equipment according to specifications by welding, brazing, cementing, soldering, and threading joints. Attach pipes to walls, structures, and fixtures, such as radiators or tanks, using brackets, clamps, tools, or welding equipment. Inspect, examine, and test installed systems and pipelines, using pressure gauge, hydrostatic testing, observation, or other methods. Measure and mark pipes for cutting and threading. Lay out full-scale drawings of pipe systems, supports, and related equipment, following blueprints. Plan pipe system layout, installation, or repair according to specifications. Select pipe sizes and types and related materials, such as supports, hangers, and hydraulic cylinders, according to specifications. Cut and bore holes in structures, such as bulkheads, decks, walls, and mains, prior to pipe installation, using hand and power tools. Modify, clean, and maintain pipe systems, units, fittings, and related machines and equipment, following specifications and using hand and power tools. Install automatic controls used to regulate pipe systems. Turn valves to shut off steam, water, or other gases or liquids from pipe sections, using valve keys or wrenches. Remove and replace worn components. Prepare cost estimates for clients. Inspect work sites for obstructions and to ensure that holes will not cause structural weakness. Operate motorized pumps to remove water from flooded manholes, basements, or facility floors. **SKILLS**—Installation; Repairing; Management of Personnel Resources; Coordination; Persuasion; Service Orientation; Time Management; Equipment Maintenance; Systems Analysis.

GOE—Interest Area: 06. Construction, Mining, and Drilling. **Work Group:** 06.02. Construction. **Other Jobs in This Work Group:** Boat Builders and Shipwrights; Boilermakers; Brattice Builders; Brickmasons and Blockmasons; Carpenters; Carpet Installers; Ceiling Tile Installers; Cement Masons and Concrete Finishers; Commercial Divers; Construction and Related Workers, All Other; Construction Carpenters; Drywall and Ceiling Tile Installers; Drywall Installers; Electricians; Explosives Workers, Ordnance Handling Experts, and Blasters; Fence Erectors; Floor Layers, Except Carpet, Wood, and Hard Tiles; Floor Sanders and Finishers; Glaziers; Grader, Bulldozer, and Scraper Operators; Hazardous Materials Removal Workers; Insulation Workers, Floor, Ceiling, and Wall; Insulation Workers, Mechanical; Manufactured Building and Mobile Home Installers; Operating Engineers; Operating Engineers and Other Construction Equipment Operators; Painters, Construction and Maintenance; Paperhangers; Paving, Surfacing, and Tamping Equipment Operators; Pile-Driver Operators; Pipelayers; Pipelaying Fitters; Plasterers and Stucco Masons; Plumbers; Plumbers, Pipefitters, and Steamfitters; Rail-Track Laying and Maintenance Equipment Operators; Refractory Materials Repairers, Except Brickmasons; Reinforcing Iron and Rebar Workers; Riggers; Roofers; Rough Carpenters; Security and Fire Alarm Systems Installers; Segmental Pavers; Sheet Metal Workers; Ship Carpenters and Joiners; Stone Cutters and Carvers; Stonemasons; Structural Iron and Steel Workers; Tapers; Terrazzo Workers and Finishers; Tile and Marble Setters.

EDUCATION/TRAINING PROGRAM(S)—Pipefitting/Pipefitter and Sprinkler Fitter; Plumbing and Related Water Supply Services, Other; Plumbing Technology/Plumber. **RELATED KNOWLEDGE/COURSES**—Building and Construction; Design; Engineering and Technology; Mechanical Devices; Economics and Accounting; Transportation.

Pipelaying Fitters

- Personality Code: R
- Growth: 18.7%
- Annual Job Openings: 56,000
- Annual Earnings: $40,950
- Education/Training Required: Moderate-term on-the-job training
- Self-Employed: 10.3%
- Part-Time: 3.4%

Align pipeline section in preparation for welding. Signal tractor driver for placement of pipeline sections in proper alignment. Insert steel spacer. Insert spacers between pipe ends. Inspect joints to ensure uniform spacing and proper alignment of pipe surfaces. Correct misalignments of pipe, using a sledgehammer. Guide pipe into trench and signal hoist operator to move pipe until alignment is achieved so that pipes can be welded together. **SKILLS**—Installation; Equipment Maintenance; Repairing.

GOE—**Interest Area:** 06. Construction, Mining, and Drilling. **Work Group:** 06.02. Construction. **Other Jobs in This Work Group:** Boat Builders and Shipwrights; Boilermakers; Brattice Builders; Brickmasons and Blockmasons; Carpenters; Carpet Installers; Ceiling Tile Installers; Cement Masons and Concrete Finishers; Commercial Divers; Construction and Related Workers, All Other; Construction Carpenters; Drywall and Ceiling Tile Installers; Drywall Installers; Electricians; Explosives Workers, Ordnance Handling Experts, and Blasters; Fence Erectors; Floor Layers, Except Carpet, Wood, and Hard Tiles; Floor Sanders and Finishers; Glaziers; Grader, Bulldozer, and Scraper Operators; Hazardous Materials Removal Workers; Insulation Workers, Floor, Ceiling, and Wall; Insulation Workers, Mechanical; Manufactured Building and Mobile Home Installers; Operating Engineers; Operating Engineers and Other Construction Equipment Operators; Painters, Construction and Maintenance; Paperhangers; Paving, Surfacing, and Tamping Equipment Operators; Pile-Driver Operators; Pipe Fitters; Pipelayers; Plasterers and Stucco Masons; Plumbers; Plumbers, Pipefitters, and Steamfitters; Rail-Track Laying and Maintenance Equipment Operators; Refractory Materials Repairers, Except Brickmasons; Reinforcing Iron and Rebar Workers; Riggers; Roofers; Rough Carpenters; Security and Fire Alarm Systems Installers; Segmental Pavers; Sheet Metal Workers; Ship Carpenters and Joiners; Stone Cutters and Carvers; Stonemasons; Structural Iron and Steel Workers; Tapers; Terrazzo Workers and Finishers; Tile and Marble Setters.

EDUCATION/TRAINING PROGRAM(S)—Pipefitting/Pipefitter and Sprinkler Fitter; Plumbing and Related Water Supply Services, Other; Plumbing Technology/Plumber. **RELATED KNOWLEDGE/COURSES**—Mechanical Devices; Building and Construction.

Plumbers

- Personality Code: R
- Growth: 18.7%
- Annual Job Openings: 56,000
- Annual Earnings: $40,950
- Education/Training Required: Long-term on-the-job training
- Self-Employed: 10.3%
- Part-Time: 3.4%

Assemble, install, and repair pipes, fittings, and fixtures of heating, water, and drainage systems according to specifications and plumbing codes. Assemble pipe sections, tubing, and fittings, using couplings; clamps; screws; bolts; cement; plastic solvent; caulking; or soldering, brazing, and welding equipment. Fill pipes or plumbing fixtures with water or air and observe pressure gauges to detect and locate leaks. Review blueprints and building codes and specifications to determine work details and procedures. Prepare written work cost estimates and negotiate contracts. Study building plans and inspect structures to assess material and equipment needs, to establish the sequence of pipe installations, and to plan installation around obstructions such as electrical wiring. Keep records of assignments and produce detailed work reports. Perform complex calculations and planning for special or very large jobs. Locate and mark the position of pipe installations, connections, passage holes, and fixtures in structures, using measuring instruments such as rulers and levels. Measure, cut, thread, and bend pipe to required angle, using hand and power tools or machines such as pipe cutters, pipe-threading machines, and pipe-bending machines. Install pipe assemblies, fittings, valves, appliances such as dishwashers and water heaters, and fixtures such as sinks and toilets, using hand and power tools. Cut openings in structures to accommodate pipes and pipe fittings, using hand and power tools. Hang steel supports from ceiling joists to hold pipes in place. Repair and maintain plumbing, replacing defective washers, replacing or mending broken pipes, and opening clogged drains. Direct workers engaged in pipe cutting and preassembly and installation of plumbing systems and components. Install underground storm, sanitary, and water piping systems and extend piping to connect fixtures and plumbing to these systems. Clear away debris in a renovation. Install oxygen and medical gas in hospitals. Use specialized techniques, equipment, or materials, such as performing computer-assisted welding of small pipes or working with the special piping used in microchip fabrication. **SKILLS**—Installation; Repairing; Troubleshooting; Management of Financial Resources; Management of Material Resources; Coordination; Equipment Selection; Management of Personnel Resources.

GOE—Interest Area: 06. Construction, Mining, and Drilling. **Work Group**: 06.02. Construction. **Other Jobs in This Work Group**: Boat Builders and Shipwrights; Boilermakers; Brattice Builders; Brickmasons and Blockmasons; Carpenters; Carpet Installers; Ceiling Tile Installers; Cement Masons and Concrete Finishers; Commercial Divers; Construction and Related Workers, All Other; Construction Carpenters; Drywall and Ceiling Tile Installers; Drywall Installers; Electricians; Explosives Workers, Ordnance Handling Experts, and Blasters; Fence Erectors; Floor Layers, Except Carpet, Wood, and Hard Tiles; Floor Sanders and Finishers; Glaziers; Grader, Bulldozer, and Scraper Operators; Hazardous Materials Removal Workers; Insulation Workers, Floor, Ceiling, and Wall; Insulation Workers, Mechanical; Manufactured Building and Mobile Home Installers; Operating Engineers; Operating Engineers and Other Construction Equipment Operators; Painters, Construction and Maintenance; Paperhangers; Paving, Surfacing, and Tamping Equipment Operators; Pile-Driver Operators; Pipe Fitters; Pipelayers; Pipelaying Fitters; Plasterers and Stucco Masons; Plumbers, Pipefitters, and Steamfitters; Rail-Track Laying and Maintenance Equipment Operators; Refractory Materials Repairers, Except Brickmasons; Reinforcing Iron and Rebar Workers; Riggers; Roofers; Rough Carpenters; Security and Fire Alarm Systems Installers; Segmental Pavers; Sheet Metal Workers; Ship Carpenters and Joiners; Stone Cutters and Carvers; Stonemasons; Structural Iron and Steel Workers; Tapers; Terrazzo Workers and Finishers; Tile and Marble Setters.

EDUCATION/TRAINING PROGRAM(S)—Pipefitting/Pipefitter and Sprinkler Fitter; Plumbing and Related Water Supply Services, Other; Plumbing Technology/Plumber. **RELATED KNOWLEDGE/COURSES**—Physics; Building and Construction; Mechanical Devices; Chemistry; Sales and Marketing; Design.

Pressure Vessel Inspectors

- Personality Code: RC
- Growth: 9.8%
- Annual Job Openings: 20,000
- Annual Earnings: $46,780
- Education/Training Required: Long-term on-the-job training
- Self-Employed: 0.9%
- Part-Time: 5.3%

Inspect pressure vessel equipment for conformance with safety laws and standards regulating their design, fabrication, installation, repair, and operation. Inspects drawings, designs, and specifications for piping, boilers, and other vessels. Performs standard tests to verify condition of equipment and calibration of meters and gauges, using test equipment and hand tools. Inspects gas mains to determine that rate of flow, pressure, location, construction, or installation conform to standards. Evaluates factors such as materials used, safety devices, regulators, construction quality, riveting, welding, pitting, corrosion, cracking, and safety valve operation. Calculates allowable limits of pressure, strength, and stresses. Examines permits and inspection records to determine that inspection schedule and remedial actions conform to procedures and regulations. Keeps records and prepares reports of inspections and investigations for administrative or legal authorities. Investigates accidents to determine causes and to develop methods of preventing recurrences. Confers with engineers, manufacturers, contractors, owners, and operators concerning problems in construction, operation, and repair. Witnesses acceptance and installation tests. Recommends or orders actions to correct violations of legal requirements or to eliminate unsafe conditions. **SKILLS**—Quality Control Analysis; Operation Monitoring; Mathematics; Science; Operations Analysis; Systems Evaluation; Writing; Troubleshooting; Systems Analysis.

GOE—Interest Area: 02. Science, Math, and Engineering. **Work Group:** 02.08. Engineering Technology. **Other Jobs in This Work Group:** Aerospace Engineering and Operations Technicians; Architectural and Civil Drafters; Architectural Drafters; Calibration and Instrumentation Technicians; Cartographers and Photogrammetrists; Civil Drafters; Civil Engineering Technicians; Construction and Building Inspectors; Drafters, All Other; Electrical and Electronic Engineering Technicians; Electrical and Electronics Drafters; Electrical Drafters; Electrical Engineering Technicians; Electro-Mechanical Technicians; Electronic Drafters; Electronics Engineering Technicians; Engineering Technicians, Except Drafters, All Other; Environmental Engineering Technicians; Industrial Engineering Technicians; Mapping Technicians; Mechanical Drafters; Mechanical Engineering Technicians; Numerical Tool and Process Control Programmers; Surveying and Mapping Technicians; Surveying Technicians; Surveyors.

EDUCATION/TRAINING PROGRAM(S)— No data available. **RELATED KNOWLEDGE/ COURSES**—Physics; Public Safety and Security; Mechanical Devices; Engineering and Technology; Law and Government; Design; Mathematics.

Radiologic Technicians

- Personality Code: RC
- Growth: 22.9%
- Annual Job Openings: 21,000
- Annual Earnings: $40,620
- Education/Training Required: Associate's degree
- Self-Employed: 0.2%
- Part-Time: 17.5%

Maintain and use equipment and supplies necessary to demonstrate portions of the human body on X-ray film or fluoroscopic screen for diagnostic

purposes. Use beam-restrictive devices and patient-shielding techniques to minimize radiation exposure to patient and staff. Position X-ray equipment and adjust controls to set exposure factors, such as time and distance. Position patient on examining table and set up and adjust equipment to obtain optimum view of specific body area as requested by physician. Determine patients' X-ray needs by reading requests or instructions from physicians. Make exposures necessary for the requested procedures, rejecting and repeating work that does not meet established standards. Process exposed radiographs, using film processors or computer generated methods. Explain procedures to patients to reduce anxieties and obtain cooperation. Perform procedures such as linear tomography; mammography; sonograms; joint and cyst aspirations; routine contrast studies; routine fluoroscopy; and examinations of the head, trunk, and extremities under supervision of physician. Prepare and set up X-ray room for patient. Assure that sterile supplies, contrast materials, catheters, and other required equipment are present and in working order, requisitioning materials as necessary. Maintain records of patients examined, examinations performed, views taken, and technical factors used. Provide assistance to physicians or other technologists in the performance of more-complex procedures. Monitor equipment operation and report malfunctioning equipment to supervisor. Provide students and other technologists with suggestions of additional views, alternate positioning, or improved techniques to ensure the images produced are of the highest quality. Coordinate work of other technicians or technologists when procedures require more than one person. Assist with on-the-job training of new employees and students and provide input to supervisors regarding training performance. Maintain a current file of examination protocols. Operate mobile X-ray equipment in operating room, in emergency room, or at patient's bedside. Provide assistance in radio-pharmaceutical administration, monitoring patients' vital signs and notifying the radiologist of any relevant changes. **SKILLS**—Service Orientation; Science; Instructing; Negotiation; Social Perceptiveness; Active Listening; Equipment Selection; Speaking; Learning Strategies; Coordination.

GOE—Interest Area: 14. Medical and Health Services. **Work Group:** 14.05. Medical Technology. **Other Jobs in This Work Group:** Cardiovascular Technologists and Technicians; Diagnostic Medical Sonographers; Health Technologists and Technicians, All Other; Medical and Clinical Laboratory Technicians; Medical and Clinical Laboratory Technologists; Medical Equipment Preparers; Nuclear Medicine Technologists; Orthotists and Prosthetists; Radiologic Technologists; Radiologic Technologists and Technicians.

EDUCATION/TRAINING PROGRAM(S)—Allied Health Diagnostic, Intervention, and Treatment Professions, Other; Medical Radiologic Technology/Science—Radiation Therapist; Radiologic Technology/Science—Radiographer. **RELATED KNOWLEDGE/COURSES**—Clerical Studies; Psychology; Medicine and Dentistry; Customer and Personal Service; Physics; English Language.

Radiologic Technologists

- Personality Code: RI
- Growth: 22.9%
- Annual Job Openings: 21,000
- Annual Earnings: $40,620
- Education/Training Required: Associate's degree
- Self-Employed: 0.2%
- Part-Time: 17.5%

Take X rays and CAT scans or administer nonradioactive materials into patient's bloodstream for diagnostic purposes. Includes technologists who specialize in other modalities, such as computed tomography, ultrasound, and magnetic resonance. Review and evaluate developed X rays, videotape, or computer-generated information to determine if images are satisfactory for diagnostic purposes. Use radiation safety measures and protection devices to comply with government regulations and to ensure safety of patients and staff. Explain procedures and observe patients to ensure safety and comfort during scan. Operate or oversee operation of radiologic and magnetic imaging equipment to produce images of the body for diagnostic purposes. Position and immobilize patient on examining table. Position imaging equipment and adjust controls to set exposure time and distance according to specification of examination. Key commands and data into computer to document and specify scan sequences, adjust transmitters and receivers, or photograph certain images. Monitor video display of area being scanned and adjust density or contrast to improve picture quality. Monitor patients' conditions and reactions, reporting abnormal signs to physician. Set up examination rooms, ensuring that all necessary equipment is ready. Prepare and administer oral or injected contrast media to patients. Take thorough and accurate patient medical histories. Remove and process film. Record, process, and maintain patient data and treatment records and prepare reports. Coordinate work with clerical personnel and other technologists. Demonstrate new equipment, procedures, and techniques to staff and provide technical assistance. Provide assistance with such tasks as dressing and changing to seriously ill, injured, or disabled patients. Move ultrasound scanner over patient's body and watch pattern produced on video screen. Measure thickness of section to be radiographed, using instruments similar to measuring tapes. Operate fluoroscope to aid physician to view and guide wire or catheter through blood vessels to area of interest. Assign duties to radiologic staff to maintain patient flows and achieve production goals. Collaborate with other medical team members, such as physicians and nurses, to conduct angiography or special vascular procedures. Perform administrative duties such as developing departmental operating budget, coordinating purchases of

supplies and equipment, and preparing work schedules. **SKILLS**—Instructing; Social Perceptiveness; Service Orientation; Reading Comprehension; Active Listening; Operation Monitoring; Speaking; Critical Thinking; Coordination.

GOE—Interest Area: 14. Medical and Health Services. **Work Group:** 14.05. Medical Technology. **Other Jobs in This Work Group:** Cardiovascular Technologists and Technicians; Diagnostic Medical Sonographers; Health Technologists and Technicians, All Other; Medical and Clinical Laboratory Technicians; Medical and Clinical Laboratory Technologists; Medical Equipment Preparers; Nuclear Medicine Technologists; Orthotists and Prosthetists; Radiologic Technicians; Radiologic Technologists and Technicians.

EDUCATION/TRAINING PROGRAM(S)— Allied Health Diagnostic, Intervention, and Treatment Professions, Other; Medical Radiologic Technology/Science—Radiation Therapist; Radiologic Technology/Science—Radiographer. **RELATED KNOWLEDGE/COURSES**—Medicine and Dentistry; Customer and Personal Service; Psychology; Physics; Biology; Chemistry.

Refractory Materials Repairers, Except Brickmasons

- Personality Code: R
- Growth: 16.3%
- Annual Job Openings: 155,000
- Annual Earnings: $36,910
- Education/Training Required: Short-term on-the-job training
- Self-Employed: 6.1%
- Part-Time: 2.1%

Realistic—R

Build or repair furnaces, kilns, cupolas, boilers, converters, ladles, soaking pits, ovens, etc., using refractory materials. Bolt sections of wooden molds together, using wrenches, and line molds with paper to prevent clay from sticking to molds. Chip slag from linings of ladles or remove linings when beyond repair, using hammers and chisels. Disassemble molds and cut, chip, and smooth clay structures such as floaters, drawbars, and L-blocks. Drill holes in furnace walls, bolt overlapping layers of plastic to walls, and hammer surfaces to compress layers into solid sheets. Dry and bake new linings by placing inverted linings over burners, by building fires in ladles, or by using blowtorches. Dump and tamp clay in molds, using tamping tools. Fasten stopper heads to rods with metal pins to assemble refractory stoppers used to plug pouring nozzles of steel ladles. Install clay structures in melting tanks and drawing kilns to control the flow and temperature of molten glass, using hoists and hand tools. Measure furnace walls to determine dimensions; then cut required number of sheets from plastic block, using saws. Mix specified amounts of sand, clay, mortar powder, and water to form refractory clay or mortar, using shovels or mixing machines. Reline or repair ladles and pouring spouts with refractory clay, using trowels. Remove worn or damaged plastic block refractory linings of furnaces, using hand tools. Spread mortar on stopper heads and rods, using trowels, and slide brick sleeves over rods to form refractory jackets. Tighten locknuts holding refractory stopper assemblies together, spread mortar on jackets to seal sleeve joints, and dry mortar in ovens. Climb scaffolding, carrying hoses, and spray surfaces of cupolas with refractory mixtures, using spray equipment. Install preformed metal scaffolding in interiors of cupolas, using hand tools. Transfer clay structures to curing ovens, melting tanks, and drawing kilns, using forklifts. **SKILLS**—Repairing; Installation; Operation and Control; Equipment Maintenance; Troubleshooting; Science; Equipment Selection; Operation Monitoring.

GOE—Interest Area: 06. Construction, Mining, and Drilling. **Work Group:** 06.02. Construction. **Other Jobs in This Work Group:** Boat Builders and Shipwrights; Boilermakers; Brattice Builders; Brickmasons and Blockmasons; Carpenters; Carpet Installers; Ceiling Tile Installers; Cement Masons and Concrete Finishers; Commercial Divers; Construction and Related Workers, All Other; Construction Carpenters; Drywall and Ceiling Tile Installers; Drywall Installers; Electricians; Explosives Workers, Ordnance Handling Experts, and Blasters; Fence Erectors; Floor Layers, Except Carpet, Wood, and Hard Tiles; Floor Sanders and Finishers; Glaziers; Grader, Bulldozer, and Scraper Operators; Hazardous Materials Removal Workers; Insulation Workers, Floor, Ceiling, and Wall; Insulation Workers, Mechanical; Manufactured Building and Mobile Home Installers; Operating Engineers; Operating Engineers and Other Construction Equipment Operators; Painters, Construction and Maintenance; Paperhangers; Paving, Surfacing, and Tamping Equipment Operators; Pile-Driver Operators; Pipe Fitters; Pipelayers; Pipelaying Fitters; Plasterers and Stucco Masons; Plumbers; Plumbers, Pipefitters, and Steamfitters; Rail-Track Laying and Maintenance Equipment Operators; Reinforcing Iron and Rebar Workers; Riggers; Roofers; Rough Carpenters; Security and Fire Alarm Systems Installers; Segmental Pavers; Sheet Metal Workers; Ship Carpenters and Joiners; Stone Cutters and Carvers; Stonemasons; Structural Iron and Steel Workers; Tapers; Terrazzo Workers and Finishers; Tile and Marble Setters.

EDUCATION/TRAINING PROGRAM(S)—Industrial Mechanics and Maintenance Technology. **RELATED KNOWLEDGE/COURSES**—Building and Construction; Mechanical Devices; Production and Processing; Fine Arts; Engineering and Technology; Chemistry.

Refrigeration Mechanics

- Personality Code: RC
- Growth: 31.8%
- Annual Job Openings: 35,000
- Annual Earnings: $35,160
- Education/Training Required: Long-term on-the-job training
- Self-Employed: 15.4%
- Part-Time: 3.1%

Install and repair industrial and commercial refrigerating systems. Braze or solder parts to repair defective joints and leaks. Observe and test system operation, using gauges and instruments. Test lines, components, and connections for leaks. Dismantle malfunctioning systems and test components, using electrical, mechanical, and pneumatic testing equipment. Adjust or replace worn or defective mechanisms and parts and reassemble repaired systems. Read blueprints to determine location, size, capacity, and type of components needed to build refrigeration system. Supervise and instruct assistants. Install wiring to connect components to an electric power source. Perform mechanical overhauls and refrigerant reclaiming. Cut, bend, thread, and connect pipe to functional components and water, power, or refrigeration system. Adjust valves according to specifications and charge system with proper type of refrigerant by pumping the specified gas or fluid into the system. Estimate, order, pick up, deliver, and install materials and supplies needed to maintain equipment in good working condition. Install expansion and control valves, using acetylene torches and wrenches. Mount compressor, condenser, and other components in specified locations on frames, using hand tools and acetylene welding equipment. Keep records of repairs and replacements made and causes of malfunctions. Lay out reference points for installation of structural and functional components, using measuring instru-

ments. Schedule work with customers and initiate work orders, house requisitions, and orders from stock. Fabricate and assemble structural and functional components of refrigeration system, using hand tools, power tools, and welding equipment. Lift and align components into position, using hoist or block and tackle. Drill holes and install mounting brackets and hangers into floor and walls of building. Insulate shells and cabinets of systems. **SKILLS**—Installation; Repairing; Equipment Maintenance; Operation Monitoring; Troubleshooting; Systems Evaluation; Science; Systems Analysis.

GOE—Interest Area: 05. Mechanics, Installers, and Repairers. **Work Group:** 05.03. Mechanical Work. **Other Jobs in This Work Group:** Aircraft Body and Bonded Structure Repairers; Aircraft Engine Specialists; Aircraft Mechanics and Service Technicians; Airframe-and-Power-Plant Mechanics; Automotive Body and Related Repairers; Automotive Glass Installers and Repairers; Automotive Master Mechanics; Automotive Service Technicians and Mechanics; Automotive Specialty Technicians; Bicycle Repairers; Bridge and Lock Tenders; Bus and Truck Mechanics and Diesel Engine Specialists; Camera and Photographic Equipment Repairers; Coin, Vending, and Amusement Machine Servicers and Repairers; Control and Valve Installers and Repairers, Except Mechanical Door; Farm Equipment Mechanics; Gas Appliance Repairers; Hand and Portable Power Tool Repairers; Heating and Air Conditioning Mechanics; Heating, Air Conditioning, and Refrigeration Mechanics and Installers; Helpers—Electricians; Helpers—Installation, Maintenance, and Repair Workers; Industrial Machinery Mechanics; Installation, Maintenance, and Repair Workers, All Other; Keyboard Instrument Repairers and Tuners; Locksmiths and Safe Repairers; Maintenance and Repair Workers, General; Maintenance Workers, Machinery; Mechanical Door Repairers; Medical Appliance Technicians; Medical Equipment Repairers; Meter Mechanics; Millwrights; Mobile Heavy Equipment Mechanics, Except Engines; Motorboat Mechanics; Motorcycle

Mechanics; Musical Instrument Repairers and Tuners; Ophthalmic Laboratory Technicians; Optical Instrument Assemblers; Outdoor Power Equipment and Other Small Engine Mechanics; Painters, Transportation Equipment; Percussion Instrument Repairers and Tuners; Precision Instrument and Equipment Repairers, All Other; Rail Car Repairers; Railroad Inspectors; Recreational Vehicle Service Technicians; Reed or Wind Instrument Repairers and Tuners; Stringed Instrument Repairers and Tuners; Tire Repairers and Changers; Valve and Regulator Repairers; Watch Repairers.

EDUCATION/TRAINING PROGRAM(S)— Heating, Air Conditioning and Refrigeration Technology/Technician (ACH/ACR/ACHR/ HRAC/HVAC/AC Technology); Heating, Air Conditioning, Ventilation, and Refrigeration Maintenance Technology/Technician (HAC, HACR, HVAC, HVACR); Solar Energy Technology/Technician. RELATED KNOWLEDGE/COURSES— Building and Construction; Mechanical Devices; Engineering and Technology; Customer and Personal Service; Physics; Design.

Roofers

- Personality Code: R
- Growth: 18.6%
- Annual Job Openings: 38,000
- Annual Earnings: $30,020
- Education/Training Required: Moderate-term on-the-job training
- Self-Employed: 31.9%
- Part-Time: 10.0%

Cover roofs of structures with shingles, slate, asphalt, aluminum, wood, and related materials. May spray roofs, sidings, and walls with material to bind, seal, insulate, or soundproof sections of structures. Fastens composition shingles or sheets to roof with asphalt, cement, or nails. Cuts roofing paper to size and nails or staples paper to roof in overlapping strips to form base for roofing materials. Cleans and maintains equipment. Removes snow, water, or debris from roofs prior to applying roofing materials. Insulates, soundproofs, and seals buildings with foam, using spray gun, air compressor, and heater. Punches holes in slate, tile, terra cotta, or wooden shingles, using punch and hammer. Applies gravel or pebbles over top layer, using rake or stiff-bristled broom. Applies alternate layers of hot asphalt or tar and roofing paper until roof covering is completed as specified. Overlaps successive layers of roofing material, determining distance of overlap, using chalkline, gauge on shingling hatchet, or lines on shingles. Cuts strips of flashing and fits them into angles formed by walls, vents, and intersecting roof surfaces. Mops or pours hot asphalt or tar onto roof base when applying asphalt or tar and gravel to roof. Aligns roofing material with edge of roof. SKILLS—Repairing; Installation; Coordination; Equipment Selection; Operation and Control.

GOE—Interest Area: 06. Construction, Mining, and Drilling. Work Group: 06.02. Construction. Other Jobs in This Work Group: Boat Builders and Shipwrights; Boilermakers; Brattice Builders; Brickmasons and Blockmasons; Carpenters; Carpet Installers; Ceiling Tile Installers; Cement Masons and Concrete Finishers; Commercial Divers; Construction and Related Workers, All Other; Construction Carpenters; Drywall and Ceiling Tile Installers; Drywall Installers; Electricians; Explosives Workers, Ordnance Handling Experts, and Blasters; Fence Erectors; Floor Layers, Except Carpet, Wood, and Hard Tiles; Floor Sanders and Finishers; Glaziers; Grader, Bulldozer, and Scraper Operators; Hazardous Materials Removal Workers; Insulation Workers, Floor, Ceiling, and Wall; Insulation Workers, Mechanical; Manufactured Building and Mobile Home Installers; Operating Engineers; Operating Engineers and Other Construction Equipment Operators; Painters, Construction and Maintenance; Paperhangers; Paving, Surfacing, and Tamping Equipment Operators; Pile-Driver Operators; Pipe Fitters; Pipelayers; Pipelaying Fitters; Plasterers and Stucco Masons; Plumbers; Plumbers, Pipefitters, and Steamfitters; Rail-Track Laying and Maintenance Equipment Operators; Refractory Materials Repairers, Except Brickmasons; Reinforcing Iron and Rebar Workers; Riggers; Rough Carpenters; Security and Fire Alarm Systems Installers; Segmental Pavers; Sheet Metal Workers; Ship Carpenters and Joiners; Stone Cutters and Carvers; Stonemasons; Structural Iron and Steel Workers; Tapers; Terrazzo Workers and Finishers; Tile and Marble Setters.

EDUCATION/TRAINING PROGRAM(S)—Roofer. **RELATED KNOWLEDGE/COURSES**—Building and Construction; Mechanical Devices.

Rough Carpenters

- ◉ Personality Code: RC
- ◉ Growth: 10.1%
- ◉ Annual Job Openings: 193,000
- ◉ Annual Earnings: $34,250
- ◉ Education/Training Required: Moderate-term on-the-job training
- ◉ Self-Employed: 29.7%
- ◉ Part-Time: 5.3%

Build rough wooden structures, such as concrete forms, scaffolds, tunnel, bridge, or sewer supports; billboard signs; and temporary frame shelters, according to sketches, blueprints, or oral instructions. Study blueprints and diagrams to determine dimensions of structure or form to be constructed. Measure materials or distances, using square, measuring tape, or rule to lay out work. Cut or saw boards, timbers, or plywood to required size, using handsaw, power saw, or woodworking machine. Assemble and fasten material together to construct wood or metal framework of structure, using bolts, nails, or screws. Anchor and brace forms and other structures in place, using nails, bolts, anchor rods,

steel cables, planks, wedges, and timbers. Mark cutting lines on materials, using pencil and scriber. Erect forms, framework, scaffolds, hoists, roof supports, or chutes, using hand tools, plumb rule, and level. Install rough door and window frames, subflooring, fixtures, or temporary supports in structures undergoing construction or repair. Examine structural timbers and supports to detect decay and replace timbers as required, using hand tools, nuts, and bolts. Bore boltholes in timber, masonry, or concrete walls, using power drill. Fabricate parts, using woodworking and metalworking machines. **SKILLS**—Repairing; Installation; Management of Personnel Resources; Equipment Selection; Coordination; Mathematics; Technology Design; Equipment Maintenance.

GOE—**Interest Area:** 06. Construction, Mining, and Drilling. **Work Group:** 06.02. Construction. **Other Jobs in This Work Group:** Boat Builders and Shipwrights; Boilermakers; Brattice Builders; Brickmasons and Blockmasons; Carpenters; Carpet Installers; Ceiling Tile Installers; Cement Masons and Concrete Finishers; Commercial Divers; Construction and Related Workers, All Other; Construction Carpenters; Drywall and Ceiling Tile Installers; Drywall Installers; Electricians; Explosives Workers, Ordnance Handling Experts, and Blasters; Fence Erectors; Floor Layers, Except Carpet, Wood, and Hard Tiles; Floor Sanders and Finishers; Glaziers; Grader, Bulldozer, and Scraper Operators; Hazardous Materials Removal Workers; Insulation Workers, Floor, Ceiling, and Wall; Insulation Workers, Mechanical; Manufactured Building and Mobile Home Installers; Operating Engineers; Operating Engineers and Other Construction Equipment Operators; Painters, Construction and Maintenance; Paperhangers; Paving, Surfacing, and Tamping Equipment Operators; Pile-Driver Operators; Pipe Fitters; Pipelayers; Pipelaying Fitters; Plasterers and Stucco Masons; Plumbers; Plumbers, Pipefitters, and Steamfitters; Rail-Track Laying and Maintenance Equipment Operators; Refractory Materials Repairers, Except Brickmasons; Reinforcing Iron and Rebar Workers; Riggers; Roofers; Security and Fire Alarm Systems Installers; Segmental

Pavers; Sheet Metal Workers; Ship Carpenters and Joiners; Stone Cutters and Carvers; Stonemasons; Structural Iron and Steel Workers; Tapers; Terrazzo Workers and Finishers; Tile and Marble Setters.

EDUCATION/TRAINING PROGRAM(S)— Carpentry/Carpenter. **RELATED KNOWL-EDGE/COURSES**—Building and Construction; Design; Engineering and Technology; Mechanical Devices; Production and Processing; Public Safety and Security.

Sheet Metal Workers

- Personality Code: R
- Growth: 19.8%
- Annual Job Openings: 30,000
- Annual Earnings: $35,000
- Education/Training Required: Moderate-term on-the-job training
- Self-Employed: 3.1%
- Part-Time: 2.7%

Fabricate, assemble, install, and repair sheet metal products and equipment, such as ducts, control boxes, drainpipes, and furnace casings. Work may involve any of the following: setting up and operating fabricating machines to cut, bend, and straighten sheet metal; shaping metal over anvils, blocks, or forms, using hammer; operating soldering and welding equipment to join sheet metal parts; inspecting, assembling, and smoothing seams and joints of burred surfaces. Drill and punch holes in metal for screws, bolts, and rivets. Fasten seams and joints together with welds, bolts, cement, rivets, solder, caulks, metal drive clips, and bonds in order to assemble components into products or to repair sheet metal items. Finish parts, using hacksaws and hand, rotary, or squaring shears. Inspect individual parts, assemblies, and installations for conformance to specifications and building

codes, using measuring instruments such as calipers, scales, and micrometers. Install assemblies, such as flashing, pipes, tubes, heating and air conditioning ducts, furnace casings, rain gutters, and downspouts, in supportive frameworks. Lay out, measure, and mark dimensions and reference lines on material, such as roofing panels, according to drawings or templates, using calculators, scribes, dividers, squares, and rulers. Select gauges and types of sheet metal or non-metallic material according to product specifications. Shape metal material over anvils, blocks, or other forms, using hand tools. Trim, file, grind, deburr, buff, and smooth surfaces, seams, and joints of assembled parts, using hand tools and portable power tools. Convert blueprints into shop drawings to be followed in the construction and assembly of sheet metal products. Develop and lay out patterns that use materials most efficiently, using computerized metalworking equipment to experiment with different layouts. Determine project requirements, including scope, assembly sequences, and required methods and materials, according to blueprints, drawings, and written or verbal instructions. Fabricate or alter parts at construction sites, using shears, hammers, punches, and drills. Fasten roof panel edges and machine-made molding to structures, nailing or welding pieces into place. Maintain equipment, making repairs and modifications when necessary. Maneuver completed units into position for installation and anchor the units. Secure metal roof panels in place; then interlock and fasten grooved panel edges. Transport prefabricated parts to construction sites for assembly and installation. **SKILLS**—Installation; Technology Design; Repairing; Equipment Selection; Quality Control Analysis; Operation and Control; Operations Analysis; Mathematics.

GOE—Interest Area: 06. Construction, Mining, and Drilling. **Work Group:** 06.02. Construction. **Other Jobs in This Work Group:** Boat Builders and Shipwrights; Boilermakers; Brattice Builders; Brickmasons and Blockmasons; Carpenters; Carpet Installers; Ceiling Tile Installers; Cement Masons and Concrete Finishers; Commercial Divers; Construction and Related Workers, All Other; Construction Carpenters; Drywall and Ceiling Tile Installers; Drywall Installers; Electricians; Explosives Workers, Ordnance Handling Experts, and Blasters; Fence Erectors; Floor Layers, Except Carpet, Wood, and Hard Tiles; Floor Sanders and Finishers; Glaziers; Grader, Bulldozer, and Scraper Operators; Hazardous Materials Removal Workers; Insulation Workers, Floor, Ceiling, and Wall; Insulation Workers, Mechanical; Manufactured Building and Mobile Home Installers; Operating Engineers; Operating Engineers and Other Construction Equipment Operators; Painters, Construction and Maintenance; Paperhangers; Paving, Surfacing, and Tamping Equipment Operators; Pile-Driver Operators; Pipe Fitters; Pipelayers; Pipelaying Fitters; Plasterers and Stucco Masons; Plumbers; Plumbers, Pipefitters, and Steamfitters; Rail-Track Laying and Maintenance Equipment Operators; Refractory Materials Repairers, Except Brickmasons; Reinforcing Iron and Rebar Workers; Riggers; Roofers; Rough Carpenters; Security and Fire Alarm Systems Installers; Segmental Pavers; Ship Carpenters and Joiners; Stone Cutters and Carvers; Stonemasons; Structural Iron and Steel Workers; Tapers; Terrazzo Workers and Finishers; Tile and Marble Setters.

EDUCATION/TRAINING PROGRAM(S)— Sheet Metal Technology/Sheetworking. **RELATED KNOWLEDGE/COURSES—**Production and Processing; Building and Construction; Design; Mechanical Devices; Computers and Electronics; Engineering and Technology.

Ship Carpenters and Joiners

- Personality Code: R
- Growth: 10.1%
- Annual Job Openings: 193,000
- Annual Earnings: $34,250
- Education/Training Required: Moderate-term on-the-job training
- Self-Employed: 29.7%
- Part-Time: 5.3%

Fabricate, assemble, install, or repair wooden furnishings in ships or boats. Reads blueprints to determine dimensions of furnishings in ships or boats. Shapes and laminates wood to form parts of ship, using steam chambers, clamps, glue, and jigs. Repairs structural woodwork and replaces defective parts and equipment, using hand tools and power tools. Shapes irregular parts and trims excess material from bulkhead and furnishings to ensure fit meets specifications. Constructs floors, doors, and partitions, using woodworking machines, hand tools, and power tools. Cuts wood or glass to specified dimensions, using hand tools and power tools. Assembles and installs hardware, gaskets, floors, furnishings, or insulation, using adhesive, hand tools, and power tools. Transfers dimensions or measurements of wood parts or bulkhead on plywood, using measuring instruments and marking devices. Greases gears and other moving parts of machines on ship. **SKILLS**—Installation; Repairing; Equipment Maintenance; Operations Analysis.

GOE—Interest Area: 06. Construction, Mining, and Drilling. **Work Group:** 06.02. Construction. **Other Jobs in This Work Group:** Boat Builders and Shipwrights; Boilermakers; Brattice Builders; Brickmasons and Blockmasons; Carpenters; Carpet Installers; Ceiling Tile Installers; Cement Masons and Concrete Finishers; Commercial Divers; Construction and Related Workers, All Other; Construction Carpenters; Drywall and Ceiling Tile

Installers; Drywall Installers; Electricians; Explosives Workers, Ordnance Handling Experts, and Blasters; Fence Erectors; Floor Layers, Except Carpet, Wood, and Hard Tiles; Floor Sanders and Finishers; Glaziers; Grader, Bulldozer, and Scraper Operators; Hazardous Materials Removal Workers; Insulation Workers, Floor, Ceiling, and Wall; Insulation Workers, Mechanical; Manufactured Building and Mobile Home Installers; Operating Engineers; Operating Engineers and Other Construction Equipment Operators; Painters, Construction and Maintenance; Paperhangers; Paving, Surfacing, and Tamping Equipment Operators; Pile-Driver Operators; Pipe Fitters; Pipelayers; Pipelaying Fitters; Plasterers and Stucco Masons; Plumbers; Plumbers, Pipefitters, and Steamfitters; Rail-Track Laying and Maintenance Equipment Operators; Refractory Materials Repairers, Except Brickmasons; Reinforcing Iron and Rebar Workers; Riggers; Roofers; Rough Carpenters; Security and Fire Alarm Systems Installers; Segmental Pavers; Sheet Metal Workers; Stone Cutters and Carvers; Stonemasons; Structural Iron and Steel Workers; Tapers; Terrazzo Workers and Finishers; Tile and Marble Setters.

EDUCATION/TRAINING PROGRAM(S)—Carpentry/Carpenter. RELATED KNOWLEDGE/COURSES—Building and Construction; Design; Engineering and Technology; Mechanical Devices.

Solderers

- Personality Code: RC
- Growth: 17.0%
- Annual Job Openings: 71,000
- Annual Earnings: $29,640
- Education/Training Required: Short-term on-the-job training
- Self-Employed: 5.6%
- Part-Time: 2.1%

Solder together components to assemble fabricated metal products, using soldering iron. Melts and applies solder along adjoining edges of workpieces to solder joints, using soldering iron, gas torch, or electric-ultrasonic equipment. Grinds, cuts, buffs, or bends edges of workpieces to be joined to ensure snug fit, using power grinder and hand tools. Removes workpieces from molten solder and holds parts together until color indicates that solder has set. Cleans workpieces, using chemical solution, file, wire brush, or grinder. Cleans tip of soldering iron, using chemical solution or cleaning compound. Melts and separates soldered joints to repair misaligned or damaged assemblies, using soldering equipment. Applies flux to workpiece surfaces in preparation for soldering. Heats soldering iron or workpiece to specified temperature for soldering, using gas flame or electric current. Dips workpieces into molten solder or places solder strip between seams and heats seam with iron to band items together. Aligns and clamps workpieces together, using rule, square, or hand tools, or positions items in fixtures, jigs, or vise. Melts and applies solder to fill holes, indentations, and seams of fabricated metal products, using soldering equipment. **SKILLS—**Operation and Control; Equipment Maintenance; Equipment Selection; Installation; Operation Monitoring; Science; Repairing.

GOE—Interest Area: 08. Industrial Production. **Work Group:** 08.03. Production Work. **Other Jobs in This Work Group:** Assemblers and Fabricators, All Other; Bakers, Manufacturing; Bindery Machine Operators and Tenders; Brazers; Cementing and Gluing Machine Operators and Tenders; Chemical Equipment Controllers and Operators; Chemical Equipment Operators and Tenders; Chemical Equipment Tenders; Cleaning, Washing, and Metal Pickling Equipment Operators and Tenders; Coating, Painting, and Spraying Machine Operators and Tenders; Coil Winders, Tapers, and Finishers; Combination Machine Tool Operators and Tenders, Metal and Plastic; Computer-Controlled Machine Tool Operators, Metal and Plastic;

Cooling and Freezing Equipment Operators and Tenders; Crushing, Grinding, and Polishing Machine Setters, Operators, and Tenders; Cutters and Trimmers, Hand; Cutting and Slicing Machine Operators and Tenders; Cutting and Slicing Machine Setters, Operators, and Tenders; Design Printing Machine Setters and Set-Up Operators; Electrolytic Plating and Coating Machine Operators and Tenders, Metal and Plastic; Electrolytic Plating and Coating Machine Setters and Set-Up Operators, Metal and Plastic; Electrotypers and Stereotypers; Embossing Machine Set-Up Operators; Engraver Set-Up Operators; Extruding and Forming Machine Operators and Tenders, Synthetic or Glass Fibers; Extruding and Forming Machine Setters, Operators, and Tenders, Synthetic and Glass Fibers; Extruding, Forming, Pressing, and Compacting Machine Operators and Tenders; Fabric and Apparel Patternmakers; Fiber Product Cutting Machine Setters and Set-Up Operators; Fiberglass Laminators and Fabricators; Film Laboratory Technicians; Fitters, Structural Metal—Precision; Food and Tobacco Roasting, Baking, and Drying Machine Operators and Tenders; Food Batchmakers; Food Cooking Machine Operators and Tenders; Furnace, Kiln, Oven, Drier, and Kettle Operators and Tenders; Glass Cutting Machine Setters and Set-Up Operators; Graders and Sorters, Agricultural Products; Grinding and Polishing Workers, Hand; Hand Compositors and Typesetters; Heaters, Metal and Plastic; Helpers—Production Workers; Job Printers; Letterpress Setters and Set-Up Operators; Marking and Identification Printing Machine Setters and Set-Up Operators; Meat, Poultry, and Fish Cutters and Trimmers; Metal Fabricators, Structural Metal Products; Metal-Refining Furnace Operators and Tenders; Mixing and Blending Machine Setters, Operators, and Tenders; Mold Makers, Hand; Molding and Casting Workers; Nonelectrolytic Plating and Coating Machine Operators and Tenders, Metal and Plastic; Nonelectrolytic Plating and Coating Machine Setters and Set-Up Operators, Metal and Plastic; Numerical Control Machine Tool Operators and Tenders,

Metal and Plastic; Offset Lithographic Press Setters and Set-Up Operators; Packaging and Filling Machine Operators and Tenders; Painting, Coating, and Decorating Workers; Photoengraving and Lithographing Machine Operators and Tenders; Photographic Hand Developers; Photographic Process Workers; Photographic Processing Machine Operators; Photographic Reproduction Technicians; Photographic Retouchers and Restorers; Plate Finishers; Platemakers; Plating and Coating Machine Setters, Operators, and Tenders, Metal and Plastic; Pourers and Casters, Metal; Precision Printing Workers; Prepress Technicians and Workers; Pressing Machine Operators and Tenders—Textile, Garment, and Related Materials; Printing Machine Operators; Printing Press Machine Operators and Tenders; Production Helpers; Production Laborers; Production Workers, All Other; Sawing Machine Operators and Tenders; Sawing Machine Setters and Set-Up Operators; Sawing Machine Setters, Operators, and Tenders, Wood; Scanner Operators; Semiconductor Processors; Separating, Filtering, Clarifying, Precipitating, and Still Machine Setters, Operators, and Tenders; Sewers, Hand; Sewing Machine Operators; Sewing Machine Operators, Garment; Sewing Machine Operators, Non-Garment; Shoe Machine Operators and Tenders; Slaughterers and Meat Packers; Soldering and Brazing Machine Operators and Tenders; Stone Sawyers; Strippers; Structural Metal Fabricators and Fitters; Team Assemblers; Textile Bleaching and Dyeing Machine Operators and Tenders; Tire Builders; Welder-Fitters; Welders and Cutters; Welders, Cutters, Solderers, and Brazers; Welders, Production; Welding Machine Operators and Tenders; Woodworking Machine Operators and Tenders, Except Sawing.

EDUCATION/TRAINING PROGRAM(S)— Welding Technology/Welder. **RELATED KNOWLEDGE/COURSES**—Building and Construction; Mechanical Devices; Production and Processing.

Surgical Technologists

- Personality Code: RS
- Growth: 27.9%
- Annual Job Openings: 13,000
- Annual Earnings: $32,130
- Education/Training Required: Postsecondary vocational training
- Self-Employed: 0%
- Part-Time: 23.0%

Assist in operations under the supervision of surgeons, registered nurses, or other surgical personnel. May help set up operating room; prepare and transport patients for surgery; adjust lights and equipment; pass instruments and other supplies to surgeons and surgeons' assistants; hold retractors; cut sutures; and help count sponges, needles, supplies, and instruments. Count sponges, needles, and instruments before and after operation. Hand instruments and supplies to surgeons and surgeons' assistants, hold retractors and cut sutures, and perform other tasks as directed by surgeon during operation. Scrub arms and hands and assist the surgical team in scrubbing and putting on gloves, masks, and surgical clothing. Position patients on the operating table and cover them with sterile surgical drapes to prevent exposure. Provide technical assistance to surgeons, surgical nurses, and anesthesiologists. Wash and sterilize equipment, using germicides and sterilizers. Prepare, care for, and dispose of tissue specimens taken for laboratory analysis. Clean and restock the operating room, placing equipment and supplies and arranging instruments according to instruction. Prepare dressings or bandages and apply or assist with their application following surgery. Operate, assemble, adjust, or monitor sterilizers, lights, suction machines, and diagnostic equipment to ensure proper operation. Monitor and continually assess operating room conditions, including patient and surgical team needs. Observe patients' vital signs to assess physical condi-

tion. Maintain supply of fluids, such as plasma, saline, blood, and glucose, for use during operations. Maintain files and records of surgical procedures. **SKILLS**—Instructing; Troubleshooting; Learning Strategies; Equipment Selection; Active Learning; Social Perceptiveness; Reading Comprehension; Coordination.

GOE—Interest Area: 14. Medical and Health Services. **Work Group:** 14.02. Medicine and Surgery. **Other Jobs in This Work Group:** Anesthesiologists; Family and General Practitioners; Healthcare Support Workers, All Other; Internists, General; Medical Assistants; Obstetricians and Gynecologists; Pediatricians, General; Pharmacists; Pharmacy Aides; Pharmacy Technicians; Physician Assistants; Physicians and Surgeons, All Other; Psychiatrists; Registered Nurses; Surgeons.

EDUCATION/TRAINING PROGRAM(S)— Pathology/Pathologist Assistant; Surgical Technology/Technologist. **RELATED KNOWLEDGE/COURSES**—Medicine and Dentistry; Customer and Personal Service; Psychology; Chemistry; Philosophy and Theology; Education and Training.

Technical Directors/Managers

- Personality Code: RA
- Growth: 18.3%
- Annual Job Openings: 10,000
- Annual Earnings: $48,200
- Education/Training Required: Long-term on-the-job training
- Self-Employed: 32.8%
- Part-Time: 9.1%

Coordinate activities of technical departments, such as taping, editing, engineering, and maintenance, to produce radio or television programs. Direct technical aspects of newscasts and other productions, checking and switching between video sources and taking responsibility for the on-air product, including camera shots and graphics. Test equipment in order to ensure proper operation. Monitor broadcasts in order to ensure that programs conform to station or network policies and regulations. Observe pictures through monitors and direct camera and video staff concerning shading and composition. Act as liaison between engineering and production departments. Supervise and assign duties to workers engaged in technical control and production of radio and television programs. Schedule use of studio and editing facilities for producers and engineering and maintenance staff. Confer with operations directors in order to formulate and maintain fair and attainable technical policies for programs. Operate equipment to produce programs or broadcast live programs from remote locations. Train workers in use of equipment such as switchers, cameras, monitors, microphones, and lights. Switch between video sources in a studio or on multi-camera remotes, using equipment such as switchers, video slide projectors, and video effects generators. Set up and execute video transitions and special effects such as fades, dissolves, cuts, keys, and supers, using computers to manipulate pictures as necessary. Collaborate with promotions directors to produce on-air station promotions. Discuss filter options, lens choices, and the visual effects of objects being filmed with photography directors and video operators. Follow instructions from production managers and directors during productions, such as commands for camera cuts, effects, graphics, and takes. **SKILLS**—Time Management; Monitoring; Operation Monitoring; Operation and Control; Coordination; Management of Personnel Resources; Instructing; Troubleshooting.

GOE—Interest Area: 01. Arts, Entertainment, and Media. **Work Group:** 01.01. Managerial Work in Arts, Entertainment, and Media. **Other Jobs in This Work Group:** Agents and Business Managers of Artists, Performers, and Athletes; Art Directors;

Athletes and Sports Competitors; Coaches and Scouts; Entertainers and Performers, Sports and Related Workers, All Other; Fitness Trainers and Aerobics Instructors; Producers; Producers and Directors; Program Directors; Umpires, Referees, and Other Sports Officials.

EDUCATION/TRAINING PROGRAM(S)— Cinematography and Film/Video Production; Directing and Theatrical Production; Drama and Dramatics/Theatre Arts, General; Dramatic/Theatre Arts and Stagecraft, Other; Film/Cinema Studies; Radio and Television; Theatre/Theatre Arts Management. **RELATED KNOWLEDGE/COURSES**—Communications and Media; Computers and Electronics; Telecommunications; Philosophy and Theology; Sales and Marketing; Customer and Personal Service.

Telecommunications Line Installers and Repairers

- Personality Code: R
- Growth: 18.8%
- Annual Job Openings: 13,000
- Annual Earnings: $39,540
- Education/Training Required: Long-term on-the-job training
- Self-Employed: 3.7%
- Part-Time: 1.4%

String and repair telephone and television cable, including fiber optics and other equipment for transmitting messages or television programming. Clean and maintain tools and test equipment. Compute impedance of wires from poles to houses in order to determine additional resistance needed for reducing signals to desired levels. Dig holes for power poles, using power augers or shovels; set poles in place with cranes; and hoist poles upright, using winches. Dig trenches for underground wires and cables. Explain cable service to subscribers after installation and collect any installation fees that are due. Fill and tamp holes, using cement, earth, and tamping devices. Participate in the construction and removal of telecommunication towers and associated support structures. Access specific areas to string lines and install terminal boxes, auxiliary equipment, and appliances, using bucket trucks or by climbing poles and ladders or entering tunnels, trenches, or crawl spaces. Inspect and test lines and cables, recording and analyzing test results to assess transmission characteristics and locate faults and malfunctions. Install equipment such as amplifiers and repeaters in order to maintain the strength of communications transmissions. Lay underground cable directly in trenches or string it through conduits running through trenches. Measure signal strength at utility poles, using electronic test equipment. Place insulation over conductors and seal splices with moisture-proof covering. Pull up cable by hand from large reels mounted on trucks; then pull lines through ducts by hand or with winches. Set up service for customers, installing, connecting, testing, and adjusting equipment. Splice cables, using hand tools, epoxy, or mechanical equipment. String cables between structures and lines from poles, towers, or trenches and pull lines to proper tension. Travel to customers' premises to install, maintain, and repair audio and visual electronic reception equipment and accessories. Use a variety of construction equipment to complete installations, including digger derricks, trenchers, and cable plows. **SKILLS**—Installation; Repairing; Troubleshooting; Equipment Maintenance; Operation Monitoring; Systems Evaluation; Mathematics; Operation and Control.

GOE—**Interest Area:** 05. Mechanics, Installers, and Repairers. **Work Group:** 05.02. Electrical and Electronic Systems. **Other Jobs in This Work Group:** Avionics Technicians; Battery Repairers; Central Office and PBX Installers and Repairers; Commu-

nication Equipment Mechanics, Installers, and Repairers; Computer, Automated Teller, and Office Machine Repairers; Data Processing Equipment Repairers; Electric Home Appliance and Power Tool Repairers; Electric Meter Installers and Repairers; Electric Motor and Switch Assemblers and Repairers; Electric Motor, Power Tool, and Related Repairers; Electrical and Electronics Installers and Repairers, Transportation Equipment; Electrical and Electronics Repairers, Commercial and Industrial Equipment; Electrical and Electronics Repairers, Powerhouse, Substation, and Relay; Electrical Parts Reconditioners; Electrical Power-Line Installers and Repairers; Electronic Equipment Installers and Repairers, Motor Vehicles; Electronic Home Entertainment Equipment Installers and Repairers; Elevator Installers and Repairers; Frame Wirers, Central Office; Home Appliance Installers; Home Appliance Repairers; Installation, Maintenance, and Repair Workers, All Other; Office Machine and Cash Register Servicers; Radio Mechanics; Signal and Track Switch Repairers; Station Installers and Repairers, Telephone; Telecommunications Equipment Installers and Repairers, Except Line Installers; Telecommunications Facility Examiners; Transformer Repairers.

EDUCATION/TRAINING PROGRAM(S)—Communications Systems Installation and Repair Technology. **RELATED KNOWLEDGE/COURSES**—Telecommunications; Computers and Electronics; Mechanical Devices; Physics; Sales and Marketing; Engineering and Technology.

Tractor-Trailer Truck Drivers

- Personality Code: RC
- Growth: 19.0%
- Annual Job Openings: 299,000
- Annual Earnings: $33,310
- Education/Training Required: Moderate-term on-the-job training
- Self-Employed: 13.1%
- Part-Time: 7.7%

Drive tractor-trailer truck to transport products, livestock, or materials to specified destinations. Drives tractor-trailer combination, applying knowledge of commercial driving regulations, to transport and deliver products, livestock, or materials, usually over long distance. Maneuvers truck into loading or unloading position, following signals from loading crew as needed. Drives truck to weigh station before and after loading and along route to document weight and conform to state regulations. Maintains driver log according to I.C.C. regulations. Inspects truck before and after trips and submits report indicating truck condition. Reads bill of lading to determine assignment. Fastens chain or binders to secure load on trailer during transit. Loads or unloads or assists in loading and unloading truck. Works as member of two-person team driving tractor with sleeper bunk behind cab. Services truck with oil, fuel, and radiator fluid to maintain tractor-trailer. Obtains customer's signature or collects payment for services. Inventories and inspects goods to be moved. Wraps goods, using pads, packing paper, and containers, and secures load to trailer wall, using straps. Gives directions to helper in packing and moving goods to trailer. **SKILLS**—Operation and Control; Equipment Maintenance; Repairing; Troubleshooting; Management of Material Resources; Operation Monitoring.

GOE—Interest Area: 07. Transportation. **Work Group:** 07.05. Truck Driving. **Other Jobs in This Work Group:** Truck Drivers, Heavy; Truck Drivers, Heavy and Tractor-Trailer; Truck Drivers, Light or Delivery Services.

EDUCATION/TRAINING PROGRAM(S)—Truck and Bus Driver/Commercial Vehicle Operation. **RELATED KNOWLEDGE/COURSES**—Transportation; Geography; Mechanical Devices; Law and Government; Public Safety and Security; Telecommunications.

Truck Drivers, Heavy

- Personality Code: R
- Growth: 19.0%
- Annual Job Openings: 299,000
- Annual Earnings: $33,310
- Education/Training Required: Short-term on-the-job training
- Self-Employed: 13.1%
- Part-Time: 7.7%

Drive truck with capacity of more than three tons to transport materials to specified destinations. Drives truck with capacity of more than three tons to transport and deliver cargo, materials, or damaged vehicle. Maintains radio or telephone contact with base or supervisor to receive instructions or be dispatched to new location. Maintains truck log according to state and federal regulations. Keeps record of materials and products transported. Position blocks and ties rope around items to secure cargo for transport. Cleans, inspects, and services vehicle. Operates equipment on vehicle to load, unload, or disperse cargo or materials. Obtains customer signature or collects payment for goods delivered and delivery charges. Assists in loading and unloading truck manually. **SKILLS**—Equipment Maintenance; Repairing; Operation Monitoring;

Operation and Control; Management of Financial Resources.

GOE—Interest Area: 07. Transportation. **Work Group:** 07.05. Truck Driving. **Other Jobs in This Work Group:** Tractor-Trailer Truck Drivers; Truck Drivers, Heavy and Tractor-Trailer; Truck Drivers, Light or Delivery Services.

EDUCATION/TRAINING PROGRAM(S)— Truck and Bus Driver/Commercial Vehicle Operation. **RELATED KNOWLEDGE/COURSES** —Transportation; Geography; Telecommunications; Mechanical Devices; Public Safety and Security; Law and Government.

Welder-Fitters

- Personality Code: RI
- Growth: 17.0%
- Annual Job Openings: 71,000
- Annual Earnings: $29,640
- Education/Training Required: Long-term on-the-job training
- Self-Employed: 5.6%
- Part-Time: 2.1%

Lay out, fit, and fabricate metal components to assemble structural forms, such as machinery frames, bridge parts, and pressure vessels, using knowledge of welding techniques, metallurgy, and engineering requirements. Includes experimental welders who analyze engineering drawings and specifications to plan welding operations where procedural information is unavailable. Lays out, positions, and secures parts and assemblies according to specifications, using straightedge, combination square, calipers, and ruler. Tack-welds or welds components and assemblies, using electric, gas, arc, or other welding equipment. Cuts workpiece, using powered saws, hand shears, or chipping knife. Melts

lead bar, wire, or scrap to add lead to joint or to extrude melted scrap into reusable form. Installs or repairs equipment, such as lead pipes, valves, floors, and tank linings. Observes tests on welded surfaces, such as hydrostatic, X-ray, and dimension tolerance, to evaluate weld quality and conformance to specifications. Inspects grooves, angles, or gap allowances, using micrometer, caliper, and precision measuring instruments. Removes rough spots from workpiece, using portable grinder, hand file, or scraper. Welds components in flat, vertical, or overhead positions. Heats, forms, and dresses metal parts, using hand tools, torch, or arc welding equipment. Ignites torch and adjusts valves, amperage, or voltage to obtain desired flame or arc. Analyzes engineering drawings and specifications to plan layout, assembly, and welding operations. Develops templates and other work aids to hold and align parts. Determines required equipment and welding method, applying knowledge of metallurgy, geometry, and welding techniques. **SKILLS—**Repairing; Installation; Equipment Maintenance; Equipment Selection; Quality Control Analysis; Mathematics; Operation Monitoring; Science.

GOE—Interest Area: 08. Industrial Production. **Work Group:** 08.03. Production Work. **Other Jobs in This Work Group:** Assemblers and Fabricators, All Other; Bakers, Manufacturing; Bindery Machine Operators and Tenders; Brazers; Cementing and Gluing Machine Operators and Tenders; Chemical Equipment Controllers and Operators; Chemical Equipment Operators and Tenders; Chemical Equipment Tenders; Cleaning, Washing, and Metal Pickling Equipment Operators and Tenders; Coating, Painting, and Spraying Machine Operators and Tenders; Coil Winders, Tapers, and Finishers; Combination Machine Tool Operators and Tenders, Metal and Plastic; Computer-Controlled Machine Tool Operators, Metal and Plastic; Cooling and Freezing Equipment Operators and Tenders; Crushing, Grinding, and Polishing Machine Setters, Operators, and Tenders; Cutters and Trimmers, Hand; Cutting and Slicing Machine

Operators and Tenders; Cutting and Slicing Machine Setters, Operators, and Tenders; Design Printing Machine Setters and Set-Up Operators; Electrolytic Plating and Coating Machine Operators and Tenders, Metal and Plastic; Electrolytic Plating and Coating Machine Setters and Set-Up Operators, Metal and Plastic; Electrotypers and Stereotypers; Embossing Machine Set-Up Operators; Engraver Set-Up Operators; Extruding and Forming Machine Operators and Tenders, Synthetic or Glass Fibers; Extruding and Forming Machine Setters, Operators, and Tenders, Synthetic and Glass Fibers; Extruding, Forming, Pressing, and Compacting Machine Operators and Tenders; Fabric and Apparel Patternmakers; Fiber Product Cutting Machine Setters and Set-Up Operators; Fiberglass Laminators and Fabricators; Film Laboratory Technicians; Fitters, Structural Metal—Precision; Food and Tobacco Roasting, Baking, and Drying Machine Operators and Tenders; Food Batchmakers; Food Cooking Machine Operators and Tenders; Furnace, Kiln, Oven, Drier, and Kettle Operators and Tenders; Glass Cutting Machine Setters and Set-Up Operators; Graders and Sorters, Agricultural Products; Grinding and Polishing Workers, Hand; Hand Compositors and Typesetters; Heaters, Metal and Plastic; Helpers—Production Workers; Job Printers; Letterpress Setters and Set-Up Operators; Marking and Identification Printing Machine Setters and Set-Up Operators; Meat, Poultry, and Fish Cutters and Trimmers; Metal Fabricators, Structural Metal Products; Metal-Refining Furnace Operators and Tenders; Mixing and Blending Machine Setters, Operators, and Tenders; Mold Makers, Hand; Molding and Casting Workers; Nonelectrolytic Plating and Coating Machine Operators and Tenders, Metal and Plastic; Nonelectrolytic Plating and Coating Machine Setters and Set-Up Operators, Metal and Plastic; Numerical Control Machine Tool Operators and Tenders, Metal and Plastic; Offset Lithographic Press Setters and Set-Up Operators; Packaging and Filling Machine Operators and Tenders; Painting, Coating, and Decorating Workers; Photoengraving and Lithographing Machine Operators and Tenders; Photographic Hand Developers; Photographic Process Workers; Photographic Processing Machine Operators; Photographic Reproduction Technicians; Photographic Retouchers and Restorers; Plate Finishers; Platemakers; Plating and Coating Machine Setters, Operators, and Tenders, Metal and Plastic; Pourers and Casters, Metal; Precision Printing Workers; Prepress Technicians and Workers; Pressing Machine Operators and Tenders—Textile, Garment, and Related Materials; Printing Machine Operators; Printing Press Machine Operators and Tenders; Production Helpers; Production Laborers; Production Workers, All Other; Sawing Machine Operators and Tenders; Sawing Machine Setters and Set-Up Operators; Sawing Machine Setters, Operators, and Tenders, Wood; Scanner Operators; Semiconductor Processors; Separating, Filtering, Clarifying, Precipitating, and Still Machine Setters, Operators, and Tenders; Sewers, Hand; Sewing Machine Operators; Sewing Machine Operators, Garment; Sewing Machine Operators, Non-Garment; Shoe Machine Operators and Tenders; Slaughterers and Meat Packers; Solderers; Soldering and Brazing Machine Operators and Tenders; Stone Sawyers; Strippers; Structural Metal Fabricators and Fitters; Team Assemblers; Textile Bleaching and Dyeing Machine Operators and Tenders; Tire Builders; Welders and Cutters; Welders, Cutters, Solderers, and Brazers; Welders, Production; Welding Machine Operators and Tenders; Woodworking Machine Operators and Tenders, Except Sawing.

EDUCATION/TRAINING PROGRAM(S)— Welding Technology/Welder. **RELATED KNOWLEDGE/COURSES—**Design; Building and Construction; Mechanical Devices; Production and Processing; Engineering and Technology; Physics.

Welders and Cutters

- Personality Code: RC
- Growth: 17.0%
- Annual Job Openings: 71,000
- Annual Earnings: $29,640
- Education/Training Required: Long-term on-the-job training
- Self-Employed: 5.6%
- Part-Time: 2.1%

Use hand welding and flame-cutting equipment to weld together metal components and parts or to cut, trim, or scarf metal objects to dimensions as specified by layouts, work orders, or blueprints. Connects and turns regulator valves to activate and adjust gas flow and pressure to obtain desired flame. Selects and installs torch, torch tip, filler rod, and flux, according to welding chart specifications or type and thickness of metal. Guides electrodes or torch along weld line at specified speed and angle to weld, melt, cut, or trim metal. Welds metal parts or components together, using brazing, gas, or arc welding equipment. Repairs broken or cracked parts, fills holes, and increases size of metal parts, using welding equipment. Welds in flat, horizontal, vertical, or overhead position. Cleans or degreases parts, using wire brush, portable grinder, or chemical bath. Inspects finished workpiece for conformance to specifications. Chips or grinds off excess weld, slag, or spatter, using hand scraper or power chipper, portable grinder, or arc-cutting equipment. Positions workpieces and clamps together or assembles in jigs or fixtures. Preheats workpiece, using hand torch or heating furnace. Ignites torch or starts power supply and strikes arc. Reviews layouts, blueprints, diagrams, or work orders in preparation for welding or cutting metal components. Selects and inserts electrode or gas nozzle into holder and connects hoses and cables to obtain gas or specified amperage, voltage, or polarity. **SKILLS**—Operation Monitoring; Repairing; Equipment Maintenance; Operation and Control; Installation; Quality Control Analysis; Mathematics; Equipment Selection.

GOE—Interest Area: 08. Industrial Production. **Work Group:** 08.03. Production Work. **Other Jobs in This Work Group:** Assemblers and Fabricators, All Other; Bakers, Manufacturing; Bindery Machine Operators and Tenders; Brazers; Cementing and Gluing Machine Operators and Tenders; Chemical Equipment Controllers and Operators; Chemical Equipment Operators and Tenders; Chemical Equipment Tenders; Cleaning, Washing, and Metal Pickling Equipment Operators and Tenders; Coating, Painting, and Spraying Machine Operators and Tenders; Coil Winders, Tapers, and Finishers; Combination Machine Tool Operators and Tenders, Metal and Plastic; Computer-Controlled Machine Tool Operators, Metal and Plastic; Cooling and Freezing Equipment Operators and Tenders; Crushing, Grinding, and Polishing Machine Setters, Operators, and Tenders; Cutters and Trimmers, Hand; Cutting and Slicing Machine Operators and Tenders; Cutting and Slicing Machine Setters, Operators, and Tenders; Design Printing Machine Setters and Set-Up Operators; Electrolytic Plating and Coating Machine Operators and Tenders, Metal and Plastic; Electrolytic Plating and Coating Machine Setters and Set-Up Operators, Metal and Plastic; Electrotypers and Stereotypers; Embossing Machine Set-Up Operators; Engraver Set-Up Operators; Extruding and Forming Machine Operators and Tenders, Synthetic or Glass Fibers; Extruding and Forming Machine Setters, Operators, and Tenders, Synthetic and Glass Fibers; Extruding, Forming, Pressing, and Compacting Machine Operators and Tenders; Fabric and Apparel Patternmakers; Fiber Product Cutting Machine Setters and Set-Up Operators; Fiberglass Laminators and Fabricators; Film Laboratory Technicians; Fitters, Structural Metal—Precision; Food and Tobacco Roasting, Baking, and Drying Machine Operators and Tenders; Food Batchmakers; Food Cooking Machine Operators and Tenders; Furnace, Kiln, Oven, Drier, and Kettle Operators and Tenders; Glass Cutting Machine Setters and

Set-Up Operators; Graders and Sorters, Agricultural Products; Grinding and Polishing Workers, Hand; Hand Compositors and Typesetters; Heaters, Metal and Plastic; Helpers—Production Workers; Job Printers; Letterpress Setters and Set-Up Operators; Marking and Identification Printing Machine Setters and Set-Up Operators; Meat, Poultry, and Fish Cutters and Trimmers; Metal Fabricators, Structural Metal Products; Metal-Refining Furnace Operators and Tenders; Mixing and Blending Machine Setters, Operators, and Tenders; Mold Makers, Hand; Molding and Casting Workers; Nonelectrolytic Plating and Coating Machine Operators and Tenders, Metal and Plastic; Nonelectrolytic Plating and Coating Machine Setters and Set-Up Operators, Metal and Plastic; Numerical Control Machine Tool Operators and Tenders, Metal and Plastic; Offset Lithographic Press Setters and Set-Up Operators; Packaging and Filling Machine Operators and Tenders; Painting, Coating, and Decorating Workers; Photoengraving and Lithographing Machine Operators and Tenders; Photographic Hand Developers; Photographic Process Workers; Photographic Processing Machine Operators; Photographic Reproduction Technicians; Photographic Retouchers and Restorers; Plate Finishers; Platemakers; Plating and Coating Machine Setters, Operators, and Tenders, Metal and Plastic; Pourers and Casters, Metal; Precision Printing Workers; Prepress Technicians and Workers; Pressing Machine Operators and Tenders—Textile, Garment, and Related Materials; Printing Machine Operators; Printing Press Machine Operators and Tenders; Production Helpers; Production Laborers; Production Workers, All Other; Sawing Machine Operators and Tenders; Sawing Machine Setters and Set-Up Operators; Sawing Machine Setters, Operators, and Tenders, Wood; Scanner Operators; Semiconductor Processors; Separating, Filtering, Clarifying, Precipitating, and Still Machine Setters, Operators, and Tenders; Sewers, Hand; Sewing Machine Operators; Sewing Machine Operators, Garment; Sewing Machine Operators, Non-Garment; Shoe Machine Operators and Tenders; Slaughterers and Meat Packers; Solderers; Soldering and Brazing Machine Operators and Tenders; Stone Sawyers; Strippers; Structural Metal Fabricators and Fitters; Team Assemblers; Textile Bleaching and Dyeing Machine Operators and Tenders; Tire Builders; Welder-Fitters; Welders, Cutters, Solderers, and Brazers; Welders, Production; Welding Machine Operators and Tenders; Woodworking Machine Operators and Tenders, Except Sawing.

EDUCATION/TRAINING PROGRAM(S)— Welding Technology/Welder. RELATED KNOWLEDGE/COURSES—Building and Construction; Mechanical Devices; Design; Production and Processing; Physics; Chemistry.

Welders, Production

- Personality Code: R
- Growth: 17.0%
- Annual Job Openings: 71,000
- Annual Earnings: $29,640
- Education/Training Required: Short-term on-the-job training
- Self-Employed: 5.6%
- Part-Time: 2.1%

Assemble and weld metal parts on production line, using welding equipment requiring only a limited knowledge of welding techniques. Welds or tack welds metal parts together, using spot welding gun or hand, electric, or gas welding equipment. Connects hoses from torch to tanks of oxygen and fuel gas and turns valves to release mixture. Ignites torch and regulates flow of gas and air to obtain desired temperature, size, and color of flame. Preheats workpieces preparatory to welding or bending, using torch. Fills cavities or corrects malformation in lead parts and hammers out bulges and bends in metal workpieces. Examines workpiece for defects and measures workpiece with straightedge or template to ensure conformance with specifications. Climbs ladders or works on scaffolds to disassemble structures. Signals crane operator to move large workpieces. Dismantles metal assemblies or cuts scrap metal, using thermal-cutting equipment such as flame-cutting torch or plasma-arc equipment. Positions and secures workpiece, using hoist, crane, wire and banding machine, or hand tools. Selects, positions, and secures torch, cutting tips, or welding rod according to type, thickness, area, and desired temperature of metal. Guides and directs flame or electrodes on or across workpiece to straighten, bend, melt, or build up metal. Fuses parts together, seals tension points, and adds metal to build up parts. **SKILLS**—Operation Monitoring; Equipment Maintenance; Operation and Control; Troubleshooting; Repairing; Installation; Quality Control Analysis; Equipment Selection.

GOE—Interest Area: 08. Industrial Production. **Work Group:** 08.03. Production Work. **Other Jobs in This Work Group:** Assemblers and Fabricators, All Other; Bakers, Manufacturing; Bindery Machine Operators and Tenders; Brazers; Cementing and Gluing Machine Operators and Tenders; Chemical Equipment Controllers and Operators; Chemical Equipment Operators and Tenders; Chemical Equipment Tenders; Cleaning, Washing, and Metal Pickling Equipment Operators and Tenders; Coating, Painting, and Spraying Machine Operators and Tenders; Coil Winders, Tapers, and Finishers; Combination Machine Tool Operators and Tenders, Metal and Plastic; Computer-Controlled Machine Tool Operators, Metal and Plastic; Cooling and Freezing Equipment Operators and Tenders; Crushing, Grinding, and Polishing Machine Setters, Operators, and Tenders; Cutters and Trimmers, Hand; Cutting and Slicing Machine Operators and Tenders; Cutting and Slicing Machine Setters, Operators, and Tenders; Design Printing Machine Setters and Set-Up Operators; Electrolytic Plating and Coating Machine Operators and Tenders, Metal and Plastic; Electrolytic Plating and Coating Machine Setters and Set-Up Operators, Metal and Plastic; Electrotypers and Stereotypers; Embossing Machine Set-Up Operators; Engraver Set-Up Operators; Extruding and Forming Machine Operators and Tenders, Synthetic or Glass Fibers; Extruding and Forming Machine Setters, Operators, and Tenders, Synthetic and Glass Fibers; Extruding, Forming, Pressing, and Compacting Machine Operators and Tenders; Fabric and Apparel Patternmakers; Fiber Product Cutting Machine Setters and Set-Up Operators; Fiberglass Laminators and Fabricators; Film Laboratory Technicians; Fitters, Structural Metal—Precision; Food and Tobacco Roasting, Baking, and Drying Machine Operators and Tenders; Food Batchmakers; Food Cooking Machine Operators and Tenders; Furnace, Kiln, Oven, Drier, and Kettle Operators and Tenders; Glass Cutting Machine Setters and Set-Up Operators; Graders and Sorters, Agricultural Products; Grinding and Polishing Workers, Hand; Hand Compositors and Typesetters; Heaters, Metal and Plastic; Helpers—Production Workers; Job Printers; Letterpress Setters and Set-Up Operators; Marking and Identification Printing Machine Setters and Set-Up Operators; Meat, Poultry, and Fish Cutters and Trimmers; Metal Fabricators, Structural Metal Products; Metal-Refining Furnace Operators and Tenders; Mixing and Blending Machine Setters, Operators, and Tenders; Mold Makers, Hand; Molding and Casting Workers; Nonelectrolytic Plating and Coating Machine Operators and Tenders, Metal and Plastic; Nonelectrolytic Plating and Coating Machine Setters and Set-Up Operators, Metal and Plastic; Numerical Control Machine Tool Operators and Tenders, Metal and Plastic; Offset Lithographic Press Setters and Set-Up Operators; Packaging and Filling Machine Operators and Tenders; Painting, Coating, and Decorating Workers; Photoengraving and Lithographing Machine Operators and Tenders; Photographic Hand Developers; Photographic Process Workers; Photographic Processing Machine Operators; Photographic Reproduction Technicians; Photographic Retouchers and Restorers; Plate Finishers; Platemakers; Plating and Coating Machine Setters, Operators, and Tenders, Metal and Plastic; Pourers and Casters, Metal; Precision Printing Workers; Prepress Technicians and Workers; Pressing Machine Operators and Tenders—Textile, Garment, and

Related Materials; Printing Machine Operators; Printing Press Machine Operators and Tenders; Production Helpers; Production Laborers; Production Workers, All Other; Sawing Machine Operators and Tenders; Sawing Machine Setters and Set-Up Operators; Sawing Machine Setters, Operators, and Tenders, Wood; Scanner Operators; Semiconductor Processors; Separating, Filtering, Clarifying, Precipitating, and Still Machine Setters, Operators, and Tenders; Sewers, Hand; Sewing Machine Operators; Sewing Machine Operators, Garment; Sewing Machine Operators, Non-Garment; Shoe Machine Operators and Tenders; Slaughterers and Meat Packers; Solderers; Soldering and Brazing Machine Operators and Tenders; Stone Sawyers; Strippers; Structural Metal Fabricators and Fitters; Team Assemblers; Textile Bleaching and Dyeing Machine Operators and Tenders; Tire Builders; Welder-Fitters; Welders and Cutters; Welders, Cutters, Solderers, and Brazers; Welding Machine Operators and Tenders; Woodworking Machine Operators and Tenders, Except Sawing.

EDUCATION/TRAINING PROGRAM(S)— Welding Technology/Welder. **RELATED KNOWLEDGE/COURSES—**Mechanical Devices; Production and Processing; Building and Construction; Physics.

Investigative Jobs

Agricultural Sciences Teachers, Postsecondary

- Personality Code: IS
- Growth: 38.1%
- Annual Job Openings: 216,000
- Annual Earnings: $65,470
- Education/Training Required: Master's degree
- Self-Employed: 0.3%
- Part-Time: 27.7%

Teach courses in the agricultural sciences. Includes teachers of agronomy, dairy sciences, fisheries management, horticultural sciences, poultry sciences, range management, and agricultural soil conservation. Evaluate and grade students' class work, laboratory work, assignments, and papers. Prepare and deliver lectures to undergraduate and/or graduate students on topics such as crop production, plant genetics, and soil chemistry. Advise students on academic and vocational curricula and on career issues. Compile, administer, and grade examinations or assign this work to others. Compile bibliographies of specialized materials for outside reading assignments. Initiate, facilitate, and moderate classroom discussions. Keep abreast of developments in their field by reading current literature, talking with colleagues, and participating in professional conferences. Maintain regularly scheduled office hours in order to advise and assist students. Maintain student attendance records, grades, and other required records. Plan, evaluate, and revise curricula, course content, and course materials and methods of instruction. Prepare course materials such as syllabi, homework assignments, and handouts. Select and obtain materials and supplies such as textbooks and laboratory equipment. Supervise laboratory sessions and field work and coordinate laboratory operations. Supervise undergraduate and/or graduate teaching, internship, and research work. Act as advisers to student organizations. Collaborate with colleagues to address teaching and research issues. Conduct research in a particular field of knowledge and publish findings in professional journals, books, and/or electronic media. Participate in campus and community events. Participate in student recruitment, registration, and placement activities. Perform administrative duties such as serving as department head. Provide professional consulting services to government and/or industry. Serve on academic or administrative committees that deal with institutional policies, departmental matters, and academic issues. Write grant proposals to procure external research funding. **SKILLS**—Science; Instructing; Learning Strategies; Reading Comprehension; Active Learning; Writing; Critical Thinking; Mathematics.

GOE—Interest Area: 12. Education and Social Service. Work Group: 12.03. Educational Services. Other Jobs in This Work Group: Adult Literacy, Remedial Education, and GED Teachers and Instructors; Anthropology and Archeology Teachers, Postsecondary; Architecture Teachers, Postsecondary; Archivists; Area, Ethnic, and Cultural Studies Teachers, Postsecondary; Art, Drama, and Music Teachers, Postsecondary; Atmospheric, Earth, Marine, and Space Sciences Teachers, Postsecondary; Audio-Visual Collections Specialists; Biological Science Teachers, Postsecondary; Business Teachers, Postsecondary; Chemistry Teachers, Postsecondary; Child Care Workers; Communications Teachers, Postsecondary; Computer Science Teachers, Postsecondary; Criminal Justice and Law Enforcement Teachers, Postsecondary; Curators; Economics Teachers, Postsecondary; Education Teachers, Postsecondary; Education, Training, and Library Workers, All Other; Educational Psychologists; Educational, Vocational, and School Counselors; Elementary School Teachers, Except Special

Education; Engineering Teachers, Postsecondary; English Language and Literature Teachers, Postsecondary; Environmental Science Teachers, Postsecondary; Farm and Home Management Advisors; Foreign Language and Literature Teachers, Postsecondary; Forestry and Conservation Science Teachers, Postsecondary; Geography Teachers, Postsecondary; Graduate Teaching Assistants; Health Specialties Teachers, Postsecondary; History Teachers, Postsecondary; Home Economics Teachers, Postsecondary; Kindergarten Teachers, Except Special Education; Law Teachers, Postsecondary; Librarians; Library Assistants, Clerical; Library Science Teachers, Postsecondary; Library Technicians; Mathematical Science Teachers, Postsecondary; Middle School Teachers, Except Special and Vocational Education; Museum Technicians and Conservators; Nannies; Nursing Instructors and Teachers, Postsecondary; Personal Financial Advisors; Philosophy and Religion Teachers, Postsecondary; Physics Teachers, Postsecondary; Political Science Teachers, Postsecondary; Postsecondary Teachers, All Other; Preschool Teachers, Except Special Education; Psychology Teachers, Postsecondary; Recreation and Fitness Studies Teachers, Postsecondary; Secondary School Teachers, Except Special and Vocational Education; Self-Enrichment Education Teachers; Social Sciences Teachers, Postsecondary, All Other; Social Work Teachers, Postsecondary; Sociology Teachers, Postsecondary; Special Education Teachers, Middle School; Special Education Teachers, Preschool, Kindergarten, and Elementary School; Special Education Teachers, Secondary School; Teacher Assistants; Teachers and Instructors, All Other; Vocational Education Teachers, Postsecondary; Vocational Education Teachers, Middle School; Vocational Education Teachers, Secondary School.

EDUCATION/TRAINING PROGRAM(S)— Agribusiness/Agricultural Business Operations; Agricultural and Domestic Animal Services, Other; Agricultural and Food Products Processing; Agricultural and Horticultural Plant Breeding; Agricultural Animal Breeding; Agricultural Business and Management, General; Agricultural Business and Management, Other; Agricultural Economics; Agricultural Mechanization, General; Agricultural Mechanization, Other; Agricultural Power Machinery Operation; Agricultural Production Operations, General; Agricultural Production Operations, Other; Agricultural Teacher Education; Agricultural/Farm Supplies Retailing and Wholesaling; Agriculture, Agriculture Operations, and Related Sciences, Other; Agriculture, General; Agronomy and Crop Science; Animal Health; Animal Nutrition; Animal Sciences, General; Animal Sciences, Other; Animal Training; Animal/Livestock Husbandry and Production; Applied Horticulture/Horticultural Business Services, Other; Applied Horticulture/Horticultural Operations, General; Aquaculture; Crop Production; Dairy Science; Equestrian/Equine Studies; Farm/Farm and Ranch Management; Food Science; Greenhouse Operations and Management; Horticultural Science; International Agriculture; Landscaping and Groundskeeping; Livestock Management; Ornamental Horticulture; Plant Nursery Operations and Management; Plant Protection and Integrated Pest Management; Plant Sciences, General; Plant Sciences, Other; Poultry Science; Range Science and Management; Soil Science and Agronomy, General; Turf and Turfgrass Management. **RELATED KNOWLEDGE/COURSES**—Biology; Education and Training; Medicine and Dentistry; Chemistry; Therapy and Counseling; Psychology.

Anesthesiologists

- Personality Code: IR
- Growth: 19.5%
- Annual Job Openings: 38,000
- Annual Earnings: more than $145,600
- Education/Training Required: First professional degree
- Self-Employed: 16.9%
- Part-Time: 8.1%

Administer anesthetics during surgery or other medical procedures. Administer anesthetic or sedation during medical procedures, using local, intravenous, spinal, or caudal methods. Confer with other medical professionals to determine type and method of anesthetic or sedation to render patient insensible to pain. Coordinate administration of anesthetics with surgeons during operation. Decide when patients have recovered or stabilized enough to be sent to another room or ward or to be sent home following outpatient surgery. Examine patient, obtain medical history, and use diagnostic tests to determine risk during surgical, obstetrical, and other medical procedures. Monitor patient before, during, and after anesthesia and counteract adverse reactions or complications. Record type and amount of anesthesia and patient condition throughout procedure. Conduct medical research to aid in controlling and curing disease, to investigate new medications, and to develop and test new medical techniques. Coordinate and direct work of nurses, medical technicians, and other health care providers. Diagnose illnesses, using examinations, tests, and reports. Inform students and staff of types and methods of anesthesia administration, signs of complications, and emergency methods to counteract reactions. Manage anesthesiological services, coordinating them with other medical activities and formulating plans and procedures. Order laboratory tests, X rays, and other diagnostic procedures. Position patient on operating table to maximize patient comfort and surgical accessibility. Provide and maintain life support and airway management and help prepare patients for emergency surgery. Provide medical care and consultation in many settings, prescribing medication and treatment and referring patients for surgery. Instruct individuals and groups on ways to preserve health and prevent disease. Schedule and maintain use of surgical suite, including operating, wash-up, waiting rooms, and anesthetic and sterilizing equipment. **SKILLS** —Operation Monitoring; Judgment and Decision Making; Reading Comprehension; Instructing; Critical Thinking; Coordination; Systems Evaluation; Active Learning; Monitoring.

GOE—Interest Area: 14. Medical and Health Services. **Work Group:** 14.02. Medicine and Surgery. **Other Jobs in This Work Group:** Family and General Practitioners; Healthcare Support Workers, All Other; Internists, General; Medical Assistants; Obstetricians and Gynecologists; Pediatricians, General; Pharmacists; Pharmacy Aides; Pharmacy Technicians; Physician Assistants; Physicians and Surgeons, All Other; Psychiatrists; Registered Nurses; Surgeons; Surgical Technologists.

EDUCATION/TRAINING PROGRAM(S)— Anesthesiology; Critical Care Anesthesiology. **RELATED KNOWLEDGE/COURSES—**Medicine and Dentistry; Biology; Chemistry; English Language; Mathematics; Physics.

Biochemists

- Personality Code: IR
- Growth: 22.9%
- Annual Job Openings: 2,000
- Annual Earnings: $62,300
- Education/Training Required: Doctoral degree
- Self-Employed: 2.6%
- Part-Time: 7.1%

Research or study chemical composition and processes of living organisms that affect vital processes such as growth and aging to determine chemical actions and effects on organisms, such as the action of foods, drugs, or other substances on body functions and tissues. Studies chemistry of living processes, such as cell development, breathing, and digestion, and living energy changes, such as growth, aging, and death. Researches methods of transferring characteristics, such as resistance to disease, from one organism to another. Examines chemical aspects of formation of antibodies and researches chemistry of cells and blood corpuscles. Develops and executes tests to detect disease, genetic disorders, or other abnormalities. Develops and tests new drugs and medications used for commercial distribution. Designs and builds laboratory equipment needed for special research projects. Analyzes foods to determine nutritional value and effects of cooking, canning, and processing on this value. Cleans, purifies, refines, and otherwise prepares pharmaceutical compounds for commercial distribution. Prepares reports and recommendations based upon research outcomes. Develops methods to process, store, and use food, drugs, and chemical compounds. Isolates, analyzes, and identifies hormones, vitamins, allergens, minerals, and enzymes and determines their effects on body functions. Researches and determines chemical action of substances such as drugs, serums, hormones, and food on tissues and vital processes. **SKILLS**—Science; Writing; Reading Comprehension; Active Learning; Programming; Critical Thinking; Mathematics; Equipment Selection.

GOE—**Interest Area:** 02. Science, Math, and Engineering. **Work Group:** 02.03. Life Sciences. **Other Jobs in This Work Group:** Agricultural and Food Science Technicians; Agricultural Technicians; Animal Scientists; Biochemists and Biophysicists; Biological Scientists, All Other; Biologists; Biophysicists; Conservation Scientists; Environmental Scientists and Specialists, Including Health; Epidemiologists; Food Science Technicians; Food Scientists and Technologists; Foresters; Life Scientists, All Other; Medical Scientists, Except Epidemiologists; Microbiologists; Plant Scientists; Range Managers; Soil and Plant Scientists; Soil Conservationists; Soil Scientists; Zoologists and Wildlife Biologists.

EDUCATION/TRAINING PROGRAM(S)— Biochemistry; Biochemistry/Biophysics and Molecular Biology; Biophysics; Cell/Cellular Biology and Anatomical Sciences, Other; Molecular Biochemistry; Molecular Biophysics; Soil Chemistry and Physics; Soil Microbiology. **RELATED KNOWLEDGE/COURSES**—Biology; Chemistry; Mathematics; Building and Construction; Engineering and Technology; English Language.

Biological Science Teachers, Postsecondary

- Personality Code: IS
- Growth: 38.1%
- Annual Job Openings: 216,000
- Annual Earnings: $55,840
- Education/Training Required: Master's degree
- Self-Employed: 0.3%
- Part-Time: 27.7%

Teach courses in biological sciences. Evaluate and grade students' class work, laboratory work, assignments, and papers. Prepare and deliver lectures to undergraduate and/or graduate students on topics such as molecular biology, marine biology, and botany. Advise students on academic and vocational curricula and on career issues. Compile, administer, and grade examinations or assign this work to others. Compile bibliographies of specialized materials for outside reading assignments. Initiate, facilitate, and moderate classroom discussions. Keep abreast of developments in their field by reading current literature, talking with colleagues, and participating in professional conferences. Maintain regularly scheduled office hours in order to advise and assist students. Maintain student attendance records, grades, and other required records. Plan, evaluate, and revise curricula, course content, and course materials and methods of instruction. Prepare course materials such as syllabi, homework assignments, and handouts. Select and obtain materials and supplies such as textbooks and laboratory equipment. Supervise students' laboratory work. Supervise undergraduate and/or graduate teaching, internship, and research work. Act as advisers to student organizations. Collaborate with colleagues to address teaching and research issues. Conduct research in a particular field of knowledge and publish findings in professional journals, books, and/or electronic media. Participate in campus and community events. Participate in student recruitment, registration, and placement activities. Perform administrative duties such as serving as department head. Provide professional consulting services to government and/or industry. Serve on academic or administrative committees that deal with institutional policies, departmental matters, and academic issues. Write grant proposals to procure external research funding. **SKILLS**—Science; Instructing; Learning Strategies; Reading Comprehension; Active Learning; Writing; Critical Thinking; Mathematics.

GOE—Interest Area: 12. Education and Social Service. **Work Group:** 12.03. Educational Services. **Other Jobs in This Work Group:** Adult Literacy, Remedial Education, and GED Teachers and Instructors; Agricultural Sciences Teachers, Postsecondary; Anthropology and Archeology Teachers, Postsecondary; Architecture Teachers, Postsecondary; Archivists; Area, Ethnic, and Cultural Studies Teachers, Postsecondary; Art, Drama, and Music Teachers, Postsecondary; Atmospheric, Earth, Marine, and Space Sciences Teachers, Postsecondary; Audio-Visual Collections Specialists; Business Teachers, Postsecondary; Chemistry Teachers, Postsecondary; Child Care Workers; Communications Teachers, Postsecondary; Computer Science Teachers, Postsecondary; Criminal Justice and Law Enforcement Teachers, Postsecondary; Curators; Economics Teachers, Postsecondary; Education Teachers, Postsecondary; Education, Training, and Library Workers, All Other; Educational Psychologists; Educational, Vocational, and School Counselors; Elementary School Teachers, Except Special Education; Engineering Teachers, Postsecondary; English Language and Literature Teachers, Postsecondary; Environmental Science Teachers, Postsecondary; Farm and Home Management Advisors; Foreign Language and Literature Teachers, Postsecondary; Forestry and Conservation Science Teachers, Postsecondary; Geography Teachers, Postsecondary; Graduate Teaching Assistants;

Health Specialties Teachers, Postsecondary; History Teachers, Postsecondary; Home Economics Teachers, Postsecondary; Kindergarten Teachers, Except Special Education; Law Teachers, Postsecondary; Librarians; Library Assistants, Clerical; Library Science Teachers, Postsecondary; Library Technicians; Mathematical Science Teachers, Postsecondary; Middle School Teachers, Except Special and Vocational Education; Museum Technicians and Conservators; Nannies; Nursing Instructors and Teachers, Postsecondary; Personal Financial Advisors; Philosophy and Religion Teachers, Postsecondary; Physics Teachers, Postsecondary; Political Science Teachers, Postsecondary; Postsecondary Teachers, All Other; Preschool Teachers, Except Special Education; Psychology Teachers, Postsecondary; Recreation and Fitness Studies Teachers, Postsecondary; Secondary School Teachers, Except Special and Vocational Education; Self-Enrichment Education Teachers; Social Sciences Teachers, Postsecondary, All Other; Social Work Teachers, Postsecondary; Sociology Teachers, Postsecondary; Special Education Teachers, Middle School; Special Education Teachers, Preschool, Kindergarten, and Elementary School; Special Education Teachers, Secondary School; Teacher Assistants; Teachers and Instructors, All Other; Vocational Education Teachers, Postsecondary; Vocational Education Teachers, Middle School; Vocational Education Teachers, Secondary School.

EDUCATION/TRAINING PROGRAM(S)— Anatomy; Animal Physiology; Biochemistry; Biological and Biomedical Sciences, Other; Biology/Biological Sciences, General; Biometry/Biometrics; Biophysics; Biotechnology; Botany/Plant Biology; Cell/Cellular Biology and Histology; Ecology; Ecology, Evolution, Systematics, and Population Biology, Other; Entomology; Evolutionary Biology; Immunology; Marine Biology and Biological Oceanography; Microbiology, General; Molecular Biology; Neuroscience; Nutrition Sciences; Parasitology; Pathology/Experimental Pathology; Pharmacology; Plant Genetics; Plant Pathology/Phytopathology; Plant Physiology; Radiation Biology/Radiobiology; Toxicology; Virology; Zoology/Animal Biology. **RELATED KNOWL-EDGE/COURSES**—Biology; Education and Training; Medicine and Dentistry; Chemistry; Therapy and Counseling; Psychology.

Biophysicists

- Personality Code: IR
- Growth: 22.9%
- Annual Job Openings: 2,000
- Annual Earnings: $62,300
- Education/Training Required: Doctoral degree
- Self-Employed: 2.6%
- Part-Time: 7.1%

Research or study physical principles of living cells and organisms, their electrical and mechanical energy, and related phenomena. Researches transformation of substances in cells, using atomic isotopes. Studies physical principles of living cells and organisms and their electrical and mechanical energy. Investigates transmission of electrical impulses along nerves and muscles. Studies absorption of light by chlorophyll in photosynthesis or by pigments of eye involved in vision. Researches cancer treatment, using radiation and nuclear particles. Analyzes functions of electronic and human brains, such as learning, thinking, and memory. Investigates dynamics of seeing and hearing. Studies spatial configuration of submicroscopic molecules, such as proteins, using X-ray and electron microscope. Researches manner in which characteristics of plants and animals are carried through successive generations. Investigates damage to cells and tissues caused by X rays and nuclear particles. **SKILLS**—Science; Reading Comprehension; Writing; Mathematics; Active Learning; Critical Thinking; Complex Problem Solving; Programming.

GOE—Interest Area: 02. Science, Math, and Engineering. **Work Group:** 02.03. Life Sciences. **Other Jobs in This Work Group:** Agricultural and Food Science Technicians; Agricultural Technicians; Animal Scientists; Biochemists; Biochemists and Biophysicists; Biological Scientists, All Other; Biologists; Conservation Scientists; Environmental Scientists and Specialists, Including Health; Epidemiologists; Food Science Technicians; Food Scientists and Technologists; Foresters; Life Scientists, All Other; Medical Scientists, Except Epidemiologists; Microbiologists; Plant Scientists; Range Managers; Soil and Plant Scientists; Soil Conservationists; Soil Scientists; Zoologists and Wildlife Biologists.

EDUCATION/TRAINING PROGRAM(S)—Biochemistry; Biochemistry/Biophysics and Molecular Biology; Biophysics; Cell/Cellular Biology and Anatomical Sciences, Other; Molecular Biochemistry; Molecular Biophysics; Soil Chemistry and Physics; Soil Microbiology. **RELATED KNOWLEDGE/COURSES**—Biology; Physics; Mathematics; Chemistry.

Chemistry Teachers, Postsecondary

- Personality Code: IS
- Growth: 38.1%
- Annual Job Openings: 216,000
- Annual Earnings: $55,420
- Education/Training Required: Master's degree
- Self-Employed: 0.3%
- Part-Time: 27.7%

Teach courses pertaining to the chemical and physical properties and compositional changes of substances. Work may include instruction in the

methods of qualitative and quantitative chemical analysis. **Includes both teachers primarily engaged in teaching and those who do a combination of both teaching and research.** Supervise undergraduate and/or graduate teaching, internship, and research work. Act as advisers to student organizations. Collaborate with colleagues to address teaching and research issues. Conduct research in a particular field of knowledge and publish findings in professional journals, books, and/or electronic media. Participate in campus and community events. Participate in student recruitment, registration, and placement activities. Perform administrative duties such as serving as department head. Provide professional consulting services to government and/or industry. Serve on academic or administrative committees that deal with institutional policies, departmental matters, and academic issues. Write grant proposals to procure external research funding. Perform administrative duties such as serving as a department head. Prepare and submit required reports related to instruction. Provide professional consulting services to government and/or industry. Evaluate and grade students' class work, laboratory performance, assignments, and papers. Prepare and deliver lectures to undergraduate and/or graduate students on topics such as organic chemistry, analytical chemistry, and chemical separation. Advise students on academic and vocational curricula and on career issues. Compile, administer, and grade examinations or assign this work to others. Compile bibliographies of specialized materials for outside reading assignments. Initiate, facilitate, and moderate classroom discussions. Keep abreast of developments in their field by reading current literature, talking with colleagues, and participating in professional conferences. Maintain regularly scheduled office hours in order to advise and assist students. Maintain student attendance records, grades, and other required records. Plan, evaluate, and revise curricula, course content, and course materials and methods of instruction. Prepare course materials such as syllabi, homework assignments, and handouts. Select and obtain materials and supplies such as textbooks and laboratory equipment.

Supervise students' laboratory work. **SKILLS**—Science; Instructing; Writing; Learning Strategies; Reading Comprehension; Active Learning; Speaking; Management of Personnel Resources.

GOE—Interest Area: 12. Education and Social Service. **Work Group:** 12.03. Educational Services. **Other Jobs in This Work Group:** Adult Literacy, Remedial Education, and GED Teachers and Instructors; Agricultural Sciences Teachers, Postsecondary; Anthropology and Archeology Teachers, Postsecondary; Architecture Teachers, Postsecondary; Archivists; Area, Ethnic, and Cultural Studies Teachers, Postsecondary; Art, Drama, and Music Teachers, Postsecondary; Atmospheric, Earth, Marine, and Space Sciences Teachers, Postsecondary; Audio-Visual Collections Specialists; Biological Science Teachers, Postsecondary; Business Teachers, Postsecondary; Child Care Workers; Communications Teachers, Postsecondary; Computer Science Teachers, Postsecondary; Criminal Justice and Law Enforcement Teachers, Postsecondary; Curators; Economics Teachers, Postsecondary; Education Teachers, Postsecondary; Education, Training, and Library Workers, All Other; Educational Psychologists; Educational, Vocational, and School Counselors; Elementary School Teachers, Except Special Education; Engineering Teachers, Postsecondary; English Language and Literature Teachers, Postsecondary; Environmental Science Teachers, Postsecondary; Farm and Home Management Advisors; Foreign Language and Literature Teachers, Postsecondary; Forestry and Conservation Science Teachers, Postsecondary; Geography Teachers, Postsecondary; Graduate Teaching Assistants; Health Specialties Teachers, Postsecondary; History Teachers, Postsecondary; Home Economics Teachers, Postsecondary; Kindergarten Teachers, Except Special Education; Law Teachers, Postsecondary; Librarians; Library Assistants, Clerical; Library Science Teachers, Postsecondary; Library Technicians; Mathematical Science Teachers, Postsecondary; Middle School Teachers, Except Special and Vocational Education; Museum Technicians and Conservators; Nannies; Nursing

Instructors and Teachers, Postsecondary; Personal Financial Advisors; Philosophy and Religion Teachers, Postsecondary; Physics Teachers, Postsecondary; Political Science Teachers, Postsecondary; Postsecondary Teachers, All Other; Preschool Teachers, Except Special Education; Psychology Teachers, Postsecondary; Recreation and Fitness Studies Teachers, Postsecondary; Secondary School Teachers, Except Special and Vocational Education; Self-Enrichment Education Teachers; Social Sciences Teachers, Postsecondary, All Other; Social Work Teachers, Postsecondary; Sociology Teachers, Postsecondary; Special Education Teachers, Middle School; Special Education Teachers, Preschool, Kindergarten, and Elementary School; Special Education Teachers, Secondary School; Teacher Assistants; Teachers and Instructors, All Other; Vocational Education Teachers, Postsecondary; Vocational Education Teachers, Middle School; Vocational Education Teachers, Secondary School.

EDUCATION/TRAINING PROGRAM(S)— Analytical Chemistry; Chemical Physics; Chemistry, General; Chemistry, Other; Geochemistry; Inorganic Chemistry; Organic Chemistry; Physical and Theoretical Chemistry; Polymer Chemistry. **RELATED KNOWLEDGE/COURSES—**Chemistry; Mathematics; Education and Training; English Language; Physics; Administration and Management.

Chiropractors

- ⊚ Personality Code: IR
- ⊚ Growth: 23.3%
- ⊚ Annual Job Openings: 3,000
- ⊚ Annual Earnings: $65,990
- ⊚ Education/Training Required: First professional degree
- ⊚ Self-Employed: 58.5%
- ⊚ Part-Time: 22.2%

Adjust spinal column and other articulations of the body to correct abnormalities of the human body believed to be caused by interference with the nervous system. Examine patient to determine nature and extent of disorder. Manipulate spine or other involved area. May utilize supplementary measures, such as exercise, rest, water, light, heat, and nutritional therapy. Advise patients about recommended courses of treatment. Consult with and refer patients to appropriate health practitioners when necessary. Counsel patients about nutrition, exercise, sleeping habits, stress management, and other matters. Diagnose health problems by reviewing patients' health and medical histories; questioning, observing and examining patients; and interpreting X rays. Evaluate the functioning of the neuromuscularskeletal system and the spine, using systems of chiropractic diagnosis. Maintain accurate case histories of patients. Obtain and record patients' medical histories. Perform a series of manual adjustments to the spine or other articulations of the body in order to correct the musculoskeletal system. Suggest and apply the use of supports such as straps, tapes, bandages, and braces if necessary. Analyze X rays in order to locate the sources of patients' difficulties and to rule out fractures or diseases as sources of problems. Arrange for diagnostic X rays to be taken. **SKILLS—**Science; Reading Comprehension; Judgment and Decision Making; Active Learning; Complex Problem Solving; Social Perceptiveness; Persuasion; Systems Analysis.

GOE—Interest Area: 14. Medical and Health Services. **Work Group:** 14.04. Health Specialties. **Other Jobs in This Work Group:** Opticians, Dispensing; Optometrists; Podiatrists.

EDUCATION/TRAINING PROGRAM(S)— Chiropractic (DC). **RELATED KNOWLEDGE/COURSES—**Medicine and Dentistry; Biology; Therapy and Counseling; English Language; Customer and Personal Service; Chemistry.

Clinical Psychologists

- Personality Code: IA
- Growth: 24.4%
- Annual Job Openings: 17,000
- Annual Earnings: $52,220
- Education/Training Required: Master's degree
- Self-Employed: 25.4%
- Part-Time: 27.2%

Diagnose or evaluate mental and emotional disorders of individuals through observation, interview, and psychological tests and formulate and administer programs of treatment. Consult reference material such as textbooks, manuals, and journals in order to identify symptoms, make diagnoses, and develop approaches to treatment. Counsel individuals and groups regarding problems such as stress, substance abuse, and family situations in order to modify behavior and/or to improve personal, social, and vocational adjustment. Develop and implement individual treatment plans, specifying type, frequency, intensity, and duration of therapy. Discuss the treatment of problems with clients. Evaluate the effectiveness of counseling or treatments and the accuracy and completeness of diagnoses; then modify plans and diagnoses as necessary. Identify psychological, emotional, or behavioral issues and diagnose disorders, using information obtained from interviews, tests, records, and reference materials. Interact with clients to assist them in gaining insight, defining goals, and planning action to achieve effective personal, social, educational, and vocational development and adjustment. Observe individuals at play, in group interactions, or in other contexts to detect indications of mental deficiency, abnormal behavior, or maladjustment. Obtain and study medical, psychological, social, and family histories by interviewing individuals, couples, or families and by reviewing records. Provide occupational, educational, and other information to individuals so that they can make educational and vocational plans. Select, administer, score, and interpret psychological tests in order to obtain information on individuals' intelligence, achievements, interests, and personalities. Utilize a variety of treatment methods such as psychotherapy, hypnosis, behavior modification, stress reduction therapy, psychodrama, and play therapy. Maintain current knowledge of relevant research. Plan, supervise, and conduct psychological research and write papers describing research results. Refer clients to other specialists, institutions, or support services as necessary. Write reports on clients and maintain required paperwork. Develop, direct, and participate in training programs for staff and students. **SKILLS**—Social Perceptiveness; Active Listening; Systems Evaluation; Persuasion; Speaking; Reading Comprehension; Systems Analysis; Science.

GOE—Interest Area: 12. Education and Social Service. **Work Group:** 12.02. Social Services. **Other Jobs in This Work Group:** Child, Family, and School Social Workers; Clergy; Clinical, Counseling, and School Psychologists; Community and Social Service Specialists, All Other; Counseling Psychologists; Counselors, All Other; Directors, Religious Activities and Education; Marriage and Family Therapists; Medical and Public Health Social Workers; Mental Health and Substance Abuse Social Workers; Mental Health Counselors; Probation Officers and Correctional Treatment Specialists; Rehabilitation Counselors; Religious Workers, All Other; Residential Advisors; Social and Human Service Assistants; Social Workers, All Other; Substance Abuse and Behavioral Disorder Counselors.

EDUCATION/TRAINING PROGRAM(S)— Clinical Child Psychology; Clinical Psychology; Counseling Psychology; Developmental and Child Psychology; Psychoanalysis and Psychotherapy; Psychology, General; School Psychology. **RELATED KNOWLEDGE/COURSES**—Therapy and Counseling; Psychology; Administration and Management; Sociology and Anthropology; Customer and Personal Service; English Language.

Compensation, Benefits, and Job Analysis Specialists

- Personality Code: IC
- Growth: 28.0%
- Annual Job Openings: 15,000
- Annual Earnings: $46,860
- Education/Training Required: Bachelor's degree
- Self-Employed: 0.8%
- Part-Time: 7.7%

Conduct programs of compensation and benefits and job analysis for employer. May specialize in specific areas, such as position classification and pension programs. Evaluate job positions, determining classification, exempt or non-exempt status, and salary. Ensure company compliance with federal and state laws, including reporting requirements. Advise managers and employees on state and federal employment regulations, collective agreements, benefit and compensation policies, personnel procedures, and classification programs. Plan, develop, evaluate, improve, and communicate methods and techniques for selecting, promoting, compensating, evaluating, and training workers. Provide advice on the resolution of classification and salary complaints. Prepare occupational classifications, job descriptions, and salary scales. Assist in preparing and maintaining personnel records and handbooks. Prepare reports, such as organization and flow charts and career path reports, to summarize job analysis and evaluation and compensation analysis information. Administer employee insurance, pension, and savings plans, working with insurance brokers and plan carriers. Negotiate collective agreements on behalf of employers or workers and mediate labor disputes and grievances. Develop, implement, administer, and evaluate personnel and labor relations programs, including performance appraisal, affirmative action, and employment equity programs. Perform multifactor data and cost analyses that may be used in areas such as support of collective bargaining agreements. Research employee benefit and health and safety practices and recommend changes or modifications to existing policies. Analyze organizational, occupational, and industrial data to facilitate organizational functions and provide technical information to business, industry, and government. Advise staff of individuals' qualifications. Assess need for and develop job analysis instruments and materials. Review occupational data on Alien Employment Certification Applications to determine the appropriate occupational title and code and provide local offices with information about immigration and occupations. Research job and worker requirements, structural and functional relationships among jobs and occupations, and occupational trends. **SKILLS**—Service Orientation; Persuasion; Coordination; Negotiation; Active Listening; Critical Thinking; Time Management; Social Perceptiveness.

GOE—Interest Area: 13. General Management and Support. **Work Group:** 13.02. Management Support. **Other Jobs in This Work Group:** Accountants; Accountants and Auditors; Appraisers and Assessors of Real Estate; Appraisers, Real Estate; Assessors; Auditors; Budget Analysts; Business Operations Specialists, All Other; Claims Adjusters, Examiners, and Investigators; Claims Examiners, Property and Casualty Insurance; Cost Estimators; Credit Analysts; Employment Interviewers, Private or Public Employment Service; Employment, Recruitment, and Placement Specialists; Financial Analysts; Human Resources, Training, and Labor Relations Specialists, All Other; Insurance Adjusters, Examiners, and Investigators; Insurance Appraisers, Auto Damage; Insurance Underwriters; Loan Counselors; Loan Officers; Logisticians; Management Analysts; Market Research Analysts; Personnel Recruiters; Purchasing Agents and Buyers, Farm Products; Purchasing Agents, Except Wholesale, Retail, and Farm Products; Tax Examiners, Collectors, and Revenue Agents; Training and

Investigative–C

Development Specialists; Wholesale and Retail Buyers, Except Farm Products.

EDUCATION/TRAINING PROGRAM(S)—Human Resources Management/Personnel Administration, General; Labor and Industrial Relations. **RELATED KNOWLEDGE/COURSES**—Personnel and Human Resources; Clerical Studies; Customer and Personal Service; English Language; Administration and Management; Education and Training.

Computer Hardware Engineers

- Personality Code: IR
- Growth: 6.1%
- Annual Job Openings: 6,000
- Annual Earnings: $75,980
- Education/Training Required: Bachelor's degree
- Self-Employed: 4.7%
- Part-Time: 3.4%

Research, design, develop, and test computer or computer-related equipment for commercial, industrial, military, or scientific use. May supervise the manufacturing and installation of computer or computer-related equipment and components. Analyze information to determine, recommend, and plan layout, including type of computers and peripheral equipment modifications. Analyze user needs and recommend appropriate hardware. Build, test, and modify product prototypes, using working models or theoretical models constructed using computer simulation. Confer with engineering staff and consult specifications to evaluate interface between hardware and software and operational and performance requirements of overall system. Design and develop computer hardware and support peripherals, including central processing units

(CPUs), support logic, microprocessors, custom integrated circuits, and printers and disk drives. Evaluate factors such as reporting formats required, cost constraints, and need for security restrictions to determine hardware configuration. Monitor functioning of equipment and make necessary modifications to ensure system operates in conformance with specifications. Specify power supply requirements and configuration, drawing on system performance expectations and design specifications. Store, retrieve, and manipulate data for analysis of system capabilities and requirements. Test and verify hardware and support peripherals to ensure that they meet specifications and requirements, analyzing and recording test data. Write detailed functional specifications that document the hardware development process and support hardware introduction. Assemble and modify existing pieces of equipment to meet special needs. Direct technicians, engineering designers, or other technical support personnel as needed. Provide technical support to designers, marketing and sales departments, suppliers, engineers, and other team members throughout the product development and implementation process. Provide training and support to system designers and users. Recommend purchase of equipment to control dust, temperature, and humidity in area of system installation. Select hardware and material, assuring compliance with specifications and product requirements. Update knowledge and skills to keep up with rapid advancements in computer technology. **SKILLS**—Programming; Troubleshooting; Installation; Science; Operations Analysis; Technology Design; Management of Material Resources; Active Learning.

GOE—Interest Area: 02. Science, Math, and Engineering. **Work Group:** 02.07. Engineering. **Other Jobs in This Work Group:** Aerospace Engineers; Agricultural Engineers; Architects, Except Landscape and Naval; Biomedical Engineers; Chemical Engineers; Civil Engineers; Computer Software Engineers, Applications; Computer Software Engineers, Systems Software; Electrical Engineers; Electronics Engineers, Except Computer; Engineers, All

Other; Environmental Engineers; Fire-Prevention and Protection Engineers; Health and Safety Engineers, Except Mining Safety Engineers and Inspectors; Industrial Engineers; Industrial Safety and Health Engineers; Landscape Architects; Marine Architects; Marine Engineers; Marine Engineers and Naval Architects; Materials Engineers; Mechanical Engineers; Mining and Geological Engineers, Including Mining Safety Engineers; Nuclear Engineers; Petroleum Engineers; Product Safety Engineers; Sales Engineers.

EDUCATION/TRAINING PROGRAM(S)— Computer Engineering, General; Computer Hardware Engineering. **RELATED KNOWLEDGE/ COURSES—**Computers and Electronics; Mathematics; Engineering and Technology; Design; Telecommunications; Education and Training.

Computer Programmers

- Personality Code: IR
- Growth: 14.6%
- Annual Job Openings: 45,000
- Annual Earnings: $61,340
- Education/Training Required: Bachelor's degree
- Self-Employed: 3.7%
- Part-Time: 4.6%

Convert project specifications and statements of problems and procedures to detailed logical flow charts for coding into computer language. Develop and write computer programs to store, locate, and retrieve specific documents, data, and information. May program Web sites. Correct errors by making appropriate changes and then rechecking the program to ensure that the desired results are produced. Conduct trial runs of programs and software applications to be sure they will produce the desired information and that the instructions are correct. Compile and write documentation of program development and subsequent revisions, inserting comments in the coded instructions so others can understand the program. Write, update, and maintain computer programs or software packages to handle specific jobs, such as tracking inventory, storing or retrieving data, or controlling other equipment. Consult with managerial, engineering, and technical personnel to clarify program intent, identify problems, and suggest changes. Perform or direct revision, repair, or expansion of existing programs to increase operating efficiency or adapt to new requirements. Write, analyze, review, and rewrite programs, using workflow chart and diagram and applying knowledge of computer capabilities, subject matter, and symbolic logic. Write or contribute to instructions or manuals to guide end users. Investigate whether networks, workstations, the central processing unit of the system, and/or peripheral equipment are responding to a program's instructions. Prepare detailed workflow charts and diagrams that describe input, output, and logical operation and convert them into a series of instructions coded in a computer language. Perform systems analysis and programming tasks to maintain and control the use of computer systems software as a systems programmer. Consult with and assist computer operators or system analysts to define and resolve problems in running computer programs. Assign, coordinate, and review work and activities of programming personnel. **SKILLS—**Programming; Operations Analysis; Technology Design; Troubleshooting; Critical Thinking; Active Learning; Complex Problem Solving; Systems Analysis.

GOE—Interest Area: 02. Science, Math, and Engineering. **Work Group:** 02.06. Mathematics and Computers. **Other Jobs in This Work Group:** Computer and Information Scientists, Research; Computer Security Specialists; Computer Specialists, All Other; Computer Support Specialists; Computer Systems Analysts; Database Administrators; Network and Computer Systems Administrators; Network Systems and Data Communications Analysts.

EDUCATION/TRAINING PROGRAM(S)— Artificial Intelligence and Robotics; Bioinformatics;

Computer Graphics; Computer Programming, Specific Applications; Computer Programming, Vendor/Product Certification; Computer Programming/Programmer, General; E-Commerce/Electronic Commerce; Management Information Systems, General; Medical Informatics; Medical Office Computer Specialist/Assistant; Web Page, Digital/Multimedia, and Information Resources Design; Web/Multimedia Management and Webmaster. **RELATED KNOWLEDGE/COURSES**— Computers and Electronics; Design; Mathematics; Telecommunications; English Language; Customer and Personal Service.

Computer Science Teachers, Postsecondary

- Personality Code: IC
- Growth: 38.1%
- Annual Job Openings: 216,000
- Annual Earnings: $51,030
- Education/Training Required: Master's degree
- Self-Employed: 0.3%
- Part-Time: 27.7%

Teach courses in computer science. May specialize in a field of computer science, such as the design and function of computers or operations and research analysis. Evaluate and grade students' class work, laboratory work, assignments, and papers. Prepare and deliver lectures to undergraduate and/or graduate students on topics such as programming, data structures, and software design. Advise students on academic and vocational curricula and on career issues. Compile, administer, and grade examinations or assign this work to others. Compile bibliographies of specialized materials for outside reading assignments. Initiate, facilitate, and moderate classroom discussions. Keep abreast of developments in their field by reading current literature, talking with colleagues, and participating in professional conferences. Maintain regularly scheduled office hours in order to advise and assist students. Maintain student attendance records, grades, and other required records. Plan, evaluate, and revise curricula, course content, and course materials and methods of instruction. Prepare course materials such as syllabi, homework assignments, and handouts. Select and obtain materials and supplies such as textbooks and laboratory equipment. Supervise students' laboratory work. Supervise undergraduate and/or graduate teaching, internship, and research work. Act as advisers to student organizations. Collaborate with colleagues to address teaching and research issues. Conduct research in a particular field of knowledge and publish findings in professional journals, books, and/or electronic media. Direct research of other teachers or of graduate students working for advanced academic degrees. Participate in campus and community events. Participate in student recruitment, registration, and placement activities. Perform administrative duties such as serving as department head. Provide professional consulting services to government and/or industry. Serve on academic or administrative committees that deal with institutional policies, departmental matters, and academic issues. Write grant proposals to procure external research funding. **SKILLS**—Programming; Instructing; Writing; Learning Strategies; Active Learning; Reading Comprehension; Mathematics; Science.

GOE—Interest Area: 12. Education and Social Service. **Work Group:** 12.03. Educational Services. **Other Jobs in This Work Group:** Adult Literacy, Remedial Education, and GED Teachers and Instructors; Agricultural Sciences Teachers, Postsecondary; Anthropology and Archeology Teachers, Postsecondary; Architecture Teachers, Postsecondary; Archivists; Area, Ethnic, and Cultural Studies Teachers, Postsecondary; Art, Drama, and Music Teachers, Postsecondary; Atmospheric, Earth, Marine, and Space Sciences Teachers, Postsecondary; Audio-Visual Collections Specialists; Biological Science Teachers, Postsecondary; Business Teachers, Postsecondary; Chemistry Teachers, Postsecondary; Child Care Workers; Communications Teachers, Postsecondary; Criminal Justice and Law Enforcement Teachers, Postsecondary; Curators; Economics Teachers, Postsecondary; Education Teachers, Postsecondary; Education, Training, and Library Workers, All Other; Educational Psychologists; Educational, Vocational, and School Counselors; Elementary School Teachers, Except Special Education; Engineering Teachers, Postsecondary; English Language and Literature Teachers, Postsecondary; Environmental Science Teachers, Postsecondary; Farm and Home Management Advisors; Foreign Language and Literature Teachers, Postsecondary; Forestry and Conservation Science Teachers, Postsecondary; Geography Teachers, Postsecondary; Graduate Teaching Assistants; Health Specialties Teachers, Postsecondary; History Teachers, Postsecondary; Home Economics Teachers, Postsecondary; Kindergarten Teachers, Except Special Education; Law Teachers, Postsecondary; Librarians; Library Assistants, Clerical; Library Science Teachers, Postsecondary; Library Technicians; Mathematical Science Teachers, Postsecondary; Middle School Teachers, Except Special and Vocational Education; Museum Technicians and Conservators; Nannies; Nursing Instructors and Teachers, Postsecondary; Personal Financial Advisors; Philosophy and Religion Teachers, Postsecondary; Physics Teachers, Postsecondary; Political Science Teachers, Postsecondary; Postsecondary Teachers, All Other; Preschool Teachers, Except Special Education; Psychology Teachers, Postsecondary; Recreation and Fitness Studies Teachers, Postsecondary; Secondary School Teachers, Except Special and Vocational Education; Self-Enrichment Education Teachers; Social Sciences Teachers, Postsecondary, All Other; Social Work Teachers, Postsecondary; Sociology Teachers, Postsecondary; Special Education Teachers, Middle School; Special Education Teachers, Preschool, Kindergarten, and Elementary School; Special Education Teachers, Secondary School; Teacher Assistants; Teachers and Instructors, All Other; Vocational Education Teachers, Postsecondary; Vocational Education Teachers, Middle School; Vocational Education Teachers, Secondary School.

EDUCATION/TRAINING PROGRAM(S)— Computer and Information Sciences, General; Computer Programming/Programmer, General; Computer Science; Computer Systems Analysis/Analyst; Information Science/Studies. **RELATED KNOWLEDGE/COURSES**—Computers and Electronics; Education and Training; Mathematics; Physics; English Language; Administration and Management; Telecommunications.

Computer Security Specialists

- Personality Code: IR
- Growth: 37.4%
- Annual Job Openings: 35,000
- Annual Earnings: $56,050
- Education/Training Required: Bachelor's degree
- Self-Employed: 0.5%
- Part-Time: 3.9%

Plan, coordinate, and implement security measures for information systems to regulate access to computer data files and prevent unauthorized modification, destruction, or disclosure of information. Confer with users to discuss issues such as computer data access needs, security violations, and programming changes. Develop plans to safeguard computer files against accidental or unauthorized modification, destruction, or disclosure and to meet emergency data processing needs. Document computer security and emergency measures policies, procedures, and tests. Encrypt data transmissions and erect firewalls to conceal confidential information as it is being transmitted and to keep out taint-

Investigative—C

ed digital transfers. Modify computer security files to incorporate new software, correct errors, or change individual access status. Monitor current reports of computer viruses to determine when to update virus protection systems. Monitor use of data files and regulate access to safeguard information in computer files. Perform risk assessments and execute tests of data processing system to ensure functioning of data processing activities and security measures. Review violations of computer security procedures and discuss procedures with violators to ensure violations are not repeated. Coordinate implementation of computer system plan with establishment personnel and outside vendors. Train users and promote security awareness to ensure system security and to improve server and network efficiency. Maintain permanent fleet cryptologic and carry-on direct support systems required in special land, sea surface, and subsurface operations. SKILLS—Programming; Technology Design; Installation; Operations Analysis; Management of Material Resources; Science; Writing; Mathematics; Quality Control Analysis.

GOE—Interest Area: 02. Science, Math, and Engineering. Work Group: 02.06. Mathematics and Computers. Other Jobs in This Work Group: Computer and Information Scientists, Research; Computer Programmers; Computer Specialists, All Other; Computer Support Specialists; Computer Systems Analysts; Database Administrators; Network and Computer Systems Administrators; Network Systems and Data Communications Analysts.

EDUCATION/TRAINING PROGRAM(S)— Computer and Information Sciences and Support Services, Other; Computer and Information Sciences, General; Computer and Information Systems Security; Computer Systems Analysis/Analyst; Computer Systems Networking and Telecommunications; Information Science/Studies; System Administration/Administrator; System, Networking, and LAN/WAN Management/Manager. RELATED KNOWLEDGE/COURSES—Computers and Electronics; Public Safety and Security; Administration and Management; Telecommunications.

Computer Software Engineers, Applications

- Personality Code: IR
- Growth: 45.5%
- Annual Job Openings: 55,000
- Annual Earnings: $72,530
- Education/Training Required: Bachelor's degree
- Self-Employed: 3.1%
- Part-Time: 2.4%

Develop, create, and modify general computer applications software or specialized utility programs. Analyze user needs and develop software solutions. Design software or customize software for client use with the aim of optimizing operational efficiency. May analyze and design databases within an application area, working individually or coordinating database development as part of a team. Confer with systems analysts, engineers, programmers, and others to design system and to obtain information on project limitations and capabilities, performance requirements, and interfaces. Modify existing software to correct errors, allow it to adapt to new hardware, or improve its performance. Analyze user needs and software requirements to determine feasibility of design within time and cost constraints. Consult with customers about software system design and maintenance. Coordinate software system installation and monitor equipment functioning to ensure specifications are met. Design, develop, and modify software systems, using scientific analysis and mathematical models to predict and measure outcome and consequences of design. Develop and direct software system testing and validation procedures, programming, and documentation. Analyze information to determine, recommend, and plan computer specifications and layouts and peripheral equipment modifications. Supervise the work of programmers, technologists and technicians, and other engineering and scientific personnel. Obtain and evaluate information on factors such as reporting formats required, costs, and security needs to determine hardware configuration. Determine system performance standards. Train users to use new or modified equipment. Store, retrieve, and manipulate data for analysis of system capabilities and requirements. **SKILLS**— Programming; Troubleshooting; Technology Design; Systems Analysis; Quality Control Analysis; Operations Analysis; Complex Problem Solving; Critical Thinking.

GOE—Interest Area: 02. Science, Math, and Engineering. **Work Group:** 02.07. Engineering. **Other Jobs in This Work Group:** Aerospace Engineers; Agricultural Engineers; Architects, Except Landscape and Naval; Biomedical Engineers; Chemical Engineers; Civil Engineers; Computer Hardware Engineers; Computer Software Engineers, Systems Software; Electrical Engineers; Electronics Engineers, Except Computer; Engineers, All Other; Environmental Engineers; Fire-Prevention and Protection Engineers; Health and Safety Engineers, Except Mining Safety Engineers and Inspectors; Industrial Engineers; Industrial Safety and Health Engineers; Landscape Architects; Marine Architects; Marine Engineers; Marine Engineers and Naval Architects; Materials Engineers; Mechanical Engineers; Mining and Geological Engineers, Including Mining Safety Engineers; Nuclear Engineers; Petroleum Engineers; Product Safety Engineers; Sales Engineers.

EDUCATION/TRAINING PROGRAM(S)— Artificial Intelligence and Robotics; Bioinformatics; Computer Engineering Technologies/Technicians, Other; Computer Engineering, General; Computer Science; Computer Software Engineering; Information Technology; Medical Illustration and Informatics, Other; Medical Informatics. **RELATED KNOWLEDGE/COURSES**—Computers and Electronics; Telecommunications; Engineering and Technology; Mathematics; Design; English Language.

Computer Software Engineers, Systems Software

- ◎ Personality Code: IR
- ◎ Growth: 45.5%
- ◎ Annual Job Openings: 39,000
- ◎ Annual Earnings: $76,240
- ◎ Education/Training Required: Bachelor's degree
- ◎ Self-Employed: 3.0%
- ◎ Part-Time: 2.4%

Research, design, develop, and test operating systems-level software, compilers, and network distribution software for medical, industrial, military, communications, aerospace, business, scientific, and general computing applications. Set operational specifications and formulate and analyze software requirements. Apply principles and techniques of computer science, engineering, and mathematical analysis. Modify existing software to correct errors, to adapt it to new hardware, or to upgrade interfaces and improve performance. Design and develop software systems, using scientific analysis and mathematical models to predict and measure outcome and consequences of design. Consult with engineering staff to evaluate interface between hardware and software, develop specifications and performance requirements, and resolve customer problems. Analyze information to determine, recommend, and plan installation of a new system or modification of an existing system. Develop and direct software system testing and validation procedures. Direct software programming and development of documentation. Consult with customers and/or other departments on project status, proposals, and technical issues such as software system design and maintenance. Advise customer about, or perform, maintenance of software system. Coordinate installation of software system. Monitor functioning of equipment to ensure system operates

Investigative-C

in conformance with specifications. Store, retrieve, and manipulate data for analysis of system capabilities and requirements. Confer with data processing and project managers to obtain information on limitations and capabilities for data processing projects. Prepare reports and correspondence concerning project specifications, activities, and status. Evaluate factors such as reporting formats required, cost constraints, and need for security restrictions to determine hardware configuration. Supervise and assign work to programmers, designers, technologists and technicians, and other engineering and scientific personnel. Train users to use new or modified equipment. Utilize microcontrollers to develop control signals, implement control algorithms, and measure process variables such as temperatures, pressures, and positions. **SKILLS**—Programming; Technology Design; Troubleshooting; Systems Analysis; Complex Problem Solving; Operations Analysis; Active Learning; Critical Thinking.

GOE—Interest Area: 02. Science, Math, and Engineering. **Work Group:** 02.07. Engineering. **Other Jobs in This Work Group:** Aerospace Engineers; Agricultural Engineers; Architects, Except Landscape and Naval; Biomedical Engineers; Chemical Engineers; Civil Engineers; Computer Hardware Engineers; Computer Software Engineers, Applications; Electrical Engineers; Electronics Engineers, Except Computer; Engineers, All Other; Environmental Engineers; Fire-Prevention and Protection Engineers; Health and Safety Engineers, Except Mining Safety Engineers and Inspectors; Industrial Engineers; Industrial Safety and Health Engineers; Landscape Architects; Marine Architects; Marine Engineers; Marine Engineers and Naval Architects; Materials Engineers; Mechanical Engineers; Mining and Geological Engineers, Including Mining Safety Engineers; Nuclear Engineers; Petroleum Engineers; Product Safety Engineers; Sales Engineers.

EDUCATION/TRAINING PROGRAM(S)— Artificial Intelligence and Robotics; Computer Engineering Technologies/Technicians, Other; Computer Engineering, General; Computer Science; Information Science/Studies; Information Technology. **RELATED KNOWLEDGE/ COURSES**—Computers and Electronics; Design; Engineering and Technology; Telecommunications; Mathematics; Education and Training.

Computer Support Specialists

- Personality Code: IC
- Growth: 30.3%
- Annual Job Openings: 71,000
- Annual Earnings: $39,440
- Education/Training Required: Associate's degree
- Self-Employed: 0.6%
- Part-Time: 6.8%

Provide technical assistance to computer system users. Answer questions or resolve computer problems for clients in person, via telephone, or from remote location. May provide assistance concerning the use of computer hardware and software, including printing, installation, word processing, electronic mail, and operating systems. Answer users' inquiries regarding computer software and hardware operation to resolve problems. Enter commands and observe system functioning to verify correct operations and detect errors. Install and perform minor repairs to hardware, software, and peripheral equipment, following design or installation specifications. Oversee the daily performance of computer systems. Set up equipment for employee use, performing or ensuring proper installation of cable, operating systems, and appropriate software. Maintain record of daily data communication transactions, problems and remedial action taken, and installation activities. Read technical manuals, confer with users, and conduct computer diagnostics to investigate and resolve problems and to provide technical assistance and support. Confer with staff, users, and management to establish requirements for new systems or modifications. Develop training materials and procedures and/or train users in the proper use of hardware and software. Refer major hardware or software problems or defective products to vendors or technicians for service. Prepare evaluations of software or hardware and recommend improvements or upgrades. Read trade magazines and technical manuals and attend conferences and seminars to maintain knowledge of hardware and software. Supervise and coordinate workers engaged in problem-solving, monitoring, and installing data communication equipment and software. Inspect equipment and read order sheets to prepare for delivery to users. Modify and customize commercial programs for internal needs. **SKILLS**—Troubleshooting; Repairing; Persuasion; Social Perceptiveness; Installation; Instructing; Equipment Maintenance; Writing; Service Orientation.

GOE—**Interest Area:** 02. Science, Math, and Engineering. **Work Group:** 02.06. Mathematics and Computers. **Other Jobs in This Work Group:** Computer and Information Scientists, Research; Computer Programmers; Computer Security Specialists; Computer Specialists, All Other; Computer Systems Analysts; Database Administrators; Network and Computer Systems Administrators; Network Systems and Data Communications Analysts.

EDUCATION/TRAINING PROGRAM(S)—Accounting and Computer Science; Agricultural Business Technology; Computer Hardware Technology/Technician; Computer Software Technology/Technician; Data Processing and Data Processing Technology/Technician; Medical Office Computer Specialist/Assistant. **RELATED KNOWLEDGE/COURSES**—Computers and Electronics; Customer and Personal Service; Telecommunications; Production and Processing; Engineering and Technology; Design.

Computer Systems Analysts

- Personality Code: IC
- Growth: 39.4%
- Annual Job Openings: 68,000
- Annual Earnings: $64,160
- Education/Training Required: Bachelor's degree
- Self-Employed: 6.4%
- Part-Time: 5.7%

Analyze science, engineering, business, and all other data processing problems for application to electronic data processing systems. Analyze user requirements, procedures, and problems to automate or improve existing systems and review computer system capabilities, workflow, and scheduling limitations. May analyze or recommend commercially available software. May supervise computer programmers. Provide staff and users with assistance solving computer-related problems, such as malfunctions and program problems. Test, maintain, and monitor computer programs and systems, including coordinating the installation of computer programs and systems. Use object-oriented programming languages, as well as client/server applications development processes and multimedia and Internet technology. Confer with clients regarding the nature of the information processing or computation needs a computer program is to address. Coordinate and link the computer systems within an organization to increase compatibility and so that information can be shared. Consult with management to ensure agreement on system principles. Expand or modify system to serve new purposes or improve work flow. Interview or survey workers, observe job performance, and/or perform the job in order to determine what information is processed and how it is processed. Determine computer software or hardware needed to set up or alter system. Train staff and users to work with comput-

Investigative—C

er systems and programs. Analyze information processing or computation needs and plan and design computer systems, using techniques such as structured analysis, data modeling, and information engineering. Assess the usefulness of pre-developed application packages and adapt them to a user environment. Define the goals of the system and devise flow charts and diagrams describing logical operational steps of programs. Develop, document, and revise system design procedures, test procedures, and quality standards. Review and analyze computer printouts and performance indicators to locate code problems; correct errors by correcting codes. Recommend new equipment or software packages. Read manuals, periodicals, and technical reports to learn how to develop programs that meet staff and user requirements. Supervise computer programmers or other systems analysts or serve as project leaders for particular systems projects. Utilize the computer in the analysis and solution of business problems such as development of integrated production and inventory control and cost analysis systems. **SKILLS**—Quality Control Analysis; Installation; Troubleshooting; Technology Design; Time Management; Service Orientation; Systems Analysis; Operations Analysis.

GOE—**Interest Area:** 02. Science, Math, and Engineering. **Work Group:** 02.06. Mathematics and Computers. **Other Jobs in This Work Group:** Computer and Information Scientists, Research; Computer Programmers; Computer Security Specialists; Computer Specialists, All Other; Computer Support Specialists; Database Administrators; Network and Computer Systems Administrators; Network Systems and Data Communications Analysts.

EDUCATION/TRAINING PROGRAM(S)— Computer and Information Sciences, General; Computer Systems Analysis/Analyst; Information Technology; Web/Multimedia Management and Webmaster. **RELATED KNOWLEDGE/COURSES**—Computers and Electronics; Customer and Personal Service; Telecommunications; Design; Education and Training; English Language.

Database Administrators

- Personality Code: IC
- Growth: 44.2%
- Annual Job Openings: 16,000
- Annual Earnings: $58,200
- Education/Training Required: Bachelor's degree
- Self-Employed: 0.6%
- Part-Time: 4.6%

Coordinate changes to computer databases; test and implement the database, applying knowledge of database management systems. May plan, coordinate, and implement security measures to safeguard computer databases. Develop standards and guidelines to guide the use and acquisition of software and to protect vulnerable information. Modify existing databases and database management systems or direct programmers and analysts to make changes. Test programs or databases, correct errors, and make necessary modifications. Plan, coordinate, and implement security measures to safeguard information in computer files against accidental or unauthorized damage, modification, or disclosure. Approve, schedule, plan, and supervise the installation and testing of new products and improvements to computer systems, such as the installation of new databases. Train users and answer questions. Establish and calculate optimum values for database parameters, using manuals and calculator. Specify users and user access levels for each segment of database. Develop data model describing data elements and how they are used, following procedures and using pen, template, or computer software. Develop methods for integrating different products so they work properly together, such as customizing commercial databases to fit specific needs. Review project requests describing database user needs to estimate time and cost required to accomplish project. Review procedures in database management system manuals for making changes to database. Work as part of a project team to coordinate database development and determine project scope and limitations. Select and enter codes to monitor database performance and to create production database. Identify and evaluate industry trends in database systems to serve as a source of information and advice for upper management. Write and code logical and physical database descriptions and specify identifiers of database to management system or direct others in coding descriptions. Review workflow charts developed by programmer analyst to understand tasks computer will perform, such as updating records. Revise company definition of data as defined in data dictionary. SKILLS—Troubleshooting; Persuasion; Operations Analysis; Instructing; Systems Evaluation; Management of Personnel Resources; Time Management; Technology Design.

GOE—Interest Area: 02. Science, Math, and Engineering. Work Group: 02.06. Mathematics and Computers. Other Jobs in This Work Group: Computer and Information Scientists, Research; Computer Programmers; Computer Security Specialists; Computer Specialists, All Other; Computer Support Specialists; Computer Systems Analysts; Network and Computer Systems Administrators; Network Systems and Data Communications Analysts.

EDUCATION/TRAINING PROGRAM(S)— Computer and Information Sciences, General; Computer and Information Systems Security; Computer Systems Analysis/Analyst; Data Modeling/Warehousing and Database Administration; Management Information Systems, General. RELATED KNOWLEDGE/COURSES—Computers and Electronics; Clerical Studies; Customer and Personal Service; Economics and Accounting; Administration and Management; Mathematics.

Dentists, General

- Personality Code: IR
- Growth: 4.1%
- Annual Job Openings: 7,000
- Annual Earnings: $120,330
- Education/Training Required: First professional degree
- Self-Employed: 39.9%
- Part-Time: 22.3%

Diagnose and treat diseases, injuries, and malformations of teeth and gums and related oral structures. May treat diseases of nerve, pulp, and other dental tissues affecting vitality of teeth. Administer anesthetics to limit the amount of pain experienced by patients during procedures. Advise and instruct patients regarding preventive dental care, the causes and treatment of dental problems, and oral health care services. Analyze and evaluate dental needs to determine changes and trends in patterns of dental disease. Apply fluoride and sealants to teeth. Bleach, clean, or polish teeth to restore natural color. Design, make, and fit prosthodontic appliances such as space maintainers, bridges, and dentures or write fabrication instructions or prescriptions for denturists and dental technicians. Diagnose and treat diseases, injuries, and malformations of teeth, gums, and related oral structures and provide preventive and corrective services. Eliminate irritating margins of fillings and correct occlusions, using dental instruments. Examine teeth, gums, and related tissues, using dental instruments, X rays, and other diagnostic equipment, to evaluate dental health, diagnose diseases or abnormalities, and plan appropriate treatments. Fill pulp chamber and canal with endodontic materials. Formulate plan of treatment for patient's teeth and mouth tissue. Manage business, employing and supervising staff and handling paperwork and insurance claims. Perform oral and periodontal surgery on the jaw or mouth. Remove diseased tissue, using surgical instruments. Treat exposure of pulp by pulp capping, removal of

Investigative—D

pulp from pulp chamber, or root canal, using dental instruments. Plan, organize, and maintain dental health programs. Produce and evaluate dental health educational materials. Write prescriptions for antibiotics and other medications. Use air turbine and hand instruments, dental appliances, and surgical implements. Use masks, gloves, and safety glasses to protect themselves and their patients from infectious diseases. **SKILLS**—Science; Reading Comprehension; Active Learning; Service Orientation; Critical Thinking; Judgment and Decision Making; Learning Strategies; Writing; Monitoring; Management of Financial Resources.

GOE—Interest Area: 14. Medical and Health Services. **Work Group:** 14.03. Dentistry. **Other Jobs in This Work Group:** Dental Assistants; Dental Hygienists; Dentists, All Other Specialists; Healthcare Support Workers, All Other; Oral and Maxillofacial Surgeons; Orthodontists; Prosthodontists.

EDUCATION/TRAINING PROGRAM(S)— Advanced General Dentistry (Cert, MS, PhD); Dental Public Health and Education (Cert, MS/MPH, PhD/DPH); Dental Public Health Specialty; Dentistry (DDS, DMD); Pediatric Dentistry/Pedodontics (Cert, MS, PhD); Pedodontics Specialty. **RELATED KNOWLEDGE/COURSES**—Medicine and Dentistry; Biology; Chemistry; English Language; Administration and Management; Psychology.

Economists

- Personality Code: IE
- Growth: 13.4%
- Annual Job Openings: 2,000
- Annual Earnings: $70,250
- Education/Training Required: Bachelor's degree
- Self-Employed: 11.5%
- Part-Time: 8.3%

Conduct research, prepare reports, or formulate plans to aid in solution of economic problems arising from production and distribution of goods and services. May collect and process economic and statistical data, using econometric and sampling techniques. Compile, analyze, and report data to explain economic phenomena and forecast market trends, applying mathematical models and statistical techniques. Develop economic guidelines and standards and prepare points of view used in forecasting trends and formulating economic policy. Forecast production and consumption of renewable resources and supply, consumption, and depletion of non-renewable resources. Study economic and statistical data in area of specialization, such as finance, labor, or agriculture. Formulate recommendations, policies, or plans to solve economic problems or to interpret markets. Provide advice and consultation on economic relationships to businesses, public and private agencies, and other employers. Supervise research projects and students' study projects. Teach theories, principles, and methods of economics. Testify at regulatory or legislative hearings concerning the estimated effects of changes in legislation or public policy and present recommendations based on cost-benefit analyses. **SKILLS**— Systems Evaluation; Systems Analysis; Persuasion; Judgment and Decision Making; Complex Problem Solving; Instructing; Writing; Learning Strategies.

GOE—Interest Area: 02. Science, Math, and Engineering. **Work Group:** 02.04. Social Sciences. **Other Jobs in This Work Group:** Anthropologists; Anthropologists and Archeologists; Archeologists; City Planning Aides; Historians; Industrial-Organizational Psychologists; Life, Physical, and Social Science Technicians, All Other; Political Scientists; Psychologists, All Other; Social Science Research Assistants; Social Scientists and Related Workers, All Other; Sociologists; Survey Researchers; Urban and Regional Planners.

EDUCATION/TRAINING PROGRAM(S)— Agricultural Economics; Applied Economics; Business/Managerial Economics; Development Economics and International Development; Econometrics and Quantitative Economics; Economics, General; Economics, Other; International Economics. **RELATED KNOWLEDGE/COURSES—** Economics and Accounting; Mathematics; Education and Training; Personnel and Human Resources; Production and Processing; Computers and Electronics.

Educational Psychologists

- Personality Code: IS
- Growth: 24.4%
- Annual Job Openings: 17,000
- Annual Earnings: $52,220
- Education/Training Required: Master's degree
- Self-Employed: 25.4%
- Part-Time: 27.2%

Investigate processes of learning and teaching and develop psychological principles and techniques applicable to educational problems. Collect and analyze data to evaluate the effectiveness of academic programs and other services, such as behavioral management systems. Collaborate with other educational professionals to develop teaching strategies and school programs. Compile and interpret students' test results, along with information from teachers and parents, in order to diagnose conditions and to help assess eligibility for special services. Design classes and programs to meet the needs of special students. Develop individualized educational plans in collaboration with teachers and other staff members. Promote an understanding of child development and its relationship to learning and behavior. Provide consultation to parents, teachers, administrators, and others on topics such as learning styles and behavior modification techniques. Provide educational programs on topics such as class-

room management, teaching strategies, or parenting skills. Refer students and their families to appropriate community agencies for medical, vocational, or social services. Select, administer, and score psychological tests. Serve as a resource to help families and schools deal with crises, such as separation and loss. Attend workshops, seminars, and/or professional meetings in order to remain informed of new developments in school psychology. Conduct research to generate new knowledge that can be used to address learning and behavior issues. Initiate and direct efforts to foster tolerance, understanding, and appreciation of diversity in school communities. Maintain student records, including special education reports, confidential records, records of services provided, and behavioral data. Report any pertinent information to the proper authorities in cases of child endangerment, neglect, or abuse. Assess an individual child's needs, limitations, and potential, using observation, review of school records, and consultation with parents and school personnel. Counsel children and families to help solve conflicts and problems in learning and adjustment. **SKILLS—**Social Perceptiveness; Systems Evaluation; Science; Learning Strategies; Systems Analysis; Writing; Complex Problem Solving; Mathematics; Service Orientation.

GOE—Interest Area: 12. Education and Social Service. **Work Group:** 12.03. Educational Services. **Other Jobs in This Work Group:** Adult Literacy, Remedial Education, and GED Teachers and Instructors; Agricultural Sciences Teachers, Postsecondary; Anthropology and Archeology Teachers, Postsecondary; Architecture Teachers, Postsecondary; Archivists; Area, Ethnic, and Cultural Studies Teachers, Postsecondary; Art, Drama, and Music Teachers, Postsecondary; Atmospheric, Earth, Marine, and Space Sciences Teachers, Postsecondary; Audio-Visual Collections Specialists; Biological Science Teachers, Postsecondary; Business Teachers, Postsecondary; Chemistry Teachers, Postsecondary; Child Care Workers; Communications Teachers, Postsecondary; Computer Science Teachers, Postsecondary; Criminal Justice and Law

Investigative—E

Enforcement Teachers, Postsecondary; Curators; Economics Teachers, Postsecondary; Education Teachers, Postsecondary; Education, Training, and Library Workers, All Other; Educational, Vocational, and School Counselors; Elementary School Teachers, Except Special Education; Engineering Teachers, Postsecondary; English Language and Literature Teachers, Postsecondary; Environmental Science Teachers, Postsecondary; Farm and Home Management Advisors; Foreign Language and Literature Teachers, Postsecondary; Forestry and Conservation Science Teachers, Postsecondary; Geography Teachers, Postsecondary; Graduate Teaching Assistants; Health Specialties Teachers, Postsecondary; History Teachers, Postsecondary; Home Economics Teachers, Postsecondary; Kindergarten Teachers, Except Special Education; Law Teachers, Postsecondary; Librarians; Library Assistants, Clerical; Library Science Teachers, Postsecondary; Library Technicians; Mathematical Science Teachers, Postsecondary; Middle School Teachers, Except Special and Vocational Education; Museum Technicians and Conservators; Nannies; Nursing Instructors and Teachers, Postsecondary; Personal Financial Advisors; Philosophy and Religion Teachers, Postsecondary; Physics Teachers, Postsecondary; Political Science Teachers, Postsecondary; Postsecondary Teachers, All Other; Preschool Teachers, Except Special Education; Psychology Teachers, Postsecondary; Recreation and Fitness Studies Teachers, Postsecondary; Secondary School Teachers, Except Special and Vocational Education; Self-Enrichment Education Teachers; Social Sciences Teachers, Postsecondary, All Other; Social Work Teachers, Postsecondary; Sociology Teachers, Postsecondary; Special Education Teachers, Middle School; Special Education Teachers, Preschool, Kindergarten, and Elementary School; Special Education Teachers, Secondary School; Teacher Assistants; Teachers and Instructors, All Other; Vocational Education Teachers, Postsecondary; Vocational Education Teachers, Middle School; Vocational Education Teachers, Secondary School.

EDUCATION/TRAINING PROGRAM(S)— Clinical Child Psychology; Clinical Psychology; Counseling Psychology; Developmental and Child Psychology; Psychoanalysis and Psychotherapy; Psychology, General; School Psychology. RELATED KNOWLEDGE/COURSES—Psychology; Education and Training; Therapy and Counseling; Sociology and Anthropology; Mathematics; English Language.

Electrical Engineers

- Personality Code: IR
- Growth: 2.5%
- Annual Job Openings: 11,000
- Annual Earnings: $69,640
- Education/Training Required: Bachelor's degree
- Self-Employed: 3.3%
- Part-Time: 2.4%

Design, develop, test, or supervise the manufacturing and installation of electrical equipment, components, or systems for commercial, industrial, military, or scientific use. Confer with engineers, customers, and others to discuss existing or potential engineering projects and products. Design, implement, maintain, and improve electrical instruments, equipment, facilities, components, products, and systems for commercial, industrial, and domestic purposes. Operate computer-assisted engineering and design software and equipment to perform engineering tasks. Direct and coordinate manufacturing, construction, installation, maintenance, support, documentation, and testing activities to ensure compliance with specifications, codes, and customer requirements. Perform detailed calculations to compute and establish manufacturing, construction, and installation standards and specifications. Inspect completed installations and observe operations to ensure conformance to design and equipment specifications and compliance with operational and safety standards. Plan and implement research methodology and procedures to apply principles of electrical theory to engineering projects. Prepare specifications for purchase of materials and equipment. Supervise and train project team members as necessary. Investigate and test vendors' and competitors' products. Oversee project production efforts to assure projects are completed satisfactorily, on time, and within budget. Prepare and study technical drawings, specifications of electrical systems, and topographical maps to ensure that installation and operations conform to standards and customer requirements. Investigate customer or public complaints, determine nature and extent of problem, and recommend remedial measures. Plan layout of electric power generating plants and distribution lines and stations. Assist in developing capital project programs for new equipment and major repairs. Develop budgets, estimating labor, material, and construction costs. **SKILLS**—Troubleshooting; Technology Design; Systems Analysis; Science; Systems Evaluation; Management of Material Resources; Complex Problem Solving; Equipment Selection.

GOE—Interest Area: 02. Science, Math, and Engineering. **Work Group:** 02.07. Engineering. **Other Jobs in This Work Group:** Aerospace Engineers; Agricultural Engineers; Architects, Except Landscape and Naval; Biomedical Engineers; Chemical Engineers; Civil Engineers; Computer Hardware Engineers; Computer Software Engineers, Applications; Computer Software Engineers, Systems Software; Electronics Engineers, Except Computer; Engineers, All Other; Environmental Engineers; Fire-Prevention and Protection Engineers; Health and Safety Engineers, Except Mining Safety Engineers and Inspectors; Industrial Engineers; Industrial Safety and Health Engineers; Landscape Architects; Marine Architects; Marine Engineers; Marine Engineers and Naval Architects; Materials Engineers; Mechanical Engineers; Mining and Geological Engineers, Including Mining Safety Engineers; Nuclear Engineers; Petroleum Engineers; Product Safety Engineers; Sales Engineers.

EDUCATION/TRAINING PROGRAM(S)—Electrical, Electronics and Communications Engineering. **RELATED KNOWLEDGE/COURSES**—Engineering and Technology; Design; Computers and Electronics; Physics; Mathematics; Telecommunications.

Electronics Engineers, Except Computer

- Personality Code: IR
- Growth: 9.4%
- Annual Job Openings: 11,000
- Annual Earnings: $71,370
- Education/Training Required: Bachelor's degree
- Self-Employed: 3.1%
- Part-Time: 2.4%

Research, design, develop, and test electronic components and systems for commercial, industrial, military, or scientific use, utilizing knowledge of electronic theory and materials properties. Design electronic circuits and components for use in fields such as telecommunications, aerospace guidance and propulsion control, acoustics, or instruments and controls. Analyze system requirements, capacity, cost, and customer needs to determine feasibility of project and develop system plan. Confer with engineers, customers, vendors, and others to discuss existing and potential engineering projects or products. Design electronic components and software, products, and systems for commercial, industrial, medical, military, and scientific applications. Develop and perform operational, maintenance, and testing procedures for electronic products, components, equipment, and systems. Direct and coordinate activities concerned with manufacture, construction, installation, maintenance, operation, and modification of electronic equipment, products, and systems. Evaluate operational systems, prototypes, and proposals and recommend repair or design modifications based on factors such as environment, service, cost, and system capabilities. Inspect electronic equipment, instruments, products, and systems to ensure conformance to specifications, safety standards, and applicable codes and regulations. Plan and develop applications and modifications for electronic properties used in components, products, and systems to improve technical performance. Plan and implement research, methodology, and procedures to apply principles of electronic theory to engineering projects. Prepare engineering sketches and specifications for construction, relocation, and installation of equipment, facilities, products, and systems. Determine material and equipment needs and order supplies. Prepare, review, and maintain maintenance schedules, design documentation, and operational reports and charts. Provide technical support and instruction to staff and customers regarding equipment standards and help solve specific, difficult in-service engineering problems. Review and evaluate work of others, inside and outside the organization, to ensure effectiveness, technical adequacy, and compatibility in the resolution of complex engineering problems. Review or prepare budget and cost estimates for equipment, construction, and installation projects and control expenditures. Operate computer-assisted engineering and design software and equipment to perform engineering tasks. **SKILLS**—Science; Mathematics; Writing; Judgment and Decision Making; Management of Financial Resources; Reading Comprehension; Technology Design; Systems Analysis.

GOE—**Interest Area:** 02. Science, Math, and Engineering. **Work Group:** 02.07. Engineering. **Other Jobs in This Work Group:** Aerospace Engineers; Agricultural Engineers; Architects, Except Landscape and Naval; Biomedical Engineers; Chemical Engineers; Civil Engineers; Computer Hardware Engineers; Computer Software Engineers, Applications; Computer Software Engineers, Systems Software; Electrical Engineers; Engineers, All Other; Environmental Engineers; Fire-Prevention and Pro-

tection Engineers; Health and Safety Engineers, Except Mining Safety Engineers and Inspectors; Industrial Engineers; Industrial Safety and Health Engineers; Landscape Architects; Marine Architects; Marine Engineers; Marine Engineers and Naval Architects; Materials Engineers; Mechanical Engineers; Mining and Geological Engineers, Including Mining Safety Engineers; Nuclear Engineers; Petroleum Engineers; Product Safety Engineers; Sales Engineers.

EDUCATION/TRAINING PROGRAM(S)—Electrical, Electronics, and Communications Engineering. **RELATED KNOWLEDGE/COURSES**—Engineering and Technology; Design; Computers and Electronics; Telecommunications; Production and Processing; Mathematics.

Engineering Teachers, Postsecondary

- Personality Code: IR
- Growth: 38.1%
- Annual Job Openings: 216,000
- Annual Earnings: $69,700
- Education/Training Required: Master's degree
- Self-Employed: 0.3%
- Part-Time: 27.7%

Teach courses pertaining to the application of physical laws and principles of engineering for the development of machines, materials, instruments, processes, and services. Includes teachers of subjects such as chemical, civil, electrical, industrial, mechanical, mineral, and petroleum engineering. Includes both teachers primarily engaged in teaching and those who do a combination of both teaching and research. Maintain regularly scheduled office hours in order to advise and assist students. Maintain student attendance records, grades, and other required records. Plan, evaluate, and revise curricula, course content, and course materials and methods of instruction. Prepare course materials such as syllabi, homework assignments, and handouts. Select and obtain materials and supplies such as textbooks and laboratory equipment. Supervise students' laboratory work. Supervise undergraduate and/or graduate teaching, internship, and research work. Act as advisers to student organizations. Collaborate with colleagues to address teaching and research issues. Conduct research in a particular field of knowledge and publish findings in professional journals, books, and/or electronic media. Participate in campus and community events. Participate in student recruitment, registration, and placement activities. Perform administrative duties such as serving as department head. Provide professional consulting services to government and/or industry. Serve on academic or administrative committees that deal with institutional policies, departmental matters, and academic issues. Write grant proposals to procure external research funding. Evaluate and grade students' class work, laboratory work, assignments, and papers. Prepare and deliver lectures to undergraduate and/or graduate students on topics such as mechanics, hydraulics, and robotics. Advise students on academic and vocational curricula and on career issues. Compile, administer, and grade examinations or assign this work to others. Compile bibliographies of specialized materials for outside reading assignments. Initiate, facilitate, and moderate class discussions. Keep abreast of developments in their field by reading current literature, talking with colleagues, and participating in professional conferences. **SKILLS**—Science; Mathematics; Instructing; Technology Design; Active Learning; Critical Thinking; Learning Strategies; Reading Comprehension; Operations Analysis.

GOE—Interest Area: 12. Education and Social Service. **Work Group:** 12.03. Educational Services. **Other Jobs in This Work Group:** Adult Literacy, Remedial Education, and GED Teachers and Instructors; Agricultural Sciences Teachers, Postsecondary; Anthropology and Archeology Teachers, Postsecondary; Architecture Teachers, Postsecondary; Archivists; Area, Ethnic, and Cultural Studies Teachers, Postsecondary; Art, Drama, and Music Teachers, Postsecondary; Atmospheric, Earth, Marine, and Space Sciences Teachers, Postsecondary; Audio-Visual Collections Specialists; Biological Science Teachers, Postsecondary; Business Teachers, Postsecondary; Chemistry Teachers, Postsecondary; Child Care Workers; Communications Teachers, Postsecondary; Computer Science Teachers, Postsecondary; Criminal Justice and Law Enforcement Teachers, Postsecondary; Curators; Economics Teachers, Postsecondary; Education Teachers, Postsecondary; Education, Training, and Library Workers, All Other; Educational Psychologists; Educational, Vocational, and School Counselors; Elementary School Teachers, Except Special Education; English Language and Literature Teachers, Postsecondary; Environmental Science Teachers, Postsecondary; Farm and Home Management Advisors; Foreign Language and Literature Teachers, Postsecondary; Forestry and Conservation Science Teachers, Postsecondary; Geography Teachers, Postsecondary; Graduate Teaching Assistants; Health Specialties Teachers, Postsecondary; History Teachers, Postsecondary; Home Economics Teachers, Postsecondary; Kindergarten Teachers, Except Special Education; Law Teachers, Postsecondary; Librarians; Library Assistants, Clerical; Library Science Teachers, Postsecondary; Library Technicians; Mathematical Science Teachers, Postsecondary; Middle School Teachers, Except Special and Vocational Education; Museum Technicians and Conservators; Nannies; Nursing Instructors and Teachers, Postsecondary; Personal Financial Advisors; Philosophy and Religion Teachers, Postsecondary; Physics Teachers, Postsecondary; Political Science Teachers, Postsecondary; Postsecondary Teachers, All Other; Preschool Teachers, Except Special Education; Psychology Teachers, Postsecondary; Recreation and Fitness Studies Teachers, Postsecondary; Secondary School Teachers, Except Special and Vocational Education; Self-Enrichment Education Teachers; Social Sciences Teachers, Postsecondary, All Other;

Investigative—E

Social Work Teachers, Postsecondary; Sociology Teachers, Postsecondary; Special Education Teachers, Middle School; Special Education Teachers, Preschool, Kindergarten, and Elementary School; Special Education Teachers, Secondary School; Teacher Assistants; Teachers and Instructors, All Other; Vocational Education Teachers, Postsecondary; Vocational Education Teachers, Middle School; Vocational Education Teachers, Secondary School.

EDUCATION/TRAINING PROGRAM(S)— Aerospace, Aeronautical, and Astronautical Engineering; Agricultural/Biological Engineering and Bioengineering; Architectural Engineering; Biomedical/Medical Engineering; Ceramic Sciences and Engineering; Chemical Engineering; Civil Engineering, General; Civil Engineering, Other; Computer Engineering, General; Computer Engineering, Other; Computer Hardware Engineering; Computer Software Engineering; Construction Engineering; Electrical, Electronics, and Communications Engineering; Engineering Mechanics; Engineering Physics; Engineering Science; Engineering, General; Engineering, Other; Environmental/Environmental Health Engineering; Forest Engineering; Geological/Geophysical Engineering; Geotechnical Engineering; Industrial Engineering; Manufacturing Engineering; Materials Engineering; Materials Science; Mechanical Engineering; Metallurgical Engineering; Mining and Mineral Engineering; Naval Architecture and Marine Engineering; Nuclear Engineering; Ocean Engineering; Petroleum Engineering; Polymer/Plastics Engineering; Structural Engineering; Surveying Engineering; Systems Engineering; Teacher Education and Professional Development, Specific Subject Areas, Other; Textile Sciences and Engineering; Transportation and Highway Engineering; Water Resources Engineering. RELATED KNOWLEDGE/COURSES—Engineering and Technology; Education and Training; Physics; Chemistry; Design; Mathematics.

Environmental Scientists and Specialists, Including Health

- Personality Code: IR
- Growth: 23.7%
- Annual Job Openings: 6,000
- Annual Earnings: $48,790
- Education/Training Required: Bachelor's degree
- Self-Employed: 2.9%
- Part-Time: 7.7%

Conduct research or perform investigation for the purpose of identifying, abating, or eliminating sources of pollutants or hazards that affect either the environment or the health of the population. Utilizing knowledge of various scientific disciplines, may collect, synthesize, study, report, and take action based on data derived from measurements or observations of air, food, soil, water, and other sources. Conduct environmental audits and inspections and investigations of violations. Evaluate violations or problems discovered during inspections in order to determine appropriate regulatory actions or to provide advice on the development and prosecution of regulatory cases. Communicate scientific and technical information through oral briefings, written documents, workshops, conferences, and public hearings. Review and implement environmental technical standards, guidelines, policies, and formal regulations that meet all appropriate requirements. Provide technical guidance, support, and oversight to environmental programs, industry, and the public. Provide advice on proper standards and regulations and the development of policies, strategies, and codes of practice for environmental management. Analyze data to determine validity, quality, and scientific significance and to interpret correlations between human activities and environmental effects. Collect, synthesize, and analyze data derived from pollution emission measurements, atmospheric monitoring, meteorological and mineralogical information, and soil or water samples. Determine data collection methods to be employed in research projects and surveys. Prepare charts or graphs from data samples and provide summary information on the environmental relevance of the data. Develop the technical portions of legal documents, administrative orders, or consent decrees. Investigate and report on accidents affecting the environment. Monitor environmental impacts of development activities. Supervise environmental technologists and technicians. Develop programs designed to obtain the most productive, non-damaging use of land. Research sources of pollution to determine their effects on the environment and to develop theories or methods of pollution abatement or control. Monitor effects of pollution and land degradation and recommend means of prevention or control. Design and direct studies to obtain technical environmental information about planned projects. Conduct applied research on topics such as waste control and treatment and pollution control methods. **SKILLS**—Service Orientation; Science; Coordination; Negotiation; Persuasion; Reading Comprehension; Active Learning; Time Management.

GOE—Interest Area: 02. Science, Math, and Engineering. **Work Group:** 02.03. Life Sciences. **Other Jobs in This Work Group:** Agricultural and Food Science Technicians; Agricultural Technicians; Animal Scientists; Biochemists; Biochemists and Biophysicists; Biological Scientists, All Other; Biologists; Biophysicists; Conservation Scientists; Epidemiologists; Food Science Technicians; Food Scientists and Technologists; Foresters; Life Scientists, All Other; Medical Scientists, Except Epidemiologists; Microbiologists; Plant Scientists; Range Managers; Soil and Plant Scientists; Soil Conservationists; Soil Scientists; Zoologists and Wildlife Biologists.

EDUCATION/TRAINING PROGRAM(S)—Environmental Science; Environmental Studies. **RELATED KNOWLEDGE/COURSES**—Biolo-gy; Geography; Law and Government; Chemistry; Customer and Personal Service; Education and Training.

Family and General Practitioners

◎ Personality Code: I

◎ Growth: 19.5%

◎ Annual Job Openings: 38,000

◎ Annual Earnings: $133,340

◎ Education/Training Required: First professional degree

◎ Self-Employed: 16.9%

◎ Part-Time: 8.1%

Diagnose, treat, and help prevent diseases and injuries that commonly occur in the general population. Advise patients and community members concerning diet, activity, hygiene, and disease prevention. Collect, record, and maintain patient information, such as medical history, reports, and examination results. Explain procedures and discuss test results or prescribed treatments with patients. Monitor the patients' conditions and progress and re-evaluate treatments as necessary. Order, perform, and interpret tests and analyze records, reports, and examination information to diagnose patients' condition. Prescribe or administer treatment, therapy, medication, vaccination, and other specialized medical care to treat or prevent illness, disease, or injury. Refer patients to medical specialists or other practitioners when necessary. Conduct research to study anatomy and develop or test medications, treatments, or procedures to prevent or control disease or injury. Coordinate work with nurses, social workers, rehabilitation therapists, pharmacists, psychologists, and other health care providers. Deliver babies. Direct and coordinate activities of nurses, students, assistants, specialists, therapists, and other medical staff. Operate on patients to remove, repair, or improve functioning of diseased or injured body parts and systems. Plan, implement, or administer health programs or standards in hospital, business, or community for information, prevention, or treatment of injury or illness. Prepare reports for government or management of birth, death, and disease statistics; workforce evaluations; or medical status of individuals. **SKILLS**—Science; Reading Comprehension; Systems Evaluation; Active Learning; Judgment and Decision Making; Management of Personnel Resources; Social Perceptiveness; Systems Analysis.

GOE—Interest Area: 14. Medical and Health Services. **Work Group:** 14.02. Medicine and Surgery. **Other Jobs in This Work Group:** Anesthesiologists; Healthcare Support Workers, All Other; Internists, General; Medical Assistants; Obstetricians and Gynecologists; Pediatricians, General; Pharmacists; Pharmacy Aides; Pharmacy Technicians; Physician Assistants; Physicians and Surgeons, All Other; Psychiatrists; Registered Nurses; Surgeons; Surgical Technologists.

EDUCATION/TRAINING PROGRAM(S)— Family Medicine; Medicine (MD); Osteopathic Medicine/Osteopathy (DO). **RELATED KNOWLEDGE/COURSES**—Medicine and Dentistry; Biology; Therapy and Counseling; Chemistry; Administration and Management; Personnel and Human Resources; Physics.

Financial Analysts

- Personality Code: IC
- Growth: 18.7%
- Annual Job Openings: 22,000
- Annual Earnings: $60,050
- Education/Training Required: Bachelor's degree
- Self-Employed: 4.8%
- Part-Time: 10.2%

Conduct quantitative analyses of information affecting investment programs of public or private institutions. Analyze financial information to produce forecasts of business, industry, and economic conditions for use in making investment decisions. Assemble spreadsheets and draw charts and graphs used to illustrate technical reports, using computer. Evaluate and compare the relative quality of various securities in a given industry. Interpret data affecting investment programs, such as price, yield, stability, future trends in investment risks, and economic influences. Maintain knowledge and stay abreast of developments in the fields of industrial technology, business, finance, and economic theory. Monitor fundamental economic, industrial, and corporate developments through the analysis of information obtained from financial publications and services, investment banking firms, government agencies, trade publications, company sources, and personal interviews. Prepare plans of action for investment based on financial analyses. Present oral and written reports on general economic trends, individual corporations, and entire industries. Recommend investments and investment timing to companies, investment firm staff, or the investing public. Collaborate with investment bankers to attract new corporate clients to securities firms. Contact brokers and purchase investments for companies according to company policy. Determine the prices at which securities should be syndicated and offered to the public. **SKILLS**—Judgment and Decision Making; Systems Analysis; Critical Thinking; Active Learning; Systems Evaluation; Reading Comprehension; Mathematics; Management of Financial Resources.

GOE—Interest Area: 13. General Management and Support. **Work Group:** 13.02. Management Support. **Other Jobs in This Work Group:** Accountants; Accountants and Auditors; Appraisers and Assessors of Real Estate; Appraisers, Real Estate; Assessors; Auditors; Budget Analysts; Business Operations Specialists, All Other; Claims Adjusters, Examiners, and Investigators; Claims Examiners, Property and Casualty Insurance; Compensation, Benefits, and Job Analysis Specialists; Cost Estimators; Credit Analysts; Employment Interviewers, Private or Public Employment Service; Employment, Recruitment, and Placement Specialists; Human Resources, Training, and Labor Relations Specialists, All Other; Insurance Adjusters, Examiners, and Investigators; Insurance Appraisers, Auto Damage; Insurance Underwriters; Loan Counselors; Loan Officers; Logisticians; Management Analysts; Market Research Analysts; Personnel Recruiters; Purchasing Agents and Buyers, Farm Products; Purchasing Agents, Except Wholesale, Retail, and Farm Products; Tax Examiners, Collectors, and Revenue Agents; Training and Development Specialists; Wholesale and Retail Buyers, Except Farm Products.

EDUCATION/TRAINING PROGRAM(S)— Accounting and Business/Management; Accounting and Finance; Finance, General. **RELATED KNOWLEDGE/COURSES**—Economics and Accounting; Mathematics; Law and Government; Computers and Electronics; Sales and Marketing; English Language.

Forestry and Conservation Science Teachers, Postsecondary

- Personality Code: IS
- Growth: 38.1%
- Annual Job Openings: 216,000
- Annual Earnings: $64,500
- Education/Training Required: Master's degree
- Self-Employed: 0.3%
- Part-Time: 27.7%

Teach courses in environmental and conservation science. Evaluate and grade students' class work, assignments, and papers. Prepare and deliver lectures to undergraduate and/or graduate students on topics such as forest resource policy, forest pathology, and mapping. Advise students on academic and vocational curricula and on career issues. Compile, administer, and grade examinations or assign this work to others. Compile bibliographies of specialized materials for outside reading assignments. Initiate, facilitate, and moderate classroom discussions. Keep abreast of developments in their field by reading current literature, talking with colleagues, and participating in professional conferences. Maintain regularly scheduled office hours in order to advise and assist students. Maintain student attendance records, grades, and other required records. Plan, evaluate, and revise curricula, course content, and course materials and methods of instruction. Prepare course materials such as syllabi, homework assignments, and handouts. Select and obtain materials and supplies such as textbooks and laboratory equipment. Supervise students' laboratory and/or field work. Supervise undergraduate and/or graduate teaching, internship, and research work. Act as advisers to student organizations. Collaborate with colleagues to address teaching and research issues. Conduct research in a particular field of knowledge and publish findings in books, professional journals, and/or electronic media. Participate in campus and community events. Participate in student recruitment, registration, and placement activities. Perform administrative duties such as serving as department head. Provide professional consulting services to government and/or industry. Serve on academic or administrative committees that deal with institutional policies, departmental matters, and academic issues. Write grant proposals to procure external research funding. **SKILLS**—Science; Instructing; Learning Strategies; Reading Comprehension; Active Learning; Writing; Critical Thinking; Mathematics.

GOE—Interest Area: 12. Education and Social Service. **Work Group:** 12.03. Educational Services. **Other Jobs in This Work Group:** Adult Literacy, Remedial Education, and GED Teachers and

Investigative—F

Instructors; Agricultural Sciences Teachers, Postsecondary; Anthropology and Archeology Teachers, Postsecondary; Architecture Teachers, Postsecondary; Archivists; Area, Ethnic, and Cultural Studies Teachers, Postsecondary; Art, Drama, and Music Teachers, Postsecondary; Atmospheric, Earth, Marine, and Space Sciences Teachers, Postsecondary; Audio-Visual Collections Specialists; Biological Science Teachers, Postsecondary; Business Teachers, Postsecondary; Chemistry Teachers, Postsecondary; Child Care Workers; Communications Teachers, Postsecondary; Computer Science Teachers, Postsecondary; Criminal Justice and Law Enforcement Teachers, Postsecondary; Curators; Economics Teachers, Postsecondary; Education Teachers, Postsecondary; Education, Training, and Library Workers, All Other; Educational Psychologists; Educational, Vocational, and School Counselors; Elementary School Teachers, Except Special Education; Engineering Teachers, Postsecondary; English Language and Literature Teachers, Postsecondary; Environmental Science Teachers, Postsecondary; Farm and Home Management Advisors; Foreign Language and Literature Teachers, Postsecondary; Geography Teachers, Postsecondary; Graduate Teaching Assistants; Health Specialties Teachers, Postsecondary; History Teachers, Postsecondary; Home Economics Teachers, Postsecondary; Kindergarten Teachers, Except Special Education; Law Teachers, Postsecondary; Librarians; Library Assistants, Clerical; Library Science Teachers, Postsecondary; Library Technicians; Mathematical Science Teachers, Postsecondary; Middle School Teachers, Except Special and Vocational Education; Museum Technicians and Conservators; Nannies; Nursing Instructors and Teachers, Postsecondary; Personal Financial Advisors; Philosophy and Religion Teachers, Postsecondary; Physics Teachers, Postsecondary; Political Science Teachers, Postsecondary; Postsecondary Teachers, All Other; Preschool Teachers, Except Special Education; Psychology Teachers, Postsecondary; Recreation and Fitness Studies Teachers, Postsecondary; Secondary School Teachers, Except Special and Vocational Education; Self-Enrichment Education Teachers;

Social Sciences Teachers, Postsecondary, All Other; Social Work Teachers, Postsecondary; Sociology Teachers, Postsecondary; Special Education Teachers, Middle School; Special Education Teachers, Preschool, Kindergarten, and Elementary School; Special Education Teachers, Secondary School; Teacher Assistants; Teachers and Instructors, All Other; Vocational Education Teachers, Postsecondary; Vocational Education Teachers, Middle School; Vocational Education Teachers, Secondary School.

EDUCATION/TRAINING PROGRAM(S)—Science Teacher Education/General Science Teacher Education. RELATED KNOWLEDGE/COURSES—Biology; Education and Training; Medicine and Dentistry; Chemistry; Therapy and Counseling; Psychology.

Geologists

- Personality Code: IR
- Growth: 11.5%
- Annual Job Openings: 2,000
- Annual Earnings: $68,460
- Education/Training Required: Bachelor's degree
- Self-Employed: 2.7%
- Part-Time: 7.7%

Study composition, structure, and history of the earth's crust; examine rocks, minerals, and fossil remains to identify and determine the sequence of processes affecting the development of the earth; apply knowledge of chemistry, physics, biology, and mathematics to explain these phenomena and to help locate mineral and petroleum deposits and underground water resources; prepare geologic reports and maps; and interpret research data to recommend further action for study. Analyze and interpret geological, geochemical, and geophysical information from sources such as survey data, well logs, boreholes, and aerial photos. Plan and conduct geological, geochemical, and geophysical field studies and surveys; sample collection; and drilling and testing programs used to collect data for research and/or application. Investigate the composition, structure, and history of the Earth's crust through the collection, examination, measurement, and classification of soils, minerals, rocks, and fossil remains. Prepare geological maps, cross-sectional diagrams, charts, and reports concerning mineral extraction, land use, and resource management, using results of field work and laboratory research. Locate and estimate probable natural gas, oil, and mineral ore deposits and underground water resources, using aerial photographs, charts, and research and survey results. Assess ground and surface water movement in order to provide advice regarding issues such as waste management, route and site selection, and the restoration of contaminated sites. Identify risks for natural disasters such as mud slides, earthquakes, and volcanic eruptions and provide advice on ways in which potential damage can be mitigated. Conduct geological and geophysical studies to provide information for use in regional development, site selection, and the development of public works projects. Inspect construction projects in order to analyze engineering problems, applying geological knowledge and using test equipment and drilling machinery. Advise construction firms and government agencies on dam and road construction, foundation design, and land use and resource management. **SKILLS**—Science; Management of Financial Resources; Time Management; Active Learning; Coordination; Critical Thinking; Persuasion; Negotiation.

GOE—Interest Area: 02. Science, Math, and Engineering. **Work Group:** 02.02. Physical Sciences. **Other Jobs in This Work Group:** Astronomers; Atmospheric and Space Scientists; Chemists; Geographers; Geoscientists, Except Hydrologists and Geographers; Hydrologists; Materials Scientists; Physical Scientists, All Other; Physicists.

EDUCATION/TRAINING PROGRAM(S)— Geochemistry; Geochemistry and Petrology; Geological and Earth Sciences/Geosciences, Other; Geology/Earth Science, General; Geophysics and Seismology; Oceanography, Chemical and Physical; Paleontology. **RELATED KNOWLEDGE/COURSES**—Geography; Physics; Chemistry; Engineering and Technology; Mathematics; Biology.

Health Specialties Teachers, Postsecondary

- Personality Code: IS
- Growth: 38.1%
- Annual Job Openings: 216,000
- Annual Earnings: $61,790
- Education/Training Required: Master's degree
- Self-Employed: 0.3%
- Part-Time: 27.7%

Teach courses in health specialties, such as veterinary medicine, dentistry, pharmacy, therapy, laboratory technology, and public health. Evaluate and grade students' class work, assignments, and papers. Prepare and deliver lectures to undergraduate and/or graduate students on topics such as public health, stress management, and worksite health promotion. Advise students on academic and vocational curricula and on career issues. Compile, administer, and grade examinations or assign this work to others. Compile bibliographies of specialized materials for outside reading assignments. Initiate, facilitate, and moderate classroom discussions. Keep abreast of developments in their field by reading current literature, talking with colleagues, and participating in professional conferences. Maintain

Investigative—H

regularly scheduled office hours in order to advise and assist students. Maintain student attendance records, grades, and other required records. Plan, evaluate, and revise curricula, course content, and course materials and methods of instruction. Prepare course materials such as syllabi, homework assignments, and handouts. Select and obtain materials and supplies such as textbooks and laboratory equipment. Supervise laboratory sessions. Supervise undergraduate and/or graduate teaching, internship, and research work. Act as advisers to student organizations. Collaborate with colleagues to address teaching and research issues. Conduct research in a particular field of knowledge and publish findings in professional journals, books, and/or electronic media. Participate in campus and community events. Participate in student recruitment, registration, and placement activities. Perform administrative duties such as serving as department head. Provide professional consulting services to government and/or industry. Serve on academic or administrative committees that deal with institutional policies, departmental matters, and academic issues. Write grant proposals to procure external research funding. **SKILLS**—Science; Instructing; Writing; Reading Comprehension; Active Learning; Critical Thinking; Learning Strategies; Speaking.

GOE—Interest Area: 12. Education and Social Service. **Work Group:** 12.03. Educational Services. **Other Jobs in This Work Group:** Adult Literacy, Remedial Education, and GED Teachers and Instructors; Agricultural Sciences Teachers, Postsecondary; Anthropology and Archeology Teachers, Postsecondary; Architecture Teachers, Postsecondary; Archivists; Area, Ethnic, and Cultural Studies Teachers, Postsecondary; Art, Drama, and Music Teachers, Postsecondary; Atmospheric, Earth, Marine, and Space Sciences Teachers, Postsecondary; Audio-Visual Collections Specialists; Biological Science Teachers, Postsecondary; Business Teachers, Postsecondary; Chemistry Teachers, Postsecondary; Child Care Workers; Communications Teachers, Postsecondary; Computer Science Teachers, Postsecondary; Criminal Justice and Law Enforcement Teachers, Postsecondary; Curators; Economics Teachers, Postsecondary; Education Teachers, Postsecondary; Education, Training, and Library Workers, All Other; Educational Psychologists; Educational, Vocational, and School Counselors; Elementary School Teachers, Except Special Education; Engineering Teachers, Postsecondary; English Language and Literature Teachers, Postsecondary; Environmental Science Teachers, Postsecondary; Farm and Home Management Advisors; Foreign Language and Literature Teachers, Postsecondary; Forestry and Conservation Science Teachers, Postsecondary; Geography Teachers, Postsecondary; Graduate Teaching Assistants; History Teachers, Postsecondary; Home Economics Teachers, Postsecondary; Kindergarten Teachers, Except Special Education; Law Teachers, Postsecondary; Librarians; Library Assistants, Clerical; Library Science Teachers, Postsecondary; Library Technicians; Mathematical Science Teachers, Postsecondary; Middle School Teachers, Except Special and Vocational Education; Museum Technicians and Conservators; Nannies; Nursing Instructors and Teachers, Postsecondary; Personal Financial Advisors; Philosophy and Religion Teachers, Postsecondary; Physics Teachers, Postsecondary; Political Science Teachers, Postsecondary; Postsecondary Teachers, All Other; Preschool Teachers, Except Special Education; Psychology Teachers, Postsecondary; Recreation and Fitness Studies Teachers, Postsecondary; Secondary School Teachers, Except Special and Vocational Education; Self-Enrichment Education Teachers; Social Sciences Teachers, Postsecondary, All Other; Social Work Teachers, Postsecondary; Sociology Teachers, Postsecondary; Special Education Teachers, Middle School; Special Education Teachers, Preschool, Kindergarten, and Elementary School; Special Education Teachers, Secondary School; Teacher Assistants; Teachers and Instructors, All Other; Vocational Education Teachers, Postsecondary; Vocational Education Teachers, Middle School; Vocational Education Teachers, Secondary School.

EDUCATION/TRAINING PROGRAM(S)— Allied Health and Medical Assisting Services, Other; Allied Health Diagnostic, Intervention, and Treatment Professions, Other; Art Therapy/Therapist; Asian Bodywork Therapy; Audiology/Audiologist and Hearing Sciences; Audiology/Audiologist and Speech-Language Pathology/Pathologist; Biostatistics; Blood Bank Technology Specialist; Cardiovascular Technology/Technologist; Chiropractic (DC); Clinical Laboratory Science/Medical Technology/Technologist; Clinical/Medical Laboratory Assistant; Clinical/Medical Laboratory Technician; Communication Disorders, General; Cytotechnology/Cytotechnologist; Dance Therapy/Therapist; Dental Assisting/Assistant; Dental Clinical Sciences, General (MS, PhD); Dental Hygiene/Hygienist; Dental Laboratory Technology/Technician; Dental Services and Allied Professions, Other; Dentistry (DDS, DMD); Diagnostic Medical Sonography/Sonographer and Ultrasound Technician; Electrocardiograph Technology/Technician; Electroneurodiagnostic/Electroencephalographic Technology/Technologist; Emergency Medical Technology/Technician (EMT Paramedic); Environmental Health; Epidemiology; Health Occupations Teacher Education; Health/Medical Physics; Health/Medical Preparatory Programs, Other; Hematology Technology/Technician; Hypnotherapy/Hypnotherapist; Massage Therapy/Therapeutic Massage; Medical Radiologic Technology/Science—Radiation Therapist; Music Therapy/Therapist; Nuclear Medical Technology/Technologist; Occupational Health and Industrial Hygiene; Occupational Therapist Assistant; Occupational Therapy/Therapist; Orthotist/Prosthetist; Perfusion Technology/Perfusionist; Pharmacy (PharmD [USA], PharmD, BS/BPharm [Canada]); Pharmacy Administration and Pharmacy Policy and Regulatory Affairs (MS, PhD); Pharmacy Technician/Assistant; Pharmacy, Pharmaceutical Sciences, and Administration, Other; Physical Therapist Assistant; Physical Therapy/Therapist; Physician Assistant; Pre-Dentistry Studies; Pre-Medicine/Pre-Medical Studies; Pre-Nursing Studies; others.

RELATED KNOWLEDGE/COURSES— Biology; Education and Training; Medicine and Dentistry; Therapy and Counseling; English Language; Chemistry.

Internists, General

- Personality Code: I
- Growth: 19.5%
- Annual Job Openings: 38,000
- Annual Earnings: more than $145,600
- Education/Training Required: First professional degree
- Self-Employed: 16.9%
- Part-Time: 8.1%

Diagnose and provide non-surgical treatment of diseases and injuries of internal organ systems. Provide care mainly for adults who have a wide range of problems associated with the internal organs. Provide consulting services to other doctors caring for patients with special or difficult problems. Plan, implement, or administer health programs in hospitals, businesses, or communities for prevention and treatment of injuries or illnesses. Prepare government or organizational reports on birth, death, and disease statistics; workforce evaluations; or the medical status of individuals. Advise patients and community members concerning diet, activity, hygiene, and disease prevention. Analyze records, reports, test results, or examination information to diagnose medical condition of patient. Collect, record, and maintain patient information, such as medical history, reports, and examination results. Make diagnoses when different illnesses occur together or in situations where the diagnosis may be obscure. Explain procedures and discuss test results or prescribed treatments with patients. Immunize patients to protect them from preventable diseases. Manage and treat common health problems, such as

Investigative—I

infections, influenza, and pneumonia, as well as serious, chronic, and complex illnesses, in adolescents, adults, and the elderly. Monitor patients' conditions and progress and re-evaluate treatments as necessary. Prescribe or administer medication, therapy, and other specialized medical care to treat or prevent illness, disease, or injury. Provide and manage long-term, comprehensive medical care, including diagnosis and non-surgical treatment of diseases, for adult patients in an office or hospital. Refer patient to medical specialist or other practitioner when necessary. Treat internal disorders, such as hypertension; heart disease; diabetes; and problems of the lung, brain, kidney, and gastrointestinal tract. Advise surgeon of a patient's risk status and recommend appropriate intervention to minimize risk. Conduct research to develop or test medications, treatments, or procedures to prevent or control disease or injury. Direct and coordinate activities of nurses, students, assistants, specialists, therapists, and other medical staff. Operate on patients to remove, repair, or improve functioning of diseased or injured body parts and systems. **SKILLS**—Science; Reading Comprehension; Systems Evaluation; Active Learning; Judgment and Decision Making; Management of Personnel Resources; Social Perceptiveness; Systems Analysis.

GOE—Interest Area: 14. Medical and Health Services. **Work Group:** 14.02. Medicine and Surgery. **Other Jobs in This Work Group:** Anesthesiologists; Family and General Practitioners; Healthcare Support Workers, All Other; Medical Assistants; Obstetricians and Gynecologists; Pediatricians, General; Pharmacists; Pharmacy Aides; Pharmacy Technicians; Physician Assistants; Physicians and Surgeons, All Other; Psychiatrists; Registered Nurses; Surgeons; Surgical Technologists.

EDUCATION/TRAINING PROGRAM(S)— Cardiology; Critical Care Medicine; Endocrinology and Metabolism; Gastroenterology; Geriatric Medicine; Hematology; Infectious Disease; Internal Medicine; Nephrology; Neurology; Nuclear Medicine; Oncology; Pulmonary Disease; Rheumatology. **RELATED KNOWLEDGE/COURSES** —Medicine and Dentistry; Biology; Therapy and Counseling; Chemistry; Administration and Management; Personnel and Human Resources; Physics.

Market Research Analysts

- Personality Code: IE
- Growth: 23.4%
- Annual Job Openings: 18,000
- Annual Earnings: $54,670
- Education/Training Required: Bachelor's degree
- Self-Employed: 7.3%
- Part-Time: 11.7%

Research market conditions in local, regional, or national areas to determine potential sales of a product or service. May gather information on competitors, prices, sales, and methods of marketing and distribution. May use survey results to create a marketing campaign based on regional preferences and buying habits. Collect and analyze data on customer demographics, preferences, needs, and buying habits to identify potential markets and factors affecting product demand. Conduct research on consumer opinions and marketing strategies, collaborating with marketing professionals, statisticians, pollsters, and other professionals. Develop and implement procedures for identifying advertising needs. Devise and evaluate methods and procedures for collecting data (such as surveys, opinion polls, or questionnaires) or arrange to obtain existing data. Forecast and track marketing and sales trends, analyzing collected data. Gather data on competitors and analyze their prices, sales, and method of marketing and distribution. Measure and assess customer and employee satisfaction. Measure the effectiveness of marketing, advertising, and communications programs and strategies. Monitor industry statistics and follow trends in trade literature. Prepare reports of findings, illustrating data graphically and translating complex findings into written text. Attend staff conferences to provide management with information and proposals concerning the promotion, distribution, design, and pricing of company products or services. Direct trained survey interviewers. Seek and provide information to help companies determine their position in the marketplace. **SKILLS**—Programming; Writing; Systems Analysis; Mathematics; Operations Analysis; Systems Evaluation; Monitoring; Active Learning; Complex Problem Solving.

GOE—Interest Area: 13. General Management and Support. **Work Group:** 13.02. Management Support. **Other Jobs in This Work Group:** Accountants; Accountants and Auditors; Appraisers and Assessors of Real Estate; Appraisers, Real Estate; Assessors; Auditors; Budget Analysts; Business Operations Specialists, All Other; Claims Adjusters, Examiners, and Investigators; Claims Examiners, Property and Casualty Insurance; Compensation, Benefits, and Job Analysis Specialists; Cost Estimators; Credit Analysts; Employment Interviewers, Private or Public Employment Service; Employment, Recruitment, and Placement Specialists; Financial Analysts; Human Resources, Training, and Labor Relations Specialists, All Other; Insurance Adjusters, Examiners, and Investigators; Insurance Appraisers, Auto Damage; Insurance Underwriters; Loan Counselors; Loan Officers; Logisticians; Management Analysts; Personnel Recruiters; Purchasing Agents and Buyers, Farm Products; Purchasing Agents, Except Wholesale, Retail, and Farm Products; Tax Examiners, Collectors, and Revenue Agents; Training and Development Specialists; Wholesale and Retail Buyers, Except Farm Products.

EDUCATION/TRAINING PROGRAM(S)— Applied Economics; Business/Managerial Economics; Econometrics and Quantitative Economics; Economics, General; International Economics;

Marketing Research. **RELATED KNOWLEDGE/COURSES**—Sales and Marketing; Psychology; Mathematics; Economics and Accounting; Computers and Electronics; Food Production.

Mathematical Science Teachers, Postsecondary

- Personality Code: IS
- Growth: 38.1%
- Annual Job Openings: 216,000
- Annual Earnings: $50,910
- Education/Training Required: Master's degree
- Self-Employed: 0.3%
- Part-Time: 27.7%

Teach courses pertaining to mathematical concepts, statistics, and actuarial science and to the application of original and standardized mathematical techniques in solving specific problems and situations. Maintain regularly scheduled office hours in order to advise and assist students. Maintain student attendance records, grades, and other required records. Plan, evaluate, and revise curricula, course content, and course materials and methods of instruction. Prepare course materials such as syllabi, homework assignments, and handouts. Select and obtain materials and supplies such as textbooks. Supervise undergraduate and/or graduate teaching, internship, and research work. Act as advisers to student organizations. Collaborate with colleagues to address teaching and research issues. Conduct research in a particular field of knowledge and publish findings in books, professional journals, and/or electronic media. Participate in campus and community events. Participate in student recruitment, registration, and placement activities. Per-

Investigative—M

form administrative duties such as serving as department head. Provide professional consulting services to government and/or industry. Serve on academic or administrative committees that deal with institutional policies, departmental matters, and academic issues. Write grant proposals to procure external research funding. Evaluate and grade students' class work, assignments, and papers. Prepare and deliver lectures to undergraduate and/or graduate students on topics such as linear algebra, differential equations, and discrete mathematics. Advise students on academic and vocational curricula and on career issues. Compile, administer, and grade examinations or assign this work to others. Compile bibliographies of specialized materials for outside reading assignments. Initiate, facilitate, and moderate classroom discussions. Keep abreast of developments in their field by reading current literature, talking with colleagues, and participating in professional conferences. **SKILLS**—Mathematics; Instructing; Learning Strategies; Active Learning; Reading Comprehension; Writing; Critical Thinking; Speaking.

GOE—Interest Area: 12. Education and Social Service. **Work Group:** 12.03. Educational Services. **Other Jobs in This Work Group:** Adult Literacy, Remedial Education, and GED Teachers and Instructors; Agricultural Sciences Teachers, Postsecondary; Anthropology and Archeology Teachers, Postsecondary; Architecture Teachers, Postsecondary; Archivists; Area, Ethnic, and Cultural Studies Teachers, Postsecondary; Art, Drama, and Music Teachers, Postsecondary; Atmospheric, Earth, Marine, and Space Sciences Teachers, Postsecondary; Audio-Visual Collections Specialists; Biological Science Teachers, Postsecondary; Business Teachers, Postsecondary; Chemistry Teachers, Postsecondary; Child Care Workers; Communications Teachers, Postsecondary; Computer Science Teachers, Postsecondary; Criminal Justice and Law Enforcement Teachers, Postsecondary; Curators; Economics Teachers, Postsecondary; Education Teachers, Postsecondary; Education, Training, and Library Workers, All Other; Educational Psychologists; Educational, Vocational, and School Counselors; Elementary School Teachers, Except Special Education; Engineering Teachers, Postsecondary; English Language and Literature Teachers, Postsecondary; Environmental Science Teachers, Postsecondary; Farm and Home Management Advisors; Foreign Language and Literature Teachers, Postsecondary; Forestry and Conservation Science Teachers, Postsecondary; Geography Teachers, Postsecondary; Graduate Teaching Assistants; Health Specialties Teachers, Postsecondary; History Teachers, Postsecondary; Home Economics Teachers, Postsecondary; Kindergarten Teachers, Except Special Education; Law Teachers, Postsecondary; Librarians; Library Assistants, Clerical; Library Science Teachers, Postsecondary; Library Technicians; Middle School Teachers, Except Special and Vocational Education; Museum Technicians and Conservators; Nannies; Nursing Instructors and Teachers, Postsecondary; Personal Financial Advisors; Philosophy and Religion Teachers, Postsecondary; Physics Teachers, Postsecondary; Political Science Teachers, Postsecondary; Postsecondary Teachers, All Other; Preschool Teachers, Except Special Education; Psychology Teachers, Postsecondary; Recreation and Fitness Studies Teachers, Postsecondary; Secondary School Teachers, Except Special and Vocational Education; Self-Enrichment Education Teachers; Social Sciences Teachers, Postsecondary, All Other; Social Work Teachers, Postsecondary; Sociology Teachers, Postsecondary; Special Education Teachers, Middle School; Special Education Teachers, Preschool, Kindergarten, and Elementary School; Special Education Teachers, Secondary School; Teacher Assistants; Teachers and Instructors, All Other; Vocational Education Teachers, Postsecondary; Vocational Education Teachers, Middle School; Vocational Education Teachers, Secondary School.

EDUCATION/TRAINING PROGRAM(S)—Algebra and Number Theory; Analysis and Functional Analysis; Applied Mathematics; Business Statistics; Geometry/Geometric Analysis; Logic; Mathematical Statistics and Probability; Mathematics and Statistics, Other; Mathematics, General; Mathematics, Other; Statistics, General; Topology and Foundations. **RELATED KNOWLEDGE/ COURSES**—Mathematics; Education and Training; English Language; Clerical Studies; Communications and Media; Administration and Management.

Medical and Clinical Laboratory Technologists

- Personality Code: IR
- Growth: 19.3%
- Annual Job Openings: 21,000
- Annual Earnings: $43,640
- Education/Training Required: Bachelor's degree
- Self-Employed: 1.6%
- Part-Time: 16.0%

Perform complex medical laboratory tests for diagnosis, treatment, and prevention of disease. May train or supervise staff. Analyze laboratory findings to check accuracy of results. Conduct chemical analysis of body fluids, including blood, urine, and spinal fluid, to determine presence of normal and abnormal components. Operate, calibrate, and maintain equipment used in quantitative and qualitative analysis, such as spectrophotometers, calorimeters, flame photometers, and computer-controlled analyzers. Enter data from analysis of medical tests and clinical results into computer for storage. Analyze samples of biological material for chemical content or reaction. Establish and monitor programs to ensure the accuracy of laboratory results. Set up, clean, and maintain laboratory equipment. Provide technical information about test results to physicians, family members, and researchers. Supervise, train, and direct lab assistants, medical and clinical laboratory technicians and technologists, and other medical laboratory workers engaged in laboratory testing. Develop, standardize, evaluate, and modify procedures, techniques, and tests used in the analysis of specimens and in medical laboratory experiments. Cultivate, isolate, and assist in identifying microbial organisms and perform various tests on these microorganisms. Study blood samples to determine the number of cells and their morphology, as well as the blood group, type, and compatibility for transfusion purposes, using microscopic technique. Obtain, cut, stain, and mount biological material on slides for microscopic study and diagnosis, following standard laboratory procedures. Select and prepare specimen and media for cell culture, using aseptic technique and knowledge of medium components and cell requirements. Conduct medical research under direction of microbiologist or biochemist. Harvest cell cultures at optimum time based on knowledge of cell cycle differences and culture conditions. **SKILLS**—Equipment Maintenance; Operation Monitoring; Quality Control Analysis; Science; Troubleshooting; Instructing; Repairing; Operation and Control.

GOE—Interest Area: 14. Medical and Health Services. **Work Group:** 14.05. Medical Technology. **Other Jobs in This Work Group:** Cardiovascular Technologists and Technicians; Diagnostic Medical Sonographers; Health Technologists and Technicians, All Other; Medical and Clinical Laboratory Technicians; Medical Equipment Preparers; Nuclear Medicine Technologists; Orthotists and Prosthetists; Radiologic Technicians; Radiologic Technologists; Radiologic Technologists and Technicians.

EDUCATION/TRAINING PROGRAM(S)— Clinical Laboratory Science/Medical Technology/ Technologist; Clinical/Medical Laboratory Science and Allied Professions, Other; Cytogenetics/Genetics/Clinical Genetics Technology/Technologist; Cytotechnology/ Cytotechnologist; Histologic Technology/

Histotechnologist; Renal/Dialysis Technologist/ Technician. **RELATED KNOWLEDGE/ COURSES**—Biology; Chemistry; Computers and Electronics; Public Safety and Security; Customer and Personal Service; Mathematics.

Medical Scientists, Except Epidemiologists

- Personality Code: IR
- Growth: 26.9%
- Annual Job Openings: 6,000
- Annual Earnings: $59,210
- Education/Training Required: Doctoral degree
- Self-Employed: 1.7%
- Part-Time: 8.8%

Conduct research dealing with the understanding of human diseases and the improvement of human health. Engage in clinical investigation or other research, production, technical writing, or related activities. Prepare and analyze organ, tissue, and cell samples to identify toxicity, bacteria, or microorganisms or to study cell structure. Standardize drug dosages, methods of immunization, and procedures for manufacture of drugs and medicinal compounds. Confer with health department, industry personnel, physicians, and others to develop health safety standards and public health improvement programs. Study animal and human health and physiological processes. Consult with and advise physicians, educators, researchers, and others regarding medical applications of physics, biology, and chemistry. Teach principles of medicine and medical and laboratory procedures to physicians, residents, students, and technicians. Use equipment such as atomic absorption spectrometers, electron microscopes, flow cytometers, and chromatography systems. Conduct research to develop methodologies, instrumentation, and procedures for medical application, analyzing data and presenting findings. Evaluate effects of drugs, gases, pesticides, parasites, and microorganisms at various levels. Follow strict safety procedures when handling toxic materials to avoid contamination. Investigate cause, progress, life cycle, or mode of transmission of diseases or parasites. Plan and direct studies to investigate human or animal disease, preventive methods, and treatments for disease. **SKILLS**—Instructing; Science; Active Learning; Systems Evaluation; Writing; Systems Analysis; Reading Comprehension; Service Orientation.

GOE—Interest Area: 02. Science, Math, and Engineering. **Work Group:** 02.03. Life Sciences. **Other Jobs in This Work Group:** Agricultural and Food Science Technicians; Agricultural Technicians; Animal Scientists; Biochemists; Biochemists and Biophysicists; Biological Scientists, All Other; Biologists; Biophysicists; Conservation Scientists; Environmental Scientists and Specialists, Including Health; Epidemiologists; Food Science Technicians; Food Scientists and Technologists; Foresters; Life Scientists, All Other; Microbiologists; Plant Scientists; Range Managers; Soil and Plant Scientists; Soil Conservationists; Soil Scientists; Zoologists and Wildlife Biologists.

EDUCATION/TRAINING PROGRAM(S)— Anatomy; Biochemistry; Biomedical Sciences, General; Biophysics; Biostatistics; Cardiovascular Science; Cell Physiology; Cell/Cellular Biology and Histology; Endocrinology; Environmental Toxicology; Epidemiology; Exercise Physiology; Human/Medical Genetics; Immunology; Medical Microbiology and Bacteriology; Medical Scientist (MS, PhD); Molecular Biology; Molecular Pharmacology; Molecular Physiology; Molecular Toxicology; Neurobiology and Neurophysiology; Neuropharmacology; Oncology and Cancer Biology; Pathology/Experimental Pathology; Pharmacology; Pharmacology and Toxicology; Pharmacology and Toxicology, Other; Physiology, General; Physiology, Pathology, and Related Sciences, Other; Reproductive Biology; Toxicology; Vision Science/Physiological Optics. **RELATED KNOWL-**

EDGE/COURSES—Biology; Medicine and Dentistry; Chemistry; Mathematics; Education and Training; Communications and Media.

Natural Sciences Managers

- Personality Code: IE
- Growth: 11.3%
- Annual Job Openings: 5,000
- Annual Earnings: $85,860
- Education/Training Required: Work experience plus degree
- Self-Employed: 1.2%
- Part-Time: 0.9%

Plan, direct, or coordinate activities in such fields as life sciences, physical sciences, mathematics, statistics, and research and development in these fields. Confer with scientists, engineers, regulators, and others to plan and review projects and to provide technical assistance. Design and coordinate successive phases of problem analysis, solution proposals, and testing. Determine scientific and technical goals within broad outlines provided by top management and make detailed plans to accomplish these goals. Develop and implement policies, standards, and procedures for the architectural, scientific, and technical work performed to ensure regulatory compliance and operations enhancement. Plan and direct research, development, and production activities. Prepare project proposals. Advise and assist in obtaining patents or meeting other legal requirements. Conduct own research in field of expertise. Develop client relationships and communicate with clients to explain proposals, present research findings, establish specifications, or discuss project status. Develop innovative technology and train staff for its implementation. Hire, supervise, and evaluate engineers, technicians, researchers, and other staff. Prepare and administer budget, approve and review expenditures, and prepare financial reports. Recruit personnel and oversee the development and maintenance of staff competence. Review project activities and prepare and review research, testing, and operational reports. Make presentations at professional meetings to further knowledge in the field. Provide for stewardship of plant and animal resources and habitats, studying land use; monitoring animal populations; and/or providing shelter, resources, and medical treatment for animals. **SKILLS**—Management of Material Resources; Management of Financial Resources; Science; Management of Personnel Resources; Coordination; Systems Analysis; Systems Evaluation; Time Management.

GOE—**Interest Area:** 02. Science, Math, and Engineering. **Work Group:** 02.01. Managerial Work in Science, Math, and Engineering. **Other Jobs in This Work Group:** Computer and Information Systems Managers; Engineering Managers.

EDUCATION/TRAINING PROGRAM(S)—Acoustics; Algebra and Number Theory; Analysis and Functional Analysis; Analytical Chemistry; Anatomy; Animal Genetics; Animal Physiology; Applied Mathematics; Applied Mathematics, Other; Astronomy; Astrophysics; Atmospheric Chemistry and Climatology; Atmospheric Physics and Dynamics; Atmospheric Sciences and Meteorology, General; Atmospheric Sciences and Meteorology, Other; Atomic/Molecular Physics; Biochemistry; Biological and Biomedical Sciences, Other; Biological and Physical Sciences; Biology/Biological Sciences, General; Biometry/Biometrics; Biophysics; Biopsychology; Biostatistics; Biotechnology; Botany/Plant Biology; Botany/Plant Biology, Other; Cell/Cellular Biology and Anatomical Sciences, Other; Cell/Cellular Biology and Histology; Chemical Physics; Chemistry, General; Chemistry, Other; Computational Mathematics; Ecology; Ecology, Evolution, Systematics, and Population Biology, Other; Elementary Particle Physics; Entomology; Evolutionary Biology; Geochemistry; Geochemistry and Petrology; Geological and Earth Sciences/Geosciences, Other;

Investigative—N

Geology/Earth Science, General; Geometry/Geometric Analysis; Geophysics and Seismology; Hydrology and Water Resources Science; Immunology; Inorganic Chemistry; Logic; Marine Biology and Biological Oceanography; Mathematics and Computer Science; Mathematics and Statistics, Other; Mathematics, General; Medical Microbiology and Bacteriology; Meteorology; Microbiology, General; Molecular Biology; Natural Sciences; Neuroscience; Nuclear Physics; Nutrition Sciences; Oceanography, Chemical and Physical; Operations Research; Optics/Optical Sciences; Organic Chemistry; Paleontology; Parasitology; Pathology/Experimental Pathology; Pharmacology; Physical and Theoretical Chemistry; Physical Sciences; Physical Sciences, Other; Physics, General; Physics, Other; Planetary Astronomy and Science; Plant Genetics; Plant Pathology/Phytopathology; Plant Physiology; Plasma and High-Temperature Physics; Polymer Chemistry; others. **RELATED KNOWLEDGE/ COURSES**—Chemistry; Administration and Management; Economics and Accounting; Physics; Law and Government; Mathematics.

Network Systems and Data Communications Analysts

- Personality Code: IR
- Growth: 57.0%
- Annual Job Openings: 29,000
- Annual Earnings: $59,120
- Education/Training Required: Bachelor's degree
- Self-Employed: 23.6%
- Part-Time: 7.9%

Analyze, design, test, and evaluate network systems, such as local area networks (LAN); wide area networks (WAN); and Internet, intranet, and other data communications systems. Perform network modeling, analysis, and planning. Research and recommend network and data communications hardware and software. Includes telecommunications specialists who deal with the interfacing of computer and communications equipment. May supervise computer programmers. Maintain needed files by adding and deleting files on the network server and backing up files to guarantee their safety in the event of problems with the network. Monitor system performance and provide security measures, troubleshooting, and maintenance as needed. Assist users in diagnosing and solving data communication problems. Set up user accounts, regulating and monitoring file access to ensure confidentiality and proper use. Design and implement network configurations, network architecture (including hardware and software technology, site locations, and integration of technologies), and systems. Maintain the peripherals, such as printers, that are connected to the network. Identify areas of operation that need upgraded equipment such as modems, fiber-optic cables, and telephone wires. Train users in use of equipment. Develop and write procedures for installation, use, and troubleshooting of communications hardware and software. Adapt and modify existing software to meet specific needs. Work with other engineers, systems analysts, programmers, technicians, scientists, and top-level managers in the design, testing, and evaluation of systems. Test and evaluate hardware and software to determine efficiency, reliability, and compatibility with existing system and make purchase recommendations. Read technical manuals and brochures to determine which equipment meets establishment requirements. Consult customers, visit workplaces, or conduct surveys to determine present and future user needs. Visit vendors, attend conferences or training, and study technical journals to keep up with changes in technology. **SKILLS**—Installation; Troubleshooting; Technology Design; Management of Material Resources; Systems Analysis; Systems Evaluation; Operations Analysis; Equipment Maintenance.

GOE—Interest Area: 02. Science, Math, and Engineering. **Work Group:** 02.06. Mathematics and

Computers. **Other Jobs in This Work Group:** Computer and Information Scientists, Research; Computer Programmers; Computer Security Specialists; Computer Specialists, All Other; Computer Support Specialists; Computer Systems Analysts; Database Administrators; Network and Computer Systems Administrators.

EDUCATION/TRAINING PROGRAM(S)— Computer and Information Sciences, General; Computer and Information Systems Security; Computer Systems Analysis/Analyst; Computer Systems Networking and Telecommunications; Information Technology. **RELATED KNOWLEDGE/COURSES**—Customer and Personal Service; Computers and Electronics; Telecommunications; Education and Training; Engineering and Technology; Design.

Obstetricians and Gynecologists

- Personality Code: I
- Growth: 19.5%
- Annual Job Openings: 38,000
- Annual Earnings: more than $145,600
- Education/Training Required: First professional degree
- Self-Employed: 16.9%
- Part-Time: 8.1%

Diagnose, treat, and help prevent diseases of women, especially those affecting the reproductive system and the process of childbirth. Conduct research to develop or test medications, treatments, or procedures to prevent or control disease or injury. Consult with, or provide consulting services to, other physicians. Direct and coordinate activities of nurses, students, assistants, specialists, therapists, and other medical staff. Plan, implement, or administer health programs in hospitals, businesses, or

communities for prevention and treatment of injuries or illnesses. Prepare government and organizational reports on birth, death, and disease statistics; workforce evaluations; or the medical status of individuals. Advise patients and community members concerning diet, activity, hygiene, and disease prevention. Analyze records, reports, test results, or examination information to diagnose medical condition of patient. Care for and treat women during prenatal, natal, and post-natal periods. Collect, record, and maintain patient information, such as medical histories, reports, and examination results. Explain procedures and discuss test results or prescribed treatments with patients. Monitor patients' condition and progress and re-evaluate treatments as necessary. Perform cesarean sections or other surgical procedures as needed to preserve patients' health and deliver babies safely. Prescribe or administer therapy, medication, and other specialized medical care to treat or prevent illness, disease, or injury. Refer patient to medical specialist or other practitioner when necessary. Treat diseases of female organs. **SKILLS**—Science; Reading Comprehension; Systems Evaluation; Active Learning; Judgment and Decision Making; Management of Personnel Resources; Social Perceptiveness; Systems Analysis.

GOE—Interest Area: 14. Medical and Health Services. **Work Group:** 14.02. Medicine and Surgery. **Other Jobs in This Work Group:** Anesthesiologists; Family and General Practitioners; Healthcare Support Workers, All Other; Internists, General; Medical Assistants; Pediatricians, General; Pharmacists; Pharmacy Aides; Pharmacy Technicians; Physician Assistants; Physicians and Surgeons, All Other; Psychiatrists; Registered Nurses; Surgeons; Surgical Technologists.

EDUCATION/TRAINING PROGRAM(S)— Neonatal-Perinatal Medicine; Obstetrics and Gynecology. **RELATED KNOWLEDGE/COURSES** —Medicine and Dentistry; Biology; Therapy and Counseling; Chemistry; Administration and Management; Personnel and Human Resources; Physics.

Optometrists

- Personality Code: IR
- Growth: 17.1%
- Annual Job Openings: 2,000
- Annual Earnings: $85,430
- Education/Training Required: First professional degree
- Self-Employed: 29.2%
- Part-Time: 25.1%

Diagnose, manage, and treat conditions and diseases of the human eye and visual system. Examine eyes and visual system, diagnose problems or impairments, prescribe corrective lenses, and provide treatment. May prescribe therapeutic drugs to treat specific eye conditions. Examine eyes, using observation, instruments, and pharmaceutical agents, to determine visual acuity and perception, focus, and coordination and to diagnose diseases and other abnormalities such as glaucoma or color blindness. Analyze test results and develop a treatment plan. Prescribe, supply, fit, and adjust eyeglasses, contact lenses, and other vision aids. Prescribe medications to treat eye diseases if state laws permit. Educate and counsel patients on contact lens care, visual hygiene, lighting arrangements, and safety factors. Consult with and refer patients to ophthalmologist or other health care practitioner if additional medical treatment is determined necessary. Remove foreign bodies from the eye. Provide patients undergoing eye surgeries, such as cataract and laser vision correction, with pre- and post-operative care. Prescribe therapeutic procedures to correct or conserve vision. Provide vision therapy and low vision rehabilitation. **SKILLS**—Science; Persuasion; Judgment and Decision Making; Management of Personnel Resources; Service Orientation; Active Listening; Reading Comprehension; Active Learning; Instructing.

GOE—Interest Area: 14. Medical and Health Services. **Work Group:** 14.04. Health Specialties.

Other Jobs in This Work Group: Chiropractors; Opticians, Dispensing; Podiatrists.

EDUCATION/TRAINING PROGRAM(S)—Optometry (OD). **RELATED KNOWLEDGE/COURSES**—Medicine and Dentistry; Biology; Psychology; Customer and Personal Service; Personnel and Human Resources; Sales and Marketing.

Oral and Maxillofacial Surgeons

- Personality Code: IR
- Growth: 4.1%
- Annual Job Openings: 7,000
- Annual Earnings: $120,330
- Education/Training Required: First professional degree
- Self-Employed: 39.9%
- Part-Time: 22.3%

Perform surgery on mouth, jaws, and related head and neck structure to execute difficult and multiple extractions of teeth, to remove tumors and other abnormal growths, to correct abnormal jaw relations by mandibular or maxillary revision, to prepare mouth for insertion of dental prosthesis, or to treat fractured jaws. Administer general and local anesthetics. Collaborate with other professionals such as restorative dentists and orthodontists in order to plan treatment. Perform surgery on the mouth and jaws in order to treat conditions such as cleft lip and palate and jaw growth problems. Perform surgery to prepare the mouth for dental implants and to aid in the regeneration of deficient bone and gum tissues. Provide emergency treatment of facial injuries, including facial lacerations, intra-oral lacerations, and fractured facial bones. Remove impacted, damaged, and non-restorable teeth. Remove tumors and other abnormal growths of the oral and facial regions, using surgical instruments.

Restore form and function by moving skin, bone, nerves, and other tissues from other parts of the body in order to reconstruct the jaws and face. Evaluate the position of the wisdom teeth in order to determine whether problems exist currently or might occur in the future. Perform minor cosmetic procedures such as chin and cheek-bone enhancements and minor facial rejuvenation procedures including the use of Botox and laser technology. Treat infections of the oral cavity, salivary glands, jaws, and neck. Treat problems affecting the oral mucosa, such as mouth ulcers and infections. Treat snoring problems, using laser surgery. **SKILLS**—Science; Reading Comprehension; Judgment and Decision Making; Critical Thinking; Active Learning; Learning Strategies; Service Orientation; Monitoring.

GOE—Interest Area: 14. Medical and Health Services. **Work Group:** 14.03. Dentistry. **Other Jobs in This Work Group:** Dental Assistants; Dental Hygienists; Dentists, All Other Specialists; Dentists, General; Healthcare Support Workers, All Other; Orthodontists; Prosthodontists.

EDUCATION/TRAINING PROGRAM(S)—Dental/Oral Surgery Specialty; Oral/Maxillofacial Surgery (Cert, MS, PhD). **RELATED KNOWLEDGE/COURSES**—Medicine and Dentistry; Chemistry; Biology; Psychology; Therapy and Counseling; English Language.

Orthodontists

- Personality Code: IR
- Growth: 4.1%
- Annual Job Openings: 7,000
- Annual Earnings: $120,330
- Education/Training Required: First professional degree
- Self-Employed: 39.9%
- Part-Time: 22.3%

Examine, diagnose, and treat dental malocclusions and oral cavity anomalies. Design and fabricate appliances to realign teeth and jaws to produce and maintain normal function and to improve appearance. Adjust dental appliances periodically in order to produce and maintain normal function. Coordinate orthodontic services with other dental and medical services. Design and fabricate appliances, such as space maintainers, retainers, and labial and lingual arch wires. Diagnose teeth and jaw or other dental-facial abnormalities. Examine patients in order to assess abnormalities of jaw development, tooth position, and other dental-facial structures. Fit dental appliances in patients' mouths in order to alter the position and relationship of teeth and jaws and to realign teeth. Prepare diagnostic and treatment records. Provide patients with proposed treatment plans and cost estimates. Study diagnostic records such as medical/dental histories, plaster models of the teeth, photos of a patient's face and teeth, and X rays in order to develop patient treatment plans. Instruct dental officers and technical assistants in orthodontic procedures and techniques. **SKILLS**—Science; Technology Design; Reading Comprehension; Active Learning; Service Orientation; Operations Analysis; Critical Thinking; Complex Problem Solving; Equipment Selection; Judgment and Decision Making.

GOE—Interest Area: 14. Medical and Health Services. **Work Group:** 14.03. Dentistry. **Other Jobs in This Work Group:** Dental Assistants; Dental Hygienists; Dentists, All Other Specialists; Dentists, General; Healthcare Support Workers, All Other; Oral and Maxillofacial Surgeons; Prosthodontists.

EDUCATION/TRAINING PROGRAM(S)—Orthodontics Specialty; Orthodontics/Orthodontology (Cert, MS, PhD). **RELATED KNOWLEDGE/COURSES**—Medicine and Dentistry; Biology; Therapy and Counseling; Chemistry; Administration and Management; Design.

Pediatricians, General

- Personality Code: I
- Growth: 19.5%
- Annual Job Openings: 38,000
- Annual Earnings: $134,170
- Education/Training Required:
  First professional degree
- Self-Employed: 16.9%
- Part-Time: 8.1%

Diagnose, treat, and help prevent children's diseases and injuries. Advise patients, parents or guardians, and community members concerning diet, activity, hygiene, and disease prevention. Collect, record, and maintain patient information, such as medical history, reports, and examination results. Examine children regularly to assess their growth and development. Examine patients or order, perform, and interpret diagnostic tests to obtain information on medical condition and determine diagnosis. Explain procedures and discuss test results or prescribed treatments with patients and parents or guardians. Monitor patients' condition and progress and re-evaluate treatments as necessary. Plan and execute medical care programs to aid in the mental and physical growth and development of children and adolescents. Prescribe or administer treatment, therapy, medication, vaccination, and other specialized medical care to treat or prevent illness, disease, or injury in infants and children. Refer patient to medical specialist or other practitioner when necessary. Treat children who have minor illnesses, acute and chronic health problems, and growth and development concerns. Conduct research to study anatomy and develop or test medications, treatments, or procedures to prevent or control disease or injury. Direct and coordinate activities of nurses, students, assistants, specialists, therapists, and other medical staff. Operate on patients to remove, repair, or improve functioning of diseased or injured body parts and systems. Plan, implement, or administer health programs or standards in hospital, business, or community for infor-

mation, prevention, or treatment of injury or illness. Provide consulting services to other physicians. Prepare reports for government or management of birth, death, and disease statistics; workforce evaluations; or medical status of individuals. **SKILLS—** Science; Reading Comprehension; Systems Evaluation; Active Learning; Judgment and Decision Making; Management of Personnel Resources; Social Perceptiveness; Systems Analysis.

GOE—Interest Area: 14. Medical and Health Services. **Work Group:** 14.02. Medicine and Surgery. **Other Jobs in This Work Group:** Anesthesiologists; Family and General Practitioners; Healthcare Support Workers, All Other; Internists, General; Medical Assistants; Obstetricians and Gynecologists; Pharmacists; Pharmacy Aides; Pharmacy Technicians; Physician Assistants; Physicians and Surgeons, All Other; Psychiatrists; Registered Nurses; Surgeons; Surgical Technologists.

EDUCATION/TRAINING PROGRAM(S)— Child/Pediatric Neurology; Family Medicine; Neonatal-Perinatal Medicine; Pediatric Cardiology; Pediatric Endocrinology; Pediatric Hemato-Oncology; Pediatric Nephrology; Pediatric Orthopedics; Pediatric Surgery; Pediatrics. **RELATED KNOWLEDGE/COURSES—**Medicine and Dentistry; Biology; Therapy and Counseling; Chemistry; Administration and Management; Personnel and Human Resources; Physics.

Pharmacists

- Personality Code: IC
- Growth: 30.1%
- Annual Job Openings: 23,000
- Annual Earnings: $80,530
- Education/Training Required:
  First professional degree
- Self-Employed: 3.4%
- Part-Time: 17.3%

Compound and dispense medications, following prescriptions issued by physicians, dentists, or other authorized medical practitioners. Review prescriptions to assure accuracy, to ascertain the needed ingredients, and to evaluate their suitability. Provide information and advice regarding drug interactions, side effects, dosage, and proper medication storage. Analyze prescribing trends to monitor patient compliance and to prevent excessive usage or harmful interactions. Order and purchase pharmaceutical supplies, medical supplies, and drugs, maintaining stock and storing and handling it properly. Maintain records such as pharmacy files, patient profiles, charge system files, inventories, control records for radioactive nuclei, and registries of poisons, narcotics, and controlled drugs. Provide specialized services to help patients manage conditions such as diabetes, asthma, smoking cessation, or high blood pressure. Advise customers on the selection of medication brands, medical equipment, and health-care supplies. Collaborate with other health care professionals to plan, monitor, review, and evaluate the quality and effectiveness of drugs and drug regimens, providing advice on drug applications and characteristics. Compound and dispense medications as prescribed by doctors and dentists by calculating, weighing, measuring, and mixing ingredients or oversee these activities. Offer health promotion and prevention activities, for example, training people to use devices such as blood pressure or diabetes monitors. Refer patients to other health professionals and agencies when appropriate. Prepare sterile solutions and infusions for use in surgical procedures, emergency rooms, or patients' homes. Plan, implement, and maintain procedures for mixing, packaging, and labeling pharmaceuticals according to policy and legal requirements to ensure quality, security, and proper disposal. Assay radiopharmaceuticals, verify rates of disintegration, and calculate the volume required to produce the desired results to ensure proper dosages. Manage pharmacy operations, hiring and supervising staff, performing administrative duties, and buying and selling non-pharmaceutical merchandise. Work in hospitals or clinics or for HMOs, dispensing prescriptions, serving as a medical team consultant, or specializing in specific drug therapy areas such as oncology or nuclear pharmacotherapy. SKILLS—Instructing; Social Perceptiveness; Reading Comprehension; Active Listening; Critical Thinking; Science; Speaking; Active Learning.

GOE—Interest Area: 14. Medical and Health Services. Work Group: 14.02. Medicine and Surgery. Other Jobs in This Work Group: Anesthesiologists; Family and General Practitioners; Healthcare Support Workers, All Other; Internists, General; Medical Assistants; Obstetricians and Gynecologists; Pediatricians, General; Pharmacy Aides; Pharmacy Technicians; Physician Assistants; Physicians and Surgeons, All Other; Psychiatrists; Registered Nurses; Surgeons; Surgical Technologists.

EDUCATION/TRAINING PROGRAM(S)— Clinical and Industrial Drug Development (MS, PhD); Clinical, Hospital, and Managed Care Pharmacy (MS, PhD); Industrial and Physical Pharmacy and Cosmetic Sciences (MS, PhD); Medicinal and Pharmaceutical Chemistry (MS, PhD); Natural Products Chemistry and Pharmacognosy (MS, PhD); Pharmaceutics and Drug Design (MS, PhD); Pharmacoeconomics/Pharmaceutical Economics (MS, PhD); Pharmacy (PharmD [USA], PharmD, BS/BPharm [Canada]); Pharmacy Administration and Pharmacy Policy and Regulatory Affairs (MS, PhD); Pharmacy, Pharmaceutical Sciences, and Administration, Other. RELATED KNOWLEDGE/COURSES—Medicine and Dentistry; Chemistry; Customer and Personal Service; Psychology; Therapy and Counseling; Mathematics.

Physician Assistants

- Personality Code: IS
- Growth: 48.9%
- Annual Job Openings: 7,000
- Annual Earnings: $65,670
- Education/Training Required: Bachelor's degree
- Self-Employed: 0.8%
- Part-Time: 16.3%

Under the supervision of a physician, provide healthcare services typically performed by a physician. Conduct complete physicals, provide treatment, and counsel patients. May, in some cases, prescribe medication. Must graduate from an accredited educational program for physician assistants. Examine patients to obtain information about their physical condition. Interpret diagnostic test results for deviations from normal. Make tentative diagnoses and decisions about management and treatment of patients. Obtain, compile, and record patient medical data, including health history, progress notes, and results of physical examination. Administer or order diagnostic tests, such as X-ray, electrocardiogram, and laboratory tests. Prescribe therapy or medication with physician approval. Perform therapeutic procedures, such as injections, immunizations, suturing and wound care, and infection management. Instruct and counsel patients about prescribed therapeutic regimens, normal growth and development, family planning, emotional problems of daily living, and health maintenance. Provide physicians with assistance during surgery or complicated medical procedures. Supervise and coordinate activities of technicians and technical assistants. Visit and observe patients on hospital rounds or house calls, updating charts, ordering therapy, and reporting back to physician. SKILLS—Social Perceptiveness; Science; Instructing; Critical Thinking; Reading Comprehension; Time Management; Active Listening; Active Learning.

GOE—Interest Area: 14. Medical and Health Services. Work Group: 14.02. Medicine and Surgery. Other Jobs in This Work Group: Anesthesiologists; Family and General Practitioners; Healthcare Support Workers, All Other; Internists, General; Medical Assistants; Obstetricians and Gynecologists; Pediatricians, General; Pharmacists; Pharmacy Aides; Pharmacy Technicians; Physicians and Surgeons, All Other; Psychiatrists; Registered Nurses; Surgeons; Surgical Technologists.

EDUCATION/TRAINING PROGRAM(S)— Physician Assistant. RELATED KNOWLEDGE/COURSES—Medicine and Dentistry; Biology; Psychology; Therapy and Counseling; Customer and Personal Service; Chemistry.

Physics Teachers, Postsecondary

- Personality Code: IS
- Growth: 38.1%
- Annual Job Openings: 216,000
- Annual Earnings: $62,880
- Education/Training Required: Master's degree
- Self-Employed: 0.3%
- Part-Time: 27.7%

Teach courses pertaining to the laws of matter and energy. Includes both teachers primarily engaged in teaching and those who do a combination of both teaching and research. Evaluate and grade students' class work, laboratory work, assignments, and papers. Prepare and deliver lectures to undergraduate and/or graduate students on topics such as quantum mechanics, particle physics, and optics. Advise students on academic and vocational curricula and on career issues. Compile, administer, and grade examinations or assign this work to others. Compile bibliographies of specialized materials for outside reading assignments. Initiate, facilitate, and moderate classroom discussions. Keep abreast of developments in their field by reading current literature, talking with colleagues, and participating in professional conferences. Maintain regularly scheduled office hours in order to advise and assist students. Maintain student attendance records, grades, and other required records. Plan, evaluate, and revise curricula, course content, and course materials and methods of instruction. Prepare course materials such as syllabi, homework assignments, and handouts. Select and obtain materials and supplies such as textbooks and laboratory equipment. Supervise students' laboratory work. Supervise undergraduate and/or graduate teaching, internship, and research work. Act as advisers to student organizations. Collaborate with colleagues to address teaching and research issues. Conduct research in a particular field of knowledge and publish findings in professional journals, books, and/or electronic media. Participate in campus and community events. Participate in student recruitment, registration, and placement activities. Perform administrative duties such as serving as department head. Provide professional consulting services to government and/or industry. Serve on academic or administrative committees that deal with institutional policies, departmental matters, and academic issues. Write grant proposals to procure external research funding. **SKILLS**—Science; Instructing; Writing; Learning Strategies; Reading Comprehension; Active Learning; Critical Thinking; Complex Problem Solving; Judgment and Decision Making.

GOE—Interest Area: 12. Education and Social Service. **Work Group:** 12.03. Educational Services. **Other Jobs in This Work Group:** Adult Literacy, Remedial Education, and GED Teachers and Instructors; Agricultural Sciences Teachers, Postsecondary; Anthropology and Archeology Teachers, Postsecondary; Architecture Teachers, Postsecondary; Archivists; Area, Ethnic, and Cultural Studies Teachers, Postsecondary; Art, Drama, and Music Teachers, Postsecondary; Atmospheric, Earth, Marine, and Space Sciences Teachers, Postsecondary; Audio-Visual Collections Specialists; Biological Science Teachers, Postsecondary; Business Teachers, Postsecondary; Chemistry Teachers, Postsecondary; Child Care Workers; Communications Teachers, Postsecondary; Computer Science Teachers, Postsecondary; Criminal Justice and Law Enforcement Teachers, Postsecondary; Curators; Economics Teachers, Postsecondary; Education Teachers, Postsecondary; Education, Training, and Library Workers, All Other; Educational Psychologists; Educational, Vocational, and School Counselors; Elementary School Teachers, Except Special Education; Engineering Teachers, Postsecondary; English Language and Literature Teachers, Postsecondary; Environmental Science Teachers, Postsecondary; Farm and Home Management Advisors; Foreign Language and Literature Teachers, Postsecondary; Forestry and Conservation Science Teachers, Postsecondary; Geography Teachers, Postsecondary; Graduate Teaching Assistants; Health Specialties Teachers, Postsecondary; History Teachers, Postsecondary; Home Economics Teachers, Postsecondary; Kindergarten Teachers, Except Special Education; Law Teachers, Postsecondary; Librarians; Library Assistants, Clerical; Library Science Teachers, Postsecondary; Library Technicians; Mathematical Science Teachers, Postsecondary; Middle School Teachers, Except Special and Vocational Education; Museum Technicians and Conservators; Nannies; Nursing Instructors and Teachers, Postsecondary; Personal Financial Advisors; Philosophy and Religion Teachers, Postsecondary; Political Science Teachers, Postsecondary; Postsecondary Teachers, All Other; Preschool Teachers, Except Special Education; Psychology Teachers, Postsecondary; Recreation and Fitness Studies Teachers, Postsecondary; Secondary School Teachers, Except Special and Vocational Education; Self-Enrichment Education Teachers; Social Sciences Teachers, Postsecondary, All Other; Social Work Teachers, Postsecondary; Sociology Teachers, Postsecondary; Special Education Teachers, Middle School; Special Education Teachers, Preschool, Kindergarten, and Elementary School; Special Education Teachers, Secondary School; Teacher Assistants; Teachers and

Instructors, All Other; Vocational Education Teachers, Postsecondary; Vocational Education Teachers, Middle School; Vocational Education Teachers, Secondary School.

EDUCATION/TRAINING PROGRAM(S)— Acoustics; Atomic/Molecular Physics; Elementary Particle Physics; Nuclear Physics; Optics/Optical Sciences; Physics, General; Physics, Other; Plasma and High-Temperature Physics; Solid State and Low-Temperature Physics; Theoretical and Mathematical Physics. RELATED KNOWLEDGE/ COURSES—Physics; Education and Training; Mathematics; English Language; Administration and Management; Chemistry.

Prosthodontists

- ◎ Personality Code: IR
- ◎ Growth: 4.1%
- ◎ Annual Job Openings: 7,000
- ◎ Annual Earnings: $120,330
- ◎ Education/Training Required: First professional degree
- ◎ Self-Employed: 39.9%
- ◎ Part-Time: 22.3%

Construct oral prostheses to replace missing teeth and other oral structures to correct natural and acquired deformation of mouth and jaws; to restore and maintain oral function, such as chewing and speaking; and to improve appearance. Repair, reline, and/or rebase dentures. Treat facial pain and jaw joint problems. Use bonding technology on the surface of the teeth in order to change tooth shape or to close gaps. Collaborate with general dentists, specialists, and other health professionals in order to develop solutions to dental and oral health concerns. Design and fabricate dental prostheses or supervise dental technicians and laboratory bench workers who construct the devices. Fit prostheses to patients, making any necessary adjust-

ments and modifications. Measure and take impressions of patients' jaws and teeth in order to determine the shape and size of dental prostheses, using face bows, dental articulators, recording devices, and other materials. Replace missing teeth and associated oral structures with permanent fixtures, such as crowns and bridges, or removable fixtures, such as dentures. Restore function and aesthetics to traumatic injury victims or to individuals with diseases or birth defects. Bleach discolored teeth in order to brighten and whiten them. Place veneers onto teeth in order to conceal defects. SKILLS—Science; Technology Design; Reading Comprehension; Critical Thinking; Judgment and Decision Making; Service Orientation; Equipment Selection; Mathematics; Active Learning; Operations Analysis.

GOE—Interest Area: 14. Medical and Health Services. Work Group: 14.03. Dentistry. Other Jobs in This Work Group: Dental Assistants; Dental Hygienists; Dentists, All Other Specialists; Dentists, General; Healthcare Support Workers, All Other; Oral and Maxillofacial Surgeons; Orthodontists.

EDUCATION/TRAINING PROGRAM(S)— Prosthodontics Specialty; Prosthodontics/Prosthodontology (Cert, MS, PhD). RELATED KNOWLEDGE/COURSES—Medicine and Dentistry; Chemistry; Biology; English Language; Design.

Psychiatrists

- ◎ Personality Code: IA
- ◎ Growth: 19.5%
- ◎ Annual Job Openings: 38,000
- ◎ Annual Earnings: $133,970
- ◎ Education/Training Required: First professional degree
- ◎ Self-Employed: 16.9%
- ◎ Part-Time: 8.1%

Diagnose, treat, and help prevent disorders of the mind. Analyze and evaluate patient data and test or examination findings to diagnose nature and extent of mental disorder. Prescribe, direct, and administer psychotherapeutic treatments or medications to treat mental, emotional, or behavioral disorders. Collaborate with physicians, psychologists, social workers, psychiatric nurses, or other professionals to discuss treatment plans and progress. Gather and maintain patient information and records, including social and medical history obtained from patients, relatives, and other professionals. Counsel outpatients and other patients during office visits. Design individualized care plans, using a variety of treatments. Examine or conduct laboratory or diagnostic tests on patient to provide information on general physical condition and mental disorder. Advise and inform guardians, relatives, and significant others of patients' conditions and treatment. Review and evaluate treatment procedures and outcomes of other psychiatrists and medical professionals. Teach, conduct research, and publish findings to increase understanding of mental, emotional, and behavioral states and disorders. Prepare and submit case reports and summaries to government and mental health agencies. Serve on committees to promote and maintain community mental health services and delivery systems. **SKILLS**—Social Perceptiveness; Persuasion; Active Learning; Science; Active Listening; Negotiation; Critical Thinking; Learning Strategies; Complex Problem Solving.

GOE—**Interest Area:** 14. Medical and Health Services. **Work Group:** 14.02. Medicine and Surgery. **Other Jobs in This Work Group:** Anesthesiologists; Family and General Practitioners; Healthcare Support Workers, All Other; Internists, General; Medical Assistants; Obstetricians and Gynecologists; Pediatricians, General; Pharmacists; Pharmacy Aides; Pharmacy Technicians; Physician Assistants; Physicians and Surgeons, All Other; Registered Nurses; Surgeons; Surgical Technologists.

EDUCATION/TRAINING PROGRAM(S)— Child Psychiatry; Physical Medical and Rehabilitation/Psychiatry; Psychiatry. **RELATED**

KNOWLEDGE/COURSES—Therapy and Counseling; Medicine and Dentistry; Psychology; Biology; Philosophy and Theology; Sociology and Anthropology.

Respiratory Therapists

- Personality Code: IR
- Growth: 34.8%
- Annual Job Openings: 10,000
- Annual Earnings: $41,150
- Education/Training Required: Associate's degree
- Self-Employed: 0%
- Part-Time: 15.5%

Assess, treat, and care for patients with breathing disorders. Assume primary responsibility for all respiratory care modalities, including the supervision of respiratory therapy technicians. Initiate and conduct therapeutic procedures; maintain patient records; and select, assemble, check, and operate equipment. Set up and operate devices such as mechanical ventilators, therapeutic gas administration apparatus, environmental control systems, and aerosol generators, following specified parameters of treatment. Provide emergency care, including artificial respiration, external cardiac massage, and assistance with cardiopulmonary resuscitation. Determine requirements for treatment, such as type, method, and duration of therapy; precautions to be taken; and medication and dosages, compatible with physicians' orders. Monitor patient's physiological responses to therapy, such as vital signs, arterial blood gases, and blood chemistry changes, and consult with physician if adverse reactions occur. Read prescription, measure arterial blood gases, and review patient information to assess patient condition. Work as part of a team of physicians, nurses, and other health care professionals to manage patient care. Enforce safety rules and ensure careful adherence to physicians' orders. Maintain charts that contain patients' pertinent identification and therapy information. Inspect, clean, test, and maintain respiratory therapy equipment to ensure equipment is functioning safely and efficiently, ordering repairs when necessary. Educate patients and their families about their conditions and teach appropriate disease management techniques, such as breathing exercises and the use of medications and respiratory equipment. Explain treatment procedures to patients to gain cooperation and allay fears. Relay blood analysis results to a physician. Perform pulmonary function and adjust equipment to obtain optimum results in therapy. Perform bronchopulmonary drainage and assist or instruct patients in performance of breathing exercises. Demonstrate respiratory care procedures to trainees and other health care personnel. Teach, train, supervise, and utilize the assistance of students, respiratory therapy technicians, and assistants. Use a variety of testing techniques to assist doctors in cardiac and pulmonary research and to diagnose disorders. Make emergency visits to resolve equipment problems. Conduct tests, such as electrocardiograms, stress testing, and lung capacity tests, to evaluate patients' cardiopulmonary functions. **SKILLS—** Instructing; Science; Active Learning; Service Orientation; Time Management; Reading Comprehension; Troubleshooting; Mathematics.

GOE—Interest Area: 14. Medical and Health Services. **Work Group:** 14.06. Medical Therapy. **Other Jobs in This Work Group:** Audiologists; Health Diagnosing and Treating Practitioners, All Other; Massage Therapists; Occupational Therapist Aides; Occupational Therapist Assistants; Occupational Therapists; Physical Therapist Aides; Physical Therapist Assistants; Physical Therapists; Radiation Therapists; Recreational Therapists; Respiratory Therapy Technicians; Speech-Language Pathologists; Therapists, All Other.

EDUCATION/TRAINING PROGRAM(S)— Respiratory Care Therapy/Therapist. **RELATED KNOWLEDGE/COURSES—**Customer and Personal Service; Medicine and Dentistry; Psychology; Biology; Education and Training; Chemistry.

Surgeons

- Personality Code: IR
- Growth: 19.5%
- Annual Job Openings: 38,000
- Annual Earnings: more than $145,600
- Education/Training Required: First professional degree
- Self-Employed: 16.9%
- Part-Time: 8.1%

Treat diseases, injuries, and deformities by invasive methods, such as manual manipulation or by using instruments and appliances. Analyze patient's medical history, medication allergies, physical condition, and examination results to verify operation's necessity and to determine best procedure. Prescribe preoperative and postoperative treatments and procedures, such as sedatives, diets, antibiotics, and preparation and treatment of the patient's operative area. Direct and coordinate activities of nurses, assistants, specialists, residents, and other medical staff. Examine patient to provide information on medical condition and surgical risk. Follow established surgical techniques during the operation. Operate on patients to correct deformities, repair injuries, prevent and treat diseases, or improve or restore patients' functions. Refer patient to medical specialist or other practitioners when necessary. Conduct research to develop and test surgical techniques that can improve operating procedures and outcomes. Examine instruments, equipment, and operating room to ensure sterility. Manage surgery services, including planning, scheduling, and coordination; determination of procedures; and procurement of supplies and equipment. Prepare case histories. Provide consultation and surgical assistance to other physicians and surgeons. Diagnose bodily disorders and orthopedic conditions and provide treatments such as medicines and surgeries in clinics, hospital wards, and operating rooms. **SKILLS—**Science; Management of Personnel Resources; Systems Evaluation; Judgment and Decision Making; Systems

Analysis; Reading Comprehension; Operation and Control; Coordination.

GOE—Interest Area: 14. Medical and Health Services. **Work Group:** 14.02. Medicine and Surgery. **Other Jobs in This Work Group:** Anesthesiologists; Family and General Practitioners; Healthcare Support Workers, All Other; Internists, General; Medical Assistants; Obstetricians and Gynecologists; Pediatricians, General; Pharmacists; Pharmacy Aides; Pharmacy Technicians; Physician Assistants; Physicians and Surgeons, All Other; Psychiatrists; Registered Nurses; Surgical Technologists.

EDUCATION/TRAINING PROGRAM(S)— Adult Reconstructive Orthopedics (Orthopedic Surgery); Colon and Rectal Surgery; Critical Care Surgery; General Surgery; Hand Surgery; Neurological Surgery/Neurosurgery; Orthopedic Surgery of the Spine; Orthopedics/Orthopedic Surgery; Otolaryngology; Pediatric Orthopedics; Pediatric Surgery; Plastic Surgery; Sports Medicine; Thoracic Surgery; Urology; Vascular Surgery. **RELATED KNOWLEDGE/COURSES—**Medicine and Dentistry; Biology; Chemistry; Administration and Management; Therapy and Counseling; Physics; Psychology.

Veterinarians

- ⊚ Personality Code: IR
- ⊚ Growth: 25.1%
- ⊚ Annual Job Openings: 4,000
- ⊚ Annual Earnings: $64,750
- ⊚ Education/Training Required: First professional degree
- ⊚ Self-Employed: 27.7%
- ⊚ Part-Time: 10.6%

Diagnose and treat diseases and dysfunctions of animals. May engage in a particular function, such as research and development, consultation, admin- istration, technical writing, sale or production of commercial products, or rendering of technical services to commercial firms or other organizations. Includes veterinarians who inspect livestock. Examine animals to detect and determine the nature of diseases or injuries. Treat sick or injured animals by prescribing medication, setting bones, dressing wounds, or performing surgery. Inoculate animals against various diseases such as rabies and distemper. Collect body tissue, feces, blood, urine, or other body fluids for examination and analysis. Operate diagnostic equipment such as radiographic and ultrasound equipment and interpret the resulting images. Advise animal owners regarding sanitary measures, feeding, and general care necessary to promote health of animals. Educate the public about diseases that can be spread from animals to humans. Train and supervise workers who handle and care for animals. Provide care to a wide range of animals or specialize in a particular species, such as horses or exotic birds. Euthanize animals. Establish and conduct quarantine and testing procedures that prevent the spread of diseases to other animals or to humans and that comply with applicable government regulations. Conduct postmortem studies and analyses to determine the causes of animals' deaths. Perform administrative duties such as scheduling appointments, accepting payments from clients, and maintaining business records. Direct the overall operations of animal hospitals, clinics, or mobile services to farms. Drive mobile clinic vans to farms so that health problems can be treated and/or prevented. Specialize in a particular type of treatment such as dentistry, pathology, nutrition, surgery, microbiology, or internal medicine. Inspect and test horses, sheep, poultry, and other animals to detect the presence of communicable diseases. Plan and execute animal nutrition and reproduction programs. Research diseases to which animals could be susceptible. Inspect animal housing facilities to determine their cleanliness and adequacy. Determine the effects of drug therapies, antibiotics, or new surgical techniques by testing them on animals. **SKILLS—**Science; Instructing; Management of Financial Resources; Reading Comprehension;

Investigative—V

Active Learning; Service Orientation; Complex Problem Solving; Judgment and Decision Making; Time Management; Management of Personnel Resources.

GOE—Interest Area: 03. Plants and Animals. **Work Group:** 03.02. Animal Care and Training. **Other Jobs in This Work Group:** Agricultural Workers, All Other; Animal Breeders; Animal Trainers; Nonfarm Animal Caretakers; Veterinary Assistants and Laboratory Animal Caretakers; Veterinary Technologists and Technicians.

EDUCATION/TRAINING PROGRAM(S)— Comparative and Laboratory Animal Medicine (Cert, MS, PhD); Laboratory Animal Medicine; Large Animal/Food Animal and Equine Surgery and Medicine (Cert, MS, PhD); Small/Companion Animal Surgery and Medicine (Cert, MS, PhD); Theriogenology; Veterinary Anatomy (Cert, MS, PhD); Veterinary Anesthesiology; Veterinary Biomedical and Clinical Sciences, Other (Cert, MS, PhD); Veterinary Dentistry; Veterinary Dermatol-ogy; Veterinary Emergency and Critical Care Medicine; Veterinary Infectious Diseases (Cert, MS, PhD); Veterinary Internal Medicine; Veterinary Medicine (DVM); Veterinary Microbiology; Veterinary Microbiology and Immunobiology (Cert, MS, PhD); Veterinary Nutrition; Veterinary Ophthalmology; Veterinary Pathology; Veterinary Pathology and Pathobiology (Cert, MS, PhD); Veterinary Physiology (Cert, MS, PhD); Veterinary Practice; Veterinary Preventive Medicine; Veterinary Preventive Medicine Epidemiology and Public Health (Cert, MS, PhD); Veterinary Radiology; Veterinary Residency Programs, Other; Veterinary Sciences/Veterinary Clinical Sciences, General (Cert, MS, PhD); Veterinary Surgery; Veterinary Toxicology; Veterinary Toxicology and Pharmacology (Cert, MS, PhD); Zoological Medicine. **RELATED KNOWLEDGE/COURSES—**Medicine and Dentistry; Biology; Customer and Personal Service; Chemistry; Sales and Marketing; Education and Training.

Artistic Jobs

Actors

- Personality Code: AE
- Growth: 17.7%
- Annual Job Openings: 8,000
- Annual Earnings: $26,460
- Education/Training Required: Long-term on-the-job training
- Self-Employed: 17.4%
- Part-Time: 28.2%

Play parts in stage, television, radio, video, or motion picture productions for entertainment, information, or instruction. Interpret serious or comic role by speech, gesture, and body movement to entertain or inform audience. May dance and sing. Attend auditions and casting calls in order to audition for roles. Collaborate with other actors as part of an ensemble. Learn about characters in scripts and their relationships to each other in order to develop role interpretations. Perform humorous and serious interpretations of emotions, actions, and situations, using body movements, facial expressions, and gestures. Portray and interpret roles, using speech, gestures, and body movements in order to entertain, inform, or instruct radio, film, television, or live audiences. Sing and/or dance during dramatic or comedic performances. Study and rehearse roles from scripts in order to interpret, learn, and memorize lines, stunts, and cues as directed. Work closely with directors, other actors, and playwrights to find the interpretation most suited to the role. Manipulate strings, wires, rods, or fingers to animate puppets or dummies in synchronization with talking, singing, or recorded programs. Perform original and stock tricks of illusion to entertain and mystify audiences, occasionally including audi-ence members as participants. Promote productions using means such as interviews about plays or movies. Read from scripts or books to narrate action or to inform or entertain audiences, utilizing few or no stage props. Tell jokes; perform comic dances, songs and skits; impersonate mannerisms and voices of others; contort face; and use other devices to amuse audiences. Work with other crewmembers responsible for lighting, costumes, makeup, and props. Write original or adapted material for dramas, comedies, puppet shows, narration, or other performances. Construct puppets and ventriloquist dummies and sew accessory clothing, using hand tools and machines. Dress in comical clown costumes and makeup and perform comedy routines to entertain audiences. Introduce performances and performers in order to stimulate excitement and coordinate smooth transition of acts during events. Prepare and perform action stunts for motion picture, television, or stage productions. **SKILLS**—Speaking; Monitoring; Social Perceptiveness; Repairing; Coordination; Active Learning; Reading Comprehension; Equipment Maintenance.

GOE—Interest Area: 01. Arts, Entertainment, and Media. **Work Group:** 01.05. Performing Arts. **Other Jobs in This Work Group:** Choreographers; Composers; Dancers; Directors—Stage, Motion Pictures, Television, and Radio; Entertainers and Performers, Sports and Related Workers, All Other; Music Arrangers and Orchestrators; Music Directors; Music Directors and Composers; Musicians and Singers; Musicians, Instrumental; Public Address System and Other Announcers; Radio and Television Announcers; Singers; Talent Directors.

EDUCATION/TRAINING PROGRAM(S)—Acting; Directing and Theatrical Production; Drama and Dramatics/Theatre Arts, General; Dramatic/Theatre Arts and Stagecraft, Other. **RELATED KNOWLEDGE/COURSES**—Fine Arts; Communications and Media; English Language.

Advertising and Promotions Managers

- Personality Code: AE
- Growth: 25.0%
- Annual Job Openings: 13,000
- Annual Earnings: $60,350
- Education/Training Required: Work experience plus degree
- Self-Employed: 2.4%
- Part-Time: 7.5%

Plan and direct advertising policies and programs or produce collateral materials, such as posters, contests, coupons, or give-aways, to create extra interest in the purchase of a product or service for a department, an entire organization, or on an account basis. Prepare budgets and submit estimates for program costs as part of campaign plan development. Plan and prepare advertising and promotional material to increase sales of products or services, working with customers, company officials, sales departments and advertising agencies. Assist with annual budget development. Inspect layouts and advertising copy and edit scripts, audio and video tapes, and other promotional material for adherence to specifications. Coordinate activities of departments, such as sales, graphic arts, media, finance, and research. Prepare and negotiate advertising and sales contracts. Identify and develop contacts for promotional campaigns and industry programs that meet identified buyer targets such as dealers, distributors, or consumers. Gather and organize information to plan advertising campaigns. Confer with department heads and/or staff to discuss topics such as contracts, selection of advertising media, or product to be advertised. Confer with clients to provide marketing or technical advice. Monitor and analyze sales promotion results to determine cost effectiveness of promotion campaigns. Read trade journals and professional literature to stay informed on trends, innovations, and changes that affect media planning. Formulate plans to extend business with established accounts and to transact business as agent for advertising accounts. Provide presentation and product demonstration support during the introduction of new products and services to field staff and customers. Direct, motivate, and monitor the mobilization of a campaign team to advance campaign goals. Plan and execute advertising policies and strategies for organizations. Track program budgets and expenses and campaign response rates to evaluate each campaign based on program objectives and industry norms. Assemble and communicate with a strong, diverse coalition of organizations and/or public figures, securing their cooperation, support and action, to further campaign goals. Train and direct workers engaged in developing and producing advertisements. Coordinate with the media to disseminate advertising. **SKILLS**—Service Orientation; Management of Financial Resources; Persuasion; Negotiation; Time Management; Coordination; Management of Personnel Resources; Monitoring.

GOE—Interest Area: 10. Sales and Marketing. **Work Group:** 10.01. Managerial Work in Sales and Marketing. **Other Jobs in This Work Group:** First-Line Supervisors/Managers of Non-Retail Sales Workers; First-Line Supervisors/Managers of Retail Sales Workers; Marketing Managers; Sales Managers.

EDUCATION/TRAINING PROGRAM(S)—Advertising; Marketing/Marketing Management, General; Public Relations/Image Management. **RELATED KNOWLEDGE/COURSES**—Sales and Marketing; Customer and Personal Service; Communications and Media; Production and Processing; Design; Clerical Studies.

Architects, Except Landscape and Naval

- Personality Code: AR
- Growth: 17.3%
- Annual Job Openings: 8,000
- Annual Earnings: $57,950
- Education/Training Required: Bachelor's degree
- Self-Employed: 21.4%
- Part-Time: 5.5%

Plan and design structures, such as private residences, office buildings, theaters, factories, and other structural property. Prepare information regarding design, structure specifications, materials, color, equipment, estimated costs, and construction time. Consult with client to determine functional and spatial requirements of structure. Direct activities of workers engaged in preparing drawings and specification documents. Plan layout of project. Prepare contract documents for building contractors. Prepare scale drawings. Integrate engineering element into unified design. Conduct periodic on-site observation of work during construction to monitor compliance with plans. Administer construction contracts. Represent client in obtaining bids and awarding construction contracts. **SKILLS**—Operations Analysis; Management of Financial Resources; Coordination; Management of Personnel Resources; Negotiation; Complex Problem Solving; Persuasion; Active Learning.

GOE—Interest Area: 02. Science, Math, and Engineering. **Work Group:** 02.07. Engineering. **Other Jobs in This Work Group:** Aerospace Engineers; Agricultural Engineers; Biomedical Engineers; Chemical Engineers; Civil Engineers; Computer Hardware Engineers; Computer Software Engineers, Applications; Computer Software Engineers, Systems Software; Electrical Engineers; Electronics Engineers, Except Computer; Engineers, All Other; Environmental Engineers; Fire-Prevention and Protection Engineers; Health and Safety Engineers, Except Mining Safety Engineers and Inspectors; Industrial Engineers; Industrial Safety and Health Engineers; Landscape Architects; Marine Architects; Marine Engineers; Marine Engineers and Naval Architects; Materials Engineers; Mechanical Engineers; Mining and Geological Engineers, Including Mining Safety Engineers; Nuclear Engineers; Petroleum Engineers; Product Safety Engineers; Sales Engineers.

EDUCATION/TRAINING PROGRAM(S)— Architectural History and Criticism, General; Architecture (BArch, BA/BS, MArch, MA/MS, PhD); Architecture and Related Services, Other; Environmental Design/Architecture. **RELATED KNOWLEDGE/COURSES**—Building and Construction; Design; Engineering and Technology; Law and Government; Public Safety and Security; Fine Arts.

Art Directors

- Personality Code: AE
- Growth: 11.4%
- Annual Job Openings: 8,000
- Annual Earnings: $62,260
- Education/Training Required: Work experience plus degree
- Self-Employed: 53.6%
- Part-Time: 23.1%

Formulate design concepts and presentation approaches, and direct workers engaged in art work, layout design, and copy writing for visual communications media, such as magazines, books, newspapers, and packaging. Formulate basic layout design or presentation approach, and specify material details, such as style and size of type, photographs, graphics, animation, video and sound.

Review and approve proofs of printed copy and art and copy materials developed by staff members. Manage own accounts and projects, working within budget and scheduling requirements. Confer with creative, art, copy-writing, or production department heads to discuss client requirements and presentation concepts, and to coordinate creative activities. Present final layouts to clients for approval. Confer with clients to determine objectives, budget, background information, and presentation approaches, styles, and techniques. Hire, train and direct staff members who develop design concepts into art layouts or who prepare layouts for printing. Work with creative directors to develop design solutions. Review illustrative material to determine if it conforms to standards and specifications. Attend photo shoots and printing sessions to ensure that the products needed are obtained. Create custom illustrations or other graphic elements. Mark up, paste, and complete layouts, and write typography instructions to prepare materials for typesetting or printing. Negotiate with printers and estimators to determine what services will be performed. Conceptualize and help design interfaces for multimedia games, products and devices. **SKILLS**—Coordination; Negotiation; Persuasion; Service Orientation; Management of Financial Resources; Instructing; Time Management; Operations Analysis.

GOE—Interest Area: 01. Arts, Entertainment, and Media. **Work Group:** 01.01. Managerial Work in Arts, Entertainment, and Media. **Other Jobs in This Work Group:** Agents and Business Managers of Artists, Performers, and Athletes; Athletes and Sports Competitors; Coaches and Scouts; Entertainers and Performers, Sports and Related Workers, All Other; Fitness Trainers and Aerobics Instructors; Producers; Producers and Directors; Program Directors; Technical Directors/Managers; Umpires, Referees, and Other Sports Officials.

EDUCATION/TRAINING PROGRAM(S)— Graphic Design; Intermedia/Multimedia. **RELATED KNOWLEDGE/COURSES—**Design; Fine Arts; Computers and Electronics; Communications

and Media; Production and Processing; Customer and Personal Service; Education and Training.

Art, Drama, and Music Teachers, Postsecondary

- Personality Code: AS
- Growth: 38.1%
- Annual Job Openings: 216,000
- Annual Earnings: $47,980
- Education/Training Required: Master's degree
- Self-Employed: 0.3%
- Part-Time: 27.7%

Teach courses in drama, music, and the arts, including fine and applied art, such as painting and sculpture or design and crafts. Serve on academic or administrative committees that deal with institutional policies, departmental matters, and academic issues. Write grant proposals to procure external research funding. Evaluate and grade students' class work, performances, projects, assignments, and papers. Prepare and deliver lectures to undergraduate and/or graduate students on topics such as acting techniques, fundamentals of music, and art history. Advise students on academic and vocational curricula, and on career issues. Compile, administer, and grade examinations, or assign this work to others. Compile bibliographies of specialized materials for outside reading assignments. Explain and demonstrate artistic techniques. Initiate, facilitate, and moderate classroom discussions. Keep abreast of developments in their field by reading current literature, talking with colleagues, and participating in professional conferences. Maintain regularly scheduled office hours in order to advise and assist students. Maintain student attendance records, grades, and other required records. Plan, evaluate, and revise curricula, course content, and course materials and methods of instruction. Prepare course materials such as syllabi, homework assignments, and handouts. Prepare students for performances, exams, or assessments. Select and obtain materials and supplies such as textbooks and performance pieces. Supervise undergraduate and/or graduate teaching, internship, and research work. Act as advisers to student organizations. Collaborate with colleagues to address teaching and research issues. Conduct research in a particular field of knowledge, and publish findings in professional journals, books, and/or electronic media. Display students' work in schools, galleries, and exhibitions. Keep students informed of community events such as plays and concerts. Organize performance groups, and direct their rehearsals. Participate in campus and community events. Participate in student recruitment, registration, and placement activities. Perform administrative duties such as serving as department head. Provide professional consulting services to government and/or industry. **SKILLS**—Instructing; Learning Strategies; Writing; Speaking; Reading Comprehension; Complex Problem Solving; Time Management; Active Learning.

GOE—Interest Area: 12. Education and Social Service. **Work Group:** 12.03. Educational Services. **Other Jobs in This Work Group:** Adult Literacy, Remedial Education, and GED Teachers and Instructors; Agricultural Sciences Teachers, Postsecondary; Anthropology and Archeology Teachers, Postsecondary; Architecture Teachers, Postsecondary; Archivists; Area, Ethnic, and Cultural Studies Teachers, Postsecondary; Atmospheric, Earth, Marine, and Space Sciences Teachers, Postsecondary; Audio-Visual Collections Specialists; Biological Science Teachers, Postsecondary; Business Teachers, Postsecondary; Chemistry Teachers, Postsecondary; Child Care Workers; Communications Teachers, Postsecondary; Computer Science Teachers, Postsecondary; Criminal Justice and Law Enforcement Teachers, Postsecondary; Curators; Economics Teachers, Postsecondary; Education

Teachers, Postsecondary; Education, Training, and Library Workers, All Other; Educational Psychologists; Educational, Vocational, and School Counselors; Elementary School Teachers, Except Special Education; Engineering Teachers, Postsecondary; English Language and Literature Teachers, Postsecondary; Environmental Science Teachers, Postsecondary; Farm and Home Management Advisors; Foreign Language and Literature Teachers, Postsecondary; Forestry and Conservation Science Teachers, Postsecondary; Geography Teachers, Postsecondary; Graduate Teaching Assistants; Health Specialties Teachers, Postsecondary; History Teachers, Postsecondary; Home Economics Teachers, Postsecondary; Kindergarten Teachers, Except Special Education; Law Teachers, Postsecondary; Librarians; Library Assistants, Clerical; Library Science Teachers, Postsecondary; Library Technicians; Mathematical Science Teachers, Postsecondary; Middle School Teachers, Except Special and Vocational Education; Museum Technicians and Conservators; Nannies; Nursing Instructors and Teachers, Postsecondary; Personal Financial Advisors; Philosophy and Religion Teachers, Postsecondary; Physics Teachers, Postsecondary; Political Science Teachers, Postsecondary; Postsecondary Teachers, All Other; Preschool Teachers, Except Special Education; Psychology Teachers, Postsecondary; Recreation and Fitness Studies Teachers, Postsecondary; Secondary School Teachers, Except Special and Vocational Education; Self-Enrichment Education Teachers; Social Sciences Teachers, Postsecondary, All Other; Social Work Teachers, Postsecondary; Sociology Teachers, Postsecondary; Special Education Teachers, Middle School; Special Education Teachers, Preschool, Kindergarten, and Elementary School; Special Education Teachers, Secondary School; Teacher Assistants; Teachers and Instructors, All Other; Vocational Education Teachers, Postsecondary; Vocational Education Teachers, Middle School; Vocational Education Teachers, Secondary School.

EDUCATION/TRAINING PROGRAM(S)— Art History, Criticism and Conservation; Art/Art

Studies, General; Arts Management; Ceramic Arts and Ceramics; Cinematography and Film/Video Production; Commercial Photography; Conducting; Crafts/Craft Design, Folk Art and Artisanry; Dance, General; Design and Applied Arts, Other; Design and Visual Communications, General; Directing and Theatrical Production; Drama and Dramatics/Theatre Arts, General; Dramatic/Theatre Arts and Stagecraft, Other; Fashion/Apparel Design; Fiber, Textile and Weaving Arts; Film/Cinema Studies; Film/Video and Photographic Arts, Other; Fine Arts and Art Studies, Other; Fine/Studio Arts, General; Graphic Design; Industrial Design; Interior Design; Intermedia/Multimedia; Jazz/Jazz Studies; Metal and Jewelry Arts; Music History, Literature, and Theory; Music Management and Merchandising; Music Pedagogy; Music Performance, General; Music Theory and Composition; Music, Other; Musicology and Ethnomusicology; Painting; Photography; Piano and Organ; Playwriting and Screenwriting; Printmaking; Sculpture; Technical Theatre/Theatre Design and Technology; Theatre Literature, History and Criticism; Theatre/Theatre Arts Management; Violin, Viola, Guitar and Other Stringed Instruments; Visual and Performing Arts, General; Visual and Performing Arts, Other; Voice and Opera. **RELATED KNOWLEDGE/COURSES**—Fine Arts; Education and Training; English Language; Communications and Media; Administration and Management; Clerical Studies.

Broadcast News Analysts

- Personality Code: AS
- Growth: 6.2%
- Annual Job Openings: 6,000
- Annual Earnings: $31,240
- Education/Training Required: Bachelor's degree
- Self-Employed: 6.3%
- Part-Time: 14.4%

Analyze, interpret, and broadcast news received from various sources. Analyze and interpret news and information received from various sources in order to be able to broadcast the information. Edit news material to ensure that it fits within available time or space. Examine news items of local, national, and international significance in order to determine topics to address, or obtain assignments from editorial staff members. Gather information and develop perspectives about news subjects through research, interviews, observation, and experience. Select material most pertinent to presentation, and organize this material into appropriate formats. Write commentaries, columns, or scripts, using computers. Coordinate and serve as an anchor on news broadcast programs. Present news stories, and introduce in-depth videotaped segments or live transmissions from on-the-scene reporters. **SKILLS**—Writing; Speaking; Reading Comprehension; Active Listening; Critical Thinking; Active Learning; Social Perceptiveness; Monitoring.

GOE—Interest Area: 01. Arts, Entertainment, and Media. **Work Group:** 01.03. News, Broadcasting and Public Relations. **Other Jobs in This Work Group:** Caption Writers; Interpreters and Translators; Public Relations Specialists; Reporters and Correspondents.

EDUCATION/TRAINING PROGRAM(S)—Broadcast Journalism; Journalism; Political Communication; Radio and Television. **RELATED KNOWLEDGE/COURSES**—Communications and Media; English Language; Telecommunications; Computers and Electronics; Geography; Sociology and Anthropology.

Camera Operators, Television, Video, and Motion Picture

- Personality Code: AR
- Growth: 13.4%
- Annual Job Openings: 4,000
- Annual Earnings: $34,330
- Education/Training Required: Moderate-term on-the-job training
- Self-Employed: 23.8%
- Part-Time: 20.4%

Operate television, video, or motion picture camera to photograph images or scenes for various purposes, such as TV broadcasts, advertising, video production, or motion pictures. Operate television or motion picture cameras to record scenes for television broadcasts, advertising, or motion pictures. Compose and frame each shot, applying the technical aspects of light, lenses, film, filters, and camera settings in order to achieve the effects sought by directors. Operate zoom lenses, changing images according to specifications and rehearsal instructions. Use cameras in any of several different camera mounts such as stationary, track-mounted, or crane-mounted. Test, clean, and maintain equipment to ensure proper working condition. Adjust positions and controls of cameras, printers, and related equipment in order to change focus, exposure, and lighting. Gather and edit raw footage on location to send to television affiliates for broadcast, using electronic news-gathering or film-production equipment.

Confer with directors, sound and lighting technicians, electricians, and other crew members to discuss assignments and determine filming sequences, desired effects, camera movements, and lighting requirements. Observe sets or locations for potential problems and to determine filming and lighting requirements. Instruct camera operators regarding camera setups, angles, distances, movement, and variables and cues for starting and stopping filming. Select and assemble cameras, accessories, equipment, and film stock to be used during filming, using knowledge of filming techniques, requirements, and computations. Label and record contents of exposed film, and note details on report forms. Read charts and compute ratios to determine variables such as lighting, shutter angles, filter factors, and camera distances. Set up cameras, optical printers, and related equipment to produce photographs and special effects. View films to resolve problems of exposure control, subject and camera movement, changes in subject distance, and related variables. Reload camera magazines with fresh raw film stock. Read and analyze work orders and specifications to determine locations of subject material, work procedures, sequences of operations, and machine setups. Receive raw film stock, and maintain film inventories. **SKILLS**—Equipment Maintenance; Troubleshooting; Operation Monitoring; Coordination; Operation and Control; Active Listening; Time Management; Persuasion.

GOE—Interest Area: 01. Arts, Entertainment, and Media. **Work Group:** 01.08. Media Technology. **Other Jobs in This Work Group:** Audio and Video Equipment Technicians; Broadcast Technicians; Film and Video Editors; Media and Communication Equipment Workers, All Other; Photographers; Professional Photographers; Radio Operators; Sound Engineering Technicians.

EDUCATION/TRAINING PROGRAM(S)—Audiovisual Communications Technologies/Technicians, Other; Cinematography and Film/Video Production; Radio and Television Broadcasting Technology/Technician. **RELATED KNOWLEDGE/COURSES**—Communications and Media;

Computers and Electronics; Telecommunications; Customer and Personal Service; Sales and Marketing; Fine Arts.

Caption Writers

- Personality Code: AS
- Growth: 16.1%
- Annual Job Openings: 23,000
- Annual Earnings: $42,330
- Education/Training Required: Moderate-term on-the-job training
- Self-Employed: 67.9%
- Part-Time: 24.2%

Write caption phrases of dialogue for hearing-impaired and foreign language–speaking viewers of movie or television productions. Writes captions to describe music and background noises. Watches production and reviews captions simultaneously to determine which caption phrases require editing. Enters commands to synchronize captions with dialogue and place on the screen. Translates foreign language dialogue into English language captions or English dialogue into foreign language captions. Operates computerized captioning system for movies or television productions for hearing-impaired and foreign language speaking viewers. Oversees encoding of captions to master tape of television production. Discusses captions with directors or producers of movie and television productions. Edits translations for correctness of grammar, punctuation, and clarity of expression. **SKILLS**—Writing; Reading Comprehension; Operation and Control; Management of Financial Resources.

GOE—**Interest Area:** 01. Arts, Entertainment, and Media. **Work Group:** 01.03. News, Broadcasting and Public Relations. **Other Jobs in This Work Group:** Broadcast News Analysts; Interpreters and

Translators; Public Relations Specialists; Reporters and Correspondents.

EDUCATION/TRAINING PROGRAM(S)— Broadcast Journalism; Business/Corporate Communications; Communication Studies/Speech Communication and Rhetoric; Communication, Journalism, and Related Programs, Other; Creative Writing; English Composition; Family and Consumer Sciences/Human Sciences Communication; Journalism; Mass Communication/Media Studies; Playwriting and Screenwriting; Technical and Business Writing. **RELATED KNOWLEDGE/ COURSES**—Foreign Language; Communications and Media; English Language; Computers and Electronics; Telecommunications.

Cartoonists

- Personality Code: AE
- Growth: 16.5%
- Annual Job Openings: 4,000
- Annual Earnings: $35,420
- Education/Training Required: Long-term on-the-job training
- Self-Employed: 55.5%
- Part-Time: 23.1%

Create original artwork using any of a wide variety of mediums and techniques, such as painting and sculpture. Sketches and submits cartoon or animation for approval. Develops personal ideas for cartoons, comic strips, or animations, or reads written material to develop ideas. Makes changes and corrections to cartoon, comic strip, or animation as necessary. Creates and prepares sketches and model drawings of characters, providing details from memory, live models, manufactured products, or reference material. Renders sequential drawings of characters or other subject material which when photographed and projected at specific speed becomes animated. Develops color patterns and moods and paints background layouts to dramatize action for animated cartoon scenes. Discusses ideas for cartoons, comic strips, or animations with editor or publisher's representative. Labels each section with designated colors when colors are used. **SKILLS**—Operations Analysis.

GOE—**Interest Area:** 01. Arts, Entertainment, and Media. **Work Group:** 01.04. Visual Arts. **Other Jobs in This Work Group:** Artists and Related Workers, All Other; Commercial and Industrial Designers; Designers, All Other; Exhibit Designers; Fashion Designers; Fine Artists, Including Painters, Sculptors, and Illustrators; Floral Designers; Graphic Designers; Interior Designers; Merchandise Displayers and Window Trimmers; Multi-Media Artists and Animators; Painters and Illustrators; Sculptors; Set and Exhibit Designers; Set Designers; Sketch Artists.

EDUCATION/TRAINING PROGRAM(S)— Art/Art Studies, General; Drawing; Fine Arts and Art Studies, Other; Fine/Studio Arts, General; Intermedia/Multimedia; Medical Illustration/ Medical Illustrator; Painting; Visual and Performing Arts, General. **RELATED KNOWLEDGE/ COURSES**—Fine Arts; Communications and Media; Sales and Marketing; Design; Telecommunications.

to suggest story, interpret emotion, or enliven show. Studies story line and music to envision and devise dance movements. Directs and stages dance presentations for various forms of entertainment. Auditions performers for one or more dance parts. Instructs cast in dance movements at rehearsals to achieve desired effect. Creates original dance routines for ballets, musicals, or other forms of entertainment. **SKILLS**—Instructing; Coordination; Monitoring; Learning Strategies.

GOE—**Interest Area:** 01. Arts, Entertainment, and Media. **Work Group:** 01.05. Performing Arts. **Other Jobs in This Work Group:** Actors; Composers; Dancers; Directors—Stage, Motion Pictures, Television, and Radio; Entertainers and Performers, Sports and Related Workers, All Other; Music Arrangers and Orchestrators; Music Directors; Music Directors and Composers; Musicians and Singers; Musicians, Instrumental; Public Address System and Other Announcers; Radio and Television Announcers; Singers; Talent Directors.

EDUCATION/TRAINING PROGRAM(S)— Dance, General; Dance, Other. **RELATED KNOWLEDGE/COURSES**—Fine Arts; Communications and Media; Personnel and Human Resources; Education and Training; Sociology and Anthropology.

Choreographers

- Personality Code: AS
- Growth: 15.8%
- Annual Job Openings: 3,000
- Annual Earnings: $31,030
- Education/Training Required: Work experience in a related occupation
- Self-Employed: 16.7%
- Part-Time: 33.8%

Create and teach dance. May direct and stage presentations. Determines dance movements designed

Commercial and Industrial Designers

- Personality Code: AR
- Growth: 14.7%
- Annual Job Openings: 7,000
- Annual Earnings: $52,320
- Education/Training Required: Bachelor's degree
- Self-Employed: 31.0%
- Part-Time: 16.5%

Develop and design manufactured products, such as cars, home appliances, and children's toys. Combine artistic talent with research on product use, marketing, and materials to create the most functional and appealing product design. Direct and coordinate the fabrication of models or samples and the drafting of working drawings and specification sheets from sketches. Modify and refine designs, using working models, to conform with customer specifications, production limitations, or changes in design trends. Prepare sketches of ideas, detailed drawings, illustrations, artwork, and/or blueprints, using drafting instruments, paints and brushes, or computer-aided design equipment. Present designs and reports to customers or design committees for approval, and discuss need for modification. Read publications, attend showings, and study competing products and design styles and motifs to obtain perspective and generate design concepts. Advise corporations on issues involving corporate image projects or problems. Evaluate feasibility of design ideas, based on factors such as appearance, safety, function, serviceability, budget, production costs/methods, and market characteristics. Fabricate models or samples in paper, wood, glass, fabric, plastic, metal, or other materials, using hand and/or power tools. Research production specifications, costs, production materials and manufacturing methods, and provide cost estimates and itemized production requirements. Supervise assistants' work throughout the design process. Develop industrial standards and regulatory guidelines. Confer with engineering, marketing, production, and/or sales departments, or with customers, to establish and evaluate design concepts for manufactured products. Coordinate the look and function of product lines. Design graphic material for use as ornamentation, illustration, or advertising on manufactured materials and packaging or containers. Develop manufacturing procedures and monitor the manufacture of their designs in a factory to improve operations and product quality. Investigate product characteristics such as the product's safety and handling qualities, its market appeal, how efficiently it can be produced, and ways of distributing, using

and maintaining it. Participate in new product planning or market research, including studying the potential need for new products. **SKILLS**—Operations Analysis; Management of Financial Resources; Active Learning; Equipment Selection; Persuasion; Systems Analysis; Systems Evaluation; Negotiation.

GOE—**Interest Area:** 01. Arts, Entertainment, and Media. **Work Group:** 01.04. Visual Arts. **Other Jobs in This Work Group:** Artists and Related Workers, All Other; Cartoonists; Designers, All Other; Exhibit Designers; Fashion Designers; Fine Artists, Including Painters, Sculptors, and Illustrators; Floral Designers; Graphic Designers; Interior Designers; Merchandise Displayers and Window Trimmers; Multi-Media Artists and Animators; Painters and Illustrators; Sculptors; Set and Exhibit Designers; Set Designers; Sketch Artists.

EDUCATION/TRAINING PROGRAM(S)— Commercial and Advertising Art; Design and Applied Arts, Other; Design and Visual Communications, General; Industrial Design. **RELATED KNOWLEDGE/COURSES**—Design; Fine Arts; Production and Processing; Sales and Marketing; English Language; Communications and Media.

Composers

- Personality Code: A
- Growth: 13.5%
- Annual Job Openings: 8,000
- Annual Earnings: $32,530
- Education/Training Required: Master's degree
- Self-Employed: 39.3%
- Part-Time: 39.5%

Compose music for orchestra, choral group, or band. Creates original musical form or writes within circumscribed musical form, such as sonata, symphony, or opera. Transcribes or records musical ideas into notes on scored music paper. Develops pattern of harmony, applying knowledge of music theory. Synthesizes ideas for melody of musical scores for choral group, or band. Creates musical and tonal structure, applying elements of music theory, such as instrumental and vocal capabilities. Determines basic pattern of melody, applying knowledge of music theory. **SKILLS**—Equipment Selection.

GOE—Interest Area: 01. Arts, Entertainment, and Media. **Work Group:** 01.05. Performing Arts. **Other Jobs in This Work Group:** Actors; Choreographers; Dancers; Directors—Stage, Motion Pictures, Television, and Radio; Entertainers and Performers, Sports and Related Workers, All Other; Music Arrangers and Orchestrators; Music Directors; Music Directors and Composers; Musicians and Singers; Musicians, Instrumental; Public Address System and Other Announcers; Radio and Television Announcers; Singers; Talent Directors.

EDUCATION/TRAINING PROGRAM(S)— Conducting; Music Management and Merchandising; Music Performance, General; Music Theory and Composition; Music, Other; Musicology and Ethnomusicology; Religious/Sacred Music; Voice and Opera. **RELATED KNOWLEDGE/COURSES**—Fine Arts; History and Archeology.

Copy Writers

- ◎ Personality Code: AE
- ◎ Growth: 16.1%
- ◎ Annual Job Openings: 23,000
- ◎ Annual Earnings: $42,330
- ◎ Education/Training Required: Bachelor's degree
- ◎ Self-Employed: 67.9%
- ◎ Part-Time: 24.2%

Write advertising copy for use by publication or broadcast media to promote sale of goods and serv-

ices. Write advertising copy for use by publication, broadcast or internet media to promote the sale of goods and services. Present drafts and ideas to clients. Discuss with the client the product, advertising themes and methods, and any changes that should be made in advertising copy. Vary language and tone of messages based on product and medium. Consult with sales, media and marketing representatives to obtain information on product or service and discuss style and length of advertising copy. Edit or rewrite existing copy as necessary, and submit copy for approval by supervisor. Write to customers in their terms and on their level so that the advertiser's sales message is more readily received. Write articles, bulletins, sales letters, speeches, and other related informative, marketing and promotional material. Invent names for products and write the slogans that appear on packaging, brochures and other promotional material. Review advertising trends, consumer surveys, and other data regarding marketing of goods and services to determine the best way to promote products. Develop advertising campaigns for a wide range of clients, working with an advertising agency's creative director and art director to determine the best way to present advertising information. Conduct research and interviews to determine which of a product's selling features should be promoted. **SKILLS**—Persuasion; Time Management; Instructing; Coordination; Negotiation; Technology Design; Critical Thinking; Active Listening.

GOE—Interest Area: 01. Arts, Entertainment, and Media. **Work Group:** 01.02. Writing and Editing. **Other Jobs in This Work Group:** Creative Writers; Editors; Media and Communication Workers, All Other; Poets and Lyricists; Technical Writers; Writers and Authors.

EDUCATION/TRAINING PROGRAM(S)— Broadcast Journalism; Business/Corporate Communications; Communication Studies/Speech Communication and Rhetoric; Communication, Journalism, and Related Programs, Other; Creative Writing; English Composition; Family and Consumer Sciences/Human Sciences Communication;

Journalism; Mass Communication/Media Studies; Playwriting and Screenwriting; Technical and Business Writing. **RELATED KNOWLEDGE/ COURSES**—Sales and Marketing; Communications and Media; Sociology and Anthropology; English Language; Computers and Electronics; Administration and Management.

Costume Attendants

- Personality Code: AR
- Growth: 27.8%
- Annual Job Openings: 66,000
- Annual Earnings: $25,410
- Education/Training Required: Moderate-term on-the-job training
- Self-Employed: 0.4%
- Part-Time: 51.9%

Select, fit, and take care of costumes for cast members, and aid entertainers. Arrange costumes in order of use to facilitate quick-change procedures for performances. Assign lockers to employees, and maintain locker rooms, dressing rooms, wig rooms, and costume storage and laundry areas. Care for non-clothing items such as flags, table skirts, and draperies. Check the appearance of costumes on-stage and under lights in order to determine whether desired effects are being achieved. Clean and press costumes before and after performances, and perform any minor repairs. Collaborate with production designers, costume designers, and other production staff in order to discuss and execute costume design details. Create worksheets for dressing lists, show notes, and costume checks. Distribute costumes and related equipment, and keep records of item status. Examine costume fit on cast members, and sketch or write notes for alterations. Inventory stock in order to determine types and conditions of available costuming. Monitor, main-

tain, and secure inventories of costumes, wigs, and makeup, providing keys or access to assigned directors, costume designers, and wardrobe mistresses/masters. Provide assistance to cast members in wearing costumes, or assign cast dressers to assist specific cast members with costume changes. Return borrowed or rented items when productions are complete and return other items to storage. Design and construct costumes or send them to tailors for construction, major repairs, or alterations. Direct the work of wardrobe crews during dress rehearsals and performances. Participate in the hiring, training, scheduling, and supervision of alteration workers. Provide managers with budget recommendations, and take responsibility for budgetary line items related to costumes, storage, and makeup needs. Purchase, rent, or requisition costumes and other wardrobe necessities. Recommend vendors and monitor their work. Review scripts or other production information in order to determine a story's locale and period, as well as the number of characters and required costumes. Study books, pictures, and examples of period clothing in order to determine styles worn during specific periods in history. **SKILLS**—Management of Financial Resources; Management of Material Resources; Repairing.

GOE—Interest Area: 01. Arts, Entertainment, and Media. **Work Group:** 01.09. Modeling and Personal Appearance. **Other Jobs in This Work Group:** Entertainers and Performers, Sports and Related Workers, All Other; Makeup Artists, Theatrical and Performance; Models.

EDUCATION/TRAINING PROGRAM(S)— No data available. **RELATED KNOWLEDGE/ COURSES**—Fine Arts; Design; Sociology and Anthropology; Geography; History and Archeology.

Creative Writers

- ⊚ Personality Code: A
- ⊚ Growth: 16.1%
- ⊚ Annual Job Openings: 23,000
- ⊚ Annual Earnings: $42,330
- ⊚ Education/Training Required: Bachelor's degree
- ⊚ Self-Employed: 67.9%
- ⊚ Part-Time: 24.2%

Create original written works, such as plays or prose, for publication or performance. Writes fiction or nonfiction prose work, such as short story, novel, biography, article, descriptive or critical analysis, or essay. Writes play or script for moving pictures or television, based on original ideas or adapted from fictional, historical, or narrative sources. Organizes material for project, plans arrangement or outline, and writes synopsis. Collaborates with other writers on specific projects. Confers with client, publisher, or producer to discuss development changes or revisions. Conducts research to obtain factual information and authentic detail, utilizing sources such as newspaper accounts, diaries, and interviews. Reviews, submits for approval, and revises written material to meet personal standards and satisfy needs of client, publisher, director, or producer. Selects subject or theme for writing project based on personal interest and writing specialty, or assignment from publisher, client, producer, or director. Develops factors, such as theme, plot, characterization, psychological analysis, historical environment, action, and dialogue, to create material. Writes humorous material for publication or performance, such as comedy routines, gags, comedy shows, or scripts for entertainers. **SKILLS**—Writing; Reading Comprehension; Coordination; Critical Thinking; Complex Problem Solving; Social Perceptiveness; Monitoring; Negotiation.

GOE—Interest Area: 01. Arts, Entertainment, and Media. **Work Group:** 01.02. Writing and Editing.

Other Jobs in This Work Group: Copy Writers; Editors; Media and Communication Workers, All Other; Poets and Lyricists; Technical Writers; Writers and Authors.

EDUCATION/TRAINING PROGRAM(S)— Broadcast Journalism; Business/Corporate Communications; Communication Studies/Speech Communication and Rhetoric; Communication, Journalism, and Related Programs, Other; Creative Writing; English Composition; Family and Consumer Sciences/Human Sciences Communication; Journalism; Mass Communication/Media Studies; Playwriting and Screenwriting; Technical and Business Writing. **RELATED KNOWLEDGE/ COURSES**—English Language; Communications and Media; Fine Arts; Sociology and Anthropology; Computers and Electronics.

Curators

- ⊚ Personality Code: AI
- ⊚ Growth: 17.0%
- ⊚ Annual Job Openings: 2,000
- ⊚ Annual Earnings: $35,660
- ⊚ Education/Training Required: Master's degree
- ⊚ Self-Employed: 3.4%
- ⊚ Part-Time: 11.8%

Administer affairs of museum and conduct research programs. Direct instructional, research, and public service activities of institution. Plan and organize the acquisition, storage, and exhibition of collections and related materials, including the selection of exhibition themes and designs. Develop and maintain an institution's registration, cataloging, and basic record-keeping systems, using computer databases. Provide information from the institution's holdings to other curators and to the public. Inspect premises to assess the need for repairs and to ensure that climate and pest-control

Artistic—C

issues are addressed. Train and supervise curatorial, fiscal, technical, research, and clerical staff, as well as volunteers or interns. Negotiate and authorize purchase, sale, exchange, or loan of collections. Plan and conduct special research projects in area of interest or expertise. Conduct or organize tours, workshops, and instructional sessions to acquaint individuals with an institution's facilities and materials. Confer with the board of directors to formulate and interpret policies, to determine budget requirements, and to plan overall operations. Attend meetings, conventions, and civic events to promote use of institution's services, to seek financing, and to maintain community alliances. Schedule events, and organize details including refreshment, entertainment, decorations, and the collection of any fees. Write and review grant proposals, journal articles, institutional reports, and publicity materials. Study, examine, and test acquisitions to authenticate their origin, composition, history, and to assess their current value. Arrange insurance coverage for objects on loan or for special exhibits, and recommend changes in coverage for the entire collection. **SKILLS**—Management of Financial Resources; Management of Personnel Resources; Time Management; Persuasion; Writing; Negotiation; Service Orientation; Monitoring.

GOE—Interest Area: 12. Education and Social Service. **Work Group:** 12.03. Educational Services. **Other Jobs in This Work Group:** Adult Literacy, Remedial Education, and GED Teachers and Instructors; Agricultural Sciences Teachers, Postsecondary; Anthropology and Archeology Teachers, Postsecondary; Architecture Teachers, Postsecondary; Archivists; Area, Ethnic, and Cultural Studies Teachers, Postsecondary; Art, Drama, and Music Teachers, Postsecondary; Atmospheric, Earth, Marine, and Space Sciences Teachers, Postsecondary; Audio-Visual Collections Specialists; Biological Science Teachers, Postsecondary; Business Teachers, Postsecondary; Chemistry Teachers, Postsecondary; Child Care Workers; Communications Teachers, Postsecondary; Computer Science Teachers, Postsecondary; Criminal Justice and Law Enforcement Teachers, Postsecondary; Economics Teachers, Postsecondary; Education Teachers, Postsecondary; Education, Training, and Library Workers, All Other; Educational Psychologists; Educational, Vocational, and School Counselors; Elementary School Teachers, Except Special Education; Engineering Teachers, Postsecondary; English Language and Literature Teachers, Postsecondary; Environmental Science Teachers, Postsecondary; Farm and Home Management Advisors; Foreign Language and Literature Teachers, Postsecondary; Forestry and Conservation Science Teachers, Postsecondary; Geography Teachers, Postsecondary; Graduate Teaching Assistants; Health Specialties Teachers, Postsecondary; History Teachers, Postsecondary; Home Economics Teachers, Postsecondary; Kindergarten Teachers, Except Special Education; Law Teachers, Postsecondary; Librarians; Library Assistants, Clerical; Library Science Teachers, Postsecondary; Library Technicians; Mathematical Science Teachers, Postsecondary; Middle School Teachers, Except Special and Vocational Education; Museum Technicians and Conservators; Nannies; Nursing Instructors and Teachers, Postsecondary; Personal Financial Advisors; Philosophy and Religion Teachers, Postsecondary; Physics Teachers, Postsecondary; Political Science Teachers, Postsecondary; Postsecondary Teachers, All Other; Preschool Teachers, Except Special Education; Psychology Teachers, Postsecondary; Recreation and Fitness Studies Teachers, Postsecondary; Secondary School Teachers, Except Special and Vocational Education; Self-Enrichment Education Teachers; Social Sciences Teachers, Postsecondary, All Other; Social Work Teachers, Postsecondary; Sociology Teachers, Postsecondary; Special Education Teachers, Middle School; Special Education Teachers, Preschool, Kindergarten, and Elementary School; Special Education Teachers, Secondary School; Teacher Assistants; Teachers and Instructors, All Other; Vocational Education Teachers, Postsecondary; Vocational Education Teachers, Middle School; Vocational Education Teachers, Secondary School.

EDUCATION/TRAINING PROGRAM(S)—Art History, Criticism and Conservation; Museology/Museum Studies; Public/Applied History and Archival Administration. **RELATED KNOWLEDGE/COURSES**—Clerical Studies; History and Archeology; Fine Arts; Sociology and Anthropology; Philosophy and Theology; Education and Training.

Directors—Stage, Motion Pictures, Television, and Radio

- Personality Code: AE
- Growth: 18.3%
- Annual Job Openings: 10,000
- Annual Earnings: $48,200
- Education/Training Required: Work experience plus degree
- Self-Employed: 32.8%
- Part-Time: 9.1%

Interpret script, conduct rehearsals, and direct activities of cast and technical crew for stage, motion pictures, television, or radio programs. Direct live broadcasts, films and recordings, or non-broadcast programming for public entertainment or education. Supervise and coordinate the work of camera, lighting, design, and sound crewmembers. Study and research scripts in order to determine how they should be directed. Cut and edit film or tape in order to integrate component parts into desired sequences. Collaborate with film and sound editors during the post-production process as films are edited and soundtracks are added. Confer with technical directors, managers, crew members, and writers to discuss details of production, such as photography, script, music, sets, and costumes. Plan details such as framing, composition, camera move-ment, sound, and actor movement for each shot or scene. Communicate to actors the approach, characterization, and movement needed for each scene in such a way that rehearsals and takes are minimized. Establish pace of programs and sequences of scenes according to time requirements and cast and set accessibility. Choose settings and locations for films and determine how scenes will be shot in these settings. Identify and approve equipment and elements required for productions, such as scenery, lights, props, costumes, choreography, and music. Compile scripts, program notes, and other material related to productions. Perform producers' duties such as securing financial backing, establishing and administering budgets, and recruiting cast and crew. Select plays or scripts for production, and determine how material should be interpreted and performed. Compile cue words and phrases, and cue announcers, cast members, and technicians during performances. Consult with writers, producers, and/or actors about script changes, or "workshop" scripts, through rehearsal with writers and actors to create final drafts. Review film daily in order to check on work in progress and to plan for future filming. Collaborate with producers in order to hire crewmembers such as art directors, cinematographers, and costumer designers. Interpret stage-set diagrams to determine stage layouts, and supervise placement of equipment and scenery. **SKILLS**—Management of Personnel Resources; Time Management; Judgment and Decision Making; Critical Thinking; Active Listening; Operations Analysis; Speaking; Active Learning.

GOE—Interest Area: 01. Arts, Entertainment, and Media. **Work Group:** 01.05. Performing Arts. **Other Jobs in This Work Group:** Actors; Choreographers; Composers; Dancers; Entertainers and Performers, Sports and Related Workers, All Other; Music Arrangers and Orchestrators; Music Directors; Music Directors and Composers; Musicians and Singers; Musicians, Instrumental; Public Address System and Other Announcers; Radio and Television Announcers; Singers; Talent Directors.

Artistic—D

EDUCATION/TRAINING PROGRAM(S)—Cinematography and Film/Video Production; Directing and Theatrical Production; Drama and Dramatics/Theatre Arts, General; Dramatic/Theatre Arts and Stagecraft, Other; Film/Cinema Studies; Radio and Television; Theatre/Theatre Arts Management. RELATED KNOWLEDGE/COURSES—Communications and Media; Telecommunications; Computers and Electronics; Geography; Education and Training; Fine Arts.

Editors

- Personality Code: AS
- Growth: 11.8%
- Annual Job Openings: 14,000
- Annual Earnings: $41,460
- Education/Training Required: Bachelor's degree
- Self-Employed: 12.9%
- Part-Time: 13.0%

Perform variety of editorial duties, such as laying out, indexing, and revising content of written materials, in preparation for final publication. Prepare, rewrite and edit copy to improve readability, or supervise others who do this work. Read copy or proof to detect and correct errors in spelling, punctuation, and syntax. Allocate print space for story text, photos, and illustrations according to space parameters and copy significance, using knowledge of layout principles. Plan the contents of publications according to the publication's style, editorial policy, and publishing requirements. Verify facts, dates, and statistics, using standard reference sources. Review and approve proofs submitted by composing room prior to publication production. Develop story or content ideas, considering reader or audience appeal. Oversee publication production, including artwork, layout, computer typesetting, and printing, ensuring adherence to deadlines and budget requirements. Confer with management and editorial staff members regarding placement and emphasis of developing news stories. Assign topics, events and stories to individual writers or reporters for coverage. Read, evaluate and edit manuscripts or other materials submitted for publication and confer with authors regarding changes in content, style or organization, or publication. Monitor news-gathering operations to ensure utilization of all news sources, such as press releases, telephone contacts, radio, television, wire services, and other reporters. Meet frequently with artists, typesetters, layout personnel, marketing directors, and production managers to discuss projects and resolve problems. Supervise and coordinate work of reporters and other editors. Make manuscript acceptance or revision recommendations to the publisher. Select local, state, national, and international news items received from wire services, based on assessment of items' significance and interest value. Interview and hire writers and reporters or negotiate contracts, royalties, and payments for authors or freelancers. SKILLS—Writing; Reading Comprehension; Active Listening; Time Management; Persuasion; Critical Thinking; Active Learning; Social Perceptiveness.

GOE—Interest Area: 01. Arts, Entertainment, and Media. Work Group: 01.02. Writing and Editing. Other Jobs in This Work Group: Copy Writers; Creative Writers; Media and Communication Workers, All Other; Poets and Lyricists; Technical Writers; Writers and Authors.

EDUCATION/TRAINING PROGRAM(S)—Broadcast Journalism; Business/Corporate Communications; Communication, Journalism, and Related Programs, Other; Creative Writing; Journalism; Mass Communication/Media Studies; Publishing; Technical and Business Writing. RELATED KNOWLEDGE/COURSES—Communications and Media; English Language; Geography; History and Archeology; Clerical Studies; Computers and Electronics.

English Language and Literature Teachers, Postsecondary

- Personality Code: AS
- Growth: 38.1%
- Annual Job Openings: 216,000
- Annual Earnings: $47,120
- Education/Training Required: Master's degree
- Self-Employed: 0.3%
- Part-Time: 27.7%

Teach courses in English language and literature, including linguistics and comparative literature. Provide professional consulting services to government and/or industry. Recruit, train, and supervise student writing instructors. Serve on academic or administrative committees that deal with institutional policies, departmental matters, and academic issues. Write grant proposals to procure external research funding. Evaluate and grade students' class work, assignments, and papers. Prepare and deliver lectures to undergraduate and/or graduate students on topics such as poetry, novel structure, and translation and adaptation. Advise students on academic and vocational curricula, and on career issues. Compile, administer, and grade examinations, or assign this work to others. Compile bibliographies of specialized materials for outside reading assignments. Initiate, facilitate, and moderate classroom discussions. Keep abreast of developments in their field by reading current literature, talking with colleagues, and participating in professional conferences. Maintain regularly scheduled office hours in order to advise and assist students. Maintain student attendance records, grades, and other required records. Plan, evaluate, and revise curricula, course content, and course materials and methods of instruction. Prepare course materials such as syllabi, homework assignments, and handouts. Select and obtain mate-rials and supplies such as textbooks. Supervise undergraduate and/or graduate teaching, internship, and research work. Provide assistance to students in college writing centers. Act as advisers to student organizations. Collaborate with colleagues to address teaching and research issues. Conduct research in a particular field of knowledge, and publish findings in professional journals, books, and/or electronic media. Participate in campus and community events. Participate in student recruitment, registration, and placement activities. Perform administrative duties such as serving as department head. **SKILLS**—Instructing; Learning Strategies; Speaking; Reading Comprehension; Writing; Critical Thinking; Active Learning; Active Listening.

GOE—Interest Area: 12. Education and Social Service. **Work Group:** 12.03. Educational Services. **Other Jobs in This Work Group:** Adult Literacy, Remedial Education, and GED Teachers and Instructors; Agricultural Sciences Teachers, Postsecondary; Anthropology and Archeology Teachers, Postsecondary; Architecture Teachers, Postsecondary; Archivists; Area, Ethnic, and Cultural Studies Teachers, Postsecondary; Art, Drama, and Music Teachers, Postsecondary; Atmospheric, Earth, Marine, and Space Sciences Teachers, Postsecondary; Audio-Visual Collections Specialists; Biological Science Teachers, Postsecondary; Business Teachers, Postsecondary; Chemistry Teachers, Postsecondary; Child Care Workers; Communications Teachers, Postsecondary; Computer Science Teachers, Postsecondary; Criminal Justice and Law Enforcement Teachers, Postsecondary; Curators; Economics Teachers, Postsecondary; Education Teachers, Postsecondary; Education, Training, and Library Workers, All Other; Educational Psychologists; Educational, Vocational, and School Counselors; Elementary School Teachers, Except Special Education; Engineering Teachers, Postsecondary; Environmental Science Teachers, Postsecondary; Farm and Home Management Advisors; Foreign Language and Literature Teachers, Postsecondary; Forestry and Conservation Science Teachers, Postsecondary; Geography Teachers, Postsecondary;

Artistic—E

Graduate Teaching Assistants; Health Specialties Teachers, Postsecondary; History Teachers, Postsecondary; Home Economics Teachers, Postsecondary; Kindergarten Teachers, Except Special Education; Law Teachers, Postsecondary; Librarians; Library Assistants, Clerical; Library Science Teachers, Postsecondary; Library Technicians; Mathematical Science Teachers, Postsecondary; Middle School Teachers, Except Special and Vocational Education; Museum Technicians and Conservators; Nannies; Nursing Instructors and Teachers, Postsecondary; Personal Financial Advisors; Philosophy and Religion Teachers, Postsecondary; Physics Teachers, Postsecondary; Political Science Teachers, Postsecondary; Postsecondary Teachers, All Other; Preschool Teachers, Except Special Education; Psychology Teachers, Postsecondary; Recreation and Fitness Studies Teachers, Postsecondary; Secondary School Teachers, Except Special and Vocational Education; Self-Enrichment Education Teachers; Social Sciences Teachers, Postsecondary, All Other; Social Work Teachers, Postsecondary; Sociology Teachers, Postsecondary; Special Education Teachers, Middle School; Special Education Teachers, Preschool, Kindergarten, and Elementary School; Special Education Teachers, Secondary School; Teacher Assistants; Teachers and Instructors, All Other; Vocational Education Teachers, Postsecondary; Vocational Education Teachers, Middle School; Vocational Education Teachers, Secondary School.

EDUCATION/TRAINING PROGRAM(S)— American Literature (Canadian); American Literature (United States); Comparative Literature; Creative Writing; English Composition; English Language and Literature, General; English Language and Literature/Letters, Other; English Literature (British and Commonwealth); Technical and Business Writing. **RELATED KNOWLEDGE/COURSES—** Foreign Language; Education and Training; English Language; Communications and Media; Therapy and Counseling; Clerical Studies.

Exhibit Designers

- Personality Code: AR
- Growth: 20.9%
- Annual Job Openings: 2,000
- Annual Earnings: $35,150
- Education/Training Required: Bachelor's degree
- Self-Employed: 32.2%
- Part-Time: 16.5%

Plan, design, and oversee construction and installation of permanent and temporary exhibits and displays. Inspects installed exhibit for conformance to specifications and satisfactory operation of special effects components. Submits plans for approval, and adapts plan to serve intended purpose or to conform to budget or fabrication restrictions. Designs, draws, paints, or sketches backgrounds and fixtures for use in windows or interior displays. Oversees preparation of artwork, construction of exhibit components, and placement of collection to ensure intended interpretation of concepts and conformance to specifications. Confers with client or staff regarding theme, interpretative or informational purpose, planned location, budget, materials, or promotion. Designs display to decorate streets, fairgrounds, building or other places for celebrations, using paper, cloth, plastic, or other materials. Prepares preliminary drawings of proposed exhibit, including detailed construction, layout, material specifications, or special effects diagrams. Arranges for acquisition of specimens or graphics, or building of exhibit structures by outside contractors to complete exhibit. **SKILLS—**Management of Financial Resources; Management of Material Resources; Negotiation; Systems Evaluation; Operations Analysis; Social Perceptiveness; Systems Analysis; Management of Personnel Resources.

GOE—Interest Area: 01. Arts, Entertainment, and Media. **Work Group:** 01.04. Visual Arts. **Other Jobs in This Work Group:** Artists and Related

Workers, All Other; Cartoonists; Commercial and Industrial Designers; Designers, All Other; Fashion Designers; Fine Artists, Including Painters, Sculptors, and Illustrators; Floral Designers; Graphic Designers; Interior Designers; Merchandise Displayers and Window Trimmers; Multi-Media Artists and Animators; Painters and Illustrators; Sculptors; Set and Exhibit Designers; Set Designers; Sketch Artists.

EDUCATION/TRAINING PROGRAM(S)—Design and Applied Arts, Other; Design and Visual Communications, General; Illustration; Technical Theatre/Theatre Design and Technology. RELATED KNOWLEDGE/COURSES—Design; Fine Arts; Building and Construction; Sales and Marketing; Computers and Electronics; Customer and Personal Service.

Fashion Designers

- Personality Code: AE
- Growth: 10.6%
- Annual Job Openings: 2,000
- Annual Earnings: $52,860
- Education/Training Required: Bachelor's degree
- Self-Employed: 29.3%
- Part-Time: 16.5%

Design clothing and accessories. Create original garments or design garments that follow well established fashion trends. May develop the line of color and kinds of materials. Test fabrics or oversee testing so that garment care labels can be created. Attend fashion shows and review garment magazines and manuals in order to gather information about fashion trends and consumer preferences. Design custom clothing and accessories for individuals, retailers, or theatrical, television, or film productions. Draw patterns for articles designed; then cut patterns, and cut material according to patterns,

using measuring instruments and scissors. Examine sample garments on and off models; then modify designs to achieve desired effects. Select materials and production techniques to be used for products. Sketch rough and detailed drawings of apparel or accessories, and write specifications such as color schemes, construction, material types, and accessory requirements. Adapt other designers' ideas for the mass market. Collaborate with other designers to coordinate special products and designs. Confer with sales and management executives or with clients in order to discuss design ideas. Determine prices for styles. Develop a group of products and/or accessories, and market them through venues such as boutiques or mail-order catalogs. Direct and coordinate workers involved in drawing and cutting patterns and constructing samples or finished garments. Identify target markets for designs, looking at factors such as age, gender, and socioeconomic status. Provide sample garments to agents and sales representatives, and arrange for showings of sample garments at sales meetings or fashion shows. Purchase new or used clothing and accessory items as needed to complete designs. Read scripts and consult directors and other production staff in order to develop design concepts and plan productions. Research the styles and periods of clothing needed for film or theatrical productions. Sew together sections of material to form mockups or samples of garments or articles, using sewing equipment. Visit textile showrooms to keep up-to-date on the latest fabrics. **SKILLS**—Persuasion; Management of Financial Resources; Operations Analysis; Systems Analysis; Negotiation; Management of Material Resources; Systems Evaluation; Coordination.

GOE—Interest Area: 01. Arts, Entertainment, and Media. **Work Group:** 01.04. Visual Arts. **Other Jobs in This Work Group:** Artists and Related Workers, All Other; Cartoonists; Commercial and Industrial Designers; Designers, All Other; Exhibit Designers; Fine Artists, Including Painters, Sculptors, and Illustrators; Floral Designers; Graphic Designers; Interior Designers; Merchandise Displayers and Window Trimmers; Multi-Media Artists and Animators; Painters and Illustrators; Sculptors; Set and Exhibit Designers; Set Designers; Sketch Artists.

EDUCATION/TRAINING PROGRAM(S)— Apparel and Textile Manufacture; Fashion and Fabric Consultant; Fashion/Apparel Design; Textile Science. RELATED KNOWLEDGE/ COURSES—Design; Fine Arts; Production and Processing; Sales and Marketing; Education and Training; Customer and Personal Service.

Film and Video Editors

- Personality Code: A
- Growth: 26.4%
- Annual Job Openings: 3,000
- Annual Earnings: $40,600
- Education/Training Required: Bachelor's degree
- Self-Employed: 21.9%
- Part-Time: 20.4%

Edit motion picture soundtracks, film, and video. Cut shot sequences to different angles at specific points in scenes, making each individual cut as fluid and seamless as possible. Study scripts to become familiar with production concepts and requirements. Edit films and videotapes to insert music, dialogue, and sound effects, to arrange films into sequences, and to correct errors, using editing equipment. Select and combine the most effective shots of each scene in order to form a logical and smoothly running story. Mark frames where a particular shot or piece of sound is to begin or end. Determine the specific audio and visual effects and music necessary to complete films. Verify key numbers and time codes on materials. Organize and string together raw footage into a continuous whole according to scripts and/or the instructions of directors and producers. Review assembled films or edited videotapes on screens or monitors in order to determine if corrections are nec-

essary. Program computerized graphic effects. Review footage sequence by sequence in order to become familiar with it before assembling it into a final product. Set up and operate computer editing systems, electronic titling systems, video switching equipment, and digital video effects units in order to produce a final product. Record needed sounds, or obtain them from sound effects libraries. Confer with producers and directors concerning layout or editing approaches needed to increase dramatic or entertainment value of productions. Manipulate plot, score, sound, and graphics to make the parts into a continuous whole, working closely with people in audio, visual, music, optical and/or special effects departments. Supervise and coordinate activities of workers engaged in film editing, assembling, and recording activities. Trim film segments to specified lengths, and reassemble segments in sequences that present stories with maximum effect. Develop post-production models for films. Piece sounds together to develop film soundtracks. Conduct film screenings for directors and members of production staffs. Collaborate with music editors to select appropriate passages of music and develop production scores. SKILLS—Equipment Selection; Coordination; Time Management; Active Learning; Operations Analysis; Equipment Maintenance; Troubleshooting; Critical Thinking.

GOE—Interest Area: 01. Arts, Entertainment, and Media. Work Group: 01.08. Media Technology. Other Jobs in This Work Group: Audio and Video Equipment Technicians; Broadcast Technicians; Camera Operators, Television, Video, and Motion Picture; Media and Communication Equipment Workers, All Other; Photographers; Professional Photographers; Radio Operators; Sound Engineering Technicians.

EDUCATION/TRAINING PROGRAM(S)— Audiovisual Communications Technologies/Technicians, Other; Cinematography and Film/Video Production; Communications Technology/Technician; Photojournalism; Radio and Television; Radio and Television Broadcasting Technology/Technician. RELATED KNOWLEDGE/COURSES—

Communications and Media; Fine Arts; Computers and Electronics; Design; Education and Training; English Language.

Floral Designers

- Personality Code: AR
- Growth: 12.4%
- Annual Job Openings: 13,000
- Annual Earnings: $19,660
- Education/Training Required: Moderate-term on-the-job training
- Self-Employed: 32.5%
- Part-Time: 16.5%

Design, cut, and arrange live, dried, or artificial flowers and foliage. Confer with clients regarding price and type of arrangement desired and the date, time, and place of delivery. Plan arrangement according to client's requirements, utilizing knowledge of design and properties of materials, or select appropriate standard design pattern. Water plants, and cut, condition, and clean flowers and foliage for storage. Select flora and foliage for arrangements, working with numerous combinations to synthesize and develop new creations. Order and purchase flowers and supplies from wholesalers and growers. Wrap and price completed arrangements. Trim material and arrange bouquets, wreaths, terrariums, and other items using trimmers, shapers, wire, pins, floral tape, foam, and other materials. Perform office and retail service duties such as keeping financial records, serving customers, answering telephones, selling giftware items and receiving payment. Inform customers about the care, maintenance, and handling of various flowers and foliage, indoor plants, and other items. Decorate or supervise the decoration of buildings, halls, churches, or other facilities for parties, weddings and other occasions. Perform general cleaning duties in the store to ensure the shop is clean and tidy. Unpack stock as it comes into the shop. Create and change in-store and window displays, designs, and looks to enhance a shop's image. Conduct classes or demonstrations, or train other workers. Grow flowers for use in arrangements or for sale in shop. SKILLS—Management of Financial Resources; Management of Material Resources; Service Orientation; Management of Personnel Resources; Social Perceptiveness; Time Management; Instructing; Learning Strategies.

GOE—**Interest Area:** 01. Arts, Entertainment, and Media. **Work Group:** 01.04. Visual Arts. **Other Jobs in This Work Group:** Artists and Related Workers, All Other; Cartoonists; Commercial and Industrial Designers; Designers, All Other; Exhibit Designers; Fashion Designers; Fine Artists, Including Painters, Sculptors, and Illustrators; Graphic Designers; Interior Designers; Merchandise Displayers and Window Trimmers; Multi-Media Artists and Animators; Painters and Illustrators; Sculptors; Set and Exhibit Designers; Set Designers; Sketch Artists.

EDUCATION/TRAINING PROGRAM(S)— Floriculture/Floristry Operations and Management. RELATED KNOWLEDGE/COURSES—Customer and Personal Service; Sales and Marketing; Fine Arts; Personnel and Human Resources; Design; Production and Processing.

Foreign Language and Literature Teachers, Postsecondary

- Personality Code: AS
- Growth: 38.1%
- Annual Job Openings: 216,000
- Annual Earnings: $46,780
- Education/Training Required: Master's degree
- Self-Employed: 0.3%
- Part-Time: 27.7%

Artistic-F

Teach courses in foreign (i.e., other than English) languages and literature. Evaluate and grade students' class work, assignments, and papers. Prepare and deliver lectures to undergraduate and/or graduate students on topics such as how to speak and write a foreign language and the cultural aspects of areas where a particular language is used. Advise students on academic and vocational curricula and on career issues. Compile, administer, and grade examinations or assign this work to others. Compile bibliographies of specialized materials for outside reading assignments. Initiate, facilitate, and moderate classroom discussions. Keep abreast of developments in their field by reading current literature, talking with colleagues, and participating in professional organizations and activities. Maintain regularly scheduled office hours in order to advise and assist students. Maintain student attendance records, grades, and other required records. Plan, evaluate, and revise curricula, course content, and course materials and methods of instruction. Prepare course materials such as syllabi, homework assignments, and handouts. Select and obtain materials and supplies such as textbooks. Supervise undergraduate and/or graduate teaching, internship, and research work. Act as advisers to student organizations. Collaborate with colleagues to address teaching and research issues. Conduct research in a particular field of knowledge and publish findings in scholarly journals, books, and/or electronic media. Participate in campus and community events. Participate in student recruitment, registration, and placement activities. Perform administrative duties such as serving as department head. Provide professional consulting services to government and/or industry. Serve on academic or administrative committees that deal with institutional policies, departmental matters, and academic issues. Write grant proposals to procure external research funding. **SKILLS**—Instructing; Learning Strategies; Speaking; Reading Comprehension; Writing; Critical Thinking; Active Learning; Active Listening.

GOE—**Interest Area:** 12. Education and Social Service. **Work Group:** 12.03. Educational Services.

Other Jobs in This Work Group: Adult Literacy, Remedial Education, and GED Teachers and Instructors; Agricultural Sciences Teachers, Postsecondary; Anthropology and Archeology Teachers, Postsecondary; Architecture Teachers, Postsecondary; Archivists; Area, Ethnic, and Cultural Studies Teachers, Postsecondary; Art, Drama, and Music Teachers, Postsecondary; Atmospheric, Earth, Marine, and Space Sciences Teachers, Postsecondary; Audio-Visual Collections Specialists; Biological Science Teachers, Postsecondary; Business Teachers, Postsecondary; Chemistry Teachers, Postsecondary; Child Care Workers; Communications Teachers, Postsecondary; Computer Science Teachers, Postsecondary; Criminal Justice and Law Enforcement Teachers, Postsecondary; Curators; Economics Teachers, Postsecondary; Education Teachers, Postsecondary; Education, Training, and Library Workers, All Other; Educational Psychologists; Educational, Vocational, and School Counselors; Elementary School Teachers, Except Special Education; Engineering Teachers, Postsecondary; English Language and Literature Teachers, Postsecondary; Environmental Science Teachers, Postsecondary; Farm and Home Management Advisors; Forestry and Conservation Science Teachers, Postsecondary; Geography Teachers, Postsecondary; Graduate Teaching Assistants; Health Specialties Teachers, Postsecondary; History Teachers, Postsecondary; Home Economics Teachers, Postsecondary; Kindergarten Teachers, Except Special Education; Law Teachers, Postsecondary; Librarians; Library Assistants, Clerical; Library Science Teachers, Postsecondary; Library Technicians; Mathematical Science Teachers, Postsecondary; Middle School Teachers, Except Special and Vocational Education; Museum Technicians and Conservators; Nannies; Nursing Instructors and Teachers, Postsecondary; Personal Financial Advisors; Philosophy and Religion Teachers, Postsecondary; Physics Teachers, Postsecondary; Political Science Teachers, Postsecondary; Postsecondary Teachers, All Other; Preschool Teachers, Except Special Education; Psychology Teachers, Postsecondary; Recreation and Fitness Studies Teachers, Postsecondary; Secondary

School Teachers, Except Special and Vocational Education; Self-Enrichment Education Teachers; Social Sciences Teachers, Postsecondary, All Other; Social Work Teachers, Postsecondary; Sociology Teachers, Postsecondary; Special Education Teachers, Middle School; Special Education Teachers, Preschool, Kindergarten, and Elementary School; Special Education Teachers, Secondary School; Teacher Assistants; Teachers and Instructors, All Other; Vocational Education Teachers, Postsecondary; Vocational Education Teachers, Middle School; Vocational Education Teachers, Secondary School.

EDUCATION/TRAINING PROGRAM(S)— African Languages, Literatures, and Linguistics; Albanian Language and Literature; American Indian/Native American Languages, Literatures, and Linguistics; Ancient Near Eastern and Biblical Languages, Literatures, and Linguistics; Ancient/Classical Greek Language and Literature; Arabic Language and Literature; Australian/Oceanic/Pacific Languages, Literatures, and Linguistics; Bahasa Indonesian/Bahasa Malay Languages and Literatures; Baltic Languages, Literatures, and Linguistics; Bengali Language and Literature; Bulgarian Language and Literature; Burmese Language and Literature; Catalan Language and Literature; Celtic Languages, Literatures, and Linguistics; Chinese Language and Literature; Classics and Classical Languages, Literatures, and Linguistics, General; Classics and Classical Languages, Literatures, and Linguistics, Other; Czech Language and Literature; Danish Language and Literature; Dutch/Flemish Language and Literature; East Asian Languages, Literatures, and Linguistics, General; East Asian Languages, Literatures, and Linguistics, Other; Filipino/Tagalog Language and Literature; Finnish and Related Languages, Literatures, and Linguistics; Foreign Languages and Literatures, General; Foreign Languages, Literatures, and Linguistics, Other; French Language and Literature; German Language and Literature; Germanic Languages, Literatures, and Linguistics, General; Germanic Languages, Literatures, and Linguistics, Other; Hebrew Language and Literature; Hindi Language and Literature; Hungarian/Magyar Language and Literature; Iranian/Persian Languages, Literatures, and Linguistics; Italian Language and Literature; Japanese Language and Literature; Khmer/Cambodian Language and Literature; Korean Language and Literature; Language Interpretation and Translation; Lao/Laotian Language and Literature; Latin Language and Literature; Latin Teacher Education; Linguistics; Middle/Near Eastern and Semitic Languages, Literatures, and Linguistics, Other; others. **RELATED KNOWLEDGE/COURSES—**Foreign Language; Education and Training; English Language; Communications and Media; Therapy and Counseling; Clerical Studies.

Graphic Designers

- Personality Code: AE
- Growth: 21.9%
- Annual Job Openings: 29,000
- Annual Earnings: $36,630
- Education/Training Required: Bachelor's degree
- Self-Employed: 31.8%
- Part-Time: 16.5%

Design or create graphics to meet specific commercial or promotional needs, such as packaging, displays, or logos. May use a variety of mediums to achieve artistic or decorative effects. Create designs, concepts, and sample layouts based on knowledge of layout principles and esthetic design concepts. Determine size and arrangement of illustrative material and copy, and select style and size of type. Use computer software to generate new images. Mark up, paste, and assemble final layouts to prepare layouts for printer. Draw and print charts, graphs, illustrations, and other artwork, using computer. Review final layouts and suggest improvements as needed. Confer with clients to discuss and determine layout design. Develop graphics and layouts for product illustrations, company logos, and Internet websites. Key information into computer equipment to create layouts for client or supervisor. Prepare illustrations or rough sketches of material, discussing them with clients and/or supervisors and making necessary changes. Study illustrations and photographs to plan presentation of materials, products, or services. Prepare notes and instructions for workers who assemble and prepare final layouts for printing. Develop negatives and prints to produce layout photographs, using negative and print developing equipment and tools. Photograph layouts, using camera, to make layout prints for supervisors or clients. Produce still and animated graphics for on-air and taped portions of television news broadcasts, using electronic video equipment. **SKILLS**—Persuasion; Time Management; Troubleshooting; Instructing; Coordination; Social Perceptiveness; Operations Analysis; Complex Problem Solving.

GOE—**Interest Area:** 01. Arts, Entertainment, and Media. **Work Group:** 01.04. Visual Arts. **Other Jobs in This Work Group:** Artists and Related Workers, All Other; Cartoonists; Commercial and Industrial Designers; Designers, All Other; Exhibit Designers; Fashion Designers; Fine Artists, Including Painters, Sculptors, and Illustrators; Floral Designers; Interior Designers; Merchandise Displayers and Window Trimmers; Multi-Media Artists and Animators; Painters and Illustrators; Sculptors; Set and Exhibit Designers; Set Designers; Sketch Artists.

EDUCATION/TRAINING PROGRAM(S)—Agricultural Communication/Journalism; Commercial and Advertising Art; Computer Graphics; Design and Visual Communications, General; Graphic Design; Industrial Design; Web Page, Digital/Multimedia and Information Resources Design. **RELATED KNOWLEDGE/COURSES**—Fine Arts; Design; Computers and Electronics; Communications and Media; Sales and Marketing; Clerical Studies.

Interior Designers

- Personality Code: AE
- Growth: 21.7%
- Annual Job Openings: 8,000
- Annual Earnings: $40,120
- Education/Training Required: Bachelor's degree
- Self-Employed: 32.2%
- Part-Time: 16.5%

Plan, design, and furnish interiors of residential, commercial, or industrial buildings. Formulate design which is practical, aesthetic, and conducive to intended purposes, such as raising productivity, selling merchandise, or improving life style. May specialize in a particular field, style, or phase of interior design. Estimate material requirements and costs, and present design to client for approval. Confer with client to determine factors affecting planning interior environments, such as budget, architectural preferences, and purpose and function. Advise client on interior design factors, such as space planning, layout and utilization of furnishings and equipment, and color coordination. Select or design, and purchase furnishings, art works, and accessories. Formulate environmental plan to be practical, esthetic, and conducive to intended purposes, such as raising productivity or selling merchandise. Subcontract fabrication, installation, and arrangement of carpeting, fixtures, accessories, draperies, paint and wall coverings, art work, furniture, and related items. Render design ideas in form of paste-ups or drawings. **SKILLS**—Installation; Persuasion; Management of Financial Resources; Active Learning; Negotiation; Speaking; Troubleshooting; Critical Thinking.

GOE—**Interest Area:** 01. Arts, Entertainment, and Media. **Work Group:** 01.04. Visual Arts. **Other Jobs in This Work Group:** Artists and Related Workers, All Other; Cartoonists; Commercial and Industrial Designers; Designers, All Other; Exhibit

Designers; Fashion Designers; Fine Artists, Including Painters, Sculptors, and Illustrators; Floral Designers; Graphic Designers; Merchandise Displayers and Window Trimmers; Multi-Media Artists and Animators; Painters and Illustrators; Sculptors; Set and Exhibit Designers; Set Designers; Sketch Artists.

EDUCATION/TRAINING PROGRAM(S)—Facilities Planning and Management; Interior Architecture; Interior Design; Textile Science. **RELATED KNOWLEDGE/COURSES—**Design; Sales and Marketing; Customer and Personal Service; Administration and Management; Clerical Studies; Building and Construction.

Interpreters and Translators

- Personality Code: AS
- Growth: 22.1%
- Annual Job Openings: 4,000
- Annual Earnings: $33,490
- Education/Training Required: Long-term on-the-job training
- Self-Employed: 19.6%
- Part-Time: 26.3%

Translate or interpret written, oral, or sign language text into another language for others. Travel with or guide tourists who speak another language. Check original texts or confer with authors to ensure that translations retain the content, meaning, and feeling of the original material. Check translations of technical terms and terminology to ensure that they are accurate and remain consistent throughout translation revisions. Compile terminology and information to be used in translations, including technical terms such as those for legal or medical material. Discuss translation requirements with clients, and determine any fees to be charged for services provided. Listen to speakers' statements in order to determine meanings and to prepare translations, using electronic listening systems as necessary. Proofread, edit, and revise translated materials. Read written materials such as legal documents, scientific works, or news reports, and rewrite material into specified languages. Refer to reference materials such as dictionaries, lexicons, encyclopedias, and computerized terminology banks as needed to ensure translation accuracy. Translate messages simultaneously or consecutively into specified languages, orally or by using hand signs, maintaining message content, context, and style as much as possible. Adapt translations to students' cognitive and grade levels, collaborating with educational team members as necessary. Follow ethical codes that protect the confidentiality of information. Identify and resolve conflicts related to the meanings of words, concepts, practices, or behaviors. Compile information about the content and context of information to be translated, as well as details of the groups for whom translation or interpretation is being performed. Adapt software and accompanying technical documents to another language and culture. Educate students, parents, staff, and teachers about the roles and functions of educational interpreters. Train and supervise other translators/interpreters. **SKILLS—**Active Listening; Writing; Reading Comprehension; Speaking; Service Orientation.

GOE—Interest Area: 01. Arts, Entertainment, and Media. **Work Group:** 01.03. News, Broadcasting and Public Relations. **Other Jobs in This Work Group:** Broadcast News Analysts; Caption Writers; Public Relations Specialists; Reporters and Correspondents.

EDUCATION/TRAINING PROGRAM(S)—African Languages, Literatures, and Linguistics; Albanian Language and Literature; American Indian/Native American Languages, Literatures, and Linguistics; Ancient Near Eastern and Biblical Languages, Literatures, and Linguistics; Ancient/Classi-

Artistic—I

cal Greek Language and Literature; Arabic Language and Literature; Australian/Oceanic/Pacific Languages, Literatures, and Linguistics; Bahasa Indonesian/Bahasa Malay Languages and Literatures; Baltic Languages, Literatures, and Linguistics; Bengali Language and Literature; Bulgarian Language and Literature; Burmese Language and Literature; Catalan Language and Literature; Celtic Languages, Literatures, and Linguistics; Chinese Language and Literature; Classics and Classical Languages, Literatures, and Linguistics, General; Classics and Classical Languages, Literatures, and Linguistics, Other; Czech Language and Literature; Danish Language and Literature; Dutch/Flemish Language and Literature; East Asian Languages, Literatures, and Linguistics, General; East Asian Languages, Literatures, and Linguistics, Other; Filipino/Tagalog Language and Literature; Finnish and Related Languages, Literatures, and Linguistics; Foreign Languages and Literatures, General; Foreign Languages, Literatures, and Linguistics, Other; French Language and Literature; German Language and Literature; Germanic Languages, Literatures, and Linguistics, General; Germanic Languages, Literatures, and Linguistics, Other; Hebrew Language and Literature; Hindi Language and Literature; Hungarian/Magyar Language and Literature; Iranian/Persian Languages, Literatures, and Linguistics; Italian Language and Literature; Japanese Language and Literature; Khmer/Cambodian Language and Literature; Korean Language and Literature; Language Interpretation and Translation; Lao/Laotian Language and Literature; Latin Language and Literature; Latin Teacher Education; Linguistics; Middle/Near Eastern and Semitic Languages, Literatures, and Linguistics, Other; others. **RELATED KNOWLEDGE/COURSES**—Foreign Language; English Language; Communications and Media; Sociology and Anthropology; Geography; History and Archeology.

Landscape Architects

- Personality Code: AR
- Growth: 22.2%
- Annual Job Openings: 2,000
- Annual Earnings: $50,480
- Education/Training Required: Bachelor's degree
- Self-Employed: 23.4%
- Part-Time: 5.5%

Plan and design land areas for such projects as parks and other recreational facilities, airports, highways, hospitals, schools, land subdivisions, and commercial, industrial, and residential sites. Prepare site plans, specifications, and cost estimates for land development, coordinating arrangement of existing and proposed land features and structures. Confer with clients, engineering personnel, and architects on overall program. Compile and analyze data on conditions, such as location, drainage, and location of structures for environmental reports and landscaping plans. Inspect landscape work to ensure compliance with specifications, approve quality of materials and work, and advise client and construction personnel. **SKILLS**—Coordination; Operations Analysis; Management of Financial Resources; Persuasion; Social Perceptiveness; Time Management; Instructing; Complex Problem Solving.

GOE—Interest Area: 02. Science, Math, and Engineering. **Work Group:** 02.07. Engineering. **Other Jobs in This Work Group:** Aerospace Engineers; Agricultural Engineers; Architects, Except Landscape and Naval; Biomedical Engineers; Chemical Engineers; Civil Engineers; Computer Hardware Engineers; Computer Software Engineers, Applications; Computer Software Engineers, Systems Software; Electrical Engineers; Electronics Engineers, Except Computer; Engineers, All Other; Environmental Engineers; Fire-Prevention and Protection Engineers; Health and Safety Engineers, Except Mining Safety Engineers and Inspectors; Industrial

Engineers; Industrial Safety and Health Engineers; Marine Architects; Marine Engineers; Marine Engineers and Naval Architects; Materials Engineers; Mechanical Engineers; Mining and Geological Engineers, Including Mining Safety Engineers; Nuclear Engineers; Petroleum Engineers; Product Safety Engineers; Sales Engineers.

EDUCATION/TRAINING PROGRAM(S)— Environmental Design/Architecture; Landscape Architecture (BS, BSLA, BLA, MSLA, MLA, PhD). **RELATED KNOWLEDGE/COURSES—**Design; Building and Construction; Geography; Engineering and Technology; Biology; Sales and Marketing.

Librarians

- ◎ Personality Code: AC
- ◎ Growth: 10.1%
- ◎ Annual Job Openings: 15,000
- ◎ Annual Earnings: $44,140
- ◎ Education/Training Required: Master's degree
- ◎ Self-Employed: 0.1%
- ◎ Part-Time: 23.1%

Administer libraries and perform related library services. Work in a variety of settings, including public libraries, schools, colleges and universities, museums, corporations, government agencies, law firms, non-profit organizations, and healthcare providers. Tasks may include selecting, acquiring, cataloguing, classifying, circulating, and maintaining library materials; and furnishing reference, bibliographical, and readers' advisory services. May perform in-depth, strategic research, and synthesize, analyze, edit, and filter information. May set up or work with databases and information systems to catalogue and access information. Search standard reference materials, including on-line sources and the Internet, in order to answer patrons'

reference questions. Analyze patrons' requests to determine needed information, and assist in furnishing or locating that information. Teach library patrons to search for information using databases. Keep records of circulation and materials. Supervise budgeting, planning, and personnel activities. Check books in and out of the library. Explain use of library facilities, resources, equipment, and services, and provide information about library policies. Review and evaluate resource material, such as book reviews and catalogs, in order to select and order print, audiovisual, and electronic resources. Code, classify, and catalog books, publications, films, audiovisual aids, and other library materials based on subject matter or standard library classification systems. Locate unusual or unique information in response to specific requests. Direct and train library staff in duties such as receiving, shelving, researching, cataloging, and equipment use. Respond to customer complaints, taking action as necessary. Organize collections of books, publications, documents, audiovisual aids, and other reference materials for convenient access. Develop library policies and procedures. Evaluate materials to determine outdated or unused items to be discarded. Develop information access aids such as indexes and annotated bibliographies, web pages, electronic pathfinders, and on-line tutorials. Plan and deliver client-centered programs and services such as special services for corporate clients, storytelling for children, newsletters, or programs for special groups. Compile lists of books, periodicals, articles, and audiovisual materials on particular subjects. Arrange for interlibrary loans of materials not available in a particular library. Assemble and arrange display materials. Confer with teachers, parents, and community organizations to develop, plan, and conduct programs in reading, viewing, and communication skills. Compile lists of overdue materials, and notify borrowers that their materials are overdue. **SKILLS—**Management of Financial Resources; Learning Strategies; Service Orientation; Instructing; Persuasion; Management of Material Resources; Monitoring; Social Perceptiveness.

Artistic—L

GOE—Interest Area: 12. Education and Social Service. **Work Group:** 12.03. Educational Services. **Other Jobs in This Work Group:** Adult Literacy, Remedial Education, and GED Teachers and Instructors; Agricultural Sciences Teachers, Postsecondary; Anthropology and Archeology Teachers, Postsecondary; Architecture Teachers, Postsecondary; Archivists; Area, Ethnic, and Cultural Studies Teachers, Postsecondary; Art, Drama, and Music Teachers, Postsecondary; Atmospheric, Earth, Marine, and Space Sciences Teachers, Postsecondary; Audio-Visual Collections Specialists; Biological Science Teachers, Postsecondary; Business Teachers, Postsecondary; Chemistry Teachers, Postsecondary; Child Care Workers; Communications Teachers, Postsecondary; Computer Science Teachers, Postsecondary; Criminal Justice and Law Enforcement Teachers, Postsecondary; Curators; Economics Teachers, Postsecondary; Education Teachers, Postsecondary; Education, Training, and Library Workers, All Other; Educational Psychologists; Educational, Vocational, and School Counselors; Elementary School Teachers, Except Special Education; Engineering Teachers, Postsecondary; English Language and Literature Teachers, Postsecondary; Environmental Science Teachers, Postsecondary; Farm and Home Management Advisors; Foreign Language and Literature Teachers, Postsecondary; Forestry and Conservation Science Teachers, Postsecondary; Geography Teachers, Postsecondary; Graduate Teaching Assistants; Health Specialties Teachers, Postsecondary; History Teachers, Postsecondary; Home Economics Teachers, Postsecondary; Kindergarten Teachers, Except Special Education; Law Teachers, Postsecondary; Library Assistants, Clerical; Library Science Teachers, Postsecondary; Library Technicians; Mathematical Science Teachers, Postsecondary; Middle School Teachers, Except Special and Vocational Education; Museum Technicians and Conservators; Nannies; Nursing Instructors and Teachers, Postsecondary; Personal Financial Advisors; Philosophy and Religion Teachers, Postsecondary; Physics Teachers, Postsecondary; Political Science Teachers, Postsecondary; Postsecondary Teachers, All Other; Preschool Teachers, Except Special Education; Psychology Teachers, Postsecondary; Recreation and Fitness Studies Teachers, Postsecondary; Secondary School Teachers, Except Special and Vocational Education; Self-Enrichment Education Teachers; Social Sciences Teachers, Postsecondary, All Other; Social Work Teachers, Postsecondary; Sociology Teachers, Postsecondary; Special Education Teachers, Middle School; Special Education Teachers, Preschool, Kindergarten, and Elementary School; Special Education Teachers, Secondary School; Teacher Assistants; Teachers and Instructors, All Other; Vocational Education Teachers, Postsecondary; Vocational Education Teachers, Middle School; Vocational Education Teachers, Secondary School.

EDUCATION/TRAINING PROGRAM(S)— Library Science, Other; Library Science/Librarianship; School Librarian/School Library Media Specialist. **RELATED KNOWLEDGE/ COURSES—**Customer and Personal Service; Clerical Studies; English Language; Personnel and Human Resources; Communications and Media; Geography.

Makeup Artists, Theatrical and Performance

- Personality Code: AR
- Growth: 18.2%
- Annual Job Openings: fewer than 500
- Annual Earnings: $29,320
- Education/Training Required: Postsecondary vocational training
- Self-Employed: 50.6%
- Part-Time: 29.5%

Apply makeup to performers to reflect period, setting, and situation of their role. Alter or maintain makeup during productions as necessary to compensate for lighting changes or to achieve continuity of effect. Analyze a script, noting events that affect each character's appearance, so that plans can be made for each scene. Apply makeup to enhance, and/or alter the appearance of people appearing in productions such as movies. Assess performers' skin-type in order to ensure that make-up will not cause break-outs or skin irritations. Attach prostheses to performers and apply makeup in order to create special features or effects such as scars, aging, or illness. Cleanse and tone the skin in order to prepare it for makeup application. Confer with stage or motion picture officials and performers in order to determine desired effects. Design rubber or plastic prostheses that can be used to change performers' appearances. Duplicate work precisely in order to replicate characters' appearances on a daily basis. Evaluate environmental characteristics such as venue size and lighting plans in order to determine makeup requirements. Examine sketches, photographs, and plaster models in order to obtain desired character image depiction. Provide performers with makeup removal assistance after performances have been completed. Requisition or acquire needed materials for special effects, including wigs, beards, and special cosmetics. Select desired makeup shades from stock, or mix oil, grease, and coloring in order to achieve specific color effects. Study production information, such as character descriptions, period settings, and situations in order to determine makeup requirements. Write makeup sheets and take photos in order to document specific looks and the products that were used to achieve the looks. Advise hairdressers on the hairstyles required for character parts. Create character drawings or models, based upon independent research, in order to augment period production files. Demonstrate products to clients, and provide instruction in makeup application. Establish budgets, and work within budgetary limits. Wash and reset wigs. **SKILLS**—Technology Design; Coordination; Management of Material Resources; Equipment Selection.

GOE—Interest Area: 01. Arts, Entertainment, and Media. **Work Group:** 01.09. Modeling and Personal Appearance. **Other Jobs in This Work Group:** Costume Attendants; Entertainers and Performers, Sports and Related Workers, All Other; Models.

EDUCATION/TRAINING PROGRAM(S)—Cosmetology/Cosmetologist, General; Make-Up Artist/Specialist; Permanent Cosmetics/Makeup and Tattooing. **RELATED KNOWLEDGE/COURSES**—Fine Arts; Sociology and Anthropology; Design; Communications and Media; History and Archeology; Geography.

Merchandise Displayers and Window Trimmers

- Personality Code: AR
- Growth: 11.3%
- Annual Job Openings: 10,000
- Annual Earnings: $22,030
- Education/Training Required: Moderate-term on-the-job training
- Self-Employed: 30.9%
- Part-Time: 16.5%

Plan and erect commercial displays, such as those in windows and interiors of retail stores and at trade exhibitions. Arrange properties, furniture, merchandise, backdrops, and other accessories, as shown in prepared sketches. Change or rotate window displays, interior display areas, and signage to reflect changes in inventory or promotion. Construct or assemble displays and display components from fabric, glass, paper, and plastic, using hand tools and woodworking power tools, according to specifications. Consult with advertising and sales staff to determine type of merchandise to be featured and time and place for each display. Cut out designs on cardboard, hardboard, and plywood, according to motif of event. Develop ideas or plans for merchandise displays or window decorations. Obtain plans from display designers or display managers, and discuss their implementation with clients or supervisors. Place prices and descriptive signs on backdrops, fixtures, merchandise, or floor. Plan and erect commercial displays to entice and appeal to customers. Prepare sketches, floor plans or models of proposed displays. Select themes, lighting, colors, and props to be used. Attend training sessions and corporate planning meetings to obtain new ideas for product launches. Collaborate with others to obtain products and other display items. Create and enhance mannequin faces by mixing and applying paint and attaching measured eyelash strips, using artist's brush, airbrush, pins, ruler, and scissors. Dress mannequins for displays. Install booths, exhibits, displays, carpets, and drapes, as guided by floor plan of building and specifications. Install decorations such as flags, banners, festive lights, and bunting on or in building, street, exhibit hall, or booth. Instruct sales staff in color-coordination of clothing racks and counter displays. Maintain props and mannequins, inspecting them for imperfections and applying preservative coatings as necessary. Store, pack, and maintain records of props and display items. Take photographs of displays and signage. Use computers to produce signage. **SKILLS**—Installation; Operations Analysis; Equipment Selection.

GOE—Interest Area: 01. Arts, Entertainment, and Media. **Work Group:** 01.04. Visual Arts. **Other Jobs in This Work Group:** Artists and Related Workers, All Other; Cartoonists; Commercial and Industrial Designers; Designers, All Other; Exhibit Designers; Fashion Designers; Fine Artists, Including Painters, Sculptors, and Illustrators; Floral Designers; Graphic Designers; Interior Designers; Multi-Media Artists and Animators; Painters and Illustrators; Sculptors; Set and Exhibit Designers; Set Designers; Sketch Artists.

EDUCATION/TRAINING PROGRAM(S)— No data available. **RELATED KNOWLEDGE/ COURSES**—Sales and Marketing; Fine Arts; Design; Sociology and Anthropology; Communications and Media; Building and Construction.

Models

- Personality Code: AE
- Growth: 14.5%
- Annual Job Openings: 1,000
- Annual Earnings: $24,270
- Education/Training Required: Moderate-term on-the-job training
- Self-Employed: 49.1%
- Part-Time: 52.5%

Model garments and other apparel to display clothing before prospective buyers at fashion shows, private showings, retail establishments, or photographer. May pose for photos to be used for advertising purposes. May pose as subject for paintings, sculptures, and other types of artistic expression. Poses as subject for paintings, sculptures, and other types of art for translation into plastic or pictorial values. Stands, turns, and walks to demonstrate features of garment to observers at fashion shows, private showings, and retail establishments. Dresses in sample or completed garments and selects own accessories. Informs prospective purchasers as to model, number, and price of garments and department where garment can be purchased. Applies makeup to face and styles hair to enhance appearance, considering such factors as color, camera techniques, and facial features. Hands out samples or presents, demonstrates toys, and converses with children and adults while dressed in costume. Wears character costumes and impersonates characters portrayed to amuse children and adults. Poses as directed or strikes suitable interpretive poses for promoting and selling merchandise or fashions during photo session. **SKILLS**—Social Perceptiveness.

GOE—**Interest Area:** 01. Arts, Entertainment, and Media. **Work Group:** 01.09. Modeling and Personal Appearance. **Other Jobs in This Work Group:** Costume Attendants; Entertainers and Performers, Sports and Related Workers, All Other; Makeup Artists, Theatrical and Performance.

EDUCATION/TRAINING PROGRAM(S)— Fashion Modeling. **RELATED KNOWLEDGE/ COURSES**—Fine Arts; Sales and Marketing; Communications and Media; Sociology and Anthropology.

Museum Technicians and Conservators

- ◉ Personality Code: AR
- ◉ Growth: 17.0%
- ◉ Annual Job Openings: 2,000
- ◉ Annual Earnings: $35,660
- ◉ Education/Training Required: Master's degree
- ◉ Self-Employed: 3.4%
- ◉ Part-Time: 11.8%

Prepare specimens, such as fossils, skeletal parts, lace, and textiles, for museum collection and exhibits. May restore documents or install, arrange, and exhibit materials. Install, arrange, assemble, and prepare artifacts for exhibition, ensuring the artifacts' safety, reporting their status and condition, and identifying and correcting any problems with the set-up. Coordinate exhibit installations, assisting with design, constructing displays, dioramas, display cases, and models, and ensuring the availability of necessary materials. Determine whether objects need repair and choose the safest and most effective method of repair. Clean objects, such as paper, textiles, wood, metal, glass, rock, pottery, and furniture, using cleansers, solvents, soap solutions, and polishes. Prepare artifacts for storage and shipping. Supervise and work with volunteers. Present public programs and tours. Specialize in particular materials or types of object, such as documents and books, paintings, decorative arts, textiles, metals, or architectural materials. Recommend preservation procedures, such as control of temperature and humidity, to curatorial and building staff. Classify and assign registration numbers to artifacts, and supervise inventory control. Direct and supervise curatorial and technical staff in the handling, mounting, care, and storage of art objects. Perform on-site field work which may involve interviewing people, inspecting and identifying artifacts, note-taking, viewing sites and collections, and repainting exhibition spaces. Repair, restore and reassemble artifacts, designing and fabricating missing or broken parts, to restore them to their original appearance and prevent deterioration. Prepare reports on the operation of conservation laboratories, documenting the condition of artifacts, treatment options, and the methods of preservation and repair used. Study object documentation or conduct standard chemical and physical tests to ascertain the object's age, composition, original appearance, need for treatment or restoration, and appropriate preservation method. Cut and weld metal sections in reconstruction or renovation of exterior structural sections and accessories of exhibits. Perform tests and examinations to establish storage and conservation requirements, policies, and procedures. **SKILLS**—Management of Material Resources; Time Management; Repairing; Critical Thinking; Instructing; Installation; Technology Design; Equipment Maintenance.

GOE—**Interest Area:** 12. Education and Social Service. **Work Group:** 12.03. Educational Services. **Other Jobs in This Work Group:** Adult Literacy, Remedial Education, and GED Teachers and Instructors; Agricultural Sciences Teachers, Postsecondary; Anthropology and Archeology Teachers, Postsecondary; Architecture Teachers, Postsecondary; Archivists; Area, Ethnic, and Cultural Studies Teachers, Postsecondary; Art, Drama, and Music Teachers, Postsecondary; Atmospheric, Earth,

Marine, and Space Sciences Teachers, Postsecondary; Audio-Visual Collections Specialists; Biological Science Teachers, Postsecondary; Business Teachers, Postsecondary; Chemistry Teachers, Postsecondary; Child Care Workers; Communications Teachers, Postsecondary; Computer Science Teachers, Postsecondary; Criminal Justice and Law Enforcement Teachers, Postsecondary; Curators; Economics Teachers, Postsecondary; Education Teachers, Postsecondary; Education, Training, and Library Workers, All Other; Educational Psychologists; Educational, Vocational, and School Counselors; Elementary School Teachers, Except Special Education; Engineering Teachers, Postsecondary; English Language and Literature Teachers, Postsecondary; Environmental Science Teachers, Postsecondary; Farm and Home Management Advisors; Foreign Language and Literature Teachers, Postsecondary; Forestry and Conservation Science Teachers, Postsecondary; Geography Teachers, Postsecondary; Graduate Teaching Assistants; Health Specialties Teachers, Postsecondary; History Teachers, Postsecondary; Home Economics Teachers, Postsecondary; Kindergarten Teachers, Except Special Education; Law Teachers, Postsecondary; Librarians; Library Assistants, Clerical; Library Science Teachers, Postsecondary; Library Technicians; Mathematical Science Teachers, Postsecondary; Middle School Teachers, Except Special and Vocational Education; Nannies; Nursing Instructors and Teachers, Postsecondary; Personal Financial Advisors; Philosophy and Religion Teachers, Postsecondary; Physics Teachers, Postsecondary; Political Science Teachers, Postsecondary; Postsecondary Teachers, All Other; Preschool Teachers, Except Special Education; Psychology Teachers, Postsecondary; Recreation and Fitness Studies Teachers, Postsecondary; Secondary School Teachers, Except Special and Vocational Education; Self-Enrichment Education Teachers; Social Sciences Teachers, Postsecondary, All Other; Social Work Teachers, Postsecondary; Sociology Teachers, Postsecondary; Special Education Teachers, Middle School; Special Education Teachers, Preschool, Kindergarten, and Elementary School; Special Education Teachers, Secondary School; Teacher Assistants; Teachers and Instructors, All Other; Vocational Education Teachers, Postsecondary; Vocational Education Teachers, Middle School; Vocational Education Teachers, Secondary School.

EDUCATION/TRAINING PROGRAM(S)— Art History, Criticism and Conservation; Museology/Museum Studies; Public/Applied History and Archival Administration. RELATED KNOWLEDGE/COURSES—History and Archeology; Sociology and Anthropology; Design; Fine Arts; Education and Training; Geography.

Music Arrangers and Orchestrators

- Personality Code: A
- Growth: 13.5%
- Annual Job Openings: 8,000
- Annual Earnings: $32,530
- Education/Training Required: Bachelor's degree
- Self-Employed: 39.3%
- Part-Time: 39.5%

Write and transcribe musical scores. Composes musical scores for orchestra, band, choral group, or individual instrumentalist or vocalist, using knowledge of music theory and instrumental and vocal capabilities. Transposes music from one voice or instrument to another to accommodate particular musician in musical group. Adapts musical composition for orchestra, band, choral group, or individual to style for which it was not originally written. Copies parts from score for individual performers. Determines voice, instrument, harmonic structure, rhythm, tempo, and tone balance to achieve desired effect. Transcribes musical parts from score written by arranger or orchestrator for each instrument or voice, using knowledge of music composition.

SKILLS—Coordination; Writing; Operations Analysis; Complex Problem Solving.

GOE—**Interest Area:** 01. Arts, Entertainment, and Media. **Work Group:** 01.05. Performing Arts. **Other Jobs in This Work Group:** Actors; Choreographers; Composers; Dancers; Directors—Stage, Motion Pictures, Television, and Radio; Entertainers and Performers, Sports and Related Workers, All Other; Music Directors; Music Directors and Composers; Musicians and Singers; Musicians, Instrumental; Public Address System and Other Announcers; Radio and Television Announcers; Singers; Talent Directors.

EDUCATION/TRAINING PROGRAM(S)—Conducting; Music Management and Merchandising; Music Performance, General; Music Theory and Composition; Music, Other; Musicology and Ethnomusicology; Religious/Sacred Music; Voice and Opera. **RELATED KNOWLEDGE/COURSES**—Fine Arts; Foreign Language.

Music Directors

- Personality Code: AS
- Growth: 13.5%
- Annual Job Openings: 8,000
- Annual Earnings: $32,530
- Education/Training Required: Master's degree
- Self-Employed: 39.3%
- Part-Time: 39.5%

Direct and conduct instrumental or vocal performances by musical groups, such as orchestras or choirs. Direct groups at rehearsals and live or recorded performances in order to achieve desired effects such as tonal and harmonic balance dynamics, rhythm, and tempo. Meet with soloists and concertmasters to discuss and prepare for performances. Plan and schedule rehearsals and performances, and arrange details such as locations, accompanists, and instrumentalists. Position members within groups to obtain balance among instrumental or vocal sections. Study scores to learn the music in detail, and to develop interpretations. Use gestures to shape the music being played, communicating desired tempo, phrasing, tone, color, pitch, volume, and other performance aspects. Assign and review staff work in such areas as scoring, arranging, and copying music, and vocal coaching. Collaborate with music librarians to ensure availability of scores. Engage services of composers to write scores. Meet with composers to discuss interpretations of their work. Perform administrative tasks such as applying for grants, developing budgets, negotiating contracts, and designing and printing programs and other promotional materials. Audition and select performers for musical presentations. Conduct guest soloists in addition to ensemble members. Consider such factors as ensemble size and abilities, availability of scores, and the need for musical variety, in order to select music to be performed. Transcribe musical compositions and melodic lines to adapt them to a particular group, or to create a particular musical style. Confer with clergy to select music for church services. Coordinate and organize tours, or hire touring companies to arrange concert dates, venues, accommodations, and transportation for longer tours. Plan and implement fund-raising and promotional activities. SKILLS—Management of Personnel Resources; Coordination; Instructing; Time Management; Monitoring; Learning Strategies; Social Perceptiveness; Operations Analysis.

GOE—**Interest Area:** 01. Arts, Entertainment, and Media. **Work Group:** 01.05. Performing Arts. **Other Jobs in This Work Group:** Actors; Choreographers; Composers; Dancers; Directors—Stage, Motion Pictures, Television, and Radio; Entertainers and Performers, Sports and Related Workers, All Other; Music Arrangers and Orchestrators; Music Directors and Composers; Musicians and Singers; Musicians, Instrumental; Public Address System and Other Announcers; Radio and Television Announcers; Singers; Talent Directors.

Artistic—M

EDUCATION/TRAINING PROGRAM(S)—Conducting; Music Management and Merchandising; Music Performance, General; Music Theory and Composition; Music, Other; Musicology and Ethnomusicology; Religious/Sacred Music; Voice and Opera. RELATED KNOWLEDGE/COURSES—Fine Arts; Personnel and Human Resources; Administration and Management; Foreign Language; Transportation; English Language.

Musicians, Instrumental

- ◉ Personality Code: A
- ◉ Growth: 17.1%
- ◉ Annual Job Openings: 25,000
- ◉ Annual Earnings: $37,380
- ◉ Education/Training Required: Long-term on-the-job training
- ◉ Self-Employed: 38.3%
- ◉ Part-Time: 39.5%

Play one or more musical instruments in recital, in accompaniment, or as members of an orchestra, band, or other musical group. Audition for orchestras, bands, or other musical groups. Improvise music during performances. Make or participate in recordings in music studios. Perform before live audiences. Play from memory or by following scores. Play musical instruments as soloists, or as members or guest artists of musical groups such as orchestras, ensembles, or bands. Practice musical instrument performances, individually or in rehearsal with other musicians, to master individual pieces of music and to maintain and improve skills. Compose original music such as popular songs, symphonies, or sonatas. Promote their own or their group's music by participating in media interviews and other activities. Provide the musical background for live shows such as ballets, operas, musical theatre, and cabarets. Sight-read musical parts during rehearsals. Transpose music to alternate keys, or to

fit individual styles or purposes. Direct bands or orchestras. Specialize in playing a specific family of instruments and/or a particular type of music. Teach music for specific instruments. SKILLS—Instructing; Coordination; Active Learning; Learning Strategies; Management of Personnel Resources; Monitoring; Systems Analysis; Management of Material Resources.

GOE—Interest Area: 01. Arts, Entertainment, and Media. Work Group: 01.05. Performing Arts. Other Jobs in This Work Group: Actors; Choreographers; Composers; Dancers; Directors—Stage, Motion Pictures, Television, and Radio; Entertainers and Performers, Sports and Related Workers, All Other; Music Arrangers and Orchestrators; Music Directors; Music Directors and Composers; Musicians and Singers; Public Address System and Other Announcers; Radio and Television Announcers; Singers; Talent Directors.

EDUCATION/TRAINING PROGRAM(S)—Jazz/Jazz Studies; Music Pedagogy; Music Performance, General; Music, General; Music, Other; Piano and Organ; Violin, Viola, Guitar and Other Stringed Instruments. RELATED KNOWLEDGE/COURSES—Fine Arts; Education and Training; Psychology; History and Archeology; Communications and Media; Sociology and Anthropology.

Painters and Illustrators

- ◉ Personality Code: AR
- ◉ Growth: 16.5%
- ◉ Annual Job Openings: 4,000
- ◉ Annual Earnings: $35,420
- ◉ Education/Training Required: Long-term on-the-job training
- ◉ Self-Employed: 55.5%
- ◉ Part-Time: 23.1%

Paint or draw subject material to produce original artwork or illustrations, using watercolors, oils, acrylics, tempera, or other paint mediums. Renders drawings, illustrations, and sketches of buildings, manufactured products, or models, working from sketches, blueprints, memory, or reference materials. Paints scenic backgrounds, murals, and portraiture for motion picture and television production sets, glass artworks, and exhibits. Etches, carves, paints, or draws artwork on material, such as stone, glass, canvas, wood, and linoleum. Develops drawings, paintings, diagrams, and models of medical or biological subjects for use in publications, exhibits, consultations, research, and teaching. Studies style, techniques, colors, textures, and materials used by artist to maintain consistency in reconstruction or retouching procedures. Removes painting from frame or paint layer from canvas to restore artwork, following specified technique and equipment. Examines surfaces of paintings and proofs of artwork, using magnifying device, to determine method of restoration or needed corrections. Installs finished stained glass in window or door frame. Assembles, leads, and solders finished glass to fabricate stained glass article. Applies select solvents and cleaning agents to clean surface of painting and remove accretions, discolorations, and deteriorated varnish. Performs tests to determine factors, such as age, structure, pigment stability, and probable reaction to various cleaning agents and solvents. Confers with professional personnel or client to discuss objectives of artwork, develop illustration ideas, and theme to be portrayed. Brushes or sprays protective or decorative finish on completed background panels, informational legends, exhibit accessories, or finished painting. Integrates and develops visual elements, such as line, space, mass, color, and perspective to produce desired effect. **SKILLS**—Operations Analysis; Management of Material Resources; Installation; Quality Control Analysis; Repairing; Active Listening; Equipment Selection.

GOE—Interest Area: 01. Arts, Entertainment, and Media. **Work Group:** 01.04. Visual Arts. **Other Jobs in This Work Group:** Artists and Related Workers, All Other; Cartoonists; Commercial and Industrial Designers; Designers, All Other; Exhibit Designers; Fashion Designers; Fine Artists, Including Painters, Sculptors, and Illustrators; Floral Designers; Graphic Designers; Interior Designers; Merchandise Displayers and Window Trimmers; Multi-Media Artists and Animators; Sculptors; Set and Exhibit Designers; Set Designers; Sketch Artists.

EDUCATION/TRAINING PROGRAM(S)—Art/Art Studies, General; Drawing; Fine Arts and Art Studies, Other; Fine/Studio Arts, General; Medical Illustration/Medical Illustrator; Painting; Visual and Performing Arts, General. **RELATED KNOWLEDGE/COURSES**—Fine Arts; Design; Chemistry; History and Archeology; Communications and Media; Engineering and Technology.

Photographers, Scientific

- Personality Code: AR
- Growth: 13.6%
- Annual Job Openings: 18,000
- Annual Earnings: $25,050
- Education/Training Required: Long-term on-the-job training
- Self-Employed: 52.5%
- Part-Time: 24.0%

Photograph variety of subject material to illustrate or record scientific/medical data or phenomena, utilizing knowledge of scientific procedures and photographic technology and techniques. Photographs variety of subject material to illustrate or record scientific or medical data or phenomena, related to an area of interest. Sights and focuses camera to take picture of subject material to illustrate or record scientific or medical data or phenomena. Plans methods and procedures for photographing

Artistic—P

subject material and set-up of required equipment. Observes and arranges subject material to desired position. Engages in research to develop new photographic procedure, materials, and scientific data. Sets up, mounts, or installs photographic equipment and cameras. Removes exposed film and develops film, using chemicals, touch up tools, and equipment. **SKILLS**—Science; Reading Comprehension; Equipment Selection; Technology Design; Active Learning; Operation and Control; Management of Material Resources; Writing.

GOE—Interest Area: 02. Science, Math, and Engineering. **Work Group:** 02.05. Laboratory Technology. **Other Jobs in This Work Group:** Biological Technicians; Chemical Technicians; Environmental Science and Protection Technicians, Including Health; Geological and Petroleum Technicians; Geological Data Technicians; Geological Sample Test Technicians; Life, Physical, and Social Science Technicians, All Other; Nuclear Equipment Operation Technicians; Nuclear Technicians.

EDUCATION/TRAINING PROGRAM(S)—Art/Art Studies, General; Commercial Photography; Film/Video and Photographic Arts, Other; Photography; Photojournalism; Visual and Performing Arts, General. **RELATED KNOWLEDGE/COURSES**—Fine Arts; Chemistry; Physics; Engineering and Technology; Medicine and Dentistry; Communications and Media.

Photographic Retouchers and Restorers

- Personality Code: AR
- Growth: 5.4%
- Annual Job Openings: 4,000
- Annual Earnings: $20,370
- Education/Training Required: Moderate-term on-the-job training
- Self-Employed: 4.0%
- Part-Time: 24.3%

Retouch or restore photographic negatives and prints to accentuate desirable features of subject, using pencils, watercolors, or airbrushes. Cuts out masking template, using shears, and positions templates on picture to mask selected areas. Wipes excess color from portrait to produce specified shade, using cotton swab. Applies paint to retouch or enhance negative or photograph, using airbrush, pen, artist's brush, cotton swab, or gloved finger. Rubs eraser or cloth over photograph to reduce gloss, remove debris, or prepare specified areas of illustration for highlighting. Paints negative with retouching medium, to ensure retouching pencil will mark surface of negative. Shades negative or photograph with pencil to smooth facial contours, conceal blemishes, stray hairs, or wrinkles, and soften highlights. Inks borders or lettering on illustration, using pen, brush, or drafting instruments. Examines drawing, negative, or photographic print to determine coloring, shading, accenting, and changes required to retouch or restore. Mixes ink or paint solutions, according to color specifications, color chart, and consistency desired. Trims edges of print to enhance appearance, using scissors or paper cutter. **SKILLS**—None met the criteria.

GOE—Interest Area: 08. Industrial Production. **Work Group:** 08.03. Production Work. **Other Jobs in This Work Group:** Assemblers and Fabricators,

All Other; Bakers, Manufacturing; Bindery Machine Operators and Tenders; Brazers; Cementing and Gluing Machine Operators and Tenders; Chemical Equipment Controllers and Operators; Chemical Equipment Operators and Tenders; Chemical Equipment Tenders; Cleaning, Washing, and Metal Pickling Equipment Operators and Tenders; Coating, Painting, and Spraying Machine Operators and Tenders; Coil Winders, Tapers, and Finishers; Combination Machine Tool Operators and Tenders, Metal and Plastic; Computer-Controlled Machine Tool Operators, Metal and Plastic; Cooling and Freezing Equipment Operators and Tenders; Crushing, Grinding, and Polishing Machine Setters, Operators, and Tenders; Cutters and Trimmers, Hand; Cutting and Slicing Machine Operators and Tenders; Cutting and Slicing Machine Setters, Operators, and Tenders; Design Printing Machine Setters and Set-Up Operators; Electrolytic Plating and Coating Machine Operators and Tenders, Metal and Plastic; Electrolytic Plating and Coating Machine Setters and Set-Up Operators, Metal and Plastic; Electrotypers and Stereotypers; Embossing Machine Set-Up Operators; Engraver Set-Up Operators; Extruding and Forming Machine Operators and Tenders, Synthetic or Glass Fibers; Extruding and Forming Machine Setters, Operators, and Tenders, Synthetic and Glass Fibers; Extruding, Forming, Pressing, and Compacting Machine Operators and Tenders; Fabric and Apparel Patternmakers; Fiber Product Cutting Machine Setters and Set-Up Operators; Fiberglass Laminators and Fabricators; Film Laboratory Technicians; Fitters, Structural Metal—Precision; Food and Tobacco Roasting, Baking, and Drying Machine Operators and Tenders; Food Batchmakers; Food Cooking Machine Operators and Tenders; Furnace, Kiln, Oven, Drier, and Kettle Operators and Tenders; Glass Cutting Machine Setters and Set-Up Operators; Graders and Sorters, Agricultural Products; Grinding and Polishing Workers, Hand; Hand Compositors and Typesetters; Heaters, Metal and Plastic; Helpers—Production Workers; Job Printers; Letterpress Setters and Set-Up Operators; Marking and Identification Printing Machine Setters and Set-Up Operators; Meat, Poultry, and Fish Cutters and Trimmers; Metal Fabricators, Structural Metal Products; Metal-Refining Furnace Operators and Tenders; Mixing and Blending Machine Setters, Operators, and Tenders; Mold Makers, Hand; Molding and Casting Workers; Nonelectrolytic Plating and Coating Machine Operators and Tenders, Metal and Plastic; Nonelectrolytic Plating and Coating Machine Setters and Set-Up Operators, Metal and Plastic; Numerical Control Machine Tool Operators and Tenders, Metal and Plastic; Offset Lithographic Press Setters and Set-Up Operators; Packaging and Filling Machine Operators and Tenders; Painting, Coating, and Decorating Workers; Photoengraving and Lithographing Machine Operators and Tenders; Photographic Hand Developers; Photographic Process Workers; Photographic Processing Machine Operators; Photographic Reproduction Technicians; Plate Finishers; Platemakers; Plating and Coating Machine Setters, Operators, and Tenders, Metal and Plastic; Pourers and Casters, Metal; Precision Printing Workers; Prepress Technicians and Workers; Pressing Machine Operators and Tenders—Textile, Garment, and Related Materials; Printing Machine Operators; Printing Press Machine Operators and Tenders; Production Helpers; Production Laborers; Production Workers, All Other; Sawing Machine Operators and Tenders; Sawing Machine Setters and Set-Up Operators; Sawing Machine Setters, Operators, and Tenders, Wood; Scanner Operators; Semiconductor Processors; Separating, Filtering, Clarifying, Precipitating, and Still Machine Setters, Operators, and Tenders; Sewers, Hand; Sewing Machine Operators; Sewing Machine Operators, Garment; Sewing Machine Operators, Non-Garment; Shoe Machine Operators and Tenders; Slaughterers and Meat Packers; Solderers; Soldering and Brazing Machine Operators and Tenders; Stone Sawyers; Strippers; Structural Metal Fabricators and Fitters; Team Assemblers; Textile Bleaching and Dyeing Machine Operators and Tenders; Tire Builders; Welder-Fitters; Welders and Cutters; Welders, Cutters, Solderers, and Brazers; Welders, Production; Welding Machine Operators and Ten-

Artistic—P

ders; Woodworking Machine Operators and Tenders, Except Sawing.

EDUCATION/TRAINING PROGRAM(S)—Photographic and Film/Video Technology/Technician and Assistant. **RELATED KNOWLEDGE/COURSES**—Fine Arts; Chemistry.

Poets and Lyricists

- Personality Code: AI
- Growth: 16.1%
- Annual Job Openings: 23,000
- Annual Earnings: $42,330
- Education/Training Required: Bachelor's degree
- Self-Employed: 67.9%
- Part-Time: 24.2%

Write poetry or song lyrics for publication or performance. Writes words to fit musical compositions, including lyrics for operas, musical plays, and choral works. Chooses subject matter and suitable form to express personal feeling and experience or ideas or to narrate story or event. Adapts text to accommodate musical requirements of composer and singer. Writes narrative, dramatic, lyric, or other types of poetry for publication. **SKILLS**—Writing; Reading Comprehension; Learning Strategies.

GOE—Interest Area: 01. Arts, Entertainment, and Media. **Work Group:** 01.02. Writing and Editing. **Other Jobs in This Work Group:** Copy Writers; Creative Writers; Editors; Media and Communication Workers, All Other; Technical Writers; Writers and Authors.

EDUCATION/TRAINING PROGRAM(S)—Broadcast Journalism; Business/Corporate Communications; Communication Studies/Speech Communication and Rhetoric; Communication, Journalism, and Related Programs, Other; Creative Writing; English Composition; Family and Con-

sumer Sciences/Human Sciences Communication; Journalism; Mass Communication/Media Studies; Playwriting and Screenwriting; Technical and Business Writing. **RELATED KNOWLEDGE/COURSES**—Fine Arts; Communications and Media; English Language.

Producers

- Personality Code: AE
- Growth: 18.3%
- Annual Job Openings: 10,000
- Annual Earnings: $48,200
- Education/Training Required: Work experience plus degree
- Self-Employed: 32.8%
- Part-Time: 9.1%

Plan and coordinate various aspects of radio, television, stage, or motion picture production, such as selecting script, coordinating writing, directing and editing, and arranging financing. Coordinate the activities of writers, directors, managers, and other personnel throughout the production process. Monitor post-production processes in order to ensure accurate completion of all details. Perform management activities such as budgeting, scheduling, planning, and marketing. Determine production size, content, and budget, establishing details such as production schedules and management policies. Compose and edit scripts, or provide screenwriters with story outlines from which scripts can be written. Conduct meetings with staff to discuss production progress and to ensure production objectives are attained. Resolve personnel problems that arise during the production process by acting as liaisons between dissenting parties when necessary. Produce shows for special occasions, such as holidays or testimonials. Edit and write news stories from information collected by reporters. Write and submit proposals to bid on contracts for projects.

Hire directors, principal cast members, and key production staff members. Arrange financing for productions. Select plays, scripts, books, or ideas to be produced. Review film, recordings, or rehearsals to ensure conformance to production and broadcast standards. Perform administrative duties such as preparing operational reports, distributing rehearsal call sheets and script copies, and arranging for rehearsal quarters. Obtain and distribute costumes, props, music, and studio equipment needed to complete productions. Negotiate contracts with artistic personnel, often in accordance with collective bargaining agreements. Maintain knowledge of minimum wages and working conditions established by unions and/or associations of actors and technicians. Plan and coordinate the production of musical recordings, selecting music and directing performers. Negotiate with parties including independent producers, and the distributors and broadcasters who will be handling completed productions. Develop marketing plans for finished products, collaborating with sales associates to supervise product distribution. Determine and direct the content of radio programming. **SKILLS**—Coordination; Negotiation; Monitoring; Management of Personnel Resources; Writing; Time Management; Social Perceptiveness; Management of Financial Resources.

GOE—Interest Area: 01. Arts, Entertainment, and Media. **Work Group:** 01.01. Managerial Work in Arts, Entertainment, and Media. **Other Jobs in This Work Group:** Agents and Business Managers of Artists, Performers, and Athletes; Art Directors; Athletes and Sports Competitors; Coaches and Scouts; Entertainers and Performers, Sports and Related Workers, All Other; Fitness Trainers and Aerobics Instructors; Producers and Directors; Program Directors; Technical Directors/Managers; Umpires, Referees, and Other Sports Officials.

EDUCATION/TRAINING PROGRAM(S)— Cinematography and Film/Video Production; Directing and Theatrical Production; Drama and Dramatics/Theatre Arts, General; Dramatic/Theatre Arts and Stagecraft, Other; Film/Cinema Studies; Radio and Television; Theatre/Theatre Arts Management. **RELATED KNOWLEDGE/ COURSES**—Communications and Media; Clerical Studies; Administration and Management; English Language; Fine Arts; Sales and Marketing.

Professional Photographers

- Personality Code: AR
- Growth: 13.6%
- Annual Job Openings: 18,000
- Annual Earnings: $25,050
- Education/Training Required: Long-term on-the-job training
- Self-Employed: 52.5%
- Part-Time: 24.0%

Photograph subjects or news worthy events, using still cameras, color or black-and-white film, and variety of photographic accessories. Frames subject matter and background in lens to capture desired image. Focuses camera and adjusts settings based on lighting, subject material, distance, and film speed. Selects and assembles equipment and required background properties, according to subject, materials, and conditions. Directs activities of workers assisting in setting up photographic equipment. Arranges subject material in desired position. Estimates or measures light level, distance, and number of exposures needed, using measuring devices and formulas. **SKILLS**—Equipment Selection; Management of Material Resources; Technology Design; Operation and Control; Management of Personnel Resources; Social Perceptiveness; Science; Monitoring; Equipment Maintenance; Systems Analysis.

GOE—Interest Area: 01. Arts, Entertainment, and Media. **Work Group:** 01.08. Media Technology. **Other Jobs in This Work Group:** Audio and Video Equipment Technicians; Broadcast Technicians;

Camera Operators, Television, Video, and Motion Picture; Film and Video Editors; Media and Communication Equipment Workers, All Other; Photographers; Radio Operators; Sound Engineering Technicians.

EDUCATION/TRAINING PROGRAM(S)— Art/Art Studies, General; Commercial Photography; Film/Video and Photographic Arts, Other; Photography; Photojournalism; Visual and Performing Arts, General. RELATED KNOWLEDGE/COURSES—Fine Arts; Communications and Media; Geography; Chemistry; Physics; Transportation.

Radio and Television Announcers

- Personality Code: AS
- Growth: –10.1%
- Annual Job Openings: 8,000
- Annual Earnings: $20,940
- Education/Training Required: Moderate-term on-the-job training
- Self-Employed: 34.4%
- Part-Time: 34.2%

Talk on radio or television. May interview guests, act as master of ceremonies, read news flashes, identify station by giving call letters, or announce song title and artist. Prepare and deliver news, sports, and/or weather reports, gathering and rewriting material so that it will convey required information and fit specific time slots. Read news flashes to inform audiences of important events. Identify stations, and introduce or close shows, using memorized or read scripts, and/or ad-libs. Select program content, in conjunction with producers and assistants, based on factors such as program specialties, audience tastes, or requests from the public. Study background information in order to prepare for programs or interviews. Comment on music and other matters, such as weather or traffic conditions. Interview show guests about their lives, their work, or topics of current interest. Discuss various topics over the telephone with viewers or listeners. Host civic, charitable, or promotional events that are broadcast over television or radio. Make promotional appearances at public or private events in order to represent their employers. Operate control consoles. Announce musical selections, station breaks, commercials, or public service information, and accept requests from listening audience. Keep daily program logs to provide information on all elements aired during broadcast, such as musical selections and station promotions. Record commercials for later broadcast. Locate guests to appear on talk or interview shows. Describe or demonstrate products that viewers may purchase through specific shows or in stores. Coordinate games, contests, or other on-air competitions, performing such duties as asking questions and awarding prizes. Attend press conferences in order to gather information for broadcast. Provide commentary and conduct interviews during sporting events, parades, conventions, and other events. Give network cues permitting selected stations to receive programs. SKILLS—Speaking; Time Management; Social Perceptiveness; Writing; Coordination; Monitoring; Persuasion; Active Listening.

GOE—Interest Area: 01. Arts, Entertainment, and Media. Work Group: 01.05. Performing Arts. Other Jobs in This Work Group: Actors; Choreographers; Composers; Dancers; Directors—Stage, Motion Pictures, Television, and Radio; Entertainers and Performers, Sports and Related Workers, All Other; Music Arrangers and Orchestrators; Music Directors; Music Directors and Composers; Musicians and Singers; Musicians, Instrumental; Public Address System and Other Announcers; Singers; Talent Directors.

EDUCATION/TRAINING PROGRAM(S)— Broadcast Journalism; Radio and Television.

RELATED KNOWLEDGE/COURSES—Communications and Media; Telecommunications; English Language; Computers and Electronics; Geography; Fine Arts.

Reporters and Correspondents

- Personality Code: AI
- Growth: 6.2%
- Annual Job Openings: 6,000
- Annual Earnings: $31,240
- Education/Training Required: Bachelor's degree
- Self-Employed: 6.3%
- Part-Time: 14.4%

Collect and analyze facts about newsworthy events by interview, investigation, or observation. Report and write stories for newspaper, news magazine, radio, or television. Report and write news stories for publication or broadcast, describing the background and details of events. Arrange interviews with people who can provide information about a particular story. Review copy and correct errors in content, grammar, and punctuation, following prescribed editorial style and formatting guidelines. Review and evaluate notes taken about event aspects in order to isolate pertinent facts and details. Determine a story's emphasis, length, and format, and organize material accordingly. Research and analyze background information related to stories in order to be able to provide complete and accurate information. Gather information about events through research, interviews, experience, and attendance at political, news, sports, artistic, social, and other functions. Investigate breaking news developments such as disasters, crimes, and human interest stories. Research and report on specialized fields such as medicine, science and technology, politics, foreign affairs, sports, arts, consumer affairs, business, religion, crime, or education. Receive assignments or evaluate leads and tips in order to develop story ideas. Discuss issues with editors in order to establish priorities and positions. Check reference materials such as books, news files, and public records in order to obtain relevant facts. Revise work in order to meet editorial approval or to fit time or space requirements. Photograph or videotape news events, or request that a photographer be assigned to provide such coverage. Develop ideas and material for columns or commentaries by analyzing and interpreting news, current issues, and personal experiences. Transmit news stories or reporting information from remote locations, using equipment such as satellite phones, telephones, fax machines, or modems. Present live or recorded commentary via broadcast media. Conduct taped or filmed interviews or narratives. Edit or assist in editing videos for broadcast. Write columns, editorials, commentaries, or reviews that interpret events or offer opinions. **SKILLS**—Writing; Active Listening; Critical Thinking; Reading Comprehension; Active Learning; Time Management; Speaking; Persuasion.

GOE—Interest Area: 01. Arts, Entertainment, and Media. **Work Group:** 01.03. News, Broadcasting and Public Relations. **Other Jobs in This Work Group:** Broadcast News Analysts; Caption Writers; Interpreters and Translators; Public Relations Specialists.

EDUCATION/TRAINING PROGRAM(S)—Agricultural Communication/Journalism; Broadcast Journalism; Journalism; Journalism, Other; Mass Communication/Media Studies; Photojournalism; Political Communication. **RELATED KNOWLEDGE/COURSES**—Communications and Media; English Language; Geography; Sociology and Anthropology; Clerical Studies; Customer and Personal Service.

Sculptors

- Personality Code: AR
- Growth: 16.5%
- Annual Job Openings: 4,000
- Annual Earnings: $35,420
- Education/Training Required: Long-term on-the-job training
- Self-Employed: 55.5%
- Part-Time: 23.1%

Design and construct three-dimensional art works, using materials such as stone, wood, plaster, and metal and employing various manual and tool techniques. Carves objects from stone, concrete, plaster, wood, or other material, using abrasives and tools, such as chisels, gouges, and mall. Models substances, such as clay or wax, using fingers and small hand tools to form objects. Cuts, bends, laminates, arranges, and fastens individual or mixed raw and manufactured materials and products to form works of art. Constructs artistic forms from metal or stone, using metalworking, welding, or masonry tools and equipment. **SKILLS**—None met the criteria.

GOE—**Interest Area:** 01. Arts, Entertainment, and Media. **Work Group:** 01.04. Visual Arts. **Other Jobs in This Work Group:** Artists and Related Workers, All Other; Cartoonists; Commercial and Industrial Designers; Designers, All Other; Exhibit Designers; Fashion Designers; Fine Artists, Including Painters, Sculptors, and Illustrators; Floral Designers; Graphic Designers; Interior Designers; Merchandise Displayers and Window Trimmers; Multi-Media Artists and Animators; Painters and Illustrators; Set and Exhibit Designers; Set Designers; Sketch Artists.

EDUCATION/TRAINING PROGRAM(S)—Art/Art Studies, General; Ceramic Arts and Ceramics; Fine Arts and Art Studies, Other; Fine/Studio Arts, General; Sculpture; Visual and Performing Arts, General. **RELATED KNOWLEDGE/**

COURSES—Fine Arts; Design; Engineering and Technology; Building and Construction.

Set Designers

- Personality Code: AR
- Growth: 20.9%
- Annual Job Openings: 2,000
- Annual Earnings: $35,150
- Education/Training Required: Bachelor's degree
- Self-Employed: 32.2%
- Part-Time: 16.5%

Design sets for theatrical, motion picture, and television productions. Integrates requirements including script, research, budget, and available locations to develop design. Presents drawings for approval and makes changes and corrections as directed. Selects furniture, draperies, pictures, lamps, and rugs for decorative quality and appearance. Confers with heads of production and direction to establish budget, schedules, and discuss design ideas. Directs and coordinates set construction, erection, or decoration activities to ensure conformance to design, budget, and schedule requirements. Assigns staff to complete design ideas and prepare sketches, illustrations, and detailed drawings of sets, or graphics and animation. Examines dressed set to ensure props and scenery do not interfere with movements of cast or view of camera. Reads script to determine location, set, or decoration requirements. Estimates costs of design materials and construction, or rental of location or props. Researches and consults experts to determine architectural and furnishing styles to depict given periods or locations. Designs and builds scale models of set design or miniature sets used in filming backgrounds or special effects. Prepares rough draft and scale working drawings of sets, including floor plans, scenery, and properties to be constructed.

SKILLS—Management of Financial Resources; Management of Material Resources; Management of Personnel Resources; Persuasion; Operations Analysis; Systems Evaluation; Negotiation; Technology Design.

GOE—Interest Area: 01. Arts, Entertainment, and Media. Work Group: 01.04. Visual Arts. Other Jobs in This Work Group: Artists and Related Workers, All Other; Cartoonists; Commercial and Industrial Designers; Designers, All Other; Exhibit Designers; Fashion Designers; Fine Artists, Including Painters, Sculptors, and Illustrators; Floral Designers; Graphic Designers; Interior Designers; Merchandise Displayers and Window Trimmers; Multi-Media Artists and Animators; Painters and Illustrators; Sculptors; Set and Exhibit Designers; Sketch Artists.

EDUCATION/TRAINING PROGRAM(S)—Design and Applied Arts, Other; Design and Visual Communications, General; Illustration; Technical Theatre/Theatre Design and Technology. RELATED KNOWLEDGE/COURSES—Fine Arts; Design; Building and Construction; Engineering and Technology; Geography; Communications and Media.

Singers

- Personality Code: AE
- Growth: 17.1%
- Annual Job Openings: 25,000
- Annual Earnings: $37,380
- Education/Training Required: Long-term on-the-job training
- Self-Employed: 38.3%
- Part-Time: 39.5%

Sing songs on stage, radio, television, or motion pictures. Sing a cappella or with musical accompaniment. Sing as a soloist or as a member of a vocal group. Collaborate with a manager or agent who handles administrative details, finds work, and negotiates contracts. Compose songs and/or create vocal arrangements. Learn acting, dancing, and other skills required for dramatic singing roles. Make or participate in recordings. Research particular roles to find out more about a character, or the time and place in which a piece is set. Interpret or modify music, applying knowledge of harmony, melody, rhythm, and voice production to individualize presentations and maintain audience interest. Memorize musical selections and routines, or sing following printed text, musical notation, or customer instructions. Observe choral leaders or prompters for cues or directions in vocal presentation. Perform before live audiences, or in television, radio, or movie productions. Practice singing exercises and study with vocal coaches, in order to develop their voices and skills and to rehearse for upcoming roles. Seek out and learn new music that is suitable for live performance and/or recording. SKILLS—None met the criteria.

GOE—Interest Area: 01. Arts, Entertainment, and Media. Work Group: 01.05. Performing Arts. Other Jobs in This Work Group: Actors; Choreographers; Composers; Dancers; Directors—Stage, Motion Pictures, Television, and Radio; Entertainers and Performers, Sports and Related Workers, All Other; Music Arrangers and Orchestrators; Music Directors; Music Directors and Composers; Musicians and Singers; Musicians, Instrumental; Public Address System and Other Announcers; Radio and Television Announcers; Talent Directors.

EDUCATION/TRAINING PROGRAM(S)—Jazz/Jazz Studies; Music Pedagogy; Music Performance, General; Music, General; Music, Other; Piano and Organ; Voice and Opera. RELATED KNOWLEDGE/COURSES—Fine Arts; Communications and Media; Foreign Language.

Artistic—S

Sketch Artists

- Personality Code: AR
- Growth: 16.5%
- Annual Job Openings: 4,000
- Annual Earnings: $35,420
- Education/Training Required: Long-term on-the-job training
- Self-Employed: 55.5%
- Part-Time: 23.1%

Sketch likenesses of subjects according to observation or descriptions either to assist law enforcement agencies in identifying suspects, to depict court room scenes, or for entertainment purposes of patrons, using mediums such as pencil, charcoal, and pastels. Draws sketch, profile, or likeness of posed subject or photograph, using pencil, charcoal, pastels, or other medium. Assembles and arranges outlines of features to form composite image, according to information provided by witness or victim. Alters copy of composite image until witness or victim is satisfied that composite is best possible representation of suspect. Poses subject to accentuate most pleasing features or profile. Classifies and codes components of image, using established system, to help identify suspect. Prepares series of simple line drawings conforming to description of suspect and presents drawings to informant for selection of sketch. Interviews crime victims and witnesses to obtain descriptive information concerning physical build, sex, nationality, and facial features of unidentified suspect. Measures distances and develops sketches of crime scene from photograph and measurements. Searches police photograph records, using classification and coding system to determine if existing photograph of suspects is available. Operates photocopy or similar machine to reproduce composite image. **SKILLS—** Active Listening; Social Perceptiveness; Speaking.

GOE—Interest Area: 01. Arts, Entertainment, and Media. **Work Group:** 01.04. Visual Arts. **Other**

Jobs in This Work Group: Artists and Related Workers, All Other; Cartoonists; Commercial and Industrial Designers; Designers, All Other; Exhibit Designers; Fashion Designers; Fine Artists, Including Painters, Sculptors, and Illustrators; Floral Designers; Graphic Designers; Interior Designers; Merchandise Displayers and Window Trimmers; Multi-Media Artists and Animators; Painters and Illustrators; Sculptors; Set and Exhibit Designers; Set Designers.

EDUCATION/TRAINING PROGRAM(S)— Art/Art Studies, General; Drawing; Fine Arts and Art Studies, Other; Fine/Studio Arts, General; Medical Illustration/Medical Illustrator; Visual and Performing Arts, General. **RELATED KNOWLEDGE/COURSES—**Fine Arts; Design.

Talent Directors

- Personality Code: AE
- Growth: 18.3%
- Annual Job Openings: 10,000
- Annual Earnings: $48,200
- Education/Training Required: Long-term on-the-job training
- Self-Employed: 32.8%
- Part-Time: 9.1%

Audition and interview performers to select most appropriate talent for parts in stage, television, radio, or motion picture productions. Arrange for and/or design screen tests or auditions for prospective performers. Attend or view productions in order to maintain knowledge of available actors. Audition and interview performers in order to match their attributes to specific roles or to increase the pool of available acting talent. Contact agents and actors in order to provide notification of audition and performance opportunities and to set up audition times. Locate performers or extras for crowd and background scenes, and stand-ins or photo doubles for actors, by direct contact or through agents. Maintain talent files that include information such as performers' specialties, past performances, and availability. Negotiate contract agreements with performers, with agents, or between performers and agents or production companies. Prepare actors for auditions by providing scripts and information about roles and casting requirements. Read scripts and confer with producers in order to determine the types and numbers of performers required for a given production. Review performer information such as photos, resumes, voice tapes, videos, and union membership, in order to decide whom to audition for parts. Select performers for roles or submit lists of suitable performers to producers or directors for final selection. Hire and supervise workers who help locate people with specified attributes and talents. Serve as liaisons between directors, actors, and agents. **SKILLS—** Negotiation; Management of Personnel Resources; Speaking; Social Perceptiveness; Persuasion; Active Listening; Writing; Reading Comprehension; Critical Thinking.

GOE—Interest Area: 01. Arts, Entertainment, and Media. **Work Group:** 01.05. Performing Arts. **Other Jobs in This Work Group:** Actors; Choreographers; Composers; Dancers; Directors—Stage, Motion Pictures, Television, and Radio; Entertainers and Performers, Sports and Related Workers, All Other; Music Arrangers and Orchestrators; Music Directors; Music Directors and Composers; Musicians and Singers; Musicians, Instrumental; Public Address System and Other Announcers; Radio and Television Announcers; Singers.

EDUCATION/TRAINING PROGRAM(S)— Cinematography and Film/Video Production; Directing and Theatrical Production; Drama and Dramatics/Theatre Arts, General; Dramatic/ Theatre Arts and Stagecraft, Other; Film/Cinema Studies; Radio and Television; Theatre/Theatre Arts Management. **RELATED KNOWLEDGE/ COURSES—**Fine Arts; Sales and Marketing; Personnel and Human Resources; Administration and Management; Communications and Media; Economics and Accounting.

Technical Writers

- Personality Code: AI
- Growth: 27.1%
- Annual Job Openings: 6,000
- Annual Earnings: $51,590
- Education/Training Required: Bachelor's degree
- Self-Employed: 7.3%
- Part-Time: 5.5%

Write technical materials, such as equipment manuals, appendices, or operating and maintenance instructions. May assist in layout work. Organize material and complete writing assignment according to set standards regarding order, clarity, conciseness, style, and terminology. Maintain records and files of work and revisions. Edit, standardize, or make changes to material prepared by other writers or establishment personnel. Confer with customer representatives, vendors, plant executives, or publisher to establish technical specifications and to determine subject material to be developed for publication. Review published materials and recommend revisions or changes in scope, format, content, and methods of reproduction and binding. Select photographs, drawings, sketches, diagrams, and charts to illustrate material. Study drawings, specifications, mockups, and product samples to integrate and delineate technology, operating procedure, and production sequence and detail. Interview production and engineering personnel and read journals and other material to become familiar with product technologies and production methods. Observe production, developmental, and experimental activities to determine operating procedure and detail. Arrange for typing, duplication, and distribution of material. Assist in laying out material

Artistic—T

for publication. Analyze developments in specific field to determine need for revisions in previously published materials and development of new material. Review manufacturer's and trade catalogs, drawings and other data relative to operation, maintenance, and service of equipment. Draw sketches to illustrate specified materials or assembly sequence. **SKILLS**—Writing; Coordination; Active Learning; Active Listening; Reading Comprehension; Service Orientation; Technology Design; Speaking; Learning Strategies.

GOE—**Interest Area:** 01. Arts, Entertainment, and Media. **Work Group:** 01.02. Writing and Editing.

Other Jobs in This Work Group: Copy Writers; Creative Writers; Editors; Media and Communication Workers, All Other; Poets and Lyricists; Writers and Authors.

EDUCATION/TRAINING PROGRAM(S)—Business/Corporate Communications; Family and Consumer Sciences/Human Sciences Communication; Technical and Business Writing. **RELATED KNOWLEDGE/COURSES**—English Language; Clerical Studies; Communications and Media; Computers and Electronics; Education and Training; Sales and Marketing.

Social Jobs

Anthropology and Archeology Teachers, Postsecondary

- Personality Code: SI
- Growth: 38.1%
- Annual Job Openings: 216,000
- Annual Earnings: $59,710
- Education/Training Required: Master's degree
- Self-Employed: 0.3%
- Part-Time: 27.7%

Teach courses in anthropology or archeology. Participate in student recruitment, registration, and placement activities. Perform administrative duties such as serving as department head. Provide professional consulting services to government and/or industry. Serve on academic or administrative committees that deal with institutional policies, departmental matters, and academic issues. Write grant proposals to procure external research funding. Evaluate and grade students' class work, assignments, and papers. Prepare and deliver lectures to undergraduate and/or graduate students on topics such as research methods, urban anthropology, and language and culture. Advise students on academic and vocational curricula, career issues, and laboratory and field research. Compile, administer, and grade examinations or assign this work to others. Compile bibliographies of specialized materials for outside reading assignments. Initiate, facilitate, and moderate classroom discussions. Keep abreast of developments in their field by reading current literature, talking with colleagues, and participating in professional conferences. Maintain regularly sched-uled office hours in order to advise and assist students. Maintain student attendance records, grades, and other required records. Plan, evaluate, and revise curricula, course content, and course materials and methods of instruction. Prepare course materials such as syllabi, homework assignments, and handouts. Select and obtain materials and supplies such as textbooks and laboratory equipment. Supervise students' laboratory or field work. Supervise undergraduate and/or graduate teaching, internship, and research work. Act as advisers to student organizations. Collaborate with colleagues to address teaching and research issues. Conduct research in a particular field of knowledge and publish findings in professional journals, books, and/or electronic media. Participate in campus and community events. **SKILLS**—Instructing; Learning Strategies; Reading Comprehension; Active Learning; Speaking; Writing; Science; Active Listening; Critical Thinking.

GOE—Interest Area: 12. Education and Social Service. **Work Group:** 12.03. Educational Services. **Other Jobs in This Work Group:** Adult Literacy, Remedial Education, and GED Teachers and Instructors; Agricultural Sciences Teachers, Postsecondary; Architecture Teachers, Postsecondary; Archivists; Area, Ethnic, and Cultural Studies Teachers, Postsecondary; Art, Drama, and Music Teachers, Postsecondary; Atmospheric, Earth, Marine, and Space Sciences Teachers, Postsecondary; Audio-Visual Collections Specialists; Biological Science Teachers, Postsecondary; Business Teachers, Postsecondary; Chemistry Teachers, Postsecondary; Child Care Workers; Communications Teachers, Postsecondary; Computer Science Teachers, Postsecondary; Criminal Justice and Law Enforcement Teachers, Postsecondary; Curators; Economics Teachers, Postsecondary; Education Teachers, Postsecondary; Education, Training, and Library Workers, All Other; Educational Psychologists; Educational, Vocational, and School Counselors; Elementary School Teachers, Except Special Education; Engineering Teachers, Postsecondary; English Language and Literature Teachers, Postsecondary; Environmental Science Teachers, Post-secondary; Farm and Home Management Advisors; Foreign Language and Literature Teachers, Postsecondary; Forestry and Conservation Science Teachers, Postsecondary; Geography Teachers, Postsecondary; Graduate Teaching Assistants; Health Specialties Teachers, Postsecondary; History Teachers, Postsecondary; Home Economics Teachers, Postsecondary; Kindergarten Teachers, Except Special Education; Law Teachers, Postsecondary; Librarians; Library Assistants, Clerical; Library Science Teachers, Postsecondary; Library Technicians; Mathematical Science Teachers, Postsecondary; Middle School Teachers, Except Special and Vocational Education; Museum Technicians and Conservators; Nannies; Nursing Instructors and Teachers, Postsecondary; Personal Financial Advisors; Philosophy and Religion Teachers, Postsecondary; Physics Teachers, Postsecondary; Political Science Teachers, Postsecondary; Postsecondary Teachers, All Other; Preschool Teachers, Except Special Education; Psychology Teachers, Postsecondary; Recreation and Fitness Studies Teachers, Postsecondary; Secondary School Teachers, Except Special and Vocational Education; Self-Enrichment Education Teachers; Social Sciences Teachers, Postsecondary, All Other; Social Work Teachers, Postsecondary; Sociology Teachers, Postsecondary; Special Education Teachers, Middle School; Special Education Teachers, Preschool, Kindergarten, and Elementary School; Special Education Teachers, Secondary School; Teacher Assistants; Teachers and Instructors, All Other; Vocational Education Teachers, Postsecondary; Vocational Education Teachers, Middle School; Vocational Education Teachers, Secondary School.

EDUCATION/TRAINING PROGRAM(S)— Anthropology; Archeology; Physical Anthropology; Social Science Teacher Education. RELATED KNOWLEDGE/COURSES—Sociology and Anthropology; History and Archeology; Education and Training; Psychology; Economics and Accounting; English Language.

Area, Ethnic, and Cultural Studies Teachers, Postsecondary

- Personality Code: SI
- Growth: 38.1%
- Annual Job Openings: 216,000
- Annual Earnings: $55,060
- Education/Training Required: Master's degree
- Self-Employed: 0.3%
- Part-Time: 27.7%

Teach courses pertaining to the culture and development of an area (e.g., Latin America), an ethnic group, or any other group (e.g., women's studies, urban affairs). Evaluate and grade students' class work, assignments, and papers. Prepare and deliver lectures to undergraduate and/or graduate students on topics such as race and ethnic relations, gender studies, and cross-cultural perspectives. Advise students on academic and vocational curricula and on career issues. Compile, administer, and grade examinations or assign this work to others. Compile bibliographies of specialized materials for outside reading assignments. Incorporate experiential/site visit components into courses. Initiate, facilitate, and moderate classroom discussions. Keep abreast of developments in their field by reading current literature, talking with colleagues, and participating in professional conferences. Maintain regularly scheduled office hours in order to advise and assist students. Maintain student attendance records, grades, and other required records. Plan, evaluate, and revise curricula, course content, and course materials and methods of instruction. Prepare course materials such as syllabi, homework assignments, and handouts. Select and obtain materials and supplies such as textbooks. Supervise undergraduate and/or graduate teaching, internship, and research work. Act as advisers to student organizations. Collaborate with colleagues to address teaching and research issues. Conduct research in a particular field of knowledge, and publish findings in professional journals, books, and/or electronic media. Participate in campus and community events. Participate in student recruitment, registration, and placement activities. Perform administrative duties such as serving as department head. Provide professional consulting services to government and/or industry. Serve on academic or administrative committees that deal with institutional policies, departmental matters, and academic issues. Write grant proposals to procure external research funding. **SKILLS**—Instructing; Learning Strategies; Reading Comprehension; Active Learning; Speaking; Writing; Science; Active Listening; Critical Thinking.

GOE—Interest Area: 12. Education and Social Service. **Work Group:** 12.03. Educational Services. **Other Jobs in This Work Group:** Adult Literacy, Remedial Education, and GED Teachers and Instructors; Agricultural Sciences Teachers, Postsecondary; Anthropology and Archeology Teachers, Postsecondary; Architecture Teachers, Postsecondary; Archivists; Art, Drama, and Music Teachers, Postsecondary; Atmospheric, Earth, Marine, and Space Sciences Teachers, Postsecondary; Audio-Visual Collections Specialists; Biological Science Teachers, Postsecondary; Business Teachers, Postsecondary; Chemistry Teachers, Postsecondary; Child Care Workers; Communications Teachers, Postsecondary; Computer Science Teachers, Postsecondary; Criminal Justice and Law Enforcement Teachers, Postsecondary; Curators; Economics Teachers, Postsecondary; Education Teachers, Postsecondary; Education, Training, and Library Workers, All Other; Educational Psychologists; Educational, Vocational, and School Counselors; Elementary School Teachers, Except Special Education; Engineering Teachers, Postsecondary; English Language and Literature Teachers, Postsecondary; Environmental Science Teachers, Postsecondary; Farm and Home Management Advisors; Foreign Language and Literature Teachers, Postsecondary; Forestry and Conservation Science Teachers, Postsecondary; Geography Teachers, Postsecondary; Graduate Teaching Assistants; Health Specialties Teachers, Postsecondary; History Teachers, Postsecondary; Home Economics Teachers, Postsecondary; Kindergarten Teachers, Except Special Education; Law Teachers, Postsecondary; Librarians; Library Assistants, Clerical; Library Science Teachers, Postsecondary; Library Technicians; Mathematical Science Teachers, Postsecondary; Middle School Teachers, Except Special and Vocational Education; Museum Technicians and Conservators; Nannies; Nursing Instructors and Teachers, Postsecondary; Personal Financial Advisors; Philosophy and Religion Teachers, Postsecondary; Physics Teachers, Postsecondary; Political Science Teachers, Postsecondary; Postsecondary Teachers, All Other; Preschool Teachers, Except Special Education; Psychology Teachers, Postsecondary; Recreation and Fitness Studies Teachers, Postsecondary; Secondary School Teachers, Except Special and Vocational Education; Self-Enrichment Education Teachers; Social Sciences Teachers, Postsecondary, All Other; Social Work Teachers, Postsecondary; Sociology Teachers, Postsecondary; Special Education Teachers, Middle School; Special Education Teachers, Preschool, Kindergarten, and Elementary School; Special Education Teachers, Secondary School; Teacher Assistants; Teachers and Instructors, All Other; Vocational Education Teachers, Postsecondary; Vocational Education Teachers, Middle School; Vocational Education Teachers, Secondary School.

EDUCATION/TRAINING PROGRAM(S)— African Studies; African-American/Black Studies; American Indian/Native American Studies; American/United States Studies/Civilization; Area Studies, Other; Area, Ethnic, Cultural, and Gender Studies, Other; Asian Studies/Civilization; Asian-American Studies; Balkans Studies; Baltic Studies; Canadian Studies; Caribbean Studies; Central/Middle and Eastern European Studies; Chinese Studies; Commonwealth Studies; East Asian Studies; Ethnic, Cultural Minority, and Gender Studies, Other;

European Studies/Civilization; French Studies; Gay/Lesbian Studies; German Studies; Hispanic-American, Puerto Rican, and Mexican-American/Chicano Studies; Intercultural/Multicultural and Diversity Studies; Islamic Studies; Italian Studies; Japanese Studies; Jewish/Judaic Studies; Korean Studies; Latin American Studies; Near and Middle Eastern Studies; Pacific Area/Pacific Rim Studies; Polish Studies; Regional Studies (U.S., Canadian, Foreign); Religion/Religious Studies, Other; Russian Studies; Scandinavian Studies; Slavic Studies; Social Studies Teacher Education; South Asian Studies; Southeast Asian Studies; Spanish and Iberian Studies; Tibetan Studies; Ukraine Studies; Ural-Altaic and Central Asian Studies; Western European Studies; Women's Studies. **RELATED KNOWLEDGE/COURSES**—Sociology and Anthropology; History and Archeology; Education and Training; Psychology; Economics and Accounting; English Language.

Child, Family, and School Social Workers

- Personality Code: S
- Growth: 23.2%
- Annual Job Openings: 45,000
- Annual Earnings: $33,810
- Education/Training Required: Bachelor's degree
- Self-Employed: 1.7%
- Part-Time: 8.7%

Provide social services and assistance to improve the social and psychological functioning of children and their families and to maximize the family well-being and the academic functioning of children. May assist single parents, arrange adoptions, and find foster homes for abandoned or abused children. In schools, they address such problems as teenage pregnancy, misbehavior, and **truancy. May also advise teachers on how to deal with problem children.** Interview clients individually, in families, or in groups, assessing their situations, capabilities, and problems, to determine what services are required to meet their needs. Counsel individuals, groups, families, or communities regarding issues including mental health, poverty, unemployment, substance abuse, physical abuse, rehabilitation, social adjustment, child care, and/or medical care. Maintain case history records and prepare reports. Counsel students whose behavior, school progress, or mental or physical impairment indicate a need for assistance, diagnosing students' problems and arranging for needed services. Consult with parents, teachers, and other school personnel to determine causes of problems such as truancy and misbehavior, and to implement solutions. Counsel parents with child rearing problems, interviewing the child and family to determine whether further action is required. Develop and review service plans in consultation with clients, and perform follow-ups assessing the quantity and quality of services provided. Collect supplementary information needed to assist client, such as employment records, medical records, or school reports. Address legal issues, such as child abuse and discipline, assisting with hearings and providing testimony to inform custody arrangements. Provide, find, or arrange for support services, such as child care, homemaker service, prenatal care, substance abuse treatment, job training, counseling, or parenting classes, to prevent more serious problems from developing. Refer clients to community resources for services such as job placement, debt counseling, legal aid, housing, medical treatment, or financial assistance, and provide concrete information, such as where to go and how to apply. Arrange for medical, psychiatric, and other tests that may disclose causes of difficulties and indicate remedial measures. Work in child and adolescent residential institutions. Administer welfare programs. Evaluate personal characteristics and home conditions of foster home or adoption applicants. Serve as liaisons between students, homes, schools, family services, child guidance clinics, courts, protective services, doctors, and other contacts, to help children who face problems such as disabilities, abuse, or poverty. **SKILLS**—Social Perceptiveness; Service Orientation; Learning Strategies; Negotiation; Monitoring; Speaking; Active Listening; Persuasion.

GOE—**Interest Area:** 12. Education and Social Service. **Work Group:** 12.02. Social Services. **Other Jobs in This Work Group:** Clergy; Clinical Psychologists; Clinical, Counseling, and School Psychologists; Community and Social Service Specialists, All Other; Counseling Psychologists; Counselors, All Other; Directors, Religious Activities and Education; Marriage and Family Therapists; Medical and Public Health Social Workers; Mental Health and Substance Abuse Social Workers; Mental Health Counselors; Probation Officers and Correctional Treatment Specialists; Rehabilitation Counselors; Religious Workers, All Other; Residential Advisors; Social and Human Service Assistants; Social Workers, All Other; Substance Abuse and Behavioral Disorder Counselors.

EDUCATION/TRAINING PROGRAM(S)—Juvenile Corrections; Social Work; Youth Services/Administration. **RELATED KNOWLEDGE/COURSES**—Therapy and Counseling; Psychology; Sociology and Anthropology; Customer and Personal Service; Law and Government; Philosophy and Theology.

Counseling Psychologists

- Personality Code: SI
- Growth: 24.4%
- Annual Job Openings: 17,000
- Annual Earnings: $52,220
- Education/Training Required: Master's degree
- Self-Employed: 25.4%
- Part-Time: 27.2%

Assess and evaluate individuals' problems through the use of case history, interview, and observation and provide individual or group counseling services to assist individuals in achieving more effective personal, social, educational, and vocational development and adjustment. Provide consulting services to schools, social service agencies, and businesses. Advise clients on how they could be helped by counseling. Analyze data such as interview notes, test results, and reference manuals in order to identify symptoms, and to diagnose the nature of clients' problems. Collect information about individuals or clients, using interviews, case histories, observational techniques, and other assessment methods. Counsel individuals, groups, or families to help them understand problems, define goals, and develop realistic action plans. Develop therapeutic and treatment plans based on clients' interests, abilities, and needs. Evaluate the results of counseling methods to determine the reliability and validity of treatments. Select, administer, and interpret psychological tests to assess intelligence, aptitudes, abilities, or interests. Consult with other professionals to discuss therapies, treatments, counseling resources, or techniques, and to share occupational information. Refer clients to specialists or to other institutions for non-counseling treatment of problems. Conduct research to develop or improve diagnostic or therapeutic counseling techniques. **SKILLS**—Social Perceptiveness; Active Listening; Learning Strategies; Critical Thinking; Persuasion; Reading Comprehension; Active Learning; Science; Monitoring.

GOE—**Interest Area:** 12. Education and Social Service. **Work Group:** 12.02. Social Services. **Other Jobs in This Work Group:** Child, Family, and School Social Workers; Clergy; Clinical Psychologists; Clinical, Counseling, and School Psychologists; Community and Social Service Specialists, All Other; Counselors, All Other; Directors, Religious Activities and Education; Marriage and Family Therapists; Medical and Public Health Social Workers; Mental Health and Substance Abuse Social Workers; Mental Health Counselors; Probation

Social—C

Officers and Correctional Treatment Specialists; Rehabilitation Counselors; Religious Workers, All Other; Residential Advisors; Social and Human Service Assistants; Social Workers, All Other; Substance Abuse and Behavioral Disorder Counselors.

EDUCATION/TRAINING PROGRAM(S)— Clinical Child Psychology; Clinical Psychology; Counseling Psychology; Developmental and Child Psychology; Psychoanalysis and Psychotherapy; Psychology, General; School Psychology. **RELATED KNOWLEDGE/COURSES—**Therapy and Counseling; Psychology; Sociology and Anthropology; Philosophy and Theology; Mathematics; Education and Training.

Dental Assistants

- Personality Code: SR
- Growth: 42.5%
- Annual Job Openings: 35,000
- Annual Earnings: $27,700
- Education/Training Required: Moderate-term on-the-job training
- Self-Employed: 0%
- Part-Time: 35.6%

Assist dentist, set up patient and equipment, and keep records. Prepare patient, sterilize and disinfect instruments, set up instrument trays, prepare materials, and assist dentist during dental procedures. Expose dental diagnostic X rays. Record treatment information in patient records. Take and record medical and dental histories and vital signs of patients. Provide postoperative instructions prescribed by dentist. Assist dentist in management of medical and dental emergencies. Pour, trim, and polish study casts. Instruct patients in oral hygiene and plaque control programs. Make preliminary impressions for study casts and occlusal registrations for mounting study casts. Clean and polish removable appliances. Clean teeth, using dental instru-

ments. Apply protective coating of fluoride to teeth. Fabricate temporary restorations and custom impressions from preliminary impressions. Schedule appointments, prepare bills and receive payment for dental services, complete insurance forms, and maintain records, manually or using computer. **SKILLS—**Social Perceptiveness; Equipment Maintenance; Instructing; Management of Material Resources; Persuasion; Service Orientation; Time Management; Operation and Control.

GOE—Interest Area: 14. Medical and Health Services. **Work Group:** 14.03. Dentistry. **Other Jobs in This Work Group:** Dental Hygienists; Dentists, All Other Specialists; Dentists, General; Healthcare Support Workers, All Other; Oral and Maxillofacial Surgeons; Orthodontists; Prosthodontists.

EDUCATION/TRAINING PROGRAM(S)— Dental Assisting/Assistant. **RELATED KNOWLEDGE/COURSES—**Medicine and Dentistry; Customer and Personal Service; Clerical Studies; Chemistry; Psychology; Computers and Electronics.

Dental Hygienists

- Personality Code: SC
- Growth: 43.1%
- Annual Job Openings: 9,000
- Annual Earnings: $56,360
- Education/Training Required: Associate's degree
- Self-Employed: 0.7%
- Part-Time: 57.8%

Clean teeth and examine oral areas, head, and neck for signs of oral disease. May educate patients on oral hygiene, take and develop X rays, or apply fluoride or sealants. Clean calcareous deposits, accretions, and stains from teeth and beneath margins of gums, using dental instruments. Feel and visually examine gums for sores and signs of disease. Chart conditions of decay and disease for diagnosis and treatment by dentist. Feel lymph nodes under patient's chin to detect swelling or tenderness that could indicate presence of oral cancer. Apply fluorides and other cavity preventing agents to arrest dental decay. Examine gums, using probes, to locate periodontal recessed gums and signs of gum disease. Expose and develop X-ray film. Provide clinical services and health education to improve and maintain oral health of school children. Remove excess cement from coronal surfaces of teeth. Make impressions for study casts. Place, carve, and finish amalgam restorations. Administer local anesthetic agents. Conduct dental health clinics for community groups to augment services of dentist. **SKILLS**—Time Management; Active Learning; Social Perceptiveness; Instructing; Persuasion; Learning Strategies; Reading Comprehension; Service Orientation.

GOE—Interest Area: 14. Medical and Health Services. **Work Group:** 14.03. Dentistry. **Other Jobs in This Work Group:** Dental Assistants; Dentists, All Other Specialists; Dentists, General; Healthcare Support Workers, All Other; Oral and Maxillofacial Surgeons; Orthodontists; Prosthodontists.

EDUCATION/TRAINING PROGRAM(S)—Dental Hygiene/Hygienist. **RELATED KNOWLEDGE/COURSES**—Biology; Medicine and Dentistry; Customer and Personal Service; Psychology; Chemistry; Sales and Marketing.

Economics Teachers, Postsecondary

- ◉ Personality Code: SI
- ◉ Growth: 38.1%
- ◉ Annual Job Openings: 216,000
- ◉ Annual Earnings: $64,950
- ◉ Education/Training Required: Master's degree
- ◉ Self-Employed: 0.3%
- ◉ Part-Time: 27.7%

Teach courses in economics. Participate in campus and community events. Participate in student recruitment, registration, and placement activities. Perform administrative duties such as serving as department head. Provide professional consulting services to government and/or industry. Serve on academic or administrative committees that deal with institutional policies, departmental matters, and academic issues. Write grant proposals to procure external research funding. Evaluate and grade students' class work, assignments, and papers. Prepare and deliver lectures to undergraduate and/or graduate students on topics such as econometrics, price theory, and macroeconomics. Advise students on academic and vocational curricula, and on career issues. Compile, administer, and grade examinations, or assign this work to others. Compile bibliographies of specialized materials for outside reading assignments. Initiate, facilitate, and moderate classroom discussions. Keep abreast of developments in their field by reading current literature, talking with colleagues, and participating in professional conferences. Maintain regularly scheduled office hours in order to advise and assist students. Maintain student attendance records, grades, and other required records. Plan, evaluate, and revise curricula, course content, and course materials and methods of instruction. Prepare course materials such as syllabi, homework assignments, and handouts. Select and obtain materials and supplies such as textbooks. Supervise undergraduate and/or graduate teaching, internship, and research work. Act as advisers to student organizations. Collaborate with colleagues to address teaching and research issues. Conduct research in a particular field of knowledge, and publish findings in professional journals, books, and/or electronic media. **SKILLS**—Instructing; Learning Strategies; Reading Comprehension; Active Learning; Speaking; Writing; Science; Active Listening; Critical Thinking.

GOE—Interest Area: 12. Education and Social Service. **Work Group:** 12.03. Educational Services. **Other Jobs in This Work Group:** Adult Literacy, Remedial Education, and GED Teachers and

Social—E

Instructors; Agricultural Sciences Teachers, Postsecondary; Anthropology and Archeology Teachers, Postsecondary; Architecture Teachers, Postsecondary; Archivists; Area, Ethnic, and Cultural Studies Teachers, Postsecondary; Art, Drama, and Music Teachers, Postsecondary; Atmospheric, Earth, Marine, and Space Sciences Teachers, Postsecondary; Audio-Visual Collections Specialists; Biological Science Teachers, Postsecondary; Business Teachers, Postsecondary; Chemistry Teachers, Postsecondary; Child Care Workers; Communications Teachers, Postsecondary; Computer Science Teachers, Postsecondary; Criminal Justice and Law Enforcement Teachers, Postsecondary; Curators; Education Teachers, Postsecondary; Education, Training, and Library Workers, All Other; Educational Psychologists; Educational, Vocational, and School Counselors; Elementary School Teachers, Except Special Education; Engineering Teachers, Postsecondary; English Language and Literature Teachers, Postsecondary; Environmental Science Teachers, Postsecondary; Farm and Home Management Advisors; Foreign Language and Literature Teachers, Postsecondary; Forestry and Conservation Science Teachers, Postsecondary; Geography Teachers, Postsecondary; Graduate Teaching Assistants; Health Specialties Teachers, Postsecondary; History Teachers, Postsecondary; Home Economics Teachers, Postsecondary; Kindergarten Teachers, Except Special Education; Law Teachers, Postsecondary; Librarians; Library Assistants, Clerical; Library Science Teachers, Postsecondary; Library Technicians; Mathematical Science Teachers, Postsecondary; Middle School Teachers, Except Special and Vocational Education; Museum Technicians and Conservators; Nannies; Nursing Instructors and Teachers, Postsecondary; Personal Financial Advisors; Philosophy and Religion Teachers, Postsecondary; Physics Teachers, Postsecondary; Political Science Teachers, Postsecondary; Postsecondary Teachers, All Other; Preschool Teachers, Except Special Education; Psychology Teachers, Postsecondary; Recreation and Fitness Studies Teachers, Postsecondary; Secondary School Teachers, Except Special and Vocational Education; Self-Enrichment Education Teachers; Social Sciences Teachers, Postsecondary, All Other; Social Work Teachers, Postsecondary; Sociology Teachers, Postsecondary; Special Education Teachers, Middle School; Special Education Teachers, Preschool, Kindergarten, and Elementary School; Special Education Teachers, Secondary School; Teacher Assistants; Teachers and Instructors, All Other; Vocational Education Teachers, Postsecondary; Vocational Education Teachers, Middle School; Vocational Education Teachers, Secondary School.

EDUCATION/TRAINING PROGRAM(S)— Applied Economics; Business/Managerial Economics; Development Economics and International Development; Econometrics and Quantitative Economics; Economics, General; Economics, Other; International Economics; Social Science Teacher Education. **RELATED KNOWLEDGE/COURSES—**Sociology and Anthropology; History and Archeology; Education and Training; Psychology; Economics and Accounting; English Language.

Education Administrators, Elementary and Secondary School

- Personality Code: SE
- Growth: 20.7%
- Annual Job Openings: 31,000
- Annual Earnings: $73,490
- Education/Training Required: Work experience plus degree
- Self-Employed: 3.2%
- Part-Time: 7.2%

Plan, direct, or coordinate the academic, clerical, or auxiliary activities of public or private elemen-

tary or secondary level schools. Write articles, manuals, and other publications, and assist in the distribution of promotional literature about facilities and programs. Advocate for new schools to be built, or for existing facilities to be repaired or remodeled. Establish, coordinate, and oversee particular programs across school districts, such as programs to evaluate student academic achievement. Plan and develop instructional methods and content for educational, vocational, or student activity programs. Prepare and submit budget requests and recommendations, or grant proposals to solicit program funding. Prepare, maintain, or oversee the preparation/maintenance of attendance, activity, planning, or personnel reports and records. Recommend personnel actions related to programs and services. Recruit, hire, train, and evaluate primary and supplemental staff. Review and approve new programs, or recommend modifications to existing programs, submitting program proposals for school board approval as necessary. Set educational standards and goals, and help establish policies and procedures to carry them out. Collect and analyze survey data, regulatory information, and data on demographic and employment trends to forecast enrollment patterns and curriculum change needs. Confer with parents and staff to discuss educational activities, policies, and student behavioral or learning problems. Counsel and provide guidance to students regarding personal, academic, vocational, or behavioral issues. Develop partnerships with businesses, communities, and other organizations to help meet identified educational needs and to provide school-to-work programs. Direct and coordinate school maintenance services and the use of school facilities. Enforce discipline and attendance rules. Organize and direct committees of specialists, volunteers, and staff to provide technical and advisory assistance for programs. Review and interpret government codes, and develop programs to ensure adherence to codes and facility safety, security, and maintenance. Teach classes or courses to students. Direct and coordinate activities of teachers, administrators, and support staff at schools, public agencies, and institutions. **SKILLS**—Management of

Financial Resources; Management of Personnel Resources; Management of Material Resources; Systems Analysis; Systems Evaluation; Coordination; Learning Strategies; Writing.

GOE—Interest Area: 12. Education and Social Service. **Work Group:** 12.01. Managerial Work in Education and Social Service. **Other Jobs in This Work Group:** Education Administrators, All Other; Education Administrators, Postsecondary; Education Administrators, Preschool and Child Care Center/Program; Instructional Coordinators; Park Naturalists; Social and Community Service Managers.

EDUCATION/TRAINING PROGRAM(S)—Educational Administration and Supervision, Other; Educational Leadership and Administration, General; Educational, Instructional, and Curriculum Supervision; Elementary and Middle School Administration/Principalship; Secondary School Administration/Principalship. **RELATED KNOWLEDGE/COURSES**—Education and Training; Sales and Marketing; Personnel and Human Resources; Administration and Management; Economics and Accounting; English Language.

Educational, Vocational, and School Counselors

- Personality Code: SA
- Growth: 15.0%
- Annual Job Openings: 32,000
- Annual Earnings: $44,640
- Education/Training Required: Master's degree
- Self-Employed: 4.4%
- Part-Time: 14.6%

Counsel individuals and provide group educational and vocational guidance services. Assess needs

Social—E

for assistance such as rehabilitation, financial aid, or additional vocational training, and refer clients to the appropriate services. Compile and study occupational, educational, and economic information to assist counselees in determining and carrying out vocational and educational objectives. Conduct follow-up interviews with counselees to determine if their needs have been met. Confer with parents or guardians, teachers, other counselors, and administrators to resolve students' behavioral, academic, and other problems. Enforce all administration policies and rules governing students. Establish and enforce behavioral rules and procedures to maintain order among students. Establish and supervise peer counseling and peer tutoring programs. Instruct individuals in career development techniques such as job search and application strategies, resume writing, and interview skills. Interview clients to obtain information about employment history, educational background, and career goals, and to identify barriers to employment. Maintain accurate and complete student records as required by laws, district policies, and administrative regulations. Meet with other professionals to discuss individual students' needs and progress. Counsel individuals to help them understand and overcome personal, social, or behavioral problems affecting their educational or vocational situations. Counsel students regarding educational issues such as course and program selection, class scheduling, school adjustment, truancy, study habits, and career planning. Evaluate individuals' abilities, interests, and personality characteristics using tests, records, interviews, and professional sources. Address community groups, faculty, and staff members to explain available counseling services. Meet with parents and guardians to discuss their children's progress, and to determine their priorities for their children and their resource needs. Observe and evaluate students' performance, behavior, social development, and physical health. Plan and conduct orientation programs and group conferences to promote the adjustment of individuals to new life experiences such as starting college. **SKILLS**—Service Orientation; Social Perceptiveness; Active Listening; Speaking; Systems Evaluation; Instructing; Reading Comprehension; Active Learning.

GOE—Interest Area: 12. Education and Social Service. **Work Group:** 12.03. Educational Services. **Other Jobs in This Work Group:** Adult Literacy, Remedial Education, and GED Teachers and Instructors; Agricultural Sciences Teachers, Postsecondary; Anthropology and Archeology Teachers, Postsecondary; Architecture Teachers, Postsecondary; Archivists; Area, Ethnic, and Cultural Studies Teachers, Postsecondary; Art, Drama, and Music Teachers, Postsecondary; Atmospheric, Earth, Marine, and Space Sciences Teachers, Postsecondary; Audio-Visual Collections Specialists; Biological Science Teachers, Postsecondary; Business Teachers, Postsecondary; Chemistry Teachers, Postsecondary; Child Care Workers; Communications Teachers, Postsecondary; Computer Science Teachers, Postsecondary; Criminal Justice and Law Enforcement Teachers, Postsecondary; Curators; Economics Teachers, Postsecondary; Education Teachers, Postsecondary; Education, Training, and Library Workers, All Other; Educational Psychologists; Elementary School Teachers, Except Special Education; Engineering Teachers, Postsecondary; English Language and Literature Teachers, Postsecondary; Environmental Science Teachers, Postsecondary; Farm and Home Management Advisors; Foreign Language and Literature Teachers, Postsecondary; Forestry and Conservation Science Teachers, Postsecondary; Geography Teachers, Postsecondary; Graduate Teaching Assistants; Health Specialties Teachers, Postsecondary; History Teachers, Postsecondary; Home Economics Teachers, Postsecondary; Kindergarten Teachers, Except Special Education; Law Teachers, Postsecondary; Librarians; Library Assistants, Clerical; Library Science Teachers, Postsecondary; Library Technicians; Mathematical Science Teachers, Postsecondary; Middle School Teachers, Except Special and Vocational Education; Museum Technicians and Conservators; Nannies; Nursing Instructors and Teachers, Postsecondary; Personal Financial Advisors; Philosophy and Religion Teachers, Postsecondary; Physics

Teachers, Postsecondary; Political Science Teachers, Postsecondary; Postsecondary Teachers, All Other; Preschool Teachers, Except Special Education; Psychology Teachers, Postsecondary; Recreation and Fitness Studies Teachers, Postsecondary; Secondary School Teachers, Except Special and Vocational Education; Self-Enrichment Education Teachers; Social Sciences Teachers, Postsecondary, All Other; Social Work Teachers, Postsecondary; Sociology Teachers, Postsecondary; Special Education Teachers, Middle School; Special Education Teachers, Preschool, Kindergarten, and Elementary School; Special Education Teachers, Secondary School; Teacher Assistants; Teachers and Instructors, All Other; Vocational Education Teachers, Postsecondary; Vocational Education Teachers, Middle School; Vocational Education Teachers, Secondary School.

EDUCATION/TRAINING PROGRAM(S)— College Student Counseling and Personnel Services; Counselor Education/School Counseling and Guidance Services. **RELATED KNOWLEDGE/ COURSES**—Therapy and Counseling; Psychology; Education and Training; Sociology and Anthropology; English Language; Personnel and Human Resources.

Elementary School Teachers, Except Special Education

- Personality Code: SA
- Growth: 15.2%
- Annual Job Openings: 183,000
- Annual Earnings: $42,160
- Education/Training Required: Bachelor's degree
- Self-Employed: 0.1%
- Part-Time: 9.2%

Teach pupils in public or private schools at the elementary level basic academic, social, and other formative skills. Plan and conduct activities for a balanced program of instruction, demonstration, and work time that provides students with opportunities to observe, question, and investigate. Plan and supervise class projects, field trips, visits by guest speakers or other experiential activities, and guide students in learning from those activities. Prepare and implement remedial programs for students requiring extra help. Prepare for assigned classes, and show written evidence of preparation upon request of immediate supervisors. Prepare materials and classrooms for class activities. Prepare objectives and outlines for courses of study, following curriculum guidelines or requirements of states and schools. Prepare reports on students and activities as required by administration. Prepare students for later grades by encouraging them to explore learning opportunities and to persevere with challenging tasks. Provide a variety of materials and resources for children to explore, manipulate and use, both in learning activities and in imaginative play. Read books to entire classes or small groups. Supervise, evaluate, and plan assignments for teacher assistants and volunteers. Establish clear objectives for all lessons, units, and projects, and communicate those objectives to students. Instruct students individually and in groups, using various teaching methods such as lectures, discussions, and demonstrations. Prepare, administer, and grade tests and assignments in order to evaluate students' progress. Assign and grade class work and homework. Adapt teaching methods and instructional materials to meet students' varying needs and interests. Confer with other staff members to plan and schedule lessons promoting learning, following approved curricula. Confer with parents or guardians, teachers, counselors, and administrators in order to resolve students' behavioral and academic problems. Enforce administration policies and rules governing students. Establish and enforce rules for behavior and procedures for maintaining order among the students for whom they are responsible. Guide and counsel students with adjustment and/or academic problems or special academic interests. SKILLS— Learning Strategies; Social Perceptiveness; Instructing; Service Orientation; Science; Speaking; Coordination; Time Management.

GOE—Interest Area: 12. Education and Social Service. Work Group: 12.03. Educational Services. Other Jobs in This Work Group: Adult Literacy, Remedial Education, and GED Teachers and Instructors; Agricultural Sciences Teachers, Postsecondary; Anthropology and Archeology Teachers, Postsecondary; Architecture Teachers, Postsecondary; Archivists; Area, Ethnic, and Cultural Studies Teachers, Postsecondary; Art, Drama, and Music Teachers, Postsecondary; Atmospheric, Earth, Marine, and Space Sciences Teachers, Postsecondary; Audio-Visual Collections Specialists; Biological Science Teachers, Postsecondary; Business Teachers, Postsecondary; Chemistry Teachers, Postsecondary; Child Care Workers; Communications Teachers, Postsecondary; Computer Science Teachers, Postsecondary; Criminal Justice and Law Enforcement Teachers, Postsecondary; Curators; Economics Teachers, Postsecondary; Education Teachers, Postsecondary; Education, Training, and Library Workers, All Other; Educational Psychologists; Educational, Vocational, and School Counselors; Engineering Teachers, Postsecondary; English Language and Literature Teachers, Postsecondary; Environmental Science Teachers, Postsecondary; Farm and Home Management Advisors; Foreign Language and Literature Teachers, Postsecondary; Forestry and Conservation Science Teachers, Postsecondary; Geography Teachers, Postsecondary; Graduate Teaching Assistants; Health Specialties Teachers, Postsecondary; History Teachers, Postsecondary; Home Economics Teachers, Postsecondary; Kindergarten Teachers, Except Special Education; Law Teachers, Postsecondary; Librarians; Library Assistants, Clerical; Library Science Teachers, Postsecondary; Library Technicians; Mathematical Science Teachers, Postsecondary; Middle School Teachers, Except Special and Vocational Education; Museum Technicians and Conservators; Nannies; Nursing Instructors and Teachers, Postsecondary; Personal Financial Advisors; Philosophy and Religion Teach-

ers, Postsecondary; Physics Teachers, Postsecondary; Political Science Teachers, Postsecondary; Postsecondary Teachers, All Other; Preschool Teachers, Except Special Education; Psychology Teachers, Postsecondary; Recreation and Fitness Studies Teachers, Postsecondary; Secondary School Teachers, Except Special and Vocational Education; Self-Enrichment Education Teachers; Social Sciences Teachers, Postsecondary, All Other; Social Work Teachers, Postsecondary; Sociology Teachers, Postsecondary; Special Education Teachers, Middle School; Special Education Teachers, Preschool, Kindergarten, and Elementary School; Special Education Teachers, Secondary School; Teacher Assistants; Teachers and Instructors, All Other; Vocational Education Teachers, Postsecondary; Vocational Education Teachers, Middle School; Vocational Education Teachers, Secondary School.

EDUCATION/TRAINING PROGRAM(S)— Elementary Education and Teaching; Teacher Education, Multiple Levels. RELATED KNOWLEDGE/COURSES—Geography; History and Archeology; Education and Training; Sociology and Anthropology; Therapy and Counseling; Psychology.

Emergency Medical Technicians and Paramedics

- ◎ Personality Code: SR
- ◎ Growth: 33.1%
- ◎ Annual Job Openings: 32,000
- ◎ Annual Earnings: $24,440
- ◎ Education/Training Required: Postsecondary vocational training
- ◎ Self-Employed: 0.8%
- ◎ Part-Time: 8.4%

Assess injuries, administer emergency medical care, and extricate trapped individuals. Transport injured or sick persons to medical facilities. Administer first-aid treatment and life-support care to sick or injured persons in prehospital setting. Operate equipment such as EKGs, external defibrillators and bag-valve mask resuscitators in advanced life-support environments. Assess nature and extent of illness or injury to establish and prioritize medical procedures. Maintain vehicles and medical and communication equipment, and replenish first-aid equipment and supplies. Observe, record, and report to physician the patient's condition or injury, the treatment provided, and reactions to drugs and treatment. Perform emergency diagnostic and treatment procedures, such as stomach suction, airway management and heart monitoring, during ambulance ride. Administer drugs, orally or by injection, and perform intravenous procedures under a physician's direction. Comfort and reassure patients. Coordinate work with other emergency medical team members and police and fire department personnel. Communicate with dispatchers and treatment center personnel to provide information about situation, to arrange reception of victims, and to receive instructions for further treatment. Immobilize patient for placement on stretcher and ambulance transport, using backboard or other spinal immobilization device. Decontaminate ambulance interior following treatment of patient with infectious disease and report case to proper authorities. Drive mobile intensive care unit to specified location, following instructions from emergency medical dispatcher. Coordinate with treatment center personnel to obtain patients' vital statistics and medical history, to determine the circumstances of the emergency, and to administer emergency treatment. **SKILLS**—Equipment Maintenance; Social Perceptiveness; Service Orientation; Coordination; Instructing; Negotiation; Critical Thinking; Speaking; Persuasion.

GOE—Interest Area: 04. Law, Law Enforcement, and Public Safety. **Work Group:** 04.04. Public Safety. **Other Jobs in This Work Group:** Agricultural

Inspectors; Aviation Inspectors; Compliance Officers, Except Agriculture, Construction, Health and Safety, and Transportation; Environmental Compliance Inspectors; Equal Opportunity Representatives and Officers; Financial Examiners; Fire Fighters; Fire Inspectors; Fire Inspectors and Investigators; Forest Fire Fighters; Forest Fire Inspectors and Prevention Specialists; Government Property Inspectors and Investigators; Licensing Examiners and Inspectors; Marine Cargo Inspectors; Municipal Fire Fighters; Nuclear Monitoring Technicians; Occupational Health and Safety Specialists; Occupational Health and Safety Technicians; Protective Service Workers, All Other; Public Transportation Inspectors.

EDUCATION/TRAINING PROGRAM(S)—Emergency Care Attendant (EMT Ambulance); Emergency Medical Technology/Technician (EMT Paramedic). **RELATED KNOWLEDGE/COURSES**—Customer and Personal Service; Medicine and Dentistry; Psychology; Public Safety and Security; Chemistry; Therapy and Counseling.

Employment Interviewers, Private or Public Employment Service

- Personality Code: SE
- Growth: 27.3%
- Annual Job Openings: 29,000
- Annual Earnings: $40,770
- Education/Training Required: Bachelor's degree
- Self-Employed: 0.8%
- Part-Time: 7.7%

Social—E

Interview job applicants in employment office and refer them to prospective employers for consideration. Search application files, notify selected applicants of job openings, and refer qualified applicants to prospective employers. Contact employers to verify referral results. Record and evaluate various pertinent data. Inform applicants of job openings and details such as duties and responsibilities, compensation, benefits, schedules, working conditions, and promotion opportunities. Interview job applicants to match their qualifications with employers' needs, recording and evaluating applicant experience, education, training, and skills. Review employment applications and job orders to match applicants with job requirements, using manual or computerized file searches. Select qualified applicants or refer them to employers, according to organization policy. Perform reference and background checks on applicants. Maintain records of applicants not selected for employment. Instruct job applicants in presenting a positive image by providing help with resume writing, personal appearance, and interview techniques. Refer applicants to services such as vocational counseling, literacy or language instruction, transportation assistance, vocational training and child care. Contact employers to solicit orders for job vacancies, determining their requirements and recording relevant data such as job descriptions. Conduct workshops and demonstrate the use of job listings to assist applicants with skill building. Search for and recruit applicants for open positions through campus job fairs and advertisements. Provide background information on organizations with which interviews are scheduled. Administer assessment tests to identify skill building needs. Conduct or arrange for skill, intelligence, or psychological testing of applicants and current employees. Hire workers and place them with employers needing temporary help. Evaluate selection and testing techniques by conducting research or follow-up activities and conferring with management and supervisory personnel. **SKILLS—** Service Orientation; Social Perceptiveness; Persuasion; Management of Personnel Resources; Negotiation; Instructing; Speaking; Time Management.

GOE—Interest Area: 13. General Management and Support. **Work Group:** 13.02. Management Support. **Other Jobs in This Work Group:** Accountants; Accountants and Auditors; Appraisers and Assessors of Real Estate; Appraisers, Real Estate; Assessors; Auditors; Budget Analysts; Business Operations Specialists, All Other; Claims Adjusters, Examiners, and Investigators; Claims Examiners, Property and Casualty Insurance; Compensation, Benefits, and Job Analysis Specialists; Cost Estimators; Credit Analysts; Employment, Recruitment, and Placement Specialists; Financial Analysts; Human Resources, Training, and Labor Relations Specialists, All Other; Insurance Adjusters, Examiners, and Investigators; Insurance Appraisers, Auto Damage; Insurance Underwriters; Loan Counselors; Loan Officers; Logisticians; Management Analysts; Market Research Analysts; Personnel Recruiters; Purchasing Agents and Buyers, Farm Products; Purchasing Agents, Except Wholesale, Retail, and Farm Products; Tax Examiners, Collectors, and Revenue Agents; Training and Development Specialists; Wholesale and Retail Buyers, Except Farm Products.

EDUCATION/TRAINING PROGRAM(S)— Human Resources Management/Personnel Administration, General; Labor and Industrial Relations. **RELATED KNOWLEDGE/COURSES—** Customer and Personal Service; Clerical Studies; Foreign Language; Personnel and Human Resources; English Language; Sales and Marketing.

Fitness Trainers and Aerobics Instructors

- Personality Code: SR
- Growth: 44.5%
- Annual Job Openings: 38,000
- Annual Earnings: $24,510
- Education/Training Required: Postsecondary vocational training
- Self-Employed: 5.4%
- Part-Time: 35.6%

Instruct or coach groups or individuals in exercise activities and the fundamentals of sports. Demonstrate techniques and methods of participation. Observe participants and inform them of corrective measures necessary to improve their skills. Those required to hold teaching degrees should be reported in the appropriate teaching category. Explain and enforce safety rules and regulations governing sports, recreational activities, and the use of exercise equipment. Offer alternatives during classes to accommodate different levels of fitness. Plan routines, choose appropriate music, and choose different movements for each set of muscles, depending on participants' capabilities and limitations. Observe participants and inform them of corrective measures necessary for skill improvement. Teach proper breathing techniques used during physical exertion. Instruct participants in maintaining exertion levels in order to maximize benefits from exercise routines. Teach and demonstrate use of gymnastic and training equipment such as trampolines and weights. Maintain fitness equipment. Conduct therapeutic, recreational, or athletic activities. Monitor participants' progress and adapt programs as needed. Evaluate individuals' abilities, needs, and physical conditions, and develop suitable training programs to meet any special requirements. Plan physical education programs to promote development of participants' physical attributes and social skills. Provide students with information and resources regarding nutrition, weight control, and lifestyle issues. Administer emergency first aid, wrap injuries, treat minor chronic disabilities, or refer injured persons to physicians. Advise clients about proper clothing and shoes. Wrap ankles, fingers, wrists, or other body parts with synthetic skin, gauze, or adhesive tape, in order to support muscles and ligaments. Teach individual and team sports to participants through instruction and demonstration, utilizing knowledge of sports techniques and of participants' physical capabilities. Promote health clubs through membership sales and record member information. Organize, lead, and referee indoor and outdoor games such as volleyball, baseball, and basketball. Maintain equipment inventories; and select, store, and issue equipment as needed. Organize and conduct competitions and tournaments. Advise participants in use of heat or ultraviolet treatments and hot baths. Massage body parts to relieve soreness, strains, and bruises. **SKILLS**—Instructing; Service Orientation; Coordination; Monitoring; Equipment Selection; Time Management; Social Perceptiveness; Learning Strategies.

GOE—Interest Area: 01. Arts, Entertainment, and Media. **Work Group:** 01.10. Sports: Coaching, Instructing, Officiating, and Performing. **Other Jobs in This Work Group:** Agents and Business Managers of Artists, Performers, and Athletes; Art Directors; Athletes and Sports Competitors; Coaches and Scouts; Entertainers and Performers, Sports and Related Workers, All Other; Producers; Producers and Directors; Program Directors; Technical Directors/Managers; Umpires, Referees, and Other Sports Officials.

EDUCATION/TRAINING PROGRAM(S)— Health and Physical Education, General; Physical Education Teaching and Coaching; Sport and Fitness Administration/Management. **RELATED KNOWLEDGE/COURSES**—Customer and Personal Service; Education and Training; Psychology; Medicine and Dentistry; Sociology and Anthropology; Fine Arts.

Social–F

Graduate Teaching Assistants

- Personality Code: SI
- Growth: 38.1%
- Annual Job Openings: 216,000
- Annual Earnings: $24,570
- Education/Training Required: Master's degree
- Self-Employed: 0.3%
- Part-Time: 27.7%

Assist department chairperson, faculty members, or other professional staff members in college or university by performing teaching or teaching-related duties, such as teaching lower level courses, developing teaching materials, preparing and giving examinations, and grading examinations or papers. Graduate assistants must be enrolled in a graduate school program. Graduate assistants who primarily perform non-teaching duties, such as laboratory research, should be reported in the occupational category related to the work performed. Provide instructors with assistance in the use of audiovisual equipment. Provide assistance to library staff in maintaining library collections. Evaluate and grade examinations, assignments, and papers, and record grades. Lead discussion sections, tutorials, and laboratory sections. Teach undergraduate level courses. Develop teaching materials such as syllabi, visual aids, answer keys, supplementary notes, and course websites. Attend lectures given by the instructor whom they are assisting. Complete laboratory projects prior to assigning them to students so that any needed modifications can be made. Copy and distribute classroom materials. Demonstrate use of laboratory equipment, and enforce laboratory rules. Inform students of the procedures for completing and submitting class work such as lab reports. Meet with supervisors to discuss students' grades, and to complete required grade-related paperwork. Notify instructors of errors or problems with assignments. Order or obtain materials needed for classes. Prepare and proctor examinations. Return assignments to students in accordance with established deadlines. Schedule and maintain regular office hours to meet with students. Arrange for supervisors to conduct teaching observations; meet with supervisors to receive feedback about teaching performance. Assist faculty members or staff with student conferences. Provide assistance to faculty members or staff with laboratory or field research. SKILLS—Instructing; Learning Strategies; Speaking; Reading Comprehension; Science; Writing; Critical Thinking; Mathematics; Active Learning.

GOE—Interest Area: 12. Education and Social Service. Work Group: 12.03. Educational Services. Other Jobs in This Work Group: Adult Literacy, Remedial Education, and GED Teachers and Instructors; Agricultural Sciences Teachers, Postsecondary; Anthropology and Archeology Teachers, Postsecondary; Architecture Teachers, Postsecondary; Archivists; Area, Ethnic, and Cultural Studies Teachers, Postsecondary; Art, Drama, and Music Teachers, Postsecondary; Atmospheric, Earth, Marine, and Space Sciences Teachers, Postsecondary; Audio-Visual Collections Specialists; Biological Science Teachers, Postsecondary; Business Teachers, Postsecondary; Chemistry Teachers, Postsecondary; Child Care Workers; Communications Teachers, Postsecondary; Computer Science Teachers, Postsecondary; Criminal Justice and Law Enforcement Teachers, Postsecondary; Curators; Economics Teachers, Postsecondary; Education Teachers, Postsecondary; Education, Training, and Library Workers, All Other; Educational Psychologists; Educational, Vocational, and School Counselors; Elementary School Teachers, Except Special Education; Engineering Teachers, Postsecondary; English Language and Literature Teachers, Postsecondary; Environmental Science Teachers, Postsecondary; Farm and Home Management Advisors; Foreign Language and Literature Teachers, Postsecondary; Forestry and Conservation Science Teachers, Postsecondary; Geography Teachers,

Postsecondary; Health Specialties Teachers, Postsecondary; History Teachers, Postsecondary; Home Economics Teachers, Postsecondary; Kindergarten Teachers, Except Special Education; Law Teachers, Postsecondary; Librarians; Library Assistants, Clerical; Library Science Teachers, Postsecondary; Library Technicians; Mathematical Science Teachers, Postsecondary; Middle School Teachers, Except Special and Vocational Education; Museum Technicians and Conservators; Nannies; Nursing Instructors and Teachers, Postsecondary; Personal Financial Advisors; Philosophy and Religion Teachers, Postsecondary; Physics Teachers, Postsecondary; Political Science Teachers, Postsecondary; Postsecondary Teachers, All Other; Preschool Teachers, Except Special Education; Psychology Teachers, Postsecondary; Recreation and Fitness Studies Teachers, Postsecondary; Secondary School Teachers, Except Special and Vocational Education; Self-Enrichment Education Teachers; Social Sciences Teachers, Postsecondary, All Other; Social Work Teachers, Postsecondary; Sociology Teachers, Postsecondary; Special Education Teachers, Middle School; Special Education Teachers, Preschool, Kindergarten, and Elementary School; Special Education Teachers, Secondary School; Teacher Assistants; Teachers and Instructors, All Other; Vocational Education Teachers, Postsecondary; Vocational Education Teachers, Middle School; Vocational Education Teachers, Secondary School.

EDUCATION/TRAINING PROGRAM(S)— No data available. RELATED KNOWLEDGE/ COURSES—Education and Training; English Language; Clerical Studies; Mathematics; Administration and Management; Computers and Electronics.

History Teachers, Postsecondary

- Personality Code: SI
- Growth: 38.1%
- Annual Job Openings: 216,000
- Annual Earnings: $52,180
- Education/Training Required: Master's degree
- Self-Employed: 0.3%
- Part-Time: 27.7%

Teach courses in human history and historiography. Perform administrative duties such as serving as department head. Provide professional consulting services to government, educational institutions, and/or industry. Serve on academic or administrative committees that deal with institutional policies, departmental matters, and academic issues. Write grant proposals to procure external research funding. Evaluate and grade students' class work, assignments, and papers. Prepare and deliver lectures to undergraduate and/or graduate students on topics such as ancient history, postwar civilizations, and the history of third-world countries. Advise students on academic and vocational curricula, and on career issues. Compile, administer, and grade examinations, or assign this work to others. Compile bibliographies of specialized materials for outside reading assignments. Initiate, facilitate, and moderate classroom discussions. Keep abreast of developments in their field by reading current literature, talking with colleagues, and participating in professional conferences. Maintain regularly scheduled office hours in order to advise and assist students. Maintain student attendance records, grades, and other required records. Plan, evaluate, and revise curricula, course content, and course materials and methods of instruction. Prepare course materials such as syllabi, homework assignments, and handouts. Select and obtain materials and supplies such as textbooks. Supervise undergraduate and/or graduate teaching, internship, and research work. Act as advisers to student organizations. Collaborate with colleagues to address teaching and research issues. Conduct research in a particular field of knowledge, and publish findings in professional journals, books, and/or electronic media. Participate in campus and community events. Participate in student recruitment, registration, and placement activities. **SKILLS—** Instructing; Learning Strategies; Reading Comprehension; Active Learning; Speaking; Writing; Science; Active Listening; Critical Thinking.

GOE—Interest Area: 12. Education and Social Service. **Work Group:** 12.03. Educational Services. **Other Jobs in This Work Group:** Adult Literacy, Remedial Education, and GED Teachers and Instructors; Agricultural Sciences Teachers, Postsecondary; Anthropology and Archeology Teachers, Postsecondary; Architecture Teachers, Postsecondary; Archivists; Area, Ethnic, and Cultural Studies Teachers, Postsecondary; Art, Drama, and Music Teachers, Postsecondary; Atmospheric, Earth, Marine, and Space Sciences Teachers, Postsecondary; Audio-Visual Collections Specialists; Biological Science Teachers, Postsecondary; Business Teachers, Postsecondary; Chemistry Teachers, Postsecondary; Child Care Workers; Communications Teachers, Postsecondary; Computer Science Teachers, Postsecondary; Criminal Justice and Law Enforcement Teachers, Postsecondary; Curators; Economics Teachers, Postsecondary; Education Teachers, Postsecondary; Education, Training, and Library Workers, All Other; Educational Psychologists; Educational, Vocational, and School Counselors; Elementary School Teachers, Except Special Education; Engineering Teachers, Postsecondary; English Language and Literature Teachers, Postsecondary; Environmental Science Teachers, Postsecondary; Farm and Home Management Advisors; Foreign Language and Literature Teachers, Postsecondary; Forestry and Conservation Science Teachers, Postsecondary; Geography Teachers, Postsecondary; Graduate Teaching Assistants; Health Specialties Teachers, Postsecondary; Home Economics Teachers, Postsecondary; Kindergarten Teachers, Except Special Education; Law Teachers, Postsecondary; Librarians; Library Assistants, Clerical; Library Science Teachers, Postsecondary; Library Technicians; Mathematical Science Teachers, Postsecondary; Middle School Teachers, Except Special and Vocational Education; Museum Technicians and Conservators; Nannies; Nursing Instructors and Teachers, Postsecondary; Personal Financial Advisors; Philosophy and Religion Teachers, Postsecondary; Physics Teachers, Postsecondary; Political Science Teachers, Postsecondary; Postsecondary Teachers, All Other; Preschool Teachers, Except Special Education; Psychology Teachers, Postsecondary; Recreation and Fitness Studies Teachers, Postsecondary; Secondary School Teachers, Except Special and Vocational Education; Self-Enrichment Education Teachers; Social Sciences Teachers, Postsecondary, All Other; Social Work Teachers, Postsecondary; Sociology Teachers, Postsecondary; Special Education Teachers, Middle School; Special Education Teachers, Preschool, Kindergarten, and Elementary School; Special Education Teachers, Secondary School; Teacher Assistants; Teachers and Instructors, All Other; Vocational Education Teachers, Postsecondary; Vocational Education Teachers, Middle School; Vocational Education Teachers, Secondary School.

EDUCATION/TRAINING PROGRAM(S)— American History (United States); Asian History; Canadian History; European History; History and Philosophy of Science and Technology; History, General; History, Other; Public/Applied History and Archival Administration. **RELATED KNOWLEDGE/COURSES—**Sociology and Anthropology; History and Archeology; Education and Training; Psychology; Economics and Accounting; English Language.

Home Health Aides

- Personality Code: SR
- Growth: 48.1%
- Annual Job Openings: 141,000
- Annual Earnings: $18,240
- Education/Training Required: Short-term on-the-job training
- Self-Employed: 1.6%
- Part-Time: 21.9%

Provide routine, personal healthcare, such as bathing, dressing, or grooming, to elderly, convalescent, or disabled persons in the home of patients or in a residential care facility. Maintain records of patient care, condition, progress, and problems in order to report and discuss observations with a supervisor or case manager. Provide patients with help moving in and out of beds, baths, wheelchairs or automobiles, and with dressing and grooming. Provide patients and families with emotional support and instruction in areas such as infant care, preparing healthy meals, independent living, and adaptation to disability or illness. Change bed linens, wash and iron patients' laundry, and clean patients' quarters. Entertain, converse with, or read aloud to patients to keep them mentally healthy and alert. Plan, purchase, prepare, and serve meals to patients and other family members, according to prescribed diets. Direct patients in simple prescribed exercises and in the use of braces or artificial limbs. Check patients' pulse, temperature and respiration. Change dressings. Perform a variety of duties as requested by client, such as obtaining household supplies and running errands. Accompany clients to doctors' offices and on other trips outside the home, providing transportation, assistance and companionship. Administer prescribed oral medications under written direction of physician or as directed by home care nurse and aide. Care for children who are disabled or who have sick or disabled parents. Massage patients and apply preparations and treatments, such as liniment, alcohol rubs, and heat-

lamp stimulation. **SKILLS**—Social Perceptiveness; Service Orientation; Instructing; Reading Comprehension; Writing; Persuasion; Active Listening; Learning Strategies; Monitoring.

GOE—Interest Area: 14. Medical and Health Services. **Work Group:** 14.07. Patient Care and Assistance. **Other Jobs in This Work Group:** Licensed Practical and Licensed Vocational Nurses; Nursing Aides, Orderlies, and Attendants; Psychiatric Aides; Psychiatric Technicians.

EDUCATION/TRAINING PROGRAM(S)—Home Health Aide/Home Attendant. **RELATED KNOWLEDGE/COURSES**—Medicine and Dentistry; Psychology; Therapy and Counseling; Philosophy and Theology; Customer and Personal Service; Public Safety and Security.

Instructional Coordinators

- Personality Code: SI
- Growth: 25.4%
- Annual Job Openings: 18,000
- Annual Earnings: $47,470
- Education/Training Required: Master's degree
- Self-Employed: 2.7%
- Part-Time: 16.5%

Develop instructional material, coordinate educational content, and incorporate current technology in specialized fields that provide guidelines to educators and instructors for developing curricula and conducting courses. Advise teaching and administrative staff in curriculum development, use of materials and equipment, and implementation of state and federal programs and procedures. Research, evaluate, and prepare recommendations on curricula, instructional methods, and materials for school systems. Update the content of educational programs to ensure that students are being trained with equipment and processes that are technologically current. Confer with members of educational committees and advisory groups to obtain knowledge of subject areas, and to relate curriculum materials to specific subjects, individual student needs, and occupational areas. Coordinate activities of workers engaged in cataloging, distributing, and maintaining educational materials and equipment in curriculum libraries and laboratories. Develop classroom-based and distance learning training courses, using needs assessments and skill level analyses. Develop instructional materials to be used by educators and instructors. Develop tests, questionnaires, and procedures that measure the effectiveness of curricula, and use these tools to determine whether program objectives are being met. Organize production and design of curriculum materials. Prepare or approve manuals, guidelines, and reports on state educational policies and practices for distribution to school districts. Recommend, order, or authorize purchase of instructional materials, supplies, equipment, and visual aids designed to meet student educational needs and district standards. Advise and teach students. Conduct or participate in workshops, committees, and conferences designed to promote the intellectual, social, and physical welfare of students. Inspect instructional equipment to determine if repairs are needed; authorize necessary repairs. Observe work of teaching staff in order to evaluate performance, and to recommend changes that could strengthen teaching skills. Plan and conduct teacher training programs and conferences dealing with new classroom procedures, instructional materials and equipment, and teaching aids. Prepare grant proposals, budgets, and program policies and goals, or assist in their preparation. **SKILLS**—Learning Strategies; Instructing; Management of Personnel Resources; Speaking; Systems Analysis; Writing; Management of Financial Resources; Systems Evaluation.

GOE—Interest Area: 12. Education and Social Service. **Work Group:** 12.01. Managerial Work in Education and Social Service. **Other Jobs in This Work**

Group: Education Administrators, All Other; Education Administrators, Elementary and Secondary School; Education Administrators, Postsecondary; Education Administrators, Preschool and Child Care Center/Program; Park Naturalists; Social and Community Service Managers.

EDUCATION/TRAINING PROGRAM(S)— Curriculum and Instruction; Educational/Instructional Media Design. **RELATED KNOWLEDGE/ COURSES**—Education and Training; Personnel and Human Resources; Psychology; Administration and Management; English Language; Economics and Accounting.

Kindergarten Teachers, Except Special Education

- Personality Code: SA
- Growth: 27.2%
- Annual Job Openings: 34,000
- Annual Earnings: $40,160
- Education/Training Required: Bachelor's degree
- Self-Employed: 2.2%
- Part-Time: 24.9%

Teach elemental natural and social science, personal hygiene, music, art, and literature to children from 4 to 6 years old. Promote physical, mental, and social development. May be required to hold State certification. Identify children showing signs of emotional, developmental, or health-related problems, and discuss them with supervisors, parents or guardians, and child development specialists. Instruct and monitor students in the use and care of equipment and materials, in order to prevent injuries and damage. Maintain accurate and complete student records, and prepare reports on children and activities, as required by laws, district policies, and administrative regulations. Meet with other professionals to discuss individual students' needs and progress. Meet with parents and guardians to discuss their children's progress, and to determine their priorities for their children and their resource needs. Organize and label materials and display children's work in a manner appropriate for their sizes and perceptual skills. Organize and lead activities designed to promote physical, mental, and social development such as games, arts and crafts, music, and storytelling. Plan and conduct activities for a balanced program of instruction, demonstration, and work time that provides students with opportunities to observe, question, and investigate. Plan and supervise class projects, field trips, visits by guests, or other experiential activities, and guide students in learning from those activities. Prepare and implement remedial programs for students requiring extra help. Prepare children for later grades by encouraging them to explore learning opportunities and to persevere with challenging tasks. Instruct students individually and in groups, adapting teaching methods to meet students' varying needs and interests. Observe and evaluate children's performance, behavior, social development, and physical health. Teach basic skills such as color, shape, number and letter recognition, personal hygiene, and social skills. Demonstrate activities to children. Assimilate arriving children to the school environment by greeting them, helping them remove outerwear, and selecting activities of interest to them. Confer with other staff members to plan and schedule lessons promoting learning, following approved curricula. **SKILLS**—Learning Strategies; Service Orientation; Social Perceptiveness; Monitoring; Instructing; Speaking; Management of Personnel Resources; Active Listening.

GOE—Interest Area: 12. Education and Social Service. **Work Group:** 12.03. Educational Services. **Other Jobs in This Work Group:** Adult Literacy, Remedial Education, and GED Teachers and Instructors; Agricultural Sciences Teachers, Postsecondary; Anthropology and Archeology Teachers, Postsecondary; Architecture Teachers, Postsecondary; Archivists; Area, Ethnic, and Cultural Studies Teachers, Postsecondary; Art, Drama, and Music Teachers, Postsecondary; Atmospheric, Earth, Marine, and Space Sciences Teachers, Postsecondary; Audio-Visual Collections Specialists; Biological Science Teachers, Postsecondary; Business Teachers, Postsecondary; Chemistry Teachers, Postsecondary; Child Care Workers; Communications Teachers, Postsecondary; Computer Science Teachers, Postsecondary; Criminal Justice and Law Enforcement Teachers, Postsecondary; Curators; Economics Teachers, Postsecondary; Education Teachers, Postsecondary; Education, Training, and Library Workers, All Other; Educational Psychologists; Educational, Vocational, and School Counselors; Elementary School Teachers, Except Special Education; Engineering Teachers, Postsecondary; English Language and Literature Teachers, Postsecondary; Environmental Science Teachers, Postsecondary; Farm and Home Management Advisors; Foreign Language and Literature Teachers, Postsecondary; Forestry and Conservation Science Teachers, Postsecondary; Geography Teachers, Postsecondary; Graduate Teaching Assistants; Health Specialties Teachers, Postsecondary; History Teachers, Postsecondary; Home Economics Teachers, Postsecondary; Law Teachers, Postsecondary; Librarians; Library Assistants, Clerical; Library Science Teachers, Postsecondary; Library Technicians; Mathematical Science Teachers, Postsecondary; Middle School Teachers, Except Special and Vocational Education; Museum Technicians and Conservators; Nannies; Nursing Instructors and Teachers, Postsecondary; Personal Financial Advisors; Philosophy and Religion Teachers, Postsecondary; Physics Teachers, Postsecondary; Political Science Teachers, Postsecondary; Postsecondary Teachers, All Other; Preschool Teachers, Except Special Education; Psychology Teachers, Postsecondary; Recreation and Fitness Studies Teachers, Postsecondary; Secondary School Teachers, Except Special and Vocational Education; Self-Enrichment Education Teachers; Social Sciences Teachers, Postsecondary, All Other; Social Work Teachers, Postsecondary; Sociology

Teachers, Postsecondary; Special Education Teachers, Middle School; Special Education Teachers, Preschool, Kindergarten, and Elementary School; Special Education Teachers, Secondary School; Teacher Assistants; Teachers and Instructors, All Other; Vocational Education Teachers, Postsecondary; Vocational Education Teachers, Middle School; Vocational Education Teachers, Secondary School.

EDUCATION/TRAINING PROGRAM(S)— Early Childhood Education and Teaching; Kindergarten/Preschool Education and Teaching. **RELATED KNOWLEDGE/COURSES—**Education and Training; Sociology and Anthropology; Psychology; Customer and Personal Service; Therapy and Counseling; History and Archeology.

Licensed Practical and Licensed Vocational Nurses

- Personality Code: SR
- Growth: 20.2%
- Annual Job Openings: 105,000
- Annual Earnings: $32,390
- Education/Training Required: Postsecondary vocational training
- Self-Employed: 0.6%
- Part-Time: 19.1%

Care for ill, injured, convalescent, or disabled persons in hospitals, nursing homes, clinics, private homes, group homes, and similar institutions. May work under the supervision of a registered nurse. Licensing required. Observe patients, charting and reporting changes in patients' conditions, such as adverse reactions to medication or treatment, and taking any necessary action. Administer prescribed medications or start intravenous fluids, and note times and amounts on patients' charts. Answer patients' calls and determine how to assist them. Measure and record patients' vital signs, such as height, weight, temperature, blood pressure, pulse and respiration. Provide basic patient care and treatments, such as taking temperatures and blood pressure, dressing wounds, treating bedsores, giving enemas, douches, alcohol rubs, and massages, or performing catheterizations. Help patients with bathing, dressing, personal hygiene, moving in bed, and standing and walking. Supervise nurses' aides and assistants. Work as part of a health care team to assess patient needs, plan and modify care and implement interventions. Record food and fluid intake and output. Evaluate nursing intervention outcomes, conferring with other health-care team members as necessary. Assemble and use equipment such as catheters, tracheotomy tubes, and oxygen suppliers. Collect samples such as blood, urine and sputum from patients, and perform routine laboratory tests on samples. Prepare patients for examinations, tests and treatments and explain procedures. Prepare food trays and examine them for conformance to prescribed diet. Apply compresses, ice bags, and hot water bottles. Clean rooms and make beds. Inventory and requisition supplies and instruments. Provide medical treatment and personal care to patients in private home settings, such as cooking, keeping rooms orderly, seeing that patients are comfortable and in good spirits, and instructing family members in simple nursing tasks. Sterilize equipment and supplies, using germicides, sterilizer, or autoclave. Assist in delivery, care, and feeding of infants. Wash and dress bodies of deceased persons. Make appointments, keep records and perform other clerical duties in doctors' offices and clinics. Set up equipment and prepare medical treatment rooms. **SKILLS—**Service Orientation; Science; Active Listening; Time Management; Judgment and Decision Making; Instructing; Management of Personnel Resources; Writing; Operation Monitoring.

GOE—Interest Area: 14. Medical and Health Services. **Work Group:** 14.07. Patient Care and Assistance. **Other Jobs in This Work Group:** Home

Health Aides; Nursing Aides, Orderlies, and Attendants; Psychiatric Aides; Psychiatric Technicians.

EDUCATION/TRAINING PROGRAM(S)— Licensed Practical /Vocational Nurse Training (LPN, LVN, Cert, Dipl, AAS). **RELATED KNOWLEDGE/COURSES**—Psychology; Customer and Personal Service; Therapy and Counseling; Medicine and Dentistry; Philosophy and Theology; Sociology and Anthropology; Education and Training.

Medical and Public Health Social Workers

- Personality Code: SI
- Growth: 28.6%
- Annual Job Openings: 18,000
- Annual Earnings: $38,430
- Education/Training Required: Bachelor's degree
- Self-Employed: 1.7%
- Part-Time: 8.7%

Provide persons, families, or vulnerable populations with the psychosocial support needed to cope with chronic, acute, or terminal illnesses, such as Alzheimer's, cancer, or AIDS. Services include advising family care givers, providing patient education and counseling, and making necessary referrals for other social services. Collaborate with other professionals to evaluate patients' medical or physical condition and to assess client needs. Investigate child abuse or neglect cases and take authorized protective action when necessary. Refer patient, client, or family to community resources to assist in recovery from mental or physical illness and to provide access to services such as financial assistance, legal aid, housing, job placement or education. Counsel clients and patients in individual and group sessions to help them overcome dependencies, recover from illness, and adjust to life. Organize support groups or counsel family members to assist them in understanding, dealing with, and supporting the client or patient. Advocate for clients or patients to resolve crises. Identify environmental impediments to client or patient progress through interviews and review of patient records. Utilize consultation data and social work experience to plan and coordinate client or patient care and rehabilitation, following through to ensure service efficacy. Modify treatment plans to comply with changes in clients' status. Monitor, evaluate, and record client progress according to measurable goals described in treatment and care plan. Supervise and direct other workers providing services to clients or patients. Develop or advise on social policy and assist in community development. Oversee Medicaid- and Medicare-related paperwork and record-keeping in hospitals. Conduct social research to advance knowledge in the social work field. Plan and conduct programs to combat social problems, prevent substance abuse, or improve community health and counseling services. **SKILLS**—Social Perceptiveness; Service Orientation; Negotiation; Coordination; Active Listening; Critical Thinking; Learning Strategies; Instructing.

GOE—Interest Area: 12. Education and Social Service. **Work Group:** 12.02. Social Services. **Other Jobs in This Work Group:** Child, Family, and School Social Workers; Clergy; Clinical Psychologists; Clinical, Counseling, and School Psychologists; Community and Social Service Specialists, All Other; Counseling Psychologists; Counselors, All Other; Directors, Religious Activities and Education; Marriage and Family Therapists; Mental Health and Substance Abuse Social Workers; Mental Health Counselors; Probation Officers and Correctional Treatment Specialists; Rehabilitation Counselors; Religious Workers, All Other; Residential Advisors; Social and Human Service Assistants; Social Workers, All Other; Substance Abuse and Behavioral Disorder Counselors.

EDUCATION/TRAINING PROGRAM(S)— Clinical/Medical Social Work. **RELATED KNOWLEDGE/COURSES**—Psychology; Thera-

Social—M

py and Counseling; Customer and Personal Service; Sociology and Anthropology; Philosophy and Theology; Medicine and Dentistry.

Medical Assistants

- Personality Code: SC
- Growth: 58.9%
- Annual Job Openings: 78,000
- Annual Earnings: $24,170
- Education/Training Required: Moderate-term on-the-job training
- Self-Employed: 2.3%
- Part-Time: 25.3%

Perform administrative and certain clinical duties under the direction of physician. Administrative duties may include scheduling appointments, maintaining medical records, billing, and coding for insurance purposes. Clinical duties may include taking and recording vital signs and medical histories, preparing patients for examination, drawing blood, and administering medications as directed by physician. Interview patients to obtain medical information and measure their vital signs, weight, and height. Show patients to examination rooms and prepare them for the physician. Record patients' medical history, vital statistics and information such as test results in medical records. Prepare and administer medications as directed by a physician. Collect blood, tissue or other laboratory specimens, log the specimens, and prepare them for testing. Explain treatment procedures, medications, diets and physicians' instructions to patients. Help physicians examine and treat patients, handing them instruments and materials or performing such tasks as giving injections and removing sutures. Authorize drug refills and provide prescription information to pharmacies. Prepare treatment rooms for patient examinations, keeping the rooms neat and clean. Clean and sterilize instruments and

dispose of contaminated supplies. Schedule appointments for patients. Change dressings on wounds. Greet and log in patients arriving at office or clinic. Contact medical facilities or departments to schedule patients for tests and/or admission. Perform general office duties such as answering telephones, taking dictation and completing insurance forms. Inventory and order medical, lab, and office supplies and equipment. Perform routine laboratory tests and sample analyses. Set up medical laboratory equipment. Keep financial records and perform other bookkeeping duties, such as handling credit and collections and mailing monthly statements to patients. Operate X-ray, electrocardiogram (EKG), and other equipment to administer routine diagnostic tests. **SKILLS**—Social Perceptiveness; Service Orientation; Instructing; Active Listening; Learning Strategies; Negotiation; Active Learning; Persuasion; Troubleshooting; Time Management.

GOE—Interest Area: 14. Medical and Health Services. **Work Group:** 14.02. Medicine and Surgery. **Other Jobs in This Work Group:** Anesthesiologists; Family and General Practitioners; Healthcare Support Workers, All Other; Internists, General; Obstetricians and Gynecologists; Pediatricians, General; Pharmacists; Pharmacy Aides; Pharmacy Technicians; Physician Assistants; Physicians and Surgeons, All Other; Psychiatrists; Registered Nurses; Surgeons; Surgical Technologists.

EDUCATION/TRAINING PROGRAM(S)—Allied Health and Medical Assisting Services, Other; Anesthesiologist Assistant; Chiropractic Assistant/Technician; Medical Administrative/Executive Assistant and Medical Secretary; Medical Insurance Coding Specialist/Coder; Medical Office Assistant/Specialist; Medical Office Management/Administration; Medical Reception/Receptionist; Medical/Clinical Assistant; Opthalmic Technician/Technologist; Optomeric Technician/Assistant; Orthoptics/Orthoptist. **RELATED KNOWLEDGE/COURSES**—Medicine and Dentistry; Customer and Personal Service; Clerical Studies; Psychology; Therapy and Counseling; English Language.

Mental Health and Substance Abuse Social Workers

- ☺ Personality Code: SI
- ☺ Growth: 34.5%
- ☺ Annual Job Openings: 17,000
- ☺ Annual Earnings: $33,020
- ☺ Education/Training Required: Master's degree
- ☺ Self-Employed: 1.6%
- ☺ Part-Time: 8.7%

Assess and treat individuals with mental, emotional, or substance abuse problems, including abuse of alcohol, tobacco, and/or other drugs. Activities may include individual and group therapy, crisis intervention, case management, client advocacy, prevention, and education. Counsel clients in individual and group sessions to assist them in dealing with substance abuse, mental and physical illness, poverty, unemployment, or physical abuse. Interview clients, review records, and confer with other professionals to evaluate mental or physical condition of client or patient. Collaborate with counselors, physicians, and nurses to plan and coordinate treatment, drawing on social work experience and patient needs. Monitor, evaluate, and record client progress with respect to treatment goals. Refer patient, client, or family to community resources for housing or treatment to assist in recovery from mental or physical illness, following through to ensure service efficacy. Counsel and aid family members to assist them in understanding, dealing with, and supporting the client or patient. Modify treatment plans according to changes in client status. Plan and conduct programs to prevent substance abuse, to combat social problems, or to improve health and counseling services in community. Supervise and direct other workers who provide services to clients or patients. Develop or advise on social policy and assist in community development. **SKILLS**—Social

Perceptiveness; Service Orientation; Negotiation; Persuasion; Active Listening; Critical Thinking; Coordination; Judgment and Decision Making.

GOE—Interest Area: 12. Education and Social Service. **Work Group:** 12.02. Social Services. **Other Jobs in This Work Group:** Child, Family, and School Social Workers; Clergy; Clinical Psychologists; Clinical, Counseling, and School Psychologists; Community and Social Service Specialists, All Other; Counseling Psychologists; Counselors, All Other; Directors, Religious Activities and Education; Marriage and Family Therapists; Medical and Public Health Social Workers; Mental Health Counselors; Probation Officers and Correctional Treatment Specialists; Rehabilitation Counselors; Religious Workers, All Other; Residential Advisors; Social and Human Service Assistants; Social Workers, All Other; Substance Abuse and Behavioral Disorder Counselors.

EDUCATION/TRAINING PROGRAM(S)—Clinical/Medical Social Work. **RELATED KNOWLEDGE/COURSES**—Psychology; Therapy and Counseling; Customer and Personal Service; Sociology and Anthropology; Medicine and Dentistry; Philosophy and Theology.

Nursing Aides, Orderlies, and Attendants

- ☺ Personality Code: SR
- ☺ Growth: 24.9%
- ☺ Annual Job Openings: 302,000
- ☺ Annual Earnings: $20,490
- ☺ Education/Training Required: Short-term on-the-job training
- ☺ Self-Employed: 1.6%
- ☺ Part-Time: 21.9%

Provide basic patient care under direction of nursing staff. Perform duties, such as feed, bathe, dress, groom, or move patients, or change linens. Turn and re-position bedridden patients, alone or with assistance, to prevent bedsores. Answer patients' call signals. Feed patients who are unable to feed themselves. Observe patients' conditions, measuring and recording food and liquid intake and output and vital signs, and report changes to professional staff. Provide patient care by supplying and emptying bed pans, applying dressings and supervising exercise routines. Provide patients with help walking, exercising, and moving in and out of bed. Bathe, groom, shave, dress, and/or drape patients to prepare them for surgery, treatment, or examination. Collect specimens such as urine, feces, or sputum. Prepare, serve, and collect food trays. Clean rooms and change linens. Transport patients to treatment units, using a wheelchair or stretcher. Deliver messages, documents and specimens. Answer phones and direct visitors. Administer medications and treatments, such as catheterizations, suppositories, irrigations, enemas, massages, and douches, as directed by a physician or nurse. Restrain patients if necessary. Maintain inventory by storing, preparing, sterilizing, and issuing supplies such as dressing packs and treatment trays. Explain medical instructions to patients and family members. Perform clerical duties such as processing documents and scheduling appointments. Work as part of a medical team that examines and treats clinic outpatients. Set up equipment such as oxygen tents, portable X-ray machines, and overhead irrigation bottles. **SKILLS**—Social Perceptiveness; Time Management; Instructing; Service Orientation; Monitoring; Coordination; Operation Monitoring; Persuasion.

GOE—Interest Area: 14. Medical and Health Services. **Work Group:** 14.07. Patient Care and Assistance. **Other Jobs in This Work Group:** Home Health Aides; Licensed Practical and Licensed Vocational Nurses; Psychiatric Aides; Psychiatric Technicians.

EDUCATION/TRAINING PROGRAM(S)— Health Aide; Nurse/Nursing Assistant/Aide and

Patient Care Assistant. **RELATED KNOWLEDGE/COURSES**—Psychology; Customer and Personal Service; Medicine and Dentistry; Education and Training; English Language; Foreign Language.

Nursing Instructors and Teachers, Postsecondary

- Personality Code: SI
- Growth: 38.1%
- Annual Job Openings: 216,000
- Annual Earnings: $50,920
- Education/Training Required: Master's degree
- Self-Employed: 0.3%
- Part-Time: 27.7%

Demonstrate and teach patient care in classroom and clinical units to nursing students. Includes both teachers primarily engaged in teaching and those who do a combination of both teaching and research. Plan, evaluate, and revise curricula, course content, and course materials and methods of instruction. Prepare course materials such as syllabi, homework assignments, and handouts. Select and obtain materials and supplies such as textbooks and laboratory equipment. Supervise students' laboratory and clinical work. Supervise undergraduate and/or graduate teaching, internship, and research work. Act as advisers to student organizations. Assess clinical education needs, and patient and client teaching needs, utilizing a variety of methods. Collaborate with colleagues to address teaching and research issues. Conduct research in a particular field of knowledge, and publish findings in professional journals, books, and/or electronic media. Coordinate training programs with area universities, clinics, hospitals, health agencies, and/or vocational schools. Participate in campus and community events. Evaluate and grade students' class work, laboratory and clinic work, assignments, and papers. Prepare and deliver lectures to undergraduate and/or graduate students on topics such as pharmacology, mental health nursing, and community health care practices. Advise students on academic and vocational curricula, and on career issues. Compile, administer, and grade examinations, or assign this work to others. Compile bibliographies of specialized materials for outside reading assignments. Demonstrate patient care in clinical units of hospitals. Initiate, facilitate, and moderate classroom discussions. Keep abreast of developments in their field by reading current literature, talking with colleagues, and participating in professional conferences. Maintain regularly scheduled office hours in order to advise and assist students. Maintain student attendance records, grades, and other required records. Participate in student recruitment, registration, and placement activities. Perform administrative duties such as serving as department head. Provide professional consulting services to government and/or industry. Serve on academic or administrative committees that deal with institutional policies, departmental matters, and academic issues. **SKILLS**—Learning Strategies; Instructing; Management of Personnel Resources; Science; Reading Comprehension; Service Orientation; Social Perceptiveness; Speaking; Time Management.

GOE—Interest Area: 12. Education and Social Service. **Work Group:** 12.03. Educational Services. **Other Jobs in This Work Group:** Adult Literacy, Remedial Education, and GED Teachers and Instructors; Agricultural Sciences Teachers, Postsecondary; Anthropology and Archeology Teachers, Postsecondary; Architecture Teachers, Postsecondary; Archivists; Area, Ethnic, and Cultural Studies Teachers, Postsecondary; Art, Drama, and Music Teachers, Postsecondary; Atmospheric, Earth, Marine, and Space Sciences Teachers, Postsecondary; Audio-Visual Collections Specialists; Biological Science Teachers, Postsecondary; Business Teachers, Postsecondary; Chemistry Teachers, Postsecondary; Child Care Workers; Communications Teachers, Postsecondary; Computer Science Teachers, Postsecondary; Criminal Justice and Law Enforcement Teachers, Postsecondary; Curators; Economics Teachers, Postsecondary; Education Teachers, Postsecondary; Education, Training, and Library Workers, All Other; Educational Psychologists; Educational, Vocational, and School Counselors; Elementary School Teachers, Except Special Education; Engineering Teachers, Postsecondary; English Language and Literature Teachers, Postsecondary; Environmental Science Teachers, Postsecondary; Farm and Home Management Advisors; Foreign Language and Literature Teachers, Postsecondary; Forestry and Conservation Science Teachers, Postsecondary; Geography Teachers, Postsecondary; Graduate Teaching Assistants; Health Specialties Teachers, Postsecondary; History Teachers, Postsecondary; Home Economics Teachers, Postsecondary; Kindergarten Teachers, Except Special Education; Law Teachers, Postsecondary; Librarians; Library Assistants, Clerical; Library Science Teachers, Postsecondary; Library Technicians; Mathematical Science Teachers, Postsecondary; Middle School Teachers, Except Special and Vocational Education; Museum Technicians and Conservators; Nannies; Personal Financial Advisors; Philosophy and Religion Teachers, Postsecondary; Physics Teachers, Postsecondary; Political Science Teachers, Postsecondary; Postsecondary Teachers, All Other; Preschool Teachers, Except Special Education; Psychology Teachers, Postsecondary; Recreation and Fitness Studies Teachers, Postsecondary; Secondary School Teachers, Except Special and Vocational Education; Self-Enrichment Education Teachers; Social Sciences Teachers, Postsecondary, All Other; Social Work Teachers, Postsecondary; Sociology Teachers, Postsecondary; Special Education Teachers, Middle School; Special Education Teachers, Preschool, Kindergarten, and Elementary School; Special Education Teachers, Secondary School; Teacher Assistants; Teachers and Instructors, All Other; Vocational Education Teachers, Postsecondary; Vocational Education Teachers, Middle School; Vocational Education Teachers, Secondary School.

Social—N

EDUCATION/TRAINING PROGRAM(S)— Adult Health Nurse/Nursing; Clinical Nurse Specialist; Family Practice Nurse/Nurse Practitioner; Maternal/Child Health and Neonatal Nurse/Nursing; Nurse Anesthetist; Nurse Midwife/Nursing Midwifery; Nursing—Registered Nurse Training (RN, ASN, BSN, MSN); Nursing Science (MS, PhD); Nursing, Other; Pediatric Nurse/Nursing; Perioperative/Operating Room and Surgical Nurse/Nursing; Pre-Nursing Studies; Psychiatric/Mental Health Nurse/Nursing; Public Health/Community Nurse/Nursing. **RELATED KNOWLEDGE/COURSES**—Education and Training; Medicine and Dentistry; Biology; Psychology; Chemistry; Therapy and Counseling.

Occupational Therapist Assistants

- Personality Code: SR
- Growth: 39.2%
- Annual Job Openings: 3,000
- Annual Earnings: $37,400
- Education/Training Required: Associate's degree
- Self-Employed: 2.9%
- Part-Time: 25.5%

Assist occupational therapists in providing occupational therapy treatments and procedures. May, in accordance with State laws, assist in development of treatment plans, carry out routine functions, direct activity programs, and document the progress of treatments. Generally requires formal training. Observe and record patients' progress, attitudes, and behavior, and maintain this information in client records. Maintain and promote a positive attitude toward clients and their treatment programs. Monitor patients' performance in therapy activities, providing encouragement. Select therapy activities to fit patients' needs and capabilities. Instruct, or assist in instructing, patients and families in home programs, basic living skills, and the care and use of adaptive equipment. Evaluate the daily living skills and capacities of physically, developmentally or emotionally disabled clients. Aid patients in dressing and grooming themselves. Implement, or assist occupational therapists with implementing, treatment plans designed to help clients function independently. Report to supervisors, verbally or in writing, on patients' progress, attitudes and behavior. Alter treatment programs to obtain better results if treatment is not having the intended effect. Work under the direction of occupational therapists to plan, implement and administer educational, vocational, and recreational programs that restore and enhance performance in individuals with functional impairments. Design, fabricate, and repair assistive devices and make adaptive changes to equipment and environments. Assemble, clean, and maintain equipment and materials for patient use. Teach patients how to deal constructively with their emotions. Perform clerical duties such as scheduling appointments, collecting data, and documenting health insurance billings. Transport patients to and from the occupational therapy work area. Demonstrate therapy techniques, such as manual and creative arts, and games. Order any needed educational or treatment supplies. Assist educational specialists or clinical psychologists in administering situational or diagnostic tests to measure client's abilities or progress. **SKILLS**—Social Perceptiveness; Instructing; Service Orientation; Persuasion; Time Management; Learning Strategies; Monitoring; Active Listening; Writing; Critical Thinking.

GOE—Interest Area: 14. Medical and Health Services. **Work Group:** 14.06. Medical Therapy. **Other Jobs in This Work Group:** Audiologists; Health Diagnosing and Treating Practitioners, All Other; Massage Therapists; Occupational Therapist Aides; Occupational Therapists; Physical Therapist Aides; Physical Therapist Assistants; Physical Therapists; Radiation Therapists; Recreational Therapists; Respiratory Therapists; Respiratory Therapy Technicians; Speech-Language Pathologists; Therapists, All Other.

EDUCATION/TRAINING PROGRAM(S)— Occupational Therapist Assistant. **RELATED KNOWLEDGE/COURSES—**Psychology; Therapy and Counseling; Sociology and Anthropology; Philosophy and Theology; Customer and Personal Service; Medicine and Dentistry.

Occupational Therapists

- Personality Code: SR
- Growth: 35.2%
- Annual Job Openings: 10,000
- Annual Earnings: $52,550
- Education/Training Required: Bachelor's degree
- Self-Employed: 4.0%
- Part-Time: 31.1%

Assess, plan, organize, and participate in rehabilitative programs that help restore vocational, homemaking, and daily living skills, as well as general independence, to disabled persons. Complete and maintain necessary records. Evaluate patients' progress and prepare reports that detail progress. Test and evaluate patients' physical and mental abilities and analyze medical data to determine realistic rehabilitation goals for patients. Select activities that will help individuals learn work and life-management skills within limits of their mental and physical capabilities. Plan, organize, and conduct occupational therapy programs in hospital, institutional, or community settings to help rehabilitate those impaired because of illness, injury or psychological or developmental problems. Recommend changes in patients' work or living environments, consistent with their needs and capabilities. Consult with rehabilitation team to select activity programs and coordinate occupational therapy with other therapeutic activities. Help clients improve decision making, abstract reasoning, memory, sequencing, coordination and perceptual skills, using computer programs. Develop and participate in health promotion programs, group activities, or discussions to promote client health, facilitate social adjustment, alleviate stress, and prevent physical or mental disability. Provide training and supervision in therapy techniques and objectives for students and nurses and other medical staff. Design and create, or requisition, special supplies and equipment, such as splints, braces and computer-aided adaptive equipment. Plan and implement programs and social activities to help patients learn work and school skills and adjust to handicaps. Lay out materials such as puzzles, scissors and eating utensils for use in therapy, and clean and repair these tools after therapy sessions. Advise on health risks in the workplace and on health-related transition to retirement. Conduct research in occupational therapy. **SKILLS—** Social Perceptiveness; Service Orientation; Instructing; Science; Coordination; Technology Design; Persuasion; Reading Comprehension; Active Learning.

GOE—Interest Area: 14. Medical and Health Services. **Work Group:** 14.06. Medical Therapy. **Other Jobs in This Work Group:** Audiologists; Health Diagnosing and Treating Practitioners, All Other; Massage Therapists; Occupational Therapist Aides; Occupational Therapist Assistants; Physical Therapist Aides; Physical Therapist Assistants; Physical Therapists; Radiation Therapists; Recreational Therapists; Respiratory Therapists; Respiratory Therapy Technicians; Speech-Language Pathologists; Therapists, All Other.

EDUCATION/TRAINING PROGRAM(S)— Occupational Therapy/Therapist. **RELATED KNOWLEDGE/COURSES—**Therapy and Counseling; Psychology; Customer and Personal Service; Medicine and Dentistry; Education and Training; Sociology and Anthropology.

Social—O

Personal and Home Care Aides

- Personality Code: SR
- Growth: 40.5%
- Annual Job Openings: 154,000
- Annual Earnings: $16,450
- Education/Training Required: Short-term on-the-job training
- Self-Employed: 7.1%
- Part-Time: 34.0%

Assist elderly or disabled adults with daily living activities at the person's home or in a daytime non-residential facility. Duties performed at a place of residence may include keeping house (making beds, doing laundry, washing dishes) and preparing meals. May provide meals and supervised activities at non-residential care facilities. May advise families, the elderly, and disabled on such things as nutrition, cleanliness, and household utilities. Perform health-care related tasks, such as monitoring vital signs and medication, under the direction of registered nurses and physiotherapists. Administer bedside and personal care, such as ambulation and personal hygiene assistance. Prepare and maintain records of client progress and services performed, reporting changes in client condition to manager or supervisor. Perform housekeeping duties, such as cooking, cleaning, washing clothes and dishes, and running errands. Care for individuals and families during periods of incapacitation, family disruption or convalescence, providing companionship, personal care and help in adjusting to new lifestyles. Instruct and advise clients on issues such as household cleanliness, utilities, hygiene, nutrition and infant care. Plan, shop for, and prepare meals, including special diets, and assist families in planning, shopping for, and preparing nutritious meals. Participate in case reviews, consulting with the team caring for the client, to evaluate the client's needs and plan for continuing

services. Transport clients to locations outside the home, such as to physicians' offices or on outings, using a motor vehicle. Train family members to provide bedside care. Provide clients with communication assistance, typing their correspondence and obtaining information for them. **SKILLS**—Social Perceptiveness; Persuasion; Service Orientation; Learning Strategies; Coordination; Instructing; Critical Thinking; Monitoring.

GOE—Interest Area: 11. Recreation, Travel, and Other Personal Services. **Work Group:** 11.08. Other Personal Services. **Other Jobs in This Work Group:** Cleaners of Vehicles and Equipment; Cooks, Private Household; Embalmers; Funeral Attendants; Personal Care and Service Workers, All Other.

EDUCATION/TRAINING PROGRAM(S)— No data available. **RELATED KNOWLEDGE/ COURSES**—Customer and Personal Service; Medicine and Dentistry; Therapy and Counseling; Psychology.

Personal Financial Advisors

- Personality Code: SE
- Growth: 34.6%
- Annual Job Openings: 18,000
- Annual Earnings: $58,700
- Education/Training Required: Bachelor's degree
- Self-Employed: 37.7%
- Part-Time: 7.0%

Advise clients on financial plans, utilizing knowledge of tax and investment strategies, securities, insurance, pension plans, and real estate. Duties include assessing clients' assets, liabilities, cash flow, insurance coverage, tax status, and financial objectives to establish investment strategies. Analyze financial information obtained from clients to determine strategies for meeting clients' financial objectives. Answer clients' questions about the purposes and details of financial plans and strategies. Build and maintain client bases, keeping current client plans up-to-date and recruiting new clients on an ongoing basis. Contact clients periodically to determine if there have been changes in their financial status. Devise debt liquidation plans that include payoff priorities and timelines. Explain and document for clients the types of services that are to be provided, and the responsibilities to be taken by the personal financial advisor. Explain to individuals and groups the details of financial assistance available to college and university students, such as loans, grants, and scholarships. Guide clients in the gathering of information such as bank account records, income tax returns, life and disability insurance records, pension plan information, and wills. Implement financial planning recommendations, or refer clients to someone who can assist them with plan implementation. Interview clients to determine their current income, expenses, insurance coverage, tax status, financial objectives, risk tolerance, and other information needed to develop a financial plan. Monitor financial market trends to ensure that plans are effective, and to identify any necessary updates. Prepare and interpret for clients information such as investment performance reports, financial document summaries, and income projections. Recommend strategies clients can use to achieve their financial goals and objectives, including specific recommendations in such areas as cash management, insurance coverage, and investment planning. Research and investigate available investment opportunities to determine whether they fit into financial plans. Review clients' accounts and plans regularly to determine whether life changes, economic changes, or financial performance indicate a need for plan reassessment. Sell financial products such as stocks, bonds, mutual funds, and insurance if licensed to do so. **SKILLS**—Service Orientation; Speaking; Management of Financial Resources; Active Listening; Judgment and Decision Making;

Mathematics; Critical Thinking; Reading Comprehension; Writing.

GOE—Interest Area: 12. Education and Social Service. **Work Group:** 12.03. Educational Services. **Other Jobs in This Work Group:** Adult Literacy, Remedial Education, and GED Teachers and Instructors; Agricultural Sciences Teachers, Postsecondary; Anthropology and Archeology Teachers, Postsecondary; Architecture Teachers, Postsecondary; Archivists; Area, Ethnic, and Cultural Studies Teachers, Postsecondary; Art, Drama, and Music Teachers, Postsecondary; Atmospheric, Earth, Marine, and Space Sciences Teachers, Postsecondary; Audio-Visual Collections Specialists; Biological Science Teachers, Postsecondary; Business Teachers, Postsecondary; Chemistry Teachers, Postsecondary; Child Care Workers; Communications Teachers, Postsecondary; Computer Science Teachers, Postsecondary; Criminal Justice and Law Enforcement Teachers, Postsecondary; Curators; Economics Teachers, Postsecondary; Education Teachers, Postsecondary; Education, Training, and Library Workers, All Other; Educational Psychologists; Educational, Vocational, and School Counselors; Elementary School Teachers, Except Special Education; Engineering Teachers, Postsecondary; English Language and Literature Teachers, Postsecondary; Environmental Science Teachers, Postsecondary; Farm and Home Management Advisors; Foreign Language and Literature Teachers, Postsecondary; Forestry and Conservation Science Teachers, Postsecondary; Geography Teachers, Postsecondary; Graduate Teaching Assistants; Health Specialties Teachers, Postsecondary; History Teachers, Postsecondary; Home Economics Teachers, Postsecondary; Kindergarten Teachers, Except Special Education; Law Teachers, Postsecondary; Librarians; Library Assistants, Clerical; Library Science Teachers, Postsecondary; Library Technicians; Mathematical Science Teachers, Postsecondary; Middle School Teachers, Except Special and Vocational Education; Museum Technicians and Conservators; Nannies; Nursing Instructors and Teachers, Postsecondary; Philosophy and Religion Teachers,

Postsecondary; Physics Teachers, Postsecondary; Political Science Teachers, Postsecondary; Postsecondary Teachers, All Other; Preschool Teachers, Except Special Education; Psychology Teachers, Postsecondary; Recreation and Fitness Studies Teachers, Postsecondary; Secondary School Teachers, Except Special and Vocational Education; Self-Enrichment Education Teachers; Social Sciences Teachers, Postsecondary, All Other; Social Work Teachers, Postsecondary; Sociology Teachers, Postsecondary; Special Education Teachers, Middle School; Special Education Teachers, Preschool, Kindergarten, and Elementary School; Special Education Teachers, Secondary School; Teacher Assistants; Teachers and Instructors, All Other; Vocational Education Teachers, Postsecondary; Vocational Education Teachers, Middle School; Vocational Education Teachers, Secondary School.

EDUCATION/TRAINING PROGRAM(S)— Finance, General; Financial Planning and Services. **RELATED KNOWLEDGE/COURSES—**Economics and Accounting; Mathematics; Administration and Management; Law and Government; Customer and Personal Service; Therapy and Counseling.

Physical Therapist Assistants

- ◉ Personality Code: SR
- ◉ Growth: 44.6%
- ◉ Annual Job Openings: 10,000
- ◉ Annual Earnings: $36,610
- ◉ Education/Training Required: Associate's degree
- ◉ Self-Employed: 0.4%
- ◉ Part-Time: 22.8%

Assist physical therapists in providing physical therapy treatments and procedures. May, in accordance with state laws, assist in the development of treatment plans, carry out routine functions, document the progress of treatment, and modify specific treatments in accordance with patient status and within the scope of treatment plans established by a physical therapist. Generally requires formal training. Instruct, motivate, safeguard and assist patients as they practice exercises and functional activities. Confer with physical therapy staff and others to discuss and evaluate patient information for planning, modifying, and coordinating treatment. Administer active and passive manual therapeutic exercises, therapeutic massage, and heat, light, sound, water, and electrical modality treatments, such as ultrasound. Observe patients during treatments to compile and evaluate data on patients' responses and progress, and report to physical therapist. Measure patients' range-of-joint motion, body parts, and vital signs to determine effects of treatments or for patient evaluations. Secure patients into or onto therapy equipment. Fit patients for orthopedic braces, prostheses, and supportive devices, such as crutches. Train patients in the use of orthopedic braces, prostheses, and supportive devices. Transport patients to and from treatment areas, lifting and transferring them according to positioning requirements. Monitor operation of equipment and record use of equipment and administration of treatment. Clean work area and check and store equipment after treatment. Assist patients to dress, undress, and put on and remove supportive devices, such as braces, splints, and slings. Administer traction to relieve neck and back pain, using intermittent and static traction equipment. Perform clerical duties, such as taking inventory, ordering supplies, answering telephone, taking messages, and filling out forms. Prepare treatment areas and electrotherapy equipment for use by physiotherapists. Perform postural drainage, percussions and vibrations, and teach deep breathing exercises to treat respiratory conditions. SKILLS—Social Perceptiveness; Service Orientation; Instructing; Time Management; Active Learning; Critical Thinking; Learning Strategies; Writing; Speaking.

GOE—**Interest Area:** 14. Medical and Health Services. **Work Group:** 14.06. Medical Therapy. **Other Jobs in This Work Group:** Audiologists; Health Diagnosing and Treating Practitioners, All Other; Massage Therapists; Occupational Therapist Aides; Occupational Therapist Assistants; Occupational Therapists; Physical Therapist Aides; Physical Therapists; Radiation Therapists; Recreational Therapists; Respiratory Therapists; Respiratory Therapy Technicians; Speech-Language Pathologists; Therapists, All Other.

EDUCATION/TRAINING PROGRAM(S)— Physical Therapist Assistant. **RELATED KNOWLEDGE/COURSES**—Psychology; Therapy and Counseling; Medicine and Dentistry; Education and Training; Customer and Personal Service; Sociology and Anthropology.

Physical Therapists

- Personality Code: SR
- Growth: 35.3%
- Annual Job Openings: 16,000
- Annual Earnings: $57,710
- Education/Training Required: Master's degree
- Self-Employed: 5.7%
- Part-Time: 23.8%

Assess, plan, organize, and participate in rehabilitative programs that improve mobility, relieve pain, increase strength, and decrease or prevent deformity of patients suffering from disease or injury. Plan, prepare and carry out individually designed programs of physical treatment to maintain, improve or restore physical functioning, alleviate pain and prevent physical dysfunction in patients. Perform and document an initial exam, evaluating the data to identify problems and determine a diagnosis prior to intervention. Evaluate effects of treatment at various stages and adjust treatments to achieve maximum benefit. Administer manual exercises, massage and/or traction to help relieve pain, increase the patient's strength, and decrease or prevent deformity and crippling. Instruct patient and family in treatment procedures to be continued at home. Confer with the patient, medical practitioners and appropriate others to plan, implement and assess the intervention program. Review physician's referral and patient's medical records to help determine diagnosis and physical therapy treatment required. Record prognosis, treatment, response, and progress in patient's chart or enter information into computer. Obtain patients' informed consent to proposed interventions. Discharge patient from physical therapy when goals or projected outcomes have been attained and provide for appropriate followup care or referrals. Test and measure patient's strength, motor development and function, sensory perception, functional capacity, and respiratory and circulatory efficiency and record data. Identify and document goals, anticipated progress and plans for reevaluation. Provide information to the patient about the proposed intervention, its material risks and expected benefits and any reasonable alternatives. Inform the patient when diagnosis reveals findings outside their scope and refer to an appropriate practitioner. Direct and supervise supportive personnel, assessing their competence, delegating specific tasks to them and establishing channels of communication. Administer treatment involving application of physical agents, using equipment, moist packs, ultraviolet and infrared lamps, and ultrasound machines. Teach physical therapy students as well as those in other health professions. Evaluate, fit, and adjust prosthetic and orthotic devices and recommend modification to orthotist. **SKILLS**—Instructing; Social Perceptiveness; Reading Comprehension; Learning Strategies; Science; Service Orientation; Time Management; Critical Thinking; Coordination.

GOE—**Interest Area:** 14. Medical and Health Services. **Work Group:** 14.06. Medical Therapy. **Other Jobs in This Work Group:** Audiologists; Health Diagnosing and Treating Practitioners, All Other;

Massage Therapists; Occupational Therapist Aides; Occupational Therapist Assistants; Occupational Therapists; Physical Therapist Aides; Physical Therapist Assistants; Radiation Therapists; Recreational Therapists; Respiratory Therapists; Respiratory Therapy Technicians; Speech-Language Pathologists; Therapists, All Other.

EDUCATION/TRAINING PROGRAM(S)— Kinesiotherapy/Kinesiotherapist; Physical Therapy/Therapist. **RELATED KNOWLEDGE/ COURSES—**Psychology; Therapy and Counseling; Customer and Personal Service; Medicine and Dentistry; Biology; Sociology and Anthropology.

Police Patrol Officers

- Personality Code: SR
- Growth: 24.7%
- Annual Job Openings: 67,000
- Annual Earnings: $44,020
- Education/Training Required: Long-term on-the-job training
- Self-Employed: 0%
- Part-Time: 1.4%

Patrol assigned area to enforce laws and ordinances, regulate traffic, control crowds, prevent crime, and arrest violators. Provide for public safety by maintaining order, responding to emergencies, protecting people and property, enforcing motor vehicle and criminal laws, and promoting good community relations. Identify, pursue, and arrest suspects and perpetrators of criminal acts. Record facts to prepare reports that document incidents and activities. Review facts of incidents to determine if criminal act or statute violations were involved. Render aid to accident victims and other persons requiring first aid for physical injuries. Testify in court to present evidence or act as witness in traffic and criminal cases. Evaluate complaint and emer-

gency-request information to determine response requirements. Patrol specific area on foot, horseback, or motorized conveyance, responding promptly to calls for assistance. Monitor, note, report, and investigate suspicious persons and situations, safety hazards, and unusual or illegal activity in patrol area. Investigate traffic accidents and other accidents to determine causes and to determine if a crime has been committed. Photograph or draw diagrams of crime or accident scenes and interview principals and eyewitnesses. Monitor traffic to ensure motorists observe traffic regulations and exhibit safe driving procedures. Relay complaint and emergency-request information to appropriate agency dispatchers. Issue citations or warnings to violators of motor vehicle ordinances. Direct traffic flow and reroute traffic in case of emergencies. Inform citizens of community services and recommend options to facilitate longer-term problem resolution. Provide road information to assist motorists. Process prisoners, and prepare and maintain records of prisoner bookings and prisoner status during booking and pre-trial process. **SKILLS—** Persuasion; Negotiation; Social Perceptiveness; Judgment and Decision Making; Service Orientation; Active Listening; Critical Thinking; Coordination.

GOE—Interest Area: 04. Law, Law Enforcement, and Public Safety. **Work Group:** 04.03. Law Enforcement. **Other Jobs in This Work Group:** Animal Control Workers; Bailiffs; Child Support, Missing Persons, and Unemployment Insurance Fraud Investigators; Correctional Officers and Jailers; Criminal Investigators and Special Agents; Crossing Guards; Detectives and Criminal Investigators; Fire Investigators; Fish and Game Wardens; Forensic Science Technicians; Gaming Surveillance Officers and Gaming Investigators; Highway Patrol Pilots; Immigration and Customs Inspectors; Lifeguards, Ski Patrol, and Other Recreational Protective Service Workers; Parking Enforcement Workers; Police and Sheriff's Patrol Officers; Police Detectives; Police Identification and Records Officers; Private Detectives and Investigators; Protective

Service Workers, All Other; Security Guards; Sheriffs and Deputy Sheriffs; Transit and Railroad Police.

EDUCATION/TRAINING PROGRAM(S)— Criminal Justice/Police Science; Criminalistics and Criminal Science. **RELATED KNOWLEDGE/ COURSES—**Public Safety and Security; Law and Government; Customer and Personal Service; Psychology; Sociology and Anthropology; Telecommunications.

Political Science Teachers, Postsecondary

- Personality Code: SI
- Growth: 38.1%
- Annual Job Openings: 216,000
- Annual Earnings: $57,340
- Education/Training Required: Master's degree
- Self-Employed: 0.3%
- Part-Time: 27.7%

Teach courses in political science, international affairs, and international relations. Evaluate and grade students' class work, assignments, and papers. Prepare and deliver lectures to undergraduate and/or graduate students on topics such as classical political thought, international relations, and democracy and citizenship. Advise students on academic and vocational curricula, and on career issues. Compile, administer, and grade examinations, or assign this work to others. Compile bibliographies of specialized materials for outside reading assignments. Initiate, facilitate, and moderate classroom discussions. Keep abreast of developments in their field by reading current literature, talking with colleagues, and participating in professional conferences. Maintain regularly scheduled office hours in order to advise and assist students. Maintain student attendance records, grades, and other required records. Plan, evaluate, and revise curricula, course content, and course materials and methods of instruction. Prepare course materials such as syllabi, homework assignments, and handouts. Select and obtain materials and supplies such as textbooks. Supervise undergraduate and/or graduate teaching, internship, and research work. Act as advisers to student organizations. Collaborate with colleagues to address teaching and research issues. Conduct research in a particular field of knowledge, and publish findings in professional journals, books, and/or electronic media. Participate in campus and community events. Participate in student recruitment, registration, and placement activities. Perform administrative duties such as serving as department head. Provide professional consulting services to government and/or industry. Serve on academic or administrative committees that deal with institutional policies, departmental matters, and academic issues. Write grant proposals to procure external research funding. **SKILLS—**Instructing; Learning Strategies; Reading Comprehension; Active Learning; Speaking; Writing; Science; Active Listening; Critical Thinking.

GOE—Interest Area: 12. Education and Social Service. **Work Group:** 12.03. Educational Services. **Other Jobs in This Work Group:** Adult Literacy, Remedial Education, and GED Teachers and Instructors; Agricultural Sciences Teachers, Postsecondary; Anthropology and Archeology Teachers, Postsecondary; Architecture Teachers, Postsecondary; Archivists; Area, Ethnic, and Cultural Studies Teachers, Postsecondary; Art, Drama, and Music Teachers, Postsecondary; Atmospheric, Earth, Marine, and Space Sciences Teachers, Postsecondary; Audio-Visual Collections Specialists; Biological Science Teachers, Postsecondary; Business Teachers, Postsecondary; Chemistry Teachers, Postsecondary; Child Care Workers; Communications Teachers, Postsecondary; Computer Science Teachers, Postsecondary; Criminal Justice and Law

Enforcement Teachers, Postsecondary; Curators; Economics Teachers, Postsecondary; Education Teachers, Postsecondary; Education, Training, and Library Workers, All Other; Educational Psychologists; Educational, Vocational, and School Counselors; Elementary School Teachers, Except Special Education; Engineering Teachers, Postsecondary; English Language and Literature Teachers, Postsecondary; Environmental Science Teachers, Postsecondary; Farm and Home Management Advisors; Foreign Language and Literature Teachers, Postsecondary; Forestry and Conservation Science Teachers, Postsecondary; Geography Teachers, Postsecondary; Graduate Teaching Assistants; Health Specialties Teachers, Postsecondary; History Teachers, Postsecondary; Home Economics Teachers, Postsecondary; Kindergarten Teachers, Except Special Education; Law Teachers, Postsecondary; Librarians; Library Assistants, Clerical; Library Science Teachers, Postsecondary; Library Technicians; Mathematical Science Teachers, Postsecondary; Middle School Teachers, Except Special and Vocational Education; Museum Technicians and Conservators; Nannies; Nursing Instructors and Teachers, Postsecondary; Personal Financial Advisors; Philosophy and Religion Teachers, Postsecondary; Physics Teachers, Postsecondary; Postsecondary Teachers, All Other; Preschool Teachers, Except Special Education; Psychology Teachers, Postsecondary; Recreation and Fitness Studies Teachers, Postsecondary; Secondary School Teachers, Except Special and Vocational Education; Self-Enrichment Education Teachers; Social Sciences Teachers, Postsecondary, All Other; Social Work Teachers, Postsecondary; Sociology Teachers, Postsecondary; Special Education Teachers, Middle School; Special Education Teachers, Preschool, Kindergarten, and Elementary School; Special Education Teachers, Secondary School; Teacher Assistants; Teachers and Instructors, All Other; Vocational Education Teachers, Postsecondary; Vocational Education Teachers, Middle School; Vocational Education Teachers, Secondary School.

EDUCATION/TRAINING PROGRAM(S)— American Government and Politics (United States);

Political Science and Government, General; Political Science and Government, Other; Social Science Teacher Education. **RELATED KNOWLEDGE/COURSES**—Sociology and Anthropology; History and Archeology; Education and Training; Psychology; Economics and Accounting; English Language.

Preschool Teachers, Except Special Education

- Personality Code: SA
- Growth: 36.2%
- Annual Job Openings: 88,000
- Annual Earnings: $19,820
- Education/Training Required: Bachelor's degree
- Self-Employed: 2.2%
- Part-Time: 24.9%

Instruct children (normally up to 5 years of age) in activities designed to promote social, physical, and intellectual growth needed for primary school in preschool, day care center, or other child development facility. May be required to hold state certification. Demonstrate activities to children. Enforce all administration policies and rules governing students. Establish and enforce rules for behavior, and procedures for maintaining order. Identify children showing signs of emotional, developmental, or health-related problems, and discuss them with supervisors, parents or guardians, and child development specialists. Maintain accurate and complete student records as required by laws, district policies, and administrative regulations. Meet with other professionals to discuss individual students' needs and progress. Meet with parents and guardians to discuss their children's progress and needs, determine their priorities for their children, and suggest ways that they can promote learning and development. Observe and evaluate children's performance, behavior, social development, and physical health. Organize and label materials, and display students' work in a manner appropriate for their ages and perceptual skills. Prepare and implement remedial programs for students requiring extra help. Prepare reports on students and activities as required by administration. Establish clear objectives for all lessons, units, and projects, and communicate those objectives to children. Organize and lead activities designed to promote physical, mental and social development, such as games, arts and crafts, music, storytelling, and field trips. Plan and conduct activities for a balanced program of instruction, demonstration, and work time that provides students with opportunities to observe, question, and investigate. Prepare materials and classrooms for class activities. Teach basic skills such as color, shape, number and letter recognition, personal hygiene, and social skills. Plan and supervise class projects, field trips, visits by guests, or other experiential activities, and guide students in learning from those activities. Adapt teaching methods and instructional materials to meet students' varying needs and interests. Arrange indoor and outdoor space to facilitate creative play, motor-skill activities, and safety. Assimilate arriving children to the school environment by greeting them, helping them remove outerwear, and selecting activities of interest to them. **SKILLS**—Social Perceptiveness; Learning Strategies; Monitoring; Instructing; Management of Personnel Resources; Speaking; Coordination; Active Listening; Service Orientation; Management of Material Resources.

GOE—Interest Area: 12. Education and Social Service. **Work Group:** 12.03. Educational Services. **Other Jobs in This Work Group:** Adult Literacy, Remedial Education, and GED Teachers and Instructors; Agricultural Sciences Teachers, Postsecondary; Anthropology and Archeology Teachers, Postsecondary; Architecture Teachers, Postsecondary; Archivists; Area, Ethnic, and Cultural Studies Teachers, Postsecondary; Art, Drama, and Music Teachers, Postsecondary; Atmospheric, Earth, Marine, and Space Sciences Teachers, Postsecondary; Audio-Visual Collections Specialists; Biological Science Teachers, Postsecondary; Business Teachers, Postsecondary; Chemistry Teachers, Postsecondary; Child Care Workers; Communications Teachers, Postsecondary; Computer Science Teachers, Postsecondary; Criminal Justice and Law Enforcement Teachers, Postsecondary; Curators; Economics Teachers, Postsecondary; Education Teachers, Postsecondary; Education, Training, and Library Workers, All Other; Educational Psychologists; Educational, Vocational, and School Counselors; Elementary School Teachers, Except Special Education; Engineering Teachers, Postsecondary; English Language and Literature Teachers, Postsecondary; Environmental Science Teachers, Postsecondary; Farm and Home Management Advisors; Foreign Language and Literature Teachers, Postsecondary; Forestry and Conservation Science Teachers, Postsecondary; Geography Teachers, Postsecondary; Graduate Teaching Assistants; Health Specialties Teachers, Postsecondary; History Teachers, Postsecondary; Home Economics Teachers, Postsecondary; Kindergarten Teachers, Except Special Education; Law Teachers, Postsecondary; Librarians; Library Assistants, Clerical; Library Science Teachers, Postsecondary; Library Technicians; Mathematical Science Teachers, Postsecondary; Middle School Teachers, Except Special and Vocational Education; Museum Technicians and Conservators; Nannies; Nursing Instructors and Teachers, Postsecondary; Personal Financial Advisors; Philosophy and Religion Teachers, Postsecondary; Physics Teachers, Postsecondary; Political Science Teachers, Postsecondary; Postsecondary Teachers, All Other; Psychology Teachers, Postsecondary; Recreation and Fitness Studies Teachers, Postsecondary; Secondary School Teachers, Except Special and Vocational Education; Self-Enrichment Education Teachers; Social Sciences Teachers, Postsecondary, All Other; Social Work Teachers, Postsecondary; Sociology Teachers, Postsecondary; Special Education Teachers, Middle School; Special Education Teachers, Preschool, Kindergarten, and Elementary School; Special Education Teachers, Secondary School;

Teacher Assistants; Teachers and Instructors, All Other; Vocational Education Teachers, Postsecondary; Vocational Education Teachers, Middle School; Vocational Education Teachers, Secondary School.

EDUCATION/TRAINING PROGRAM(S)— Child Care and Support Services Management; Early Childhood Education and Teaching; Kindergarten/Preschool Education and Teaching. **RELATED KNOWLEDGE/COURSES—**Customer and Personal Service; Education and Training; Psychology; Therapy and Counseling; Sociology and Anthropology; Fine Arts.

Psychology Teachers, Postsecondary

- Personality Code: SI
- Growth: 38.1%
- Annual Job Openings: 216,000
- Annual Earnings: $54,170
- Education/Training Required: Master's degree
- Self-Employed: 0.3%
- Part-Time: 27.7%

Teach courses in psychology, such as child, clinical, and developmental psychology, and psychological counseling. Evaluate and grade students' class work, laboratory work, assignments, and papers. Prepare and deliver lectures to undergraduate and/or graduate students on topics such as abnormal psychology, cognitive processes, and work motivation. Advise students on academic and vocational curricula, and on career issues. Compile, administer, and grade examinations, or assign this work to others. Compile bibliographies of specialized materials for outside reading assignments. Initiate, facilitate, and moderate classroom discussions. Keep abreast of developments in their field by reading current liter-

ature, talking with colleagues, and participating in professional conferences. Maintain regularly scheduled office hours in order to advise and assist students. Maintain student attendance records, grades, and other required records. Plan, evaluate, and revise curricula, course content, and course materials and methods of instruction. Prepare course materials such as syllabi, homework assignments, and handouts. Select and obtain materials and supplies such as textbooks. Supervise students' laboratory work. Supervise undergraduate and/or graduate teaching, internship, and research work. Act as advisers to student organizations. Collaborate with colleagues to address teaching and research issues. Conduct research in a particular field of knowledge, and publish findings in professional journals, books, and/or electronic media. Participate in campus and community events. Participate in student recruitment, registration, and placement activities. Perform administrative duties such as serving as department head. Provide professional consulting services to government and/or industry. Serve on academic or administrative committees that deal with institutional policies, departmental matters, and academic issues. Write grant proposals to procure external research funding. **SKILLS—**Instructing; Learning Strategies; Reading Comprehension; Active Learning; Speaking; Writing; Science; Active Listening; Critical Thinking.

GOE—Interest Area: 12. Education and Social Service. **Work Group:** 12.03. Educational Services. **Other Jobs in This Work Group:** Adult Literacy, Remedial Education, and GED Teachers and Instructors; Agricultural Sciences Teachers, Postsecondary; Anthropology and Archeology Teachers, Postsecondary; Architecture Teachers, Postsecondary; Archivists; Area, Ethnic, and Cultural Studies Teachers, Postsecondary; Art, Drama, and Music Teachers, Postsecondary; Atmospheric, Earth, Marine, and Space Sciences Teachers, Postsecondary; Audio-Visual Collections Specialists; Biological Science Teachers, Postsecondary; Business Teachers, Postsecondary; Chemistry Teachers, Postsecondary; Child Care Workers; Communications Teachers, Postsecondary; Computer Science Teachers, Postsecondary; Criminal Justice and Law Enforcement Teachers, Postsecondary; Curators; Economics Teachers, Postsecondary; Education Teachers, Postsecondary; Education, Training, and Library Workers, All Other; Educational Psychologists; Educational, Vocational, and School Counselors; Elementary School Teachers, Except Special Education; Engineering Teachers, Postsecondary; English Language and Literature Teachers, Postsecondary; Environmental Science Teachers, Postsecondary; Farm and Home Management Advisors; Foreign Language and Literature Teachers, Postsecondary; Forestry and Conservation Science Teachers, Postsecondary; Geography Teachers, Postsecondary; Graduate Teaching Assistants; Health Specialties Teachers, Postsecondary; History Teachers, Postsecondary; Home Economics Teachers, Postsecondary; Kindergarten Teachers, Except Special Education; Law Teachers, Postsecondary; Librarians; Library Assistants, Clerical; Library Science Teachers, Postsecondary; Library Technicians; Mathematical Science Teachers, Postsecondary; Middle School Teachers, Except Special and Vocational Education; Museum Technicians and Conservators; Nannies; Nursing Instructors and Teachers, Postsecondary; Personal Financial Advisors; Philosophy and Religion Teachers, Postsecondary; Physics Teachers, Postsecondary; Political Science Teachers, Postsecondary; Postsecondary Teachers, All Other; Preschool Teachers, Except Special Education; Recreation and Fitness Studies Teachers, Postsecondary; Secondary School Teachers, Except Special and Vocational Education; Self-Enrichment Education Teachers; Social Sciences Teachers, Postsecondary, All Other; Social Work Teachers, Postsecondary; Sociology Teachers, Postsecondary; Special Education Teachers, Middle School; Special Education Teachers, Preschool, Kindergarten, and Elementary School; Special Education Teachers, Secondary School; Teacher Assistants; Teachers and Instructors, All Other; Vocational Education Teachers, Postsecondary; Vocational Education Teachers, Middle School; Vocational Education Teachers, Secondary School.

EDUCATION/TRAINING PROGRAM(S)— Clinical Psychology; Cognitive Psychology and Psy-

cholinguistics; Community Psychology; Comparative Psychology; Counseling Psychology; Developmental and Child Psychology; Educational Psychology; Experimental Psychology; Industrial and Organizational Psychology; Marriage and Family Therapy/Counseling; Personality Psychology; Physiological Psychology/Psychobiology; Psychology Teacher Education; Psychology, General; Psychology, Other; Psychometrics and Quantitative Psychology; School Psychology; Social Psychology; Social Science Teacher Education. **RELATED KNOWLEDGE/COURSES—**Sociology and Anthropology; History and Archeology; Education and Training; Psychology; Economics and Accounting; English Language.

Radiation Therapists

◎ Personality Code: SR

◎ Growth: 31.6%

◎ Annual Job Openings: 1,000

◎ Annual Earnings: $54,190

◎ Education/Training Required: Associate's degree

◎ Self-Employed: 0%

◎ Part-Time: 14.2%

Provide radiation therapy to patients as prescribed by a radiologist according to established practices and standards. Duties may include reviewing prescription and diagnosis; acting as liaison with physician and supportive care personnel; preparing equipment, such as immobilization, treatment, and protection devices; and maintaining records, reports, and files. May assist in dosimetry procedures and tumor localization. Administer prescribed doses of radiation to specific body parts, using radiation therapy equipment according to established practices and standards. Position patients for treatment with accuracy according to prescription. Enter data into computer and set controls to operate and adjust equipment and regulate dosage. Follow principles of radiation protection for patient, self, and others. Maintain records, reports and files as required, including such information as radiation dosages, equipment settings and patients' reactions. Review prescription, diagnosis, patient chart, and identification. Conduct most treatment sessions independently, in accordance with the long-term treatment plan and under the general direction of the patient's physician. Check radiation therapy equipment to ensure proper operation. Observe and reassure patients during treatment and report unusual reactions to physician or turn equipment off if unexpected adverse reactions occur. Check for side effects such as skin irritation, nausea and hair loss to assess patients' reaction to treatment. Educate, prepare and reassure patients and their families by answering questions, providing physical assistance, and reinforcing physicians' advice regarding treatment reactions and post-treatment care. Calculate actual treatment dosages delivered during each session. Prepare and construct equipment, such as immobilization, treatment, and protection devices. Photograph treated area of patient and process film. Help physicians, radiation oncologists and clinical physicists to prepare physical and technical aspects of radiation treatment plans, using information about patient condition and anatomy. Train and supervise student or subordinate radiotherapy technologists. Act as liaison with physicist and supportive care personnel. Provide assistance to other health-care personnel during dosimetry procedures and tumor localization. Implement appropriate follow-up care plans. Store, sterilize, or prepare the special applicators containing the radioactive substance implanted by the physician. Assist in the preparation of sealed radioactive materials, such as cobalt, radium, cesium and isotopes, for use in radiation treatments. **SKILLS**—Operation Monitoring; Technology Design; Operation and Control; Time Management; Instructing; Service Orientation; Management of Personnel Resources; Social Perceptiveness.

GOE—Interest Area: 14. Medical and Health Services. **Work Group:** 14.06. Medical Therapy. **Other Jobs in This Work Group:** Audiologists; Health Diagnosing and Treating Practitioners, All Other;

Massage Therapists; Occupational Therapist Aides; Occupational Therapist Assistants; Occupational Therapists; Physical Therapist Aides; Physical Therapist Assistants; Physical Therapists; Recreational Therapists; Respiratory Therapists; Respiratory Therapy Technicians; Speech-Language Pathologists; Therapists, All Other.

EDUCATION/TRAINING PROGRAM(S)— Medical Radiologic Technology/Science— Radiation Therapist. **RELATED KNOWLEDGE/COURSES**—Medicine and Dentistry; Customer and Personal Service; Psychology; Biology; Physics; Mathematics.

Registered Nurses

- Personality Code: SI
- Growth: 27.3%
- Annual Job Openings: 215,000
- Annual Earnings: $49,550
- Education/Training Required: Associate's degree
- Self-Employed: 1.2%
- Part-Time: 22.0%

Assess patient health problems and needs, develop and implement nursing care plans, and maintain medical records. Administer nursing care to ill, injured, convalescent, or disabled patients. May advise patients on health maintenance and disease prevention or provide case management. Licensing or registration required. Includes advance practice nurses such as: nurse practitioners, clinical nurse specialists, certified nurse midwives, and certified registered nurse anesthetists. Advanced practice nursing is practiced by RNs who have specialized formal, post-basic education and who function in highly autonomous and specialized roles. Maintain accurate, detailed reports and records. Monitor, record and report symptoms and changes in patients' conditions. Record patients' medical information and vital signs. Modify patient treatment plans as indicated by patients' responses and conditions. Consult and coordinate with health care team members to assess, plan, implement and evaluate patient care plans. Order, interpret, and evaluate diagnostic tests to identify and assess patient's condition. Monitor all aspects of patient care, including diet and physical activity. Direct and supervise less skilled nursing/health care personnel, or supervise a particular unit on one shift. Prepare patients for, and assist with, examinations and treatments. Observe nurses and visit patients to ensure that proper nursing care is provided. Assess the needs of individuals, families and/or communities, including assessment of individuals' home and/or work environments to identify potential health or safety problems. Instruct individuals, families and other groups on topics such as health education, disease prevention and childbirth, and develop health improvement programs. Prepare rooms, sterile instruments, equipment and supplies, and ensure that stock of supplies is maintained. Inform physician of patient's condition during anesthesia. Deliver infants and provide prenatal and postpartum care and treatment under obstetrician's supervision. Administer local, inhalation, intravenous, and other anesthetics. Provide health care, first aid, immunizations and assistance in convalescence and rehabilitation in locations such as schools, hospitals, and industry. Perform physical examinations, make tentative diagnoses, and treat patients en route to hospitals or at disaster site triage centers. Conduct specified laboratory tests. Hand items to surgeons during operations. Prescribe or recommend drugs, medical devices or other forms of treatment, such as physical therapy, inhalation therapy, or related therapeutic procedures. Direct and coordinate infection control programs, advising and consulting with specified personnel about necessary precautions. **SKILLS**—Social Perceptiveness; Service Orientation; Instructing; Time Management; Critical Thinking; Learning Strategies; Coordination; Active Learning; Monitoring.

GOE—Interest Area: 14. Medical and Health Services. **Work Group:** 14.02. Medicine and Surgery. **Other Jobs in This Work Group:** Anesthesiologists;

Family and General Practitioners; Healthcare Support Workers, All Other; Internists, General; Medical Assistants; Obstetricians and Gynecologists; Pediatricians, General; Pharmacists; Pharmacy Aides; Pharmacy Technicians; Physician Assistants; Physicians and Surgeons, All Other; Psychiatrists; Surgeons; Surgical Technologists.

EDUCATION/TRAINING PROGRAM(S)— Adult Health Nurse/Nursing; Clinical Nurse Specialist; Critical Care Nursing; Family Practice Nurse/Nurse Practitioner; Maternal/Child Health and Neonatal Nurse/Nursing; Nurse Anesthetist; Nurse Midwife/Nursing Midwifery; Nursing— Registered Nurse Training (RN, ASN, BSN, MSN); Nursing Science (MS, PhD); Nursing, Other; Occupational and Environmental Health Nursing; Pediatric Nurse/Nursing; Perioperative/ Operating Room and Surgical Nurse/Nursing; Psychiatric/Mental Health Nurse/Nursing; Public Health/Community Nurse/Nursing. **RELATED KNOWLEDGE/COURSES**—Psychology; Medicine and Dentistry; Customer and Personal Service; Therapy and Counseling; Sociology and Anthropology; Philosophy and Theology.

Secondary School Teachers, Except Special and Vocational Education

- Personality Code: SA
- Growth: 18.2%
- Annual Job Openings: 118,000
- Annual Earnings: $44,580
- Education/Training Required: Bachelor's degree
- Self-Employed: 0%
- Part-Time: 8.8%

Social—S

Instruct students in secondary public or private schools in one or more subjects at the secondary level, such as English, mathematics, or social studies. May be designated according to subject matter specialty, such as typing instructors, commercial teachers, or English teachers. Instruct through lectures, discussions, and demonstrations in one or more subjects such as English, mathematics, or social studies. Prepare, administer, and grade tests and assignments to evaluate students' progress. Assign and grade class work and homework. Adapt teaching methods and instructional materials to meet students' varying needs and interests. Confer with other staff members to plan and schedule lessons promoting learning, following approved curricula. Confer with parents or guardians, other teachers, counselors, and administrators in order to resolve students' behavioral and academic problems. Enforce all administration policies and rules governing students. Establish and enforce rules for behavior and procedures for maintaining order among the students for whom they are responsible. Guide and counsel students with adjustment and/or academic problems, or special academic interests. Instruct and monitor students in the use and care of equipment and materials, in order to prevent injuries and damage. Maintain accurate and complete student records as required by laws, district policies, and administrative regulations. Establish clear objectives for all lessons, units, and projects, and communicate those objectives to students. Meet with other professionals to discuss individual students' needs and progress. Meet with parents and guardians to discuss their children's progress, and to determine their priorities for their children and their resource needs. Observe and evaluate students' performance, behavior, social development, and physical health. Plan and conduct activities for a balanced program of instruction, demonstration, and work time that provides students with opportunities to observe, question, and investigate. Plan and supervise class projects, field trips, visits by guest speakers, or other experiential activities, and guide students in learning from those activities. Prepare and implement remedial programs for students requiring extra help. Prepare for assigned classes, and show written evidence of preparation upon request of immediate supervisors. Prepare materials and classrooms for class activities. **SKILLS**—Learning Strategies; Instructing; Speaking; Social Perceptiveness; Mathematics; Reading Comprehension; Monitoring; Active Learning.

GOE—Interest Area: 12. Education and Social Service. **Work Group:** 12.03. Educational Services. **Other Jobs in This Work Group:** Adult Literacy, Remedial Education, and GED Teachers and Instructors; Agricultural Sciences Teachers, Postsecondary; Anthropology and Archeology Teachers, Postsecondary; Architecture Teachers, Postsecondary; Archivists; Area, Ethnic, and Cultural Studies Teachers, Postsecondary; Art, Drama, and Music Teachers, Postsecondary; Atmospheric, Earth, Marine, and Space Sciences Teachers, Postsecondary; Audio-Visual Collections Specialists; Biological Science Teachers, Postsecondary; Business Teachers, Postsecondary; Chemistry Teachers, Postsecondary; Child Care Workers; Communications Teachers, Postsecondary; Computer Science Teachers, Postsecondary; Criminal Justice and Law Enforcement Teachers, Postsecondary; Curators; Economics Teachers, Postsecondary; Education Teachers, Postsecondary; Education, Training, and Library Workers, All Other; Educational Psychologists; Educational, Vocational, and School Counselors; Elementary School Teachers, Except Special Education; Engineering Teachers, Postsecondary; English Language and Literature Teachers, Postsecondary; Environmental Science Teachers, Postsecondary; Farm and Home Management Advisors; Foreign Language and Literature Teachers, Postsecondary; Forestry and Conservation Science Teachers, Postsecondary; Geography Teachers, Postsecondary; Graduate Teaching Assistants; Health Specialties Teachers, Postsecondary; History Teachers, Postsecondary; Home Economics Teachers, Postsecondary; Kindergarten Teachers, Except Special Education; Law Teachers, Postsecondary; Librarians; Library Assistants, Clerical; Library Science Teachers, Postsecondary; Library Technicians; Mathematical Science Teachers, Postsecondary; Middle School Teachers, Except Special and Vocational Education; Museum Technicians and Conservators; Nannies; Nursing Instructors and Teachers, Postsecondary; Personal Financial Advisors; Philosophy and Religion Teachers, Postsecondary; Physics Teachers, Postsecondary; Political Science Teachers, Postsecondary; Postsecondary Teachers, All Other; Preschool Teachers, Except Special Education; Psychology Teachers, Postsecondary; Recreation and Fitness Studies Teachers, Postsecondary; Self-Enrichment Education Teachers; Social Sciences Teachers, Postsecondary, All Other; Social Work Teachers, Postsecondary; Sociology Teachers, Postsecondary; Special Education Teachers, Middle School; Special Education Teachers, Preschool, Kindergarten, and Elementary School; Special Education Teachers, Secondary School; Teacher Assistants; Teachers and Instructors, All Other; Vocational Education Teachers, Postsecondary; Vocational Education Teachers, Middle School; Vocational Education Teachers, Secondary School.

EDUCATION/TRAINING PROGRAM(S)— Agricultural Teacher Education; Art Teacher Education; Biology Teacher Education; Business Teacher Education; Chemistry Teacher Education; Computer Teacher Education; Drama and Dance Teacher Education; Driver and Safety Teacher Education; English/Language Arts Teacher Education; Family and Consumer Sciences/Home Economics Teacher Education; Foreign Language Teacher Education; French Language Teacher Education; Geography Teacher Education; German Language Teacher Education; Health Occupations Teacher Education; Health Teacher Education; History Teacher Education; Junior High/Intermediate/Middle School Education and Teaching; Latin Teacher Education; Mathematics Teacher Education; Music Teacher Education; Physical Education Teaching and Coaching; Physics Teacher Education; Reading Teacher Education; Sales and Marketing Operations/Marketing and Distribution Teacher Education; Science Teacher Education/General Science

Teacher Education; Secondary Education and Teaching; Social Science Teacher Education; Social Studies Teacher Education; Spanish Language Teacher Education; Speech Teacher Education; Teacher Education and Professional Development, Specific Subject Areas, Other; Teacher Education, Multiple Levels; Technology Teacher Education/Industrial Arts Teacher Education. **RELATED KNOWLEDGE/COURSES**—Education and Training; Therapy and Counseling; English Language; History and Archeology; Sociology and Anthropology; Geography.

Security Guards

- Personality Code: SE
- Growth: 31.9%
- Annual Job Openings: 228,000
- Annual Earnings: $19,660
- Education/Training Required: Short-term on-the-job training
- Self-Employed: 0.9%
- Part-Time: 15.1%

Guard, patrol, or monitor premises to prevent theft, violence, or infractions of rules. Patrol industrial and commercial premises to prevent and detect signs of intrusion and ensure security of doors, windows, and gates. Answer alarms and investigate disturbances. Monitor and authorize entrance and departure of employees, visitors, and other persons to guard against theft and maintain security of premises. Write reports of daily activities and irregularities, such as equipment or property damage, theft, presence of unauthorized persons, or unusual occurrences. Call police or fire departments in cases of emergency, such as fire or presence of unauthorized persons. Circulate among visitors, patrons, and employees to preserve order and protect property. Answer telephone calls to take messages, answer questions, and provide information during

Social—S

non-business hours or when switchboard is closed. Warn persons of rule infractions or violations, and apprehend or evict violators from premises, using force when necessary. Operate detecting devices to screen individuals and prevent passage of prohibited articles into restricted areas. Escort or drive motor vehicle to transport individuals to specified locations and to provide personal protection. Inspect and adjust security systems, equipment, and machinery to ensure operational use and to detect evidence of tampering. Drive and guard armored vehicle to transport money and valuables to prevent theft and ensure safe delivery. **SKILLS**—Social Perceptiveness; Negotiation; Learning Strategies; Speaking; Time Management; Monitoring; Active Listening; Critical Thinking.

GOE—Interest Area: 04. Law, Law Enforcement, and Public Safety. **Work Group:** 04.03. Law Enforcement. **Other Jobs in This Work Group:** Animal Control Workers; Bailiffs; Child Support, Missing Persons, and Unemployment Insurance Fraud Investigators; Correctional Officers and Jailers; Criminal Investigators and Special Agents; Crossing Guards; Detectives and Criminal Investigators; Fire Investigators; Fish and Game Wardens; Forensic Science Technicians; Gaming Surveillance Officers and Gaming Investigators; Highway Patrol Pilots; Immigration and Customs Inspectors; Lifeguards, Ski Patrol, and Other Recreational Protective Service Workers; Parking Enforcement Workers; Police and Sheriff's Patrol Officers; Police Detectives; Police Identification and Records Officers; Police Patrol Officers; Private Detectives and Investigators; Protective Service Workers, All Other; Sheriffs and Deputy Sheriffs; Transit and Railroad Police.

EDUCATION/TRAINING PROGRAM(S)—Securities Services Administration/Management; Security and Loss Prevention Services. **RELATED KNOWLEDGE/COURSES**—Public Safety and Security; Customer and Personal Service; Law and Government; Clerical Studies; Telecommunications; English Language.

Self-Enrichment Education Teachers

- Personality Code: SA
- Growth: 40.1%
- Annual Job Openings: 39,000
- Annual Earnings: $29,820
- Education/Training Required: Work experience in a related occupation
- Self-Employed: 19.9%
- Part-Time: 41.0%

Teach or instruct courses other than those that normally lead to an occupational objective or degree. Courses may include self-improvement, nonvocational, and nonacademic subjects. Teaching may or may not take place in a traditional educational institution. Review instructional content, methods, and student evaluations in order to assess strengths and weaknesses, and to develop recommendations for course revision, development, or elimination. Attend professional meetings, conferences, and workshops in order to maintain and improve professional competence. Attend staff meetings, and serve on committees as required. Meet with parents and guardians to discuss their children's progress, and to determine their priorities for their children. Observe and evaluate the performance of other instructors. Organize and supervise games and other recreational activities to promote physical, mental, and social development. Participate in publicity planning and student recruitment. Schedule class times to ensure maximum attendance. Select, order, and issue books, materials, and supplies for courses or projects. Write instructional articles on designated subjects. Use computers, audiovisual aids, and other equipment and materials to supplement presentations. Conduct classes, workshops, and demonstrations, and provide individual instruction to teach topics and skills such as cooking, dancing, writing, physical fitness, photography, personal finance, and flying.

Instruct students individually and in groups, using various teaching methods such as lectures, discussions, and demonstrations. Adapt teaching methods and instructional materials to meet students' varying needs and interests. Assign and grade class work and homework. Confer with other teachers and professionals to plan and schedule lessons promoting learning and development. Enforce policies and rules governing students. Establish clear objectives for all lessons, units, and projects, and communicate those objectives to students. Instruct and monitor students in use and care of equipment and materials, in order to prevent injury and damage. Maintain accurate and complete student records as required by administrative policy. Meet with other instructors to discuss individual students and their progress. Monitor students' performance in order to make suggestions for improvement, and to ensure that they satisfy course standards, training requirements, and objectives. **SKILLS**—Instructing; Writing; Speaking; Learning Strategies; Service Orientation; Systems Evaluation; Reading Comprehension; Active Listening; Judgment and Decision Making; Management of Material Resources.

GOE—**Interest Area:** 12. Education and Social Service. **Work Group:** 12.03. Educational Services. **Other Jobs in This Work Group:** Adult Literacy, Remedial Education, and GED Teachers and Instructors; Agricultural Sciences Teachers, Postsecondary; Anthropology and Archeology Teachers, Postsecondary; Architecture Teachers, Postsecondary; Archivists; Area, Ethnic, and Cultural Studies Teachers, Postsecondary; Art, Drama, and Music Teachers, Postsecondary; Atmospheric, Earth, Marine, and Space Sciences Teachers, Postsecondary; Audio-Visual Collections Specialists; Biological Science Teachers, Postsecondary; Business Teachers, Postsecondary; Chemistry Teachers, Postsecondary; Child Care Workers; Communications Teachers, Postsecondary; Computer Science Teachers, Postsecondary; Criminal Justice and Law Enforcement Teachers, Postsecondary; Curators; Economics Teachers, Postsecondary; Education Teachers, Postsecondary; Education, Training, and Library Workers, All Other; Educational Psychologists; Educational, Vocational, and School Counselors; Elementary School Teachers, Except Special Education; Engineering Teachers, Postsecondary; English Language and Literature Teachers, Postsecondary; Environmental Science Teachers, Postsecondary; Farm and Home Management Advisors; Foreign Language and Literature Teachers, Postsecondary; Forestry and Conservation Science Teachers, Postsecondary; Geography Teachers, Postsecondary; Graduate Teaching Assistants; Health Specialties Teachers, Postsecondary; History Teachers, Postsecondary; Home Economics Teachers, Postsecondary; Kindergarten Teachers, Except Special Education; Law Teachers, Postsecondary; Librarians; Library Assistants, Clerical; Library Science Teachers, Postsecondary; Library Technicians; Mathematical Science Teachers, Postsecondary; Middle School Teachers, Except Special and Vocational Education; Museum Technicians and Conservators; Nannies; Nursing Instructors and Teachers, Postsecondary; Personal Financial Advisors; Philosophy and Religion Teachers, Postsecondary; Physics Teachers, Postsecondary; Political Science Teachers, Postsecondary; Postsecondary Teachers, All Other; Preschool Teachers, Except Special Education; Psychology Teachers, Postsecondary; Recreation and Fitness Studies Teachers, Postsecondary; Secondary School Teachers, Except Special and Vocational Education; Social Sciences Teachers, Postsecondary, All Other; Social Work Teachers, Postsecondary; Sociology Teachers, Postsecondary; Special Education Teachers, Middle School; Special Education Teachers, Preschool, Kindergarten, and Elementary School; Special Education Teachers, Secondary School; Teacher Assistants; Teachers and Instructors, All Other; Vocational Education Teachers, Postsecondary; Vocational Education Teachers, Middle School; Vocational Education Teachers, Secondary School.

EDUCATION/TRAINING PROGRAM(S)— Adult and Continuing Education and Teaching. **RELATED KNOWLEDGE/COURSES**—Education and Training; English Language; Philosophy and Theology; Sociology and Anthropology; History and Archeology; Economics and Accounting.

Social—S

Sheriffs and Deputy Sheriffs

- Personality Code: SE
- Growth: 24.7%
- Annual Job Openings: 67,000
- Annual Earnings: $44,020
- Education/Training Required: Long-term on-the-job training
- Self-Employed: 0%
- Part-Time: 1.4%

Enforce law and order in rural or unincorporated districts or serve legal processes of courts. May patrol courthouse, guard court or grand jury, or escort defendants. Investigate illegal or suspicious activities. Notify patrol units to take violators into custody or to provide needed assistance or medical aid. Question individuals entering secured areas to determine their business, directing and rerouting individuals as necessary. Record daily activities, and submit logs and other related reports and paperwork to appropriate authorities. Serve statements of claims, subpoenas, summonses, jury summonses, orders to pay alimony, and other court orders. Take control of accident scenes to maintain traffic flow, to assist accident victims, and to investigate causes. Verify that the proper legal charges have been made against law offenders. Patrol and guard courthouses, grand jury rooms, or assigned areas, in order to provide security, enforce laws, maintain order, and arrest violators. Locate and confiscate real or personal property, as directed by court order. Manage jail operations, and tend to jail inmates. Place people in protective custody. Drive vehicles or patrol specific areas to detect law violators, issue citations, and make arrests. Execute arrest warrants, locating and taking persons into custody. Transport or escort prisoners and defendants en route to courtrooms, prisons or jails, attorneys' offices, or medical facilities. **SKILLS**—Social Perceptiveness; Service Orientation; Active Listening; Speaking; Coordination; Judgment and Decision Making; Writing; Critical Thinking.

GOE—Interest Area: 04. Law, Law Enforcement, and Public Safety. **Work Group:** 04.03. Law Enforcement. **Other Jobs in This Work Group:** Animal Control Workers; Bailiffs; Child Support, Missing Persons, and Unemployment Insurance Fraud Investigators; Correctional Officers and Jailers; Criminal Investigators and Special Agents; Crossing Guards; Detectives and Criminal Investigators; Fire Investigators; Fish and Game Wardens; Forensic Science Technicians; Gaming Surveillance Officers and Gaming Investigators; Highway Patrol Pilots; Immigration and Customs Inspectors; Lifeguards, Ski Patrol, and Other Recreational Protective Service Workers; Parking Enforcement Workers; Police and Sheriff's Patrol Officers; Police Detectives; Police Identification and Records Officers; Police Patrol Officers; Private Detectives and Investigators; Protective Service Workers, All Other; Security Guards; Transit and Railroad Police.

EDUCATION/TRAINING PROGRAM(S)— Criminal Justice/Police Science; Criminalistics and Criminal Science. **RELATED KNOWLEDGE/ COURSES**—Public Safety and Security; Law and Government; Psychology; Geography; Sociology and Anthropology; Clerical Studies.

Social and Community Service Managers

- Personality Code: SE
- Growth: 27.7%
- Annual Job Openings: 19,000
- Annual Earnings: $45,450
- Education/Training Required: Bachelor's degree
- Self-Employed: 6.6%
- Part-Time: 10.7%

Plan, organize, or coordinate the activities of a social service program or community outreach organization. Oversee the program or organization's budget and policies regarding participant involvement, program requirements, and benefits. Work may involve directing social workers, counselors, or probation officers. Establish and maintain relationships with other agencies and organizations in community in order to meet community needs and to ensure that services are not duplicated. Prepare and maintain records and reports, such as budgets, personnel records, or training manuals. Direct activities of professional and technical staff members and volunteers. Evaluate the work of staff and volunteers in order to ensure that programs are of appropriate quality and that resources are used effectively. Establish and oversee administrative procedures to meet objectives set by boards of directors or senior management. Participate in the determination of organizational policies regarding such issues as participant eligibility, program requirements, and program benefits. Research and analyze member or community needs in order to determine program directions and goals. Speak to community groups to explain and interpret agency purposes, programs, and policies. Recruit, interview, and hire or sign up volunteers and staff. Represent organizations in relations with governmental and media institutions. Plan and administer budgets for programs, equipment and support services. Analyze proposed legislation, regulations, or rule changes in order to determine how agency services could be impacted. Act as consultants to agency staff and other community programs regarding the interpretation of program-related federal, state, and county regulations and policies. Implement and evaluate staff training programs. Direct fund-raising activities and the preparation of public relations materials. **SKILLS**—Social Perceptiveness; Service Orientation; Negotiation; Management of Personnel Resources; Persuasion; Instructing; Monitoring; Learning Strategies; Time Management.

GOE—**Interest Area:** 12. Education and Social Service. **Work Group:** 12.01. Managerial Work in Edu-

cation and Social Service. **Other Jobs in This Work Group:** Education Administrators, All Other; Education Administrators, Elementary and Secondary School; Education Administrators, Postsecondary; Education Administrators, Preschool and Child Care Center/Program; Instructional Coordinators; Park Naturalists.

EDUCATION/TRAINING PROGRAM(S)—Business Administration and Management, General; Business, Management, Marketing, and Related Support Services, Other; Business/Commerce, General; Community Organization and Advocacy; Entrepreneurship/Entrepreneurial Studies; Human Services, General; Non-Profit/Public/Organizational Management; Public Administration. **RELATED KNOWLEDGE/COURSES**—Customer and Personal Service; Sociology and Anthropology; Psychology; Education and Training; Clerical Studies; Therapy and Counseling.

Social and Human Service Assistants

- Personality Code: SC
- Growth: 48.7%
- Annual Job Openings: 63,000
- Annual Earnings: $23,860
- Education/Training Required: Moderate-term on-the-job training
- Self-Employed: 0.2%
- Part-Time: 10.6%

Assist professionals from a wide variety of fields, such as psychology, rehabilitation, or social work, to provide client services, as well as support for families. May assist clients in identifying available benefits and social and community services and help clients obtain them. May assist social workers with developing, organizing, and conducting programs to prevent and resolve problems relevant to substance abuse, human relationships, rehabilitation, or adult daycare. Provide information on and refer individuals to public or private agencies and community services for assistance. Keep records and prepare reports for owner or management concerning visits with clients. Visit individuals in homes or attend group meetings to provide information on agency services, requirements and procedures. Advise clients regarding food stamps, child care, food, money management, sanitation, and housekeeping. Submit to and review reports and problems with superior. Oversee day-to-day group activities of residents in institution. Interview individuals and family members to compile information on social, educational, criminal, institutional, or drug history. Meet with youth groups to acquaint them with consequences of delinquent acts. Transport and accompany clients to shopping area and to appointments, using automobile. Explain rules established by owner or management, such as sanitation and maintenance requirements, and parking regulations. Observe and discuss meal preparation and suggest alternate methods of food preparation. Demonstrate use and care of equipment for tenant use. Consult with supervisor concerning programs for individual families. Monitor free, supplementary meal program to ensure cleanliness of facility and that eligibility guidelines are met for persons receiving meals. Observe clients' food selections and recommend alternate economical and nutritional food choices. Inform tenants of facilities, such as laundries and playgrounds. Care for children in client's home during client's appointments. Assist in locating housing for displaced individuals. Assist clients with preparation of forms, such as tax or rent forms. Assist in planning of food budget, utilizing charts and sample budgets. SKILLS—Social Perceptiveness; Service Orientation; Management of Financial Resources; Time Management; Instructing; Learning Strategies; Active Listening; Speaking; Critical Thinking.

GOE—Interest Area: 12. Education and Social Service. Work Group: 12.02. Social Services. Other Jobs in This Work Group: Child, Family, and

School Social Workers; Clergy; Clinical Psychologists; Clinical, Counseling, and School Psychologists; Community and Social Service Specialists, All Other; Counseling Psychologists; Counselors, All Other; Directors, Religious Activities and Education; Marriage and Family Therapists; Medical and Public Health Social Workers; Mental Health and Substance Abuse Social Workers; Mental Health Counselors; Probation Officers and Correctional Treatment Specialists; Rehabilitation Counselors; Religious Workers, All Other; Residential Advisors; Social Workers, All Other; Substance Abuse and Behavioral Disorder Counselors.

EDUCATION/TRAINING PROGRAM(S)— Mental and Social Health Services and Allied Professions, Other. RELATED KNOWLEDGE/ COURSES—Therapy and Counseling; Psychology; Customer and Personal Service; Clerical Studies; Sociology and Anthropology; Philosophy and Theology.

Sociology Teachers, Postsecondary

- Personality Code: SI
- Growth: 38.1%
- Annual Job Openings: 216,000
- Annual Earnings: $52,770
- Education/Training Required: Master's degree
- Self-Employed: 0.3%
- Part-Time: 27.7%

Teach courses in sociology. Evaluate and grade students' class work, assignments, and papers. Prepare and deliver lectures to undergraduate and/or graduate students on topics such as race and ethnic relations, measurement and data collection, and workplace social relations. Advise students on academic and vocational curricula, and on career issues.

Compile, administer, and grade examinations, or assign this work to others. Compile bibliographies of specialized materials for outside reading assignments. Initiate, facilitate, and moderate classroom discussions. Keep abreast of developments in their field by reading current literature, talking with colleagues, and participating in professional conferences. Maintain regularly scheduled office hours in order to advise and assist students. Maintain student attendance records, grades, and other required records. Plan, evaluate, and revise curricula, course content, and course materials and methods of instruction. Prepare course materials such as syllabi, homework assignments, and handouts. Select and obtain materials and supplies such as textbooks and laboratory equipment. Supervise students' laboratory and field work. Supervise undergraduate and/or graduate teaching, internship, and research work. Act as advisers to student organizations. Collaborate with colleagues to address teaching and research issues. Conduct research in a particular field of knowledge, and publish findings in professional journals, books, and/or electronic media. Participate in campus and community events. Participate in student recruitment, registration, and placement activities. Perform administrative duties such as serving as department head. Provide professional consulting services to government and/or industry. Serve on academic or administrative committees that deal with institutional policies, departmental matters, and academic issues. Write grant proposals to procure external research funding. **SKILLS—** Instructing; Learning Strategies; Reading Comprehension; Active Learning; Speaking; Writing; Science; Active Listening; Critical Thinking.

GOE—Interest Area: 12. Education and Social Service. **Work Group:** 12.03. Educational Services. **Other Jobs in This Work Group:** Adult Literacy, Remedial Education, and GED Teachers and Instructors; Agricultural Sciences Teachers, Postsecondary; Anthropology and Archeology Teachers, Postsecondary; Architecture Teachers, Postsecondary; Archivists; Area, Ethnic, and Cultural Studies Teachers, Postsecondary; Art, Drama, and Music Teachers, Postsecondary; Atmospheric, Earth, Marine, and Space Sciences Teachers, Postsecondary; Audio-Visual Collections Specialists; Biological Science Teachers, Postsecondary; Business Teachers, Postsecondary; Chemistry Teachers, Postsecondary; Child Care Workers; Communications Teachers, Postsecondary; Computer Science Teachers, Postsecondary; Criminal Justice and Law Enforcement Teachers, Postsecondary; Curators; Economics Teachers, Postsecondary; Education Teachers, Postsecondary; Education, Training, and Library Workers, All Other; Educational Psychologists; Educational, Vocational, and School Counselors; Elementary School Teachers, Except Special Education; Engineering Teachers, Postsecondary; English Language and Literature Teachers, Postsecondary; Environmental Science Teachers, Postsecondary; Farm and Home Management Advisors; Foreign Language and Literature Teachers, Postsecondary; Forestry and Conservation Science Teachers, Postsecondary; Geography Teachers, Postsecondary; Graduate Teaching Assistants; Health Specialties Teachers, Postsecondary; History Teachers, Postsecondary; Home Economics Teachers, Postsecondary; Kindergarten Teachers, Except Special Education; Law Teachers, Postsecondary; Librarians; Library Assistants, Clerical; Library Science Teachers, Postsecondary; Library Technicians; Mathematical Science Teachers, Postsecondary; Middle School Teachers, Except Special and Vocational Education; Museum Technicians and Conservators; Nannies; Nursing Instructors and Teachers, Postsecondary; Personal Financial Advisors; Philosophy and Religion Teachers, Postsecondary; Physics Teachers, Postsecondary; Political Science Teachers, Postsecondary; Postsecondary Teachers, All Other; Preschool Teachers, Except Special Education; Psychology Teachers, Postsecondary; Recreation and Fitness Studies Teachers, Postsecondary; Secondary School Teachers, Except Special and Vocational Education; Self-Enrichment Education Teachers; Social Sciences Teachers, Postsecondary, All Other; Social Work Teachers, Postsecondary; Special Education Teachers, Middle School; Special Education Teachers, Preschool, Kindergarten, and Elementary

Social—S

School; Special Education Teachers, Secondary School; Teacher Assistants; Teachers and Instructors, All Other; Vocational Education Teachers, Postsecondary; Vocational Education Teachers, Middle School; Vocational Education Teachers, Secondary School.

EDUCATION/TRAINING PROGRAM(S)— Social Science Teacher Education; Sociology. **RELATED KNOWLEDGE/COURSES—**Sociology and Anthropology; History and Archeology; Education and Training; Psychology; Economics and Accounting; English Language.

Special Education Teachers, Middle School

- Personality Code: SA
- Growth: 30.0%
- Annual Job Openings: 59,000
- Annual Earnings: $42,010
- Education/Training Required: Bachelor's degree
- Self-Employed: 0.3%
- Part-Time: 9.3%

Teach middle school subjects to educationally and physically handicapped students. Includes teachers who specialize and work with audibly and visually handicapped students and those who teach basic academic and life processes skills to the mentally impaired. Observe and evaluate students' performance, behavior, social development, and physical health. Organize and label materials, and display students' work. Organize and supervise games and other recreational activities to promote physical, mental, and social development. Plan and conduct activities for a balanced program of instruction, demonstration, and work time that provides students with opportunities to observe, question, and investigate. Plan and supervise class projects, field

trips, visits by guest speakers, or other experiential activities, and guide students in learning from those activities. Prepare for assigned classes, and show written evidence of preparation upon request of immediate supervisors. Prepare materials and classrooms for class activities. Prepare objectives and outlines for courses of study, following curriculum guidelines or requirements of states and schools. Prepare, administer, and grade tests and assignments to evaluate students' progress. Provide additional instruction in vocational areas. Provide interpretation and transcription of regular classroom materials through Braille and sign language. Develop and implement strategies to meet the needs of students with a variety of handicapping conditions. Instruct students in daily living skills required for independent maintenance and self-sufficiency, such as hygiene, safety, and food preparation. Instruct through lectures, discussions, and demonstrations in one or more subjects such as English, mathematics, or social studies. Confer with parents, administrators, testing specialists, social workers, and professionals to develop individual educational plans designed to promote students' educational, physical, and social development. Employ special educational strategies and techniques during instruction to improve the development of sensory- and perceptual-motor skills, language, cognition, and memory. Modify the general education curriculum for special-needs students based upon a variety of instructional techniques and instructional technology. Confer with other staff members to plan and schedule lessons promoting learning, following approved curricula. **SKILLS—**Learning Strategies; Social Perceptiveness; Instructing; Monitoring; Speaking; Active Listening; Writing; Service Orientation; Complex Problem Solving.

GOE—Interest Area: 12. Education and Social Service. **Work Group:** 12.03. Educational Services. **Other Jobs in This Work Group:** Adult Literacy, Remedial Education, and GED Teachers and Instructors; Agricultural Sciences Teachers, Postsecondary; Anthropology and Archeology Teachers, Postsecondary; Architecture Teachers, Postsecondary; Archivists; Area, Ethnic, and Cultural Studies Teachers, Postsecondary; Art, Drama, and Music Teachers, Postsecondary; Atmospheric, Earth, Marine, and Space Sciences Teachers, Postsecondary; Audio-Visual Collections Specialists; Biological Science Teachers, Postsecondary; Business Teachers, Postsecondary; Chemistry Teachers, Postsecondary; Child Care Workers; Communications Teachers, Postsecondary; Computer Science Teachers, Postsecondary; Criminal Justice and Law Enforcement Teachers, Postsecondary; Curators; Economics Teachers, Postsecondary; Education Teachers, Postsecondary; Education, Training, and Library Workers, All Other; Educational Psychologists; Educational, Vocational, and School Counselors; Elementary School Teachers, Except Special Education; Engineering Teachers, Postsecondary; English Language and Literature Teachers, Postsecondary; Environmental Science Teachers, Postsecondary; Farm and Home Management Advisors; Foreign Language and Literature Teachers, Postsecondary; Forestry and Conservation Science Teachers, Postsecondary; Geography Teachers, Postsecondary; Graduate Teaching Assistants; Health Specialties Teachers, Postsecondary; History Teachers, Postsecondary; Home Economics Teachers, Postsecondary; Kindergarten Teachers, Except Special Education; Law Teachers, Postsecondary; Librarians; Library Assistants, Clerical; Library Science Teachers, Postsecondary; Library Technicians; Mathematical Science Teachers, Postsecondary; Middle School Teachers, Except Special and Vocational Education; Museum Technicians and Conservators; Nannies; Nursing Instructors and Teachers, Postsecondary; Personal Financial Advisors; Philosophy and Religion Teachers, Postsecondary; Physics Teachers, Postsecondary; Political Science Teachers, Postsecondary; Postsecondary Teachers, All Other; Preschool Teachers, Except Special Education; Psychology Teachers, Postsecondary; Recreation and Fitness Studies Teachers, Postsecondary; Secondary School Teachers, Except Special and Vocational Education; Self-Enrichment Education Teachers; Social Sciences Teachers, Postsecondary, All Other; Social Work Teachers, Postsecondary; Sociology Teachers, Postsecondary; Special Education Teachers, Preschool, Kindergarten, and Elementary School; Special Education Teachers, Secondary School; Teacher Assistants; Teachers and Instructors, All Other; Vocational Education Teachers, Postsecondary; Vocational Education Teachers, Middle School; Vocational Education Teachers, Secondary School.

EDUCATION/TRAINING PROGRAM(S)— Special Education and Teaching, General. **RELATED KNOWLEDGE/COURSES—**Therapy and Counseling; Education and Training; Psychology; Medicine and Dentistry; English Language; Customer and Personal Service.

Special Education Teachers, Preschool, Kindergarten, and Elementary School

- Personality Code: SA
- Growth: 30.0%
- Annual Job Openings: 59,000
- Annual Earnings: $42,920
- Education/Training Required: Bachelor's degree
- Self-Employed: 0.3%
- Part-Time: 9.3%

Teach elementary and preschool school subjects to educationally and physically handicapped students. Includes teachers who specialize and work with audibly and visually handicapped students and those who teach basic academic and life processes skills to the mentally impaired. Develop and implement strategies to meet the needs of stu-

Social—S

dents with a variety of handicapping conditions. Instruct students in academic subjects, using a variety of techniques such as phonetics, multisensory learning, and repetition, in order to reinforce learning and to meet students' varying needs and interests. Prepare objectives and outlines for courses of study, following curriculum guidelines or requirements of states and schools. Prepare students for later grades by encouraging them to explore learning opportunities and to persevere with challenging tasks. Prepare, administer, and grade tests and assignments to evaluate students' progress. Provide interpretation and transcription of regular classroom materials through Braille and sign language. Supervise, evaluate, and plan assignments for teacher assistants and volunteers. Teach socially acceptable behavior, employing techniques such as behavior modification and positive reinforcement. Teach students personal development skills such as goal setting, independence, and self-advocacy. Administer standardized ability and achievement tests, and interpret results to determine students' strengths and areas of need. Attend professional meetings, educational conferences, and teacher training workshops in order to maintain and improve professional competence. Attend staff meetings, and serve on committees as required. Collaborate with other teachers and administrators in the development, evaluation, and revision of preschool, kindergarten, or elementary school programs. Instruct students in daily living skills required for independent maintenance and self-sufficiency, such as hygiene, safety, and food preparation. Confer with parents, administrators, testing specialists, social workers, and professionals to develop individual educational plans designed to promote students' educational, physical, and social development. Modify the general education curriculum for special-needs students based upon a variety of instructional techniques and technologies. Confer with other staff members to plan and schedule lessons promoting learning, following approved curricula. **SKILLS**—Learning Strategies; Social Perceptiveness; Instructing; Monitoring; Speaking; Active Listening; Writing; Service Orientation; Complex Problem Solving.

GOE—Interest Area: 12. Education and Social Service. **Work Group:** 12.03. Educational Services. **Other Jobs in This Work Group:** Adult Literacy, Remedial Education, and GED Teachers and Instructors; Agricultural Sciences Teachers, Postsecondary; Anthropology and Archeology Teachers, Postsecondary; Architecture Teachers, Postsecondary; Archivists; Area, Ethnic, and Cultural Studies Teachers, Postsecondary; Art, Drama, and Music Teachers, Postsecondary; Atmospheric, Earth, Marine, and Space Sciences Teachers, Postsecondary; Audio-Visual Collections Specialists; Biological Science Teachers, Postsecondary; Business Teachers, Postsecondary; Chemistry Teachers, Postsecondary; Child Care Workers; Communications Teachers, Postsecondary; Computer Science Teachers, Postsecondary; Criminal Justice and Law Enforcement Teachers, Postsecondary; Curators; Economics Teachers, Postsecondary; Education Teachers, Postsecondary; Education, Training, and Library Workers, All Other; Educational Psychologists; Educational, Vocational, and School Counselors; Elementary School Teachers, Except Special Education; Engineering Teachers, Postsecondary; English Language and Literature Teachers, Postsecondary; Environmental Science Teachers, Postsecondary; Farm and Home Management Advisors; Foreign Language and Literature Teachers, Postsecondary; Forestry and Conservation Science Teachers, Postsecondary; Geography Teachers, Postsecondary; Graduate Teaching Assistants; Health Specialties Teachers, Postsecondary; History Teachers, Postsecondary; Home Economics Teachers, Postsecondary; Kindergarten Teachers, Except Special Education; Law Teachers, Postsecondary; Librarians; Library Assistants, Clerical; Library Science Teachers, Postsecondary; Library Technicians; Mathematical Science Teachers, Postsecondary; Middle School Teachers, Except Special and Vocational Education; Museum Technicians and Conservators; Nannies; Nursing Instructors and Teachers, Postsecondary; Personal Financial Advisors; Philosophy and Religion Teachers, Postsecondary; Physics Teachers, Postsecondary; Political Science Teachers, Postsecondary; Postsecondary Teachers, All Other; Preschool Teachers, Except Special Education; Psychology Teachers, Postsecondary; Recreation and Fitness Studies Teachers, Postsecondary; Secondary School Teachers, Except Special and Vocational Education; Self-Enrichment Education Teachers; Social Sciences Teachers, Postsecondary, All Other; Social Work Teachers, Postsecondary; Sociology Teachers, Postsecondary; Special Education Teachers, Middle School; Special Education Teachers, Secondary School; Teacher Assistants; Teachers and Instructors, All Other; Vocational Education Teachers, Postsecondary; Vocational Education Teachers, Middle School; Vocational Education Teachers, Secondary School.

EDUCATION/TRAINING PROGRAM(S)— Education/Teaching of Individuals with Autism; Education/Teaching of Individuals with Emotional Disturbances; Education/Teaching of Individuals with Hearing Impairments, Including Deafness; Education/Teaching of Individuals with Mental Retardation; Education/Teaching of Individuals with Multiple Disabilities; Education/Teaching of Individuals with Orthopedic and Other Physical Health Impairments; Education/Teaching of Individuals with Specific Learning Disabilities; Education/Teaching of Individuals with Speech or Language Impairments; Education/Teaching of Individuals with Traumatic Brain Injuries; Education/Teaching of Individuals with Vision Impairments, Including Blindness; Special Education and Teaching, General; Special Education and Teaching, Other. RELATED KNOWLEDGE/COURSES— Therapy and Counseling; Education and Training; Psychology; Medicine and Dentistry; English Language; Customer and Personal Service.

Special Education Teachers, Secondary School

- Personality Code: SA
- Growth: 30.0%
- Annual Job Openings: 59,000
- Annual Earnings: $44,240
- Education/Training Required: Bachelor's degree
- Self-Employed: 0.3%
- Part-Time: 9.3%

Teach secondary school subjects to educationally and physically handicapped students. Includes teachers who specialize and work with audibly and visually handicapped students and those who teach basic academic and life processes skills to the mentally impaired. Establish clear objectives for all lessons, units, and projects, and communicate those objectives to students. Guide and counsel students with adjustment and/or academic problems, or special academic interests. Instruct and monitor students in the use and care of equipment and materials, in order to prevent injuries and damage. Maintain accurate and complete student records, and prepare reports on children and activities, as required by laws, district policies, and administrative regulations. Meet with other professionals to discuss individual students' needs and progress. Meet with parents and guardians to discuss their children's progress, and to determine their priorities for their children and their resource needs. Meet with parents and guardians to provide guidance in using community resources, and to teach skills for dealing with students' impairments. Observe and evaluate students' performance, behavior, social development, and physical health. Plan and conduct activities for a balanced program of instruction, demonstration, and work time that provides students with opportunities to observe, question, and investigate. Plan and supervise class projects, field trips, visits by guest speakers, or other experiential activities, and guide students in learning from those activities. Prepare for assigned classes, and show written evidence of preparation upon request of immediate supervisors. Develop and implement strategies to meet the needs of students with a variety of handicapping conditions. Instruct students in daily living skills required for independent maintenance and self-sufficiency, such as hygiene, safety, and food preparation. Instruct through lectures, discussions, and demonstrations in one or more subjects such as English, mathematics, or social studies. Confer with parents, administrators, testing specialists, social workers, and professionals to develop individual educational plans designed to promote students' educational, physical, and social development. Modify the general education curriculum for special-needs students, based upon a variety of instructional techniques and technologies. **SKILLS**—Learning Strategies; Social Perceptiveness; Instructing; Monitoring; Speaking; Active Listening; Writing; Service Orientation; Complex Problem Solving.

GOE—Interest Area: 12. Education and Social Service. **Work Group:** 12.03. Educational Services. **Other Jobs in This Work Group:** Adult Literacy, Remedial Education, and GED Teachers and Instructors; Agricultural Sciences Teachers, Postsecondary; Anthropology and Archeology Teachers, Postsecondary; Architecture Teachers, Postsecondary; Archivists; Area, Ethnic, and Cultural Studies Teachers, Postsecondary; Art, Drama, and Music Teachers, Postsecondary; Atmospheric, Earth, Marine, and Space Sciences Teachers, Postsecondary; Audio-Visual Collections Specialists; Biological Science Teachers, Postsecondary; Business Teachers, Postsecondary; Chemistry Teachers, Postsecondary; Child Care Workers; Communications Teachers, Postsecondary; Computer Science Teachers, Postsecondary; Criminal Justice and Law Enforcement Teachers, Postsecondary; Curators; Economics Teachers, Postsecondary; Education Teachers, Postsecondary; Education, Training, and Library Workers, All Other; Educational Psycholo-gists; Educational, Vocational, and School Counselors; Elementary School Teachers, Except Special Education; Engineering Teachers, Postsecondary; English Language and Literature Teachers, Postsecondary; Environmental Science Teachers, Postsecondary; Farm and Home Management Advisors; Foreign Language and Literature Teachers, Postsecondary; Forestry and Conservation Science Teachers, Postsecondary; Geography Teachers, Postsecondary; Graduate Teaching Assistants; Health Specialties Teachers, Postsecondary; History Teachers, Postsecondary; Home Economics Teachers, Postsecondary; Kindergarten Teachers, Except Special Education; Law Teachers, Postsecondary; Librarians; Library Assistants, Clerical; Library Science Teachers, Postsecondary; Library Technicians; Mathematical Science Teachers, Postsecondary; Middle School Teachers, Except Special and Vocational Education; Museum Technicians and Conservators; Nannies; Nursing Instructors and Teachers, Postsecondary; Personal Financial Advisors; Philosophy and Religion Teachers, Postsecondary; Physics Teachers, Postsecondary; Political Science Teachers, Postsecondary; Postsecondary Teachers, All Other; Preschool Teachers, Except Special Education; Psychology Teachers, Postsecondary; Recreation and Fitness Studies Teachers, Postsecondary; Secondary School Teachers, Except Special and Vocational Education; Self-Enrichment Education Teachers; Social Sciences Teachers, Postsecondary, All Other; Social Work Teachers, Postsecondary; Sociology Teachers, Postsecondary; Special Education Teachers, Middle School; Special Education Teachers, Preschool, Kindergarten, and Elementary School; Teacher Assistants; Teachers and Instructors, All Other; Vocational Education Teachers, Postsecondary; Vocational Education Teachers, Middle School; Vocational Education Teachers, Secondary School.

EDUCATION/TRAINING PROGRAM(S)—Special Education and Teaching, General. **RELATED KNOWLEDGE/COURSES**—Therapy and Counseling; Education and Training; Psychology; Medicine and Dentistry; English Language; Customer and Personal Service.

Speech-Language Pathologists

- Personality Code: SI
- Growth: 27.2%
- Annual Job Openings: 10,000
- Annual Earnings: $50,050
- Education/Training Required: Master's degree
- Self-Employed: 8.2%
- Part-Time: 28.1%

Assess and treat persons with speech, language, voice, and fluency disorders. May select alternative communication systems and teach their use. May perform research related to speech and language problems. Monitor patients' progress and adjust treatments accordingly. Evaluate hearing and speech/language test results and medical or background information to diagnose and plan treatment for speech, language, fluency, voice, and swallowing disorders. Administer hearing or speech/language evaluations, tests, or examinations to patients to collect information on type and degree of impairments, using written and oral tests and special instruments. Record information on the initial evaluation, treatment, progress, and discharge of clients. Develop and implement treatment plans for problems such as stuttering, delayed language, swallowing disorders, and inappropriate pitch or harsh voice problems, based on own assessments and recommendations of physicians, psychologists, and social workers. Develop individual or group programs in schools to deal with speech or language problems. Instruct clients in techniques for more effective communication, including sign language, lip reading, and voice improvement. Teach clients to control or strengthen tongue, jaw, face muscles, and breathing mechanisms. Develop speech exercise programs to reduce disabilities. Consult with and advise educators or medical staff on speech or hearing topics such as communication strategies and speech and language stimulation. Instruct patients and family members in strategies to cope with or avoid communication-related misunderstandings. Design, develop, and employ alternative diagnostic or communication devices and strategies. Conduct lessons and direct educational or therapeutic games to assist teachers dealing with speech problems. Refer clients to additional medical or educational services if needed. Participate in conferences or training, or publish research results, to share knowledge of new hearing or speech disorder treatment methods or technologies. Communicate with non-speaking students, using sign language or computer technology. Provide communication instruction to dialect speakers or students with limited English proficiency. Use computer applications to identify and assist with communication disabilities. **SKILLS**—Instructing; Social Perceptiveness; Learning Strategies; Service Orientation; Time Management; Active Learning; Coordination; Speaking.

GOE—Interest Area: 14. Medical and Health Services. **Work Group:** 14.06. Medical Therapy. **Other Jobs in This Work Group:** Audiologists; Health Diagnosing and Treating Practitioners, All Other; Massage Therapists; Occupational Therapist Aides; Occupational Therapist Assistants; Occupational Therapists; Physical Therapist Aides; Physical Therapist Assistants; Physical Therapists; Radiation Therapists; Recreational Therapists; Respiratory Therapists; Respiratory Therapy Technicians; Therapists, All Other.

EDUCATION/TRAINING PROGRAM(S)—Audiology/Audiologist and Speech-Language Pathology/Pathologist; Communication Disorders Sciences and Services, Other; Communication Disorders, General; Speech-Language Pathology/Pathologist. **RELATED KNOWLEDGE/COURSES**—Therapy and Counseling; Psychology; Education and Training; English Language; Sociology and Anthropology; Medicine and Dentistry.

Social—S

Teacher Assistants

- Personality Code: SC
- Growth: 23.0%
- Annual Job Openings: 259,000
- Annual Earnings: $19,000
- Education/Training Required: Short-term on-the-job training
- Self-Employed: 0.3%
- Part-Time: 41.1%

Perform duties that are instructional in nature or deliver direct services to students or parents. Serve in a position for which a teacher or another professional has ultimate responsibility for the design and implementation of educational programs and services. Provide disabled students with assistive devices, supportive technology, and assistance accessing facilities such as restrooms. Requisition and stock teaching materials and supplies. Type, file, and duplicate materials. Use computers, audiovisual aids, and other equipment and materials to supplement presentations. Discuss assigned duties with classroom teachers in order to coordinate instructional efforts. Prepare lesson materials, bulletin board displays, exhibits, equipment, and demonstrations. Present subject matter to students under the direction and guidance of teachers, using lectures, discussions, or supervised role-playing methods. Tutor and assist children individually or in small groups in order to help them master assignments and to reinforce learning concepts presented by teachers. Supervise students in classrooms, halls, cafeterias, school yards, and gymnasiums, or on field trips. Conduct demonstrations to teach such skills as sports, dancing, and handicrafts. Distribute teaching materials such as textbooks, workbooks, papers, and pencils to students. Distribute tests and homework assignments, and collect them when they are completed. Enforce administration policies and rules governing students. Grade homework and tests, and compute and record results, using answer sheets or electronic marking devices. Instruct and monitor students in the use and care of equipment and materials, in order to prevent injuries and damage. Observe students' performance, and record relevant data to assess progress. Organize and label materials, and display students' work in a manner appropriate for their eye levels and perceptual skills. Organize and supervise games and other recreational activities to promote physical, mental, and social development. Participate in teacher-parent conferences regarding students' progress or problems. Plan, prepare, and develop various teaching aids such as bibliographies, charts, and graphs. Prepare lesson outlines and plans in assigned subject areas, and submit outlines to teachers for review. Provide extra assistance to students with special needs, such as non-English-speaking students or those with physical and mental disabilities. **SKILLS**—Instructing; Learning Strategies; Service Orientation; Speaking; Active Listening; Social Perceptiveness; Reading Comprehension; Writing.

GOE—Interest Area: 12. Education and Social Service. **Work Group:** 12.03. Educational Services. **Other Jobs in This Work Group:** Adult Literacy, Remedial Education, and GED Teachers and Instructors; Agricultural Sciences Teachers, Postsecondary; Anthropology and Archeology Teachers, Postsecondary; Architecture Teachers, Postsecondary; Archivists; Area, Ethnic, and Cultural Studies Teachers, Postsecondary; Art, Drama, and Music Teachers, Postsecondary; Atmospheric, Earth, Marine, and Space Sciences Teachers, Postsecondary; Audio-Visual Collections Specialists; Biological Science Teachers, Postsecondary; Business Teachers, Postsecondary; Chemistry Teachers, Postsecondary; Child Care Workers; Communications Teachers, Postsecondary; Computer Science Teachers, Postsecondary; Criminal Justice and Law Enforcement Teachers, Postsecondary; Curators; Economics Teachers, Postsecondary; Education Teachers, Postsecondary; Education, Training, and Library Workers, All Other; Educational Psychologists; Educational, Vocational, and School Counselors; Elementary School Teachers, Except Special Education; Engineering Teachers, Postsecondary;

English Language and Literature Teachers, Postsecondary; Environmental Science Teachers, Postsecondary; Farm and Home Management Advisors; Foreign Language and Literature Teachers, Postsecondary; Forestry and Conservation Science Teachers, Postsecondary; Geography Teachers, Postsecondary; Graduate Teaching Assistants; Health Specialties Teachers, Postsecondary; History Teachers, Postsecondary; Home Economics Teachers, Postsecondary; Kindergarten Teachers, Except Special Education; Law Teachers, Postsecondary; Librarians; Library Assistants, Clerical; Library Science Teachers, Postsecondary; Library Technicians; Mathematical Science Teachers, Postsecondary; Middle School Teachers, Except Special and Vocational Education; Museum Technicians and Conservators; Nannies; Nursing Instructors and Teachers, Postsecondary; Personal Financial Advisors; Philosophy and Religion Teachers, Postsecondary; Physics Teachers, Postsecondary; Political Science Teachers, Postsecondary; Postsecondary Teachers, All Other; Preschool Teachers, Except Special Education; Psychology Teachers, Postsecondary; Recreation and Fitness Studies Teachers, Postsecondary; Secondary School Teachers, Except Special and Vocational Education; Self-Enrichment Education Teachers; Social Sciences Teachers, Postsecondary, All Other; Social Work Teachers, Postsecondary; Sociology Teachers, Postsecondary; Special Education Teachers, Middle School; Special Education Teachers, Preschool, Kindergarten, and Elementary School; Special Education Teachers, Secondary School; Teachers and Instructors, All Other; Vocational Education Teachers, Postsecondary; Vocational Education Teachers, Middle School; Vocational Education Teachers, Secondary School.

EDUCATION/TRAINING PROGRAM(S)— Teacher Assistant/Aide; Teaching Assistants/Aides, Other. **RELATED KNOWLEDGE/COURSES—** Education and Training; English Language; History and Archeology; Psychology; Sociology and Anthropology; Philosophy and Theology.

Training and Development Specialists

- Personality Code: SE
- Growth: 27.9%
- Annual Job Openings: 35,000
- Annual Earnings: $44,160
- Education/Training Required: Bachelor's degree
- Self-Employed: 0.8%
- Part-Time: 7.7%

Conduct training and development programs for employees. Keep up with developments in area of expertise by reading current journals, books and magazine articles. Present information, using a variety of instructional techniques and formats such as role playing, simulations, team exercises, group discussions, videos and lectures. Schedule classes based on availability of classrooms, equipment, and instructors. Organize and develop, or obtain, training procedure manuals and guides and course materials such as handouts and visual materials. Offer specific training programs to help workers maintain or improve job skills. Monitor, evaluate and record training activities and program effectiveness. Attend meetings and seminars to obtain information for use in training programs, or to inform management of training program status. Coordinate recruitment and placement of training program participants. Evaluate training materials prepared by instructors, such as outlines, text, and handouts. Develop alternative training methods if expected improvements are not seen. Assess training needs through surveys, interviews with employees, focus groups, and/or consultation with managers, instructors or customer representatives. Screen, hire, and assign workers to positions based on qualifications. Select and assign instructors to conduct training. Devise programs to develop executive potential among employees in lower-level positions. Design, plan, organize and direct orientation and training for employees or cus-

Social—T

tomers of industrial or commercial establishment. Negotiate contracts with clients, including desired training outcomes, fees and expenses. Supervise instructors, evaluate instructor performance, and refer instructors to classes for skill development. Monitor training costs to ensure budget is not exceeded, and prepare budget reports to justify expenditures. Refer trainees to employer relations representatives, to locations offering job placement assistance, or to appropriate social services agencies if warranted. SKILLS—Service Orientation; Instructing; Social Perceptiveness; Writing; Persuasion; Active Learning; Speaking; Time Management.

GOE—Interest Area: 13. General Management and Support. Work Group: 13.02. Management Support. Other Jobs in This Work Group: Accountants; Accountants and Auditors; Appraisers and Assessors of Real Estate; Appraisers, Real Estate; Assessors; Auditors; Budget Analysts; Business Operations Specialists, All Other; Claims Adjusters, Examiners, and Investigators; Claims Examiners, Property and Casualty Insurance; Compensation, Benefits, and Job Analysis Specialists; Cost Estimators; Credit Analysts; Employment Interviewers, Private or Public Employment Service; Employment, Recruitment, and Placement Specialists; Financial Analysts; Human Resources, Training, and Labor Relations Specialists, All Other; Insurance Adjusters, Examiners, and Investigators; Insurance Appraisers, Auto Damage; Insurance Underwriters; Loan Counselors; Loan Officers; Logisticians; Management Analysts; Market Research Analysts; Personnel Recruiters; Purchasing Agents and Buyers, Farm Products; Purchasing Agents, Except Wholesale, Retail, and Farm Products; Tax Examiners, Collectors, and Revenue Agents; Wholesale and Retail Buyers, Except Farm Products.

EDUCATION/TRAINING PROGRAM(S)— Human Resources Management/Personnel Administration, General; Organizational Behavior Studies. RELATED KNOWLEDGE/COURSES—Customer and Personal Service; Psychology; Sociology and Anthropology; Personnel and Human Resources; Education and Training; Clerical Studies; Public Safety and Security.

Vocational Education Teachers, Postsecondary

- Personality Code: SR
- Growth: 38.1%
- Annual Job Openings: 216,000
- Annual Earnings: $39,740
- Education/Training Required: Work experience in a related occupation
- Self-Employed: 0.3%
- Part-Time: 27.7%

Teach or instruct vocational or occupational subjects at the postsecondary level (but at less than the baccalaureate) to students who have graduated or left high school. Includes correspondence school instructors; industrial, commercial and government training instructors; and adult education teachers and instructors who prepare persons to operate industrial machinery and equipment and transportation and communications equipment. Teaching may take place in public or private schools whose primary business is education or in a school associated with an organization whose primary business is other than education. Conduct on-the-job training, classes, or training sessions to teach and demonstrate principles, techniques, procedures, and/or methods of designated subjects. Present lectures and conduct discussions to increase students' knowledge and competence, using visual aids such as graphs, charts, videotapes, and slides. Administer oral, written, or performance tests in order to measure progress, and to evaluate training effectiveness. Advise students on course selection, career decisions, and other academic and vocational concerns. Determine training needs of students or workers. Develop curricula, and plan course content and methods of instruction. Integrate academic and vocational curricula so that students can obtain a variety of skills. Observe and evaluate students' work to determine progress, provide feedback, and make suggestions for improvement. Participate in conferences, seminars, and training sessions to keep abreast of developments in the field; and integrate relevant information into training programs. Prepare outlines of instructional programs and training schedules, and establish course goals. Provide individualized instruction and tutorial and/or remedial instruction. Select and assemble books, materials, supplies, and equipment for training, courses, or projects. Supervise and monitor students' use of tools and equipment. Supervise independent or group projects, field placements, laboratory work, or other training. Arrange for lectures by experts in designated fields. Develop teaching aids such as instructional software, multimedia visual aids, or study materials. Prepare reports and maintain records such as student grades, attendance rolls, and training activity details. Review enrollment applications, and correspond with applicants to obtain additional information. Serve on faculty and school committees concerned with budgeting, curriculum revision, and course and diploma requirements. **SKILLS**—Instructing; Service Orientation; Writing; Speaking; Learning Strategies; Judgment and Decision Making; Active Listening; Reading Comprehension; Complex Problem Solving; Technology Design.

GOE—Interest Area: 12. Education and Social Service. **Work Group:** 12.03. Educational Services. **Other Jobs in This Work Group:** Adult Literacy, Remedial Education, and GED Teachers and Instructors; Agricultural Sciences Teachers, Postsecondary; Anthropology and Archeology Teachers, Postsecondary; Architecture Teachers, Postsecondary; Archivists; Area, Ethnic, and Cultural Studies Teachers, Postsecondary; Art, Drama, and Music Teachers, Postsecondary; Atmospheric, Earth, Marine, and Space Sciences Teachers, Postsecondary; Audio-Visual Collections Specialists; Biological Science Teachers, Postsecondary; Business Teachers, Postsecondary; Chemistry Teachers, Postsecondary; Child Care Workers; Communications Teachers, Postsecondary; Computer Science Teachers, Postsecondary; Criminal Justice and Law Enforcement Teachers, Postsecondary; Curators; Economics Teachers, Postsecondary; Education Teachers, Postsecondary; Education, Training, and Library Workers, All Other; Educational Psychologists; Educational, Vocational, and School Counselors; Elementary School Teachers, Except Special Education; Engineering Teachers, Postsecondary; English Language and Literature Teachers, Postsecondary; Environmental Science Teachers, Postsecondary; Farm and Home Management Advisors; Foreign Language and Literature Teachers, Postsecondary; Forestry and Conservation Science Teachers, Postsecondary; Geography Teachers, Postsecondary; Graduate Teaching Assistants; Health Specialties Teachers, Postsecondary; History Teachers, Postsecondary; Home Economics Teachers, Postsecondary; Kindergarten Teachers, Except Special Education; Law Teachers, Postsecondary; Librarians; Library Assistants, Clerical; Library Science Teachers, Postsecondary; Library Technicians; Mathematical Science Teachers, Postsecondary; Middle School Teachers, Except Special and Vocational Education; Museum Technicians and Conservators; Nannies; Nursing Instructors and Teachers, Postsecondary; Personal Financial Advisors; Philosophy and Religion Teachers, Postsecondary; Physics Teachers, Postsecondary; Political Science Teachers, Postsecondary; Postsecondary Teachers, All Other; Preschool Teachers, Except Special Education; Psychology Teachers, Postsecondary; Recreation and Fitness Studies Teachers, Postsecondary; Secondary School Teachers, Except Special and Vocational Education; Self-Enrichment Education Teachers; Social Sciences Teachers, Postsecondary, All Other; Social Work Teachers, Postsecondary; Sociology Teachers, Postsecondary; Special Education Teachers, Middle School; Special Education Teachers, Preschool, Kindergarten, and Elementary School; Special Edu-

Social–V

cation Teachers, Secondary School; Teacher Assistants; Teachers and Instructors, All Other; Vocational Education Teachers, Middle School; Vocational Education Teachers, Secondary School.

EDUCATION/TRAINING PROGRAM(S)— Agricultural Teacher Education; Business Teacher Education; Health Occupations Teacher Education; Sales and Marketing Operations/Marketing and Distribution Teacher Education; Teacher Education and Professional Development, Specific Subject Areas, Other; Technical Teacher Education; Technology Teacher Education/Industrial Arts Teacher Education; Trade and Industrial Teacher Education. **RELATED KNOWLEDGE/COURSES—**Education and Training; English Language; Philosophy and Theology; Sociology and Anthropology; Communications and Media; Administration and Management.

Enterprising Jobs

Administrative Services Managers

- Personality Code: EC
- Growth: 19.8%
- Annual Job Openings: 40,000
- Annual Earnings: $56,940
- Education/Training Required: Work experience plus degree
- Self-Employed: 0.2%
- Part-Time: 4.6%

Plan, direct, or coordinate supportive services of an organization, such as recordkeeping, mail distribution, telephone operator/receptionist, and other office support services. May oversee facilities planning and maintenance and custodial operations. Monitor the facility to ensure that it remains safe, secure, and well-maintained. Direct or coordinate the supportive services department of a business, agency, or organization. Set goals and deadlines for the department. Prepare and review operational reports and schedules to ensure accuracy and efficiency. Analyze internal processes and recommend and implement procedural or policy changes to improve operations, such as supply changes or the disposal of records. Acquire, distribute, and store supplies. Plan, administer, and control budgets for contracts, equipment, and supplies. Oversee construction and renovation projects to improve efficiency and to ensure that facilities meet environmental, health, and security standards and comply with government regulations. Hire and terminate clerical and administrative personnel. Oversee the maintenance and repair of machinery, equipment, and electrical and mechanical systems. Manage leasing of facility space. **SKILLS**—Man-

agement of Personnel Resources; Service Orientation; Coordination; Management of Financial Resources; Monitoring; Social Perceptiveness; Speaking; Time Management.

GOE—Interest Area: 09. Business Detail. **Work Group:** 09.01. Managerial Work in Business Detail. **Other Jobs in This Work Group:** First-Line Supervisors, Administrative Support; First-Line Supervisors, Customer Service; First-Line Supervisors/Managers of Office and Administrative Support Workers.

EDUCATION/TRAINING PROGRAM(S)—Business Administration and Management, General; Business/Commerce, General; Medical/Health Management and Clinical Assistant/Specialist; Public Administration; Purchasing, Procurement/Acquisitions and Contracts Management. **RELATED KNOWLEDGE/COURSES**—Personnel and Human Resources; Clerical Studies; Customer and Personal Service; Economics and Accounting; Administration and Management; Public Safety and Security; Law and Government.

Agents and Business Managers of Artists, Performers, and Athletes

- Personality Code: ES
- Growth: 27.8%
- Annual Job Openings: 2,000
- Annual Earnings: $54,640
- Education/Training Required: Work experience plus degree
- Self-Employed: 27.0%
- Part-Time: 15.2%

Represent and promote artists, performers, and athletes to prospective employers. May handle contract negotiation and other business matters for clients. Arrange meetings concerning issues involving their clients. Collect fees, commissions, or other payments, according to contract terms. Conduct auditions or interviews in order to evaluate potential clients. Confer with clients to develop strategies for their careers, and to explain actions taken on their behalf. Develop contacts with individuals and organizations, and apply effective strategies and techniques to ensure their clients' success. Keep informed of industry trends and deals. Manage business and financial affairs for clients, such as arranging travel and lodging, selling tickets, and directing marketing and advertising activities. Negotiate with managers, promoters, union officials, and other persons regarding clients' contractual rights and obligations. Obtain information about and/or inspect performance facilities, equipment, and accommodations to ensure that they meet specifications. Schedule promotional or performance engagements for clients. Advise clients on financial and legal matters such as investments and taxes. Hire trainers or coaches to advise clients on performance matters such as training techniques or performance presentations. Prepare periodic accounting statements for clients. **SKILLS**—Negotiation; Management of Financial Resources; Management of Personnel Resources; Time Management; Service Orientation; Speaking; Coordination; Persuasion.

GOE—Interest Area: 01. Arts, Entertainment, and Media. **Work Group:** 01.01. Managerial Work in Arts, Entertainment, and Media. **Other Jobs in This Work Group:** Art Directors; Athletes and Sports Competitors; Coaches and Scouts; Entertainers and Performers, Sports and Related Workers, All Other; Fitness Trainers and Aerobics Instructors; Producers; Producers and Directors; Program Directors; Technical Directors/Managers; Umpires, Referees, and Other Sports Officials.

EDUCATION/TRAINING PROGRAM(S)— Arts Management; Purchasing, Procurement/ Acquisitions and Contracts Management. **RELATED KNOWLEDGE/COURSES**—Sales and Marketing; Economics and Accounting; Personnel and Human Resources; Administration and Management; Fine Arts; Law and Government.

Child Support, Missing Persons, and Unemployment Insurance Fraud Investigators

- Personality Code: ES
- Growth: 22.4%
- Annual Job Openings: 11,000
- Annual Earnings: $52,390
- Education/Training Required: Work experience in a related occupation
- Self-Employed: 0%
- Part-Time: 0.5%

Conduct investigations to locate, arrest, and return fugitives and persons wanted for non-payment of support payments and unemployment insurance fraud, and to locate missing persons. Serves warrants and makes arrests to return persons sought in connection with crimes or for non-payment of child support. Computes amount of child support payments. Testifies in court to present evidence regarding cases. Examines medical and dental X rays, fingerprints, and other information to identify bodies held in morgue. Examines case file to determine that divorce decree and court-ordered judgment for payment are in order. Completes reports to document information acquired during criminal and child support cases, and actions taken. Monitors child support payments awarded by court to ensure compliance and enforcement of child support laws. Determines types of court jurisdiction, according to facts and circumstances surrounding case, and files court action. Confers with prosecuting attorney to prepare court case and with court clerk to obtain arrest warrant and schedule court date. Interviews client to obtain information, such as relocation of absent parent, amount of child support awarded, and names of witnesses. Interviews and discusses case with parent charged with nonpayment of support to resolve issues in lieu of filing court proceedings. Reviews files and criminal records to develop possible leads, such as previous addresses and aliases. Prepares file indicating data, such as wage records of accused, witnesses, and blood test results. Obtains extradition papers to bring about return of fugitive. Contacts employers, neighbors, relatives, and law enforcement agencies to locate person sought and verify information gathered about case. **SKILLS**— Negotiation; Active Listening; Speaking; Critical Thinking; Reading Comprehension; Judgment and Decision Making; Writing; Persuasion.

GOE—Interest Area: 04. Law, Law Enforcement, and Public Safety. **Work Group:** 04.03. Law Enforcement. **Other Jobs in This Work Group:** Animal Control Workers; Bailiffs; Correctional Officers and Jailers; Criminal Investigators and Special Agents; Crossing Guards; Detectives and Criminal Investigators; Fire Investigators; Fish and Game Wardens; Forensic Science Technicians; Gaming Surveillance Officers and Gaming Investigators; Highway Patrol Pilots; Immigration and Customs Inspectors; Lifeguards, Ski Patrol, and Other Recreational Protective Service Workers; Parking Enforcement Workers; Police and Sheriff's Patrol Officers; Police Detectives; Police Identification and Records Officers; Police Patrol Officers; Private Detectives and Investigators; Protective Service Workers, All Other; Security Guards; Sheriffs and Deputy Sheriffs; Transit and Railroad Police.

EDUCATION/TRAINING PROGRAM(S)— Criminal Justice/Police Science; Criminalistics and Criminal Science. **RELATED KNOWLEDGE/COURSES**—Law and Government; Public Safety and Security; Geography; English Language; Economics and Accounting; Sociology and Anthropology.

Compensation and Benefits Managers

- Personality Code: ES
- Growth: 19.4%
- Annual Job Openings: 21,000
- Annual Earnings: $68,800
- Education/Training Required: Work experience plus degree
- Self-Employed: 0%
- Part-Time: 3.7%

Plan, direct, or coordinate compensation and benefits activities and staff of an organization. Advise management on such matters as equal employment opportunity, sexual harassment and discrimination. Direct preparation and distribution of written and verbal information to inform employees of benefits, compensation, and personnel policies. Administer, direct, and review employee benefit programs, including the integration of benefit programs following mergers and acquisition. Plan and conduct new employee orientations to foster positive attitude toward organizational objectives. Plan, direct, supervise, and coordinate work activities of subordinates and staff relating to employment, compensation, labor relations, and employee relations. Identify and implement benefits to increase the quality of life for employees, by working with brokers and researching benefits issues. Design, evaluate and modify benefits policies to ensure that programs are current, competitive and in compliance with legal requirements.

Enterprising—C

Analyze compensation policies, government regulations, and prevailing wage rates to develop competitive compensation plan. Formulate policies, procedures and programs for recruitment, testing, placement, classification, orientation, benefits and compensation, and labor and industrial relations. Mediate between benefits providers and employees, such as by assisting in handling employees' benefits-related questions or taking suggestions. Fulfill all reporting requirements of all relevant government rules and regulations, including the Employee Retirement Income Security Act (ERISA). Maintain records and compile statistical reports concerning personnel-related data such as hires, transfers, performance appraisals, and absenteeism rates. Analyze statistical data and reports to identify and determine causes of personnel problems and develop recommendations for improvement of organization's personnel policies and practices. Develop methods to improve employment policies, processes, and practices, and recommend changes to management. Negotiate bargaining agreements. Investigate and report on industrial accidents for insurance carriers. Represent organization at personnel-related hearings and investigations. **SKILLS**—Management of Personnel Resources; Management of Financial Resources; Time Management; Social Perceptiveness; Monitoring; Instructing; Management of Material Resources; Negotiation.

GOE—**Interest Area:** 13. General Management and Support. **Work Group:** 13.01. General Management Work and Management of Support Functions. **Other Jobs in This Work Group:** Business Operations Specialists, All Other; Chief Executives; Farm, Ranch, and Other Agricultural Managers; Financial Managers; Financial Managers, Branch or Department; Financial Specialists, All Other; Funeral Directors; General and Operations Managers; Government Service Executives; Human Resources Managers; Human Resources Managers, All Other; Legislators; Managers, All Other; Postmasters and Mail Superintendents; Private Sector Executives; Property, Real Estate, and Community Association Managers; Public Relations Managers; Purchasing Managers; Storage and Distribution Managers; Training and Development Managers; Transportation, Storage, and Distribution Managers; Treasurers, Controllers, and Chief Financial Officers.

EDUCATION/TRAINING PROGRAM(S)—Human Resources Management/Personnel Administration, General; Labor and Industrial Relations. **RELATED KNOWLEDGE/COURSES**—Personnel and Human Resources; Clerical Studies; Administration and Management; Economics and Accounting; Law and Government; Education and Training.

Computer and Information Systems Managers

- Personality Code: EC
- Growth: 36.1%
- Annual Job Openings: 39,000
- Annual Earnings: $89,740
- Education/Training Required: Work experience plus degree
- Self-Employed: 1.1%
- Part-Time: 1.8%

Plan, direct, or coordinate activities in such fields as electronic data processing, information systems, systems analysis, and computer programming. Manage backup, security and user help systems. Consult with users, management, vendors, and technicians to assess computing needs and system requirements. Direct daily operations of department, analyzing workflow, establishing priorities, developing standards and setting deadlines. Assign and review the work of systems analysts, programmers, and other computer-related workers. Stay abreast of advances in technology. Develop computer information resources, providing for data security and control, strategic computing, and disaster recovery. Review and approve all systems charts and programs prior to their implementation. Evaluate the organization's technology use and needs and recommend improvements, such as hardware and software upgrades. Control operational budget and expenditures. Meet with department heads, managers, supervisors, vendors, and others, to solicit cooperation and resolve problems. Develop and interpret organizational goals, policies, and procedures. Recruit, hire, train and supervise staff, and/or participate in staffing decisions. Review project plans in order to plan and coordinate project activity. Evaluate data processing proposals to assess project feasibility and requirements. Prepare and review operational reports or project progress reports. Purchase necessary equipment. **SKILLS**—Management of Financial Resources; Negotiation; Operations Analysis; Persuasion; Programming; Management of Material Resources; Systems Analysis; Technology Design; Systems Evaluation.

GOE—**Interest Area:** 02. Science, Math, and Engineering. **Work Group:** 02.01. Managerial Work in Science, Math, and Engineering. **Other Jobs in This Work Group:** Engineering Managers; Natural Sciences Managers.

EDUCATION/TRAINING PROGRAM(S)— Computer and Information Sciences, General; Computer Science; Information Resources Management/CIO Training; Information Science/Studies; Knowledge Management; Management Information Systems, General; Operations Management and Supervision; System Administration/Administrator. **RELATED KNOWLEDGE/COURSES**— Clerical Studies; Computers and Electronics; Economics and Accounting; Engineering and Technology; Administration and Management; Design.

Construction Managers

- Personality Code: ER
- Growth: 12.0%
- Annual Job Openings: 47,000
- Annual Earnings: $66,470
- Education/Training Required: Bachelor's degree
- Self-Employed: 46.9%
- Part-Time: 3.6%

Plan, direct, coordinate, or budget, usually through subordinate supervisory personnel, activities concerned with the construction and maintenance of structures, facilities, and systems. Participate in the conceptual development of a construction project and oversee its organization, scheduling, and implementation. Confer with supervisory personnel, owners, contractors, and design professionals to discuss and resolve matters such as work procedures, complaints, and construction problems. Plan, organize, and direct activities concerned with the construction and maintenance of structures, facilities, and systems. Schedule the project in logical steps and budget time required to meet deadlines. Determine labor requirements and dispatch workers to construction sites. Inspect and review projects to monitor compliance with building and safety codes, and other regulations. Interpret and explain plans and contract terms to administrative staff, workers, and clients, representing the owner or developer. Prepare contracts and negotiate revisions, changes and additions to contractual agreements with architects, consultants, clients, suppliers and subcontractors. Obtain all necessary permits and licenses. Direct and supervise workers. Study job specifications to determine appropriate construction methods. Select, contract, and oversee workers who complete specific pieces of the project, such as painting or plumbing. Requisition supplies and materials to complete construction projects. Prepare and submit budget estimates and progress and cost tracking reports. Develop and implement quality control programs. Take actions to deal with the results of delays, bad weather, or emergencies at construction site. Investigate damage, accidents, or delays at construction sites, to ensure that proper procedures are being carried out. Evaluate construction methods and determine cost-effectiveness of plans, using computers. **SKILLS**—Coordination; Negotiation; Troubleshooting; Installation; Repairing; Instructing; Management of Material Resources; Persuasion; Management of Financial Resources.

GOE—Interest Area: 06. Construction, Mining, and Drilling. **Work Group:** 06.01. Managerial Work in Construction, Mining, and Drilling. **Other Jobs in This Work Group:** First-Line Supervisors and Manager/Supervisors—Construction Trades Workers; First-Line Supervisors and Manager/Supervisors—Extractive Workers; First-Line Supervisors/Managers of Construction Trades and Extraction Workers.

EDUCATION/TRAINING PROGRAM(S)— Business Administration and Management, General; Business/Commerce, General; Construction Engineering Technology/Technician; Operations Management and Supervision. **RELATED KNOWLEDGE/COURSES**—Building and Construction; Design; Administration and Management; Public Safety and Security; Customer and Personal Service; Mechanical Devices.

Criminal Investigators and Special Agents

- Personality Code: EI
- Growth: 22.4%
- Annual Job Openings: 11,000
- Annual Earnings: $52,390
- Education/Training Required: Work experience in a related occupation
- Self-Employed: 0%
- Part-Time: 0.5%

Investigate alleged or suspected criminal violations of federal, state, or local laws to determine if evidence is sufficient to recommend prosecution. Collaborate with other offices and agencies in order to exchange information and coordinate activities. Collect and record physical information about arrested suspects, including fingerprints, height and weight measurements, and photographs. Compare crime scene fingerprints with those from suspects or fingerprint files to identify perpetrators, using computers. Investigate organized crime, public corruption, financial crime, copyright infringement, civil rights violations, bank robbery, extortion, kidnapping, and other violations of federal or state statutes. Manage security programs designed to protect personnel, facilities, and information. Record evidence and documents, using equipment such as cameras and photocopy machines. Search for and collect evidence such as fingerprints, using investigative equipment. Serve subpoenas or other official papers. Testify before grand juries concerning criminal activity investigations. Administer counter-terrorism and counter-narcotics reward programs. Issue security clearances. Determine scope, timing, and direction of investigations. Develop relationships with informants in order to obtain information related to cases. Examine records in order to locate links in chains of evidence or information. Identify case issues and evidence needed, based on analysis of charges, complaints, or allegations of law violations. Obtain and use search and arrest warrants. Obtain and verify evidence by interviewing and observing suspects and witnesses, or by analyzing records. Perform undercover assignments and maintain surveillance, including monitoring authorized wiretaps. Prepare reports that detail investigation findings. Analyze evidence in laboratories, or in the field. Collaborate with other authorities on activities such as surveillance, transcription and research. Provide protection for individuals such as government leaders, political candidates and visiting foreign dignitaries. Train foreign civilian police. **SKILLS**—Social Perceptiveness; Speaking; Persuasion; Active Listening; Writing; Critical Thinking; Coordination; Judgment and Decision Making.

GOE—**Interest Area:** 04. Law, Law Enforcement, and Public Safety. **Work Group:** 04.03. Law Enforcement. **Other Jobs in This Work Group:** Animal Control Workers; Bailiffs; Child Support, Missing Persons, and Unemployment Insurance Fraud Investigators; Correctional Officers and Jailers; Crossing Guards; Detectives and Criminal Investigators; Fire Investigators; Fish and Game Wardens; Forensic Science Technicians; Gaming Surveillance Officers and Gaming Investigators; Highway Patrol Pilots; Immigration and Customs Inspectors; Lifeguards, Ski Patrol, and Other Recreational Protective Service Workers; Parking Enforcement Workers; Police and Sheriff's Patrol Officers; Police Detectives; Police Identification and Records Officers; Police Patrol Officers; Private Detectives and Investigators; Protective Service Workers, All Other; Security Guards; Sheriffs and Deputy Sheriffs; Transit and Railroad Police.

EDUCATION/TRAINING PROGRAM(S)— Criminal Justice/Police Science; Criminalistics and Criminal Science. **RELATED KNOWLEDGE/ COURSES—**Public Safety and Security; Law and Government; Psychology; Sociology and Anthropology; Telecommunications; Geography.

Education Administrators, Postsecondary

- Personality Code: ES
- Growth: 25.9%
- Annual Job Openings: 19,000
- Annual Earnings: $66,640
- Education/Training Required: Work experience plus degree
- Self-Employed: 2.6%
- Part-Time: 7.2%

Plan, direct, or coordinate research, instructional, student administration and services, and other educational activities at postsecondary institutions, including universities, colleges, and junior and community colleges. Direct activities of administrative departments such as admissions, registration, and career services. Direct, coordinate, and evaluate the activities of personnel engaged in administering academic institutions, departments, and/or alumni organizations. Establish operational policies and procedures and make any necessary modifications, based on analysis of operations, demographics, and other research information. Appoint individuals to faculty positions, and evaluate their performance. Confer with other academic staff to explain and formulate admission requirements and course credit policies. Develop curricula, and recommend curricula revisions and additions. Participate in faculty and college committee activities. Participate in student recruitment, selection, and admission, making admissions recommendations when required to do so. Plan, administer, and control budgets, maintain financial records, and produce financial reports. Provide assistance to faculty and staff in duties such as teaching classes, conducting orientation programs, issuing transcripts, and scheduling events. Recruit, hire, train, and terminate departmental personnel. Represent institutions at community and campus events, in meetings with other institution personnel, and during accreditation processes. Review registration statistics, and consult with faculty officials to develop registration policies. Audit the financial status of student organizations and facility accounts. Coordinate the production and dissemination of university publications such as course catalogs and class schedules. Determine course schedules, and coordinate teaching assignments and room assignments in order to ensure optimum use of buildings and equipment. Direct and participate in institutional fundraising activities, and encourage alumni participation in such activities. Direct scholarship, fellowship, and loan programs, performing activities such as selecting recipients and distributing aid. Plan and promote sporting events and social, cultural, and recreational activities. Review student misconduct reports requiring disciplinary action, and counsel students regarding such reports. SKILLS—Management of Financial Resources; Systems Evaluation; Management of Personnel Resources; Management of Material Resources; Coordination; Negotiation; Systems Analysis; Judgment and Decision Making.

GOE—Interest Area: 12. Education and Social Service. Work Group: 12.01. Managerial Work in Education and Social Service. Other Jobs in This Work Group: Education Administrators, All Other; Education Administrators, Elementary and Secondary School; Education Administrators, Preschool and Child Care Center/Program; Instructional Coordinators; Park Naturalists; Social and Community Service Managers.

EDUCATION/TRAINING PROGRAM(S)— Community College Education; Educational Administration and Supervision, Other; Educational Leadership and Administration, General; Educational, Instructional, and Curriculum Supervision; Higher Education/Higher Education Administration. RELATED KNOWLEDGE/COURSES— Education and Training; Administration and Management; Economics and Accounting; Personnel and Human Resources; Law and Government; English Language.

Engineering Managers

- Personality Code: ER
- Growth: 9.2%
- Annual Job Openings: 16,000
- Annual Earnings: $94,470
- Education/Training Required: Work experience plus degree
- Self-Employed: 0.1%
- Part-Time: 1.0%

Plan, direct, or coordinate activities in such fields as architecture and engineering or research and development in these fields. Confer with management, production, and marketing staff to discuss project specifications and procedures. Coordinate and direct projects, making detailed plans to accomplish goals and directing the integration of technical activities. Analyze technology, resource needs, and market demand, to plan and assess the feasibility of projects. Plan and direct the installation, testing, operation, maintenance, and repair of facilities and equipment. Direct, review, and approve product design and changes. Recruit employees); assign, direct, and evaluate their work); and oversee the development and maintenance of staff competence. Prepare budgets, bids, and contracts, and direct the negotiation of research contracts. Develop and implement policies, standards and procedures for the engineering and technical work performed in the department, service, laboratory or firm. Perform administrative functions such as reviewing and writing reports, approving expenditures, enforcing rules, and making decisions about the purchase of materials or services. Review and recommend or approve contracts and cost estimates. Present and explain proposals, reports, and findings to clients. Consult or negotiate with clients to prepare project specifications. Set scientific and technical goals within broad outlines provided by top management. Administer highway planning, construction, and maintenance. Direct the engineering of water control, treatment, and distribution projects. Plan, direct, and coordinate survey work with other staff activities, certifying survey work, and writing land legal descriptions. Confer with and report to officials and the public to provide information and solicit support for projects. SKILLS—Technology Design; Operations Analysis; Science; Management of Financial Resources; Installation; Negotiation; Persuasion; Time Management.

GOE—Interest Area: 02. Science, Math, and Engineering. Work Group: 02.01. Managerial Work in Science, Math, and Engineering. Other Jobs in

This Work Group: Computer and Information Systems Managers; Natural Sciences Managers.

EDUCATION/TRAINING PROGRAM(S)—Aerospace, Aeronautical and Astronautical Engineering; Agricultural/Biological Engineering and Bioengineering; Architectural Engineering; Architecture (BArch, BA/BS, MArch, MA/MS, PhD); Biomedical/Medical Engineering; Ceramic Sciences and Engineering; Chemical Engineering; City/Urban, Community and Regional Planning; Civil Engineering, General; Civil Engineering, Other; Computer Engineering, General; Computer Engineering, Other; Computer Hardware Engineering; Computer Software Engineering; Construction Engineering; Electrical, Electronics and Communications Engineering; Engineering Mechanics; Engineering Physics; Engineering Science; Engineering, General; Engineering, Other; Environmental Design/Architecture; Environmental/Environmental Health Engineering; Forest Engineering; Geological/Geophysical Engineering; Geotechnical Engineering; Industrial Engineering; Interior Architecture; Landscape Architecture (BS, BSLA, BLA, MSLA, MLA, PhD); Manufacturing Engineering; Materials Engineering; Materials Science; Mechanical Engineering; Metallurgical Engineering; Mining and Mineral Engineering; Naval Architecture and Marine Engineering; Nuclear Engineering; Ocean Engineering; Petroleum Engineering; Polymer/Plastics Engineering; Structural Engineering; Surveying Engineering; Systems Engineering; Textile Sciences and Engineering; Transportation and Highway Engineering; Water Resources Engineering. **RELATED KNOWLEDGE/COURSES**—Engineering and Technology; Design; Physics; Mathematics; Personnel and Human Resources; Administration and Management; Building and Construction.

Financial Managers, Branch or Department

- Personality Code: EC
- Growth: 18.3%
- Annual Job Openings: 71,000
- Annual Earnings: $77,300
- Education/Training Required: Work experience plus degree
- Self-Employed: 3.1%
- Part-Time: 4.8%

Direct and coordinate financial activities of workers in a branch, office, or department of an establishment, such as branch bank, brokerage firm, risk and insurance department, or credit department. Examine, evaluate, and process loan applications. Monitor order flow and transactions that brokerage firm executes on the floor of exchange. Recruit staff members, and oversee training programs. Review collection reports to determine the status of collections and the amounts of outstanding balances. Review reports of securities transactions and price lists in order to analyze market conditions. Submit delinquent accounts to attorneys or outside agencies for collection. Analyze and classify risks and investments to determine their potential impacts on companies. Approve or reject, or coordinate the approval and rejection of, lines of credit and commercial, real estate, and personal loans. Develop and analyze information to assess the current and future financial status of firms. Establish procedures for custody and control of assets, records, loan collateral, and securities, in order to ensure safekeeping. Evaluate data pertaining to costs in order to plan budgets. Evaluate financial reporting systems, accounting and collection procedures, and investment activities, and make recommendations for changes to procedures, operating systems, budgets, and other financial control functions. Network within communities to find and attract new business. Oversee the flow of cash and financial instruments. Plan, direct, and coordinate risk and insurance programs of establishments to control risks and losses. Plan, direct, and coordinate the activities of workers in branches, offices, or departments of such establishments as branch banks, brokerage firms, risk and insurance departments, or credit departments. Prepare financial and regulatory reports required by laws, regulations, and boards of directors. Prepare operational and risk reports for management analysis. Communicate with stockholders and other investors to provide information, and to raise capital. Direct floor operations of brokerage firm engaged in buying and selling securities at exchange. Direct insurance negotiations, select insurance brokers and carriers, and place insurance. Establish and maintain relationships with individual and business customers, and provide assistance with problems these customers may encounter. SKILLS—Management of Financial Resources; Management of Personnel Resources; Systems Analysis; Systems Evaluation; Judgment and Decision Making; Monitoring; Writing; Negotiation.

GOE—Interest Area: 13. General Management and Support. Work Group: 13.01. General Management Work and Management of Support Functions. Other Jobs in This Work Group: Business Operations Specialists, All Other; Chief Executives; Compensation and Benefits Managers; Farm, Ranch, and Other Agricultural Managers; Financial Managers; Financial Specialists, All Other; Funeral Directors; General and Operations Managers; Government Service Executives; Human Resources Managers; Human Resources Managers, All Other; Legislators; Managers, All Other; Postmasters and Mail Superintendents; Private Sector Executives; Property, Real Estate, and Community Association Managers; Public Relations Managers; Purchasing Managers; Storage and Distribution Managers; Training and Development Managers; Transportation, Storage, and Distribution Managers; Treasurers, Controllers, and Chief Financial Officers.

EDUCATION/TRAINING PROGRAM(S)—Accounting and Business/Management; Accounting and Finance; Credit Management; Finance and Financial Management Services, Other; Finance, General; International Finance; Public Finance. RELATED KNOWLEDGE/COURSES—Economics and Accounting; Administration and Management; Law and Government; Mathematics; Personnel and Human Resources; Psychology.

First-Line Supervisors and Manager/Supervisors— Construction Trades Workers

- Personality Code: ER
- Growth: 14.1%
- Annual Job Openings: 67,000
- Annual Earnings: $48,730
- Education/Training Required: Work experience in a related occupation
- Self-Employed: 20.1%
- Part-Time: 2.1%

Directly supervise and coordinate activities of construction trades workers and their helpers. Manager/Supervisors are generally found in smaller establishments where they perform both supervisory and management functions, such as accounting, marketing, and personnel work and may also engage in the same construction trades work as the workers they supervise. Supervises and coordinates activities of construction trades workers. Directs and leads workers engaged in construction activities. Assigns work to employees, using material and worker requirements data. Confers with staff and worker to ensure production and personnel problems are resolved. Suggests and initiates personnel actions, such as promotions, transfers, and hires. Analyzes and resolves worker problems and recommends motivational plans. Examines and inspects work progress, equipment and construction sites to verify safety and ensure that specifications are met. Estimates material and worker requirements to complete job. Reads specifications, such as blueprints and data, to determine construction requirements. Analyzes and plans installation and construction of equipment and structures. Locates, measures, and marks location and placement of structures and equipment. Records information, such as personnel, production, and operational data, on specified forms and reports. Trains workers in construction methods and operation of equipment. Recommends measures to improve production methods and equipment performance to increase efficiency and safety. Assists workers engaged in construction activities, using hand tools and equipment. **SKILLS**—Management of Personnel Resources; Management of Material Resources; Installation; Time Management; Coordination; Persuasion; Instructing; Quality Control Analysis; Systems Evaluation.

GOE—Interest Area: 06. Construction, Mining, and Drilling. **Work Group:** 06.01. Managerial Work in Construction, Mining, and Drilling. **Other Jobs in This Work Group:** Construction Managers; First-Line Supervisors and Manager/Supervisors—Extractive Workers; First-Line Supervisors/Managers of Construction Trades and Extraction Workers.

EDUCATION/TRAINING PROGRAM(S)—Building/Construction Finishing, Management, and Inspection, Other; Building/Construction Site Management/Manager; Building/Home/Construction Inspection/Inspector; Building/Property Maintenance and Management; Carpentry/Carpenter; Concrete Finishing/Concrete Finisher; Construction Trades, Other; Drywall Installation/Drywaller; Electrical and Power Trans-

mission Installation/Installer, General; Electrical and Power Transmission Installers, Other; Electrician; Glazier; Lineworker; Mason/Masonry; Painting/Painter and Wall Coverer; Plumbing Technology/Plumber; Roofer; Well Drilling/Driller. **RELATED KNOWLEDGE/COURSES**—Building and Construction; Personnel and Human Resources; Administration and Management; Design; Engineering and Technology; Mechanical Devices.

First-Line Supervisors and Manager/Supervisors— Extractive Workers

- Personality Code: ER
- Growth: 14.1%
- Annual Job Openings: 67,000
- Annual Earnings: $48,730
- Education/Training Required: Work experience in a related occupation
- Self-Employed: 20.1%
- Part-Time: 2.1%

Directly supervise and coordinate activities of extractive workers and their helpers. Manager/Supervisors are generally found in smaller establishments where they perform both supervisory and management functions, such as accounting, marketing, and personnel work, and may also engage in the same extractive work as the workers they supervise. Supervises and coordinates activities of workers engaged in the extraction of geological materials. Directs and leads workers engaged in extraction of geological materials. Assigns work to employees, using material and worker requirements data. Confers with staff and

Enterprising—F

workers to ensure production personnel problems are resolved. Analyzes and resolves worker problems and recommends motivational plans. Analyzes and plans extraction process of geological materials. Trains workers in construction methods and operation of equipment. Examines and inspects equipment, site, and materials, to verify specifications are met. Recommends measures to improve production methods and equipment performance to increase efficiency and safety. Suggests and initiates personnel actions, such as promotions, transfers, and hires. Records information, such as personnel, production, and operational data on specified forms. Assists workers engaged in extraction activities, using hand tools and equipment. Locates, measures, and marks, materials and site location, using measuring and marking equipment. Orders materials, supplies and repair of equipment and machinery. **SKILLS**—Management of Personnel Resources; Instructing; Management of Material Resources; Systems Evaluation; Coordination; Systems Analysis; Time Management; Negotiation.

GOE—**Interest Area:** 06. Construction, Mining, and Drilling. **Work Group:** 06.01. Managerial Work in Construction, Mining, and Drilling. **Other Jobs in This Work Group:** Construction Managers; First-Line Supervisors and Manager/Supervisors—Construction Trades Workers; First-Line Supervisors/Managers of Construction Trades and Extraction Workers.

EDUCATION/TRAINING PROGRAM(S)— Blasting/Blaster; Well Drilling/Driller. **RELATED KNOWLEDGE/COURSES**—Personnel and Human Resources; Administration and Management; Engineering and Technology; Physics; Production and Processing; Mechanical Devices; Education and Training.

First-Line Supervisors, Administrative Support

- Personality Code: EC
- Growth: 6.6%
- Annual Job Openings: 140,000
- Annual Earnings: $39,490
- Education/Training Required: Work experience in a related occupation
- Self-Employed: 0.9%
- Part-Time: 6.7%

Supervise and coordinate activities of workers involved in providing administrative support. Trains employees in work and safety procedures and company policies. Computes figures, such as balances, totals, and commissions. Analyzes financial activities of establishment or department and assists in planning budget. Inspects equipment for defects and notifies maintenance personnel or outside service contractors for repairs. Plans layout of stockroom, warehouse, or other storage areas, considering turnover, size, weight, and related factors pertaining to items stored. Compiles reports and information required by management or governmental agencies. Identifies and resolves discrepancies or errors. Maintains records of such matters as inventory, personnel, orders, supplies, and machine maintenance. Examines procedures and recommends changes to save time, labor, and other costs and to improve quality control and operating efficiency. Participates in work of subordinates to facilitate productivity or overcome difficult aspects of work. Supervises and coordinates activities of workers engaged in clerical or administrative support activities. Plans, prepares, and revises work schedules and duty assignments according to budget allotments, customer needs, problems, work-loads, and statistical forecasts. Verifies completeness and accuracy of subordinates' work, computations, and records. Interviews, selects, and discharges employees. Oversees, coordinates, or performs activities associated with shipping, receiving, distribution, and transportation. Evaluates subordinate job performance and conformance to regulations, and recommends appropriate personnel action. Consults with supervisor and other personnel to resolve problems, such as equipment performance, output quality, and work schedules. Requisitions supplies. Reviews records and reports pertaining to such activities as production, operation, pay roll, customer accounts, and shipping. **SKILLS**—Management of Personnel Resources; Management of Financial Resources; Management of Material Resources; Social Perceptiveness; Time Management; Monitoring; Instructing; Systems Evaluation.

GOE—Interest Area: 09. Business Detail. **Work Group:** 09.01. Managerial Work in Business Detail. **Other Jobs in This Work Group:** Administrative Services Managers; First-Line Supervisors, Customer Service; First-Line Supervisors/Managers of Office and Administrative Support Workers.

EDUCATION/TRAINING PROGRAM(S)— Agricultural Business Technology; Customer Service Management; Medical/Health Management and Clinical Assistant/Specialist; Office Management and Supervision. **RELATED KNOWLEDGE/ COURSES**—Clerical Studies; Personnel and Human Resources; Transportation; Economics and Accounting; Administration and Management; Law and Government.

First-Line Supervisors/Managers of Food Preparation and Serving Workers

- Personality Code: ER
- Growth: 15.5%
- Annual Job Openings: 154,000
- Annual Earnings: $24,700
- Education/Training Required: Work experience in a related occupation
- Self-Employed: 4.5%
- Part-Time: 14.7%

Supervise workers engaged in preparing and serving food. Compile and balance cash receipts at the end of the day or shift. Resolve customer complaints regarding food service. Train workers in food preparation, and in service, sanitation, and safety procedures. Inspect supplies, equipment, and work areas in order to ensure efficient service and conformance to standards. Control inventories of food, equipment, smallware, and liquor, and report shortages to designated personnel. Observe and evaluate workers and work procedures in order to ensure quality standards and service. Assign duties, responsibilities, and work stations to employees in accordance with work requirements. Estimate ingredients and supplies required to prepare a recipe. Perform personnel actions such as hiring and firing staff, consulting with other managers as necessary. Analyze operational problems, such as theft and wastage, and establish procedures to alleviate these problems. Specify food portions and courses, production and time sequences, and workstation and equipment arrangements. Recommend measures for improving work procedures and worker performance in order to increase service quality and enhance job safety. Greet and seat guests, and present menus and wine lists. Present bills and accept payments. Forecast

Enterprising—F

staff, equipment, and supply requirements based on a master menu. Perform serving duties such as carving meat, preparing flambe dishes, or serving wine and liquor. Record production and operational data on specified forms. Purchase or requisition supplies and equipment needed to ensure quality and timely delivery of services. Collaborate with other personnel in order to plan menus, serving arrangements, and related details. Supervise and check the assembly of regular and special diet trays and the delivery of food trolleys to hospital patients. Schedule parties and take reservations. Develop departmental objectives, budgets, policies, procedures, and strategies. Develop equipment maintenance schedules and arrange for repairs. Evaluate new products for usefulness and suitability. SKILLS—Management of Personnel Resources; Management of Financial Resources; Instructing; Equipment Maintenance; Learning Strategies; Monitoring; Service Orientation; Negotiation.

GOE—Interest Area: 11. Recreation, Travel, and Other Personal Services. Work Group: 11.01. Managerial Work in Recreation, Travel, and Other Personal Services. Other Jobs in This Work Group: Aircraft Cargo Handling Supervisors; First-Line Supervisors/Managers of Housekeeping and Janitorial Workers; First-Line Supervisors/Managers of Personal Service Workers; Food Service Managers; Gaming Managers; Gaming Supervisors; Housekeeping Supervisors; Janitorial Supervisors; Lodging Managers; Meeting and Convention Planners.

EDUCATION/TRAINING PROGRAM(S)— Cooking and Related Culinary Arts, General; Foodservice Systems Administration/Management; Restaurant, Culinary, and Catering Management/Manager. RELATED KNOWLEDGE/ COURSES—Customer and Personal Service; Food Production; Administration and Management; Sales and Marketing; Personnel and Human Resources; Education and Training.

First-Line Supervisors/Managers of Mechanics, Installers, and Repairers

- Personality Code: ER
- Growth: 15.4%
- Annual Job Openings: 42,000
- Annual Earnings: $48,620
- Education/Training Required: Work experience in a related occupation
- Self-Employed: 0.1%
- Part-Time: 1.3%

Supervise and coordinate the activities of mechanics, installers, and repairers. Determine schedules, sequences, and assignments for work activities, based on work priority, quantity of equipment and skill of personnel. Patrol and monitor work areas and examine tools and equipment in order to detect unsafe conditions or violations of procedures or safety rules. Monitor employees' work levels and review work performance. Examine objects, systems, or facilities); and analyze information to determine needed installations, services, or repairs. Participate in budget preparation and administration, coordinating purchasing and documentation, and monitoring departmental expenditures. Counsel employees about work-related issues and assist employees to correct job-skill deficiencies. Requisition materials and supplies, such as tools, equipment, and replacement parts. Compute estimates and actual costs of factors such as materials, labor, and outside contractors. Interpret specifications, blueprints, and job orders in order to construct templates and lay out reference points for workers. Conduct or arrange for worker training in safety, repair, and maintenance techniques); operational procedures); and equipment use. Investigate accidents and injuries, and prepare reports of findings. Confer with personnel, such as management, engineering, quality control, customer, and union workers' representatives, in order to coordinate work activities, resolve employee grievances, and identify and review resource needs. Recommend or initiate personnel actions, such as hires, promotions, transfers, discharges, and disciplinary measures. Perform skilled repair and maintenance operations, using equipment such as hand and power tools, hydraulic presses and shears, and welding equipment. Compile operational and personnel records, such as time and production records, inventory data, repair and maintenance statistics, and test results. Develop, implement, and evaluate maintenance policies and procedures. Monitor tool inventories and the condition and maintenance of shops in order to ensure adequate working conditions. Inspect, test, and measure completed work, using devices such as hand tools and gauges to verify conformance to standards and repair requirements. **SKILLS**—Management of Personnel Resources; Installation; Management of Financial Resources; Management of Material Resources; Repairing; Equipment Maintenance; Negotiation; Troubleshooting.

GOE—**Interest Area:** 05. Mechanics, Installers, and Repairers. **Work Group:** 05.01. Managerial Work in Mechanics, Installers, and Repairers. **Other Jobs in This Work Group:** None.

EDUCATION/TRAINING PROGRAM(S)—Operations Management and Supervision. **RELATED KNOWLEDGE/COURSES**—Mechanical Devices; Building and Construction; Personnel and Human Resources; Design; Administration and Management; Customer and Personal Service.

First-Line Supervisors/Managers of Non-Retail Sales Workers

- Personality Code: EC
- Growth: 6.8%
- Annual Job Openings: 72,000
- Annual Earnings: $55,690
- Education/Training Required: Work experience in a related occupation
- Self-Employed: 44.7%
- Part-Time: 5.7%

Directly supervise and coordinate activities of sales workers other than retail sales workers. May perform duties, such as budgeting, accounting, and personnel work, in addition to supervisory duties. Analyze details of sales territories to assess their growth potential, and to set quotas. Direct and supervise employees engaged in sales, inventory-taking, reconciling cash receipts, or performing specific services such as pumping gasoline for customers. Hire, train, and evaluate personnel. Inventory stock, and reorder when inventories drop to specified levels. Keep records pertaining to purchases, sales, and requisitions. Listen to and resolve customer complaints regarding services, products, or personnel. Monitor sales staff performance to ensure that goals are met. Plan and prepare work schedules, and assign employees to specific duties. Prepare sales and inventory reports for management and budget departments. Provide staff with assistance in performing difficult or complicated duties. Attend company meetings to exchange product information and coordinate work activities with other departments. Confer with company officials to develop methods and procedures to increase sales, expand markets, and promote business. Coordinate sales promotion activities, and prepare merchandise

Enterprising—F

displays and advertising copy. Examine merchandise to ensure correct pricing and display, and that it functions as advertised. Examine products purchased for resale or received for storage to determine product condition. Formulate pricing policies on merchandise according to profitability requirements. Prepare rental or lease agreements, specifying charges and payment procedures for use of machinery, tools, or other items. Visit retailers and sales representatives to promote products and gather information. **SKILLS**—Management of Personnel Resources; Management of Financial Resources; Management of Material Resources; Systems Evaluation; Systems Analysis; Negotiation; Coordination; Social Perceptiveness.

GOE—**Interest Area:** 10. Sales and Marketing. **Work Group:** 10.01. Managerial Work in Sales and Marketing. **Other Jobs in This Work Group:** Advertising and Promotions Managers; First-Line Supervisors/Managers of Retail Sales Workers; Marketing Managers; Sales Managers.

EDUCATION/TRAINING PROGRAM(S)— Business, Management, Marketing, and Related Support Services, Other; General Merchandising, Sales, and Related Marketing Operations, Other; Special Products Marketing Operations; Specialized Merchandising, Sales, and Related Marketing Operations, Other. **RELATED KNOWLEDGE/ COURSES**—Sales and Marketing; Economics and Accounting; Personnel and Human Resources; Administration and Management; Mathematics; Customer and Personal Service.

First-Line Supervisors/Managers of Police and Detectives

- Personality Code: ES
- Growth: 15.3%
- Annual Job Openings: 14,000
- Annual Earnings: $62,350
- Education/Training Required: Work experience in a related occupation
- Self-Employed: 0%
- Part-Time: 1.4%

Supervise and coordinate activities of members of police force. Explain police operations to subordinates to assist them in performing their job duties. Inform personnel of changes in regulations and policies, implications of new or amended laws, and new techniques of police work. Supervise and coordinate the investigation of criminal cases, offering guidance and expertise to investigators, and ensuring that procedures are conducted in accordance with laws and regulations. Investigate and resolve personnel problems within organization and charges of misconduct against staff. Train staff in proper police work procedures. Maintain logs, prepare reports, and direct the preparation, handling, and maintenance of departmental records. Monitor and evaluate the job performance of subordinates, and authorize promotions and transfers. Direct collection, preparation, and handling of evidence and personal property of prisoners. Develop, implement and revise departmental policies and procedures. Conduct raids and order detention of witnesses and suspects for questioning. Prepare work schedules and assign duties to subordinates. Discipline staff for violation of department rules and regulations. Cooperate with court personnel and officials from other law enforcement agencies and testify in court as necessary. Review contents of written orders to ensure adherence to legal requirements. Inspect facilities, supplies, vehicles, and equipment to ensure conformance to standards. Prepare news releases and respond to police correspondence. Requisition and issue equipment and supplies. Meet with civic, educational, and community groups to develop community programs and events, and to discuss law enforcement subjects. Direct release or transfer of prisoners. Prepare budgets and manage expenditures of department funds. **SKILLS**—Management of Personnel Resources; Persuasion; Negotiation; Social Perceptiveness; Service Orientation; Monitoring; Instructing; Coordination.

GOE—Interest Area: 04. Law, Law Enforcement, and Public Safety. **Work Group:** 04.01. Managerial Work in Law, Law Enforcement, and Public Safety. **Other Jobs in This Work Group:** Emergency Management Specialists; First-Line Supervisors/Managers of Correctional Officers; First-Line Supervisors/Managers of Fire Fighting and Prevention Workers; First-Line Supervisors/Managers, Protective Service Workers, All Other; Forest Fire Fighting and Prevention Supervisors; Municipal Fire Fighting and Prevention Supervisors.

EDUCATION/TRAINING PROGRAM(S)—Corrections; Criminal Justice/Law Enforcement Administration; Criminal Justice/Safety Studies. **RELATED KNOWLEDGE/COURSES**—Public Safety and Security; Psychology; Law and Government; Customer and Personal Service; Personnel and Human Resources; Education and Training.

First-Line Supervisors/Managers of Production and Operating Workers

- Personality Code: ER
- Growth: 9.5%
- Annual Job Openings: 66,000
- Annual Earnings: $43,720
- Education/Training Required: Work experience in a related occupation
- Self-Employed: 2.2%
- Part-Time: 1.9%

Supervise and coordinate the activities of production and operating workers, such as inspectors, precision workers, machine setters and operators, assemblers, fabricators, and plant and system operators. Calculate labor and equipment requirements and production specifications, using standard formulas. Confer with management or subordinates to resolve worker problems, complaints, or grievances. Confer with other supervisors to coordinate operations and activities within or between departments. Demonstrate equipment operations and work and safety procedures to new employees, or assign employees to experienced workers for training. Direct and coordinate the activities of employees engaged in the production or processing of goods, such as inspectors, machine setters, and fabricators. Inspect materials, products, or equipment to detect defects or malfunctions. Interpret specifications, blueprints, job orders, and company policies and procedures for workers. Maintain operations data such as time, production, and cost records, and prepare management reports of production results. Observe work, and monitor gauges, dials, and other indicators to ensure that operators conform to production or processing standards. Plan and establish work schedules, assignments, and production

Enterprising—F

sequences to meet production goals. Recommend or implement measures to motivate employees and to improve production methods, equipment performance, product quality, or efficiency. Requisition materials, supplies, equipment parts, or repair services. Determine standards, budgets, production goals, and rates, based on company policies, equipment and labor availability, and workloads. Enforce safety and sanitation regulations. Plan and develop new products and production processes. Read and analyze charts, work orders, production schedules, and other records and reports, in order to determine production requirements and to evaluate current production estimates and outputs. Recommend personnel actions such as hirings and promotions. Set up and adjust machines and equipment. **SKILLS**—Management of Personnel Resources; Management of Material Resources; Systems Analysis; Negotiation; Coordination; Management of Financial Resources; Social Perceptiveness; Instructing; Operation Monitoring.

GOE—Interest Area: 08. Industrial Production. **Work Group:** 08.01. Managerial Work in Industrial Production. **Other Jobs in This Work Group:** First-Line Supervisors/Managers of Helpers, Laborers, and Material Movers, Hand; Industrial Production Managers.

EDUCATION/TRAINING PROGRAM(S)— Operations Management and Supervision. **RELATED KNOWLEDGE/COURSES**—Production and Processing; Personnel and Human Resources; Administration and Management; Economics and Accounting; Psychology; Mathematics.

Government Service Executives

- ◉ Personality Code: EC
- ◉ Growth: 16.7%
- ◉ Annual Job Openings: 63,000
- ◉ Annual Earnings: $134,740
- ◉ Education/Training Required: Work experience plus degree
- ◉ Self-Employed: 14.6%
- ◉ Part-Time: 5.3%

Determine and formulate policies and provide overall direction of federal, state, local, or international government activities. Plan, direct, and coordinate operational activities at the highest level of management with the help of subordinate managers. Directs organization charged with administering and monitoring regulated activities to interpret and clarify laws and ensure compliance with laws. Administers, interprets, and explains policies, rules, regulations, and laws to organizations and individuals under authority of commission or applicable legislation. Develops, plans, organizes, and administers policies and procedures for organization to ensure administrative and operational objectives are met. Directs and coordinates activities of workers in public organization to ensure continuing operations, maximize returns on investments, and increase productivity. Negotiates contracts and agreements with federal and state agencies and other organizations and prepares budget for funding and implementation of programs. Implements corrective action plan to solve problems. Reviews and analyzes legislation, laws, and public policy and recommends changes to promote and support interests of general population, as well as special groups. Develops, directs, and coordinates testing, hiring, training, and evaluation of staff personnel. Establishes and maintains comprehensive and current record keeping system of activities and operational procedures in business office. Testifies in court, before control or review board, or at legislature. Participates in activities to promote business and expand services, and provides technical assistance in conducting of conferences, seminars, and workshops. Delivers speeches, writes articles, and presents information for organization at meetings or conventions to promote services, exchange ideas, and accomplish objectives. Plans, promotes, organizes, and coordinates public community service program and maintains cooperative working relationships among public and agency participants. Conducts or directs investigations or hearings to resolve complaints and violations of laws. Prepares, reviews, and submits reports concerning activities, expenses, budget, government statutes and rulings, and other items affecting business or program services. Directs, coordinates, and conducts activities between United States government and foreign entities to provide information to promote international interest and harmony. **SKILLS**—Management of Financial Resources; Systems Evaluation; Coordination; Systems Analysis; Management of Personnel Resources; Judgment and Decision Making; Negotiation; Persuasion.

GOE—Interest Area: 13. General Management and Support. **Work Group:** 13.01. General Management Work and Management of Support Functions. **Other Jobs in This Work Group:** Business Operations Specialists, All Other; Chief Executives; Compensation and Benefits Managers; Farm, Ranch, and Other Agricultural Managers; Financial Managers; Financial Managers, Branch or Department; Financial Specialists, All Other; Funeral Directors; General and Operations Managers; Human Resources Managers; Human Resources Managers, All Other; Legislators; Managers, All Other; Postmasters and Mail Superintendents; Private Sector Executives; Property, Real Estate, and Community Association Managers; Public Relations Managers; Purchasing Managers; Storage and Distribution Managers; Training and Development Managers; Transportation, Storage, and Distribution Managers; Treasurers, Controllers, and Chief Financial Officers.

EDUCATION/TRAINING PROGRAM(S)—Business Administration and Management, General; Business/Commerce, General; Entrepreneurship/Entrepreneurial Studies; International Business/Trade/Commerce; Public Administration; Public Administration and Social Service Professions, Other; Public Policy Analysis. **RELATED KNOWLEDGE/COURSES**—Administration and Management; Law and Government; Personnel and Human Resources; Economics and Accounting; Education and Training; Psychology.

Hosts and Hostesses, Restaurant, Lounge, and Coffee Shop

- Personality Code: ES
- Growth: 16.4%
- Annual Job Openings: 95,000
- Annual Earnings: $15,380
- Education/Training Required: Short-term on-the-job training
- Self-Employed: 0.6%
- Part-Time: 66.9%

Welcome patrons, seat them at tables or in lounge, and help ensure quality of facilities and service. Provide guests with menus. Greet guests and seat them at tables or in waiting areas. Assign patrons to tables suitable for their needs. Inspect dining and serving areas to ensure cleanliness and proper setup. Speak with patrons to ensure satisfaction with food and service, and to respond to complaints. Receive and record patrons' dining reservations. Maintain contact with kitchen staff, management, serving staff, and customers to ensure that dining details are handled properly and customers' concerns are addressed. Inform patrons of establishment specialties and features. Direct patrons to coatrooms and waiting areas such as lounges. Operate cash registers to accept payments for food and beverages. Prepare cash receipts after establishments close, and make bank deposits. Supervise and coordinate activities of dining room staff to ensure that patrons receive prompt and courteous service. Prepare staff work schedules. Order or requisition supplies and equipment for tables and serving stations. Hire, train, and supervise food and beverage service staff. Plan parties or other special events and services. Confer with other staff to help plan establishments' menus. Perform marketing and advertising services. **SKILLS—** Service Orientation; Persuasion; Instructing; Social Perceptiveness; Negotiation; Learning Strategies.

GOE—Interest Area: 11. Recreation, Travel, and Other Personal Services. **Work Group:** 11.05. Food and Beverage Services. **Other Jobs in This Work Group:** Bakers; Bakers, Bread and Pastry; Bartenders; Butchers and Meat Cutters; Chefs and Head Cooks; Combined Food Preparation and Serving Workers, Including Fast Food; Cooks, All Other; Cooks, Fast Food; Cooks, Institution and Cafeteria; Cooks, Restaurant; Cooks, Short Order; Counter Attendants, Cafeteria, Food Concession, and Coffee Shop; Dining Room and Cafeteria Attendants and Bartender Helpers; Dishwashers; Food Preparation and Serving Related Workers, All Other; Food Preparation Workers; Food Servers, Nonrestaurant; Waiters and Waitresses.

EDUCATION/TRAINING PROGRAM(S)— Food Service, Waiter/Waitress, and Dining Room Management/Manager. **RELATED KNOWLEDGE/COURSES—**Customer and Personal Service; Food Production; Sales and Marketing; Administration and Management; Public Safety and Security.

Human Resources Managers

- Personality Code: ES
- Growth: 19.4%
- Annual Job Openings: 21,000
- Annual Earnings: $68,800
- Education/Training Required: Work experience plus degree
- Self-Employed: 0%
- Part-Time: 3.7%

Plan, direct, and coordinate human resource management activities of an organization to maximize the strategic use of human resources and maintain functions such as employee compensation, recruitment, personnel policies, and regulatory compliance. Administer compensation, benefits and performance management systems, and safety and recreation programs. Identify staff vacancies and recruit, interview and select applicants. Allocate human resources, ensuring appropriate matches between personnel. Provide current and prospective employees with information about policies, job duties, working conditions, wages, opportunities for promotion and employee benefits. Perform difficult staffing duties, including dealing with understaffing, refereeing disputes, firing employees, and administering disciplinary procedures. Advise managers on organizational policy matters such as equal employment opportunity and sexual harassment, and recommend needed changes. Analyze and modify compensation and benefits policies to establish competitive programs and ensure compliance with legal requirements. Plan and conduct new employee orientation to foster positive attitude toward organizational objectives. Serve as a link between management and employees by handling questions, interpreting and administering contracts and helping resolve work-related problems. Plan, direct, supervise, and coordinate work activities of subordinates and staff relating to employment, compensation, labor relations, and employee relations. Analyze training needs to design employee development, language training and health and safety programs. Maintain records and compile statistical reports concerning personnel-related data such as hires, transfers, performance appraisals, and absenteeism rates. Analyze statistical data and reports to identify and determine causes of personnel problems and develop recommendations for improvement of organization's personnel policies and practices. Plan, organize, direct, control or coordinate the personnel, training, or labor relations activities of an organization. Conduct exit interviews to identify reasons for employee termination. Investigate and report on industrial accidents for insurance carriers. Represent organization at personnel-related hearings and investigations. Negotiate bargaining agreements and help interpret labor contracts. **SKILLS**—Management of Personnel Resources; Negotiation; Persuasion; Time Management; Social Perceptiveness; Learning Strategies; Active Listening; Management of Financial Resources.

GOE—Interest Area: 13. General Management and Support. **Work Group:** 13.01. General Management Work and Management of Support Functions. **Other Jobs in This Work Group:** Business Operations Specialists, All Other; Chief Executives; Compensation and Benefits Managers; Farm, Ranch, and Other Agricultural Managers; Financial Managers; Financial Managers, Branch or Department; Financial Specialists, All Other; Funeral Directors; General and Operations Managers; Government Service Executives; Human Resources Managers, All Other; Legislators; Managers, All Other; Postmasters and Mail Superintendents; Private Sector Executives; Property, Real Estate, and Community Association Managers; Public Relations Managers; Purchasing Managers; Storage and Distribution Managers; Training and Development Managers; Transportation, Storage, and Distribution Managers; Treasurers, Controllers, and Chief Financial Officers.

EDUCATION/TRAINING PROGRAM(S)— Human Resources Development; Human Resources

Management/Personnel Administration, General; Labor and Industrial Relations; Labor Studies. **RELATED KNOWLEDGE/COURSES**—Personnel and Human Resources; Clerical Studies; Education and Training; Law and Government; Customer and Personal Service; Economics and Accounting.

Insurance Adjusters, Examiners, and Investigators

- Personality Code: EI
- Growth: 14.2%
- Annual Job Openings: 31,000
- Annual Earnings: $44,040
- Education/Training Required: Long-term on-the-job training
- Self-Employed: 1.9%
- Part-Time: 4.9%

Investigate, analyze, and determine the extent of insurance company's liability concerning personal, casualty, or property loss or damages, and attempt to effect settlement with claimants. Correspond with or interview medical specialists, agents, witnesses, or claimants to compile information. Calculate benefit payments and approve payment of claims within a certain monetary limit. Interview or correspond with claimant and witnesses, consult police and hospital records, and inspect property damage to determine extent of liability. Investigate and assess damage to property. Examine claims form and other records to determine insurance coverage. Analyze information gathered by investigation and report findings and recommendations. Negotiate claim settlements and recommend litigation when settlement cannot be negotiated. Prepare report of findings of investigation. Collect evidence to support contested claims in court. Interview or correspond with agents and claimants to correct errors or omissions and to investigate questionable claims. Refer questionable claims to investigator or claims adjuster for investigation or settlement. Examine titles to property to determine validity and act as company agent in transactions with property owners. Obtain credit information from banks and other credit services. Communicate with former associates to verify employment record and to obtain background information regarding persons or businesses applying for credit. SKILLS—Negotiation; Persuasion; Time Management; Judgment and Decision Making; Social Perceptiveness; Service Orientation; Management of Financial Resources; Critical Thinking.

GOE—Interest Area: 13. General Management and Support. Work Group: 13.02. Management Support. Other Jobs in This Work Group: Accountants; Accountants and Auditors; Appraisers and Assessors of Real Estate; Appraisers, Real Estate; Assessors; Auditors; Budget Analysts; Business Operations Specialists, All Other; Claims Adjusters, Examiners, and Investigators; Claims Examiners, Property and Casualty Insurance; Compensation, Benefits, and Job Analysis Specialists; Cost Estimators; Credit Analysts; Employment Interviewers, Private or Public Employment Service; Employment, Recruitment, and Placement Specialists; Financial Analysts; Human Resources, Training, and Labor Relations Specialists, All Other; Insurance Appraisers, Auto Damage; Insurance Underwriters; Loan Counselors; Loan Officers; Logisticians; Management Analysts; Market Research Analysts; Personnel Recruiters; Purchasing Agents and Buyers, Farm Products; Purchasing Agents, Except Wholesale, Retail, and Farm Products; Tax Examiners, Collectors, and Revenue Agents; Training and Development Specialists; Wholesale and Retail Buyers, Except Farm Products.

EDUCATION/TRAINING PROGRAM(S)— Health/Medical Claims Examiner; Insurance. RELATED KNOWLEDGE/COURSES—Customer and Personal Service; Clerical Studies; Computers and Electronics; Law and Government; English Language; Mathematics.

Lawn Service Managers

- Personality Code: ER
- Growth: 21.6%
- Annual Job Openings: 18,000
- Annual Earnings: $33,770
- Education/Training Required: Work experience in a related occupation
- Self-Employed: 34.7%
- Part-Time: 5.9%

Plan, direct, and coordinate activities of workers engaged in pruning trees and shrubs, cultivating lawns, and applying pesticides and other chemicals according to service contract specifications. Supervises workers who provide grounds-keeping services on a contract basis. Investigates customer complaints. Prepares work activity and personnel reports. Suggests changes in work procedures and orders corrective work done. Spot checks completed work to improve quality of service and to ensure contract compliance. Schedules work for crew according to weather conditions, availability of equipment, and seasonal limitations. Reviews contracts to ascertain service, machine, and work force requirements for job. Prepares service cost estimates for customers. Answers customers' questions about grounds-keeping care requirements. SKILLS— Management of Personnel Resources; Time Management; Management of Financial Resources; Coordination; Systems Evaluation; Management of Material Resources; Negotiation; Systems Analysis.

GOE—Interest Area: 03. Plants and Animals. Work Group: 03.01. Managerial Work in Plants and Animals. Other Jobs in This Work Group: Agricultural Crop Farm Managers; Farm Labor Contractors; Farmers and Ranchers; First-Line Supervisors and Manager/Supervisors—Agricultural Crop Workers; First-Line Supervisors and Manager/Supervisors—Animal Care Workers, Except Livestock; First-Line Supervisors and Manager/Supervisors—Animal Husbandry Workers; First-Line Supervisors and Manager/Supervisors—Fishery Workers; First-Line Supervisors and Manager/Supervisors—Horticultural Workers; First-Line Supervisors and Manager/Supervisors—Landscaping Workers; First-Line Supervisors and Manager/Supervisors—Logging Workers; First-Line Supervisors/Managers of Farming, Fishing, and Forestry Workers; First-Line Supervisors/Managers of Landscaping, Lawn Service, and Groundskeeping Workers; Fish Hatchery Managers; Nursery and Greenhouse Managers.

EDUCATION/TRAINING PROGRAM(S)— Landscaping and Groundskeeping; Ornamental Horticulture; Turf and Turfgrass Management. **RELATED KNOWLEDGE/COURSES—** Administration and Management; Personnel and Human Resources; Customer and Personal Service; Economics and Accounting; Sales and Marketing; Geography.

Lawyers

- ◎ Personality Code: EC
- ◎ Growth: 17.0%
- ◎ Annual Job Openings: 53,000
- ◎ Annual Earnings: $91,490
- ◎ Education/Training Required: First professional degree
- ◎ Self-Employed: 26.8%
- ◎ Part-Time: 6.2%

Represent clients in criminal and civil litigation and other legal proceedings, draw up legal documents, and manage or advise clients on legal transactions. May specialize in a single area or may practice broadly in many areas of law. Advise clients concerning business transactions, claim liability, advisability of prosecuting or defending lawsuits, or legal rights and obligations. Interpret laws, rulings and regulations for individuals and businesses. Analyze the probable outcomes of cases, using knowledge of legal precedents. Present and summarize cases to judges and juries. Evaluate findings and develop strategies and arguments in preparation for presentation of cases. Gather evidence to formulate defense or to initiate legal actions, by such means as interviewing clients and witnesses to ascertain the facts of a case. Represent clients in court or before government agencies. Examine legal data to determine advisability of defending or prosecuting lawsuit. Select jurors, argue motions, meet with judges and question witnesses during the course of a trial. Present evidence to defend clients or prosecute defendants in criminal or civil litigation. Study Constitution, statutes, decisions, regulations, and ordinances of quasi-judicial bodies to determine ramifications for cases. Prepare and draft legal documents, such as wills, deeds, patent applications, mortgages, leases, and contracts. Prepare legal briefs and opinions, and file appeals in state and federal courts of appeal. Negotiate settlements of civil disputes. Confer with colleagues with specialties in appropriate areas of legal issue to establish and verify bases for legal proceedings. Search for and examine public and other legal records to write opinions or establish ownership. Supervise legal assistants. Perform administrative and management functions related to the practice of law. Act as agent, trustee, guardian, or executor for businesses or individuals. Probate wills and represent and advise executors and administrators of estates. Help develop federal and state programs, draft and interpret laws and legislation, and establish enforcement procedures. Work in environmental law, representing public interest groups, waste disposal companies, or construction firms in their dealings with state and federal agencies. **SKILLS—**Persuasion; Negotiation; Critical Thinking; Active Learning; Social Perceptiveness; Writing; Judgment and Decision Making; Time Management.

GOE—Interest Area: 04. Law, Law Enforcement, and Public Safety. **Work Group:** 04.02. Law. **Other Jobs in This Work Group:** Administrative Law Judges, Adjudicators, and Hearing Officers; Arbitrators, Mediators, and Conciliators; Judges, Magistrate Judges, and Magistrates; Law Clerks; Legal Support Workers, All Other; Paralegals and Legal Assistants; Title Examiners and Abstractors; Title Examiners, Abstractors, and Searchers; Title Searchers.

EDUCATION/TRAINING PROGRAM(S)— Advanced Legal Research/Studies, General (LL.M., M.C.L., M.L.I., M.S.L., J.S.D./S.J.D.); American/U.S. Law/Legal Studies/Jurisprudence (LL.M., M.C.J., J.S.D./S.J.D.); Banking, Corporate, Finance, and Securities Law (LL.M., J.S.D./S.J.D.); Canadian Law/Legal Studies/Jurisprudence (LL.M., M.C.J., J.S.D./S.J.D.); Comparative Law (LL.M., M.C.L., J.S.D./S.J.D.); Energy, Environment, and Natural Resources Law (LL.M., M.S., J.S.D./S.J.D.); Health Law (LL.M., M.J., J.S.D./S.J.D.); International Business, Trade, and Tax Law (LL.M., J.S.D./S.J.D.); International Law and Legal Studies (LL.M., J.S.D./S.J.D.); Law (LL.B., J.D.); Legal Professions and Studies, Other; Legal Research and Advanced Professional Studies, Other; Programs for Foreign Lawyers (LL.M., M.C.L.); Tax Law/Taxation (LL.M., J.S.D./S.J.D.). **RELATED KNOWLEDGE/COURSES**—Law and Government; English Language; Customer and Personal Service; Personnel and Human Resources; Administration and Management; Psychology.

Loan Officers

◎ Personality Code: ES

◎ Growth: 18.8%

◎ Annual Job Openings: 30,000

◎ Annual Earnings: $46,640

◎ Education/Training Required: Bachelor's degree

◎ Self-Employed: 2.3%

◎ Part-Time: 5.0%

Evaluate, authorize, or recommend approval of commercial, real estate, or credit loans. Advise borrowers on financial status and methods of payments. Includes mortgage loan officers and agents, collection analysts, loan servicing officers, and loan underwriters. Approve loans within specified limits, and refer loan applications outside those limits to management for approval. Meet with applicants to obtain information for loan applications and to answer questions about the process. Analyze applicants' financial status, credit, and property evaluations to determine feasibility of granting loans. Explain to customers the different types of loans and credit options that are available, as well as the terms of those services. Obtain and compile copies of loan applicants' credit histories, corporate financial statements, and other financial information. Review and update credit and loan files. Review loan agreements to ensure that they are complete and accurate according to policy. Compute payment schedules. Stay abreast of new types of loans and other financial services and products in order to better meet customers' needs. Submit applications to credit analysts for verification and recommendation. Handle customer complaints and take appropriate action to resolve them. Work with clients to identify their financial goals and to find ways of reaching those goals. Confer with underwriters to aid in resolving mortgage application problems. Negotiate payment arrangements with customers who have delinquent loans. Market bank products to individuals and firms, promoting bank services that may meet customers' needs. Supervise loan personnel. Set credit policies, credit lines, procedures and standards in conjunction with senior managers. Provide special services such as investment banking for clients with more specialized needs. Analyze potential loan markets and develop referral networks in order to locate prospects for loans. Prepare reports to send to customers whose accounts are delinquent, and forward irreconcilable accounts for collector action. Arrange for maintenance and liquidation of delinquent properties. Interview, hire, and train new employees. Petition courts to transfer titles and deeds of collateral to banks. **SKILLS**—Persuasion; Social Perceptiveness; Service Orientation; Instructing; Negotiation; Learning Strategies; Complex Problem Solving; Coordination.

GOE—**Interest Area:** 13. General Management and Support. **Work Group:** 13.02. Management Support. **Other Jobs in This Work Group:** Accountants; Accountants and Auditors; Appraisers and Assessors of Real Estate; Appraisers, Real Estate; Assessors; Auditors; Budget Analysts; Business Operations Specialists, All Other; Claims Adjusters, Examiners, and Investigators; Claims Examiners, Property and Casualty Insurance; Compensation, Benefits, and Job Analysis Specialists; Cost Estimators; Credit Analysts; Employment Interviewers, Private or Public Employment Service; Employment, Recruitment, and Placement Specialists; Financial Analysts; Human Resources, Training, and Labor Relations Specialists, All Other; Insurance Adjusters, Examiners, and Investigators; Insurance Appraisers, Auto Damage; Insurance Underwriters; Loan Counselors; Logisticians; Management Analysts; Market Research Analysts; Personnel Recruiters; Purchasing Agents and Buyers, Farm Products; Purchasing Agents, Except Wholesale, Retail, and Farm Products; Tax Examiners, Collectors, and Revenue Agents; Training and Development Specialists; Wholesale and Retail Buyers, Except Farm Products.

EDUCATION/TRAINING PROGRAM(S)— Credit Management; Finance, General. **RELATED KNOWLEDGE/COURSES**—Economics and Accounting; Sales and Marketing; Customer and Personal Service; Law and Government; English Language; Mathematics.

Management Analysts

- Personality Code: EC
- Growth: 30.4%
- Annual Job Openings: 78,000
- Annual Earnings: $62,580
- Education/Training Required: Work experience plus degree
- Self-Employed: 29.8%
- Part-Time: 14.0%

Conduct organizational studies and evaluations, design systems and procedures, conduct work simplifications and measurement studies, and prepare operations and procedures manuals to assist management in operating more efficiently and effectively. Includes program analysts and management consultants. Review forms and reports, and confer with management and users about format, distribution, and purpose, and to identify problems and improvements. Develop and implement records management program for filing, protection, and retrieval of records, and assure compliance with program. Interview personnel and conduct on-site observation to ascertain unit functions, work performed, and methods, equipment, and personnel used. Prepare manuals and train workers in use of new forms, reports, procedures or equipment, according to organizational policy. Design, evaluate, recommend, and approve changes of forms and reports. Recommend purchase of storage equipment, and design area layout to locate equipment in space available. Plan study of work problems and procedures, such as organizational change, communications, information flow, integrated production methods, inventory control, or cost analysis. Gather and organize information on problems or procedures. Analyze data gathered and develop solutions or alternative methods of proceeding. Document findings of study and prepare recommendations for implementation of new systems, procedures, or organizational changes. Confer with personnel concerned to ensure successful functioning of newly implemented systems or procedures. **SKILLS**—Systems Evaluation; Management of Personnel Resources; Systems Analysis; Management of Material Resources; Operations Analysis; Judgment and Decision Making; Monitoring; Complex Problem Solving.

GOE—**Interest Area:** 13. General Management and Support. **Work Group:** 13.02. Management Support. **Other Jobs in This Work Group:** Accountants; Accountants and Auditors; Appraisers and Assessors of Real Estate; Appraisers, Real Estate; Assessors; Auditors; Budget Analysts; Business Operations Specialists, All Other; Claims Adjusters, Examiners, and Investigators; Claims Examiners, Property and Casualty Insurance; Compensation, Benefits, and Job Analysis Specialists; Cost Estimators; Credit Analysts; Employment Interviewers, Private or Public Employment Service; Employment, Recruitment, and Placement Specialists; Financial Analysts; Human Resources, Training, and Labor Relations Specialists, All Other; Insurance Adjusters, Examiners, and Investigators; Insurance Appraisers, Auto Damage; Insurance Underwriters; Loan Counselors; Loan Officers; Logisticians; Market Research Analysts; Personnel Recruiters; Purchasing Agents and Buyers, Farm Products; Purchasing Agents, Except Wholesale, Retail, and Farm Products; Tax Examiners, Collectors, and Revenue Agents; Training and Development Specialists; Wholesale and Retail Buyers, Except Farm Products.

EDUCATION/TRAINING PROGRAM(S)— Business Administration and Management, General; Business/Commerce, General. **RELATED KNOWLEDGE/COURSES**—Administration and Management; Personnel and Human Resources; Education and Training; Economics and Accounting; Clerical Studies; English Language.

Marketing Managers

- Personality Code: EC
- Growth: 21.3%
- Annual Job Openings: 30,000
- Annual Earnings: $83,210
- Education/Training Required: Work experience plus degree
- Self-Employed: 3.1%
- Part-Time: 4.7%

Determine the demand for products and services offered by a firm and its competitors and identify potential customers. Develop pricing strategies with the goal of maximizing the firm's profits or share of the market while ensuring the firm's customers are satisfied. Oversee product development or monitor trends that indicate the need for new products and services. Develop pricing strategies, balancing firm objectives and customer satisfaction. Identify, develop, and evaluate marketing strategy, based on knowledge of establishment objectives, market characteristics, and cost and markup factors. Evaluate the financial aspects of product development, such as budgets, expenditures, research and development appropriations, and return-on-investment and profit-loss projections. Formulate, direct and coordinate marketing activities and policies to promote products and services, working with advertising and promotion managers. Direct the hiring, training, and performance evaluations of marketing and sales staff and oversee their daily activities. Negotiate contracts with vendors and distributors to manage product distribution, establishing distribution networks and developing distribution strategies. Consult with product development personnel on product specifications such as design, color, and packaging. Compile lists describing product or service offerings. Use sales forecasting and strategic planning to ensure the sale and profitability of products, lines, or services, analyzing business developments and monitoring market trends. Select products and accessories to be displayed at trade or special production shows. Confer with legal staff to resolve problems, such as copyright infringement and royalty sharing with outside producers and distributors. Coordinate and participate in promotional activities and trade shows, working with developers, advertisers, and production managers, to market products and services. Advise business and other groups on local, national, and international factors affecting the buying and selling of products and services. Initiate market research studies and analyze their findings. Consult with buying personnel to gain advice regarding the types of products or services expected to be in demand. Conduct economic and commercial surveys to identify potential markets for products and services. **SKILLS**—Management of Financial Resources; Management of Personnel Resources; Negotiation; Operations Analysis; Persuasion; Coordination; Instructing; Time Management.

GOE—Interest Area: 10. Sales and Marketing. **Work Group:** 10.01. Managerial Work in Sales and Marketing. **Other Jobs in This Work Group:** Advertising and Promotions Managers; First-Line Supervisors/Managers of Non-Retail Sales Workers; First-Line Supervisors/Managers of Retail Sales Workers; Sales Managers.

EDUCATION/TRAINING PROGRAM(S)— Apparel and Textile Marketing Management; Consumer Merchandising/Retailing Management; International Marketing; Marketing Research; Marketing, Other; Marketing/Marketing Management, General. **RELATED KNOWLEDGE/COURSES**—Sales and Marketing; Customer and Personal Service; Administration and Management; Personnel and Human Resources; Education and Training; English Language.

Medical and Health Services Managers

- Personality Code: ES
- Growth: 29.3%
- Annual Job Openings: 33,000
- Annual Earnings: $64,550
- Education/Training Required: Work experience plus degree
- Self-Employed: 5.3%
- Part-Time: 5.4%

Plan, direct, or coordinate medicine and health services in hospitals, clinics, managed care organizations, public health agencies, or similar organizations. Direct, supervise and evaluate work activities of medical, nursing, technical, clerical, service, maintenance, and other personnel. Establish objectives and evaluative or operational criteria for units they manage. Direct or conduct recruitment, hiring and training of personnel. Develop and maintain computerized record management systems to store and process data, such as personnel activities and information, and to produce reports. Develop and implement organizational policies and procedures for the facility or medical unit. Conduct and administer fiscal operations, including accounting, planning budgets, authorizing expenditures, establishing rates for services, and coordinating financial reporting. Establish work schedules and assignments for staff, according to workload, space and equipment availability. Maintain communication between governing boards, medical staff, and department heads by attending board meetings and coordinating interdepartmental functioning. Monitor the use of diagnostic services, inpatient beds, facilities, and staff to ensure effective use of resources and assess the need for additional staff, equipment, and services. Maintain awareness of advances in medicine, computerized diagnostic and treatment equipment, data processing technology, government regulations, health insurance changes,

Enterprising—M

and financing options. Manage change in integrated health care delivery systems, such as work restructuring, technological innovations, and shifts in the focus of care. Prepare activity reports to inform management of the status and implementation plans of programs, services, and quality initiatives. Plan, implement and administer programs and services in a health care or medical facility, including personnel administration, training, and coordination of medical, nursing and physical plant staff. Consult with medical, business, and community groups to discuss service problems, respond to community needs, enhance public relations, coordinate activities and plans, and promote health programs. Inspect facilities and recommend building or equipment modifications to ensure emergency readiness and compliance to access, safety, and sanitation regulations. **SKILLS**—Persuasion; Management of Personnel Resources; Service Orientation; Management of Material Resources; Monitoring; Social Perceptiveness; Management of Financial Resources; Critical Thinking; Learning Strategies.

GOE—Interest Area: 14. Medical and Health Services. **Work Group:** 14.01. Managerial Work in Medical and Health Services. **Other Jobs in This Work Group:** Coroners.

EDUCATION/TRAINING PROGRAM(S)— Community Health and Preventive Medicine; Health and Medical Administrative Services, Other; Health Information/Medical Records Administration/Administrator; Health Services Administration; Health Unit Manager/Ward Supervisor; Health/Health Care Administration/Management; Hospital and Health Care Facilities Administration/Management; Medical Staff Services Technology/Technician; Nursing Administration (MSN, MS, PhD); Public Health, General (MPH, DPH). **RELATED KNOWLEDGE/COURSES**—Therapy and Counseling; Customer and Personal Service; Personnel and Human Resources; Medicine and Dentistry; Psychology; Sociology and Anthropology; Education and Training; Philosophy and Theology.

Paralegals and Legal Assistants

- Personality Code: EC
- Growth: 28.7%
- Annual Job Openings: 29,000
- Annual Earnings: $37,930
- Education/Training Required: Associate's degree
- Self-Employed: 2.3%
- Part-Time: 10.8%

Assist lawyers by researching legal precedent, investigating facts, or preparing legal documents. Conduct research to support a legal proceeding, to formulate a defense, or to initiate legal action. Prepare legal documents, including briefs, pleadings, appeals, wills, contracts, and real estate closing statements. Prepare affidavits or other documents, maintain document file, and file pleadings with court clerk. Gather and analyze research data, such as statutes, decisions, and legal articles, codes, and documents. Investigate facts and law of cases to determine causes of action and to prepare cases. Call upon witnesses to testify at hearing. Direct and coordinate law office activity, including delivery of subpoenas. Arbitrate disputes between parties and assist in real estate closing process. Keep and monitor legal volumes to ensure that law library is up-to-date. Appraise and inventory real and personal property for estate planning. **SKILLS**—Time Management; Instructing; Active Listening; Writing; Speaking; Monitoring; Social Perceptiveness; Service Orientation.

GOE—Interest Area: 04. Law, Law Enforcement, and Public Safety. **Work Group:** 04.02. Law. **Other Jobs in This Work Group:** Administrative Law Judges, Adjudicators, and Hearing Officers; Arbitrators, Mediators, and Conciliators; Judges, Magistrate Judges, and Magistrates; Law Clerks; Lawyers; Legal Support Workers, All Other; Title Examiners and Abstractors; Title Examiners, Abstractors, and Searchers; Title Searchers.

EDUCATION/TRAINING PROGRAM(S)— Legal Assistant/Paralegal. **RELATED KNOWL-EDGE/COURSES—**Clerical Studies; Law and Government; Customer and Personal Service; Computers and Electronics; English Language; Personnel and Human Resources.

Personnel Recruiters

- Personality Code: ES
- Growth: 27.3%
- Annual Job Openings: 29,000
- Annual Earnings: $40,770
- Education/Training Required: Bachelor's degree
- Self-Employed: 0.8%
- Part-Time: 7.7%

Seek out, interview, and screen applicants to fill existing and future job openings and promote career opportunities within an organization. Establish and maintain relationships with hiring managers to stay abreast of current and future hiring and business needs. Interview applicants to obtain information on work history, training, education, and job skills. Maintain current knowledge of Equal Employment Opportunity (EEO) and affirmative action guidelines and laws, such as the Americans with Disabilities Act. Perform searches for qualified candidates according to relevant job criteria, using computer databases, networking, Internet recruiting resources, cold calls, media, recruiting firms, and employee referrals. Prepare and maintain employment records. Contact applicants to inform them of employment possibilities, consideration, and selection. Inform potential applicants about facilities, operations, benefits, and job or career opportunities in organizations. Screen and refer applicants to hiring personnel in the organization, making hiring recommendations when appropriate. Arrange for interviews and provide travel arrangements as necessary. Advise managers and employees on staffing policies and procedures. Review and evaluate applicant qualifications or eligibility for specified licensing, according to established guidelines and designated licensing codes. Hire applicants and authorize paperwork assigning them to positions. Conduct reference and background checks on applicants. Evaluate recruitment and selection criteria to ensure conformance to professional, statistical, and testing standards, recommending revision as needed. Recruit applicants for open positions, arranging job fairs with college campus representatives. Advise management on organizing, preparing, and implementing recruiting and retention programs. Supervise personnel clerks performing filing, typing and record-keeping duties. Project yearly recruitment expenditures for budgetary consideration and control. **SKILLS—**Management of Personnel Resources; Negotiation; Persuasion; Service Orientation; Time Management; Management of Financial Resources; Monitoring; Social Perceptiveness.

GOE—Interest Area: 13. General Management and Support. **Work Group:** 13.02. Management Support. **Other Jobs in This Work Group:** Accountants; Accountants and Auditors; Appraisers and Assessors of Real Estate; Appraisers, Real Estate; Assessors; Auditors; Budget Analysts; Business Operations Specialists, All Other; Claims Adjusters, Examiners, and Investigators; Claims Examiners, Property and Casualty Insurance; Compensation, Benefits, and Job Analysis Specialists; Cost Estimators; Credit Analysts; Employment Interviewers, Private or Public Employment Service; Employment, Recruitment, and Placement Specialists; Financial Analysts; Human Resources, Training, and Labor Relations Specialists, All Other; Insurance Adjusters, Examiners, and Investigators; Insurance Appraisers, Auto Damage; Insurance Underwriters; Loan Counselors; Loan Officers; Logisticians; Management Analysts; Market Research Analysts; Purchasing Agents and Buyers, Farm Products; Purchasing Agents, Except Wholesale, Retail, and Farm Products; Tax Examiners, Collectors, and Revenue Agents; Training and Development Specialists; Wholesale and Retail Buyers, Except Farm Products.

Enterprising–P

EDUCATION/TRAINING PROGRAM(S)—
Human Resources Management/Personnel Admin-
istration, General; Labor and Industrial Relations.
RELATED KNOWLEDGE/COURSES—Person-
nel and Human Resources; Clerical Studies; Educa-
tion and Training; Sales and Marketing;
Administration and Management; Computers and
Electronics.

Police Detectives

- Personality Code: ES
- Growth: 22.4%
- Annual Job Openings: 11,000
- Annual Earnings: $52,390
- Education/Training Required: Work
  experience in a related occupation
- Self-Employed: 0%
- Part-Time: 0.5%

**Conduct investigations to prevent crimes or solve
criminal cases.** Examine crime scenes to obtain
clues and evidence, such as loose hairs, fibers, clothing, or weapons. Secure deceased body and obtain
evidence from it, preventing bystanders from tampering with it prior to medical examiner's arrival.
Obtain evidence from suspects. Provide testimony
as a witness in court. Analyze completed police
reports to determine what additional information
and investigative work is needed. Prepare charges or
responses to charges, or information for court cases,
according to formalized procedures. Note, mark,
and photograph location of objects found, such as
footprints, tire tracks, bullets and bloodstains, and
take measurements of the scene. Obtain facts or
statements from complainants, witnesses, and
accused persons and record interviews, using recording device. Obtain summary of incident from officer in charge at crime scene, taking care to avoid
disturbing evidence. Examine records and governmental agency files to find identifying data about
suspects. Prepare and serve search and arrest warrants. Block or rope off scene and check perimeter
to ensure that entire scene is secured. Summon
medical help for injured individuals and alert medical personnel to take statements from them. Provide information to lab personnel concerning the
source of an item of evidence and tests to be performed. Monitor conditions of victims who are
unconscious so that arrangements can be made to
take statements if consciousness is regained. Secure
persons at scene, keeping witnesses from conversing
or leaving the scene before investigators arrive. Preserve, process, and analyze items of evidence
obtained from crime scenes and suspects, placing
them in proper containers and destroying evidence
no longer needed. Record progress of investigation,
maintain informational files on suspects, and submit reports to commanding officer or magistrate to
authorize warrants. Take photographs from all
angles of relevant parts of a crime scene, including
entrance and exit routes and streets and intersec-
tions. Organize scene search, assigning specific tasks
and areas of search to individual officers and obtaining adequate lighting as necessary. **SKILLS**—Persuasion; Negotiation; Social Perceptiveness;
Coordination; Service Orientation; Active Listening; Speaking; Critical Thinking; Time Management.

GOE—Interest Area: 04. Law, Law Enforcement,
and Public Safety. **Work Group:** 04.03. Law
Enforcement. **Other Jobs in This Work Group:**
Animal Control Workers; Bailiffs; Child Support,
Missing Persons, and Unemployment Insurance
Fraud Investigators; Correctional Officers and Jail-
ers; Criminal Investigators and Special Agents;
Crossing Guards; Detectives and Criminal Investi-
gators; Fire Investigators; Fish and Game Wardens;
Forensic Science Technicians; Gaming Surveillance
Officers and Gaming Investigators; Highway Patrol
Pilots; Immigration and Customs Inspectors; Life-
guards, Ski Patrol, and Other Recreational Protec-
tive Service Workers; Parking Enforcement
Workers; Police and Sheriff's Patrol Officers; Police
Identification and Records Officers; Police Patrol
Officers; Private Detectives and Investigators; Pro-

tective Service Workers, All Other; Security Guards; Sheriffs and Deputy Sheriffs; Transit and Railroad Police.

EDUCATION/TRAINING PROGRAM(S)— Criminal Justice/Police Science; Criminalistics and Criminal Science. **RELATED KNOWLEDGE/ COURSES**—Public Safety and Security; Law and Government; Psychology; Customer and Personal Service; Education and Training; Philosophy and Theology.

Private Sector Executives

◎ Personality Code: EC

◎ Growth: 16.7%

◎ Annual Job Openings: 63,000

◎ Annual Earnings: $134,740

◎ Education/Training Required: Work experience plus degree

◎ Self-Employed: 14.6%

◎ Part-Time: 5.3%

Determine and formulate policies and business strategies and provide overall direction of private sector organizations. Plan, direct, and coordinate operational activities at the highest level of management with the help of subordinate managers. Directs, plans, and implements policies and objectives of organization or business in accordance with charter and board of directors. Directs activities of organization to plan procedures, establish responsibilities, and coordinate functions among departments and sites. Analyzes operations to evaluate performance of company and staff and to determine areas of cost reduction and program improvement. Confers with board members, organization officials, and staff members to establish policies and formulate plans. Reviews financial statements and sales and activity reports to ensure that organization's objectives are achieved. Assigns or delegates responsibilities to subordinates. Directs and coordinates activities of business involved with buying and selling investment products and financial services. Establishes internal control procedures. Presides over or serves on board of directors, management committees, or other governing boards. Directs inservice training of staff. Administers program for selection of sites, construction of buildings, and provision of equipment and supplies. Screens, selects, hires, transfers, and discharges employees. Promotes objectives of institution or business before associations, public, government agencies, or community groups. Negotiates or approves contracts with suppliers and distributors, and with maintenance, janitorial, and security providers. Prepares reports and budgets. Directs non-merchandising departments of business, such as advertising, purchasing, credit, and accounting. Directs and coordinates activities of business or department concerned with production, pricing, sales, and/or distribution of products. Directs and coordinates organization's financial and budget activities to fund operations, maximize investments, and increase efficiency. **SKILLS—** Management of Financial Resources; Systems Evaluation; Systems Analysis; Management of Personnel Resources; Coordination; Judgment and Decision Making; Management of Material Resources; Negotiation.

GOE—Interest Area: 13. General Management and Support. **Work Group:** 13.01. General Management Work and Management of Support Functions. **Other Jobs in This Work Group:** Business Operations Specialists, All Other; Chief Executives; Compensation and Benefits Managers; Farm, Ranch, and Other Agricultural Managers; Financial Managers; Financial Managers, Branch or Department; Financial Specialists, All Other; Funeral Directors; General and Operations Managers; Government Service Executives; Human Resources Managers; Human Resources Managers, All Other; Legislators; Managers, All Other; Postmasters and Mail Superintendents; Property, Real Estate, and Community Association Managers; Public Relations Managers; Purchasing Managers; Storage and

Distribution Managers; Training and Development Managers; Transportation, Storage, and Distribution Managers; Treasurers, Controllers, and Chief Financial Officers.

EDUCATION/TRAINING PROGRAM(S)—Business Administration and Management, General; Business/Commerce, General; Entrepreneurship/Entrepreneurial Studies; International Business/Trade/Commerce; Public Administration; Public Administration and Social Service Professions, Other; Public Policy Analysis. **RELATED KNOWLEDGE/COURSES**—Economics and Accounting; Production and Processing; Administration and Management; Sales and Marketing; Personnel and Human Resources; Psychology.

Program Directors

- Personality Code: EA
- Growth: 18.3%
- Annual Job Openings: 10,000
- Annual Earnings: $48,200
- Education/Training Required: Work experience plus degree
- Self-Employed: 32.8%
- Part-Time: 9.1%

Direct and coordinate activities of personnel engaged in preparation of radio or television station program schedules and programs such as sports or news. Check completed program logs for accuracy and conformance with FCC rules and regulations and resolve program log inaccuracies. Confer with directors and production staff to discuss issues such as production and casting problems, budgets, policies, and news coverage. Coordinate activities between departments, such as news and programming. Cue announcers, actors, performers, and guests. Develop promotions for current programs and specials. Direct and coordinate activities of personnel engaged in broadcast news, sports, or

programming. Establish work schedules and assign work to staff members. Evaluate new and existing programming for suitability and in order to assess the need for changes, using information such as audience surveys and feedback. Monitor and review programming in order to ensure that schedules are met, guidelines are adhered to, and performances are of adequate quality. Monitor network transmissions for advisories concerning daily program schedules, program content, special feeds, and/or program changes. Perform personnel duties such as hiring staff and evaluating work performance. Plan and schedule programming and event coverage based on broadcast length, time availability, and other factors such as community needs, ratings data, and viewer demographics. Act as a liaison between talent and directors, providing information that performers/guests need to prepare for appearances and communicating relevant information from guests, performers, or staff to directors. Conduct interviews for broadcasts. Develop budgets for programming and broadcasting activities and monitor expenditures to ensure that they remain within budgetary limits. Develop ideas for programs and features that a station could produce. Operate and maintain on-air and production audio equipment. Prepare copy and edit tape so that material is ready for broadcasting. Read news, read and/or record public service and promotional announcements, and otherwise participate as a member of an on-air shift as required. Review information about programs and schedules in order to ensure accuracy and provide such information to local media outlets as necessary. **SKILLS**—Management of Personnel Resources; Coordination; Management of Financial Resources; Management of Material Resources; Writing; Time Management; Active Learning; Reading Comprehension.

GOE—Interest Area: 01. Arts, Entertainment, and Media. **Work Group:** 01.01. Managerial Work in Arts, Entertainment, and Media. **Other Jobs in This Work Group:** Agents and Business Managers of Artists, Performers, and Athletes; Art Directors; Athletes and Sports Competitors; Coaches and

Scouts; Entertainers and Performers, Sports and Related Workers, All Other; Fitness Trainers and Aerobics Instructors; Producers; Producers and Directors; Technical Directors/Managers; Umpires, Referees, and Other Sports Officials.

EDUCATION/TRAINING PROGRAM(S)— Cinematography and Film/Video Production; Directing and Theatrical Production; Drama and Dramatics/Theatre Arts, General; Dramatic/Theatre Arts and Stagecraft, Other; Film/Cinema Studies; Radio and Television; Theatre/Theatre Arts Management. **RELATED KNOWLEDGE/COURSES—** Communications and Media; Administration and Management; Personnel and Human Resources; Economics and Accounting; Telecommunications; English Language.

Public Relations Specialists

- ◉ Personality Code: EA
- ◉ Growth: 32.9%
- ◉ Annual Job Openings: 28,000
- ◉ Annual Earnings: $42,590
- ◉ Education/Training Required: Bachelor's degree
- ◉ Self-Employed: 6.1%
- ◉ Part-Time: 12.5%

Engage in promoting or creating good will for individuals, groups, or organizations by writing or selecting favorable publicity material and releasing it through various communications media. May prepare and arrange displays, and make speeches. Prepare or edit organizational publications for internal and external audiences, including employee newsletters and stockholders' reports. Respond to requests for information from the media or designate another appropriate spokesperson or information source. Establish and maintain cooperative relationships with representatives of community, consumer, employee, and public interest groups. Plan and direct development and communication of informational programs to maintain favorable public and stockholder perceptions of an organization's accomplishments and agenda. Confer with production and support personnel to produce or coordinate production of advertisements and promotions. Arrange public appearances, lectures, contests, or exhibits for clients to increase product and service awareness and to promote goodwill. Study the objectives, promotional policies and needs of organizations to develop public relations strategies that will influence public opinion or promote ideas, products and services. Confer with other managers to identify trends and key group interests and concerns or to provide advice on business decisions. Consult with advertising agencies or staff to arrange promotional campaigns in all types of media for products, organizations, or individuals. Coach client representatives in effective communication with the public and with employees. Prepare and deliver speeches to further public relations objectives. Purchase advertising space and time as required to promote client's product or agenda. Plan and conduct market and public opinion research to test products or determine potential for product success, communicating results to client or management. **SKILLS—**Persuasion; Service Orientation; Negotiation; Social Perceptiveness; Coordination; Management of Financial Resources; Monitoring; Writing; Time Management.

GOE—Interest Area: 01. Arts, Entertainment, and Media. **Work Group:** 01.03. News, Broadcasting and Public Relations. **Other Jobs in This Work Group:** Broadcast News Analysts; Caption Writers; Interpreters and Translators; Reporters and Correspondents.

EDUCATION/TRAINING PROGRAM(S)— Communication Studies/Speech Communication and Rhetoric; Family and Consumer Sciences/Human Sciences Communication; Health Communication; Political Communication; Public Relations/Image Management. **RELATED**

KNOWLEDGE/COURSES—Sales and Marketing; Customer and Personal Service; Communications and Media; Administration and Management; Clerical Studies; English Language.

Retail Salespersons

- Personality Code: ES
- Growth: 14.6%
- Annual Job Openings: 1,014,000
- Annual Earnings: $18,090
- Education/Training Required: Short-term on-the-job training
- Self-Employed: 4.3%
- Part-Time: 32.6%

Sell merchandise, such as furniture, motor vehicles, appliances, or apparel in a retail establishment. Greet customers and ascertain what each customer wants or needs. Open and close cash registers, performing tasks such as counting money, separating charge slips, coupons, and vouchers, balancing cash drawers, and making deposits. Maintain knowledge of current sales and promotions, policies regarding payment and exchanges, and security practices. Compute sales prices, total purchases and receive and process cash or credit payment. Maintain records related to sales. Watch for and recognize security risks and thefts, and know how to prevent or handle these situations. Recommend, select, and help locate or obtain merchandise based on customer needs and desires. Answer questions regarding the store and its merchandise. Describe merchandise and explain use, operation, and care of merchandise to customers. Ticket, arrange and display merchandise to promote sales. Prepare sales slips or sales contracts. Place special orders or call other stores to find desired items. Demonstrate use or operation of merchandise. Clean shelves, counters, and tables. Exchange merchandise for customers and accept returns. Bag or package purchases, and wrap gifts. Help customers try on or fit merchandise. Inventory stock and requisition new stock. Prepare merchandise for purchase or rental. Sell or arrange for delivery, insurance, financing, or service contracts for merchandise. Estimate and quote trade-in allowances. SKILLS—Social Perceptiveness; Writing; Speaking; Critical Thinking; Negotiation; Instructing; Management of Personnel Resources; Service Orientation.

GOE—Interest Area: 10. Sales and Marketing. Work Group: 10.03. General Sales. Other Jobs in This Work Group: Parts Salespersons; Real Estate Brokers; Real Estate Sales Agents; Sales and Related Workers, All Other; Sales Representatives, Wholesale and Manufacturing, Except Technical and Scientific Products; Service Station Attendants; Stock Clerks, Sales Floor; Travel Agents.

EDUCATION/TRAINING PROGRAM(S)—Floriculture/Floristry Operations and Management; Retailing and Retail Operations; Sales, Distribution, and Marketing Operations, General; Selling Skills and Sales Operations. RELATED KNOWLEDGE/COURSES—Sales and Marketing; Customer and Personal Service; Administration and Management; Education and Training; Personnel and Human Resources; Clerical Studies.

Sales Agents, Financial Services

- Personality Code: EC
- Growth: 13.0%
- Annual Job Openings: 39,000
- Annual Earnings: $60,530
- Education/Training Required: Bachelor's degree
- Self-Employed: 12.8%
- Part-Time: 6.0%

Sell financial services, such as loan, tax, and securities counseling to customers of financial institutions and business establishments. Contact prospective customers in order to present information and explain available services. Determine customers' financial services needs, and prepare proposals to sell services that address these needs. Develop prospects from current commercial customers, referral leads, and sales and trade meetings. Prepare forms or agreements to complete sales. Sell services and equipment, such as trusts, investments, and check processing services. Evaluate costs and revenue of agreements in order to determine continued profitability. Make presentations on financial services to groups in order to attract new clients. Review business trends in order to advise customers regarding expected fluctuations. **SKILLS**—Persuasion; Systems Analysis; Management of Financial Resources; Service Orientation; Negotiation; Systems Evaluation; Active Learning; Monitoring.

GOE—**Interest Area:** 10. Sales and Marketing. **Work Group:** 10.02. Sales Technology. **Other Jobs in This Work Group:** Advertising Sales Agents; Insurance Sales Agents; Sales Agents, Securities and Commodities; Sales and Related Workers, All Other; Sales Representatives, Agricultural; Sales Representatives, Chemical and Pharmaceutical; Sales Representatives, Electrical/Electronic; Sales Representatives, Instruments; Sales Representatives, Mechanical Equipment and Supplies; Sales Representatives, Medical; Sales Representatives, Services, All Other; Sales Representatives, Wholesale and Manufacturing, Technical and Scientific Products; Securities, Commodities, and Financial Services Sales Agents.

EDUCATION/TRAINING PROGRAM(S)— Business and Personal/Financial Services Marketing Operations; Financial Planning and Services; Investments and Securities. **RELATED KNOWLEDGE/COURSES**—Economics and Accounting; Sales and Marketing; Computers and Electronics; Mathematics; Law and Government; Communications and Media.

Sales Agents, Securities and Commodities

- Personality Code: EC
- Growth: 13.0%
- Annual Job Openings: 39,000
- Annual Earnings: $60,530
- Education/Training Required: Bachelor's degree
- Self-Employed: 12.8%
- Part-Time: 6.0%

Buy and sell securities in investment and trading firms and develop and implement financial plans for individuals, businesses, and organizations. Record transactions accurately, and keep clients informed about transactions. Analyze market conditions in order to determine optimum times to execute securities transactions. Review financial periodicals, stock and bond reports, business publications and other material in order to identify potential investments for clients and to keep abreast of trends affecting market conditions. Read corporate reports and calculate ratios to determine best prospects for profit on stock purchases and to monitor client accounts. Interview clients to determine clients' assets, liabilities, cash flow, insurance coverage, tax status, and financial objectives. Review all securities transactions to ensure accuracy of information and that trades conform to regulations of governing agencies. Prepare documents needed to implement plans selected by clients. Complete sales order tickets and submit for processing of client requested transactions. Inform and advise concerned parties regarding fluctuations and securities transactions affecting plans or accounts. Prepare financial reports to monitor client or corporate finances. Identify potential clients, using advertising campaigns, mailing lists, and personal contacts. Contact prospective customers to determine customer needs, present information, and explain available services. Explain stock market terms and

Enterprising—S

trading practices to clients. Offer advice on the purchase or sale of particular securities. Supply the latest price quotes on any security, as well as information on the activities and financial positions of the corporations issuing these securities. Calculate costs for billings and commissions purposes. Develop financial plans based on analysis of clients' financial status, and discuss financial options with clients. Relay buy or sell orders to securities exchanges or to firm trading departments. **SKILLS**—Management of Financial Resources; Systems Analysis; Systems Evaluation; Persuasion; Service Orientation; Negotiation; Active Learning; Judgment and Decision Making.

GOE—Interest Area: 10. Sales and Marketing. **Work Group:** 10.02. Sales Technology. **Other Jobs in This Work Group:** Advertising Sales Agents; Insurance Sales Agents; Sales Agents, Financial Services; Sales and Related Workers, All Other; Sales Representatives, Agricultural; Sales Representatives, Chemical and Pharmaceutical; Sales Representatives, Electrical/Electronic; Sales Representatives, Instruments; Sales Representatives, Mechanical Equipment and Supplies; Sales Representatives, Medical; Sales Representatives, Services, All Other; Sales Representatives, Wholesale and Manufacturing, Technical and Scientific Products; Securities, Commodities, and Financial Services Sales Agents.

EDUCATION/TRAINING PROGRAM(S)—Business and Personal/Financial Services Marketing Operations; Financial Planning and Services; Investments and Securities. **RELATED KNOWLEDGE/COURSES**—Economics and Accounting; Sales and Marketing; Mathematics; Computers and Electronics; Customer and Personal Service; Personnel and Human Resources.

Sales Engineers

- Personality Code: ER
- Growth: 19.9%
- Annual Job Openings: 7,000
- Annual Earnings: $67,790
- Education/Training Required: Bachelor's degree
- Self-Employed: 0.6%
- Part-Time: 0.8%

Sell business goods or services, the selling of which requires a technical background equivalent to a baccalaureate degree in engineering. Arrange for demonstrations or trial installations of equipment. Attend company training seminars to become familiar with product lines. Collaborate with sales teams to understand customer requirements, to promote the sale of company products, and to provide sales support. Confer with customers and engineers to assess equipment needs, and to determine system requirements. Create sales or service contracts for products or services. Develop sales plans to introduce products in new markets. Develop, present, or respond to proposals for specific customer requirements, including request for proposal responses and industry-specific solutions. Identify resale opportunities, and support them to achieve sales plans. Keep informed on industry news and trends, products, services, competitors, relevant information about legacy, existing, and emerging technologies, and the latest product-line developments. Plan and modify product configurations to meet customer needs. Prepare and deliver technical presentations that explain products or services to customers and prospective customers. Recommend improved materials or machinery to customers, documenting how such changes will lower costs or increase production. Research and identify potential customers for products or services. Secure and renew orders and arrange delivery. Sell products requiring extensive technical expertise and support for installation and use, such as material handling equipment, numerical-control machinery, and computer systems. Visit prospective buyers at commercial, industrial, or other establishments to show samples or catalogs, and to inform them about product pricing, availability, and advantages. Attend trade shows and seminars to promote products or to learn about industry developments. Diagnose problems with installed equipment. Document account activities, generate reports, and keep records of business transactions with customers and suppliers. Maintain sales forecasting reports. Provide information needed for the development of custom-made machinery. Provide technical and non-technical support and services to clients or other staff members regarding the use, operation, and maintenance of equipment. SKILLS—Technology Design; Troubleshooting; Operations Analysis; Persuasion; Negotiation; Management of Material Resources; Service Orientation; Speaking.

GOE—Interest Area: 02. Science, Math, and Engineering. Work Group: 02.07. Engineering. Other Jobs in This Work Group: Aerospace Engineers; Agricultural Engineers; Architects, Except Landscape and Naval; Biomedical Engineers; Chemical Engineers; Civil Engineers; Computer Hardware Engineers; Computer Software Engineers, Applications; Computer Software Engineers, Systems Software; Electrical Engineers; Electronics Engineers, Except Computer; Engineers, All Other; Environmental Engineers; Fire-Prevention and Protection Engineers; Health and Safety Engineers, Except Mining Safety Engineers and Inspectors; Industrial Engineers; Industrial Safety and Health Engineers; Landscape Architects; Marine Architects; Marine Engineers; Marine Engineers and Naval Architects; Materials Engineers; Mechanical Engineers; Mining and Geological Engineers, Including Mining Safety Engineers; Nuclear Engineers; Petroleum Engineers; Product Safety Engineers.

EDUCATION/TRAINING PROGRAM(S)— Selling Skills and Sales Operations. RELATED KNOWLEDGE/COURSES—Sales and Marketing; Design; Engineering and Technology; Production and Processing; Physics; Customer and Personal Service.

Sales Managers

- Personality Code: EC
- Growth: 30.5%
- Annual Job Openings: 54,000
- Annual Earnings: $80,470
- Education/Training Required: Work experience plus degree
- Self-Employed: 3.0%
- Part-Time: 4.7%

Direct the actual distribution or movement of a product or service to the customer. Coordinate sales distribution by establishing sales territories, quotas, and goals and establish training programs for sales representatives. Analyze sales statistics gathered by staff to determine sales potential and inventory requirements and monitor the preferences of customers. Resolve customer complaints regarding sales and service. Monitor customer preferences to determine focus of sales efforts. Direct and coordinate activities involving sales of manufactured products, services, commodities, real estate or other subjects of sale. Determine price schedules and discount rates. Review operational records and reports to project sales and determine profitability. Direct, coordinate, and review activities in sales and service accounting and record keeping, and in receiving and shipping operations. Confer or consult with department heads to plan advertising services and to secure information on equipment and customer specifications. Advise dealers and distributors on policies and operating procedures to ensure functional effectiveness of business. Prepare budgets and approve budget expenditures. Represent company at trade association meetings to promote products. Plan and direct staffing, training, and performance evaluations to develop and control sales and service programs. Visit franchised dealers to stimulate interest in establishment or expansion of leasing programs. Confer with potential customers regarding equipment needs and advise customers on types of equipment to purchase. Oversee

Enterprising—S

regional and local sales managers and their staffs. Direct clerical staff to keep records of export correspondence, bid requests, and credit collections, and to maintain current information on tariffs, licenses, and restrictions. Direct foreign sales and service outlets of an organization. **SKILLS**—Negotiation; Service Orientation; Persuasion; Management of Personnel Resources; Time Management; Monitoring; Instructing; Social Perceptiveness.

GOE—Interest Area: 10. Sales and Marketing. **Work Group:** 10.01. Managerial Work in Sales and Marketing. **Other Jobs in This Work Group:** Advertising and Promotions Managers; First-Line Supervisors/Managers of Non-Retail Sales Workers; First-Line Supervisors/Managers of Retail Sales Workers; Marketing Managers.

EDUCATION/TRAINING PROGRAM(S)— Business Administration and Management, General; Business/Commerce, General; Consumer Merchandising/Retailing Management; Marketing, Other; Marketing/Marketing Management, General. **RELATED KNOWLEDGE/COURSES**—Sales and Marketing; Computers and Electronics; Mathematics; Customer and Personal Service; Administration and Management; Law and Government.

Sales Representatives, Agricultural

- Personality Code: ER
- Growth: 19.3%
- Annual Job Openings: 44,000
- Annual Earnings: $57,120
- Education/Training Required: Moderate-term on-the-job training
- Self-Employed: 4.6%
- Part-Time: 8.1%

Sell agricultural products and services, such as animal feeds, farm and garden equipment, and dairy, poultry, and veterinarian supplies. Solicits orders from customers in person or by phone. Demonstrates use of agricultural equipment or machines. Recommends changes in customer use of agricultural products to improve production. Prepares reports of business transactions. Informs customer of estimated delivery schedule, service contracts, warranty, or other information pertaining to purchased products. Displays or shows customer agricultural related products. Compiles lists of prospective customers for use as sales leads. Prepares sales contracts for orders obtained. Consults with customer regarding installation, set-up, or layout of agricultural equipment and machines. Quotes prices and credit terms. **SKILLS**—Persuasion; Negotiation; Speaking; Writing; Active Listening; Mathematics; Instructing; Service Orientation.

GOE—Interest Area: 10. Sales and Marketing. **Work Group:** 10.02. Sales Technology. **Other Jobs in This Work Group:** Advertising Sales Agents; Insurance Sales Agents; Sales Agents, Financial Services; Sales Agents, Securities and Commodities; Sales and Related Workers, All Other; Sales Representatives, Chemical and Pharmaceutical; Sales Representatives, Electrical/Electronic; Sales Representatives, Instruments; Sales Representatives, Mechanical Equipment and Supplies; Sales Representatives, Medical; Sales Representatives, Services, All Other; Sales Representatives, Wholesale and Manufacturing, Technical and Scientific Products; Securities, Commodities, and Financial Services Sales Agents.

EDUCATION/TRAINING PROGRAM(S)— Business, Management, Marketing, and Related Support Services, Other; Selling Skills and Sales Operations. **RELATED KNOWLEDGE/COURSES**—Sales and Marketing; Economics and Accounting; Mathematics; Food Production; Telecommunications; Communications and Media.

Sales Representatives, Chemical and Pharmaceutical

- Personality Code: ES
- Growth: 19.3%
- Annual Job Openings: 44,000
- Annual Earnings: $57,120
- Education/Training Required: Moderate-term on-the-job training
- Self-Employed: 4.6%
- Part-Time: 8.1%

Sell chemical or pharmaceutical products or services, such as acids, industrial chemicals, agricultural chemicals, medicines, drugs, and water treatment supplies. Promotes and sells pharmaceutical and chemical products to potential customers. Explains water treatment package benefits to customer and sells chemicals to treat and resolve water process problems. Estimates and advises customer of service costs to correct water-treatment process problems. Discusses characteristics and clinical studies pertaining to pharmaceutical products with physicians, dentists, hospitals, and retail/wholesale establishments. Distributes drug samples to customer and takes orders for pharmaceutical supply items from customer. Inspects, tests, and observes chemical changes in water system equipment, utilizing test kit, reference manual, and knowledge of chemical treatment. **SKILLS**—Persuasion; Science; Speaking; Social Perceptiveness; Negotiation; Active Listening; Critical Thinking; Instructing.

GOE—Interest Area: 10. Sales and Marketing. **Work Group:** 10.02. Sales Technology. **Other Jobs in This Work Group:** Advertising Sales Agents; Insurance Sales Agents; Sales Agents, Financial Services; Sales Agents, Securities and Commodities; Sales and Related Workers, All Other; Sales Representatives, Agricultural; Sales Representatives, Elec-

trical/Electronic; Sales Representatives, Instruments; Sales Representatives, Mechanical Equipment and Supplies; Sales Representatives, Medical; Sales Representatives, Services, All Other; Sales Representatives, Wholesale and Manufacturing, Technical and Scientific Products; Securities, Commodities, and Financial Services Sales Agents.

EDUCATION/TRAINING PROGRAM(S)—Business, Management, Marketing, and Related Support Services, Other; Selling Skills and Sales Operations. **RELATED KNOWLEDGE/COURSES**—Sales and Marketing; Chemistry; Biology; Mathematics; Medicine and Dentistry; Economics and Accounting.

Sales Representatives, Electrical/Electronic

- Personality Code: ER
- Growth: 19.3%
- Annual Job Openings: 44,000
- Annual Earnings: $57,120
- Education/Training Required: Moderate-term on-the-job training
- Self-Employed: 4.6%
- Part-Time: 8.1%

Sell electrical, electronic, or related products or services, such as communication equipment, radiographic-inspection equipment and services, ultrasonic equipment, electronics parts, computers, and EDP systems. Analyzes communication needs of customer and consults with staff engineers regarding technical problems. Trains establishment personnel in equipment use, utilizing knowledge of electronics and product sold. Recommends equipment to meet customer requirements, considering salable features, such as flexibility, cost, capacity, and economy of operation. Negotiates terms of sale and services with customer. Sells electrical or electronic equipment,

Enterprising—S

such as computers, data processing and radiographic equipment to businesses and industrial establishments. **SKILLS**—Persuasion; Negotiation; Instructing; Operations Analysis; Active Listening; Equipment Selection; Speaking; Technology Design.

GOE—Interest Area: 10. Sales and Marketing. **Work Group:** 10.02. Sales Technology. **Other Jobs in This Work Group:** Advertising Sales Agents; Insurance Sales Agents; Sales Agents, Financial Services; Sales Agents, Securities and Commodities; Sales and Related Workers, All Other; Sales Representatives, Agricultural; Sales Representatives, Chemical and Pharmaceutical; Sales Representatives, Instruments; Sales Representatives, Mechanical Equipment and Supplies; Sales Representatives, Medical; Sales Representatives, Services, All Other; Sales Representatives, Wholesale and Manufacturing, Technical and Scientific Products; Securities, Commodities, and Financial Services Sales Agents.

EDUCATION/TRAINING PROGRAM(S)— Business, Management, Marketing, and Related Support Services, Other; Selling Skills and Sales Operations. **RELATED KNOWLEDGE/COURSES**—Sales and Marketing; Computers and Electronics; Education and Training; Economics and Accounting; Telecommunications; Mathematics.

Sales Representatives, Instruments

- Personality Code: ER
- Growth: 19.3%
- Annual Job Openings: 44,000
- Annual Earnings: $57,120
- Education/Training Required: Moderate-term on-the-job training
- Self-Employed: 4.6%
- Part-Time: 8.1%

Sell precision instruments, such as dynamometers and spring scales, and laboratory, navigation, and surveying instruments. Assists customer with product selection, utilizing knowledge of engineering specifications and catalog resources. Evaluates customer needs and emphasizes product features based on technical knowledge of product capabilities and limitations. Sells weighing and other precision instruments, such as spring scales, dynamometers, and laboratory, navigational, and surveying instruments to customer. **SKILLS**—Persuasion; Service Orientation; Active Listening; Speaking; Negotiation; Instructing.

GOE—Interest Area: 10. Sales and Marketing. **Work Group:** 10.02. Sales Technology. **Other Jobs in This Work Group:** Advertising Sales Agents; Insurance Sales Agents; Sales Agents, Financial Services; Sales Agents, Securities and Commodities; Sales and Related Workers, All Other; Sales Representatives, Agricultural; Sales Representatives, Chemical and Pharmaceutical; Sales Representatives, Electrical/Electronic; Sales Representatives, Mechanical Equipment and Supplies; Sales Representatives, Medical; Sales Representatives, Services, All Other; Sales Representatives, Wholesale and Manufacturing, Technical and Scientific Products; Securities, Commodities, and Financial Services Sales Agents.

EDUCATION/TRAINING PROGRAM(S)— Business, Management, Marketing, and Related Support Services, Other; Selling Skills and Sales Operations. **RELATED KNOWLEDGE/ COURSES**—Sales and Marketing; Engineering and Technology; Customer and Personal Service.

Sales Representatives, Mechanical Equipment and Supplies

- Personality Code: ER
- Growth: 19.3%
- Annual Job Openings: 44,000
- Annual Earnings: $57,120
- Education/Training Required: Moderate-term on-the-job training
- Self-Employed: 4.6%
- Part-Time: 8.1%

Sell mechanical equipment, machinery, materials, and supplies, such as aircraft and railroad equipment and parts, construction machinery, material-handling equipment, industrial machinery, and welding equipment. Recommends and sells textile, industrial, construction, railroad, and oil field machinery, equipment, materials, and supplies, and services utilizing knowledge of machine operations. Computes installation or production costs, estimates savings, and prepares and submits bid specifications to customer for review and approval. Submits orders for product and follows-up on order to verify material list accuracy and delivery schedule meets project deadline. Appraises equipment and verifies customer credit rating to establish trade-in value and contract terms. Reviews existing machinery/equipment placement and diagrams proposal to illustrate efficient space utilization, using standard measuring devices and templates. Attends sales and trade meetings and reads related publications to obtain current market condition information, business trends, and industry developments. Inspects establishment premises to verify installation feasibility, and obtains building blueprints and elevator specifications to submit to engineering department for bid. Demonstrates and explains use of installed equipment and production processes. Arranges for installation and test-operation of machinery and recommends solutions to product-related problems.

Contacts current and potential customers, visits establishments to evaluate needs, and promotes sale of products and services. SKILLS—Operations Analysis; Persuasion; Negotiation; Equipment Selection; Instructing; Active Listening; Speaking; Reading Comprehension.

GOE—Interest Area: 10. Sales and Marketing. Work Group: 10.02. Sales Technology. Other Jobs in This Work Group: Advertising Sales Agents; Insurance Sales Agents; Sales Agents, Financial Services; Sales Agents, Securities and Commodities; Sales and Related Workers, All Other; Sales Representatives, Agricultural; Sales Representatives, Chemical and Pharmaceutical; Sales Representatives, Electrical/Electronic; Sales Representatives, Instruments; Sales Representatives, Medical; Sales Representatives, Services, All Other; Sales Representatives, Wholesale and Manufacturing, Technical and Scientific Products; Securities, Commodities, and Financial Services Sales Agents.

EDUCATION/TRAINING PROGRAM(S)—Business, Management, Marketing, and Related Support Services, Other; Selling Skills and Sales Operations. RELATED KNOWLEDGE/COURSES—Sales and Marketing; Mathematics; Economics and Accounting; Design; Telecommunications; Engineering and Technology.

Sales Representatives, Medical

- Personality Code: ES
- Growth: 19.3%
- Annual Job Openings: 44,000
- Annual Earnings: $57,120
- Education/Training Required: Moderate-term on-the-job training
- Self-Employed: 4.6%
- Part-Time: 8.1%

Enterprising—S

Sell medical equipment, products, and services. Does not include pharmaceutical sales representatives. Promotes sale of medical and dental equipment, supplies, and services to doctors, dentists, hospitals, medical schools, and retail establishments. Writes specifications to order custom-made surgical appliances, using customer measurements and physician prescriptions. Advises customer regarding office layout, legal and insurance regulations, cost analysis, and collection methods. Designs and fabricates custom-made medical appliances. Selects surgical appliances from stock and fits and sells appliance to customer. Studies data describing new products to accurately recommend purchase of equipment and supplies. **SKILLS**—Technology Design; Persuasion; Negotiation; Operations Analysis; Active Listening; Writing; Speaking; Service Orientation.

GOE—Interest Area: 10. Sales and Marketing. **Work Group:** 10.02. Sales Technology. **Other Jobs in This Work Group:** Advertising Sales Agents; Insurance Sales Agents; Sales Agents, Financial Services; Sales Agents, Securities and Commodities; Sales and Related Workers, All Other; Sales Representatives, Agricultural; Sales Representatives, Chemical and Pharmaceutical; Sales Representatives, Electrical/Electronic; Sales Representatives, Instruments; Sales Representatives, Mechanical Equipment and Supplies; Sales Representatives, Services, All Other; Sales Representatives, Wholesale and Manufacturing, Technical and Scientific Products; Securities, Commodities, and Financial Services Sales Agents.

EDUCATION/TRAINING PROGRAM(S)— Business, Management, Marketing, and Related Support Services, Other; Selling Skills and Sales Operations. **RELATED KNOWLEDGE/ COURSES**—Sales and Marketing; Design; Mathematics; Economics and Accounting; Engineering and Technology; Medicine and Dentistry.

Sales Representatives, Wholesale and Manufacturing, Except Technical and Scientific Products

- Personality Code: ES
- Growth: 19.1%
- Annual Job Openings: 160,000
- Annual Earnings: $43,860
- Education/Training Required: Moderate-term on-the-job training
- Self-Employed: 4.6%
- Part-Time: 8.1%

Sell goods for wholesalers or manufacturers to businesses or groups of individuals. Work requires substantial knowledge of items sold. Answer customers' questions about products, prices, availability, product uses, and credit terms. Arrange and direct delivery and installation of products and equipment. Contact regular and prospective customers to demonstrate products, explain product features, and solicit orders. Estimate or quote prices, credit or contract terms, warranties, and delivery dates. Forward orders to manufacturers. Identify prospective customers by using business directories, following leads from existing clients, participating in organizations and clubs, and attending trade shows and conferences. Monitor market conditions, product innovations, and competitors' products, prices, and sales. Negotiate details of contracts and payments, and prepare sales contracts and order forms. Prepare drawings, estimates, and bids that meet specific customer needs. Provide customers with product samples and catalogs. Recommend products to customers, based on customers' needs and interests. Buy products from manufacturers or brokerage firms, and distribute them to wholesale and retail clients. Check stock levels and reorder merchandise as necessary. Consult with clients after sales or contract signings in order to resolve problems and to provide ongoing support. Negotiate with retail merchants to improve product exposure such as shelf positioning and advertising. Obtain credit information about prospective customers. Perform administrative duties, such as preparing sales budgets and reports, keeping sales records, and filing expense account reports. Plan, assemble, and stock product displays in retail stores, or make recommendations to retailers regarding product displays, promotional programs, and advertising. Train customers' employees to operate and maintain new equipment. **SKILLS**—Negotiation; Management of Material Resources; Persuasion; Service Orientation; Speaking; Social Perceptiveness; Instructing; Writing.

GOE—**Interest Area:** 10. Sales and Marketing. **Work Group:** 10.03. General Sales. **Other Jobs in This Work Group:** Parts Salespersons; Real Estate Brokers; Real Estate Sales Agents; Retail Salespersons; Sales and Related Workers, All Other; Service Station Attendants; Stock Clerks, Sales Floor; Travel Agents.

EDUCATION/TRAINING PROGRAM(S)—Apparel and Accessories Marketing Operations; Business, Management, Marketing, and Related Support Services, Other; Fashion Merchandising; General Merchandising, Sales, and Related Marketing Operations, Other; Sales, Distribution, and Marketing Operations, General; Special Products Marketing Operations; Specialized Merchandising, Sales, and Related Marketing Operations, Other. **RELATED KNOWLEDGE/COURSES**—Sales and Marketing; Customer and Personal Service; Communications and Media; Transportation; Economics and Accounting; Psychology.

Storage and Distribution Managers

- Personality Code: EC
- Growth: 19.7%
- Annual Job Openings: 13,000
- Annual Earnings: $63,590
- Education/Training Required: Work experience in a related occupation
- Self-Employed: 1.1%
- Part-Time: 2.4%

Plan, direct, and coordinate the storage and distribution operations within an organization or the activities of organizations that are engaged in storing and distributing materials and products. Supervise the activities of workers engaged in receiving, storing, testing, and shipping products or materials. Plan, develop, and implement warehouse safety and security programs and activities. Review invoices, work orders, consumption reports, and demand forecasts in order to estimate peak delivery periods and to issue work assignments. Schedule and monitor air or surface pickup, delivery, or distribution of products or materials. Interview, select, and train warehouse and supervisory personnel. Confer with department heads to coordinate warehouse activities, such as production, sales, records control, and purchasing. Respond to customers' or shippers' questions and complaints regarding storage and distribution services. Inspect physical conditions of warehouses, vehicle fleets and equipment, and order testing, maintenance, repair, or replacement as necessary. Develop and document standard and emergency operating procedures for receiving, handling, storing, shipping, or salvaging products or materials. Examine products or materials in order to estimate quantities or weight and type of container required for storage or transport. Negotiate with carriers, warehouse operators and insurance company representatives for services and preferential rates. Issue shipping instructions and provide routing

Enterprising—S

information to ensure that delivery times and locations are coordinated. Examine invoices and shipping manifests for conformity to tariff and customs regulations. Prepare and manage departmental budgets. Prepare or direct preparation of correspondence, reports, and operations, maintenance, and safety manuals. Arrange for necessary shipping documentation, and contact customs officials in order to effect release of shipments. Advise sales and billing departments of transportation charges for customers' accounts. Evaluate freight costs and the inventory costs associated with transit times in order to ensure that costs are appropriate. Participate in setting transportation and service rates. Track and trace goods while they are en route to their destinations, expediting orders when necessary. **SKILLS—** Management of Personnel Resources; Operations Analysis; Monitoring; Persuasion; Service Orientation; Management of Material Resources; Social Perceptiveness; Negotiation.

GOE—Interest Area: 13. General Management and Support. **Work Group:** 13.01. General Management Work and Management of Support Functions. **Other Jobs in This Work Group:** Business Operations Specialists, All Other; Chief Executives; Compensation and Benefits Managers; Farm, Ranch, and Other Agricultural Managers; Financial Managers; Financial Managers, Branch or Department; Financial Specialists, All Other; Funeral Directors; General and Operations Managers; Government Service Executives; Human Resources Managers; Human Resources Managers, All Other; Legislators; Managers, All Other; Postmasters and Mail Superintendents; Private Sector Executives; Property, Real Estate, and Community Association Managers; Public Relations Managers; Purchasing Managers; Training and Development Managers; Transportation, Storage, and Distribution Managers; Treasurers, Controllers, and Chief Financial Officers.

EDUCATION/TRAINING PROGRAM(S)— Aeronautics/Aviation/Aerospace Science and Technology, General; Aviation/Airway Management and Operations; Business Administration and Management, General; Business/Commerce, General; Logistics and Materials Management; Public Administration. **RELATED KNOWLEDGE/ COURSES—**Customer and Personal Service; Administration and Management; Sales and Marketing; Personnel and Human Resources; Education and Training; Production and Processing.

Training and Development Managers

- Personality Code: ES
- Growth: 19.4%
- Annual Job Openings: 21,000
- Annual Earnings: $68,800
- Education/Training Required: Work experience plus degree
- Self-Employed: 0%
- Part-Time: 3.7%

Plan, direct, or coordinate the training and development activities and staff of an organization. Conduct orientation sessions and arrange on-the-job training for new hires. Evaluate instructor performance and the effectiveness of training programs, providing recommendations for improvement. Develop testing and evaluation procedures. Conduct or arrange for ongoing technical training and personal development classes for staff members. Confer with management and conduct surveys to identify training needs based on projected production processes, changes, and other factors. Develop and organize training manuals, multimedia visual aids, and other educational materials. Plan, develop, and provide training and staff development programs, using knowledge of the effectiveness of methods such as classroom training, demonstrations, on-the-job training, meetings, conferences, and workshops. Analyze training needs to develop new training programs or modify and improve existing programs. Review and evaluate training and apprenticeship programs for compliance with government standards. Train instructors and supervisors in techniques and skills for training and dealing with employees. Coordinate established courses with technical and professional courses provided by community schools and designate training procedures. Prepare training budget for department or organization. **SKILLS**—Management of Personnel Resources; Management of Financial Resources; Learning Strategies; Negotiation; Instructing; Service Orientation; Social Perceptiveness; Persuasion.

GOE—**Interest Area:** 13. General Management and Support. **Work Group:** 13.01. General Management Work and Management of Support Functions. **Other Jobs in This Work Group:** Business Operations Specialists, All Other; Chief Executives; Compensation and Benefits Managers; Farm, Ranch, and Other Agricultural Managers; Financial Managers; Financial Managers, Branch or Department; Financial Specialists, All Other; Funeral Directors; General and Operations Managers; Government Service Executives; Human Resources Managers; Human Resources Managers, All Other; Legislators; Managers, All Other; Postmasters and Mail Superintendents; Private Sector Executives; Property, Real Estate, and Community Association Managers; Public Relations Managers; Purchasing Managers; Storage and Distribution Managers; Transportation, Storage, and Distribution Managers; Treasurers, Controllers, and Chief Financial Officers.

EDUCATION/TRAINING PROGRAM(S)— Human Resources Development; Human Resources Management/Personnel Administration, General. **RELATED KNOWLEDGE/COURSES**—Clerical Studies; Personnel and Human Resources; Administration and Management; Education and Training; Psychology; Computers and Electronics.

Transportation Managers

- Personality Code: EC
- Growth: 19.7%
- Annual Job Openings: 13,000
- Annual Earnings: $63,590
- Education/Training Required: Work experience in a related occupation
- Self-Employed: 1.1%
- Part-Time: 2.4%

Plan, direct, and coordinate the transportation operations within an organization or the activities of organizations that provide transportation services. Direct activities related to dispatching, routing, and tracking transportation vehicles, such as aircraft and railroad cars. Plan, organize and manage the work of subordinate staff to ensure that the work is accomplished in a manner consistent with organizational requirements. Direct investigations to verify and resolve customer or shipper complaints. Serve as contact persons for all workers within assigned territories. Implement schedule and policy changes. Collaborate with other managers and staff members in order to formulate and implement policies, procedures, goals, and objectives. Monitor operations to ensure that staff members comply with administrative policies and procedures, safety rules, union contracts, and government regulations. Promote safe work activities by conducting safety audits, attending company safety meetings, and meeting with individual staff members. Develop criteria, application instructions, procedural manuals, and contracts for federal and state public transportation programs. Monitor spending to ensure that expenses are consistent with approved budgets. Direct and coordinate, through subordinates, activities of operations department in order to obtain use of equipment, facilities, and human resources. Direct activities of staff performing repairs and maintenance to equipment, vehicles, and facilities. Conduct investigations in cooperation with government agencies to determine causes of transportation accidents and to improve safety procedures. Analyze expenditures and other financial information in order to develop plans, policies, and budgets for increasing profits and improving services. Negotiate and authorize contracts with equipment and materials suppliers, and monitor contract fulfillment. Supervise workers assigning tariff classifications and preparing billing. Set operations policies and standards, including determination of safety procedures for the handling of dangerous goods. Recommend or authorize capital expenditures for acquisition of new equipment or property in order to increase efficiency and services of operations department. Prepare management recommendations, such as proposed fee and tariff increases or schedule changes. **SKILLS**—Negotiation; Time Management; Coordination; Instructing; Monitoring; Critical Thinking; Management of Financial Resources; Active Learning.

GOE—Interest Area: 07. Transportation. **Work Group:** 07.01. Managerial Work in Transportation. **Other Jobs in This Work Group:** First-Line Supervisors/Managers of Transportation and Material-Moving Machine and Vehicle Operators; Railroad Conductors and Yardmasters.

EDUCATION/TRAINING PROGRAM(S)— Aeronautics/Aviation/Aerospace Science and Technology, General; Aviation/Airway Management and Operations; Business Administration and Management, General; Business/Commerce, General; Logistics and Materials Management; Public Administration. **RELATED KNOWLEDGE/ COURSES**—Transportation; Customer and Personal Service; Clerical Studies; Sales and Marketing; Administration and Management; Psychology.

Treasurers, Controllers, and Chief Financial Officers

- Personality Code: EC
- Growth: 18.3%
- Annual Job Openings: 71,000
- Annual Earnings: $77,300
- Education/Training Required: Work experience plus degree
- Self-Employed: 3.1%
- Part-Time: 4.8%

Plan, direct, and coordinate the financial activities of an organization at the highest level of management. Includes financial reserve officers. Coordinate and direct the financial planning, budgeting, procurement, or investment activities of all or part of an organization. Develop internal control policies, guidelines, and procedures for activities such as budget administration, cash and credit management, and accounting. Prepare or direct preparation of financial statements, business activity reports, financial position forecasts, annual budgets, and/or reports required by regulatory agencies. Advise management on short-term and long-term financial objectives, policies, and actions. Analyze the financial details of past, present, and expected operations in order to identify development opportunities and areas where improvement is needed. Delegate authority for the receipt, disbursement, banking, protection, and custody of funds, securities, and financial instruments. Evaluate needs for procurement of funds and investment of surpluses, and make appropriate recommendations. Lead staff training and development in budgeting and financial management areas. Maintain current knowledge of organizational policies and procedures, federal and state policies and directives, and current accounting standards. Supervise employees performing financial reporting, accounting, billing, collections, payroll, and budgeting duties. Conduct or coordinate audits of company accounts and financial transactions to ensure compliance with state and federal requirements and statutes. Develop and maintain relationships with banking, insurance, and non-organizational accounting personnel in order to facilitate financial activities. Monitor and evaluate the performance of accounting and other financial staff; recommend and implement personnel actions such as promotions and dismissals. Monitor financial activities and details such as reserve levels to ensure that all legal and regulatory requirements are met. Perform tax planning work. Provide direction and assistance to other organizational units regarding accounting and budgeting policies and procedures, and efficient control and utilization of financial resources. Receive and record requests for disbursements; authorize disbursements in accordance with policies and procedures. **SKILLS**—Management of Financial Resources; Systems Analysis; Systems Evaluation; Judgment and Decision Making; Complex Problem Solving; Mathematics; Management of Personnel Resources; Critical Thinking.

GOE—Interest Area: 13. General Management and Support. **Work Group:** 13.01. General Man-

agement Work and Management of Support Functions. **Other Jobs in This Work Group:** Business Operations Specialists, All Other; Chief Executives; Compensation and Benefits Managers; Farm, Ranch, and Other Agricultural Managers; Financial Managers; Financial Managers, Branch or Department; Financial Specialists, All Other; Funeral Directors; General and Operations Managers; Government Service Executives; Human Resources Managers; Human Resources Managers, All Other; Legislators; Managers, All Other; Postmasters and Mail Superintendents; Private Sector Executives; Property, Real Estate, and Community Association Managers; Public Relations Managers; Purchasing Managers; Storage and Distribution Managers; Training and Development Managers; Transportation, Storage, and Distribution Managers.

EDUCATION/TRAINING PROGRAM(S)— Accounting and Business/Management; Accounting and Finance; Credit Management; Finance and Financial Management Services, Other; Finance, General; International Finance; Public Finance. **RELATED KNOWLEDGE/COURSES**—Economics and Accounting; Administration and Management; Law and Government; Mathematics; English Language; Personnel and Human Resources.

Conventional Jobs

Accountants

- Personality Code: CE
- Growth: 19.5%
- Annual Job Openings: 119,000
- Annual Earnings: $49,060
- Education/Training Required: Bachelor's degree
- Self-Employed: 10.6%
- Part-Time: 8.8%

Analyze financial information and prepare financial reports to determine or maintain record of assets, liabilities, profit and loss, tax liability, or other financial activities within an organization. Prepare, examine, and analyze accounting records, financial statements, and other financial reports to assess accuracy, completeness, and conformance to reporting and procedural standards. Compute taxes owed and prepare tax returns, ensuring compliance with payment, reporting, and other tax requirements. Analyze business operations, trends, costs, revenues, financial commitments, and obligations to project future revenues and expenses or to provide advice. Report to management regarding the finances of establishment. Establish tables of accounts and assign entries to proper accounts. Develop, maintain, and analyze budgets, preparing periodic reports that compare budgeted costs to actual costs. Develop, implement, modify, and document record-keeping and accounting systems, making use of current computer technology. Prepare forms and manuals for accounting and book-keeping personnel and direct their work activities. Survey operations to ascertain accounting needs and to recommend, develop, and maintain solutions to business and financial problems. Work as Internal Revenue Service agents. Advise management about issues such as resource utilization, tax strategies, and the assumptions underlying budget forecasts. Provide internal and external auditing services for businesses and individuals. Advise clients in areas such as compensation, employee health care benefits, the design of accounting and data processing systems, and long-range tax and estate plans. Investigate bankruptcies and other complex financial transactions and prepare reports summarizing the findings. Represent clients before taxing authorities and provide support during litigation involving financial issues. Appraise, evaluate, and inventory real property and equipment, recording information such as the property's description, value, and location. Maintain and examine the records of government agencies. **SKILLS**—Management of Financial Resources; Systems Evaluation; Systems Analysis; Operations Analysis; Judgment and Decision Making; Time Management; Monitoring; Negotiation.

GOE—Interest Area: 13. General Management and Support. **Work Group:** 13.02. Management Support. **Other Jobs in This Work Group:** Accountants and Auditors; Appraisers and Assessors of Real Estate; Appraisers, Real Estate; Assessors; Auditors; Budget Analysts; Business Operations Specialists, All Other; Claims Adjusters, Examiners, and Investigators; Claims Examiners, Property and Casualty Insurance; Compensation, Benefits, and Job Analysis Specialists; Cost Estimators; Credit Analysts; Employment Interviewers, Private or Public Employment Service; Employment, Recruitment, and Placement Specialists; Financial Analysts; Human Resources, Training, and Labor Relations Specialists, All Other; Insurance Adjusters, Examiners, and Investigators; Insurance Appraisers, Auto Damage; Insurance Underwriters; Loan Counselors; Loan Officers; Logisticians; Management Analysts; Market Research Analysts; Personnel Recruiters; Purchasing Agents and Buyers, Farm Products; Purchasing Agents, Except Wholesale, Retail, and Farm Products; Tax Examiners, Collectors, and Revenue Agents; Training and Development Specialists; Wholesale and Retail Buyers, Except Farm Products.

EDUCATION/TRAINING PROGRAM(S)— Accounting; Accounting and Business/Management; Accounting and Computer Science; Accounting and Finance; Auditing; Taxation. RELATED KNOWLEDGE/COURSES—Economics and Accounting; Clerical Studies; Mathematics; Law and Government; Customer and Personal Service; Computers and Electronics.

Actuaries

- Personality Code: CI
- Growth: 14.9%
- Annual Job Openings: 2,000
- Annual Earnings: $72,520
- Education/Training Required: Work experience plus degree
- Self-Employed: 1.4%
- Part-Time: 6.4%

Analyze statistical data, such as mortality, accident, sickness, disability, and retirement rates and construct probability tables to forecast risk and liability for payment of future benefits. May ascertain premium rates required and cash reserves necessary to ensure payment of future benefits. Ascertain premium rates required and cash reserves and liabilities necessary to ensure payment of future benefits. Analyze statistical information to estimate mortality, accident, sickness, disability, and retirement rates. Design, review, and help administer insurance, annuity and pension plans, determining financial soundness and calculating premiums. Collaborate with programmers, underwriters, accounts, claims experts, and senior management to help companies develop plans for new lines of business or improving existing business. Determine or help determine company policy, and explain complex technical matters to company executives, government officials, shareholders, policyholders, and/or the public. Testify before public agencies on proposed legislation affect-

ing businesses. Provide advice to clients on a contract basis, working as a consultant. Testify in court as expert witness or to provide legal evidence on matters such as the value of potential lifetime earnings of a person who is disabled or killed in an accident. Construct probability tables for events such as fires, natural disasters, and unemployment, based on analysis of statistical data and other pertinent information. Determine policy contract provisions for each type of insurance. SKILLS—Mathematics; Programming; Active Learning; Complex Problem Solving; Critical Thinking; Operations Analysis; Monitoring; Instructing.

GOE—Interest Area: 02. Science, Math, and Engineering. Work Group: 02.06. Mathematics and Computers. Other Jobs in This Work Group: Mathematical Science Occupations, All Other; Mathematical Technicians; Mathematicians; Operations Research Analysts; Statistical Assistants; Statisticians.

EDUCATION/TRAINING PROGRAM(S)— Actuarial Science. RELATED KNOWLEDGE/ COURSES—Mathematics; Economics and Accounting; Computers and Electronics; Sales and Marketing; English Language; Personnel and Human Resources.

Adjustment Clerks

- Personality Code: CE
- Growth: 24.3%
- Annual Job Openings: 419,000
- Annual Earnings: $26,500
- Education/Training Required: Moderate-term on-the-job training
- Self-Employed: 0.5%
- Part-Time: 14.8%

Investigate and resolve customers' inquiries concerning merchandise, service, billing, or credit rating. Examine pertinent information to determine accuracy of customers' complaints and responsibility for errors. Notify customers and appropriate personnel of findings, adjustments, and recommendations, such as exchange of merchandise, refund of money, credit to customers' accounts, or adjustment to customers' bills. Reviews claims adjustments with dealer, examines parts claimed to be defective and approves or disapproves of dealer's claim. Notifies customer and designated personnel of findings and recommendations, such as exchanging merchandise or refunding money, or adjustment of bill. Examines weather conditions, number of days in billing period, and reviews meter accounts for errors which might explain high utility charges. Writes work order. Prepares reports showing volume, types, and disposition of claims handled. Compares merchandise with original requisition and information on invoice and prepares invoice for returned goods. Orders tests to detect product malfunction and determines if defect resulted from faulty construction. Trains dealers or service personnel in construction of products, service operations, and customer service. **SKILLS**—Instructing; Speaking; Writing; Service Orientation; Active Listening; Persuasion; Negotiation; Critical Thinking.

GOE—Interest Area: 09. Business Detail. **Work Group:** 09.05. Customer Service. **Other Jobs in This Work Group:** Bill and Account Collectors; Cashiers; Counter and Rental Clerks; Customer Service Representatives; Customer Service Representatives, Utilities; Gaming Cage Workers; Gaming Change Persons and Booth Cashiers; New Accounts Clerks; Order Clerks; Receptionists and Information Clerks; Tellers; Travel Clerks.

EDUCATION/TRAINING PROGRAM(S)— Customer Service Support/Call Center/Teleservice Operation; Receptionist. **RELATED KNOWLEDGE/COURSES**—Economics and Accounting; Clerical Studies; Education and Training; Customer and Personal Service.

Air Traffic Controllers

- Personality Code: CR
- Growth: 12.6%
- Annual Job Openings: 2,000
- Annual Earnings: $96,260
- Education/Training Required: Long-term on-the-job training
- Self-Employed: 0%
- Part-Time: 3.6%

Control air traffic on and within vicinity of airport and movement of air traffic between altitude sectors and control centers according to established procedures and policies. Authorize, regulate, and control commercial airline flights according to government or company regulations to expedite and ensure flight safety. Analyze factors such as weather reports, fuel requirements, and maps in order to determine air routes. Check conditions and traffic at different altitudes in response to pilots' requests for altitude changes. Conduct pre-flight briefings on weather conditions, suggested routes, altitudes, indications of turbulence, and other flight safety information. Contact pilots by radio to provide meteorological, navigational, and other information. Determine the timing and procedures for flight vector changes. Direct ground traffic, including taxiing aircraft, maintenance and baggage vehicles, and airport workers. Direct pilots to runways when space is available, or direct them to maintain a traffic pattern until there is space for them to land. Inform pilots about nearby planes as well as potentially hazardous conditions such as weather, speed and direction of wind, and visibility problems. Issue landing and take-off authorizations and instructions. Maintain radio and telephone contact with adjacent control towers, terminal control units, and other area control centers in order to coordinate aircraft movement. Monitor aircraft within a specific airspace, using radar, computer equipment, and visual references. Monitor and direct the movement of aircraft within an assigned air space and on the ground at airports to minimize delays and maximize safety. Organize flight plans and traffic management plans to prepare for planes about to enter assigned airspace. Provide flight path changes or directions to emergency landing fields for pilots traveling in bad weather or in emergency situations. Compile information about flights from flight plans, pilot reports, radar, and observations. Relay to control centers such air traffic information as courses, altitudes, and expected arrival times. Transfer control of departing flights to traffic control centers and accept control of arriving flights. Complete daily activity reports and keep records of messages from aircraft. Initiate and coordinate searches for missing aircraft. Inspect, adjust, and control radio equipment and airport lights. Review records and reports for clarity and completeness, and maintain records and reports as required under federal law. **SKILLS**—Operation and Control; Operation Monitoring; Active Listening; Coordination; Critical Thinking; Active Learning; Troubleshooting; Judgment and Decision Making; Systems Analysis.

GOE—**Interest Area:** 07. Transportation. **Work Group:** 07.02. Vehicle Expediting and Coordinating. **Other Jobs in This Work Group:** Airfield Operations Specialists; Railroad Brake, Signal, and Switch Operators; Traffic Technicians.

EDUCATION/TRAINING PROGRAM(S)—Air Traffic Controller. **RELATED KNOWLEDGE/ COURSES**—Transportation; Physics; Telecommunications; Geography; Computers and Electronics; Clerical Studies.

Assessors

- Personality Code: CE
- Growth: 17.6%
- Annual Job Openings: 11,000
- Annual Earnings: $43,610
- Education/Training Required: Postsecondary vocational training
- Self-Employed: 34.8%
- Part-Time: 8.9%

Appraise real and personal property to determine its fair value. May assess taxes in accordance with prescribed schedules. Determine taxability and value of properties, using methods such as field inspection, structural measurement, calculation, sales analysis, market trend studies, and income and expense analysis. Inspect new construction and major improvements to existing structures in order to determine values. Explain assessed values to property owners and defend appealed assessments at public hearings. Inspect properties, considering factors such as market value, location, and building or replacement costs to determine appraisal value. Prepare and maintain current data on each parcel assessed, including maps of boundaries, inventories of land and structures, property characteristics, and any applicable exemptions. Identify the ownership of each piece of taxable property. Conduct regular reviews of property within jurisdictions in order to determine changes in property due to construction or demolition. Complete and maintain assessment rolls that show the assessed values and status of all property in a municipality. Issue notices of assessments and taxes. Review information about transfers of property to ensure its accuracy, checking basic information on buyers, sellers, and sales prices and making corrections as necessary. Maintain familiarity with aspects of local real estate markets. Analyze trends in sales prices, construction costs, and rents, in order to assess property values and/or determine the accuracy of assessments. Approve applications for property tax exemptions or deductions. Establish uniform and equitable systems for assessing all classes and kinds of property. Write and submit appraisal and tax reports for public record. Serve on assessment review boards. Hire staff members. Provide sales analyses to be used for equalization of school aid. Calculate tax bills for properties by multiplying assessed values by jurisdiction tax rates. **SKILLS**—Negotiation; Social Perceptiveness; Persuasion; Mathematics; Active Listening; Speaking; Service Orientation; Instructing.

GOE—Interest Area: 13. General Management and Support. **Work Group:** 13.02. Management Support. **Other Jobs in This Work Group:** Accountants; Accountants and Auditors; Appraisers and Assessors of Real Estate; Appraisers, Real Estate; Auditors; Budget Analysts; Business Operations Specialists, All Other; Claims Adjusters, Examiners, and Investigators; Claims Examiners, Property and Casualty Insurance; Compensation, Benefits, and Job Analysis Specialists; Cost Estimators; Credit Analysts; Employment Interviewers, Private or Public Employment Service; Employment, Recruitment, and Placement Specialists; Financial Analysts; Human Resources, Training, and Labor Relations Specialists, All Other; Insurance Adjusters, Examiners, and Investigators; Insurance Appraisers, Auto Damage; Insurance Underwriters; Loan Counselors; Loan Officers; Logisticians; Management Analysts; Market Research Analysts; Personnel Recruiters; Purchasing Agents and Buyers, Farm Products; Purchasing Agents, Except Wholesale, Retail, and Farm Products; Tax Examiners, Collectors, and Revenue Agents; Training and Development Specialists; Wholesale and Retail Buyers, Except Farm Products.

EDUCATION/TRAINING PROGRAM(S)— Real Estate. **RELATED KNOWLEDGE/COURSES—**Customer and Personal Service; Clerical Studies; Building and Construction; Law and Government; Mathematics; Computers and Electronics.

Audio and Video Equipment Technicians

- Personality Code: CS
- Growth: 26.7%
- Annual Job Openings: 5,000
- Annual Earnings: $30,810
- Education/Training Required: Long-term on-the-job training
- Self-Employed: 9.1%
- Part-Time: 12.5%

Set up or set up and operate audio and video equipment including microphones, sound speakers, video screens, projectors, video monitors, recording equipment, connecting wires and cables, sound and mixing boards, and related electronic equipment for concerts, sports events, meetings and conventions, presentations, and news conferences. May also set up and operate associated spotlights and other custom lighting systems. Notify supervisors when major equipment repairs are needed. Monitor incoming and outgoing pictures and sound feeds to ensure quality, and notify directors of any possible problems. Mix and regulate sound inputs and feeds, or coordinate audio feeds with television pictures. Install, adjust, and operate electronic equipment used to record, edit, and transmit radio and television programs, cable programs, and motion pictures. Design layouts of audio and video equipment, and perform upgrades and maintenance. Perform minor repairs and routine cleaning of audio and video equipment. Diagnose and resolve media system problems in classrooms. Switch sources of video input from one camera or studio to another, from film to live programming, or from network to local programming. Meet with directors and senior members of camera crews to discuss assignments and determine filming sequences, camera movements, and picture composition. Construct and position properties, sets, lighting equipment, and other equipment. Compress, digitize, duplicate, and store audio and video data. Obtain, set up, and load videotapes for scheduled productions or broadcasts. Edit videotapes by erasing and removing portions of programs and adding video and/or sound as required. Direct and coordinate activities of assistants and other personnel during production. Plan and develop pre-production ideas into outlines, scripts, story boards, and graphics, using own ideas or specifications of assignments. Maintain inventories of audio and video tapes and related supplies. Determine formats, approaches, content, levels, and mediums to effectively meet objectives within budgetary constraints, utilizing research, knowledge, and training. Record and edit audio material such as movie soundtracks, using audio recording and editing equipment. Inform users of audio and videotaping service policies and procedures. Obtain and preview musical performance programs prior to events in order to become familiar with the order and approximate times of pieces. Produce rough and finished graphics and graphic designs. Locate and secure settings, properties, effects, and other production necessities. **SKILLS**—Troubleshooting; Installation; Equipment Maintenance; Operation and Control; Service Orientation; Operation Monitoring; Repairing; Technology Design; Time Management.

GOE—**Interest Area:** 01. Arts, Entertainment, and Media. **Work Group:** 01.08. Media Technology. **Other Jobs in This Work Group:** Broadcast Technicians; Camera Operators, Television, Video, and Motion Picture; Film and Video Editors; Media and Communication Equipment Workers, All Other; Photographers; Professional Photographers; Radio Operators; Sound Engineering Technicians.

EDUCATION/TRAINING PROGRAM(S)— Agricultural Communication/Journalism; Photographic and Film/Video Technology/Technician and Assistant; Recording Arts Technology/Technician. **RELATED KNOWLEDGE/COURSES**— Computers and Electronics; Telecommunications; Engineering and Technology; Communications and Media; Mechanical Devices; Customer and Personal Service.

Audio-Visual Collections Specialists

- Personality Code: CS
- Growth: 16.3%
- Annual Job Openings: 2,000
- Annual Earnings: $32,590
- Education/Training Required: Moderate-term on-the-job training
- Self-Employed: 3.1%
- Part-Time: 16.5%

Prepare, plan, and operate audio-visual teaching aids for use in education. May record, catalogue, and file audio-visual materials. Set up, adjust, and operate audiovisual equipment such as cameras, film and slide projectors, and recording equipment, for meetings, events, classes, seminars and video conferences. Offer presentations and workshops on the role of multimedia in effective presentations. Attend conventions and conferences, read trade journals, and communicate with industry insiders in order to keep abreast of industry developments. Instruct users in the selection, use, and design of audiovisual materials, and assist them in the preparation of instructional materials and the rehearsal of presentations. Maintain hardware and software, including computers, scanners, color copiers, and color laser printers. Confer with teachers in order to select course materials and to determine which training aids are best suited to particular grade levels. Perform simple maintenance tasks such as cleaning monitors and lenses and changing batteries and light bulbs. Develop manuals, texts, workbooks, or related materials for use in conjunction with production materials. Direct and coordinate activities of assistants and other personnel during production. Determine formats, approaches, content, levels, and mediums necessary to meet production objectives effectively and within budgetary constraints. Acquire, catalog, and maintain collections of audio-visual material such as films, video- and audio-tapes, photographs, and software programs. Narrate presentations and productions. Construct and position properties, sets, lighting equipment, and other equipment. Develop preproduction ideas and incorporate them into outlines, scripts, story boards, and graphics. **SKILLS**—Troubleshooting; Instructing; Technology Design; Installation; Equipment Selection; Operations Analysis; Writing; Active Learning.

GOE—Interest Area: 12. Education and Social Service. **Work Group:** 12.03. Educational Services. **Other Jobs in This Work Group:** Adult Literacy, Remedial Education, and GED Teachers and Instructors; Agricultural Sciences Teachers, Postsecondary; Anthropology and Archeology Teachers, Postsecondary; Architecture Teachers, Postsecondary; Archivists; Area, Ethnic, and Cultural Studies Teachers, Postsecondary; Art, Drama, and Music Teachers, Postsecondary; Atmospheric, Earth, Marine, and Space Sciences Teachers, Postsecondary; Biological Science Teachers, Postsecondary; Business Teachers, Postsecondary; Chemistry Teachers, Postsecondary; Child Care Workers; Communications Teachers, Postsecondary; Computer Science Teachers, Postsecondary; Criminal Justice and Law Enforcement Teachers, Postsecondary; Curators; Economics Teachers, Postsecondary; Education Teachers, Postsecondary; Education, Training, and Library Workers, All Other; Educational Psychologists; Educational, Vocational, and School Counselors; Elementary School Teachers, Except Special Education; Engineering Teachers, Postsecondary; English Language and Literature Teachers, Postsecondary; Environmental Science Teachers, Postsecondary; Farm and Home Management Advisors; Foreign Language and Literature Teachers, Postsecondary; Forestry and Conservation Science Teachers, Postsecondary; Geography Teachers, Postsecondary; Graduate Teaching Assistants; Health Specialties Teachers, Postsecondary; History Teachers, Postsecondary; Home Economics Teachers, Postsecondary; Kindergarten Teachers, Except Special Education; Law Teachers, Postsecondary; Librarians; Library Assistants, Clerical; Library Science Teachers, Postsecondary; Library Technicians; Mathematical Science Teachers, Postsecondary;

Middle School Teachers, Except Special and Vocational Education; Museum Technicians and Conservators; Nannies; Nursing Instructors and Teachers, Postsecondary; Personal Financial Advisors; Philosophy and Religion Teachers, Postsecondary; Physics Teachers, Postsecondary; Political Science Teachers, Postsecondary; Postsecondary Teachers, All Other; Preschool Teachers, Except Special Education; Psychology Teachers, Postsecondary; Recreation and Fitness Studies Teachers, Postsecondary; Secondary School Teachers, Except Special and Vocational Education; Self-Enrichment Education Teachers; Social Sciences Teachers, Postsecondary, All Other; Social Work Teachers, Postsecondary; Sociology Teachers, Postsecondary; Special Education Teachers, Middle School; Special Education Teachers, Preschool, Kindergarten, and Elementary School; Special Education Teachers, Secondary School; Teacher Assistants; Teachers and Instructors, All Other; Vocational Education Teachers, Postsecondary; Vocational Education Teachers, Middle School; Vocational Education Teachers, Secondary School.

EDUCATION/TRAINING PROGRAM(S)— No data available. **RELATED KNOWLEDGE/ COURSES**—Education and Training; Customer and Personal Service; Communications and Media; Computers and Electronics; Telecommunications; Clerical Studies.

Auditors

- Personality Code: CE
- Growth: 19.5%
- Annual Job Openings: 119,000
- Annual Earnings: $49,060
- Education/Training Required: Bachelor's degree
- Self-Employed: 10.6%
- Part-Time: 8.8%

Examine and analyze accounting records to determine financial status of establishment and prepare financial reports concerning operating procedures. Collect and analyze data to detect deficient controls, duplicated effort, extravagance, fraud, or non-compliance with laws, regulations, and management policies. Report to management about asset utilization and audit results, and recommend changes in operations and financial activities. Prepare detailed reports on audit findings. Review data about material assets, net worth, liabilities, capital stock, surplus, income, and expenditures. Inspect account books and accounting systems for efficiency, effectiveness, and use of accepted accounting procedures to record transactions. Examine and evaluate financial and information systems, recommending controls to ensure system reliability and data integrity. Supervise auditing of establishments, and determine scope of investigation required. Prepare, analyze, and verify annual reports, financial statements, and other records, using accepted accounting and statistical procedures to assess financial condition and facilitate financial planning. Confer with company officials about financial and regulatory matters. Inspect cash on hand, notes receivable and payable, negotiable securities, and canceled checks to confirm records are accurate. Examine inventory to verify journal and ledger entries. Examine whether the organization's objectives are reflected in its management activities, and whether employees understand the objectives. Examine records and interview workers to ensure recording of transactions and compliance with laws and regulations. Direct activities of personnel engaged in filing, recording, compiling and transmitting financial records. Produce up-to-the-minute information, using internal computer systems, to allow management to base decisions on actual, not historical, data. Conduct pre-implementation audits to determine if systems and programs under development will work as planned. **SKILLS**—Management of Financial Resources; Time Management; Instructing; Negotiation; Service Orientation; Writing; Critical Thinking; Persuasion.

GOE—Interest Area: 13. General Management and Support. **Work Group:** 13.02. Management Support. **Other Jobs in This Work Group:** Accountants; Accountants and Auditors; Appraisers and Assessors of Real Estate; Appraisers, Real Estate; Assessors; Budget Analysts; Business Operations Specialists, All Other; Claims Adjusters, Examiners, and Investigators; Claims Examiners, Property and Casualty Insurance; Compensation, Benefits, and Job Analysis Specialists; Cost Estimators; Credit Analysts; Employment Interviewers, Private or Public Employment Service; Employment, Recruitment, and Placement Specialists; Financial Analysts; Human Resources, Training, and Labor Relations Specialists, All Other; Insurance Adjusters, Examiners, and Investigators; Insurance Appraisers, Auto Damage; Insurance Underwriters; Loan Counselors; Loan Officers; Logisticians; Management Analysts; Market Research Analysts; Personnel Recruiters; Purchasing Agents and Buyers, Farm Products; Purchasing Agents, Except Wholesale, Retail, and Farm Products; Tax Examiners, Collectors, and Revenue Agents; Training and Development Specialists; Wholesale and Retail Buyers, Except Farm Products.

EDUCATION/TRAINING PROGRAM(S)— Accounting; Accounting and Business/Management; Accounting and Computer Science; Accounting and Finance; Auditing; Taxation. **RELATED KNOWLEDGE/COURSES**—Economics and Accounting; Customer and Personal Service; Mathematics; Sales and Marketing; Law and Government; Computers and Electronics.

Bill and Account Collectors

- Personality Code: CE
- Growth: 24.5%
- Annual Job Openings: 76,000
- Annual Earnings: $27,000
- Education/Training Required: Short-term on-the-job training
- Self-Employed: 0.9%
- Part-Time: 11.3%

Locate and notify customers of delinquent accounts by mail, telephone, or personal visit to solicit payment. Duties include receiving payment and posting amount to customer's account; preparing statements to credit department if customer fails to respond; initiating repossession proceedings or service disconnection; keeping records of collection and status of accounts. Receive payments and post amounts paid to customer accounts. Locate and monitor overdue accounts, using computers and a variety of automated systems. Record information about financial status of customers and status of collection efforts. Locate and notify customers of delinquent accounts by mail, telephone, or personal visits in order to solicit payment. Confer with customers by telephone or in person to determine reasons for overdue payments and to review the terms of sales, service, or credit contracts. Advise customers of necessary actions and strategies for debt repayment. Persuade customers to pay amounts due on credit accounts, damage claims, or nonpayable checks, or to return merchandise. Sort and file correspondence, and perform miscellaneous clerical duties such as answering correspondence and writing reports. Perform various administrative functions for assigned accounts, such as recording address changes and purging the records of deceased customers. Arrange for debt repayment or establish repayment schedules, based on customers' financial situations. Negotiate credit extensions when necessary. Trace delinquent customers to new addresses by inquiring at post offices, telephone companies, credit bureaus, or through the questioning of neighbors. Notify credit departments, order merchandise repossession or service disconnection, and turn over account records to attorneys when customers fail to respond to collection attempts. SKILLS—Social Perceptiveness; Time Management; Management of Financial Resources; Service Orientation; Persuasion; Management of Personnel Resources; Speaking; Instructing; Judgment and Decision Making.

GOE—Interest Area: 09. Business Detail. Work Group: 09.05. Customer Service. Other Jobs in This Work Group: Adjustment Clerks; Cashiers; Counter and Rental Clerks; Customer Service Representatives; Customer Service Representatives, Utilities; Gaming Cage Workers; Gaming Change Persons and Booth Cashiers; New Accounts Clerks; Order Clerks; Receptionists and Information Clerks; Tellers; Travel Clerks.

EDUCATION/TRAINING PROGRAM(S)—Banking and Financial Support Services. RELATED KNOWLEDGE/COURSES—Clerical Studies; Customer and Personal Service; Computers and Electronics; Law and Government; Economics and Accounting; Personnel and Human Resources.

Billing, Cost, and Rate Clerks

- Personality Code: CE
- Growth: 7.9%
- Annual Job Openings: 78,000
- Annual Earnings: $26,290
- Education/Training Required: Short-term on-the-job training
- Self-Employed: 2.2%
- Part-Time: 16.1%

Compile data, compute fees and charges, and prepare invoices for billing purposes. Duties include computing costs and calculating rates for goods, services, and shipment of goods; posting data; and keeping other relevant records. May involve use of computer or typewriter, calculator, and adding and bookkeeping machines. Verify accuracy of billing data and revise any errors. Operate typing, adding, calculating, and billing machines. Prepare itemized statements, bills, or invoices; and record amounts due for items purchased or services rendered. Review documents such as purchase orders, sales tickets, charge slips, or hospital records in order to compute fees and charges due. Perform bookkeeping work, including posting data and keeping other records concerning costs of goods and services and the shipment of goods. Keep records of invoices and support documents. Resolve discrepancies in accounting records. Type billing documents, shipping labels, credit memorandums, and credit forms, using typewriters or computers. Contact customers in order to obtain or relay account information. Compute credit terms, discounts, shipment charges, and rates for goods and services in order to complete billing documents. Answer mail and telephone inquiries regarding rates, routing, and procedures. Track accumulated hours and dollar amounts charged to each client job in order to calculate client fees for professional services such as legal and accounting services. Review compiled data on operating costs and revenues in order to set rates. Compile reports of cost factors, such as labor, production, storage, and equipment. Consult sources such as rate books, manuals, and insurance company representatives in order to determine specific charges and information such as rules, regulations, and government tax and tariff information. Update manuals when rates, rules, or regulations are amended. Estimate market value of products or services. **SKILLS**—Instructing; Service Orientation; Active Listening; Social Perceptiveness; Writing; Reading Comprehension; Negotiation; Learning Strategies.

GOE—Interest Area: 09. Business Detail. **Work Group:** 09.03. Bookkeeping, Auditing, and Accounting. **Other Jobs in This Work Group:** Billing and Posting Clerks and Machine Operators; Bookkeeping, Accounting, and Auditing Clerks; Brokerage Clerks; Office and Administrative Support Workers, All Other; Payroll and Timekeeping Clerks; Statement Clerks; Tax Preparers.

EDUCATION/TRAINING PROGRAM(S)— Accounting Technology/Technician and Bookkeeping. **RELATED KNOWLEDGE/COURSES** —Clerical Studies; Computers and Electronics; Customer and Personal Service; Economics and Accounting; English Language; Mathematics.

Billing, Posting, and Calculating Machine Operators

- Personality Code: CR
- Growth: 7.9%
- Annual Job Openings: 78,000
- Annual Earnings: $26,290
- Education/Training Required: Short-term on-the-job training
- Self-Employed: 2.2%
- Part-Time: 16.1%

Operate machines that automatically perform mathematical processes, such as addition, subtraction, multiplication, and division, to calculate and record billing, accounting, statistical, and other numerical data. Duties include operating special billing machines to prepare statements, bills, and invoices, and operating bookkeeping machines to copy and post data, make computations, and compile records of transactions. Assign purchase order numbers to invoices, requisitions, and formal and informal bids. Bundle sorted documents to prepare those drawn on other banks for collection. Clean machines, and replace ribbons, film, and tape. Compile, code, and verify requisition, production, statistical, mileage, and other reports which require specialized knowledge in selecting the totals used. Compute and record inventory data from audio transcription, using transcribing machines and calculators. Maintain ledgers and registers, posting charges and refunds to individual funds, and computing and verifying balances. Prepare transmittal reports for changes to assessment and tax rolls, redemption file changes, and for warrants, deposits, and invoices. Sort and list items for proof or collection. Train other calculating machine operators, and review their work. Verify and post to ledgers purchase orders, reports of goods received, invoices, paid vouchers, and other information. Operate bookkeeping machines to copy and post data, make computations, and compile records of transactions. Balance and reconcile batch control totals with source documents or computer listings in order to locate errors, encode correct amounts, or prepare correction records. Compute monies due on personal and real property, inventories, redemption payments and other amounts, applying specialized knowledge of tax rates, formulas, interest rates, and other relevant information. Compute payroll and retirement amounts, applying knowledge of payroll deductions, actuarial tables, disability factors, and survivor allowances. Encode and add amounts of transaction documents, such as checks or money orders, using encoding machines. Enter into machines all information needed for bill generation. Observe operation of sorters to locate documents that machines cannot read, and manually record amounts of these documents. Reconcile and post receipts for cash received by various departments. Send completed bills to billing clerks for information verification. Sort and microfilm transaction documents, such as checks, using sorting machines. Transcribe data from office records, using specified forms, billing machines, and transcribing machines. **SKILLS**—Mathematics; Management of Financial Resources; Operation and Control; Operation Monitoring.

GOE—Interest Area: 09. Business Detail. **Work Group:** 09.09. Clerical Machine Operation. **Other Jobs in This Work Group:** Automatic Teller Machine Servicers; Computer Operators; Data Entry Keyers; Duplicating Machine Operators; Mail Clerks and Mail Machine Operators, Except Postal Service; Mail Machine Operators, Preparation and Handling; Office and Administrative Support Workers, All Other; Office Machine Operators, Except Computer; Postal Service Clerks; Typesetting and Composing Machine Operators and Tenders; Word Processors and Typists.

EDUCATION/TRAINING PROGRAM(S)— Accounting Technology/Technician and Bookkeeping. **RELATED KNOWLEDGE/COURSES** —Clerical Studies; Economics and Accounting; Computers and Electronics; Mathematics.

Bookkeeping, Accounting, and Auditing Clerks

- Personality Code: CE
- Growth: 3.0%
- Annual Job Openings: 274,000
- Annual Earnings: $27,760
- Education/Training Required: Moderate-term on-the-job training
- Self-Employed: 7.9%
- Part-Time: 25.0%

Compute, classify, and record numerical data to keep financial records complete. Perform any combination of routine calculating, posting, and verifying duties to obtain primary financial data for use in maintaining accounting records. May also check the accuracy of figures, calculations, and postings pertaining to business transactions recorded by other workers. Check figures, postings, and documents for correct entry, mathematical accuracy, and proper codes. Operate computers programmed with accounting software to record, store, and analyze information. Comply with federal, state, and company policies, procedures, and regulations. Debit, credit, and total accounts on computer spreadsheets and databases, using specialized accounting software. Classify, record, and summarize numerical and financial data in order to compile and keep financial records, using journals and ledgers or computers. Calculate, prepare, and issue bills, invoices, account statements, and other financial statements according to established procedures. Compile statistical, financial, accounting or auditing reports and tables pertaining to such matters as cash receipts, expenditures, accounts payable and receivable, and profits and losses. Code documents according to company procedures. Access computerized financial information to answer general questions as well as those related to specific accounts.

Operate 10-key calculators, typewriters, and copy machines to perform calculations and produce documents. Reconcile or note and report discrepancies found in records. Perform financial calculations such as amounts due, interest charges, balances, discounts, equity, and principal. Perform general office duties such as filing, answering telephones, and handling routine correspondence. Prepare bank deposits by compiling data from cashiers, verifying and balancing receipts, and sending cash, checks, or other forms of payment to banks. Receive, record, and bank cash, checks, and vouchers. Calculate and prepare checks for utilities, taxes, and other payments. Compare computer printouts to manually maintained journals in order to determine if they match. Reconcile records of bank transactions. Prepare trial balances of books. Monitor status of loans and accounts to ensure that payments are up to date. Transfer details from separate journals to general ledgers and/or data processing sheets. Compile budget data and documents, based on estimated revenues and expenses and previous budgets. **SKILLS**—Management of Financial Resources; Time Management; Instructing; Critical Thinking; Negotiation; Active Learning; Persuasion; Mathematics; Learning Strategies.

GOE—Interest Area: 09. Business Detail. **Work Group:** 09.03. Bookkeeping, Auditing, and Accounting. **Other Jobs in This Work Group:** Billing and Posting Clerks and Machine Operators; Billing, Cost, and Rate Clerks; Brokerage Clerks; Office and Administrative Support Workers, All Other; Payroll and Timekeeping Clerks; Statement Clerks; Tax Preparers.

EDUCATION/TRAINING PROGRAM(S)— Accounting and Related Services, Other; Accounting Technology/Technician and Bookkeeping. **RELATED KNOWLEDGE/COURSES**—Clerical Studies; Economics and Accounting; Computers and Electronics; Mathematics; Customer and Personal Service; English Language.

Budget Analysts

- Personality Code: CE
- Growth: 14.0%
- Annual Job Openings: 8,000
- Annual Earnings: $54,520
- Education/Training Required: Bachelor's degree
- Self-Employed: 0%
- Part-Time: 4.7%

Examine budget estimates for completeness, accuracy, and conformance with procedures and regulations. Analyze budgeting and accounting reports for the purpose of maintaining expenditure controls. Analyze monthly department budgeting and accounting reports to maintain expenditure controls. Direct the preparation of regular and special budget reports. Consult with managers to ensure that budget adjustments are made in accordance with program changes. Match appropriations for specific programs with appropriations for broader programs, including items for emergency funds. Provide advice and technical assistance with cost analysis, fiscal allocation, and budget preparation. Summarize budgets and submit recommendations for the approval or disapproval of funds requests. Seek new ways to improve efficiency and increase profits. Review operating budgets to analyze trends affecting budget needs. Examine budget estimates for completeness, accuracy, and conformance with procedures and regulations. Perform cost-benefits analyses to compare operating programs, review financial requests, and explore alternative financing methods. Interpret budget directives and establish policies for carrying out directives. Compile and analyze accounting records and other data to determine the financial resources required to implement a program. Testify before examining and fund-granting authorities, clarifying and promoting the proposed budgets. **SKILLS**—Management of Financial Resources; Operations Analysis; Mathematics; Service Orientation; Negotiation; Time Management; Active Learning; Monitoring.

GOE—Interest Area: 13. General Management and Support. **Work Group:** 13.02. Management Support. **Other Jobs in This Work Group:** Accountants; Accountants and Auditors; Appraisers and Assessors of Real Estate; Appraisers, Real Estate; Assessors; Auditors; Business Operations Specialists, All Other; Claims Adjusters, Examiners, and Investigators; Claims Examiners, Property and Casualty Insurance; Compensation, Benefits, and Job Analysis Specialists; Cost Estimators; Credit Analysts; Employment Interviewers, Private or Public Employment Service; Employment, Recruitment, and Placement Specialists; Financial Analysts; Human Resources, Training, and Labor Relations Specialists, All Other; Insurance Adjusters, Examiners, and Investigators; Insurance Appraisers, Auto Damage; Insurance Underwriters; Loan Counselors; Loan Officers; Logisticians; Management Analysts; Market Research Analysts; Personnel Recruiters; Purchasing Agents and Buyers, Farm Products; Purchasing Agents, Except Wholesale, Retail, and Farm Products; Tax Examiners, Collectors, and Revenue Agents; Training and Development Specialists; Wholesale and Retail Buyers, Except Farm Products.

EDUCATION/TRAINING PROGRAM(S)— Accounting; Finance, General. **RELATED KNOWLEDGE/COURSES—**Economics and Accounting; Administration and Management; Clerical Studies; Computers and Electronics; Mathematics; English Language.

Cargo and Freight Agents

- Personality Code: CR
- Growth: 15.5%
- Annual Job Openings: 8,000
- Annual Earnings: $31,990
- Education/Training Required: Moderate-term on-the-job training
- Self-Employed: 0.1%
- Part-Time: 5.5%

Expedite and route movement of incoming and outgoing cargo and freight shipments in airline, train, and trucking terminals, and shipping docks. Take orders from customers and arrange pickup of freight and cargo for delivery to loading platform. Prepare and examine bills of lading to determine shipping charges and tariffs. Advise clients on transportation and payment methods. Arrange insurance coverage for goods. Check import/export documentation to determine cargo contents, and classify goods into different fee or tariff groups, using a tariff coding system. Contact vendors and/or claims adjustment departments in order to resolve problems with shipments, or contact service depots to arrange for repairs. Determine method of shipment, and prepare bills of lading, invoices, and other shipping documents. Direct delivery trucks to shipping doors or designated marshalling areas, and help load and unload goods safely. Direct or participate in cargo loading in order to ensure completeness of load and even distribution of weight. Enter shipping information into a computer by hand or by using a hand-held scanner that reads bar codes on goods. Estimate freight or postal rates, and record shipment costs and weights. Inspect and count items received and check them against invoices or other documents, recording shortages and rejecting damaged goods. Keep records of all goods shipped, received, and stored. Negotiate and arrange transport of goods with shipping or freight companies. Notify consignees, passengers, or customers of the arrival of freight or baggage, and arrange for delivery. Retrieve stored items and trace lost shipments as necessary. Route received goods to first available flight or to appropriate storage areas or departments, using forklifts, handtrucks, or other equipment. Assemble containers and crates used to transport items such as machines or vehicles. Attach address labels, identification codes, and shipping instructions to containers. Coordinate and supervise activities of workers engaged in packing and shipping merchandise. Inspect trucks and vans to ensure cleanliness when shipping such items as grain, flour, and milk. Install straps, braces, and padding to loads in order to prevent shifting or damage during shipment. Maintain a supply of packing materials. Obtain flight numbers, airplane numbers, and names of crew members from dispatchers and record data on airplane flight papers. Open cargo containers and unwrap contents, using steel cutters, crowbars, or other hand tools. **SKILLS**—Service Orientation; Operation and Control; Coordination.

GOE—Interest Area: 09. Business Detail. **Work Group:** 09.08. Records and Materials Processing. **Other Jobs in This Work Group:** Couriers and Messengers; Mail Clerks, Except Mail Machine Operators and Postal Service; Marking Clerks; Office and Administrative Support Workers, All Other; Order Fillers, Wholesale and Retail Sales; Postal Service Mail Carriers; Postal Service Mail Sorters, Processors, and Processing Machine Operators; Shipping, Receiving, and Traffic Clerks; Stock Clerks and Order Fillers; Stock Clerks—Stockroom, Warehouse, or Storage Yard; Weighers, Measurers, Checkers, and Samplers, Recordkeeping.

EDUCATION/TRAINING PROGRAM(S)— General Office Occupations and Clerical Services. **RELATED KNOWLEDGE/COURSES**—Transportation; Geography; Clerical Studies; Telecommunications; Customer and Personal Service.

Cartographers and Photogrammetrists

- Personality Code: CR
- Growth: 15.1%
- Annual Job Openings: 1,000
- Annual Earnings: $44,170
- Education/Training Required: Bachelor's degree
- Self-Employed: 3.3%
- Part-Time: 7.7%

Collect, analyze, and interpret geographic information provided by geodetic surveys, aerial photographs, and satellite data. Research, study, and prepare maps and other spatial data in digital or graphic form for legal, social, political, educational, and design purposes. May work with Geographic Information Systems (GIS). May design and evaluate algorithms, data structures, and user interfaces for GIS and mapping systems. Identify, scale, and orient geodetic points, elevations, and other planimetric or topographic features, applying standard mathematical formulas. Collect information about specific features of the Earth, using aerial photography and other digital remote sensing techniques. Revise existing maps and charts, making all necessary corrections and adjustments. Compile data required for map preparation, including aerial photographs, survey notes, records, reports, and original maps. Inspect final compositions in order to ensure completeness and accuracy. Determine map content and layout, as well as production specifications such as scale, size, projection, and colors, and direct production in order to ensure that specifications are followed. Examine and analyze data from ground surveys, reports, aerial photographs, and satellite images in order to prepare topographic maps, aerial-photograph mosaics, and related charts. Select aerial photographic and remote sensing techniques and plotting equipment needed to meet required standards of accuracy. Delineate aerial pho-

Conventional—C

tographic detail, such as control points, hydrography, topography, and cultural features, using precision stereoplotting apparatus or drafting instruments. Build and update digital databases. Prepare and alter trace maps, charts, tables, detailed drawings, and three-dimensional optical models of terrain, using stereoscopic plotting and computer graphics equipment. Determine guidelines that specify which source material is acceptable for use. Study legal records in order to establish boundaries of local, national, and international properties. Travel over photographed areas in order to observe, identify, record, and verify all relevant features. **SKILLS**—Active Learning; Technology Design; Science; Mathematics; Troubleshooting; Critical Thinking; Reading Comprehension; Complex Problem Solving.

GOE—**Interest Area:** 02. Science, Math, and Engineering. **Work Group:** 02.08. Engineering Technology. **Other Jobs in This Work Group:** Aerospace Engineering and Operations Technicians; Architectural and Civil Drafters; Architectural Drafters; Calibration and Instrumentation Technicians; Civil Drafters; Civil Engineering Technicians; Construction and Building Inspectors; Drafters, All Other; Electrical and Electronic Engineering Technicians; Electrical and Electronics Drafters; Electrical Drafters; Electrical Engineering Technicians; Electro-Mechanical Technicians; Electronic Drafters; Electronics Engineering Technicians; Engineering Technicians, Except Drafters, All Other; Environmental Engineering Technicians; Industrial Engineering Technicians; Mapping Technicians; Mechanical Drafters; Mechanical Engineering Technicians; Numerical Tool and Process Control Programmers; Pressure Vessel Inspectors; Surveying and Mapping Technicians; Surveying Technicians; Surveyors.

EDUCATION/TRAINING PROGRAM(S)—Cartography; Surveying Technology/Surveying. **RELATED KNOWLEDGE/COURSES**—Geography; Design; Computers and Electronics; Engineering and Technology; Mathematics; Production and Processing.

Cashiers

- Personality Code: CE
- Growth: 13.2%
- Annual Job Openings: 1,221,000
- Annual Earnings: $15,760
- Education/Training Required: Short-term on-the-job training
- Self-Employed: 1.0%
- Part-Time: 44.8%

Receive and disburse money in establishments other than financial institutions. Usually involves use of electronic scanners, cash registers, or related equipment. Often involved in processing credit or debit card transactions and validating checks. Receive payment by cash, check, credit cards, vouchers, or automatic debits. Issue receipts, refunds, credits, or change due to customers. Count money in cash drawers at the beginning of shifts to ensure that amounts are correct and that there is adequate change. Greet customers entering establishments. Maintain clean and orderly checkout areas. Establish or identify prices of goods, services or admission, and tabulate bills using calculators, cash registers, or optical price scanners. Issue trading stamps, and redeem food stamps and coupons. Resolve customer complaints. Answer customers' questions, and provide information on procedures or policies. Cash checks for customers. Weigh items sold by weight in order to determine prices. Calculate total payments received during a time period, and reconcile this with total sales. Compute and record totals of transactions. Sell tickets and other items to customers. Keep periodic balance sheets of amounts and numbers of transactions. Bag, box, wrap, or gift-wrap merchandise, and prepare packages for shipment. Sort, count, and wrap currency and coins. Process merchandise returns and exchanges. Pay company bills by cash, vouchers, or checks. Request information or assistance using paging systems. Stock shelves, and mark prices on shelves and items. Compile and maintain non-monetary reports and records. Monitor checkout stations to ensure that they have adequate cash available and that they are staffed appropriately. Post charges against guests' or patients' accounts. Offer customers carry-out service at the completion of transactions. **SKILLS**—Social Perceptiveness; Service Orientation; Learning Strategies; Management of Personnel Resources; Instructing; Negotiation; Persuasion; Systems Analysis.

GOE—**Interest Area:** 09. Business Detail. **Work Group:** 09.05. Customer Service. **Other Jobs in This Work Group:** Adjustment Clerks; Bill and Account Collectors; Counter and Rental Clerks; Customer Service Representatives; Customer Service Representatives, Utilities; Gaming Cage Workers; Gaming Change Persons and Booth Cashiers; New Accounts Clerks; Order Clerks; Receptionists and Information Clerks; Tellers; Travel Clerks.

EDUCATION/TRAINING PROGRAM(S)— Retailing and Retail Operations. **RELATED KNOWLEDGE/COURSES**—Customer and Personal Service; Education and Training; Foreign Language; English Language; Administration and Management; Mathematics.

Claims Examiners, Property and Casualty Insurance

- Personality Code: CE
- Growth: 14.2%
- Annual Job Openings: 31,000
- Annual Earnings: $44,040
- Education/Training Required: Long-term on-the-job training
- Self-Employed: 1.9%
- Part-Time: 4.9%

Review settled insurance claims to determine that payments and settlements have been made in accordance with company practices and procedures. Report overpayments, underpayments, and other irregularities. Confer with legal counsel on claims requiring litigation. Resolve complex, severe exposure claims, using high service oriented file handling. Supervise claims adjusters to ensure that adjusters have followed proper methods. Verify and analyze data used in settling claims to ensure that claims are valid and that settlements are made according to company practices and procedures. Conduct detailed bill reviews to implement sound litigation management and expense control. Enter claim payments, reserves and new claims on computer system, inputting concise yet sufficient file documentation. Maintain claim files, such as records of settled claims and an inventory of claims requiring detailed analysis. Prepare reports to be submitted to company's data processing department. Adjust reserves and provide reserve recommendations to ensure reserving activities consistent with corporate policies. Communicate with reinsurance brokers to obtain information necessary for processing claims. Confer with legal counsel on claims requiring litigation. Contact and/or interview claimants, doctors, medical specialists, or employers to get additional information. Examine claims investigated by insurance adjusters, further investigating questionable claims to determine whether to authorize payments. Investigate, evaluate and settle claims, applying technical knowledge and human relations skills to effect fair and prompt disposal of cases and to contribute to a reduced loss ratio. Pay and process claims within designated authority level. Present cases and participate in their discussion at claim committee meetings. Report overpayments, underpayments, and other irregularities. **SKILLS**—Mathematics; Reading Comprehension; Writing; Judgment and Decision Making; Monitoring; Critical Thinking; Systems Evaluation; Speaking.

GOE—**Interest Area:** 13. General Management and Support. **Work Group:** 13.02. Management

Support. **Other Jobs in This Work Group:** Accountants; Accountants and Auditors; Appraisers and Assessors of Real Estate; Appraisers, Real Estate; Assessors; Auditors; Budget Analysts; Business Operations Specialists, All Other; Claims Adjusters, Examiners, and Investigators; Compensation, Benefits, and Job Analysis Specialists; Cost Estimators; Credit Analysts; Employment Interviewers, Private or Public Employment Service; Employment, Recruitment, and Placement Specialists; Financial Analysts; Human Resources, Training, and Labor Relations Specialists, All Other; Insurance Adjusters, Examiners, and Investigators; Insurance Appraisers, Auto Damage; Insurance Underwriters; Loan Counselors; Loan Officers; Logisticians; Management Analysts; Market Research Analysts; Personnel Recruiters; Purchasing Agents and Buyers, Farm Products; Purchasing Agents, Except Wholesale, Retail, and Farm Products; Tax Examiners, Collectors, and Revenue Agents; Training and Development Specialists; Wholesale and Retail Buyers, Except Farm Products.

EDUCATION/TRAINING PROGRAM(S)— Health/Medical Claims Examiner; Insurance. **RELATED KNOWLEDGE/COURSES—**Law and Government; Mathematics; Economics and Accounting; Communications and Media.

Construction and Building Inspectors

- Personality Code: CR
- Growth: 13.8%
- Annual Job Openings: 10,000
- Annual Earnings: $42,650
- Education/Training Required: Work experience in a related occupation
- Self-Employed: 8.1%
- Part-Time: 5.9%

Inspect structures using engineering skills to determine structural soundness and compliance with specifications, building codes, and other regulations. Inspections may be general in nature or may be limited to a specific area, such as electrical systems or plumbing. Use survey instruments, metering devices, tape measures, and test equipment, such as concrete strength measurers, to perform inspections. Inspect bridges, dams, highways, buildings, wiring, plumbing, electrical circuits, sewers, heating systems, and foundations during and after construction for structural quality, general safety and conformance to specifications and codes. Maintain daily logs and supplement inspection records with photographs. Review and interpret plans, blueprints, site layouts, specifications, and construction methods to ensure compliance to legal requirements and safety regulations. Inspect and monitor construction sites to ensure adherence to safety standards, building codes, and specifications. Measure dimensions and verify level, alignment, and elevation of structures and fixtures to ensure compliance to building plans and codes. Issue violation notices and stop-work orders, conferring with owners, violators, and authorities to explain regulations and recommend rectifications. Issue permits for construction, relocation, demolition and occupancy. Approve and sign plans that meet required specifications. Compute estimates of work completed or of needed renovations or upgrades, and approve payment for contractors. Monitor installation of plumbing, wiring, equipment, and appliances to ensure that installation is performed properly and is in compliance with applicable regulations. Examine lifting and conveying devices, such as elevators, escalators, moving sidewalks, lifts and hoists, inclined railways, ski lifts, and amusement rides to ensure safety and proper functioning. Train, direct and supervise other construction inspectors. Evaluate premises for cleanliness, including proper garbage disposal and lack of vermin infestation. **SKILLS—**Persuasion; Time Management; Mathematics; Coordination; Active Learning; Instructing; Negotiation; Critical Thinking.

GOE—**Interest Area:** 02. Science, Math, and Engineering. **Work Group:** 02.08. Engineering Technology. **Other Jobs in This Work Group:** Aerospace Engineering and Operations Technicians; Architectural and Civil Drafters; Architectural Drafters; Calibration and Instrumentation Technicians; Cartographers and Photogrammetrists; Civil Drafters; Civil Engineering Technicians; Drafters, All Other; Electrical and Electronic Engineering Technicians; Electrical and Electronics Drafters; Electrical Drafters; Electrical Engineering Technicians; Electro-Mechanical Technicians; Electronic Drafters; Electronics Engineering Technicians; Engineering Technicians, Except Drafters, All Other; Environmental Engineering Technicians; Industrial Engineering Technicians; Mapping Technicians; Mechanical Drafters; Mechanical Engineering Technicians; Numerical Tool and Process Control Programmers; Pressure Vessel Inspectors; Surveying and Mapping Technicians; Surveying Technicians; Surveyors.

EDUCATION/TRAINING PROGRAM(S)—Building/Home/Construction Inspection/Inspector. RELATED KNOWLEDGE/COURSES—Building and Construction; Design; Engineering and Technology; Public Safety and Security; Customer and Personal Service; Administration and Management; Computers and Electronics.

Cost Estimators

- Personality Code: CE
- Growth: 18.6%
- Annual Job Openings: 25,000
- Annual Earnings: $48,290
- Education/Training Required: Bachelor's degree
- Self-Employed: 1.7%
- Part-Time: 5.9%

Prepare cost estimates for product manufacturing, construction projects, or services to aid management in bidding on or determining price of product or service. May specialize according to particular service performed or type of product manufactured. Analyze blueprints and other documentation to prepare time, cost, materials, and labor estimates. Assess cost effectiveness of products, projects or services, tracking actual costs relative to bids as the project develops. Consult with clients, vendors, personnel in other departments or construction foremen to discuss and formulate estimates and resolve issues. Confer with engineers, architects, owners, contractors and subcontractors on changes and adjustments to cost estimates. Prepare estimates used by management for purposes such as planning, organizing, and scheduling work. Prepare estimates for use in selecting vendors or subcontractors. Review material and labor requirements, to decide whether it is more cost-effective to produce or purchase components. Prepare cost and expenditure statements and other necessary documentation at regular intervals for the duration of the project. Prepare and maintain a directory of suppliers, contractors and subcontractors. Set up cost monitoring and reporting systems and procedures. Establish and maintain tendering process, and conduct negotiations. Conduct special studies to develop and establish standard hour and related cost data or to effect cost reduction. Visit site and record information about access, drainage and topography, and availability of services such as water and electricity. SKILLS—Management of Financial Resources; Negotiation; Coordination; Management of Personnel Resources; Persuasion; Time Management; Mathematics; Active Listening.

GOE—**Interest Area:** 13. General Management and Support. **Work Group:** 13.02. Management Support. **Other Jobs in This Work Group:** Accountants; Accountants and Auditors; Appraisers and Assessors of Real Estate; Appraisers, Real Estate; Assessors; Auditors; Budget Analysts; Business Operations Specialists, All Other; Claims Adjusters, Examiners, and Investigators; Claims Examiners, Property and Casu-

Conventional–C

alty Insurance; Compensation, Benefits, and Job Analysis Specialists; Credit Analysts; Employment Interviewers, Private or Public Employment Service; Employment, Recruitment, and Placement Specialists; Financial Analysts; Human Resources, Training, and Labor Relations Specialists, All Other; Insurance Adjusters, Examiners, and Investigators; Insurance Appraisers, Auto Damage; Insurance Underwriters; Loan Counselors; Loan Officers; Logisticians; Management Analysts; Market Research Analysts; Personnel Recruiters; Purchasing Agents and Buyers, Farm Products; Purchasing Agents, Except Wholesale, Retail, and Farm Products; Tax Examiners, Collectors, and Revenue Agents; Training and Development Specialists; Wholesale and Retail Buyers, Except Farm Products.

EDUCATION/TRAINING PROGRAM(S)— Business Administration and Management, General; Business/Commerce, General; Construction Engineering; Construction Engineering Technology/ Technician; Manufacturing Engineering; Materials Engineering; Mechanical Engineering. **RELATED KNOWLEDGE/COURSES—**Administration and Management; Sales and Marketing; Production and Processing; Clerical Studies; Economics and Accounting; Personnel and Human Resources; Mathematics.

Counter and Rental Clerks

- Personality Code: CE
- Growth: 26.3%
- Annual Job Openings: 144,000
- Annual Earnings: $17,640
- Education/Training Required: Short-term on-the-job training
- Self-Employed: 1.3%
- Part-Time: 35.9%

Receive orders for repairs, rentals, and services. May describe available options, compute cost, and accept payment. Compute charges for merchandise or services and receive payments. Prepare merchandise for display, or for purchase or rental. Recommend and provide advice on a wide variety of products and services. Answer telephones to provide information and receive orders. Greet customers and discuss the type, quality and quantity of merchandise sought for rental. Keep records of transactions, and of the number of customers entering an establishment. Prepare rental forms, obtaining customer signature and other information, such as required licenses. Receive, examine, and tag articles to be altered, cleaned, stored, or repaired. Inspect and adjust rental items to meet needs of customer. Explain rental fees, policies and procedures. Reserve items for requested times and keep records of items rented. Receive orders for services, such as rentals, repairs, dry cleaning, and storage. Rent items, arrange for provision of services to customers and accept returns. Provide information about rental items, such as availability, operation or description. Advise customers on use and care of merchandise. **SKILLS—**Instructing; Service Orientation.

GOE—Interest Area: 09. Business Detail. **Work Group:** 09.05. Customer Service. **Other Jobs in This Work Group:** Adjustment Clerks; Bill and Account Collectors; Cashiers; Customer Service Representatives; Customer Service Representatives, Utilities; Gaming Cage Workers; Gaming Change Persons and Booth Cashiers; New Accounts Clerks; Order Clerks; Receptionists and Information Clerks; Tellers; Travel Clerks.

EDUCATION/TRAINING PROGRAM(S)— Selling Skills and Sales Operations. **RELATED KNOWLEDGE/COURSES—**Administration and Management; Food Production; Sales and Marketing; Personnel and Human Resources; English Language; Clerical Studies; Mathematics.

Court Clerks

- Personality Code: CE
- Growth: 12.3%
- Annual Job Openings: 14,000
- Annual Earnings: $27,450
- Education/Training Required: Short-term on-the-job training
- Self-Employed: 2.6%
- Part-Time: 8.3%

Perform clerical duties in court of law; prepare docket of cases to be called; secure information for judges; and contact witnesses, attorneys, and litigants to obtain information for court. Prepare dockets or calendars of cases to be called, using typewriters or computers. Record case dispositions, court orders, and arrangements made for payment of court fees. Answer inquiries from the general public regarding judicial procedures, court appearances, trial dates, adjournments, outstanding warrants, summonses, subpoenas, witness fees, and payment of fines. Prepare and issue orders of the court, including probation orders, release documentation, sentencing information, and summonses. Prepare documents recording the outcomes of court proceedings. Instruct parties about timing of court appearances. Explain procedures or forms to parties in cases or to the general public. Search files, and contact witnesses, attorneys, and litigants, in order to obtain information for the court. Follow procedures to secure courtrooms and exhibits such as money, drugs, and weapons. Amend indictments when necessary, and endorse indictments with pertinent information. Read charges and related information to the court and, if necessary, record defendants' pleas. Swear in jury members, interpreters, witnesses and defendants. Collect court fees or fines, and record amounts collected. Direct support staff in handling of paperwork processed by clerks' offices. Prepare and mark all applicable court exhibits and evidence. Examine legal documents submitted to courts for adherence to laws or court procedures. Record court proceedings, using recording equipment, or record minutes of court proceedings using stenotype machines or shorthand. Prepare courtrooms with paper, pens, water, easels, and electronic equipment, and ensure that recording equipment is working. Conduct roll calls, and poll jurors. Open courts, calling them to order and announcing judges. Meet with judges, lawyers, parole officers, police, and social agency officials in order to coordinate the functions of the court. **SKILLS**—Instructing; Service Orientation; Active Listening; Coordination; Critical Thinking; Learning Strategies; Time Management; Writing.

GOE—Interest Area: 09. Business Detail. **Work Group:** 09.02. Administrative Detail. **Other Jobs in This Work Group:** Claims Takers, Unemployment Benefits; Court, Municipal, and License Clerks; Eligibility Interviewers, Government Programs; Executive Secretaries and Administrative Assistants; Interviewers, Except Eligibility and Loan; Legal Secretaries; License Clerks; Loan Interviewers and Clerks; Medical Secretaries; Municipal Clerks; Office and Administrative Support Workers, All Other; Secretaries, Except Legal, Medical, and Executive; Welfare Eligibility Workers and Interviewers.

EDUCATION/TRAINING PROGRAM(S)—General Office Occupations and Clerical Services. **RELATED KNOWLEDGE/COURSES**—Clerical Studies; Customer and Personal Service; Law and Government; Computers and Electronics; English Language; Public Safety and Security.

Credit Analysts

- Personality Code: CE
- Growth: 18.7%
- Annual Job Openings: 9,000
- Annual Earnings: $45,020
- Education/Training Required: Bachelor's degree
- Self-Employed: 0%
- Part-Time: 4.1%

Conventional—C

Analyze current credit data and financial statements of individuals or firms to determine the degree of risk involved in extending credit or lending money. Prepare reports with this credit information for use in decision-making. Analyze credit data and financial statements to determine the degree of risk involved in extending credit or lending money. Prepare reports that include the degree of risk involved in extending credit or lending money. Evaluate customer records and recommend payment plans based on earnings, savings data, payment history, and purchase activity. Confer with credit association and other business representatives to exchange credit information. Complete loan applications, including credit analyses and summaries of loan requests, and submit to loan committees for approval. Generate financial ratios, using computer programs, to evaluate customers' financial status. Review individual or commercial customer files to identify and select delinquent accounts for collection. Compare liquidity, profitability, and credit histories of establishments being evaluated with those of similar establishments in the same industries and geographic locations. Consult with customers to resolve complaints and verify financial and credit transactions. Analyze financial data such as income growth, quality of management, and market share to determine expected profitability of loans. **SKILLS**—Speaking; Negotiation; Writing; Instructing; Social Perceptiveness; Active Listening; Monitoring; Service Orientation; Operations Analysis; Judgment and Decision Making.

GOE—Interest Area: 13. General Management and Support. **Work Group:** 13.02. Management Support. **Other Jobs in This Work Group:** Accountants; Accountants and Auditors; Appraisers and Assessors of Real Estate; Appraisers, Real Estate; Assessors; Auditors; Budget Analysts; Business Operations Specialists, All Other; Claims Adjusters, Examiners, and Investigators; Claims Examiners, Property and Casualty Insurance; Compensation, Benefits, and Job Analysis Specialists; Cost Estimators; Employment Interviewers, Private or Public Employment Service; Employment, Recruitment, and Placement Specialists; Financial Analysts; Human Resources, Training, and Labor Relations Specialists, All Other; Insurance Adjusters, Examiners, and Investigators; Insurance Appraisers, Auto Damage; Insurance Underwriters; Loan Counselors; Loan Officers; Logisticians; Management Analysts; Market Research Analysts; Personnel Recruiters; Purchasing Agents and Buyers, Farm Products; Purchasing Agents, Except Wholesale, Retail, and Farm Products; Tax Examiners, Collectors, and Revenue Agents; Training and Development Specialists; Wholesale and Retail Buyers, Except Farm Products.

EDUCATION/TRAINING PROGRAM(S)—Accounting; Credit Management; Finance, General. **RELATED KNOWLEDGE/COURSES**—Economics and Accounting; Clerical Studies; Mathematics; Customer and Personal Service; Administration and Management; English Language; Law and Government.

Customer Service Representatives, Utilities

- Personality Code: CE
- Growth: 24.3%
- Annual Job Openings: 419,000
- Annual Earnings: $26,500
- Education/Training Required: Moderate-term on-the-job training
- Self-Employed: 0.5%
- Part-Time: 14.8%

Interview applicants for water, gas, electric, or telephone service. Talk with customer by phone or in person and receive orders for installation, turn-on, discontinuance, or change in services. Determines charges for service requested and collects deposits.

Solicits sale of new or additional utility services. Resolves billing or service complaints and refers grievances to designated departments for investigation. Confers with customer by phone or in person to receive orders for installation, turn-on, discontinuance, or change in service. Completes contract forms, prepares change of address records, and issues discontinuance orders, using computer. **SKILLS—** Service Orientation; Active Listening; Speaking; Negotiation.

GOE—Interest Area: 09. Business Detail. **Work Group:** 09.05. Customer Service. **Other Jobs in This Work Group:** Adjustment Clerks; Bill and Account Collectors; Cashiers; Counter and Rental Clerks; Customer Service Representatives; Gaming Cage Workers; Gaming Change Persons and Booth Cashiers; New Accounts Clerks; Order Clerks; Receptionists and Information Clerks; Tellers; Travel Clerks.

EDUCATION/TRAINING PROGRAM(S)— Customer Service Support/Call Center/Teleservice Operation; Receptionist. **RELATED KNOWLEDGE/COURSES—**Sales and Marketing; Customer and Personal Service; Economics and Accounting; Clerical Studies; Telecommunications.

Dispatchers, Except Police, Fire, and Ambulance

- Personality Code: CR
- Growth: 14.4%
- Annual Job Openings: 28,000
- Annual Earnings: $30,390
- Education/Training Required: Moderate-term on-the-job training
- Self-Employed: 0.6%
- Part-Time: 8.5%

Schedule and dispatch workers, work crews, equipment, or service vehicles for conveyance of materials, freight, or passengers, or for normal installation, service, or emergency repairs rendered outside the place of business. Duties may include using radio, telephone, or computer to transmit assignments and compiling statistics and reports on work progress. Schedule and dispatch workers, work crews, equipment, or service vehicles to appropriate locations according to customer requests, specifications, or needs, using radios or telephones. Arrange for necessary repairs in order to restore service and schedules. Relay work orders, messages, and information to or from work crews, supervisors, and field inspectors using telephones or two-way radios. Confer with customers or supervising personnel in order to address questions, problems, and requests for service or equipment. Prepare daily work and run schedules. Receive or prepare work orders. Oversee all communications within specifically assigned territories. Monitor personnel and/or equipment locations and utilization in order to coordinate service and schedules. Record and maintain files and records of customer requests, work or services performed, charges, expenses, inventory, and other dispatch information. Determine types or amounts of equipment, vehicles, materials, or personnel required according to work orders or specifications. Advise personnel about traffic problems such as construction areas, accidents, congestion, weather conditions, and other hazards. Ensure timely and efficient movement of trains according to train orders and schedules. Order supplies and equipment, and issue them to personnel. **SKILLS—** Service Orientation; Operations Analysis; Management of Personnel Resources; Critical Thinking; Learning Strategies; Instructing; Social Perceptiveness; Troubleshooting; Time Management.

GOE—Interest Area: 09. Business Detail. **Work Group:** 09.06. Communications. **Other Jobs in This Work Group:** Central Office Operators; Communications Equipment Operators, All Other; Directory Assistance Operators; Police, Fire, and Ambulance Dispatchers; Switchboard Operators, Including Answering Service; Telephone Operators.

Conventional—D

EDUCATION/TRAINING PROGRAM(S)—No data available. **RELATED KNOWLEDGE/ COURSES**—Transportation; Clerical Studies; Public Safety and Security; Customer and Personal Service; Computers and Electronics; Geography; Communications and Media.

Executive Secretaries and Administrative Assistants

- Personality Code: CE
- Growth: 8.7%
- Annual Job Openings: 210,000
- Annual Earnings: $34,080
- Education/Training Required: Moderate-term on-the-job training
- Self-Employed: 1.6%
- Part-Time: 17.5%

Provide high-level administrative support by conducting research, preparing statistical reports, handling information requests, and performing clerical functions such as preparing correspondence, receiving visitors, arranging conference calls, and scheduling meetings. May also train and supervise lower-level clerical staff. Manage and maintain executives' schedules. Prepare invoices, reports, memos, letters, financial statements and other documents, using word processing, spreadsheet, database, and/or presentation software. Read and analyze incoming memos, submissions, and reports in order to determine their significance and plan their distribution. Open, sort, and distribute incoming correspondence, including faxes and email. File and retrieve corporate documents, records, and reports. Greet visitors and determine whether they should be given access to specific individuals. Prepare responses to correspondence containing routine inquiries. Perform general office duties such as ordering supplies, maintaining records management systems, and performing basic bookkeeping work. Prepare agendas and make arrangements for committee, board, and other meetings. Make travel arrangements for executives. Conduct research, compile data, and prepare papers for consideration and presentation by executives, committees and boards of directors. Compile, transcribe, and distribute minutes of meetings. Attend meetings in order to record minutes. Coordinate and direct office services, such as records and budget preparation, personnel, and housekeeping, in order to aid executives. Meet with individuals, special interest groups and others on behalf of executives, committees and boards of directors. Set up and oversee administrative policies and procedures for offices and/or organizations. Supervise and train other clerical staff. Review operating practices and procedures in order to determine whether improvements can be made in areas such as workflow, reporting procedures, or expenditures. Interpret administrative and operating policies and procedures for employees. **SKILLS**—Time Management; Active Listening; Writing; Speaking; Instructing; Service Orientation; Management of Financial Resources; Critical Thinking; Management of Material Resources.

GOE—Interest Area: 09. Business Detail. **Work Group:** 09.02. Administrative Detail. **Other Jobs in This Work Group:** Claims Takers, Unemployment Benefits; Court Clerks; Court, Municipal, and License Clerks; Eligibility Interviewers, Government Programs; Interviewers, Except Eligibility and Loan; Legal Secretaries; License Clerks; Loan Interviewers and Clerks; Medical Secretaries; Municipal Clerks; Office and Administrative Support Workers, All Other; Secretaries, Except Legal, Medical, and Executive; Welfare Eligibility Workers and Interviewers.

EDUCATION/TRAINING PROGRAM(S)—Administrative Assistant and Secretarial Science, General; Executive Assistant/Executive Secretary; Medical Administrative/Executive Assistant and Medical Secretary. **RELATED KNOWLEDGE/**

COURSES—Clerical Studies; Customer and Personal Service; English Language; Computers and Electronics; Communications and Media; Administration and Management; Personnel and Human Resources.

Freight Inspectors

- Personality Code: CR
- Growth: 7.7%
- Annual Job Openings: 5,000
- Annual Earnings: $49,590
- Education/Training Required: Work experience in a related occupation
- Self-Employed: 0.4%
- Part-Time: 3.2%

Inspect freight for proper storage according to specifications. Inspects shipment to ascertain that freight is securely braced and blocked. Observes loading of freight to ensure that crews comply with procedures. Monitors temperature and humidity of freight storage area. Records freight condition and handling, and notifies crews to reload freight or insert additional bracing or packing. Measures height and width of loads that will pass over bridges or through tunnels. Notifies workers of special treatment required for shipments. Prepares and submits report after trip. Posts warning signs on vehicles containing explosives or inflammatory or radioactive materials. **SKILLS**—Writing; Mathematics; Systems Analysis.

GOE—Interest Area: 07. Transportation. **Work Group:** 07.08. Support Work. **Other Jobs in This Work Group:** Railroad Yard Workers; Stevedores, Except Equipment Operators; Train Crew Members; Transportation Inspectors; Transportation Workers, All Other.

EDUCATION/TRAINING PROGRAM(S)— No data available. **RELATED KNOWLEDGE/ COURSES**—Transportation; Public Safety and Security; Production and Processing; Geography.

Hotel, Motel, and Resort Desk Clerks

- Personality Code: CE
- Growth: 23.9%
- Annual Job Openings: 46,000
- Annual Earnings: $17,450
- Education/Training Required: Short-term on-the-job training
- Self-Employed: 0%
- Part-Time: 27.2%

Accommodate hotel, motel, and resort patrons by registering and assigning rooms to guests, issuing room keys, transmitting and receiving messages, keeping records of occupied rooms and guests' accounts, making and confirming reservations, and presenting statements to and collecting payments from departing guests. Greet, register, and assign rooms to guests of hotels or motels. Verify customers' credit, and establish how the customer will pay for the accommodation. Keep records of room availability and guests' accounts, manually or using computers. Compute bills, collect payments, and make change for guests. Perform simple bookkeeping activities, such as balancing cash accounts. Issue room keys and escort instructions to bellhops. Review accounts and charges with guests during the check out process. Post charges, such those for rooms, food, liquor, or telephone calls, to ledgers manually, or by using computers. Transmit and receive messages, using telephones or telephone switchboards. Contact housekeeping or maintenance staff when guests report problems. Make and confirm reservations. Answer inquiries pertaining to hotel services, registration of guests, and shopping, dining, entertainment, and travel directions. Record guest comments or complaints, referring customers to managers as necessary. Advise housekeeping staff when rooms have been vacated and are ready for cleaning. Arrange tours, taxis, and restaurants for customers. Deposit guests' valuables in hotel safes or safe-deposit boxes. Date-stamp, sort, and rack incoming mail and messages. **SKILLS**—Service Orientation; Instructing; Critical Thinking; Learning Strategies; Social Perceptiveness; Persuasion; Negotiation; Active Listening.

GOE—Interest Area: 11. Recreation, Travel, and Other Personal Services. **Work Group:** 11.03. Transportation and Lodging Services. **Other Jobs in This Work Group:** Baggage Porters and Bellhops; Concierges; Flight Attendants; Reservation and Transportation Ticket Agents; Reservation and Transportation Ticket Agents and Travel Clerks; Transportation Attendants, Except Flight Attendants and Baggage Porters.

EDUCATION/TRAINING PROGRAM(S)— Selling Skills and Sales Operations. **RELATED KNOWLEDGE/COURSES**—Customer and Personal Service; Clerical Studies; Sales and Marketing; Computers and Electronics; Administration and Management; Geography.

Human Resources Assistants, Except Payroll and Timekeeping

- Personality Code: CE
- Growth: 19.3%
- Annual Job Openings: 36,000
- Annual Earnings: $31,060
- Education/Training Required: Short-term on-the-job training
- Self-Employed: 0%
- Part-Time: 15.1%

Compile and keep personnel records. Record data for each employee, such as address, weekly earnings, absences, amount of sales or production, supervisory reports on ability, and date of and reason for termination. Compile and type reports from employment records. File employment records. Search employee files and furnish information to authorized persons. Explain company personnel policies, benefits, and procedures to employees or job applicants. Process, verify, and maintain documentation relating to personnel activities such as staffing, recruitment, training, grievances, performance evaluations, and classifications. Record data for each employee, including such information as addresses, weekly earnings, absences, amount of sales or production, supervisory reports on performance, and dates of and reasons for terminations. Process and review employment applications in order to evaluate qualifications or eligibility of applicants. Answer questions regarding examinations, eligibility, salaries, benefits, and other pertinent information. Examine employee files to answer inquiries and provide information for personnel actions. Gather personnel records from other departments and/or employees. Search employee files in order to obtain information for authorized persons and organizations, such as credit bureaus and finance companies. Interview job applicants to obtain and verify information used to screen and evaluate them. Request information from law enforcement officials, previous employers, and other references in order to determine applicants' employment acceptability. Compile and prepare reports and documents pertaining to personnel activities. Inform job applicants of their acceptance or rejection of employment. Select applicants meeting specified job requirements and refer them to hiring personnel. Arrange for in-house and external training activities. Arrange for advertising or posting of job vacancies, and notify eligible workers of position availability. Provide assistance in administering employee benefit programs and worker's compensation plans. Prepare badges, passes, and identification cards, and perform other security-related duties. Administer and score applicant and employee aptitude, personality, and interest assessment instruments. **SKILLS**—Active Listening;

Social Perceptiveness; Time Management; Management of Personnel Resources; Service Orientation; Instructing; Writing; Critical Thinking.

GOE—Interest Area: 09. Business Detail. **Work Group:** 09.07. Records Processing. **Other Jobs in This Work Group:** Correspondence Clerks; Court Reporters; Credit Authorizers; Credit Authorizers, Checkers, and Clerks; Credit Checkers; File Clerks; Information and Record Clerks, All Other; Insurance Claims and Policy Processing Clerks; Insurance Claims Clerks; Insurance Policy Processing Clerks; Medical Records and Health Information Technicians; Medical Transcriptionists; Office and Administrative Support Workers, All Other; Office Clerks, General; Procurement Clerks; Proofreaders and Copy Markers.

EDUCATION/TRAINING PROGRAM(S)— General Office Occupations and Clerical Services. **RELATED KNOWLEDGE/COURSES—**Clerical Studies; Personnel and Human Resources; Customer and Personal Service; Computers and Electronics; Education and Training; English Language.

Immigration and Customs Inspectors

- Personality Code: CE
- Growth: 22.4%
- Annual Job Openings: 11,000
- Annual Earnings: $52,390
- Education/Training Required: Work experience in a related occupation
- Self-Employed: 0%
- Part-Time: 0.5%

Investigate and inspect persons, common carriers, goods, and merchandise, arriving in or departing from the United States or between states to detect violations of immigration and customs laws and regulations. Investigate applications for duty refunds, and petition for remission or mitigation of penalties when warranted. Locate and seize contraband, undeclared merchandise, and vehicles, aircraft, or boats that contain such merchandise. Record and report job-related activities, findings, transactions, violations, discrepancies, and decisions. Collect samples of merchandise for examination, appraisal, or testing. Institute civil and criminal prosecutions, and cooperate with other law enforcement agencies in the investigation and prosecution of those in violation of immigration or customs laws. Testify regarding decisions at immigration appeals or in federal court. Detain persons found to be in violation of customs or immigration laws, and arrange for legal action such as deportation. Determine duty and taxes to be paid on goods. Examine immigration applications, visas, and passports, and interview persons in order to determine eligibility for admission, residence, and travel in U.S. Inspect cargo, baggage, and personal articles entering or leaving U.S. for compliance with revenue laws and U.S. Customs Service regulations. Interpret and explain laws and regulations to travelers, prospective immigrants, shippers, and manufacturers. **SKILLS**—Writing; Speaking; Negotiation; Judgment and Decision Making; Systems Analysis.

GOE—Interest Area: 04. Law, Law Enforcement, and Public Safety. **Work Group:** 04.03. Law Enforcement. **Other Jobs in This Work Group:** Animal Control Workers; Bailiffs; Child Support, Missing Persons, and Unemployment Insurance Fraud Investigators; Correctional Officers and Jailers; Criminal Investigators and Special Agents; Crossing Guards; Detectives and Criminal Investigators; Fire Investigators; Fish and Game Wardens; Forensic Science Technicians; Gaming Surveillance Officers and Gaming Investigators; Highway Patrol Pilots; Lifeguards, Ski Patrol, and Other Recreational Protective Service Workers; Parking Enforcement Workers; Police and Sheriff's Patrol Officers; Police Detectives; Police Identification and Records Officers; Police Patrol Officers; Private Detectives and Investigators; Protective Service Workers, All Other;

Security Guards; Sheriffs and Deputy Sheriffs; Transit and Railroad Police.

EDUCATION/TRAINING PROGRAM(S)— Criminal Justice/Police Science; Criminalistics and Criminal Science. **RELATED KNOWLEDGE/ COURSES—**Law and Government; Geography; Public Safety and Security; Foreign Language; Transportation; Communications and Media.

Insurance Claims Clerks

- Personality Code: CE
- Growth: 3.6%
- Annual Job Openings: 41,000
- Annual Earnings: $28,520
- Education/Training Required: Moderate-term on-the-job training
- Self-Employed: 0.3%
- Part-Time: 10.3%

Obtain information from insured or designated persons for purpose of settling claim with insurance carrier. Apply insurance rating systems. Calculate amount of claim. Contact insured or other involved persons to obtain missing information. Post or attach information to claim file. Prepare and review insurance-claim forms and related documents for completeness. Provide customer service, such as giving limited instructions on how to proceed with claims or providing referrals to auto repair facilities or local contractors. Review insurance policy to determine coverage. Transmit claims for payment or further investigation. Organize and work with detailed office or warehouse records, using computers to enter, access, search and retrieve data. Pay small claims. **SKILLS—**Speaking; Active Listening; Reading Comprehension; Mathematics.

GOE—Interest Area: 09. Business Detail. **Work Group:** 09.07. Records Processing. **Other Jobs in This Work Group:** Correspondence Clerks; Court Reporters; Credit Authorizers; Credit Authorizers, Checkers, and Clerks; Credit Checkers; File Clerks; Human Resources Assistants, Except Payroll and Timekeeping; Information and Record Clerks, All Other; Insurance Claims and Policy Processing Clerks; Insurance Policy Processing Clerks; Medical Records and Health Information Technicians; Medical Transcriptionists; Office and Administrative Support Workers, All Other; Office Clerks, General; Procurement Clerks; Proofreaders and Copy Markers.

EDUCATION/TRAINING PROGRAM(S)— General Office Occupations and Clerical Services. **RELATED KNOWLEDGE/COURSES—**Clerical Studies; Law and Government; Economics and Accounting; Telecommunications; Geography; Mathematics.

Insurance Policy Processing Clerks

- Personality Code: CE
- Growth: 3.6%
- Annual Job Openings: 41,000
- Annual Earnings: $28,520
- Education/Training Required: Moderate-term on-the-job training
- Self-Employed: 0.3%
- Part-Time: 10.3%

Process applications for, changes to, reinstatement of, and cancellation of insurance policies. Duties include reviewing insurance applications to ensure that all questions have been answered, compiling data on insurance policy changes, changing policy records to conform to insured party's specifications, compiling data on lapsed insurance policies to determine automatic reinstatement according to company policies, canceling insurance policies as requested by agents, and verifying the accuracy of insurance company records. Modify, update, and process existing policies and claims to reflect any change in beneficiary, amount of coverage, or type of insurance. Process and record new insurance policies and claims. Review and verify data, such as age, name, address, and principal sum and value of property on insurance applications and policies. Organize and work with detailed office or warehouse records, maintaining files for each policyholder, including policies that are to be reinstated or cancelled. Examine letters from policyholders or agents, original insurance applications, and other company documents to determine if changes are needed and effects of changes. Correspond with insured or agent to obtain information or inform them account status or changes. Transcribe data to worksheets and enter data into computer for use in preparing documents and adjusting accounts. Notify insurance agent and accounting department of policy cancellation. Interview clients and take their calls in order to provide customer service and obtain information on claims. Compare information from application to criteria for policy reinstatement and approve reinstatement when criteria are met. Process, prepare, and submit business or government forms, such as submitting applications for coverage to insurance carriers. Collect initial premiums and issue receipts. Calculate premiums, refunds, commissions, adjustments, and new reserve requirements, using insurance rate standards. Obtain computer printout of policy cancellations or retrieve cancellation cards from file. Compose business correspondence for supervisors, managers and professionals. Check computations of interest accrued, premiums due, and settlement surrender on loan values. **SKILLS**— Critical Thinking; Social Perceptiveness; Learning Strategies; Service Orientation; Instructing; Active Learning; Coordination; Reading Comprehension.

GOE—Interest Area: 09. Business Detail. **Work Group:** 09.07. Records Processing. **Other Jobs in**

This Work Group: Correspondence Clerks; Court Reporters; Credit Authorizers; Credit Authorizers, Checkers, and Clerks; Credit Checkers; File Clerks; Human Resources Assistants, Except Payroll and Timekeeping; Information and Record Clerks, All Other; Insurance Claims and Policy Processing Clerks; Insurance Claims Clerks; Medical Records and Health Information Technicians; Medical Transcriptionists; Office and Administrative Support Workers, All Other; Office Clerks, General; Procurement Clerks; Proofreaders and Copy Markers.

EDUCATION/TRAINING PROGRAM(S)— General Office Occupations and Clerical Services. **RELATED KNOWLEDGE/COURSES**—Clerical Studies; Customer and Personal Service; Computers and Electronics; Sales and Marketing; Economics and Accounting; Production and Processing.

Insurance Underwriters

- Personality Code: CE
- Growth: 10.0%
- Annual Job Openings: 12,000
- Annual Earnings: $47,330
- Education/Training Required: Bachelor's degree
- Self-Employed: 1.0%
- Part-Time: 4.5%

Review individual applications for insurance to evaluate degree of risk involved and determine acceptance of applications. Examine documents to determine degree of risk from such factors as applicant financial standing and value and condition of property. Decline excessive risks. Write to field representatives, medical personnel, and others to obtain further information, quote rates, or explain company underwriting policies. Evaluate possibility of losses due to catastrophe or excessive insurance.

Decrease value of policy when risk is substandard and specify applicable endorsements or apply rating to ensure safe profitable distribution of risks, using reference materials. Review company records to determine amount of insurance in force on single risk or group of closely related risks. Authorize reinsurance of policy when risk is high. **SKILLS**—Service Orientation; Writing; Active Learning; Learning Strategies; Persuasion; Active Listening; Monitoring; Negotiation.

GOE—Interest Area: 13. General Management and Support. **Work Group:** 13.02. Management Support. **Other Jobs in This Work Group:** Accountants; Accountants and Auditors; Appraisers and Assessors of Real Estate; Appraisers, Real Estate; Assessors; Auditors; Budget Analysts; Business Operations Specialists, All Other; Claims Adjusters, Examiners, and Investigators; Claims Examiners, Property and Casualty Insurance; Compensation, Benefits, and Job Analysis Specialists; Cost Estimators; Credit Analysts; Employment Interviewers, Private or Public Employment Service; Employment, Recruitment, and Placement Specialists; Financial Analysts; Human Resources, Training, and Labor Relations Specialists, All Other; Insurance Adjusters, Examiners, and Investigators; Insurance Appraisers, Auto Damage; Loan Counselors; Loan Officers; Logisticians; Management Analysts; Market Research Analysts; Personnel Recruiters; Purchasing Agents and Buyers, Farm Products; Purchasing Agents, Except Wholesale, Retail, and Farm Products; Tax Examiners, Collectors, and Revenue Agents; Training and Development Specialists; Wholesale and Retail Buyers, Except Farm Products.

EDUCATION/TRAINING PROGRAM(S)—Insurance. **RELATED KNOWLEDGE/COURSES**—Customer and Personal Service; Clerical Studies; Sales and Marketing; Economics and Accounting; Computers and Electronics; Law and Government.

Interviewers, Except Eligibility and Loan

- Personality Code: CS
- Growth: 28.0%
- Annual Job Openings: 46,000
- Annual Earnings: $22,590
- Education/Training Required: Short-term on-the-job training
- Self-Employed: 0.7%
- Part-Time: 30.4%

Interview persons by telephone, by mail, in person, or by other means for the purpose of completing forms, applications, or questionnaires. Ask specific questions, record answers, and assist persons with completing form. May sort, classify, and file forms. Ask questions in accordance with instructions to obtain various specified information, such as person's name, address, age, religious preference, and state of residency. Identify and resolve inconsistencies in interviewees' responses by means of appropriate questioning and/or explanation. Compile, record and code results and data from interview or survey, using computer or specified form. Review data obtained from interview for completeness and accuracy. Contact individuals to be interviewed at home, place of business, or field location, by telephone, mail, or in person. Assist individuals in filling out applications or questionnaires. Ensure payment for services by verifying benefits with the person's insurance provider or working out financing options. Identify and report problems in obtaining valid data. Explain survey objectives and procedures to interviewees, and interpret survey questions to help interviewees' comprehension. Perform patient services, such as answering the telephone and assisting patients with financial and medical questions. Prepare reports to provide answers in response to specific problems. Locate and list addresses and households. Perform other office duties as needed, such as telemarketing and customer service inquiries, billing patients and receiving payments. Meet with supervisor daily to submit completed assignments and discuss progress. Collect and analyze data, such as studying old records, tallying the number of outpatients entering each day or week, or participating in federal, state, or local population surveys as a Census Enumerator. SKILLS— Service Orientation; Social Perceptiveness; Speaking; Persuasion; Active Listening; Negotiation; Learning Strategies; Writing; Critical Thinking.

GOE—Interest Area: 09. Business Detail. **Work Group:** 09.02. Administrative Detail. **Other Jobs in This Work Group:** Claims Takers, Unemployment Benefits; Court Clerks; Court, Municipal, and License Clerks; Eligibility Interviewers, Government Programs; Executive Secretaries and Administrative Assistants; Legal Secretaries; License Clerks; Loan Interviewers and Clerks; Medical Secretaries; Municipal Clerks; Office and Administrative Support Workers, All Other; Secretaries, Except Legal, Medical, and Executive; Welfare Eligibility Workers and Interviewers.

EDUCATION/TRAINING PROGRAM(S)— Receptionist. **RELATED KNOWLEDGE/ COURSES**—Customer and Personal Service; Therapy and Counseling; Sales and Marketing; Education and Training; Psychology; Philosophy and Theology.

Legal Secretaries

- Personality Code: CE
- Growth: 18.8%
- Annual Job Openings: 39,000
- Annual Earnings: $35,660
- Education/Training Required: Postsecondary vocational training
- Self-Employed: 1.7%
- Part-Time: 17.5%

Perform secretarial duties utilizing legal terminology, procedures, and documents. Prepare legal papers and correspondence, such as summonses, complaints, motions, and subpoenas. May also assist with legal research. Prepare and process legal documents and papers, such as summonses, subpoenas, complaints, appeals, motions, and pretrial agreements. Mail, fax, or arrange for delivery of legal correspondence to clients, witnesses, and court officials. Receive and place telephone calls. Schedule and make appointments. Make photocopies of correspondence, document, and other printed matter. Organize and maintain law libraries and document and case files. Assist attorneys in collecting information such as employment, medical, and other records. Attend legal meetings, such as client interviews, hearings, or depositions, and take notes. Draft and type office memos. Review legal publications and perform data base searches to identify laws and court decisions relevant to pending cases. Submit articles and information from searches to attorneys for review and approval for use. Complete various forms, such as accident reports, trial and courtroom requests, and applications for clients. SKILLS—Time Management; Writing; Social Perceptiveness; Reading Comprehension; Negotiation; Learning Strategies; Persuasion; Active Learning; Instructing.

GOE—Interest Area: 09. Business Detail. **Work Group:** 09.02. Administrative Detail. **Other Jobs in This Work Group:** Claims Takers, Unemployment Benefits; Court Clerks; Court, Municipal, and License Clerks; Eligibility Interviewers, Government Programs; Executive Secretaries and Administrative Assistants; Interviewers, Except Eligibility and Loan; License Clerks; Loan Interviewers and Clerks; Medical Secretaries; Municipal Clerks; Office and Administrative Support Workers, All Other; Secretaries, Except Legal, Medical, and Executive; Welfare Eligibility Workers and Interviewers.

EDUCATION/TRAINING PROGRAM(S)— Legal Administrative Assistant/Secretary. **RELATED KNOWLEDGE/COURSES**—Clerical Studies; Law and Government; Customer and Personal Service; Economics and Accounting; Computers and Electronics; English Language.

Library Assistants, Clerical

- Personality Code: CR
- Growth: 21.5%
- Annual Job Openings: 27,000
- Annual Earnings: $19,930
- Education/Training Required: Short-term on-the-job training
- Self-Employed: 0.1%
- Part-Time: 50.4%

Compile records, sort and shelve books, and issue and receive library materials such as pictures, cards, slides and microfilm. Locate library materials for loan and replace material in shelving area, stacks, or files according to identification number and title. Register patrons to permit them to borrow books, periodicals, and other library materials. Lend and collect books, periodicals, videotapes, and other materials at circulation desks. Enter and update patrons' records on computers. Process new materials including books, audiovisual materials, and computer software. Sort books, publications, and other items according to established procedure and return them to shelves, files, or other designated storage areas. Locate library materials for patrons, including books, periodicals, tape cassettes, Braille volumes, and pictures. Instruct patrons on how to use reference sources, card catalogs, and automated information systems. Inspect returned books for condition and due-date status, and compute any applicable fines. Answer routine inquiries, and refer patrons in need of professional assistance to librarians. Maintain records of items received, stored, issued, and returned, and file catalog cards according to system used. Perform clerical activities such as filing, typing, word processing, photocopying and mailing out material, and mail sorting. Provide assistance to librarians in the maintenance of collections of books, periodicals, magazines, newspapers, and audiovisual and other materials. Take action to deal with disruptive or problem patrons. Classify and catalog items according to content and purpose. Register new patrons and issue borrower identification cards that permit patrons to borrow books and other materials. Send out notices and accept fine payments for lost or overdue books. Operate small branch libraries, under the direction of off-site librarian supervisors. Prepare, store, and retrieve classification and catalog information, lecture notes, or other information related to stored documents, using computers. Schedule and supervise clerical workers, volunteers, and student assistants. Operate and maintain audiovisual equipment. Review records, such as microfilm and issue cards, in order to identify titles of overdue materials and delinquent borrowers. Select substitute titles when requested materials are unavailable following criteria such as age, education, and interests. Repair books, using mending tape, paste, and brushes. SKILLS—Service Orientation; Instructing; Reading Comprehension; Time Management; Learning Strategies; Social Perceptiveness; Active Listening; Writing.

GOE—Interest Area: 12. Education and Social Service. Work Group: 12.03. Educational Services. Other Jobs in This Work Group: Adult Literacy, Remedial Education, and GED Teachers and Instructors; Agricultural Sciences Teachers, Postsecondary; Anthropology and Archeology Teachers, Postsecondary; Architecture Teachers, Postsecondary; Archivists; Area, Ethnic, and Cultural Studies Teachers, Postsecondary; Art, Drama, and Music Teachers, Postsecondary; Atmospheric, Earth, Marine, and Space Sciences Teachers, Postsecondary; Audio-Visual Collections Specialists; Biological Science Teachers, Postsecondary; Business Teachers, Postsecondary; Chemistry Teachers, Postsecondary; Child Care Workers; Communications Teachers, Postsecondary; Computer Science Teachers, Postsecondary; Criminal Justice and Law Enforcement Teachers, Postsecondary; Curators; Economics Teachers, Postsecondary; Education

Teachers, Postsecondary; Education, Training, and Library Workers, All Other; Educational Psychologists; Educational, Vocational, and School Counselors; Elementary School Teachers, Except Special Education; Engineering Teachers, Postsecondary; English Language and Literature Teachers, Postsecondary; Environmental Science Teachers, Postsecondary; Farm and Home Management Advisors; Foreign Language and Literature Teachers, Postsecondary; Forestry and Conservation Science Teachers, Postsecondary; Geography Teachers, Postsecondary; Graduate Teaching Assistants; Health Specialties Teachers, Postsecondary; History Teachers, Postsecondary; Home Economics Teachers, Postsecondary; Kindergarten Teachers, Except Special Education; Law Teachers, Postsecondary; Librarians; Library Science Teachers, Postsecondary; Library Technicians; Mathematical Science Teachers, Postsecondary; Middle School Teachers, Except Special and Vocational Education; Museum Technicians and Conservators; Nannies; Nursing Instructors and Teachers, Postsecondary; Personal Financial Advisors; Philosophy and Religion Teachers, Postsecondary; Physics Teachers, Postsecondary; Political Science Teachers, Postsecondary; Postsecondary Teachers, All Other; Preschool Teachers, Except Special Education; Psychology Teachers, Postsecondary; Recreation and Fitness Studies Teachers, Postsecondary; Secondary School Teachers, Except Special and Vocational Education; Self-Enrichment Education Teachers; Social Sciences Teachers, Postsecondary, All Other; Social Work Teachers, Postsecondary; Sociology Teachers, Postsecondary; Special Education Teachers, Middle School; Special Education Teachers, Preschool, Kindergarten, and Elementary School; Special Education Teachers, Secondary School; Teacher Assistants; Teachers and Instructors, All Other; Vocational Education Teachers, Postsecondary; Vocational Education Teachers, Middle School; Vocational Education Teachers, Secondary School.

EDUCATION/TRAINING PROGRAM(S)— Library Assistant/Technician. **RELATED KNOWLEDGE/COURSES—**Clerical Studies; Computers and Electronics; Customer and Personal Service; English Language; History and Archeology; Geography; Communications and Media.

Licensing Examiners and Inspectors

- Personality Code: CE
- Growth: 9.8%
- Annual Job Openings: 20,000
- Annual Earnings: $46,780
- Education/Training Required: Long-term on-the-job training
- Self-Employed: 0.9%
- Part-Time: 5.3%

Examine, evaluate, and investigate eligibility for, conformity with, or liability under licenses or permits. Administer oral, written, road, or flight tests to license applicants. Advise licensees and other individuals or groups concerning licensing, permit, or passport regulations. Evaluate applications, records, and documents in order to gather information about eligibility or liability issues. Issue licenses to individuals meeting standards. Prepare correspondence to inform concerned parties of licensing decisions and of appeals processes. Prepare reports of activities, evaluations, recommendations, and decisions. Report law or regulation violations to appropriate boards and agencies. Score tests and observe equipment operation and control in order to rate ability of applicants. Confer with and interview officials, technical or professional specialists, and applicants, in order to obtain information or to clarify facts relevant to licensing decisions. Visit establishments to verify that valid licenses and permits are displayed, and that licensing standards are being upheld. Warn violators of infractions or penalties. **SKILLS—**Speaking; Monitoring; Reading Comprehension; Active Listening; Writing; Judgment and Decision Making; Critical Thinking; Mathematics.

Conventional—L

GOE—**Interest Area:** 04. Law, Law Enforcement, and Public Safety. **Work Group:** 04.04. Public Safety. **Other Jobs in This Work Group:** Agricultural Inspectors; Aviation Inspectors; Compliance Officers, Except Agriculture, Construction, Health and Safety, and Transportation; Emergency Medical Technicians and Paramedics; Environmental Compliance Inspectors; Equal Opportunity Representatives and Officers; Financial Examiners; Fire Fighters; Fire Inspectors; Fire Inspectors and Investigators; Forest Fire Fighters; Forest Fire Inspectors and Prevention Specialists; Government Property Inspectors and Investigators; Marine Cargo Inspectors; Municipal Fire Fighters; Nuclear Monitoring Technicians; Occupational Health and Safety Specialists; Occupational Health and Safety Technicians; Protective Service Workers, All Other; Public Transportation Inspectors.

EDUCATION/TRAINING PROGRAM(S)— No data available. **RELATED KNOWLEDGE/ COURSES**—Law and Government; Transportation; Clerical Studies; English Language; Communications and Media.

Mapping Technicians

- Personality Code: CR
- Growth: 23.1%
- Annual Job Openings: 10,000
- Annual Earnings: $29,520
- Education/Training Required: Moderate-term on-the-job training
- Self-Employed: 5.5%
- Part-Time: 7.0%

Calculate mapmaking information from field notes, and draw and verify accuracy of topographical maps. Monitor mapping work and the updating of maps in order to ensure accuracy, the inclusion of new and/or changed information, and compliance with rules and regulations. Produce and update overlay maps in order to show information boundaries, water locations, and topographic features on various base maps and at different scales. Redraw and correct maps, such as revising parcel maps to reflect tax code area changes, using information from official records and surveys. Trace contours and topographic details in order to generate maps that denote specific land and property locations and geographic attributes. Trim, align, and join prints in order to form photographic mosaics, maintaining scaled distances between reference points. Complete detailed source and method notes detailing the location of routine and complex land parcels. Create survey description pages and historical records related to the mapping activities and specifications of section plats. Determine scales, line sizes, and colors to be used for hard copies of computerized maps, using plotters. Enter GPS data, legal deeds, field notes, and land survey reports into GIS workstations so that information can be transformed into graphic land descriptions, such as maps and drawings. Identify and compile database information in order to create maps in response to requests. Identify, research, and resolve anomalies in legal land descriptions, referring issues to title and survey experts as appropriate. Analyze aerial photographs in order to detect and interpret significant military, industrial, resource, or topographical data. Calculate latitudes, longitudes, angles, areas, and other information for mapmaking, using survey field notes and reference tables. Check all layers of maps in order to ensure accuracy, identifying and marking errors and making corrections. Compare topographical features and contour lines with images from aerial photographs, old maps, and other reference materials in order to verify the accuracy of their identification. Compute and measure scaled distances between reference points in order to establish relative positions of adjoining prints and enable the creation of photographic mosaics. **SKILLS**—Mathematics; Technology Design; Management of Personnel Resources; Operations Analysis; Active Learning; Monitoring.

GOE—Interest Area: 02. Science, Math, and Engineering. Work Group: 02.08. Engineering Technology. Other Jobs in This Work Group: Aerospace Engineering and Operations Technicians; Architectural and Civil Drafters; Architectural Drafters; Calibration and Instrumentation Technicians; Cartographers and Photogrammetrists; Civil Drafters; Civil Engineering Technicians; Construction and Building Inspectors; Drafters, All Other; Electrical and Electronic Engineering Technicians; Electrical and Electronics Drafters; Electrical Drafters; Electrical Engineering Technicians; Electro-Mechanical Technicians; Electronic Drafters; Electronics Engineering Technicians; Engineering Technicians, Except Drafters, All Other; Environmental Engineering Technicians; Industrial Engineering Technicians; Mechanical Drafters; Mechanical Engineering Technicians; Numerical Tool and Process Control Programmers; Pressure Vessel Inspectors; Surveying and Mapping Technicians; Surveying Technicians; Surveyors.

EDUCATION/TRAINING PROGRAM(S)—Cartography; Surveying Technology/Surveying. RELATED KNOWLEDGE/COURSES—Geography; Design; Mathematics; Computers and Electronics; Administration and Management; Engineering and Technology.

Marine Cargo Inspectors

- Personality Code: CR
- Growth: 7.7%
- Annual Job Openings: 5,000
- Annual Earnings: $49,590
- Education/Training Required: Work experience in a related occupation
- Self-Employed: 0.4%
- Part-Time: 3.2%

Inspect cargoes of seagoing vessels to certify compliance with health and safety regulations in cargo handling and stowage. Inspects loaded cargo in holds and cargo-handling devices to determine compliance with regulations and need for maintenance. Reads vessel documents to ascertain cargo capabilities according to design and cargo regulations. Calculates gross and net tonnage, hold capacities, volume of stored fuel and water, cargo weight, and ship stability factors, using mathematical formulas. Determines type of license and safety equipment required and computes applicable tolls and wharfage fees. Examines blueprints of ship and takes physical measurements to determine capacity and depth of vessel in water, using measuring instruments. Writes certificates of admeasurement, listing details such as design, length, depth, and breadth of vessel and method of propulsion. Issues certificate of compliance when violations are not detected or recommends remedial procedures to correct deficiencies. Times roll of ship, using stopwatch. Analyzes data, formulates recommendations, and writes reports of findings. Advises crew in techniques of stowing dangerous and heavy cargo according to knowledge of hazardous cargo. SKILLS—Mathematics; Writing; Systems Evaluation; Reading Comprehension; Speaking; Critical Thinking; Persuasion; Judgment and Decision Making.

GOE—Interest Area: 04. Law, Law Enforcement, and Public Safety. Work Group: 04.04. Public Safety. Other Jobs in This Work Group: Agricultural Inspectors; Aviation Inspectors; Compliance Officers, Except Agriculture, Construction, Health and Safety, and Transportation; Emergency Medical Technicians and Paramedics; Environmental Compliance Inspectors; Equal Opportunity Representatives and Officers; Financial Examiners; Fire Fighters; Fire Inspectors; Fire Inspectors and Investigators; Forest Fire Fighters; Forest Fire Inspectors and Prevention Specialists; Government Property Inspectors and Investigators; Licensing Examiners and Inspectors; Municipal Fire Fighters; Nuclear Monitoring Technicians; Occupational Health and Safety Specialists; Occupational Health and Safety

Conventional—M

Technicians; Protective Service Workers, All Other; Public Transportation Inspectors.

EDUCATION/TRAINING PROGRAM(S)—No data available. **RELATED KNOWLEDGE/ COURSES**—Public Safety and Security; Mathematics; Transportation; Design; Physics; Law and Government.

Medical Records and Health Information Technicians

- Personality Code: C
- Growth: 46.8%
- Annual Job Openings: 24,000
- Annual Earnings: $24,520
- Education/Training Required: Associate's degree
- Self-Employed: 1.1%
- Part-Time: 17.6%

Compile, process, and maintain medical records of hospital and clinic patients in a manner consistent with medical, administrative, ethical, legal, and regulatory requirements of the health care system. Process, maintain, compile, and report patient information for health requirements and standards. Protect the security of medical records to ensure that confidentiality is maintained. Process patient admission and discharge documents. Review records for completeness, accuracy and compliance with regulations. Compile and maintain patients' medical records to document condition and treatment and to provide data for research or cost control and care improvement efforts. Enter data, such as demographic characteristics, history and extent of disease, diagnostic procedures and treatment into computer. Release information to persons and agencies according to regulations. Plan, develop, main-

tain and operate a variety of health record indexes and storage and retrieval systems to collect, classify, store and analyze information. Manage the department and supervise clerical workers, directing and controlling activities of personnel in the medical records department. Transcribe medical reports. Identify, compile, abstract and code patient data, using standard classification systems. Resolve/clarify codes and diagnoses with conflicting, missing, or unclear information by consulting with doctors or others to get additional information and by participating in the coding team's regular meetings. Train medical records staff. Assign the patient to one of several hundred "diagnosis-related groups," or DRGs, using appropriate computer software. Post medical insurance billings. Process and prepare business and government forms. Contact discharged patients, their families, and physicians to maintain registry with follow-up information, such as quality of life and length of survival of cancer patients. Prepare statistical reports, narrative reports and graphic presentations of information such as tumor registry data for use by hospital staff, researchers, and other users. Consult classification manuals to locate information about disease processes. Compile medical care and census data for statistical reports on diseases treated, surgery performed, and use of hospital beds. Develop in-service educational materials. **SKILLS**—Instructing; Systems Evaluation; Time Management; Active Listening; Critical Thinking; Learning Strategies; Service Orientation; Reading Comprehension; Active Learning; Social Perceptiveness.

GOE—Interest Area: 09. Business Detail. **Work Group:** 09.07. Records Processing. **Other Jobs in This Work Group:** Correspondence Clerks; Court Reporters; Credit Authorizers; Credit Authorizers, Checkers, and Clerks; Credit Checkers; File Clerks; Human Resources Assistants, Except Payroll and Timekeeping; Information and Record Clerks, All Other; Insurance Claims and Policy Processing Clerks; Insurance Claims Clerks; Insurance Policy Processing Clerks; Medical Transcriptionists; Office and Administrative Support Workers, All Other;

Office Clerks, General; Procurement Clerks; Proof-readers and Copy Markers.

EDUCATION/TRAINING PROGRAM(S)—
Health Information/Medical Records Technology/Technician; Medical Insurance Coding Specialist/Coder. **RELATED KNOWLEDGE/ COURSES—**Clerical Studies; Customer and Personal Service; Personnel and Human Resources; Medicine and Dentistry; Administration and Management; Computers and Electronics.

Medical Secretaries

- ◉ Personality Code: CE
- ◉ Growth: 17.2%
- ◉ Annual Job Openings: 50,000
- ◉ Annual Earnings: $26,000
- ◉ Education/Training Required: Postsecondary vocational training
- ◉ Self-Employed: 1.6%
- ◉ Part-Time: 17.5%

Perform secretarial duties utilizing specific knowledge of medical terminology and hospital, clinic, or laboratory procedures. Duties include scheduling appointments, billing patients, and compiling and recording medical charts, reports, and correspondence. Schedule and confirm patient diagnostic appointments, surgeries and medical consultations. Compile and record medical charts, reports, and correspondence, using typewriter or personal computer. Answer telephones, and direct calls to appropriate staff. Receive and route messages and documents such as laboratory results to appropriate staff. Greet visitors, ascertain purpose of visit, and direct them to appropriate staff. Interview patients in order to complete documents, case histories, and forms such as intake and insurance forms. Maintain medical records, technical library and correspondence files. Operate office equipment

such as voice mail messaging systems, and use word processing, spreadsheet, and other software applications to prepare reports, invoices, financial statements, letters, case histories and medical records. Transmit correspondence and medical records by mail, e-mail, or fax. Perform various clerical and administrative functions, such as ordering and maintaining an inventory of supplies. Arrange hospital admissions for patients. Transcribe recorded messages and practitioners' diagnoses and recommendations into patients' medical records. Perform bookkeeping duties, such as credits and collections, preparing and sending financial statements and bills, and keeping financial records. Complete insurance and other claim forms. Prepare correspondence and assist physicians or medical scientists with preparation of reports, speeches, articles and conference proceedings. **SKILLS—**Social Perceptiveness; Instructing; Active Listening; Time Management; Writing; Management of Personnel Resources; Reading Comprehension; Speaking; Management of Material Resources.

GOE—Interest Area: 09. Business Detail. **Work Group:** 09.02. Administrative Detail. **Other Jobs in This Work Group:** Claims Takers, Unemployment Benefits; Court Clerks; Court, Municipal, and License Clerks; Eligibility Interviewers, Government Programs; Executive Secretaries and Administrative Assistants; Interviewers, Except Eligibility and Loan; Legal Secretaries; License Clerks; Loan Interviewers and Clerks; Municipal Clerks; Office and Administrative Support Workers, All Other; Secretaries, Except Legal, Medical, and Executive; Welfare Eligibility Workers and Interviewers.

EDUCATION/TRAINING PROGRAM(S)—
Medical Administrative/Executive Assistant and Medical Secretary; Medical Insurance Specialist/ Medical Biller; Medical Office Assistant/Specialist. **RELATED KNOWLEDGE/COURSES—** Customer and Personal Service; Clerical studies; Telecommunications; English Language; Computers and Electronics; Communications and Media.

Conventional—M

Office Clerks, General

- Personality Code: C
- Growth: 10.4%
- Annual Job Openings: 550,000
- Annual Earnings: $22,450
- Education/Training Required: Short-term on-the-job training
- Self-Employed: 0.5%
- Part-Time: 25.7%

Perform duties too varied and diverse to be classified in any specific office clerical occupation, requiring limited knowledge of office management systems and procedures. Clerical duties may be assigned in accordance with the office procedures of individual establishments and may include a combination of answering telephones, bookkeeping, typing or word processing, stenography, office machine operation, and filing. Collect, count, and disburse money, do basic bookkeeping and complete banking transactions. Communicate with customers, employees, and other individuals to answer questions, disseminate or explain information, take orders and address complaints. Answer telephones, direct calls and take messages. Compile, copy, sort, and file records of office activities, business transactions, and other activities. Complete and mail bills, contracts, policies, invoices, or checks. Operate office machines, such as photocopiers and scanners, facsimile machines, voice mail systems and personal computers. Compute, record, and proofread data and other information, such as records or reports. Maintain and update filing, inventory, mailing, and database systems, either manually or using a computer. Open, sort and route incoming mail, answer correspondence, and prepare outgoing mail. Review files, records, and other documents to obtain information to respond to requests. Deliver messages and run errands. Inventory and order materials, supplies, and services. Complete work schedules, manage calendars and arrange appointments. Process and prepare documents, such as business or government forms and expense reports. Monitor and direct the work of lower-level clerks. Type, format, proofread and edit correspondence and other documents, from notes or dictating machines, using computers or typewriters. Count, weigh, measure, and/or organize materials. Train other staff members to perform work activities, such as using computer applications. Prepare meeting agendas, attend meetings, and record and transcribe minutes. Troubleshoot problems involving office equipment, such as computer hardware and software. **SKILLS—** Active Listening; Reading Comprehension; Social Perceptiveness; Service Orientation; Writing; Speaking; Time Management; Learning Strategies.

GOE—**Interest Area:** 09. Business Detail. **Work Group:** 09.07. Records Processing. **Other Jobs in This Work Group:** Correspondence Clerks; Court Reporters; Credit Authorizers; Credit Authorizers, Checkers, and Clerks; Credit Checkers; File Clerks; Human Resources Assistants, Except Payroll and Timekeeping; Information and Record Clerks, All Other; Insurance Claims and Policy Processing Clerks; Insurance Claims Clerks; Insurance Policy Processing Clerks; Medical Records and Health Information Technicians; Medical Transcriptionists; Office and Administrative Support Workers, All Other; Procurement Clerks; Proofreaders and Copy Markers.

EDUCATION/TRAINING PROGRAM(S)— General Office Occupations and Clerical Services. **RELATED KNOWLEDGE/COURSES—**Clerical Studies; Customer and Personal Service; Economics and Accounting; Personnel and Human Resources; Computers and Electronics; English Language.

Pharmacy Technicians

- Personality Code: CR
- Growth: 28.8%
- Annual Job Openings: 39,000
- Annual Earnings: $22,760
- Education/Training Required: Moderate-term on-the-job training
- Self-Employed: 0%
- Part-Time: 23.0%

Prepare medications under the direction of a pharmacist. May measure, mix, count out, label, and record amounts and dosages of medications. Receive written prescription or refill requests and verify that information is complete and accurate. Maintain proper storage and security conditions for drugs. Answer telephones, responding to questions or requests. Fill bottles with prescribed medications and type and affix labels. Assist customers by answering simple questions, locating items or referring them to the pharmacist for medication information. Price and file prescriptions that have been filled. Clean, and help maintain, equipment and work areas, and sterilize glassware according to prescribed methods. Establish and maintain patient profiles, including lists of medications taken by individual patients. Order, label, and count stock of medications, chemicals, and supplies, and enter inventory data into computer. Receive and store incoming supplies, verify quantities against invoices, and inform supervisors of stock needs and shortages. Transfer medication from vials to the appropriate number of sterile, disposable syringes, using aseptic techniques. Add measured drugs or nutrients to intravenous solutions under sterile conditions to prepare intravenous (IV) packs under pharmacist supervision. Supply and monitor robotic machines that dispense medicine into containers, and label the containers. Prepare and process medical insurance claim forms and records. Mix pharmaceutical preparations according to written prescriptions. Operate cash registers to accept payment from customers. Compute charges for medication and equipment dispensed to hospital patients, and enter data in computer. Deliver medications and pharmaceutical supplies to patients, nursing stations or surgery. Price stock and mark items for sale. Maintain and merchandise home health-care products and services. **SKILLS**— Instructing; Service Orientation; Active Listening; Active Learning; Critical Thinking; Speaking; Mathematics; Troubleshooting.

GOE—Interest Area: 14. Medical and Health Services. **Work Group:** 14.02. Medicine and Surgery. **Other Jobs in This Work Group:** Anesthesiologists; Family and General Practitioners; Healthcare Support Workers, All Other; Internists, General; Medical Assistants; Obstetricians and Gynecologists; Pediatricians, General; Pharmacists; Pharmacy Aides; Physician Assistants; Physicians and Surgeons, All Other; Psychiatrists; Registered Nurses; Surgeons; Surgical Technologists.

EDUCATION/TRAINING PROGRAM(S)— Pharmacy Technician/Assistant. **RELATED KNOWLEDGE/COURSES**—Customer and Personal Service; Chemistry; Medicine and Dentistry; Mathematics; Clerical Studies; Therapy and Counseling.

Police Identification and Records Officers

- Personality Code: CR
- Growth: 22.4%
- Annual Job Openings: 11,000
- Annual Earnings: $52,390
- Education/Training Required: Work experience in a related occupation
- Self-Employed: 0%
- Part-Time: 0.5%

Collect evidence at crime scene, classify and identify fingerprints, and photograph evidence for use

Conventional—P

in criminal and civil cases. Photograph crime or accident scenes for evidence records. Testify in court and present evidence. Dust selected areas of crime scene and lift latent fingerprints, adhering to proper preservation procedures. Look for trace evidence, such as fingerprints, hairs, fibers, or shoe impressions, using alternative light sources when necessary. Analyze and process evidence at crime scenes and in the laboratory, wearing protective equipment and using powders and chemicals. Package, store and retrieve evidence. Serve as technical advisor and coordinate with other law enforcement workers to exchange information on crime scene collection activities. Perform emergency work during off-hours. Submit evidence to supervisors. Process film and prints from crime or accident scenes. Identify, classify, and file fingerprints, using systems such as the Henry Classification system. **SKILLS**—Persuasion; Negotiation; Service Orientation; Judgment and Decision Making; Social Perceptiveness; Critical Thinking; Time Management; Learning Strategies; Coordination.

GOE—Interest Area: 04. Law, Law Enforcement, and Public Safety. **Work Group:** 04.03. Law Enforcement. **Other Jobs in This Work Group:** Animal Control Workers; Bailiffs; Child Support, Missing Persons, and Unemployment Insurance Fraud Investigators; Correctional Officers and Jailers; Criminal Investigators and Special Agents; Crossing Guards; Detectives and Criminal Investigators; Fire Investigators; Fish and Game Wardens; Forensic Science Technicians; Gaming Surveillance Officers and Gaming Investigators; Highway Patrol Pilots; Immigration and Customs Inspectors; Lifeguards, Ski Patrol, and Other Recreational Protective Service Workers; Parking Enforcement Workers; Police and Sheriff's Patrol Officers; Police Detectives; Police Patrol Officers; Private Detectives and Investigators; Protective Service Workers, All Other; Security Guards; Sheriffs and Deputy Sheriffs; Transit and Railroad Police.

EDUCATION/TRAINING PROGRAM(S)— Criminal Justice/Police Science; Criminalistics and Criminal Science. **RELATED KNOWLEDGE/ COURSES**—Law and Government; Customer and

Personal Service; Public Safety and Security; Telecommunications; Computers and Electronics; Psychology; English Language.

Postal Service Mail Carriers

- Personality Code: CR
- Growth: –0.5%
- Annual Job Openings: 20,000
- Annual Earnings: $39,620
- Education/Training Required: Short-term on-the-job training
- Self-Employed: 0%
- Part-Time: 6.5%

Sort mail for delivery. Deliver mail on established route by vehicle or on foot. Bundle mail in preparation for delivery or transportation to relay boxes. Deliver mail to residences and business establishments along specified routes by walking and/or driving, using a combination of satchels, carts, cars, and small trucks. Enter change of address orders into computers that process forwarding address stickers. Hold mail for customers who are away from delivery locations. Leave notices telling patrons where to collect mail that could not be delivered. Maintain accurate records of deliveries. Meet schedules for the collection and return of mail. Record address changes and redirect mail for those addresses. Return incorrectly addressed mail to senders. Return to the post office with mail collected from homes, businesses, and public mailboxes. Sign for cash-on-delivery and registered mail before leaving the post office. Sort mail for delivery, arranging it in delivery sequence. Travel to post offices to pick up the mail for routes and/or pick up mail from postal relay boxes. Turn in money and receipts collected along mail routes. Answer customers' questions about postal services and regulations. Complete forms that notify publishers of address

changes. Obtain signed receipts for registered, certified, and insured mail; collect associated charges;
and complete any necessary paperwork. Provide
customers with change of address cards and other
forms. Register, certify, and insure parcels and letters. Report any unusual circumstances concerning
mail delivery, including the condition of street letter
boxes. Sell stamps and money orders. SKILLS—
None met the criteria.

GOE—Interest Area: 09. Business Detail. Work
Group: 09.08. Records and Materials Processing.
Other Jobs in This Work Group: Cargo and
Freight Agents; Couriers and Messengers; Mail
Clerks, Except Mail Machine Operators and Postal
Service; Marking Clerks; Office and Administrative
Support Workers, All Other; Order Fillers, Whole-
sale and Retail Sales; Postal Service Mail Sorters,
Processors, and Processing Machine Operators;
Shipping, Receiving, and Traffic Clerks; Stock
Clerks and Order Fillers; Stock Clerks—Stockroom,
Warehouse, or Storage Yard; Weighers, Measurers,
Checkers, and Samplers, Recordkeeping.

EDUCATION/TRAINING PROGRAM(S)—
General Office Occupations and Clerical Services.
RELATED KNOWLEDGE/COURSES—Trans-
portation; Geography; Clerical Studies.

Production, Planning, and Expediting Clerks

- Personality Code: CE
- Growth: 14.1%
- Annual Job Openings: 51,000
- Annual Earnings: $34,820
- Education/Training Required: Short-term on-the-job training
- Self-Employed: 0.4%
- Part-Time: 9.3%

Coordinate and expedite the flow of work and
materials within or between departments of an
establishment according to production schedule.
Duties include reviewing and distributing production, work, and shipment schedules; conferring
with department supervisors to determine progress
of work and completion dates; and compiling
reports on progress of work, inventory levels, costs,
and production problems. Maintains files, such as
maintenance records, bills of lading, and cost
reports. Arranges for delivery and distributes supplies
and parts to expedite flow of materials to meet production schedules. Examines documents, materials,
and products, and monitors work processes for completeness, accuracy, and conformance to standards
and specifications. Completes status reports, such as
production progress, customer information, and
materials inventory. Confers with establishment personnel, vendors, and customers to coordinate processing and shipping, and to resolve complaints.
Reviews documents, such as production schedules,
staffing tables, and specifications to obtain information, such as materials, priorities, and personnel
requirements. Compiles schedules and orders, such
as personnel assignments, production, work flow,
transportation, and maintenance and repair. Monitors work progress, provides services, such as furnishing permits, tickets, and union information, and
directs workers to expedite work flow. Requisitions
and maintains inventory of materials and supplies to
meet production demands. Calculates figures, such
as labor and materials amounts, manufacturing
costs, and wages, using pricing schedules, adding
machine, or calculator. SKILLS—Management of
Material Resources; Management of Personnel
Resources; Management of Financial Resources; Systems Analysis; Time Management; Systems Evaluation; Service Orientation; Negotiation.

GOE—Interest Area: 09. Business Detail. Work
Group: 09.04. Material Control. Other Jobs in
This Work Group: Meter Readers, Utilities.

EDUCATION/TRAINING PROGRAM(S)—
Parts, Warehousing, and Inventory Management
Operations. RELATED KNOWLEDGE/

COURSES—Clerical Studies; Production and Processing; Economics and Accounting; Mathematics; Computers and Electronics; Administration and Management.

Receptionists and Information Clerks

- Personality Code: CE
- Growth: 29.5%
- Annual Job Openings: 296,000
- Annual Earnings: $21,320
- Education/Training Required: Short-term on-the-job training
- Self-Employed: 1.2%
- Part-Time: 31.5%

Answer inquiries and obtain information for general public, customers, visitors, and other interested parties. Provide information regarding activities conducted at establishment; location of departments, offices, and employees within organization. Operate telephone switchboard to answer, screen and forward calls, providing information, taking messages and scheduling appointments. Receive payment and record receipts for services. Perform administrative support tasks such as proofreading, transcribing handwritten information, and operating calculators or computers to work with pay records, invoices, balance sheets and other documents. Greet persons entering establishment, determine nature and purpose of visit, and direct or escort them to specific destinations. Hear and resolve complaints from customers and public. File and maintain records. Transmit information or documents to customers, using computer, mail, or facsimile machine. Schedule appointments, and maintain and update appointment calendars. Analyze data to determine answers to questions from customers or members of the public. Provide infor-

mation about establishment, such as location of departments or offices, employees within the organization, or services provided. Keep a current record of staff members' whereabouts and availability. Collect, sort, distribute and prepare mail, messages and courier deliveries. Calculate and quote rates for tours, stocks, insurance policies, and other products and services. Take orders for merchandise or materials and send them to the proper departments to be filled. Process and prepare memos, correspondence, travel vouchers, or other documents. Schedule space and equipment for special programs and prepare lists of participants. Enroll individuals to participate in programs and notify them of their acceptance. SKILLS—Service Orientation; Social Perceptiveness; Active Listening; Writing; Critical Thinking; Reading Comprehension; Speaking; Persuasion.

GOE—Interest Area: 09. Business Detail. Work Group: 09.05. Customer Service. Other Jobs in This Work Group: Adjustment Clerks; Bill and Account Collectors; Cashiers; Counter and Rental Clerks; Customer Service Representatives; Customer Service Representatives, Utilities; Gaming Cage Workers; Gaming Change Persons and Booth Cashiers; New Accounts Clerks; Order Clerks; Tellers; Travel Clerks.

EDUCATION/TRAINING PROGRAM(S)—General Office Occupations and Clerical Services; Health Unit Coordinator/Ward Clerk; Medical Reception/Receptionist; Receptionist. RELATED KNOWLEDGE/COURSES—Customer and Personal Service; Clerical Studies; Computers and Electronics; Transportation; Administration and Management; English Language.

Reservation and Transportation Ticket Agents

- Personality Code: CE
- Growth: 12.2%
- Annual Job Openings: 35,000
- Annual Earnings: $26,220
- Education/Training Required: Short-term on-the-job training
- Self-Employed: 1.1%
- Part-Time: 15.7%

Make and confirm reservations for passengers and sell tickets for transportation agencies such as airlines, bus companies, railroads, and steamship lines. May check baggage and direct passengers to designated concourse, pier, or track. Determines whether space is available on travel dates requested by customer. Arranges reservations and routing for passengers at request of Ticket Agent. Examines passenger ticket or pass to direct passenger to specified area for loading. Plans route and computes ticket cost, using schedules, rate books, and computer. Reads coded data on tickets to ascertain destination, marks tickets, and assigns boarding pass. Assists passengers requiring special assistance to board or depart conveyance. Informs travel agents in other locations of space reserved or available. Sells travel insurance. Announces arrival and departure information, using public-address system. Telephones customer or Ticket Agent to advise of changes with travel conveyance or to confirm reservation. Sells and assembles tickets for transmittal or mailing to customers. Answers inquiries made to travel agencies or transportation firms, such as airlines, bus companies, railroad companies, and steamship lines. Checks baggage and directs passenger to designated location for loading. Assigns specified space to customers and maintains computerized inventory of passenger space available. **SKILLS**—Service Orientation; Active Listening; Speaking.

GOE—**Interest Area:** 11. Recreation, Travel, and Other Personal Services. **Work Group:** 11.03. Transportation and Lodging Services. **Other Jobs in This Work Group:** Baggage Porters and Bellhops; Concierges; Flight Attendants; Hotel, Motel, and Resort Desk Clerks; Reservation and Transportation Ticket Agents and Travel Clerks; Transportation Attendants, Except Flight Attendants and Baggage Porters.

EDUCATION/TRAINING PROGRAM(S)— Selling Skills and Sales Operations; Tourism and Travel Services Marketing Operations; Tourism Promotion Operations. **RELATED KNOWLEDGE/COURSES**—Geography; Transportation; Sales and Marketing; Clerical Studies; Computers and Electronics; Foreign Language; Telecommunications; Communications and Media.

Statement Clerks

- Personality Code: CE
- Growth: 7.9%
- Annual Job Openings: 78,000
- Annual Earnings: $26,290
- Education/Training Required: Short-term on-the-job training
- Self-Employed: 2.2%
- Part-Time: 16.1%

Prepare and distribute bank statements to customers, answer inquiries, and reconcile discrepancies in records and accounts. Compare previously prepared bank statements with canceled checks, and reconcile discrepancies. Encode and cancel checks, using bank machines. Load machines with statements, cancelled checks, and envelopes in order to prepare statements for distribution to customers, or stuff envelopes by hand. Maintain files of canceled checks and customers' signatures. Match statements with batches of canceled checks by account numbers. Monitor equipment in order to ensure proper

Conventional—S

operation. Retrieve checks returned to customers in error, adjusting customer accounts and answering inquiries about errors as necessary. Route statements for mailing or over-the-counter delivery to customers. Verify signatures and required information on checks. Weigh envelopes containing statements in order to determine correct postage and affix postage using stamps or metering equipment. Fix minor problems, such as equipment jams, and notify repair personnel of major equipment problems. Post stop-payment notices in order to prevent payment of protested checks. Take orders for imprinted checks. **SKILLS**—Active Listening; Reading Comprehension; Mathematics.

GOE—Interest Area: 09. Business Detail. **Work Group:** 09.03. Bookkeeping, Auditing, and Accounting. **Other Jobs in This Work Group:** Billing and Posting Clerks and Machine Operators; Billing, Cost, and Rate Clerks; Bookkeeping, Accounting, and Auditing Clerks; Brokerage Clerks; Office and Administrative Support Workers, All Other; Payroll and Timekeeping Clerks; Tax Preparers.

EDUCATION/TRAINING PROGRAM(S)— Accounting Technology/Technician and Bookkeeping. **RELATED KNOWLEDGE/COURSES** —Clerical Studies; Computers and Electronics; Economics and Accounting; Telecommunications.

Tax Preparers

- Personality Code: CE
- Growth: 23.2%
- Annual Job Openings: 11,000
- Annual Earnings: $26,530
- Education/Training Required: Moderate-term on-the-job training
- Self-Employed: 26.2%
- Part-Time: 20.3%

Prepare tax returns for individuals or small businesses but do not have the background or responsibilities of an accredited or certified public accountant. Check data input or verify totals on forms prepared by others to detect errors in arithmetic, data entry, or procedures. Compute taxes owed or overpaid, using adding machines or personal computers, and complete entries on forms, following tax form instructions and tax tables. Interview clients to obtain additional information on taxable income and deductible expenses and allowances. Prepare or assist in preparing simple to complex tax returns for individuals or small businesses. Review financial records such as income statements and documentation of expenditures in order to determine forms needed to prepare tax returns. Use all appropriate adjustments, deductions, and credits to keep clients' taxes to a minimum. Calculate form preparation fees according to return complexity and processing time required. Consult tax law handbooks or bulletins in order to determine procedures for preparation of atypical returns. Furnish taxpayers with sufficient information and advice in order to ensure correct tax form completion. **SKILLS**—Mathematics; Reading Comprehension; Active Listening; Speaking; Active Learning; Judgment and Decision Making; Monitoring; Service Orientation.

GOE—Interest Area: 09. Business Detail. **Work Group:** 09.03. Bookkeeping, Auditing, and Accounting. **Other Jobs in This Work Group:** Billing and Posting Clerks and Machine Operators; Billing, Cost, and Rate Clerks; Bookkeeping, Accounting, and Auditing Clerks; Brokerage Clerks; Office and Administrative Support Workers, All Other; Payroll and Timekeeping Clerks; Statement Clerks.

EDUCATION/TRAINING PROGRAM(S)— Accounting Technology/Technician and Bookkeeping; Taxation. **RELATED KNOWLEDGE/ COURSES**—Economics and Accounting; Law and Government; Clerical Studies; Mathematics; Computers and Electronics.

Travel Clerks

- Personality Code: CS
- Growth: 12.2%
- Annual Job Openings: 35,000
- Annual Earnings: $26,220
- Education/Training Required: Short-term on-the-job training
- Self-Employed: 1.1%
- Part-Time: 15.7%

Provide tourists with travel information, such as points of interest, restaurants, rates, and emergency service. Duties include answering inquiries, offering suggestions, and providing literature pertaining to trips, excursions, sporting events, concerts and plays. May make reservations, deliver tickets, arrange for visas, or contact individuals and groups to inform them of package tours. Provides customers with travel suggestions and information such as guides, directories, brochures, and maps. Contacts motel, hotel, resort, and travel operators by mail or telephone to obtain advertising literature. Studies maps, directories, routes, and rate tables to determine travel route and cost and availability of accommodations. Calculates estimated travel rates and expenses, using items such as rate tables and calculators. Informs client of travel dates, times, connections, baggage limits, medical and visa requirements, and emergency information. Obtains reservations for air, train, or car travel and hotel or other housing accommodations. Confirms travel arrangements and reservations. Assists client in preparing required documents and forms for travel, such as visas. Plans itinerary for travel and accommodations, using knowledge of routes, types of carriers, and regulations. Provides information concerning fares, availability of travel, and accommodations, either orally or by using guides, brochures, and maps. Confers with customers by telephone, writing, or in person to answer questions regarding services and determine travel preferences. **SKILLS**—Service Orientation; Speaking; Active Listening; Social Perceptiveness; Coordination; Mathematics.

GOE—Interest Area: 09. Business Detail. **Work Group:** 09.05. Customer Service. **Other Jobs in This Work Group:** Adjustment Clerks; Bill and Account Collectors; Cashiers; Counter and Rental Clerks; Customer Service Representatives; Customer Service Representatives, Utilities; Gaming Cage Workers; Gaming Change Persons and Booth Cashiers; New Accounts Clerks; Order Clerks; Receptionists and Information Clerks; Tellers.

EDUCATION/TRAINING PROGRAM(S)—Selling Skills and Sales Operations; Tourism and Travel Services Marketing Operations; Tourism Promotion Operations. **RELATED KNOWLEDGE/COURSES**—Geography; Transportation; Customer and Personal Service; Clerical Studies; Telecommunications.

Conventional—T

PART V

Appendixes

Appendix A:
Occupations Ordered by Two-Letter Personality Codes

Appendix B:
Definitions of Skills

Appendix C:
GOE Interest Fields and Groups

Appendix D:
Definitions of Related Knowledge/Courses

Appendix A: Occupations Ordered by Two-Letter Personality Codes

This listing is based on the coding used by the O*NET database of the U.S. Department of Labor. Other publishers may not create the exact same set of linkages between personality codes and occupations. For example, some sales jobs that are coded as Social by Psychological Assessment Resources, Inc., the publisher of the *Self-Directed Search,* are coded as Enterprising by O*NET.

Realistic

Personality Code	Job
R	Brattice Builders
R	Brickmasons and Blockmasons
R	Ceiling Tile Installers
R	Cement Masons and Concrete Finishers
R	Construction Carpenters
R	Drywall Installers
R	Pipe Fitters
R	Pipelaying Fitters
R	Plumbers
R	Refractory Materials Repairers, Except Brickmasons
R	Roofers
R	Sheet Metal Workers
R	Ship Carpenters and Joiners
R	Telecommunications Line Installers and Repairers
R	Truck Drivers, Heavy
R	Welders, Production
RA	Technical Directors/Managers
RC	Automotive Master Mechanics
RC	Automotive Specialty Technicians
RC	Boat Builders and Shipwrights
RC	Brazers
RC	Bus and Truck Mechanics and Diesel Engine Specialists
RC	Calibration and Instrumentation Technicians
RC	Carpenter Assemblers and Repairers
RC	Grader, Bulldozer, and Scraper Operators
RC	Heating and Air Conditioning Mechanics
RC	Maintenance and Repair Workers, General
RC	Pressure Vessel Inspectors
RC	Radiologic Technicians
RC	Refrigeration Mechanics
RC	Rough Carpenters
RC	Solderers
RC	Tractor-Trailer Truck Drivers
RC	Welders and Cutters

RE	Airline Pilots, Copilots, and Flight Engineers
RE	First-Line Supervisors and Manager/ Supervisors—Landscaping Workers
RE	Forest Fire Fighting and Prevention Supervisors
RE	Highway Patrol Pilots
RE	Municipal Fire Fighting and Prevention Supervisors
RI	Civil Engineers
RI	Electrical Engineering Technicians
RI	Electricians
RI	Electronics Engineering Technicians
RI	Operating Engineers
RI	Radiologic Technologists
RI	Welder-Fitters
RS	Correctional Officers and Jailers
RS	Forest Fire Fighters
RS	Municipal Fire Fighters
RS	Surgical Technologists

Investigative

Personality Code	Job
I	Family and General Practitioners
I	Internists, General
I	Obstetricians and Gynecologists
I	Pediatricians, General
IA	Clinical Psychologists
IA	Psychiatrists
IC	Compensation, Benefits, and Job Analysis Specialists
IC	Computer Science Teachers, Postsecondary
IC	Computer Support Specialists
IC	Computer Systems Analysts
IC	Database Administrators
IC	Financial Analysts
IC	Pharmacists
IE	Economists
IE	Market Research Analysts

IE	Natural Sciences Managers
IR	Anesthesiologists
IR	Biochemists
IR	Biophysicists
IR	Chiropractors
IR	Computer Hardware Engineers
IR	Computer Programmers
IR	Computer Security Specialists
IR	Computer Software Engineers, Applications
IR	Computer Software Engineers, Systems Software
IR	Dentists, General
IR	Electrical Engineers
IR	Electronics Engineers, Except Computer
IR	Engineering Teachers, Postsecondary
IR	Environmental Scientists and Specialists, Including Health
IR	Geologists
IR	Medical and Clinical Laboratory Technologists
IR	Medical Scientists, Except Epidemiologists
IR	Network Systems and Data Communications Analysts
IR	Optometrists
IR	Oral and Maxillofacial Surgeons
IR	Orthodontists
IR	Prosthodontists
IR	Respiratory Therapists
IR	Surgeons
IR	Veterinarians
IS	Agricultural Sciences Teachers, Postsecondary
IS	Biological Science Teachers, Postsecondary
IS	Chemistry Teachers, Postsecondary
IS	Educational Psychologists
IS	Forestry and Conservation Science Teachers, Postsecondary
IS	Health Specialties Teachers, Postsecondary

IS	Mathematical Science Teachers, Postsecondary
IS	Physician Assistants
IS	Physics Teachers, Postsecondary

Artistic

Personality Code	Job
A	Composers
A	Creative Writers
A	Film and Video Editors
A	Music Arrangers and Orchestrators
A	Musicians, Instrumental
AC	Librarians
AE	Actors
AE	Advertising and Promotions Managers
AE	Art Directors
AE	Cartoonists
AE	Copy Writers
AE	Directors—Stage, Motion Pictures, Television, and Radio
AE	Fashion Designers
AE	Graphic Designers
AE	Interior Designers
AE	Models
AE	Producers
AE	Singers
AE	Talent Directors
AI	Curators
AI	Poets and Lyricists
AI	Reporters and Correspondents
AI	Technical Writers
AR	Architects, Except Landscape and Naval
AR	Camera Operators, Television, Video, and Motion Picture
AR	Commercial and Industrial Designers
AR	Costume Attendants
AR	Exhibit Designers
AR	Floral Designers
AR	Landscape Architects

AR	Makeup Artists, Theatrical and Performance
AR	Merchandise Displayers and Window Trimmers
AR	Museum Technicians and Conservators
AR	Painters and Illustrators
AR	Photographers, Scientific
AR	Photographic Retouchers and Restorers
AR	Professional Photographers
AR	Sculptors
AR	Set Designers
AR	Sketch Artists
AS	Art, Drama, and Music Teachers, Postsecondary
AS	Broadcast News Analysts
AS	Caption Writers
AS	Choreographers
AS	Editors
AS	English Language and Literature Teachers, Postsecondary
AS	Foreign Language and Literature Teachers, Postsecondary
AS	Interpreters and Translators
AS	Music Directors
AS	Radio and Television Announcers

Social

Personality Code	Job
S	Child, Family, and School Social Workers
SA	Educational, Vocational, and School Counselors
SA	Elementary School Teachers, Except Special Education
SA	Kindergarten Teachers, Except Special Education
SA	Preschool Teachers, Except Special Education
SA	Secondary School Teachers, Except Special and Vocational Education

SA	Self-Enrichment Education Teachers
SA	Special Education Teachers, Middle School
SA	Special Education Teachers, Preschool, Kindergarten, and Elementary School
SA	Special Education Teachers, Secondary School
SC	Dental Hygienists
SC	Medical Assistants
SC	Social and Human Service Assistants
SC	Teacher Assistants
SE	Education Administrators, Elementary and Secondary School
SE	Employment Interviewers, Private or Public Employment Service
SE	Personal Financial Advisors
SE	Security Guards
SE	Sheriffs and Deputy Sheriffs
SE	Social and Community Service Managers
SE	Training and Development Specialists
SI	Anthropology and Archeology Teachers, Postsecondary
SI	Area, Ethnic, and Cultural Studies Teachers, Postsecondary
SI	Counseling Psychologists
SI	Economics Teachers, Postsecondary
SI	Graduate Teaching Assistants
SI	History Teachers, Postsecondary
SI	Instructional Coordinators
SI	Medical and Public Health Social Workers
SI	Mental Health and Substance Abuse Social Workers
SI	Nursing Instructors and Teachers, Postsecondary
SI	Political Science Teachers, Postsecondary
SI	Psychology Teachers, Postsecondary
SI	Registered Nurses
SI	Sociology Teachers, Postsecondary
SI	Speech-Language Pathologists
SR	Dental Assistants

SR	Emergency Medical Technicians and Paramedics
SR	Fitness Trainers and Aerobics Instructors
SR	Home Health Aides
SR	Licensed Practical and Licensed Vocational Nurses
SR	Nursing Aides, Orderlies, and Attendants
SR	Occupational Therapist Assistants
SR	Occupational Therapists
SR	Personal and Home Care Aides
SR	Physical Therapist Assistants
SR	Physical Therapists
SR	Police Patrol Officers
SR	Radiation Therapists
SR	Vocational Education Teachers, Postsecondary

Enterprising

Personality Code	Job
EA	Program Directors
EA	Public Relations Specialists
EC	Administrative Services Managers
EC	Computer and Information Systems Managers
EC	Financial Managers, Branch or Department
EC	First-Line Supervisors, Administrative Support
EC	First-Line Supervisors/Managers of Non-Retail Sales Workers
EC	Government Service Executives
EC	Lawyers
EC	Management Analysts
EC	Marketing Managers
EC	Paralegals and Legal Assistants
EC	Private Sector Executives
EC	Sales Agents, Financial Services

EC	Sales Agents, Securities and Commodities
EC	Sales Managers
EC	Storage and Distribution Managers
EC	Transportation Managers
EC	Treasurers, Controllers, and Chief Financial Officers
EI	Criminal Investigators and Special Agents
EI	Insurance Adjusters, Examiners, and Investigators
ER	Construction Managers
ER	Engineering Managers
ER	First-Line Supervisors and Manager/Supervisors—Construction Trades Workers
ER	First-Line Supervisors and Manager/Supervisors—Extractive Workers
ER	First-Line Supervisors/Managers of Food Preparation and Serving Workers
ER	First-Line Supervisors/Managers of Mechanics, Installers, and Repairers
ER	First-Line Supervisors/Managers of Production and Operating Workers
ER	Lawn Service Managers
ER	Sales Engineers
ER	Sales Representatives, Agricultural
ER	Sales Representatives, Electrical/Electronic
ER	Sales Representatives, Instruments
ER	Sales Representatives, Mechanical Equipment and Supplies
ES	Agents and Business Managers of Artists, Performers, and Athletes
ES	Child Support, Missing Persons, and Unemployment Insurance Fraud Investigators
ES	Compensation and Benefits Managers
ES	Education Administrators, Postsecondary
ES	First-Line Supervisors/Managers of Police and Detectives
ES	Hosts and Hostesses, Restaurant, Lounge, and Coffee Shop

ES	Human Resources Managers
ES	Loan Officers
ES	Medical and Health Services Managers
ES	Personnel Recruiters
ES	Police Detectives
ES	Retail Salespersons
ES	Sales Representatives, Chemical and Pharmaceutical
ES	Sales Representatives, Medical
ES	Sales Representatives, Wholesale and Manufacturing, Except Technical and Scientific Products
ES	Training and Development Managers

Conventional

Personality Code	Job
C	Medical Records and Health Information Technicians
C	Office Clerks, General
CE	Accountants
CE	Adjustment Clerks
CE	Assessors
CE	Auditors
CE	Bill and Account Collectors
CE	Billing, Cost, and Rate Clerks
CE	Bookkeeping, Accounting, and Auditing Clerks
CE	Budget Analysts
CE	Cashiers
CE	Claims Examiners, Property and Casualty Insurance
CE	Cost Estimators
CE	Counter and Rental Clerks
CE	Court Clerks
CE	Credit Analysts
CE	Customer Service Representatives, Utilities
CE	Executive Secretaries and Administrative Assistants
CE	Hotel, Motel, and Resort Desk Clerks

CE	Human Resources Assistants, Except Payroll and Timekeeping	CR	Cargo and Freight Agents
CE	Immigration and Customs Inspectors	CR	Cartographers and Photogrammetrists
CE	Insurance Claims Clerks	CR	Construction and Building Inspectors
CE	Insurance Policy Processing Clerks	CR	Dispatchers, Except Police, Fire, and Ambulance
CE	Insurance Underwriters	CR	Freight Inspectors
CE	Legal Secretaries	CR	Library Assistants, Clerical
CE	Licensing Examiners and Inspectors	CR	Mapping Technicians
CE	Medical Secretaries	CR	Marine Cargo Inspectors
CE	Production, Planning, and Expediting Clerks	CR	Pharmacy Technicians
CE	Receptionists and Information Clerks	CR	Police Identification and Records Officers
CE	Reservation and Transportation Ticket Agents	CR	Postal Service Mail Carriers
CE	Statement Clerks	CS	Audio and Video Equipment Technicians
CE	Tax Preparers	CS	Audio-Visual Collections Specialists
CI	Actuaries	CS	Interviewers, Except Eligibility and Loan
CR	Air Traffic Controllers	CS	Travel Clerks
CR	Billing, Posting, and Calculating Machine Operators		

Appendix B: Definitions of Skills

This table provides definitions for the skills in the job descriptions in Part IV.

Skill	Definition
Basic Skills—Content	**Background structures needed to work with and acquire more specific skills in a variety of different domains.**
Active Listening	Giving full attention to what other people are saying, taking time to understand the points being made, asking questions as appropriate, and not interrupting at inappropriate times.
Mathematics	Using mathematics to solve problems.
Reading Comprehension	Understanding written sentences and paragraphs in work-related documents.
Science	Using scientific rules and methods to solve problems.
Speaking	Talking to others to convey information effectively.
Writing	Communicating effectively in writing as appropriate for the needs of the audience.
Basic Skills—Process	**Procedures that contribute to the more rapid acquisition of knowledge and skill across a variety of domains.**
Active Learning	Understanding the implications of new information for both current and future problem-solving and decision-making.
Critical Thinking	Using logic and reasoning to identify the strengths and weaknesses of alternative solutions, conclusions, or approaches to problems.
Learning Strategies	Selecting and using training/instructional methods and procedures appropriate for the situation when learning or teaching new things.
Monitoring	Monitoring/assessing performance of yourself, other individuals, or organizations to make improvements or take corrective action.
Social Skills	**Developed capacities used to work with people to achieve goals.**
Coordination	Adjusting actions in relation to others' actions.
Instructing	Teaching others how to do something.
Negotiation	Bringing others together and trying to reconcile differences.
Persuasion	Persuading others to change their minds or behavior.
Service Orientation	Actively looking for ways to help people.
Social Perceptiveness	Being aware of others' reactions and understanding why they react as they do.
Complex Problem-Solving Skills	**Developed capacities used to solve novel, ill-defined problems in complex, real-world settings.**
Complex Problem Solving	Identifying complex problems and reviewing related information to develop and evaluate options and implement solutions.

(continued)

(continued)

Skill	Definition
Technical Skills	**Developed capacities used to design, set up, operate, and correct malfunctions involving application of machines or technological systems.**
Equipment Maintenance	Performing routine maintenance on equipment and determining when and what kind of maintenance is needed.
Equipment Selection	Determining the kind of tools and equipment needed to do a job.
Installation	Installing equipment, machines, wiring, or programs to meet specifications.
Operation and Control	Controlling operations of equipment or systems.
Operation Monitoring	Watching gauges, dials, or other indicators to make sure a machine is working properly.
Operations Analysis	Analyzing needs and product requirements to create a design.
Programming	Writing computer programs for various purposes.
Quality Control Analysis	Conducting tests and inspections of products, services, or processes to evaluate quality or performance.
Repairing	Repairing machines or systems, using the needed tools.
Technology Design	Generating or adapting equipment and technology to serve user needs.
Troubleshooting	Determining causes of operating errors and deciding what to do about them.
Systems Skills	**Developed capacities used to understand, monitor, and improve socio-technical systems.**
Judgment and Decision Making	Considering the relative costs and benefits of potential actions to choose the most appropriate one.
Systems Analysis	Determining how a system should work and how changes in conditions, operations, and the environment will affect outcomes.
Systems Evaluation	Identifying measures or indicators of system performance and the actions needed to improve or correct performance relative to the goals of the system.
Time Management	Managing one's own time and the time of others.
Resource Management Skills	**Developed capacities used to allocate resources efficiently.**
Management of Financial Resources	Determining how money will be spent to get the work done and accounting for these expenditures.
Management of Material Resources	Obtaining and seeing to the appropriate use of equipment, facilities, and materials needed to do certain work.
Management of Personnel Resources	Motivating, developing, and directing people as they work, identifying the best people for the job.

Appendix C: GOE Interest Fields and Groups

This table provides descriptions of the GOE interest fields and groups.

Field/Group Code	Field/Group Name	Definition
01	Arts, Entertainment, and Media	An interest in creatively expressing feelings or ideas, in communicating news or information, or in performing.
01.01	Managerial Work in Arts, Entertainment, and Media	These workers manage people who work in the field of arts, entertainment, and media. They oversee performers and performances in the arts and sports. They work for radio, television, and motion picture production companies and for artists and athletes.
01.02	Writing and Editing	These workers write or edit prose or poetry. Some use knowledge of a technical field to write manuals. Most work for publishers, in radio and television studios, and in the theatre and motion picture industries. Some are self-employed and sell their stories and plays directly to publishers.
01.03	News, Broadcasting, and Public Relations	These workers write, edit, translate, and report factual or persuasive information. They use their language skills and knowledge of special writing techniques to communicate facts or convince people of a point of view. They find employment with radio and television stations, newspapers, publishing firms, and advertising agencies. Some translators travel with visiting foreign businesspeople or diplomats; others work in courtrooms and law firms.
01.04	Visual Arts	These workers draw, paint, or sculpt works of art or design consumer goods in which visual appeal is important. They work for advertising agencies, printing and publishing firms, television and motion picture studios, museums, and restoration laboratories. They also work for manufacturers and in retail and wholesale trade. Many operate their own commercial art studios or do freelance work.
01.05	Performing Arts	These workers direct or perform for the public in works of drama, music, dance, or spectacle. They are employed by motion picture, television, and radio studios; stock companies; nightclubs; theaters; orchestras; bands; choral groups; music publishing and recording companies; traveling carnivals or circuses; and perma-

(continued)

(continued)

Field/Group Code	Field/Group Name	Definition
		nently located amusement parks. They may compose, arrange, or orchestrate musical compositions; choreograph dance routines; or plan the presentation of performances. Besides the time spent on stage, performers must spend a large portion of their time practicing their craft, auditioning for parts, and rehearsing their performances.
01.06	Craft Arts	These workers create visually appealing objects from clay, glass, fabric, and other materials. Their jobs demand considerable skill. Some are employed by manufacturing firms, but many are self-employed, selling items they have made through galleries and gift shops.
01.07	Graphic Arts	These workers produce printed materials, specializing in text, in pictures, or in combining both. Some of them use precision engraving and etching equipment and use considerable manual dexterity. Others use computerized or photographic equipment and rely more on technical skills. All of them have a good sense of what is visually appealing. They are employed by manufacturing firms, printing and publishing companies, and the publications departments in businesses of all kinds.
01.08	Media Technology	These workers perform the technical tasks that create the photographs, movies and videos, radio and television broadcasts, and sound recordings that provide entertainment and information for all of us. They are employed by local and network broadcasters, film studios and independent film or video production companies, recording studios, and photography studios.
01.09	Modeling and Personal Appearance	These workers pose before a camera or a live audience or they prepare the makeup or costuming for models or performers. Models display clothing, hairstyles, and commercial products; appear in fashion shows and other public or private product exhibitions; and pose for artists and photographers. They and their makeup artists work for manufacturers, wholesalers, and retailers. Some are employed by motion picture and television studios; others work in nightclubs. Many models are self-employed or get jobs through model agencies or unions. Makeup artists and costume attendants who attend to performers work for theaters and motion picture and television studios.
01.10	Sports: Coaching, Instructing, Officiating, and Performing	These workers participate in professional sporting events such as football, baseball, and horse racing. Included are contestants, trainers, coaches, referees, and umpires. Some work at private recreational facilities such as ski resorts, tennis courts, and gymnasiums.
02	Science, Math, and Engineering	An interest in discovering, collecting, and analyzing information about the natural world; in applying scientific research findings; in imagining and manipulating quantitative data; and in applying technology.

Field/Group Code	Field/Group Name	Definition
02.01	Managerial Work in Science, Math, and Engineering	These workers manage scientists who are doing research and engineers who are applying scientific principles to solve real-world problems. They set goals, oversee financial and technical resources, and evaluate outcomes. They work for industries, government agencies, universities, and hospitals.
02.02	Physical Sciences	These workers are concerned mostly with non-living things, such as chemicals, rocks, metals, and movements of the earth and stars. They conduct scientific studies and perform other activities requiring a knowledge of math, physics, or chemistry. Some workers investigate, discover, and test new theories. Some develop new or improved materials or processes for use in production and construction. Some do research in such fields as geology, astronomy, oceanography, and meteorology. Workers base their conclusions on information that can be measured or proved. Industries, government agencies, and large universities employ most of these workers in research facilities.
02.03	Life Sciences	These workers do research and conduct experiments to find out more about plants, animals, and other living things. Some study methods of producing better species of plants or animals; some work to find ways of preserving the natural balance in the environment. Others conduct research to improve medicine, health, and living conditions for human beings. These jobs are found in manufacturing plants, government agencies, universities, and hospitals.
02.04	Social Sciences	These workers gather, study, and analyze information about individuals, groups, or entire societies. They conduct research into all aspects of human behavior, including abnormal behavior, language, work, politics, lifestyle, and cultural expression. They are employed by schools and colleges, government agencies, businesses, museums, and private research foundations.
02.05	Laboratory Technology	These workers use special laboratory techniques and equipment to perform tests in such fields as chemistry, biology, and physics; then they record information resulting from their experiments and tests. These reports are used by scientists, medical doctors, researchers, and engineers. Hospitals, government agencies, universities, and private industries employ these workers in their laboratories and research activities.
02.06	Mathematics and Computers	These workers use advanced math, statistics, and computer programs to solve problems and conduct research. They analyze and interpret numerical data for planning and decision making. Some of these workers determine how computers may best be used to solve problems or process information. Businesses and industries, colleges, research organizations, and government agencies

(continued)

(continued)

Field/Group Code	Field/Group Name	Definition
		hire these workers. Some programmers work as consultants on changing assignments.
02.07	Engineering	These workers plan, design, and direct the development and construction of buildings, bridges, roads, airports, dams, sewage systems, air conditioning systems, mining machinery, and other structures and equipment. They utilize scientific principles to develop processes and techniques for generating and transmitting electrical power, for manufacturing chemicals, for extracting metals from ores, and for controlling the quality of products being made. Workers specialize in one or more kinds of engineering, such as civil, electrical, mechanical, mining, and safety. Some are hired by industrial plants, petroleum and mining companies, research laboratories, and construction companies. Others find employment with federal, state, and local governments.
02.08	Engineering Technology	These workers perform a variety of technical tasks. They make detailed drawings and work plans; measure and prepare maps of land and water areas; operate complex communications equipment; inspect buildings and equipment for structural, mechanical, or electrical problems; and schedule and control production and transportation operations. Many work in industrial plants, oilfields and mines, research laboratories, and construction sites. Engineering firms; manufacturers; and federal, state, and local governments hire these workers.
03	Plants and Animals	An interest in working with plants and animals, usually outdoors.
03.01	Managerial Work in Plants and Animals	These workers operate or manage farms, ranches, hatcheries, nurseries, forests, and other plant and animal businesses. Some breed specialty plants and animals. Others provide services to increase production or beautify land areas. Many work in rural areas or woodlands and on farms, ranches, and forest preserves. Others find employment with commercial nurseries, landscaping firms, business services, or government agencies located in large and small communities all over the country. Many are self-employed, operating their own large or small businesses.
03.02	Animal Care and Training	These workers care for and train animals of many kinds. They work in pet shops, pet grooming parlors, testing laboratories, animal shelters, and veterinary offices. Some are employed by zoos, aquariums, circuses, and other places where animals are exhibited or used in entertainment acts. Others work for animal training or obedience schools, stables, kennels, race tracks, or riding academies. This group does not include workers

Field/Group Code	Field/Group Name	Definition
		employed on farms, ranches, or other places where animals are raised for food.
03.03	Hands-on Work in Plants and Animals	These workers perform strenuous tasks with plants or animals, usually outdoors in a non-factory setting. They work with their hands, use tools and equipment, or operate machinery. They work on farms or ranches; at logging camps or fish hatcheries; in forests or game preserves; or with commercial fishing businesses, onshore or in fishing boats. In cities and towns they usually work in parks, gardens, or nurseries.
04	Law, Law Enforcement, and Public Safety	An interest in upholding people's rights or in protecting people and property by using authority, inspecting, or monitoring.
04.01	Managerial Work in Law, Law Enforcement, and Public Safety	These workers manage fire and police departments. They set goals and policies, oversee financial and human resources, evaluate outcomes, and represent their departments to the public and the governments of the jurisdictions they serve. They work for cites and towns. Supervisors of forest fire fighters mostly work for the federal government.
04.02	Law	These workers provide legal advice and representation to clients, hear and make decisions on court cases, help individuals and groups reach agreements, and conduct investigations into legal matters. Although they specialize in many different fields, all of them apply knowledge of laws and regulations to the problems they must solve. They work for law firms, courts, businesses, government agencies, and legislators.
04.03	Law Enforcement	These workers enforce laws and regulations to protect people, animals, and property. They investigate suspicious persons and acts; prevent crimes; and identify the causes of fires, working for federal, state, and local governments. Some are hired by private businesses, such as factories and stores. They operate in a variety of settings, such as railroads, hotels, lumberyards, industrial plants, and amusement establishments.
04.04	Public Safety	These workers protect the public by responding to emergencies and by assuring that people are not exposed to unsafe products or facilities. Some respond hastily to emergencies, stabilizing sick or injured people en route to a hospital or acting quickly to put out fires and evacuate people from burning buildings. Dealing with sudden crises requires them to have both technical skills and the ability to keep a cool head. Others investigate business practices; examine records; and inspect materials, products, workplaces, utilities, and transportation equipment for compliance with government regulations or conformance to company policies. They may impound records, close down businesses, or

(continued)

(continued)

Field/Group Code	Field/Group Name	Definition
		bring other pressures to bear against individuals or organizations which they find to be in violation of rules. Although they are not involved directly with construction, installation, or processing operations, they must know the technical principles to be able to measure and evaluate the quality of the materials and equipment they inspect.
04.05	Military	These workers serve in the Armed Forces of the United States: the Air Force, Army, Coast Guard, Marines, Navy, and National Guard. Although workers in the Armed Forces perform almost every occupation found in the civilian workforce, the occupations in this subgroup are unique to the military and have no civilian counterparts. The purpose of workers in the military is to ensure peace and protect the nation in times of war. In unusual cases, the military must assist in national emergencies or to restore order in events of civil disobedience.
05	Mechanics, Installers, and Repairers	An interest in applying mechanical and electrical/electronic principles to practical situations by use of machines or hand tools.
05.01	Managerial Work in Mechanics, Installers, and Repairers	These workers directly supervise and coordinate activities of mechanics, repairers, and installers and their helpers. They are generally found in smaller establishments, where they perform both supervisory and management functions, such as accounting, marketing, and personnel work, and may also engage in the same repair and installation work as the workers they supervise.
05.02	Electrical and Electronic Systems	These workers repair and install electrical devices and systems such as motors, transformers, appliances, and power lines and electronic devices and systems such as radios, computers, and telephone networks. They work for manufacturers, utilities, and service companies. Since electrical and electronic equipment is used almost everywhere, they may work in almost any kind of location, as well as in repair shops.
05.03	Mechanical Work	These workers install, service, and repair various kinds of machinery. Some are large, such as bodies and engines of cars, trucks, buses, airplanes, and ships; furnaces and air conditioners; office machines; and home appliances. Others are small, such as locks, watches, medical instruments, power tools, and musical instruments. These workers are hired by manufacturers, service companies, and businesses that use machines.
05.04	Hands-on Work in Mechanics, Installers, and Repairers	These workers perform a variety of tasks requiring little skill, such as moving materials, repairing simple machines and equipment, and helping skilled workers. These jobs are found in a variety of settings, mostly other than in factories.
06	Construction, Mining, and Drilling	An interest in assembling components of buildings and other structures or in using mechanical devices to drill or excavate.

Field/Group Code	Field/Group Name	Definition
06.01	Managerial Work in Construction, Mining, and Drilling	These workers directly supervise and coordinate activities of the workers who construct buildings, roads, or other structures or who drill or dig for oil and minerals. They are responsible for setting and meeting goals and for bringing together the people and equipment needed to get the work done.
06.02	Construction	These workers construct buildings and other large structures. Besides laying the foundations and putting up the framework, walls, floors, and roof, they also install plumbing and electric conduits, windows, and insulation and finish interior surfaces with paint, paper, and carpeting. Outside, they may install driveways, parking lots, fences, and swimming pools. They may also apply their skills to servicing or refurbishing components of buildings. General construction companies and specialized installation and service firms employ these workers.
06.03	Mining and Drilling	These workers operate drilling or other excavating and pumping equipment, usually in oilfields, quarries, or mines. They are hired by large energy or extractive companies or by small drilling contractors that do work for the large companies.
06.04	Hands-on Work in Construction, Extraction, and Maintenance	These workers perform a variety of tasks requiring little skill, such as moving materials, cleaning work areas, doing routine installations, operating simple tools, and helping skilled workers. They work at construction sites, oilfields, quarries, and mines.
07	Transportation	An interest in operations that move people or materials.
07.01	Managerial Work in Transportation	These workers manage transportation services. They may be responsible for a whole airline, rail line, bus line, or subway system; they may oversee a fleet of trucks or cargo vessels; or they may coordinate the activities of the crew on one large train. They have a good knowledge of the transportation equipment for which they are responsible, and they understand how to plan for and react to factors that might affect whether the vehicles complete their routes safely, on schedule, and within budget. Most of them work within basic guidelines of policy and goals set by their employers.
07.02	Vehicle Expediting and Coordinating	These workers monitor and control the movements of vehicles. They work at airports or along rail lines, routing vehicles so they keep on schedule but also keep a safe distance from other vehicles. Traffic technicians work under the direction of a traffic engineer to conduct field studies of traffic volume, signals, lighting, and other factors that influence the flow of vehicles.
07.03	Air Vehicle Operation	These workers pilot airplanes or helicopters or train or supervise pilots. Most are hired by commercial airlines. Some find jobs piloting planes for private companies, such as package delivery services or crop-dusting services, or for individuals.

(continued)

(continued)

Field/Group Code	Field/Group Name	Definition
07.04	Water Vehicle Operation	These workers operate ships, boats, and barges. They steer them, operate motor equipment, maintain the vessel, and see that passengers and/or cargo are handled well. Most are hired by freight shipping companies, although some work for cruise lines, fishing fleets, or individuals.
07.05	Truck Driving	These workers drive large trucks, small trucks, or delivery vans. They may cover long distances or a familiar local route. Most of these jobs are found with trucking companies or with wholesale and retail companies that do deliveries.
07.06	Rail Vehicle Operation	These workers drive locomotives, subways, and streetcars. Most of these jobs are found with railroads and city transit authorities.
07.07	Other Services Requiring Driving	These workers drive ambulances, taxis, buses (city, intercity, or school), or other small vehicles, mostly to take people from place to place. Some drive a route to sell or deliver items, such as ice cream bars, take-out food, or newspapers. Some park cars on parking lots.
07.08	Support Work	These workers provide support for routine operations at airports, railroads, and docks. They load and unload cargo, secure cargo inside vehicles, and refuel and clean vehicles.
08	Industrial Production	An interest in repetitive, concrete, organized activities most often done in a factory setting.
08.01	Managerial Work in Industrial Production	These workers manage industrial processing and manufacturing plants. They make decisions about policy and operation in accordance with overall company policy and goals. They must have working knowledge of the equipment and methods for the activity that they direct.
08.02	Production Technology	These workers perform highly skilled hand and/or machine work requiring special techniques, training, and experience. Some set up machines for others to operate or set up and perform a variety of machine operations on their own. Some do precision handwork. Some inspect and test the work of others to make sure it meets standards of quality. Production technology workers mostly are employed on assembly lines, but the materials they work with may be as big as airplane bodies or as small as gemstones.
08.03	Production Work	These workers use hands and hand tools with skill to make or process materials, products, and parts. They follow established procedures and techniques. Although their jobs are found most often in manufacturing plants, they are also found in places we might not ordinarily think of as factories, such as printing and publishing companies, slaughterhouses, and canneries.
08.04	Metal and Plastics Machining Technology	These workers cut and grind metal and plastic parts to desired shapes and measurements, usually following specifications that require very precise work. They create the patterns, molds, and

Field/Group Code	Field/Group Name	Definition
		models that manufacturers then use to mass-produce products of all kinds. Most work in machine shops of manufacturing plants.
08.05	Woodworking Technology	These workers follow specifications as they cut, shape, and finish wood products such as furniture and cabinets. Some create wooden models of products that will be mass-produced out of wood, metal, or plastic. Although most work in manufacturing plants, some work in homes and offices to custom-make cabinets.
08.06	Systems Operation	These workers operate and maintain equipment in systems that generate and distribute electricity, provide water and process wastewater, and pump oil and gas from oil fields to storage tanks. These jobs are found in utility companies, refineries, ships, industrial plants, and large apartment houses.
08.07	Hands-on Work: Loading, Moving, Hoisting, and Conveying	These workers use their hands, machinery, tools, and other equipment to package or move products or materials. They work in a variety of settings, including offices, mailrooms, manufacturing plants, water treatment plants, and construction sites. They may work with small packages or computer chips or with huge containers or structural components of buildings.
09	Business Detail	An interest in organized, clearly defined activities requiring accuracy and attention to details, primarily in an office setting.
09.01	Managerial Work in Business Detail	These workers supervise and coordinate certain high-level business activities: contracts for buying or selling goods and services, office support services, facilities planning and maintenance, customer service, and administrative support. Within the general policies and goals of their organization, they make plans, oversee financial and technical resources, and evaluate outcomes. They work in the offices of every kind of business, government agency, and school.
09.02	Administrative Detail	These workers do high-level clerical work requiring special skills and knowledge, as well as some low-level managerial work. They work in the offices of businesses, industries, courts of law, and government agencies, as well as in medicine, law, and other professions.
09.03	Bookkeeping, Auditing, and Accounting	These workers collect, organize, compute, and record the numerical information used in business and financial transactions. They use both clerical and math skills, and some use machines. They work in banks, finance companies, accounting firms, payroll and inventory control departments in business and government agencies, and other places.
09.04	Material Control	These workers monitor the production of a business or the use of utilities. They examine documents or meters and maintain records of consumption or production. Some order raw materials and supplies and arrange for shipping of output. Workers find

(continued)

(continued)

Field/Group Code	Field/Group Name	Definition
		jobs for water works, electricity and gas suppliers, institutions, industrial plants, government agencies, factories, transportation companies, department stores, hotels, restaurants, hospitals, laundries, and dry-cleaning plants.
09.05	Customer Service	These workers deal with people in person, often standing behind a window or in a booth. They may receive payment; collect information; give out change, cash, or merchandise; provide information in answer to questions; or help customers fill out forms. Many keep written records of the information or money they receive or perform other clerical duties. Private businesses, banks, institutions such as schools and hospitals, and government agencies hire them to work in offices and reception areas.
09.06	Communications	These workers talk with people by telephone or by using other communication equipment to give and receive information. Some deal with the public; some interact only with fellow workers. Many keep written records of the information they receive or perform other clerical duties. Private businesses, hotels, telephone companies, institutions such as schools and hospitals, and government agencies hire them to work in offices.
09.07	Records Processing	These workers prepare, review, file, and coordinate recorded information. Some check records and schedules for accuracy. Some schedule the activities of people or the use of equipment. Jobs in this group are found in most businesses, institutions, and government agencies.
09.08	Records and Materials Processing	These workers routinely file, sort, route, or deliver items such as letters, packages, or messages. Some of their work may be done with machines and computer terminals. Their jobs are found in most businesses, factories, and government agencies and in the U.S. Postal Service and various private courier services.
09.09	Clerical Machine Operation	These workers use business machines to record or process data. They operate machines that type, print, sort, compute, send, or receive information. Their jobs are found in businesses, factories, and government agencies and wherever else large amounts of data are handled.
10	Sales and Marketing	An interest in bringing others to a particular point of view by personal persuasion, using sales and promotional techniques.
10.01	Managerial Work in Sales and Marketing	These workers direct or manage various kinds of selling and/or advertising operations—either a department within a business or a specialized business firm that contracts to provide selling and/or advertising services. These workers usually carry out their activities according to policies and procedures determined by owners, boards of directors, administrators, and other persons with higher authority.

Field/Group Code	Field/Group Name	Definition
10.02	Sales Technology	These workers sell products such as industrial machinery, data processing equipment, and pharmaceuticals, plus services such as investment counseling, insurance, and advertising. They advise customers of the capabilities, uses, and other important features of these products and services and help customers choose those best suited to their needs. They work for manufacturers, wholesalers, insurance companies, financial institutions, and business service establishments. Some are self-employed.
10.03	General Sales	These workers sell, demonstrate, and solicit orders for products and services of many kinds. They are hired by retail and wholesale firms, manufacturers and distributors, business services, and nonprofit organizations. Some spend all their time in a single location, such as a department store or automobile agency. Others call on businesses or individuals to sell products or services or follow up on earlier sales.
10.04	Personal Soliciting	These workers appeal to people directly and sell them merchandise or services. In most cases they do not build a long-term relationship with the buyer. They may sell products on the street, staying in one location or moving through business and residential areas. They may call potential buyers by telephone. They may demonstrate a product in a mall or other place with a lot of foot traffic.
11	Recreation, Travel, and Other Personal Services	An interest in catering to the personal wishes and needs of others so that they may enjoy cleanliness, good food and drink, comfortable lodging away from home, and enjoyable recreation.
11.01	Managerial Work in Recreation, Travel, and Other Personal Services	These workers manage, through lower-level personnel, all or part of the activities in restaurants, hotels, resorts, and other places where people expect good personal service. Some of them manage services that keep a building clean. Within the guidelines of their organization, they set goals, monitor resources, and evaluate the work of others.
11.02	Recreational Services	These workers provide services to help people enjoy their leisure activities. They may lead people in recreational activities such as exercise, crafts, music, or camping or they may help people engaged in recreation by performing such services as dealing cards, guiding tourists, taking tickets, or operating thrill rides.
11.03	Transportation and Lodging Services	These workers help visitors, travelers, and customers get acquainted with and feel at ease in an unfamiliar setting. They are charged with the safety and comfort of people who are traveling or vacationing. They may register travelers at hotels, book trips for passengers, or carry travelers' luggage. These workers find employment with air, rail, and water transportation companies; hotels and restaurants; retirement homes; and related establishments.

(continued)

(continued)

11.04	Barber and Beauty Services	These workers cut and style hair and provide a variety of other services to improve people's appearance or physical condition. They may specialize in one activity or perform many different duties.
11.05	Food and Beverage Services	These workers prepare and serve food. Some of them cook or do other tasks to prepare food in kitchens of restaurants or institutional cafeterias. Others aid in the preparation process by cutting meat, baking bread and pastries, or decorating cakes. The various kinds of workers who serve food and drink may wait on tables, serve diners at a counter, bring meals outside at drive-ins, or tend bar. Other workers play a supporting role by greeting diners as they enter a restaurant, by washing dishes, or by keeping the dining room set up with clean linens and silverware.
11.06	Apparel, Shoes, Leather, and Fabric Care	These workers clean, alter, restore, and repair clothing, shoes, or other items made from fabric or leather. Their jobs are found in clothing stores; manufacturing plants; and specialty cleaning, alteration, and repair shops.
11.07	Cleaning and Building Services	These workers maintain the cleanliness of houses, various kinds of buildings, vehicles, and large equipment. They use detergents and other cleaning agents, vacuum cleaners, brushes, and specialized equipment to remove dirt, spills, and trash so the living or working environment is healthy, safe, and pleasant to be in. Some cleaners also do minor repairs, such as fixing leaky faucets. In hospitals they may disinfect equipment and supplies. Some of these workers provide other services for the convenience of people working or seeking recreation in a building, such as retrieving people's personal items in a locker room.
11.08	Other Personal Services	These workers provide personal services to people who need a lot of attention: young children, people with chronic health problems, people in mourning, or very busy people. They provide such services as companionship, bathing and grooming, simple meal preparation, organizing the household, running errands, and basic emotional support.
12	Education and Social Service	An interest in teaching people or improving their social or spiritual well-being.
12.01	Managerial Work in Education and Social Service	These workers are employed at colleges, school districts, corporations, parks, and social service agencies. They are responsible for planning, budgeting, evaluating results, and supervising workers. They need to balance their financial responsibilities against the educational and social service goals of their organizations and sometimes must make trade-offs. They enjoy helping people achieve their learning and social goals, but they are content to do so behind the scenes.
12.02	Social Services	These workers help people deal with their problems and major life events. They may work on a person-to-person basis or with groups of people. Workers sometimes specialize in problems that

Field/Group Code	Field/Group Name	Definition
		are personal, social, vocational, physical, educational, or spiritual in nature. Schools, rehabilitation centers, mental health clinics, guidance centers, and religious institutions employ these workers. Jobs are also found in public and private welfare and employment services, juvenile courts, and vocational rehabilitation programs.
12.03	Educational Services	These workers do general and specialized teaching, vocational training, and advising about education, career planning, or finances. Some provide library and museum services. Jobs are found in schools, colleges, libraries, and museums.
13	General Management and Support	An interest in making an organization run smoothly.
13.01	General Management Work and Management of Support Functions	These workers are top-level and middle-level administrators who direct, through lower-level personnel, all or part of the activities in business establishments, government agencies, and labor unions. They set policies, make important decisions, and determine priorities. They use a variety of skills, including math, critical thinking, communications, insight into human nature, and computer applications. They have a good knowledge of how their industry operates and what laws and regulations they must follow.
13.02	Management Support	These workers plan, manage, analyze, evaluate, and make decisions about personnel, purchases, and financial transactions and records. They use mathematics, logic, psychology, computerized tools, and knowledge of industry practices and government regulations that apply to their specific fields. They provide information and recommendations that help higher management accomplish the goals of the organization. They supervise clerical and sometimes technical staff that support them.
14	Medical and Health Services	An interest in helping people be healthy.
14.01	Managerial Work in Medical and Health Services	These workers manage medical activities. Some primarily supervise doctors, nurses, therapists, and other health care workers. Others provide leadership for all aspects of a hospital or nursing home, including finance and physical facilities. Some make decisions about how an autopsy is to be conducted. They do planning, budgeting, staffing, and evaluation of outcomes. They work for hospitals, health insurers, and government agencies.
14.02	Medicine and Surgery	These workers diagnose and treat human diseases, disorders, and injuries. They work in such places as hospitals, clinics, health facilities, industrial plants, pharmacies, and government agencies. Some are professionals who make life-and-death decisions, perform invasive procedures, and prescribe drugs. They may specialize or work in general practice. Many are self-employed and have their own offices. Other workers in this group provide care under the supervision of professionals.

(continued)

(continued)

Field/Group Code	Field/Group Name	Definition
14.03	Dentistry	These workers provide health care for patients' teeth and mouth tissues. Most dentists are general practitioners, performing a variety of oral care tasks. Others specialize: Orthodontists straighten teeth; prosthodontists make artificial teeth and dentures; oral and maxillofacial surgeons operate on the mouth and jaws. Dental hygienists clean teeth and teach people how to take care of their teeth. Dental assistants provide chairside help, get the patient and equipment ready, and keep records.
14.04	Health Specialties	These workers are health professionals and technicians who specialize in certain parts of the human body. They are employed in private practices, vision-care chains, hospitals, and long-term health care facilities. Optometrists diagnose various diseases, disorders, and injuries of the eye, but opticians specialize in using lenses to correct imperfections in how the eye focuses. Podiatrists maintain the health of the feet and lower extremities. Chiropractors adjust the spinal column and other joints to prevent disease and correct abnormalities of the human body believed to be caused by interference with the nervous system.
14.05	Medical Technology	These workers use technology mostly to detect signs of disease. They are employed by hospitals, long-term health care facilities, HMOs, physicians' offices, and specialized diagnostic laboratories and practices. They perform tests requested by physicians, and the findings they report help the physicians to diagnose disease and formulate a therapy.
14.06	Medical Therapy	These workers care for, treat, or train people to improve their physical and emotional well-being. Most persons in this group work with people who are sick, injured, or disabled. Hospitals, nursing homes, and rehabilitation centers hire workers in this group, as do schools, industrial plants, doctors' offices, and sports organizations.
14.07	Patient Care and Assistance	These workers are concerned with the physical needs and welfare of others. They may assist professional workers. These workers care for people who are very old, very young, or have handicaps, frequently helping people do the things they cannot do for themselves. Jobs are found in hospitals, clinics, daycare centers, nurseries, schools, private homes, and centers for disabled people.
14.08	Health Protection and Promotion	These workers help people maintain good health and fitness. They educate and advise people to help them live healthier lifestyles, eat well, and get into better physical condition.

Appendix D: Definitions of Related Knowledge/Courses

This table provides definitions for the related knowledge/courses items in the job descriptions in Part IV.

Knowledge/Course	Definition
Administration and Management	Knowledge of business and management principles involved in strategic planning, resource allocation, human resources modeling, leadership techniques, production methods, and coordination of people and resources.
Biology	Knowledge of plant and animal organisms and their tissues, cells, functions, interdependencies, and interactions with each other and the environment.
Building and Construction	Knowledge of materials, methods, and the tools involved in the construction or repair of houses, buildings, or other structures such as highways and roads.
Chemistry	Knowledge of the chemical composition, structure, and properties of substances and of the chemical processes and transformations that they undergo. This includes uses of chemicals and their danger signs, production techniques, and disposal methods.
Clerical Practices	Knowledge of administrative and clerical procedures and systems such as word processing, managing files and records, stenography and transcription, designing forms, and other office procedures and terminology.
Communications and Media	Knowledge of media production, communication, and dissemination techniques and methods. This includes alternative ways to inform and entertain via written, oral, and visual media.
Computers and Electronics	Knowledge of circuit boards, processors, chips, electronic equipment, and computer hardware and software, including applications and programming.
Customer and Personal Service	Knowledge of principles and processes for providing customer and personal services. This includes customer needs assessment, meeting quality standards for services, and evaluation of customer satisfaction.
Design	Knowledge of design techniques, tools, and principles involved in production of precision technical plans, blueprints, drawings, and models.
Economics and Accounting	Knowledge of economic and accounting principles and practices, the financial markets, banking, and the analysis and reporting of financial data.
Education and Training	Knowledge of principles and methods for curriculum and training design, teaching and instruction for individuals and groups, and the measurement of training effects.

(continued)

(continued)

Knowledge/Course	Definition
Engineering and Technology	Knowledge of the practical application of engineering science and technology. This includes applying principles, techniques, procedures, and equipment to the design and production of various goods and services.
English Language	Knowledge of the structure and content of the English language, including the meaning and spelling of words, rules of composition, and grammar.
Fine Arts	Knowledge of the theory and techniques required to compose, produce, and perform works of music, dance, visual arts, drama, and sculpture.
Food Production	Knowledge of techniques and equipment for planting, growing, and harvesting food products (both plant and animal) for consumption, including storage/handling techniques.
Foreign Language	Knowledge of the structure and content of a foreign (non-English) language, including the meaning and spelling of words, rules of composition and grammar, and pronunciation.
Geography	Knowledge of principles and methods for describing the features of land, sea, and air masses, including their physical characteristics; locations; interrelationships; and distribution of plant, animal, and human life.
History and Archeology	Knowledge of historical events and their causes, indicators, and effects on civilizations and cultures.
Law and Government	Knowledge of laws, legal codes, court procedures, precedents, government regulations, executive orders, agency rules, and the democratic political process.
Mathematics	Knowledge of arithmetic, algebra, geometry, calculus, and statistics and their applications.
Mechanical Devices	Knowledge of machines and tools, including their designs, uses, repair, and maintenance.
Medicine and Dentistry	Knowledge of the information and techniques needed to diagnose and treat human injuries, diseases, and deformities. This includes symptoms, treatment alternatives, drug properties and interactions, and preventive health-care measures.
Personnel and Human Resources	Knowledge of principles and procedures for personnel recruitment, selection, training, compensation and benefits, labor relations and negotiation, and personnel information systems.
Philosophy and Theology	Knowledge of different philosophical systems and religions. This includes their basic principles, values, ethics, ways of thinking, customs, practices, and impact on human culture.
Physics	Knowledge and prediction of physical principles and laws and their interrelationships and applications to understanding fluid, material, and atmospheric dynamics and mechanical, electrical, atomic, and subatomic structures and processes.
Production and Processing	Knowledge of raw materials, production processes, quality control, costs, and other techniques for maximizing the effective manufacture and distribution of goods.

Knowledge/Course	Definition
Psychology	Knowledge of human behavior and performance; individual differences in ability, personality, and interests; learning and motivation; psychological research methods; and the assessment and treatment of behavioral and affective disorders.
Public Safety and Security	Knowledge of relevant equipment, policies, procedures, and strategies to promote effective local, state, or national security operations for the protection of people, data, property, and institutions.
Sales and Marketing	Knowledge of principles and methods for showing, promoting, and selling products or services. This includes marketing strategy and tactics, product demonstration, sales techniques, and sales control systems.
Sociology and Anthropology	Knowledge of group behavior and dynamics, societal trends and influences, human migrations, ethnicity, and cultures and their history and origins.
Telecommunications	Knowledge of transmission, broadcasting, switching, control, and operation of telecommunications systems.
Therapy and Counseling	Knowledge of principles, methods, and procedures for diagnosis, treatment, and rehabilitation of physical and mental dysfunctions and for career counseling and guidance.
Transportation	Knowledge of principles and methods for moving people or goods by air, rail, sea, or road, including the relative costs and benefits.

Index

B

D

E

F